Library of Congress Cataloging-in-Publication Data

Leccese, Arthur P.
    Drugs and society : behavioral medicines and abusable drugs /
Arthur P. Leccese.
        p.   cm.
    Includes bibliographical references and index.
    ISBN 0-13-221623-X
    1. Psychopharmacology. 2. Drug abuse. I. Title.
RM315.L364 1991   90-22532
615'.78--dc20   CIP

Editorial/production supervision and interior design: Elaine Lynch
Manufacturing buyers: Debra Kesar and Mary Ann Gloriande
Cover design: Mike Fender

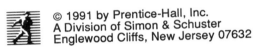 © 1991 by Prentice-Hall, Inc.
A Division of Simon & Schuster
Englewood Cliffs, New Jersey 07632

Printed in the United States of America
10 9 8 7 6 5 4 3 2 1

ISBN 0-13-221623-X

Prentice-Hall International (UK) Limited, London
Prentice-Hall of Australia Pty. Limited, Sydney
Prentice-Hall Canada Inc., Toronto
Prentice-Hall Hispanoamericana, S.A., Mexico
Prentice-Hall of India Private Limited, New Delhi
Prentice-Hall of Japan, Inc., Tokyo
Simon & Schuster Asia Pte. Ltd., Singapore
Editora Prentice-Hall do Brasil, Ltda., Rio de Janeiro

This book is dedicated to two groups of people. The first group includes the two most important women in my life, Linda M. (Buechner) Leccese, my wife, and Doris M. (Braun) Leccese, my mother. The second group consists of my teachers, including especially Mrs. Lundgren, Dr. Cathy Galizio, Dr. Aaron Snyder, Dr. Doug Grant, Dr. Elton E. Quinton, and Dr. William Lyness.

CONTENTS

PREFACE   xv

PART A   PSYCHOPHARMACOLOGY

CHAPTER 1   CELLS, CHEMICALS, AND NEURONAL COMMUNICATION   1

Synaptic Anatomy: A Specialized Cell   1
Typical Intracellular Structures   2
Neuronal Membrane   2
Convergence and Divergence   4
Non-Neuronal Cells of the Nervous System   4
The Blood-Brain Barrier   5
Action Potentials   6
Resting Potential   6
Sequence of Events during AP   6
Ionic Basis of AP   6
EPSPs and IPSPs   7
Definitions and Descriptions of Events   7
Ionic Basis   7
Neurotransmitters (NTs) and Neuromodulators (NMs)   7
Two Forms of Information Transfer   7
List of Common NTs and NMs   8
Enzymes in Synthesis and Degradation   9
Chapter Summary   10
Review Essay Questions   10
References   11

CHAPTER 2   NERVOUS SYSTEM ANATOMY   12

Nervous System Gross Anatomy   12
Peripheral Nervous System   13
The Central Nervous System   16
Endocrine System   18
Nervous System Organization   22
Chapter Summary   22
Review Essay Questions   23
References   23

CHAPTER 3   BASIC PHARMACOLOGY   **25**

Methods of Drug Administration   25
   Oral   25
   Oral, Anal, or Vaginal Insertion   26
   Inhalation   26
   Insufflation   27
   Injection   27
   New Technologies   27
Methods of Drug Preparation   29
Drug Absorption   29
Drug Distribution   30
Metabolism and Excretion   31
   Half-Life   31
   Active Metabolites   32
Importance of Basic Pharmacology   33
Chapter Summary   34
Review Essay Questions   34
References   35

CHAPTER 4   DETERMINANTS AND DESCRIPTIONS OF DRUG ACTIONS   **36**

Mechanism of Action   36
   Target Effects vs. Side Effects   36
   Efficacy vs. Potency   37
Agonists and Antagonists   37
   Types of Short-Term Agonist Actions   38
   Types of Short-Term Antagonist Action   40
   Long-Term Effects of Agonists and Antagonists   42
Other Factors Influencing Drug Effects   44
   Physical Status of Consumer   44
   Drug Interactions   45
   Previous Drug Use   45
   Set and Setting   45
Dose-Response Curves   46
   Qualitative and Quantitative Changes   47
   Toxicity and Therapeutic Windows   47
   Potency and Efficacy   47
Chapter Summary   49
Review Essay Questions   50
References   50

CHAPTER 5   TOLERANCE, SENSITIZATION AND PHYSICAL DEPENDENCY   **52**

Tolerance   52
Differential and Cross Tolerance   53
Sensitization   55
Mechanisms of Tolerance and Sensitization   56
   Pharmacokinetic   56
   Pharmacodynamic   57

     Behavioral   58
    User Control Over Development of Tolerance and Sensitization   59
    Dependency and Cross-Dependency   60
    Cessation Phenomena   60
    Physical Dependency vs. Compulsive Use   61
    User Control over Development of Dependency and Compulsive Use   62
    Chapter Summary   63
    Review Essay Questions   64
    References   64

PART B   BEHAVIORAL MEDICINES

    CHAPTER 6   HISTORY, RESEARCH METHODOLOGY, AND CONTROVERSIES   67
       Brief History   67
          Folk Medicine: Witchcraft and Shamanism   67
          Modern Behavioral Medicines   68
       Evaluating the Effectiveness of Behavioral Medicines   68
          False Positives and False Negatives   68
          Characteristics of an Adequate Study   69
       Stigmatizing Label, Psychological Disorder, or Mental Illness?   72
          Tom Szasz and *The Myth of Mental Illness*   73
          The Medicalization of Deviance   73
          The Abnormal Nervous System   73
          The Meaning of Effective Behavioral Medicines   74
       Underuse by Patients   75
          Side Effects   75
          Wounded Sense of Autonomy   75
          Symptom of Behavioral Disorder   75
       Overuse by Patients   76
       Underuse or Overuse by Physicians   76
          Who Can Diagnose and Prescribe   76
          Psychiatric Calvinism and Underuse   76
       Chapter Summary   77
       Review Essay Questions   77
       References   78

    CHAPTER 7   SCHIZOPHRENIA   80
       The Disorder   80
          Basic Symptoms   80
          Differential Diagnosis and the DSM-IIIR   81
          Incidence and Subtypes   82
          Nervous System Abnormalities: The Dopamine Hypothesis   82
       Basic Pharmacology   83
       Effects on Symptoms of Schizophrenia   84
          Amelioration of Specific Symptoms   84
          Delayed Therapeutic Onset   85
       Interactions with Endogenous Systems   85

Suspected Mechanism of Therapeutic Action   85
Mesolimbic Dopamine Blockade   85
Minor Side Effects   86
Major Side Effects   87
   Acute Dyskinesias   87
   Tardive Dyskinesias   89
   Neuroleptic Malignant Syndrome   92
Toxicity   92
Which Antipsychotic Is Best?   92
Long-Term Maintenance   93
   The Role of Psychotherapy   93
   Side Effects   93
   Tolerance and Dependency   93
   Compliance Problems   93
   When to Stop Drug Treatment   94
Chapter Summary   94
Review Essay Questions   95
References   95

CHAPTER 8   DEPRESSION   98

The Disorder   98
   Incidence   98
   Differential Diagnosis, Subtypes, and the DSM-IIIR   99
   Nervous System Abnormalities: The Monoamine Deficiency Hypothesis   100
Tricyclic Antidepressants for Depression   100
   Basic Pharmacology   100
   Effects on Symptoms of Depression   101
   Interactions with Endogenous Systems   103
   Suspected Mechanism of Therapeutic Action   104
   Side Effects   105
   Toxicity   105
Monoamine Oxidase Inhibitors (MAOIs) for Depression   106
   Basic Pharmacology   106
   Effects on Symptoms of Depression   107
   Interaction with Endogenous Systems and Suspected Mechanism of Action   107
   Side Effects   107
   Toxicity   108
Other Drug Treatments for Depression   108
Long-Term Antidepressant Treatment   109
   The Role of Psychotherapy   109
   Which Antidepressant Is Best?   110
   Compliance Problems   111
   Tolerance and Dependency   111
   Drug Holidays   112
   When to Stop Drug Treatment   112
Chapter Summary   113
Review Essay Questions   114
References   114

CHAPTER 9   MANIA   **119**

The Disorder   119
Basic Symptoms   119
Differential Diagnosis and the DSM-IIIR   120
Incidence and Subtypes   120
Nervous System Abnormalities   121
Basic Pharmacology of Lithium   121
Effects of Lithium on Symptoms of Bipolar Affective Disorder (BAD)   122
Acute Depression   122
Acute Mania   122
Relapse   123
Interactions with Endogenous Systems   123
Effects of Neurotransmitters   123
Effects on Second Messengers   123
Suspected Mechanism of Therapeutic Action   123
Side Effects   124
Toxicity   125
Toxicity from Overdose   126
Treatment for Toxicity   126
Long-Term Use of Lithium   126
The Role of Psychotherapy   126
Therapeutic Onset   127
Importance of Plasma Levels vs. Dose   127
Drug Interactions   128
Compliance, Tolerance, and Dependency   128
Drug Holidays and when to Stop Treatment   128
Other Drugs for Mania and/or BAD   128
Chapter Summary   129
Review Essay Questions   129
References   130

CHAPTER 10   GENERALIZED ANXIETY DISORDER   **133**

The Disorder   133
Differential Diagnosis and the DSM-IIIR   133
Nervous System Abnormalities in GAD   134
Benzodiazapine Treatment of GAD   135
Basic Pharmacology   135
Effects on Symptoms of GAD   137
Interactions with Endogenous Systems   138
Suspected Mechanism of Action: Neuromodulation of GABA   138
Side Effects   139
Toxicity   140
Long-Term Use of Benzodiazapines   140
Nonbenzodiazapine Treatment of GAD   143
Chapter Summary   144
Review Essay Questions   144
References   145

CHAPTER 11   ATTENTION DEFICIT DISORDER   **148**

The Disorder 148
Basic Symptoms 148
Differential Diagnosis and the DSM-IIIR 148
Nervous System Abnormalities in ADD 150
Basic Pharmacology of Methylphenidate 150
Effects on Symptoms of ADD and Hyperactivity 151
Amelioration of Symptoms 151
"Paradoxical Effect" 152
Rate-Dependent Effects 152
Effectiveness in Adolescents and Adults 152
Interaction with Endogenous Systems 153
Suspected Mechanism of Action 154
Monamine Agonist Effect 154
General Stimulant Effect 154
Side Effects 155
Toxicity 156
Long-Term Use of Methylphenidate 156
The Role of Psychotherapy 156
Compliance 156
Tolerance and Dependency 156
Drug Holidays 157
When to Stop Treatment 157
Other Drugs Used to Treat ADD 158
Chapter Summary 159
Review Essay Questions 160
References 160

CHAPTER 12   DRUG ABUSE   **164**

The Disorder 164
Stigmatizing Label, Psychological Problem, or Mental Illness? 164
Risks of Pharmacological Treatment 166
Varieties of Techniques to Aid Cessation or Reduction of Drug Use 166
Technique 1. Substitute For "Safer" Intoxication and/or to Avoid Withdrawal 167
Technique 2. Suppress Symptoms of Drug Cessation 168
Technique 3. Block Drug Effects 168
Technique 4. Punish Drug Consumption 168
Technique 5. Treat Underlying Disorder 168
Treatment of Heroin Abuse 169
Psychopharmacotherapeutics 169
Methadone 169
Naltrexone 170
Clonidine 172
Summary of Drug Treatment of Heroin Abuse 174
Treatment of Alcohol Abuse 175
Lithium and Antidepressants 175
Antianxiety Agents 175
Antabuse 176
Summary of Drug Treatment of Alcohol Abuse 178

Treatment of Nicotine Abuse   179
　Nicotine-Containing Chewing Gum   179
　Summary of Drug Treatment of Nicotine Abuse   180
Treatment of Cocaine Abuse   181
　Lithium   181
　Methylphenidate   182
　Tricyclic Antidepressants   182
　Dopaminergic Agonists   183
　Summary of Drug Treatment of Cocaine Abuse   183
Chapter Summary   184
Review Essay Questions   184
References   185

PART C   ABUSABLE DRUGS

CHAPTER 13   MOTIVATIONS FOR USE AND PRIMARY DANGERS   190
Problems in Developing Scientific Theories of Drug Use and Abuse   190
　An Emotion-Charged Issue   190
　Lack of Agreement in the Scientific Community   191
　Changeability in Motivators for Drug Use   191
　Various Levels of Drug Use   192
Theories of Drug Use and Abuse   193
　Personality   194
　Social and Cultural Factors   194
　Learning   194
　Neurobiology   195
　Combined Approaches   195
　Summary of Theories of Motivation for Drug Use   196
Primary Dangers of Acute Use   196
　Drug Interactions   196
　Behavioral Toxicity   197
　Organ Toxicity   197
　Overdose   197
　Summary of Primary Dangers of Acute Use   198
Primary Dangers of Chronic Use   198
　Tolerance and Sensitization   198
　Compulsive Use and Physical Dependency   198
　Brain and Other Organ Damage   199
　Violence and/or Psychosis   199
　Summary of Primary Dangers of Chronic Use   200
Chapter Summary   201
Review Essay Questions   201
References   201

**CHAPTER 14   RESEARCH METHODOLOGY AND A SYSTEM
OF CATEGORIZATION   206**
Research Methodology   206
　Retrospective Studies   207
　Pharmacoepidemiology   208

Prospective Studies   209
Summary of Research Methodology   211

Categories of Drugs   211
Categorization by Legal Status   212
Categorization Based on Full Dose-Response Curves   213
Summary of Categorization of Drugs   216

Chapter Summary   217

Review Essay Questions   217

References   218

CHAPTER 15   STIMULANTS   220

Commonalities and Differences   220
A Partial List of Stimulants   220
The Full Dose-Response Curve Revisited   221
Time- and Place-Dependent Differences   221
True Within-Class Differences   222
Summary of Commonalities and Differences   223

Basic Pharmacology   223
Cocaine   223
Caffeine   224
Nicotine   225
Strychnine   225
Summary of Basic Pharmacology of Stimulants   226

Sites and Mechanisms of Stimulant Action   226
Cocaine   226
Caffeine   227
Nicotine   228
Strychnine   228
Summary of Sites and Mechanisms of Stimulant Action   229

Acute Side Effects at Low and Medium Doses   230
Cocaine   231
Caffeine   231
Nicotine   232
Strychnine   232
Summary of Acute Side Effects At Low and Medium Doses   232

Overdose   233
Differential Symptoms and Treatment   233
Summary of Overdose   235

Interactions   235

Chronic Effects   236
Brain and Other Organ Damage   236
Tolerance and Sensitization   237
Cross-Tolerance and Cross-Sensitization   237
Physical Dependency/Compulsive Use   238
Stimulant-Induced Violence and/or Psychosis   239
Summary of Chronic Effects   241

Chapter Summary   241

Review Essay Questions   242

References   242

CHAPTER 16   DEPRESSANTS   **245**

Commonalities and Differences 245
   Characteristics of Depressants   245
   Subcategories 246
   True Within-Class Differences   247
   Summary of Commonalities and Differences   247
Basic Pharmacology   247
   Ethyl Alcohol   247
   Morphine 248
   Pentobarbital 249
   Summary of Basic Pharmacology 250
Sites and Mechanisms of Depressant Action   251
   Ethyl Alcohol   251
   Morphine 252
   Pentobarbital 254
   Summary of Sites and Mechanisms of Action   254
Acute Side Effects at Low and Medium Doses   255
   Ethyl Alcohol   255
   Morphine 256
   Pentobarbital 257
   Summary of Acute Side Effects at Low and Medium Doses   257
Overdose 258
Interactions 259
Chronic Effects 259
   Ethyl Alcohol   259
   Morphine 261
   Pentobarbital   263
   Summary of Chronic Effects   264
Chapter Summary 265
Review Essay Questions 265
References 265

CHAPTER 17   HALLUCINOGENS   **272**

Commonalities and Differences 272
   The Labeling Problem   273
   Summary of Commonalities and Differences   274
Basic Pharmacology 274
   Marijuana 274
   LSD   275
   MDMA 276
   Summary of Basic Pharmacology 277
Sites and Mechanisms of Action   277
   Marijuana 277
   LSD   278
   MDMA 278
   Summary of Sites and Mechanisms of Action   279
Acute Side Effects at Low and Medium Doses   279
   Marijuana 280
   LSD   281

MDMA   281
Summary of Acute Side Effects at Low and Medium Doses   282
Overdose   283
Chronic Effects   284
Marijuana   284
LSD   287
MDMA   290
Summary of Chronic Effects   290
Chapter Summary   291
Review Essay Questions   292
References   292

CHAPTER 18   PHENCYCLINOIDS   299
Brief History   299
Chemical Diversity   300
Basic Pharmacology   301
Sites and Mechanisms of Action   303
Acute Side Effects at Low and Medium Doses   303
Overdose   304
Chronic Effects   306
Tolerance and Sensitization   306
Physical Dependency/Compulsive Use   306
Violence and/or Psychosis   306
Brain and Other Organ Damage   308
Chapter Summary   308
Review Essay Questions   309
References   309

INDEX   313

PREFACE

Discussions of the effects of drugs on human behavior and society often result in heated arguments that make scientific evidence less important than emotion, prejudice, and mystical notions about the powers of "drugs." The purpose of this text is to introduce you to the methodology and results of research aimed at providing scientific answers to the emotional questions surrounding study of the effects of drugs on human behavior and society. To accomplish this end, it is necessary to cover the widest possible range of drugs. Many textbooks cover only those drugs that are used and abused by the general population for recreational purposes. Other textbooks cover only those drugs whose physical and psychological effects are said to be therapeutic for behavioral disorders. This text provides a unique perspective on drugs that effect society and human behavior by applying a rigorously scientific approach to both of these categories of drugs.

In order to enable you to maintain a scientific perspective throughout the reading of this text, coverage of behavioral medicines precedes coverage of recreational drug use and abuse. This approach enables a clearer understanding of behavioral medicines by allowing discussion of key concepts without some of the emotional distractions associated with discussions of drug abuse. When these same concepts are reintroduced in later chapters dealing with recreational drug use and abuse, the scientific perspective gained in early exposures may allow you to more easily apply this perspective despite previous bias and prejudice. For example, by first focusing on why some patients refuse to take medication that is known to be effective in reducing the symptoms of a distressing behavioral disorder, it becomes easier to later understand the motivations of individuals who self-administer drugs sometimes in the face of obvious and profound negative effects. Consideration of the effect of method of adminstration upon the therapeutic effectiveness of a behavioral medicine can enable greater understanding of later discussions of the effects of method of administration upon the acute and chronic consequences of recreational drug use and abuse. An understanding of how societal views of behavioral medicines can increase or decrease their effectiveness can ease the task of determining which effects of abused drugs are influenced by the way these compounds are viewed by the general society. For a final example, early chapters provide knowledge about the influence of basic pharmacology and interactions with endogenous systems upon the side effects and long-term use of behavioral medicine. This can later allow an easier grasp of the principle that understanding of the side effects and long-term consequences of recreational drug use and abuse also requires knowledge of a particular abusable drug's basic pharmacology and interactions with endogenous system.

No text covering such complicated issues can stand alone in the education of the individual. The text is designed to gently introduce the reader to facts from the fields of research design, abnormal psychology, learning theory, and physiological psychology that are necessary for a sophisticated understanding of the effects of drugs upon human behavior and the society in which we live. The first portion of the text provides a basic overview of the science of psychopharmacology. The first two chapters discuss the anatomy and characteristics of individual cells of the nervous system, as well as the way that these cells are organized within the anatomy of the nervous system. While these chapters are no substitute for a more thorough course on human anatomy and physiological psychology, they provide enough information for any reader to obtain full advantage of facts presented later. An entire chapter is then devoted to revealing the importance of understanding the basic pharmacology of any drug. All subsequent discussions of particular drugs include summaries of the basic pharmacology of that drug. A chapter that describes the ways in which drug effects occur and the ways in which scientists describe drug effects is followed by a chapter that discusses tolerance, sensitization, and physical dependence.

The second major portion of this book covers behavioral medicines used by physicians to treat behavioral disorders. An initial chapter details the history of treatment of behavioral disorders, the research methods employed in determining whether a medicine is safe and effective, and the various controversies that surround the issue of treating behavioral disorders with drugs. This initial coverage is followed by detailed presentations of facts and experiments about drugs used for a variety of behavioral disorders, including schizophrenia, depression, mania, anxiety, and hyperactivity. Although some other texts mention the use of psychiatric medicines in the treatment of drug abuse, this text is unique in that an entire chapter is devoted to this topic. There is a special emphasis upon applying the scientific methods used when studying other behavioral disorders to the special problems of using drugs to treat a disorder involving excessive self-administration of a recreational drug.

Further understanding of the use of drugs for the treatment of drug abuse can be gained by examining the final chapters of the text. In the first chapters of this final section, theories of motivations for use and abuse, medical assessments of the primary dangers of acute and chronic drug use, and the research methodology and system of classification employed by scientists to study these drugs are presented to remind you of the appropriateness of maintaining a scientific perspective. Subsequent chapters investigate the commonalities and similarities among and within different classes of abused recreational drugs. The text provides specific examples using representative compounds that reveal the characteristics of stimulants, depressants, hallucinogens, and phencyclinoids.

There is simply no way around the fact that a complete understanding of the effects of drugs on human behavior requires the memorizing of specific facts, the acquisition of knowledge about research methods used to obtain these facts, and practice at applying these facts about drugs to questions about the impact of drugs upon society and the behavior of individuals. Readers who take the time to memorize facts about basic pharmacology and interactions with endogenous systems will be rewarded for their efforts. Tables and figures have been strategically placed throughout the text to help you decide which facts must be memorized and to provide you with visual images that will aid your memory. Section summaries, chapter summaries, and review essay questions can help you decide whether you have paid sufficient attention to specific facts and their application to issues.

Throughout the text, your ability to comprehend information in any one chapter is based upon the assumption that you have understood material in previous chapters. Unless you have a strong background in learning theory, abnormal psychology, research methodology, and physiological psychology, it would be unwise to attempt to read any of Chapters 7 through 12 without having first read Chapters 1 through 6. Similarly, Chapters 15 through 18 are best read after having studied, at least, the materials in Chapter 1 through 6 as well as Chapters 13 and 14.

Some of what is stated in this book may be contrary to messages you have heard before from the media, your teachers, and drug abuse "experts." Whenever possible, references to the published literature accompanies statements of fact or interpretations of data. You are encouraged to examine this original literature at every opportunity. Doing so will provide you with a wealth of additional information, and will allow you to verify the accuracy of the presentation of information in this text. It is hoped that the study of this text will be only the beginning of your involvement in the scientific literature pertaining to behavioral medicines, abusable recreational drugs, and their effects upon individuals and society.

ACKNOWLEDGMENTS

The staff at the Olin-Chalmers Library at Kenyon College was of great help in acquiring the information contained in this text. Special thanks to Carol Singer, Carol Marshall, and Allan Bosch. Drs. Michael Levine and Jon Williams read early drafts and made many valuable comments. Special efforts in the reading of the text, and encouragement throughout the writing process, were provided by Dr. Charles Rice. Of course, any errors or omissions in the text are the sole responsibility of the author. This text would have been impossible without the aid and encouragement of the staff at Prentice Hall, including especially Mr. Robert Thoreson, Ms. Susan Finnemore, Ms. Elaine Lynch, and the following people who served as reviewers for the publisher: Ray Goldberg, Ph.D., SUNY - Cortland; Mitchell J. Picker, Ph.D., Department of Psychology, University of North Carolina at Chapel Hill; John H. Hannigan, Ph.D., Center for Behavioral Teratology, SUNY-Albany; John P. Broida, Department of Psychology, University of Southern Maine; James S. MacDonall, Department of Psychology, Fordham University; and S.W. Sadava, Ph.D., Department of Psychology, Brock University. Finally, and most importantly, I acknowledge the invaluable contribution made by Mr. Charles Beneke, who created all the figures in this text, and thus painstakingly converted my jumbled ideas into graceful works of art.

Chapter 1

CELLS, CHEMICALS, AND NEURONAL COMMUNICATION

The purposes of this chapter are to:

1. Introduce the anatomy of the special cells called neurons,

2. Present the nature and function of some non-neuronal cells of the nervous system,

3. Explain the electrical activities of neurons, including action potentials, EPSPs, and IPSPs, and

4. Discuss neurotransmitters and neuromodulators, including their function, names, synthesis, and degradation.

SYNAPTIC ANATOMY: A SPECIALIZED CELL

The most important effect of drugs on the body is their influence on the activity of highly specialized cells called **neurons**. The connections between neurons form the basic unit of communication in the human body. Since neurons are cells, they have all the usual subcellular structures (such as the nucleus, Golgi bodies, and mitochondria) needed by any cell in the human body. However, neurons are specialized cells and therefore have additional characteristics.

Typical Intracellular Structures

Figure 1.1 presents a schematic drawing of a typical neuron with **dendrites** at one end, the **axon** at the other end, and the **cell body** in the middle. The cell body contains most of the life-sustaining structures common to all cells.

Neuronal Membrane

The **neuronal membrane** is a baglike structure that contains the cell body, dendrites, and axon[12]. The neuronal membrane separates the contents of the neuron from the surrounding environment. The special electrical characteristics of this membrane enable the neuron to perform its role as the basic unit of communication in the nervous system.

Dendrites. There is a unique anatomy to the neuron[11]. At one end (see Figure 1.1) is an extensive branching, which reminded early neuroanatomists of the branches of a tree. Thus, the structures at this end of the neuron are named dendrites, from the Latin word for branches. Information from other neurons arrives at the dendrites of the typical neuron. **Receptors**, large and very specific molecules in the neuronal membrane of the dendrites, receive and react to this information, transmitting it to other parts of the neuron.

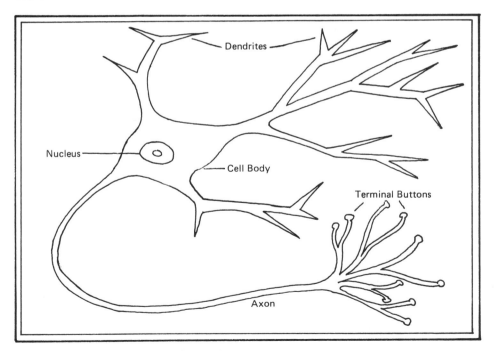

Figure 1.1. Schematic of neuron, showing dendrites, axon, and cell body.

Axon.   At the other end of the neuron in Figure 1.1 is the axon, with less extensive branching and the addition of a round nodule at the end of each branch. Information usually travels from the axon of one neuron to the dendrites of the next neuron. The axon begins at the **axon hillock**, a structure which can't be seen with the eye. It is, however, easy to identify by its special electrical characteristics. The rounded nodules at the end of the axons are **terminal buttons**.

Vesicles.   Inside the terminal buttons are sacs, called **vesicles**, that contain **neurotransmitters** or **neuromodulators**. Neurotransmitters and neuromodulators are the chemicals that neurons use to communicate with one another. The neurotransmitters are produced in the cell body of the neuron and travel down to the terminal buttons of the **axon**, where they are packaged in the vesicles. The names, purpose, production, and breakdown of these chemicals will be discussed in detail later in this chapter.

The Synapse.   The point at which two neurons meet and communicate with each other is the **synapse** (see Figure 1.2). A synapse is usually formed at the junction of the axon of one neuron and the dendrites of another neuron. The area between the two neurons is the **synaptic gap** or **synaptic cleft.** The neuron that contributes the axon, and

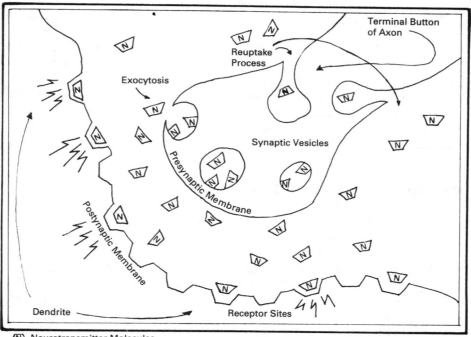

/N\ Neurotransmitter Molecules

Figure 1.2. Schematic synapse, showing dendrites, axon, and synaptic gap or cleft. A schematic neuron similar to this one will be used throughout the text to illustrate the mechanism(s) of action of specific drugs.

is thus sending the information, is the **presynaptic neuron,** while the neuron that receives information through its dendrites is the **postsynaptic neuron.** When certain conditions are met in the presynaptic neuron, the neurotransmitters contained in the vesicles of the axon's terminal buttons are released into the synaptic cleft. This process, called **exocytosis,** occurs when the vesicles literally move to and fuse with the membrane of the terminal buttons, thus spilling their contents into the synaptic cleft.

  Receptors. The neurotransmitters move through the synaptic cleft and **bind** to receptors on the dendrites of the postsynaptic neuron. This bond is not permanent. After the neurotransmitter exerts its effect, it is let go and either destroyed or recycled. The action of the neurotransmitter upon the receptor influences the electrical activity of the postsynaptic neuron. Depending upon a number of conditions, the postsynaptic neuron will then either release or fail to release its own neurotransmitters onto the dendrites of the next neuron.

Convergence and Divergence

  Since each neuron has both dendrites and an axon, it can act as either a presynaptic or postsynaptic neuron. To keep things simple, the discussion of communication among neurons has so far had one neuron sending information and one neuron receiving information. In reality, a postsynaptic neuron receives a **convergence** of information from a large number of neurons, each of which sends an axon to the dendrites of the postsynaptic neuron. In addition, each presynaptic neuron has a **divergence** of outputs. That is, the terminal buttons of the presynaptic neuron are likely to connect to the dendrites of a number of different postsynaptic neurons. Figure 1.3 presents a model neuron accepting a convergence of incoming information from a number of presynaptic neurons. This model neuron is also sending out a divergence of information to many postsynaptic neurons. The complexity of the convergence and divergence of neuronal connections accounts for the remarkable variations in thought and behavior of humans.

NON-NEURONAL CELLS OF THE NERVOUS SYSTEM

There are a number of cells in the nervous system that are not neurons. These **non-neuronal cells** perform a variety of roles necessary for the proper functioning of the nervous system. Although each type of non-neuronal cell has a different name, the general term for all the different types is **glia.** This name, which is Latin for "glue," reflects the fact that early anatomists thought that the sole function of these cells was to hold neurons in their permanent positions. In fact, the earliest name for these cells was the German word "Nervenkitt," which is probably best translated as "nerve putty"[14]. However, it is now known that glial cells do things in addition to "gluing" neurons into position. Glial cells also insulate the neuron, particularly the axon, from the electrical activity of other neurons. In addition, they scavenge dead neurons, and are perhaps the physical basis of the **blood-brain barrier**[10].

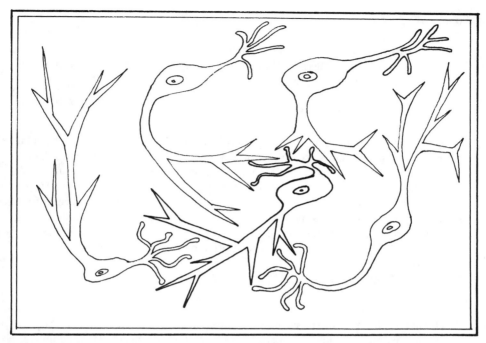

Figure 1.3. Schematic neurons showing convergence and divergence. Note that the neuron in the middle receives input from a number of other neurons and also sends output to many other neurons.

The Blood-Brain Barrier

The idea of the blood-brain barrier came about because some drugs were unable to effect the brain but did effect other areas of the body. This was initially explained by assuming that some impenetrable barrier existed between the blood and the brain. A more thorough understanding of drug action has revealed that the blood-brain barrier is far from absolute. That is, drugs said not to cross the blood-brain barrier are merely much less likely to get to the brain than drugs that are able to cross the barrier. Most drugs usually thought to not cross the barrier are able to gain access to the brain if the drug is given in a sufficiently large dose[5].

Each neuron is provided with oxygen and nutrients by the tiny capillaries of blood vessels. The physical basis of the blood-brain barrier is a special type of glial cell that is in the space between these blood vessels and the neuron. The glial cell allows oxygen and nutrients to freely pass from blood vessel to neuron. Drugs that cross the blood-brain barrier can easily get from the blood vessel, through the glial cell, into the neuron. Drugs that are not able to pass the barrier are less capable of passing through the glial cell, and are thus less capable of gaining access to the neuron[4].

ACTION POTENTIALS

The release of neurotransmitter by the presynaptic neuron is triggered by the occurrence of an **action potential**. An action potential (AP) occurs when the normal concentration of ions in and around the neuron changes significantly.

Resting Potential

The neuronal membrane maintains a **disequilibrium**, or lack of balance, in the concentrations of certain charged molecules (ions) in the neuron and in the extracellular fluid around it. The most important imbalances are the excess of sodium outside the cell and the excess of potassium inside the cell. These two cause a **polarity**, an electrical difference between the inside and outside of the neuron. This electrical difference is the **resting potential**, measured in thousandths of a volt (mV). While the resting potential varies from neuron to neuron, if the outside of the neuron is, for reference purposes, set at zero then the inside of the axon will often be found to be at about -70 mV.

Sequence of Events during AP

When presynaptic neurons send the proper information, the resting potential at the axon hillock of the postsynaptic neuron becomes less negative. If this change in the resting potential reaches a specific level, that is, if **threshold** is achieved, an action potential occurs. The action potential is described by the **all-or-none law.** This law holds that if the change in resting potential does not reach threshold, no action potential occurs. In addition, the action potential is always of the same magnitude. Changes in resting potentials that exceed threshold do not result in bigger, stronger, or more intense action potentials. Thus, a neuron either gets *all* of the typical action potential *or* it gets *none* of it. If an action potential occurs at the axon hillock, it is transmitted all the way down the axon and results in **exocytosis**, the release of neurotransmitter from the vesicles of the terminal buttons into the synaptic cleft.

Ionic Basis of AP

During the action potential, a complicated series of events results in the membrane allowing sodium to rush into the neuron. This is followed by a period of time during which the membrane allows potassium to leave the neuron. When the action potential in any particular neuron ends with the release of neurotransmitter, the neuron does not simply return to the resting potential. There is a short period of time when the inside of the neuron is even more negative than it was before. This is the **refractory period**. The refractory period is ended when the **sodium-potassium "pump"** restores the original balance of sodium and potassium and thus restores the original resting potential. The entire process of the action potential, from the hitting of threshold in the axon hillock to the beginning of exocytosis in the terminal button, takes approximately 150 thousandths of a second[2].

EPSPs and IPSPs

Definitions and Descriptions of Events

When the neurotransmitters of the presynaptic neuron interact with the receptors of the postsynaptic neuron, they do one of two things. They may cause the resting potential (-70 mV) of the dendrites to become less negative. This makes the neuron less polarized (**hypopolarized**). This change in the resting potential can then spread through the synaptic membrane from the dendrites to the cell body to the axon, causing the axon hillock to approach threshold. A hypopolarization at the dendrite, which excites the entire postsynaptic neuron, is referred to as an **EPSP**, for **E**xcitatory **P**ost**S**ynaptic **P**otential. On the other hand, the neurotransmitter/receptor interaction may cause the dendrites to become more negative than the -70 mV resting potential. This makes the neuron more polarized (**hyperpolarized**). The spread of this disturbance will make it less likely that the axon hillock of the postsynaptic neuron will generate an action potential. A hyperpolarization at the dendrite, which inhibits the entire postsynaptic neuron, is referred to as an **IPSP**, for **I**nhibitory **P**ost**S**ynaptic **P**otential[7].

Ionic Basis

The resting potential at the axon hillock fluctuates as the many presynaptic neurons converging on the single postsynaptic neuron cause IPSPs or EPSPs. Unlike action potentials, EPSPs and IPSPs are **graded potentials** that do not follow the all-or-none law. Postsynaptic potentials may be small or large and they **dissipate**, or fade away, over time and space. No single postsynaptic potential is likely to be enough to achieve threshold. However, the postsynaptic neuron acts as a little calculator, **summating** (adding and subtracting) the influences of the various EPSPs and IPSPs. If there is enough depolarization, threshold is reached and the postsynaptic neuron experiences an action potential. The postsynaptic neuron then exerts its own influence on the many neurons to which it diverges. If there is insufficient depolarization or an excess of IPSPs, threshold is not reached and no action potential occurs in the postsynaptic neuron[13].

NEUROTRANSMITTERS (NTs) AND NEUROMODULATORS (NMs)

Two Forms of Information Transfer

Neurotransmitters are frequently labeled as either excitatory or inhibitory, depending on whether they cause EPSPs or IPSPs, respectively, in the postsynaptic neuron. However, the postsynaptic receptor is equally important in determining whether the neurotransmitter causes EPSPs or IPSPs. One neurotransmitter may bind to more than one type of receptor. A neurotransmitter may cause an EPSP when it interacts with one kind of receptor and yet cause an IPSP at a different receptor on a different postsynaptic neuron. In addition, any one neuron may contain more than one chemical in the vesicles in the terminal buttons(colocalization)[9], but all the vesicles of any single neuron contain the same combination of chemicals.

In future chapters, the way specific drugs affect the body and behavior are described in sections on "Mechanisms of Action." In most cases, the effects of drugs can be explained by saying that the drug mimics and/or prevents the interaction of various neurotransmitters with their specific receptor(s). It is important to remember that these drugs then affect behavior by influencing the balance of sodium and potassium and thus increase or decrease the EPSPs or IPSPs that would normally occur at these synapses.

However, EPSPs and IPSPs are not the only way that the contents of synaptic vesicles influence the resting potential of the postsynaptic neuron. Some vesicles contain **neuromodulators**, compounds that do not themselves induce EPSPs or IPSPs, but instead modulate the influence of neurotransmitters[3,8]. That is, if a postsynaptic neuron has had a neuromodulator attached to specific receptors, the EPSPs or IPSPs caused by the binding of neurotransmitters to other receptors will be either enhanced or weakened.

An analogy helps explain the role of neuromodulation. If someone inexperienced with televisions came upon one that wasn't turned on, she might investigate the device by spinning a number of the attractive dials that protrude from its surface. After spinning the dial marked, "volume," she might decide that it accomplishes absolutely nothing. If someone else then turned on the television, she would discover that the volume dial does indeed have an effect. If, and only if, the television is on could the volume dial increase or decrease the intensity of sound coming from the device. When scientists first attempted to discover the function of certain chemicals found in the nervous system, the scientists thought the chemicals served no function because they induced no EPSPs or IPSPs. However, it was later discovered that the substances could influence the electrical potential of neurons, but only in the presence of EPSPs and IPSPs induced by other chemicals. These neuromodulators were therefore like the apparently useless volume dial on the television which exerted no effect unless the television was turned on and receiving signals.

Neuromodulators may be released into the synaptic cleft either by presynaptic neurons that contain only that chemical or as the result of release of colocalized chemicals. The complexity of neuronal communication is, however, enhanced by the fact that neuromodulators can also be released into the bloodstream from organs outside the nervous system. For example, some of the behavioral effects of puberty can be explained as the result of blood-borne hormones that gain access to the brain and exert a modulating effect upon ongoing EPSPs and IPSPs[6].

Common NTs and NMs

A large number of chemicals found in the body have been proposed to be neurotransmitters and/or neuromodulators. Table 1.1 presents a partial list of some of the best understood of these chemicals. It is often incorrect to claim that a chemical is exclusively one or the other. A substance that acts as a neuromodulator at one receptor

Table 1.1
A Partial List of Neurotransmitters and Neuromodulators

Acetylcholine	Glycine	Vasopressin
Dopamine	Adenosine	ACTH
Epinephrine	Glutamate	Endorphins
Norepinephrine	GABA	Enkaphalins
Serotonin		

may actually induce EPSPs or IPSPs at other receptors, thus making it a neurotransmitter as well[3]. Whether neurotransmitters or neuromodulators, these molecules are natural chemicals, constructed in the body mainly from raw materials found in food. Since they are made in the body, they are referred to as **endogenous compounds**. Throughout this book, they will be contrasted with **exogenous drugs**, compounds from outside the body that are nonetheless capable of influencing neuronal communication. Exogenous drugs can only influence behavior if they influence the activity of these endogenous compounds. When the specifics of these influences are better understood, it may be possible to induce the behavioral effects of drugs by directly influencing endogenous compounds through diet, exercise, meditation etc. Thus, drug effects may be obtainable without taking drugs[15].

Enzymes in Synthesis and Degradation

For many of these endogenous compounds, we know the way the body puts the compounds together (**synthesis**) and the way these compounds are broken apart (**metabolism**). A thorough understanding of these processes makes it easier to understand how some drugs can interfere with the normal actions of neurotransmitters and neuromodulators. The body starts with a **precursor**, the raw material, and uses **enzymes** to change the precursor into a **product**. Enzymes are special protein molecules that help convert precursors into products. Enzymes themselves are not changed by this reaction, so as soon as they are finished, they release the product and can begin another conversion. The product of this enzymatic effort then sometimes becomes the precursor for the next step in synthesis. Metabolism also is done by enzymes. The precursor in this case is the product of previous synthesis. The products of metabolism are called **metabolites**[1]. They are frequently easier for the body to dispose of than the original compound. Figure 1.4 is a schematic diagram showing the role of precursors, products, and enzymes in the synthesis and metabolism of endogenous substances.

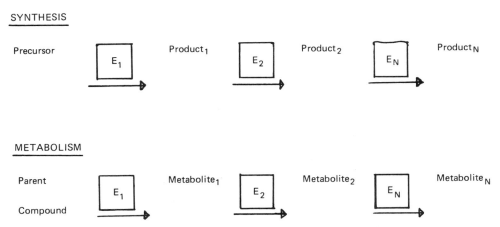

Figure 1.4. The role of precursors, products, and enzymes in the synthesis and metabolism of endogenous substances. Synthesis and metabolism might require only one step involving only one enzyme, or may instead require many steps involving many different enzymes.

CHAPTER SUMMARY

Along with non-neuronal cells that provide support functions of various types, the nervous system contains specialized cells called neurons. Unique electrical characteristics and special cellular structures enable neurons to communicate with one another. Divergence describes the fact that any single neuron will release neurotransmitters and/or neuromodulators onto many different postsynaptic neurons. Convergence describes the fact that any one postsynaptic neuron will be influenced by neurotransmitters and neuromodulators from many different presynaptic neurons. The inputs received by the postsynaptic neuron involve the interaction of presynaptic neurotransmitters and neuromodulators with receptors on the postsynaptic neuron. These interactions lead to either EPSPs or IPSPs, which push the postsynaptic neuron either towards or away from having an action potential, respectively. If the sum of all converging inputs causes the postsynaptic neuron to have an action potential, then it becomes one of many presynaptic neurons influencing the next neuron in the chain of communication.

REVIEW ESSAY QUESTIONS

1. Name the special parts of the neuron that enable it to perform its function as the basic unit of communication in the nervous system.

2. List and discuss the functions of the non-neuronal cells of the nervous system.

3. Discuss the characteristics of the action potential, including the concept of threshold, the all-or-none law, the role of the resting membrane potential and the sodium-potassium "pump."

4. Present the similarities and differences of EPSPs and IPSPs. Include information about how they each differ from action potentials.

5. Describe the differences between and similarities of neurotransmitters and neuromodulators.

REFERENCES

1. Bloom, F.E. Neurohormonal transmission and the central nervous system. In A.G. Goodman, L.S. Goodman, T.W. Rall, and F. Murad (Eds.) *The pharmacological basis of therapeutics* (7th ed.). New York: Macmillan, 236-259, 1985.

2. Catterall, W.A. The molecular basis of neuronal excitability. *Science*, 1984, 223, 653-660.

3. Elliott, G.R., & Barchas, J.D. Changing concepts about neuroregulation: Neurotransmitters and neuromodulators. In D. de Wied and P.A. Van Keep (Eds.) *Hormones and the brain*. Baltimore, MD: University Park Press, 1980.

4. Fenstermacher, J. D. Current models of blood-brain transfer. *Trends in Neuroscience*, 1985, 8, 449-453.

5. Goldstein, G.W., & Getz, A.L. The blood-brain barrier. *Scientific American*, 1986, 255, 74-83.

6. *Grumbach, M.M. The neuroendocrinology of puberty. In D.T. Krieger, and J. C. Hughes (Eds.) *Neuroendocrinology*, Sunderland, MA: Sinauer Associates, 1980.

7. Hille, B. Electrical excitability and ionic channels. In G.J. Siegel, R.W. Albers, B.W. Agranoff, and R. Katzman (Eds.) *Basic neurochemistry: Molecular, cellular and medical aspects (3rd ed.)*. Boston: Little, Brown and Co., 1981.

8. Krieger, D.T. Brain peptides: What, where and why? In P.H. Abelson, E. Butz, and S.H. Snyder (Eds.) *Neuroscience*, Washington, D.C.: AAAS, 1985.

9. Lal, H., LaBella, F., & Lane, J. *Endocoids*. New York: Alan R. Liss, 1985.

10. Neuwelt, E.A. *Implications of the blood-brain barrier and its manipulation*. Summit, NJ: Plenum Press, 1988.

11. Raine, C.S. Neurocellular anatomy. In G.J. Siegel, R.W. Albers, B.W. Agranoff, and R. Katzman (Eds.) *Basic neurochemistry: Molecular, cellular and medical aspects (3rd ed.)* Boston, MA: Little, Brown and Co., 1981.

12. Singer, S.J., & Nicolson, G.L. The fluid mosaic model of the structure of cell membranes. *Science*, 1972, 175, 720-731.

13. Snyder, S.H. Drug and neurotransmitter receptors in the brain. In P.H. Abelson, E. Butz, and S.H. Snyder (Eds.) *Neuroscience*, Washington, D.C.: AAAS, 332-352, 1985.

14. Somjen, G.G. Nervenkitt: Notes on the history of the concept of neuroglia. *Glia*, 1988, 1, 2-9.

15. *Weil, A., & Rosen, W. *Chocolate to Morphine: Understanding Mind-Active Drugs*, Boston: Houghton Mifflin Company, 1986.

*Introductory or intermediate material.

Chapter 2

NERVOUS SYSTEM ANATOMY

The purposes of this chapter are to:

1. Present the basic divisions of the human nervous system,

2. Discuss in detail the peripheral nervous system, especially the neurotransmitters involved in the balance between the sympathetic and parasympathetic nervous system,

3. Provide details about the central nervous system, its major subdivisions, and the location of major neurotransmitters and neuromodulators,

4. Explain the complexities of the endocrine system, and

5. Describe how the divisions of the nervous system influence each other through parallel processing and a system of hierarchies.

NERVOUS SYSTEM GROSS ANATOMY

The anatomy of the nervous system is best approached by dividing and subdividing the nervous system into increasingly more specialized systems. Table 2.1 shows how this approach can be used to ease the memorization of the **gross anatomy** of the nervous system. Gross anatomy does not refer to the study of vile and disgusting body parts. Instead, the term is used to distinguish the study of easily observable body parts from the **microanatomy** that involves the study of cells and their components. The most general division in the gross anatomy of the nervous system is the separation into the **peripheral nervous system**, the **central nervous system**, and the **endocrine system**.

Table 2.1
Nervous System

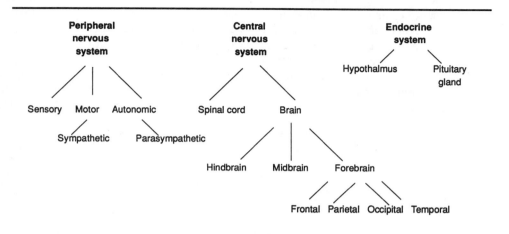

Peripheral Nervous System

Sensory, motor, and autonomic.   The peripheral nervous system can be divided into three parts, the sensory system, the motor system, and the autonomic nervous system. The **sensory system** involves all the sense organs that collect information about events in the outside world and occurrences within the body. This information is sent through **sensory nerves** (bundles of neurons) to the central nervous system. The **motor system** involves all the **motor nerves** that send information out to the muscles of the body, telling them to contract or to relax. The **autonomic nervous system** is a complex system that can be further subdivided into two parts, the **sympathetic nervous system** and the **parasympathetic nervous system**. Both of these branches of the autonomic nervous system are capable of having widespread effects throughout the body[22].

Sympathetic and parasympathetic.   The sympathetic nervous system is involved in what is often referred to as "fight or flight" emergency reactions. When activated, the sympathetic nervous system causes an increase in heart rate, an increase in attention or arousal, an increase in the utilization of energy, and an increase of blood flow to the lungs, heart, and brain. The sympathetic nervous system is activated under conditions of excitement when energy demands are high, ranging from an argument with parents, to a close encounter with a speeding automobile, to the thrill of love at first sight. While the sympathetic nervous system is active when energy needs to be used, the parasympathetic nervous system is active when things are quieter and energy is being stored. For example, the parasympathetic nervous system is activated when the individual is relaxed, such as after a meal or in the aftermath of a sexual encounter.

The two branches of the autonomic nervous system perform opposite functions. Sensibly enough, the relationship between them is one of **reciprocal inhibition**. That is, when the parasympathetic nervous system is activated, it directly suppresses, or inhibits, the level of activity in the sympathetic nervous system. When the situation demands that energy be used, the sympathetic nervous system becomes activated, and it then inhibits the level of activity in the parasympathetic nervous system. The nature and intensity of activity in the autonomic nervous system is therefore the result of the delicate balance between the two divisions of the system[9,20].

Figure 2.1 shows the anatomy and neurochemistry of both branches of the autonomic nervous system. Table 2.2 summarizes the major differences between these two branches. Each branch has its own **ganglia**, which are collections of the cell bodies

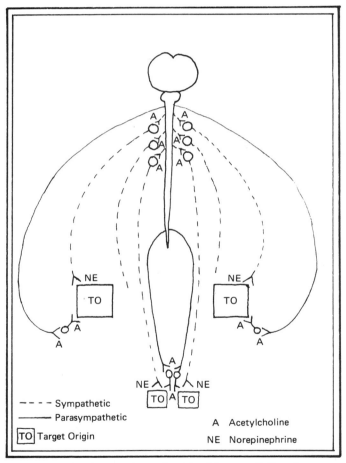

Figure 2.1 The anatomy and neurochemistry of the sympathetic and parasympathetic branches of the autonomic nervous system. Note the differences in location of the ganglia, the length of pre- and post-ganglionic fibers, and the neurotransmitters used by the two branches.

of neurons. These ganglia are connected to the central nervous system by **preganglionic fibers** (bundles of axons) attached to neurons from the spinal cord. The neurons whose cell bodies are in the ganglia send out **postganglionic fibers** to the **target organs**. Target organs are those parts of the body, including the heart, lungs, intestines, genitalia, blood vessels, etc., that are controlled by the autonomic nervous system.

The prefix "para" means "around," accurately describing the fact that the sympathetic nervous system comes from the middle area of the body, while the parasympathetic nervous system is both above and below the sympathetic branch. The sympathetic ganglia are very close to the spinal cord in the area between the lower part of the neck to just above the waist. The parasympathetic ganglia come from the area above the bottom of the neck and also from the area below the waist. Unlike the sympathetic ganglia, the ganglia of the parasympathetic branch are close to the target organ instead of close to the spinal cord.

For both the sympathetic and parasympathetic branches of the autonomic nervous system, the neurotransmitter contained within the vesicles of preganglionic fibers is acetylcholine. The receptors on the dendrites of cells that form the postganglionic fibers of both branches contain receptors for acetylcholine. Thus, drugs that mimic the action of acetylcholine will excite the postganglionic neurons of both branches, causing both of them to release neurotransmitter onto target organs. However, the two branches each use different neurotransmitters to communicate with target organs. In the sympathetic branch, the postganglionic fibers release norepinephrine onto target organs. Drugs that act like norepinephrine are sometimes called **sympathomimetics** because they cause target organs to use energy just as if there were naturally occurring activation of

Table 2.2
Differences between the Sympathetic and Parasympathetic Branches of the Autonomic Nervous System

	SYMPATHETIC	PARASYMPATHETIC
Function	Uses stored energy	Stores energy
Location	Between neck and waist	Above neck, below waist
Ganglia	Near spinal cord	Near target organs
Pregaglionic fibers	Short	Long
Postgaglionic fibers	Long	Short
Pregaglionic NT	Acetylcholine	Acetylcholine
Postgaglionic NT	Norepinephrine	Acetylcholine

the sympathetic branch[3]. The postganglionic fibers of the parasympathetic branch release acetylcholine onto their target organs. Drugs that act like acetylcholine will cause the target organs to act as if they were being stimulated by the natural influences of the parasympathetic branch. One complicating factor in the parasympathetic branch is that the receptors on the target organs are slightly different from those acetylcholine receptors that exist within the ganglion (and, incidentally, also those acetylcholine receptors that are on muscle). While endogenous acetylcholine stimulates receptors at all three sites, the receptors within the ganglion and on muscle are called **nicotinic** because they respond most strongly to nicotine (see Chapter 15). Receptors on target organs are called **muscarinic** because they respond most strongly to the drug muscarine[15].

The Central Nervous System

Brain and spinal cord. Except for information from the eyes, ears, nose, and a few other structures, all the information coming in from the sensory nerves, and going out from the motor nerves, passes through the **spinal cord.** The spinal cord, along with the **brain,** form the central nervous system. The spinal cord is the first point at which the peripheral nervous system gets access to the brain. The spinal cord is also the last point before the brain connects with the peripheral nervous system. The entire central nervous system, brain and spinal cord, is surrounded by a three-layered membrane called the **meninges.**

Hindbrain, midbrain, and forebrain. The brain can be divided into a number of different levels. These include the **hindbrain, midbrain** and **forebrain.** The hindbrain is nearest to the spinal cord, the forebrain is on top of the brain, and, obviously, the midbrain is in the middle. There are a large number of structures at each level of the brain, and there is a complicated anatomy where each part connects to many others in complex ways[4]. A thorough knowledge of brain anatomy will make it much easier to understand the complex effects of drugs that influence behavior. However, it is possible to gain some understanding of drug action by knowing only a few of the more important facts about central nervous system anatomy.

Reticular activating system. One important brain structure is a set of neurons called the **reticular activating system** or **RAS.** The RAS is a network of neurons that extends from the hindbrain, through the midbrain, to all the parts of the forebrain. There are a number of collections of cell bodies in the hindbrain that form the RAS, including a collection called the **locus coruleus.** The main neurotransmitter in the locus coruleus is norepinephrine, the same neurotransmitter released by the sympathetic postganglionic neurons onto target organs of the autonomic nervous system. It shouldn't be too surprising, then, to learn that the RAS is involved in the use of, rather than the storage of, energy. The RAS is responsible for determining the most basic levels of awareness, or consciousness, of the individual. People with extensive damage to the RAS usually die, or are at best in a coma. Drugs that act like norepinephrine will mimic the action of the RAS, causing alertness and preventing sleep[3].

Cerebral cortex. While the hindbrain determines the level of consciousness because it contains the RAS, the forebrain contains extremely important structures that determine the complexity of human interaction with the environment. In humans, a significant part of the forebrain is devoted to **cerebral cortex**, the outermost and most sophisticated portion of the brain. The cortex is split into two **cerebral hemispheres.** Figure 2.2 shows the side view of one of the cerebral hemispheres. You should note that each cerebral hemisphere consists of four sections, or **lobes**. These are, from top front to back to bottom, the **frontal, parietal, occipital,** and **temporal lobes.** While its important to avoid gross overgeneralization, it is possible to summarize the primary functions of each of these lobes. The frontal lobe is involved with movement and planning, the parietal lobe with the experience of sensory stimulation including especially the sense of touch, the occipital lobe with vision and the temporal lobe with hearing and memory[11].

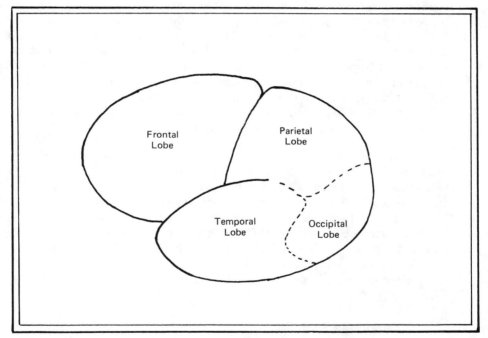

Figure 2.2   A side view of the left cerebral hemisphere, showing the location of the frontal, parietal, occipital, and temporal lobes.

The two hemispheres are connected by neurons that form thick bundles as they cross from one hemisphere to the other. The largest of these is the **corpus callosum.** The corpus callosum is sometimes cut to prevent the spread of epilepsy. These so-called **split-brain patients** have had much to do with our understanding of the different specialties of the two cerebral hemispheres. Of course, in normal humans, both hemispheres are involved in all activities that require the use of the brain[24].

The brain uses about one-quarter of the body's blood supply, even at rest. Four major arteries provide the brain with its blood supply. These include the two **vertebral arteries** and the two **internal carotids**. These four arteries form the **circle of Willis** at the base of the brain. They then branch out into specific arteries that supply blood to specific areas of the brain. In particular, the **basilar** arteries supply the hindbrain, the **anterior cerebral branches** supply the middle portions of each hemisphere, the **posterior cerebral branches** supply the back part of each hemisphere, and the **middle cerebral branches** take care of the rest of the brain. After circulating through the brain, blood with waste products pools in a variety of **venous sinuses** prior to passing out of the brain via a system of **veins**[2,22].

Ventricles, CSF, and meninges. The brain is not a solid structure. There is within the brain a series of interconnected open spaces called **ventricles**. These ventricles connect to a **central canal** that extends to the end of the spinal column. Special cells in the ventricles, called **ependymal cells**, produce a fluid called **cerebrospinal fluid** or **CSF**. This fluid circulates through the ventricles and down the central canal to exit points. CSF surrounds the entire central nervous system by circulating between the layers of the **meninges**, special membranes that surround the central nervous system. The CSF performs two main functions. First, it acts as a fluid cushion to protect the delicate brain and spinal cord from colliding with the hard bones of the skull and spinal column. Second, it helps remove waste products from the brain and spinal cord, delivering them to the venous sinuses to be carried away to urine and feces[22].

Major NTs and NMs. Figure 2.3 presents a highly simplified view of the location of a number of major neurotransmitters within the central nervous system. Some neurotransmitters are found in almost all areas of the central nervous system, while others are highly localized in specific areas[18,19]. For example, the neurotransmitter dopamine is found mainly in sharply defined pathways connecting major structures. Two of the more important of these pathways are the forebrain mesolimbic and nigrostriatal pathways. The mesolimbic pathway connects the "primitive" structures of the hindbrain and midbrain that are concerned with emotion to the "sophisticated" areas of the frontal lobes[10]. The nigrostriatal pathway, on the other hand, connects two areas that are very important in movement[23].

Endocrine System

Along with the peripheral nervous system, the endocrine system enables the brain and the rest of the body to interact with each other. Even though it is technically a part of the brain, the **hypothalamus** controls the rest of the endocrine system. Neurotransmitters such as dopamine, norepinephrine, and serotonin are all utilized by the brain to control the activity of the hypothalamus[13,25]. The hypothalamus then determines the activity of the **pituitary gland**[21]. The pituitary gland dangles from beneath the brain and releases specialized chemical messengers, called **hormones,** into the bloodstream. Once in the bloodstream, these hormones act at **target organs** in the rest of the body. Target organs for different hormones range from bones, to adrenal glands, to sexual organs[12].

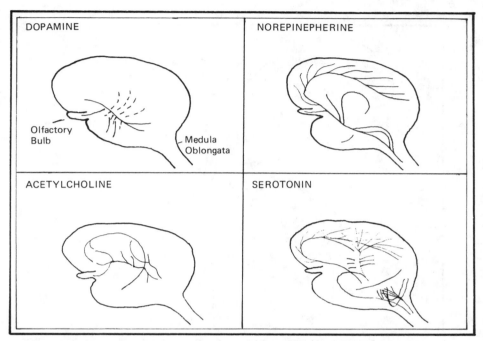

Figure 2.3 A simplified view of the location(s) of dopamine, serotonin, acetylcholine, and norepinephrine within the human brain.

The easiest way to understand the endocrine system is to view hormones as neurotransmitters and neuromodulators. Instead of crossing synaptic clefts to gain access to postsynaptic receptors, hormones get to target organs through the bloodstream. Target organs can be compared to postsynaptic neurons. Target organs have specific receptors, and can be influenced by hormones acting as either neurotransmitters or neuromodulators[16].

Close examination of the connections between the hypothalamus and the pituitary gland reveals that there are really two parts to the pituitary gland, the **anterior pituitary** and the **posterior pituitary**. Figure 2.4 presents a view of the connections of the hypothalamus to each portion of the pituitary gland.

Anterior pituitary. The anterior pituitary is that portion closest to the front of the head. It has a **vascular connection** to the hypothalamus. That is, the hypothalamus releases hormones into blood vessels that go directly to the anterior pituitary. Hormones from the hypothalamus tell the anterior pituitary to release, or to not release, specific types of anterior pituitary hormones. Table 2.3 summarizes the names and target organs of anterior pituitary hormones. An important aspect of the anterior pituitary system is that the target organs themselves often produce hormones that are released into the bloodstream. For example, anterior pituitary hormones like FSH and LH cause the ovaries of females to produce the hormones **estrogen** and **progesterone**, while they cause the testicles of males to produce the hormone **testosterone**[1].

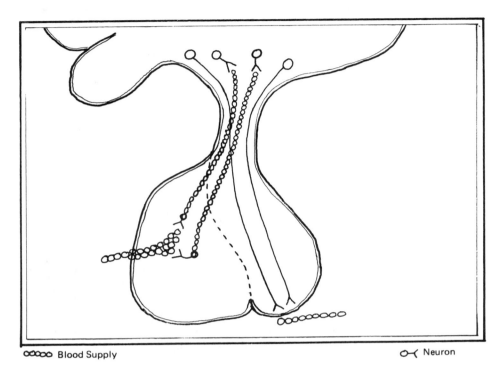

Figure 2.4. The differing hypothalamic connections to the anterior versus the posterior pituitary. Note that the connections from the hypothalamus to the anterior pituitary are made via a system of blood vessels called the portal system. On the other hand, the posterior pituitary contains the axons of neurons whose cell bodies lie in the hypothalamus.

Table 2.3
Anterior Pituitary Hormones

NAME	TARGET ORGAN(S)
Adrenocorticotropic hormone (ACTH)	Adrenal cortex
Thyroid stimulating hormone (TSH)	Thyroid gland
Follicle stimulating hormone (FSH)	Ovaries, testicles
Luteinizing hormone (LH)	Ovaries, testicles
Prolactin	Ovaries, breasts
Somatotropic hormone (STH)	Bones, muscle, pancreas
Melanocyte stimulating hormone (MSH)	Melanocytes in skin

The blood supply carries all the hormones produced by the hypothalamus, anterior pituitary and target organs to all parts of the body, including the brain. This enables control of the system through the use of **inhibitory feedback loops**[7]. Furnaces with thermostats work through inhibitory feedback loops. When the temperature goes down, the furnace goes on. The thermostat senses the heat, and shuts down the furnace. The thermostat uses the presence of heat to start a feedback loop that inhibits the furnace from producing even more heat.

Inhibitory feedback loops enable each level of the endocrine system to influence the action of the remaining levels. As mentioned above, the ovaries of a female release the hormones **estrogen** and **progesterone** in response to specific anterior pituitary hormones that were themselves released because of specific hypothalamic hormones. Estrogen and progesterone circulate in the bloodstream and eventually interact with the hypothalamus and pituitary gland. The presence of estrogen and progesterone in the blood supplied to the hypothalamus and pituitary gland means that the message to produce the hormones has been received and acted upon by the ovaries. Since the appointed task has been completed, the hypothalamus and pituitary no longer need to send signals to the ovaries. Thus, the hormones produced by the ovaries feedback to inhibit the activity of the hypothalamus and pituitary[5].

Posterior pituitary.   The remaining part of the pituitary gland is called the **posterior pituitary**. The posterior pituitary has a direct neuronal connection to the hypothalamus. That is, instead of having hypothalamic hormones reach it through the bloodstream, the posterior pituitary contains the axons of neurons with cell bodies that are actually within the hypothalamus (see Figure 2.4). When stimulated by the brain, the hypothalamic neurons have an action potential which spreads down the axon, causing the terminal buttons located in the posterior pituitary to release their hormones into the bloodstream. Only two hormones are released by the posterior pituitary. **Oxytocin** is a hormone that is responsible for the contractions of the uterus that occur during childbirth. The other hormone is known as either **vasopressin** or **antidiuretic hormone (ADH)**. This hormone results in elevated blood pressure and prevents the loss of bodily fluids through urine. Both oxytocin and vasopressin have central nervous system effects in addition to their effects on target organs. In particular, they have each been shown to have an influence on memory and mood[6].

While there are many target organs for the different hormones, the most important target organ of the endocrine system is the brain itself. Diseases of the endocrine system can have specific effects on behavior[8] and this has led to the development of hormonal treatment for some behavioral disorders[14]. Ordinary changes in the levels of various hormones can sometimes have profound effects upon behavior, as evidenced by the emotional storms suffered by adolescents during puberty. Finally, many drugs taken for their specific effect on the central nervous system have hormonal side effects that can, in turn, induce unwanted effects upon the central nervous system and behavior. Even worse, the same hormonal effects may also cause a wide range of non-behavioral effects. The influences of drugs on the hormonal system can have consequences that range from relatively minor, to bizarre, to life-threatening[17].

NERVOUS SYSTEM ORGANIZATION

The organization of the nervous system is complex and still somewhat mysterious. We do know, however, that the nervous system is organized **hierarchically** and that there is a simultaneous **parallel processing** of information[11]. "Higher" portions of the nervous system, particularly the brain, are further up in the hierarchy, or chain of command, than are the "lower" parts of the nervous system, including the sensory nerves, spinal cord, etc. Saying that a particular anatomical structure is a "higher" structure usually means that it analyzes the information collected from "lower" structures and simultaneously controls the activity of these "lower" structures. Parallel processing of information in the nervous system occurs because different levels of the hierarchy are simultaneously analyzing the same input. Each of the different structures performs a special analysis of the information. The type of analysis is determined by whether the processing is being done by a "higher" or "lower" structure. The incredible capacity of the human brain to analyze information and solve problems is due, in part, to the fact that information undergoes this parallel processing by structures arranged in a precise hierarchy.

It is relatively simple to determine the position of a part of the nervous system in the hierarchy. The three divisions of the peripheral nervous system alternate their position relative to each other, depending on the activity of the individual. However, any portion of the peripheral nervous system is always lower in the hierarchy than any particular part of the central nervous system. Of course, each part of the endocrine system controls the other through feedback loops, but it is safe to say that the hypothalamus, which is in the brain, controls the pituitary gland and that the pituitary gland controls the hormone producing organs of the body.

Conveniently enough, since humans stand upright, the position within the body of a part of the central nervous system tells whether it is higher or lower in the hierarchy than some other part. The closer a structure is to the top of the head, the higher it is in the hierarchy. For example, the forebrain is "higher" than the hindbrain, while the spinal cord is "lower" than the midbrain. The lobes of the cerebral cortex are at the top of the nervous system hierarchy. As with the divisions of the peripheral nervous system, the different lobes alternate their position relative to each other, depending upon the activity of the individual.

CHAPTER SUMMARY

The gross anatomy of the nervous system reveals that it can be divided into three major parts, the peripheral nervous system, the central nervous system and the endocrine system. Each of these systems can be further divided into components that interact with one another, and with the two other systems, in complex ways. The simplest and most powerful unifying principle of nervous system function suggests that the many different components are organized both in parallel and hierarchically.

REVIEW ESSAY QUESTIONS

1. Summarize the anatomical and neurochemical differences between the sympathetic and parasympathetic branches of the autonomic nervous system.

2. Link the anatomy of the ventricular system to the two functions of cerebrospinal fluid (CSF).

3. Compare the connections between the hypothalamus and each portion of the pituitary gland.

4. Discuss the role of inhibitory feedback loops in the regulation of the endocrine system.

5. What does it mean to say that the nervous system is organized hierarchically and it engages in simultaneous parallel processing of information?

REFERENCES

1. Adler, N. T. *Neuroendocrinology of Reproduction*, New York: Plenum Press, 1981.
2. Cartmill, M., Hylander, W.L., & Shafland, J. *Human Structure*. Cambridge, MA: Harvard University Press, 1987.
3. Coyle, J.J., & Snyder, S.H. Catecholamines. In G.J. Siegel, R.W. Albers, B.W. Agranoff & R. Katzman (Eds.) *Basic Neurochemistry: Molecular, Cellular and Medical Aspects, (3rd ed.)*. Boston: Little, Brown and Co., 205-217, 1981.
4. DeArmond, S.J., Fusco, M.M., & Dewey, M.M. *Structure of the Human Brain: A Photograpic Atlas, (3rd ed.)*. New York: Oxford University Press, 1989.
5. Donovan, B.T. *Hormones and Human Behavior*. London: Cambridge University Press, 1985.
6. Gash, D.M., & Boer, G.J. *Vasopressin: Principles and Properties*. New York: Plenum Press, 1987.
7. Hadley, M.E. *Endocrinology*. Englewood Cliffs, NJ: Prentice Hall, 1984.
8. Halbrecht, J.D. *Hormones and Depression*. New York: Raven Press, 1987.
9. Kalat, J. W. *Biological Psychology (3rd ed.)*. Belmont, CA: Wadsworth Publishing Company, 1988.
10. Kalivas, P.W., & Nemeroff, C.B. *The Mesocorticolimbic Dopamine System*. New York: New York Academy of Sciences, 1988.
11. Kolb, B., & Wishaw, I. Q. *Fundamentals of Human Neuropsychology*, New York: W. H. Freeman, 1985.
12. Krieger, D. T., & Hughes, J. C. *Neuroendocrinology*, Sunderland, MA: Sinauer Associates, 1980.
13. Krulich, L. Central neurotransmitters and the secretion of prolactin, GH, LH and TSH. *Annual Review of Physiology*, 1979, 41, 603-616.
14. Lal, H., LaBella, F., & Lane, J. *Endocoids*, New York: Alan R. Liss, 1985.
15. MacIntosh, F.C. Acetylcholine. In G.J. Siegel, R.W. Albers, B.W. Agranoff and R. Katzman (Eds.) *Basic Neurochemistry: Molecular, Cellular and Medical Aspects, 3rd Edition*, Boston: Little, Brown and Co., 183-204, 1981.
16. Martin, J.B., Brownstein, M.J., & Krieger, D.T. *Brain Peptides Update: Volume 1*. Somerset, NJ: Wiley, 1987.
17. McEwen, B.S. Endocrine effects on the brain and their relationship to behavior. In G.J. Siegel, R.W. Albers, B.W. Agranoff, & R. Katzman (Eds.) *Basic Neurochemistry: Molecular, Cellular and Medical Aspects, (3rd ed.)*, Boston: Little, Brown and Co., 775-799, 1981.

18. Moore, R.Y., & Bloom, F.E. Central catecholamine neuron systems: Anatomy and physiology of the dopamine system. *Annual Review of Neuroscience*, 1978, 1, 129-169.

19. Moore, R.Y., & Bloom, F.E. Central catecholamine neuron systems: Anatomy and physiology of the norepinephrine and epinephrine systems. *Annual Review of Neuroscience*, 1979, 2, 113-168.

20. Nauta, W. J. H., & Feirtag, M. *Fundamental Neuroanatomy*, New York: W. H. Freeman, 1986.

21. Negro-Vilar, A., & Conn, P.M. *Peptide hormones: Effects and Mechanisms of Action*. Boca Raton, FL:
CRC Press, 1988.

22. Netter, F. H. *CIBA Medical Collection of Medical Illustrations, Vol. 1, Nervous System*, New York:
CIBA, 1983.

23. Sourkes, T.L. Parkinson's Disease and other disorders of the Basal Ganglia. In G.J. Siegel, R.W. Albers,
B.W. Agranoff and R. Katzman (Eds.) *Basic Neurochemistry: Molecular, Cellular and Medical Aspects,
(3rd ed.)* Boston: Little, Brown and Co., 719-722, 1981.

24. Sperry, R. W. Some effects of disconnecting the cerebral hemispheres. *Science*, 1982, 217, 1223-1226.

25. Weiner, R.I. and Ganong, W.F. Role of brain monamines and histamine in the regulation of anterior pituitary secretion. *Physiological Review*, 1978, 58, 905-976.

Chapter 3

BASIC PHARMACOLOGY

The purposes of this chapter are to:

1. Familiarize you with the many ways that drugs can be administered and the variety of ways in which they can be prepared, and

2. Teach the basic pharmacology that is applicable to all drugs, namely, absorption, distribution, metabolism, and excretion.

METHODS OF DRUG ADMINISTRATION

There are six typical ways of getting drugs into the body, and three more that are especially important because they result from recent advances in technology that enable **continuous drug administration**. The traditional ways of administering drugs involve **intermittent drug administration**, and include **oral consumption**, **injection**, **insufflation** into the nostrils, **inhalation**, absorption via **anal or vaginal suppositories**, and **absorption in the mouth**. The three means of continuous drug administration include **transdermal** (across the skin) **patches**, **subcutaneous** (underneath the skin) **implants**, and **subcutaneous pumps**. Each method of drug administration leads to different rates of **drug effect onset**. Each method also has particular advantages and disadvantages[8]. Knowing the predictable effects of administering the same drug in different ways can enable more rational decisions about personal drug use, the prescription of drugs, and policy decisions regarding drug regulation[5].

Oral

Taking a drug orally leads to the slowest onset of drug effects. If there is food in the stomach, onset of drug action can be greatly delayed, and sometimes the food can make the drug completely inactive. Once the drug is absorbed into the bloodstream, it is immediately passed through the liver before circulating to the rest of the body, including the brain. This leads to a breakdown of at least some of the drug and is referred to as **first-pass metabolism**. Sometimes this can completely eliminate the active drug before any of it gets to the brain, and there is no drug effect. With other methods of administration, first-pass metabolism is avoided and the drug has access to the brain before any breakdown in the liver occurs.

If excessive amounts of a drug are taking orally, there is the possibility that the individual will vomit. Anyone who has swallowed a large quantity of alcohol knows that vomiting is sometimes automatic. Certain areas of the brain outside of the blood-brain barrier can detect poisonous compounds in the bloodstream. These **emetic** (or **vomiting**) **centers** are an evolutionary mechanism that deals with the occasional eating of bad foods. Bad foods bring poisons into the bloodstream, and once a poison is detected by the brain, the signal to vomit is sent to the stomach. These vomiting centers are comparable to the canaries that coal miners brought down into the mines: If the rapidly breathing canaries fell over, that meant that the miners better leave before the fumes effected them as well. If the vomiting centers of the brain detect poison in the bloodstream, vomiting occurs and no more of the offending substance is absorbed. Of course, no system is perfect. The system is supposed to deal with food and nutritional liquids that are taken in gradually and in limited quantities. If a liquid drug is drunk rapidly and in large quantity, the system may not detect the high blood levels until a lethal dose has already been absorbed into the bloodstream.

Oral, Anal, or Vaginal Absorption

Since there is a substantial amount of blood vessels in the pink skin of the anus or vagina, it is said that these areas are **highly vascularized**. Drugs can be prepared in suppository form so that they can be inserted into one of these areas and rapidly absorbed into the bloodstream. The **sublingual** (under the tongue) and **buccal** (between cheek and gum) areas of the mouth are also highly vascularized. Drugs placed under the tongue or between cheek and gum are also rapidly absorbed into the bloodstream. The blood does not go first to the liver from any of these areas, so whatever is absorbed into the bloodstream has the potential to get to the brain and to affect behavior. If excessively high levels of the drug are absorbed into the bloodstream, vomiting will be induced. Unfortunately, it is unlikely that any beneficial removal of drug occurs, since the drug is not being absorbed from the stomach, but instead from the anus, vagina, or mouth area.

Inhalation

Inhalation is an extremely effective way to rapidly get substantial amounts of a drug into the body. The lungs cover an incredible amount of area and each section is highly vascularized. This insures that inhalations bring in large amounts of oxygen and exhalations get rid of large amounts of carbon dioxide. When inhalations include little particles of drug, the drug is taken into the bloodstream along with the oxygen. Coughing is due to irritation of the lungs and throat, as well as the bronchial tubes that lead to the lungs. While this can eliminate the drug from that particular inhalation, drugs are absorbed so rapidly from the lungs that substantial amounts can be taken in before coughing starts. Smokers eventually get used to this irritation and no longer cough with each inhalation. Excessively high levels of drugs taken in by inhalation may lead to vomiting. Most smokers remember, and yet were not stopped by, the intense nausea that followed their first cigarette. Of course, vomiting does no good, since the drug is being absorbed from the lungs.

Insufflation

The nose is another highly vascularized area of the body. Drugs taken through insufflation can be rapidly absorbed into the bloodstream. Vomiting may occur, but again, it's not very helpful, since the drug is in the nose and not in the stomach. Some people think that automatic sneezing will prevent the absorption of excessive amounts of drug. Sneezing, however, comes about as a result of irritation of the nasal passages. Additives to insufflated drugs may make them less irritating to the nasal passages, enabling the comfortable administration of dangerous amounts of drugs.

Injection

Finally, the injection of drugs can be achieved in a number of ways, but is usually done under the skin (**subcutaneously**), into a muscle (**intramuscularly**) or into a vein (**intravenously**). Intravenous injection is the most rapid of the three ways. This can be used to great advantage by physicians who face medical emergencies where it is important to get as much drug as possible into the body as rapidly as possible. Unfortunately, this can also be used to their own disadvantages by people who take non-prescription or street drugs by injection. There is no mechanism for the body to rapidly clear drugs injected into the bloodstream. In addition, any contaminants (including the deadly **AIDS virus**) in the syringe or on the needle are also injected directly into the bloodstream. No amount of vomiting, coughing, or sneezing will help rid the body of contaminants or dangerously high levels of the injected drug.

New Technologies

By definition, intermittent drug administration requires that the drug be given in well-timed intervals. Unfortunately, people often forget to take their medicine at the times they are supposed to. In addition, intermittent drug administration leads to excessively high levels of drug followed at some time by low levels that mean another dose must be taken. Continuous administration of drugs eliminates these **peaks and valleys** as well as the need for persons to carefully time their drug intake. Figure 3.1 compares the influence of time on the blood levels of a drug administered intermittently versus the same drug administered continuously. So far, none of these technological advances has been exploited by those who use drugs for non-medical purposes. However, technological advances in drug administration have, in the past, rapidly spread from medical use to illicit drug use[13].

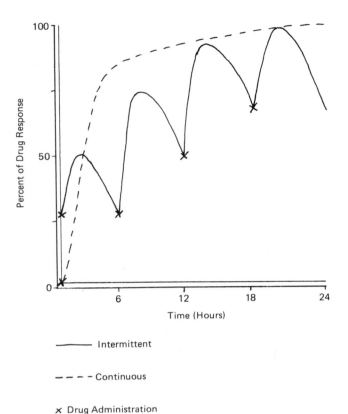

Figure 3.1. The effects of time on a drug's effect after continuous versus intermittent administration of the same drug. Note that continuous administration enables a continuous maximum effect of the drug, while intermittent drug administration leads to "peaks" and "valleys" in drug effects.

The skin is an effective barrier between the inside of the person and the outside world. However, even the ancient Greeks were aware that medicines could gain access to the inside of the body through placing drug-containing plasters onto, or rubbing ointments into, the skin[6]. Today, these fairly messy procedures have been replaced by the transdermal patch. The transdermal patch is a small, drug-soaked piece of material with an outer barrier that looks much like the outer portion of a band-aid. There is no barrier on the inside layer of the patch, and the drug is specially prepared so that it can cross the skin and be slowly absorbed into the bloodstream. This remarkably slow process is a highly effective way to deliver a steady amount of drug over a long period of time. While the technique is, of course, useless in emergencies, it is an excellent and proven means of administering certain drugs that an individual must take for a lengthy, or even life long, medical problem[4].

Unfortunately, some drugs cannot be prepared in a way that enables them to be used in a transdermal patch. The body is, however, capable of breaking down certain plastic materials. It is sometimes possible to cover some drug molecules with only a few layers of this plastic material and to cover others with more layers. These plastic-covered molecules can then be formed into a single mass that can be surgically implanted under the skin. The drug contained in this subcutaneous implant will then be slowly released as the body first exposes that drug encased in only a few layers and later exposes drug molecules encased in more layers. The success of this technique requires careful planning, and only a few drugs are presently available as subcutaneous implants[8].

Finally, the most sophisticated means of continuous drug administration is the use of an intravenous injection controlled by a pump. When hospitals need to continuously administer extremely precise amounts of potentially harmful medications, they use intravenous injections controlled by bulky pumps that are outside the body. Efforts are presently underway to develop pumps so small that they can fit underneath the skin of the patient. These subcutaneous pumps would continuously inject precise amounts of drug directly into the bloodstream. Hopefully, continued research will enable correction of problems with this technique, which include movement of the needle from the appropriate injection site, irritation or infection at the injection site, pump failure, leaking, and clogs[12].

METHODS OF DRUG PREPARATION

Different methods of drug preparation lead naturally to different means of drug administration. Although there are exceptions, it is usually possible to make any drug available in any form. The exceptions to this rule, though few, are extremely important and are discussed whenever specific drugs are covered in detail.

Drugs prescribed by physicians are manufactured by drug companies under the control of federal and state regulations. Whenever a drug is put into some form that requires additional materials, as happens for example when the drug is made into a pill, sweet-tasting liquid, suppository or injectable fluid, these materials are also tested for safety[7].

DRUG ABSORPTION

The ways in which a drug is administered has a powerful influence on how fast the drug is **absorbed,** or gains access to the bloodstream. Another important influence on the rate of absorption of a drug is the **lipid solubility** of the drug[1]. Drugs that are lipid soluble prefer to be in fats (**lipids**) rather than in fluids. It is simplest to think of the drug as having to deal with two different bodily components. One is made up of fluids like blood, sweat, tears, and urine. The other part of the body, including especially the brain and lungs, is made up of greater amounts of lipids. If taken orally, a lipid soluble drug will easily pass through the fatty lining of the stomach and intestines, gaining access to the bloodstream. A drug with low lipid solubility will take a long time to pass through this fatty area. If the lipid solubility is exceptionally low, the drug will simply be passed out of the body in feces before any of it is absorbed. Therefore, drugs with very low lipid solubility are not effective when taken orally, and must be administered by a method that allows easier access to the bloodstream.

No matter what the method of administration is, the lipid solubility of a drug determines how fast it leaves the bloodstream and enters the fatty parts of the body. The brain has substantial amounts of lipids. Drugs that are not lipid soluble take longer to reach the brain and are more quickly removed from the body. This leads to the need for larger and more frequent doses in individuals who must take low lipid soluble medicines for long periods of time. Lipid soluble drugs, on the other hand, gain quicker access to the brain and tend to accumulate there. This has enormously important implications for those who must take lipid soluble medicines for long periods of time, since substantial quantities of the drug can build up in the brain. Negative behavioral effects of lipid soluble medicines may continue for long periods of time after an individual has stopped taking the drug.

Perhaps the most important benefit of a thorough understanding of drug absorption is the development of sensible ways to treat overdoses[2]. A drug that is not very lipid soluble can be removed from the bloodstream by the emergency use of **dialysis**. In effect, an artificial kidney is used to cleanse the blood of the drugs. On the other hand, lipid soluble drugs are concentrated in high lipid areas like the brain. Even after all the drug is removed from the patient's bloodstream with dialysis, there can still be significant amounts of the drug stored in, and having a bad effect on, the brain.

DRUG DISTRIBUTION

Television commercials have given the impression that drugs act as magic bullets. If someone with a sore shoulder takes aspirin, the commercials imply, the drug will go straight from the stomach to the shoulder. Unfortunately, this is not the case. The bloodstream goes to the entire body, providing each cell with nourishment and oxygen and removing waste products. Therefore, once a drug gets into the circulation it has potential access to each part of the body. However, three major factors limit the access of the drug to particular cells and body areas while increasing the amount of drug that gets to other cells and body areas.

First, some drugs simply float around in the bloodstream while others are bound to **blood-borne carrier proteins**[9]. These are huge protein molecules in the blood that grab onto the drug. Even though the blood goes to all parts of the body, only some parts are capable of stripping the drug off the carrier proteins. As the blood passes through the body, these areas remove the drug, which can then have an effect on these areas. Parts of the body that can't take the drug off the protein sit idly by, as the drug floats off to another cell.

The second factor influencing distribution of a drug is the drug's lipid solubility. Areas of the body, and parts of the brain, that are high in lipids obtain more of lipid-soluble drugs. Areas of the body, and parts of the brain, that are low in lipids instead obtain more of drugs that are not lipid soluble. The third factor which influences the distribution of drug within the brain, is the blood-brain barrier (see Chapter 1).

A final barrier to complete distribution of drug throughout the entire body is the **placental barrier** that controls the transfer of materials to the developing fetus. While the placental barrier, like the blood-brain barrier, is not absolute, some drugs are better capable of crossing the placental barrier and affecting the fetus. Drugs that cross the barrier may have no obvious effect on the fetus, or they may instead induce birth defects. Drugs that induce birth defects are referred to as **teratogens** (literally, "monster makers")[3,11].

METABOLISM AND EXCRETION

Just as neurotransmitters are broken down by enzymes, drugs also are broken down, or **metabolized**, by enzymes. These enzymes can exist in a number of different places, including the blood, brain, and lungs. However, for most drugs the most important place for metabolism is the **liver.** Metabolized drugs can be removed from the body in tears, sweat, saliva, exhaled breath, and feces. However, most metabolized drugs are excreted by the **kidney** into the urine. Some drugs have to undergo multiple steps in their metabolism before they exit the body[10].

Since urine is primarily water, the most efficient way to get drugs out of the body is to make them less lipid soluble and more water soluble. Drugs that are metabolized by the body are converted from things that are more **lipophilic** (fat loving) to more **hydrophilic** (water loving). If metabolism by liver enzymes has made the drug very hydrophilic, the drug goes into the urine and leaves the body. If the drug is still not very hydrophilic, it remains in the bloodstream. Even though its not hydrophilic enough to leave the blood and enter the urine, the first steps in metabolism may have made it hydrophilic enough that it doesn't get taken up by the fatty areas of the brain. This explains how large quantities of a drug can be found in the blood of individuals who show no behavioral signs of drug effect.

Half-Life

The amount of time needed for one half of the dose given to be removed from the body is called the **half-life** or **t 1/2** of the drug[1]. By definition, after the passage of time equivalent to one half-life, half the drug has been metabolized. Each additional half-life removes an additional one-half of the remaining drug. Logically, this situation leads to increasingly small amounts of the drug, but never results in complete elimination. Nonetheless, since about 95% of the drug is removed from the body after six half-lives, most pharmacologists agree that it is then safe to say that the drug has been completely metabolized and eliminated. Figure 3.2 shows the importance of considering the t 1/2 of a drug when deciding the frequency of intermittent drug administration.

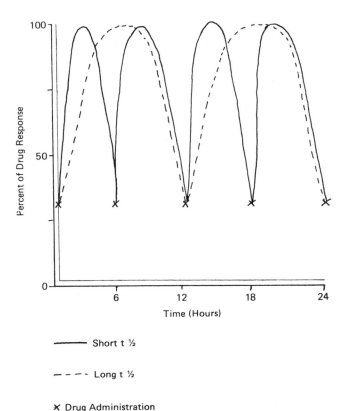

— Short t ½

– – – · Long t ½

✗ Drug Administration

Figure 3.2. The importance of t 1/2 when deciding the frequency of intermittent drug administration. Note that the drug with the longer half-life has a longer duration of action, and can thus be taken less frequently than the drug with the shorter half-life.

Active Metabolites

Knowing the half-life of a drug can enable an educated guess about how long a drug effect will last. This has enormous importance for deciding how often to have a patient take a drug or for deciding how long after halting a drug a patient is likely to experience negative side effects. Unfortunately, some drugs have metabolites that are still psychologically active. Although metabolism has made these **active metabolites** less lipophilic than the original, or **parent compound**, the active metabolites are still sufficiently lipophilic to gain access to the brain and to effect behavior. Sometimes the half-life of these active metabolites can be extremely long. It may initially appear that a drug with a t 1/2 of 4 hours would, for all practical purposes, be eliminated from the body in 24 hours (or six half-lives). However, if the drug had an active metabolite with a t 1/2 of 12 hours, an individual wouldn't be free from behavioral effects for at least three whole days. Figure 3.3 demonstrates the impact of active metabolites on the duration of a drug effect.

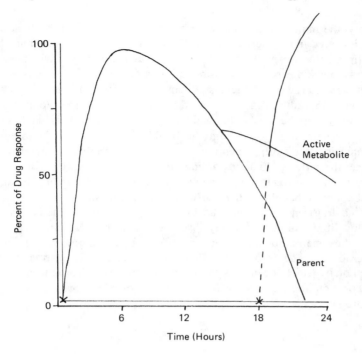

x Drug Administration

Figure 3.3. The impact of active metabolites on the duration of a drug's effect. Note that the presence of active metabolites can cause a second drug administration to result in drug effects that are in excess of the desired effect (that is, overdose).

IMPORTANCE OF BASIC PHARMACOLOGY

As this chapter reveals, the basic pharmacology of a drug has a powerful effect on the consequences of different means of administration, the rate of absorption of the drug, characteristics of distribution, and the drug's metabolism and excretion. Thus, for nearly all of the specific drugs discussed in the remainder of the text, special attention will be paid to the basic pharmacology of the drug. A full understanding of between-drug differences and similarities in basic pharmacology will enable a greater understanding of the specifics of how a drug is used and/or abused.

The importance of the various aspects of basic pharmacology is made clear when looking at a number of different drugs which are all administered in the same way. The ways in which lipid solubility and method of administration interact can enable easy predictions about the speed of the onset of drug effects. For example, if the method of administration is by intravenous injection, it can be expected that both a low lipid soluble and a high lipid soluble drug will quickly induce their effects. However, if a comparison is made between onset of drug effects when taken orally, the drug with high lipid solubility will induce its effects much faster than the drug with low lipid solubility.

Similarly, the importance of basic pharmacology can be seen by looking at a single drug administered in a variety of ways. For example, the onset of effects from a drug with low lipid solubility will be much slower when the drug is taken orally, as compared to intravenous injection. The more rapidly a drug exerts its effects, the more likely it is to cause an intense effect due to simultaneous influence on a relatively greater number of neurons. In addition, a drug gaining quick access to the bloodstream via injection might overwhelm the number of available carrier proteins. This would result in a greater distribution of drug away from the bloodstream and into the brain, thus enhancing the intensity of this drug when it is injected versus orally consumed. It might appear at first that the different methods of administering this one drug will have little effect on the duration of the drug effect. However, the duration of the effect of the injected drug is likely to be shorter than that of the orally consumed drug, simply because enzymes that metabolize the drug can quickly gain access to a great amount of the injected drug. When a drug of low lipid solubility is slowly absorbed into the bloodstream, enzymes can only break down that small amount of drug available at any one moment, and must wait for the remainder to finally get into the bloodstream. Thus, the basic pharmacology of a drug and the method by which the drug is administered can have a profound effect on the delay between consumption and drug effect, the intensity of the drug effect, and the duration of the drug effect.

CHAPTER SUMMARY

There are a variety of ways that drugs can be administered, including methods that result in intermittent administrations and others that result in continuous administrations. Each method has specific advantages and disadvantages. The lipid solubility of a drug is a powerful determinant of which methods will lead to rapid and effective drug effects. The absorption of a drug into the bloodstream and the distribution of the drug to various parts of the body, including the brain, are also powerfully influenced by the lipid solubility of the drug. Drugs are removed from the body via metabolism and excretion. Metabolism involves the use of enzymes to change drugs into relatively more water soluble compounds that can be excreted in the urine, although there are other routes from which drugs may leave the body. A thorough understanding of the effects of lipid solubility on absorption, distribution, metabolism, and excretion of drugs can enable predictions about the effects of one drug administered in a number of different ways or the effects of many different drugs all administered in a single manner.

REVIEW ESSAY QUESTIONS

1. Discuss how different ways of administering drugs can influence the speed at which drug effects occur.

2. Discuss the mechanism and efficiency of the body's methods for eliminating excessive amounts of drugs taken in by each of the different methods of drug administration.

3. What are the three presently available means of continuous drug administration, and what are the advantages of each?

4. Explain the importance of lipid solubility in the absorption and distribution of drugs in the body.

5. What is the importance of the relative degree of hydrophilicity versus lipophilicity in metabolism and excretion of drugs?

REFERENCES

1. Benet, L. Z., & Sheiner, L. B. Pharmacokinetics: The dynamics of drug absorption, distribution, and elimination. In A. G. Gilman, L. S. Goodman, T. W. Rall, and F. Murad (Eds.) *The Pharmacological Basis of Therapeutics* (7th ed.), New York: Macmillan Publishing Company, 1985.

2. Bourne, P. D. *Acute drug abuse emergencies: A treatment manual*, New York: Academic Press, 1976.

3. Braude, M.C., & Zimmerman, A.M. *Genetic and perinatal effects of abused substances*. New York: Academic Press, 1987.

4. Brown, L.B., & Langer, R. Transdermal delivery of drugs. *Annual Review of Medicine*, 1988, 39, 221-229.

5. Janowsky, D. S., Addario, D., & Risch, S. C. *Psychopharmacology case studies* (2nd ed.), New York: The Guilford Press, 1987.

6. Kligman, A.M. Skin permeability: Dermatologic aspects of transdermal drug delivery. *American Heart Journal*, 1984, 108, 200-206.

7. Leber, P. FDA: The federal regulation of drug development. In H.Y. Meltzer (Ed.) *Psychopharmacology: The Third Generation of Progress*, New York: Raven Press, 1987.

8. Lemberger, L., Schildcrout, S., & Cuff, G. Drug delivery systems: Applicability to neuropsychopharmacology. In H.Y. Meltzer (Ed.) *Psychopharmacology: The Third Generation of Progress*, New York: Raven Press, 1987.

9. Levy, R. & Shand, D. Clinical implications of drug-protein binding. *Clinical Pharmacokinetics*, 1984, 9, 1-104.

10. Mitchell, J.R., & Horning, M.G. *Drug metabolism and drug toxicity*. New York: Raven Press, 1981.

11. *Norwood, C. *At highest risk: Environmental hazards to young and unborn children*. New York: McGraw Hill, 1980.

12. Penn, R.D. *Neurological applications of implanted drugs*. New York: New York Academy of Sciences, 1988.

13. *Zinberg, N. E. *Drug, set and setting: The basis for controlled intoxicant use*, New Haven, CT: Yale University Press, 1984.

*Introductory or intermediate reading

Chapter 4

DETERMINANTS AND DESCRIPTIONS OF DRUG ACTIONS

The purposes of this chapter are to:

1. Discuss the mechanism of action of drugs,

2. Define and describe the various short- and long-term effects of agonists and antagonists,

3. Explain how dose-response curves provide an accurate and readily grasped summary of the full range of a drug's effects, and

4. Discuss a number of pharmacological and nonpharmacological factors that can influence an individual's response to a particular drug.

MECHANISM OF ACTION

Although some clinically and socially relevant drugs act on the membrane of the neuron, most of the drugs discussed in this book act on dendrites or axons. That is, for these drugs to act, they have to be distributed to the proper part of the body and/or brain and then gain access to an appropriate synaptic cleft.

Target Effects Vs. Side Effects

It's typical that discussions of drug action refer to **target effects** and **side effects**. As they are usually used, target effects refer to what the doctor and patient want the drug to do, and side effects refer to drug effects that they wish didn't occur. Most drugs have a variety of actions at a number of different types of neurons. So, a drug that is taken for a target effect that involves blockade of dopamine receptors may also block a number of other types of receptors, and may even stimulate dopamine or other receptors in different parts of the brain. In addition, drugs can have effects at many different levels of the nervous system hierarchy.

The labeling of one of the drug's actions as a target effect and the others as side effects is often an arbitrary decision that is very dependent upon circumstances. For example, when the drug Valium is taken to reduce anxiety, the drowsiness that often occurs is seen as a side effect that can interfere with driving. When taken at night, this same drowsiness may be seen as the target effect of the Valium. Despite this apparent arbitrariness, it is nonetheless useful and important to state what the target effect is, because that determines why an individual takes the drug. In addition, the development of new drugs that may have fewer or less severe side effects requires an understanding of the specific drug-receptor interaction(s) responsible for the target effect[9].

Efficacy Versus Potency

Another important distinction is the difference between **efficacy** and **potency**[16]. Efficacy refers to whether a drug is capable of causing a particular target effect, while potency refers to the **effective dose**, the specific amount of a drug, needed to get that effect. Two drugs may be equally efficacious while differing widely in potency, or strength. That is, both drugs can cause the effect, but with one drug a larger dose is required to get that effect. Sometimes a person with a behavioral disorder is allergic to a particular drug and is switched from this more potent drug to a less potent one. Explaining to the patient the difference between efficacy and potency can correct the erroneous impression that the increased dose of the second drug means that the physician thinks he or she is more ill than before.

AGONISTS AND ANTAGONISTS

The effects of drugs upon behavior are determined by a large number of factors. One of the most important things to determine first is whether a drug acts, in the short-term, to increase or decrease the activity of an endogenous neurotransmitter or neuromodulator system. If a drug increases the activity of an endogenous system, it is referred to as an **agonist** for that neurotransmitter system. On the other hand, if a drug decreases the activity of an endogenous system, it is referred to as an **antagonist** for that neurotransmitter system[16].

It is important to clear up two misconceptions that can easily develop when students are first presented with the concepts of agonists and antagonists. First, it is incorrect to assume that all agonists induce EPSPs while all antagonists induce IPSPs. Table 4.1 demonstrates the combined effect that drug type and usual postsynaptic event have on the likelihood of action potentials.

Table 4.1

DRUG TYPE	USUAL POST-SYNAPTIC EVENT	PROBABILITY OF AN ACTION POTENTIAL
Agonist	EPSP	Increased
Agonist	IPSP	Decreased
Antagonist	EPSP	Decreased
Antagonist	IPSP	Increased

As Table 4.1 reveals, things become complicated under two conditions. The first complication occurs when an agonist acts at a synapse where the presynaptic neuron usually causes IPSPs in the postsynaptic neuron. This agonist will cause an increase in the intensity or number of IPSPs induced. Thus, the agonist will make it less likely that the postsynaptic neuron will have an action potential. The second complication occurs when an antagonist acts at a synapse where IPSPs normally occur. This causes a decrease in events that usually push the postsynaptic neuron away from an action potential. This then results in an actual increase in the probability that a postsynaptic neuron will have an action potential. The action of an antagonist at a synapse where IPSPs usually occur is consistent with a basic rule of mathematics: The multiplication of two negative numbers results in a positive one.

The second misconception about agonists and antagonists arises because a drug that is known, for example, to block a postsynaptic receptor for neurotransmitter X is called an "X antagonist." This leads some to erroneously conclude that all the behavioral and physical effects arise because the drug is an antagonist for neurotransmitter X. However, a drug might be an agonist for a neurotransmitter at one place in the nervous system and an antagonist for that same neurotransmitter at another site. This is because the important thing is the interaction between the neurotransmitter and the postsynaptic receptor, rather than the effect of either one alone. Additionally, a drug usually affects more than one neurotransmitter or neuromodulator. A drug can be an antagonist for one chemical messenger and an agonist for another. Thus, drugs have multiple actions at different receptors. Calling a drug an "X antagonist" does not necessarily mean that all, or even the most important, effects of the drug come about because it is an antagonist for the neurotransmitter X[17].

Types of Short-Term Agonist Actions

Exogenous precursors. One way to have an agonist drug effect is to administer extra amounts of the precursor needed to synthesize a neurotransmitter. Loading the body with **exogenous precursors** can sometimes lead to the production of greater than usual amounts of neurotransmitter. When the vesicles release this greater than usual amount of neurotransmitter into the synaptic cleft, there is a greater than usual number of neurotransmitter/receptor interactions (there are always extra postsynaptic receptors waiting to be stimulated by chemicals from the presynaptic neuron). Foods contain the precursors for a number of neurotransmitters, making the study of the effects of food on brain function[13] as well as normal and abnormal behavior[27] a legitimate part of the study of the behavioral effects of drugs. Exogenous precursors can also be used to decrease the symptoms caused when neuronal death leads to a reduction of activity in a neurotransmitter system. For example, the drug **L-DOPA** is used in treating Parkinson's disease, which is caused by the death of dopamine neurons in the brain[18].

Facilitated release. Each action potential causes the release of a specific number of presynaptic vesicles into the synaptic gap. An agonist effect can be obtained by administering a drug that causes a greater than usual number of vesicles to release their contents. This drug effect is called **facilitated release**. The anti-hyperactive drug Ritalin (see Chapter 11) is effective, at least in part, because it facilitates the release of neurotransmitters like dopamine, norepinephrine, and serotonin.

Direct agonist. If a receptor is thought of as a lock and the endogenous neurotransmitter as a key, then the **direct agonist** is comparable to a skeleton key that opens the lock as easily as the original key. These drugs can exert an agonist effect because their physical structure is similar to the endogenous chemical messenger. The receptor can't tell the difference between the endogenous neurotransmitter and the drug, so the direct agonist causes EPSPs or IPSPs without the natural input from the presynaptic neuron. In fact, the direct agonist is the first drug discussed so far that can work even if presynaptic neurons are dead or have lost their ability to synthesize neurotransmitter. Direct agonists for dopamine receptors are useful in the advanced stages of Parkinson's disease, when L-DOPA is ineffective due to the small number of remaining dopamine-synthesizing neurons.

Blockade of reuptake. As mentioned at the end of Chapter 1, the natural means for limiting the availability of the neurotransmitter for interaction with the postsynaptic receptor is to remove the neurotransmitter from the synaptic cleft. This is accomplished in one of two ways. One method involves **reuptake**, or recycling. In reuptake, the neurotransmitter is taken up by the presynaptic neuron and repackaged into a synaptic vesicle. **Blockade of reuptake** results in an agonist action. Since the neurotransmitter is not taken up by the presynaptic neuron, it spends a greater than usual amount of time available for interaction with postsynaptic receptors. The antidepressant tricyclic drugs (see Chapter 8) probably have their therapeutic effect because they block the reuptake of serotonin and/or norepinephrine.

Inhibition of enzymatic degradation. The other method of limiting the availability of the neurotransmitter for interaction with the postsynaptic neuron involves **enzymatic degradation.** Just as enzymes are involved in synthesis, other enzymes break down neurotransmitters into materials that can no longer interact with postsynaptic receptors. Agonist action results from interference with this mechanism for removal of the neurotransmitter from the synaptic cleft. **Inhibition of enzymatic degradation** can occur by two different mechanisms. **Reversible inhibition** occurs when the physical structure of the drug is so similar to that of the neurotransmitter that the enzymes waste effort trying to break down the drug, rather than the endogenous neurotransmitter. **Irreversible inhibition** occurs when the drug binds to and permanently changes the structure of the enzyme so that the enzyme can no longer act on the endogenous neurotransmitter. Either mechanism results in greater than usual numbers of EPSPs or IPSPs because the neurotransmitter remains in the synaptic gap, ready to interact with receptors, for an extended period of time. This particular mechanism of agonist action has led to the development of powerful poisons that have been used as insecticides and, unfortunately, as "nerve gas" to kill humans in wars starting with World War I[22].

Types of Short-Term Antagonist Action

False precursors. One way to exert an antagonist action is to give **false precursors**. These drugs are similar in physical shape to the real precursor for a certain neurotransmitter. Enzymes involved in the synthesis of the neurotransmitter are diverted from their usual task as they attempt to transform the false precursor into the neurotransmitter. However, the false precursor is not exactly the same as the real precursor, and the enzymes are unable to transform the molecule. The enzymes spend so much futile time trying to transform the false precursor that very little of the real precursor gets converted into a neurotransmitter. This can lead to a shortage of neurotransmitter. Consequently, when an action potential arrives at the terminal button, the vesicles released into the synaptic cleft have a less than normal amount of neurotransmitter and the number of EPSPs or IPSPs is reduced. It is possible that the behavioral effects of some foods may be mediated by the presence of false precursors[27].

Deactivation of synthetic enzymes. Another way to influence the synthesis of new neurotransmitter is to cause a generalized **deactivation of synthetic enzymes**. Rather than simply tying up the enzymes with false precursors, these antagonists change the enzymes so that they can no longer perform their normal role in the synthesis of neurotransmitters. The agonist and antagonist drug actions discussed so far have been specific to one neurotransmitter or class of neurotransmitters. Deactivation of synthetic enzymes is **non-specific**, that is, it results in low levels of many different types of neurotransmitters. This type of antagonist action is, therefore, usually seen as an unfortunate side effect, rather than as a useful drug action.

Destruction of vesicle integrity. The two antagonist drug actions discussed so far have involved reduction in the amount of neurotransmitter that is inside synaptic vesicles. Another antagonist action is caused by drugs that **destroy the integrity of synaptic vesicles**. Some drugs can make synaptic vesicles "leaky," so that the neurotransmitter contents of the vesicle flow out into the area within the synaptic membrane that forms the terminal button. When the synaptic vesicle is later called upon to release its contents into the synaptic cleft, there is less neurotransmitter ejected, and fewer EPSPs or IPSPs occur. Prior to the development of more effective antipsychotic drugs (see Chapter 7), the best treatment for the severe behavioral disorder of schizophrenia was the vesicle destroying drug reserpine[6].

Direct antagonists. Just as there are direct agonists, there are **direct antagonists.** Direct antagonists are similar enough to the real neurotransmitter to bind to the postsynaptic receptor, but this binding does not cause EPSPs or IPSPs. The presence of the direct antagonist in the receptor prevents the real neurotransmitter from activating the receptor. Direct antagonists are therefore sometimes referred to as **blockers.** While some direct antagonists permanently occupy the receptor, most are just like the real neurotransmitter in that they bind to the receptor and then are let go. The direct antagonists are then either destroyed by enzymes or bind to the same or another receptor at a later time. There are periodic changes in the relative success of the neurotransmitter and the agonist in their **competition** for the postsynaptic receptor. These are responsible for a number of the more bizarre side effects associated with antipsychotic drugs (see Chapter 7).

Stimulation of autoreceptors. The release of drugs from the synapse is oftentimes controlled by feedback inhibition similar to that controlling the release of hormones by the endocrine system (see Chapter 1). When a presynaptic neuron releases neurotransmitter into the synaptic cleft, some of the neurotransmitter finds its way back to the membrane of the presynaptic neuron. There are **autoreceptors** on the presynaptic neuron to which the neurotransmitters can bind. Stimulation of autoreceptors by the neurotransmitter provides evidence that there must be neurotransmitter in the cleft that is stimulating postsynaptic receptors. This leads to a reduction in the production of neurotransmitter by the presynaptic neuron, thus avoiding excessive stimulation of the postsynaptic neuron[25]. Drugs that have an *agonist* effect at the autoreceptor mimic the action of the neurotransmitter on the presynaptic neuron and decrease the production of neurotransmitter. Subsequent exocytosis results in the release of a less than normal amount of neurotransmitter, and thus these autoreceptor agonists have an actual *antagonist* effect on the postsynaptic neuron[12]. Figure 4.1 illustrates how the autoreceptor agonist has an antagonist effect upon the postsynaptic neuron.

Stabilization of membrane potentials. Finally, it is possible to affect behavior with drugs that do not act exclusively at or near the synapse. Some drugs act as antagonists by **stabilizing the membrane potential** of the cell body and axon of the postsynaptic neuron. When the neuronal membrane is stabilized, the EPSPs or IPSPs caused by the activity at the synapse are prevented from spreading down the axon and influencing whether or not threshold is reached[20]. **Local anesthetics** that block the transmission of information regarding pain often work by this method.

Table 4.2 summarizes the many ways in which drugs can act as agonists and antagonists; it emphasizes whether the drug acts at the presynaptic neuron, the synaptic cleft, or the postsynaptic neuron.

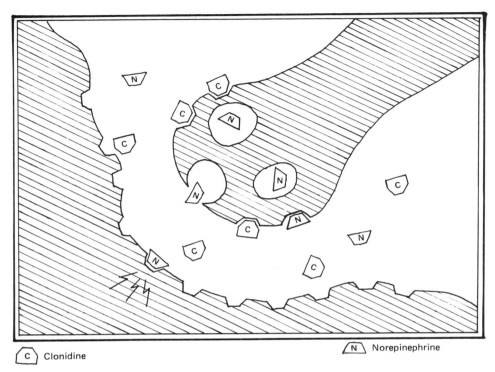

 Clonidine   Norepinephrine

Figure 4.1. An autoreceptor agonist acting as a synaptic antagonist. By stimulating presynaptic receptors that reduce the numbers of neurotransmitter molecules localized in and released from the synaptic vesicles, the autoreceptor agonist results in fewer neurotransmitter molecules being available to stimulate postsynaptic receptors. The net result of autoreceptor agonist activity is thus a postsynaptic antagonist action.

Long-Term Effects of Agonists and Antagonists

The body attempts to limit the effects of drugs in order to maintain the balance that is the basis of normal behavior. The process of maintaining balance, or **homeostasis**, occurs whenever natural or artificial changes require the body to compensate for those changes. The attempt to maintain homeostasis is the process underlying many of the **chronic** (or long-term), as opposed to **acute** (or short-term), effects of drugs. Some chronic effects of drugs represent the body's successful attempts to maintain homeostasis. However, since drugs may induce changes that are many times more powerful than those caused by more natural experiences, the body may be unable to maintain homeostasis in the face of drug-induced changes. Therefore, other chronic drug effects arise, not from success, but instead from a failure of the body's attempts to maintain homeostasis[17]. Specific examples of each of these possible consequences of chronic drug use are cited in later chapters where the long-term use of behavioral medicines and/or recreational drugs is discussed.

Table 4.2

NAME	TYPE	SITE
Exogenous precursor	Agonist	Presynaptic neuron
False precursor	Antagonist	Presynaptic neuron
Enzyme inactivation	Antagonist	Presynaptic neuron
Vesicle destruction	Antagonist	Presynaptic neuron
Facilitated release	Agonist	Presynaptic neuron
Autoreceptor stimulation	Antagonist	Presynaptic neuron
Blocked reuptake	Agonist	Synaptic cleft
Inhibited degradation	Agonist	Synaptic cleft
Direct agonist	Agonist	Postsynaptic neuron
Direct antagonist	Antagonist	Postsynaptic neuron
Membrane stabilization	Antagonist	Postsynaptic neuron

Depletion of neurotransmitter. If an agonist that acts through facilitation of neurotransmitter release is administered over a long period of time, there will eventually be a **depletion of neurotransmitter**. The agonist drug may have been causing the neuron to release the neurotransmitter contents of unusually large numbers of synaptic vesicles for a long period of time. The synthetic enzymes often are unable to keep up with this excess synthesis requirement, and neurotransmitter levels thus become abnormally low. When the drug is no longer taken, the low levels of presynaptic neurotransmitter produce a decreased effect on the postsynaptic neuron.

Increased synthesis of neurotransmitter. Chronic use of a direct antagonist can, on the other hand, lead to **increased synthesis of neurotransmitter**. When postsynaptic receptors are blocked by the direct antagonist, the postsynaptic neuron informs the presynaptic neuron that something is wrong and that subnormal levels of receptor stimulation are occurring. The presynaptic neuron attempts to compensate for the lack of postsynaptic EPSPs and IPSPs by synthesizing more neurotransmitter. When the drug is no longer taken, there is an excessive effect on the postsynaptic neuron.

Receptor supersensitivity. Chronic administration of any antagonist also causes a homeostatic increase in the sensitivity of the postsynaptic receptors. This is called **receptor supersensitivity**. When drug use is halted, receptors that have been blocked for a long period of time will, when finally stimulated by the neurotransmitter, cause a more powerful EPSP or IPSP than they did before.

Cell death. Finally, the most extreme consequence of chronic use of a drug is **cell death**. At sufficient doses for a sufficient period of time, any type of agonist or antagonist can cause the death of a neuron[11]. Unfortunately, the impact on behavior is compounded by the effect on the surviving neuron as it experiences convergence from or divergence to other neurons. If the presynaptic neuron dies, the postsynaptic neuron experiences receptor supersensitivity, just as it would if an antagonist were present. Consequently, the input of other presynaptic neurons converging on the postsynaptic neuron will then be abnormally enhanced. If the postsynaptic neuron dies, the surviving presynaptic neuron produces excess levels of neurotransmitter, just as it would if the postsynaptic neuron were subjected to a regular antagonist. Divergence insures that there is an abnormally enhanced effect upon all the remaining postsynaptic neurons with which the surviving presynaptic neuron has contact.

OTHER FACTORS INFLUENCING DRUG EFFECTS

Determining the mechanism by which a drug induces a behavioral effect requires a description of the drug's effect as an agonist or antagonist with every possible known neurotransmitter. However, additional factors can have a powerful influence over the behavioral effect of a drug. Some of these factors, such as the sex and weight of the individual, are obviously "physical." Others might be more typically categorized as "social," "cultural," or "psychological." However, any factor that influences behavior must do so through an interaction with the nervous system (see Chapter 1). Theoretically, scientists will some day understand the human body well enough to explain the influences of "social," "cultural," and "psychological" variables by detailing alterations in neuro-transmitters and neuromodulators[1].

Physical Status of Consumer

Some of the easily observable and well understood physical variables that can influence the effect of a drug include weight, sex, age, and general health. The amount of drug given (or **dose**) is normally expressed in metric terms that reveal the weight of drug in relation to the body weight of the individual taking the drug. This is most often expressed with the abbreviation **mg/kg**, which means the weight of the drug in milligrams per kilogram of body weight. Since calculations of dose employ body weight as a denominator, a heavier person who takes a certain weight of drug is actually getting a smaller dose than a lighter person taking the same weight of drug[16]. By expressing dose in terms of mg/kg, weight differences between individuals are already taken into account.

Sex differences in responses to a drug can often be explained solely by the fact that men usually weigh more than women. However, men and women also differ in the rate at which they metabolize and excrete specific drugs, and the additional layers of subcutaneous fat that women have can lead to greater dilution of lipophilic drugs[2].

Age influences on a drug effect usually occur at the extremes of age. Young children, and even adolescents, have immature nervous systems that are especially sensitive to certain drug effects and immature bodily organs that are not as good at metabolism and excretion as are adult bodily organs[4,26]. The elderly, on the other hand, may suffer from impaired metabolism and excretion due to the decreases in efficiency that hamper older bodily organs[23,24].

Finally, an individual's general health can have a profound influence on drug effects. Any illness-caused impairment of bodily organs important in absorption, distribution, metabolism, or excretion can have a strong effect on a drug effect. Diseases of the brain or nervous system have a particularly powerful effect upon the behavioral actions of drugs[21].

Drug Interactions

Drug interactions arise when one drug influences the absorption, distribution, metabolism, or excretion of another drug[10,14]. Drug interactions usually influence potency, but can occasionally influence efficacy by creating novel negative effects or by rendering one drug therapeutically useless. Drug interactions can occur in a variety of ways. Among the more common mechanisms of drug interaction are: (a) a chemical reaction in which one drug changes the physical shape of the other, (b) one drug influencing the absorption of another, (c) competition for blood-borne carrier proteins, or (d) one drug enhancing or decreasing the metabolism and/or excretion of another[19].

Previous Drug Use

A further complication is that drugs can interact with themselves. In Chapter 5, the phenomenon of tolerance, sensitization, and physical dependency are discussed as cases of chronic consumption of a drug later influencing the effect of that drug.

Set and Setting

Despite the major influence of "physical" variables like age, sex, drug interactions, etc., on drug effects, **psychological and social factors** can be very powerful. In fact, at low doses, these factors may actually determine the nature of a drug effect. Since most people understand that behavior is influenced by many things, they often can accept the influence of social and psychological factors on the behavioral effects of drugs. In fact, these same factors can often have a profound influence on "physical" effects, such as the induction of vomiting or sweating. Drug effects on neurotransmitters, synapses, and behavior can, and should be, considered to be influenced as much by previous experience as by other behaviors[7]. In a review of "nonpharmacological factors" that influence the behavioral effects of drugs, it was concluded that "because behavioral variables are so critical in determining the effects of drugs, an understanding of those variables is as fundamental to drug action as is the understanding of traditional pharmacological mechanisms"[1]. This point will become particularly clear in Chapter 12, which discusses medicines that can aid the reduction or cessation of drug abuse.

The influence of psychological and social variables on a drug effect are often summarized as the total effect of **set and setting**[5,28]. Set refers to the individual's expectation, which arises from what he or she has been told by physician, friends, school, the media, etc., about what can be expected from a particular drug[8]. Especially at low doses, an individual will likely experience the behavioral effects that he or she has learned to expect. The **placebo** effect refers to the fact that a drug effect usually obtainable only because a drug has a specific action at certain synapses can sometimes be obtained when a useless compound is given to someone who truly believes that the "drug" will have that effect[3]. In other cases, a useful drug can be rendered ineffective simply because the person taking the drug has strong doubts about the compound's effectiveness[15]. Setting refers to the physical environment in which the drug is administered. Drug effects can be diminished or enhanced by the environment in which they are consumed. Even the dose of a drug necessary to cause death can be influenced by the physical setting in which the drug is taken[28].

DOSE-RESPONSE CURVES

The large number of variables influencing the effects, particularly the behavioral effects, of drugs makes it difficult for researchers to link the basic pharmacology and agonist and/or antagonist actions of a drug with specific effects. However, this difficult task is greatly aided by a device that at least enables accurate identification of the influence of

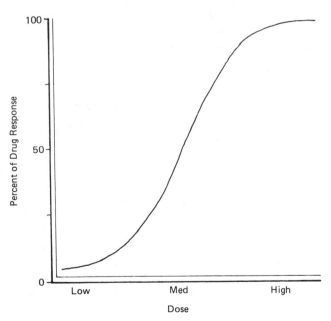

Figure 4.2 A typical dose-response curve, demonstrating little drug effect at low doses, a rapid increase in drug effect throughout the middle doses, and a leveling off (asymptote) of drug effect at high doses.

the *dose* of the drug on the *response* of the individual. Dose-response curves reveal that all drug effects are **dose-dependent**. That is, while other factors can drastically change an individual's response to a drug, it will always be the case that there is (a) some low dose below which no drug effect can be obtained and (b) some high dose at which negative consequences will occur[16].

Figure 4.2 presents a typical **dose-response curve**. The dose-response curve shows at a glance the doses needed to induce a response to a drug. The left side of the dose-response curve shows the effects of smaller doses while the right side shows the effects of larger doses. The dose-response curve shows that there is always some dose of a drug (represented by the far left of the dose-response curve) which will have no effect on that particular response. As the dose of the drug is increased (the viewer's gaze shifts farther to the right of the dose-response curve), the intensity of the drug effect increases.

Qualitative and Quantitative Changes

Sometimes, different effects occur at higher doses than at lower doses. When an increase in dose leads to more of the same effect obtained at a lower dose, a **quantitative change** has occurred. If an increase in dose leads to an effect not present at lower doses, than a **qualitative change** has occurred and it will be necessary to create a new dose-response curve for this newly observed effect.

Toxicity and Therapeutic Windows

Near the top, and usually to the far right, of the dose-response curve is a special case of a drug-induced side effect. When damage to the brain or other vital organs arises from a particular dose of a drug, the drug is said to have caused a poisoning or **toxicity**. That is, the dose used is a **toxic dose**. No matter how beneficial a medicine may appear, and no matter how safe it may be at usual doses, when a drug is taken at a dose represented by the extreme right of the dose-response curve, the toxic effect of death can occur.

The dose-response curve reveals much about a drug and even enables comparisons to be made between different drugs. The dose-response curve, for example, can be used to determine the range between the dose necessary to achieve some specific beneficial effect and the dose that will induce toxic side effects. This range is referred to as the **therapeutic window**.   As a general rule of thumb, medicines with a large therapeutic window are preferable to those with a small therapeutic window. It is, however, always important to remember that the size of this window can be influenced in a particular individual by the host of factors listed above.

Potency and Efficacy

The great utility of the dose-response curve is clearest when it is desirable to make comparisons between drugs. Between-drug comparisons can be made by superimposing the dose-response curves of two different medicines for the same disorder. This

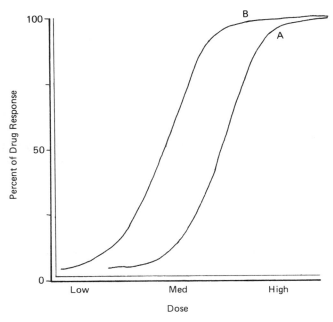

Figure 4.3. Dose-response curves for two different drugs, with Drug A less potent than Drug B, but Drug A and Drug B equally efficacious. Note that more of Drug A must be given in order to obtain the same effect obtained with a lower dose of Drug B. Note also that by giving enough of Drug A, any effect of Drug B can be duplicated.

enables scientists to determine if differences between the drugs are due to potency or efficacy (see Chapter 3). Figures 4.3 and 4.4 compare two different drugs, A and B, each used to treat depression. In Figure 4.3 Drug A and Drug B are equally efficacious, but Drug B is more potent. Thus, since Drug B could be given at lower doses or less frequently, it would be preferable in most cases. However, if someone had an allergy to Drug B but not to Drug A, Drug A could be effectively substituted, although at a higher dose than would be needed with Drug B. In Figure 4.4 Drug A is less potent than Drug B but more efficacious. That is, a comparatively small dose of Drug B eliminates most of the depression, but leaves the patient still feeling inappropriately sad. No matter how high the dosage, the depression is never completely eliminated. Drug A, on the other hand, must be given at a comparatively larger dose just to bring the person the same amount of relief offered by small doses of Drug B. However, a slight increase in the dose of Drug A enables a complete elimination of the depression, rendering it preferable to the less potent Drug B. As will be seen throughout the remainder of this text, much confusion about similarities and differences between drugs can be cleared up by a sound use of dose-response curves.

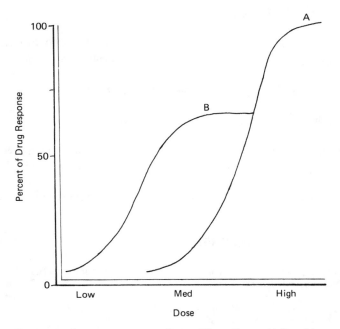

Figure 4.4. Dose response curves for two different drugs, with Drug A less potent than Drug B, but with Drug A nonetheless more efficacious than Drug B. Note that the lesser potency of Drug A means that much more of Drug A, compared to Drug B, is needed to get from 0-50% of the desired drug effect. Note also that since Drug A is more efficacious, large amounts of Drug A produce drug effects in excess of what can be produced by any amount of Drug B.

CHAPTER SUMMARY

When discussing the effects of drugs, it is important to appreciate that distinctions between the target effect and the side effect depend upon the intended use of the drug. It is also important, when comparing drugs, to clearly identify whether between-drug differences are differences in efficacy or differences in potency. Understanding how a particular drug exerts its effects begins with determining that a particular behavioral or physical effect arises because the drug is an agonist or antagonist for some particular neurotransmitter system. An in-depth understanding requires a further determination as to which of the various agonist and antagonist actions summarized in Table 4.2 are responsible for a particular drug effect. An understanding of the acute agonist or antagonist effect of the drug will aid in predictions of possible long-term effects of the drug.

A variety of factors other than the agonist or antagonist effect on certain neurotransmitter systems can influence the effects of drugs. These factors include, but are not limited to, dose, set, and setting. The dose-response curve shows the consequences of many points along the full dose range. Careful analysis of the dose-response curve can provide easy access to a wealth of information about the effects of a drug.

REVIEW ESSAY QUESTIONS

1. Why is it wrong to say that agonists cause EPSPs and antagonists cause IPSPs? Why might it be misleading to refer to a particular drug as "a neurotransmitter X antagonist"?

2. Name and describe the five listed ways that a drug can have an agonist effect.

3. Name and describe the five listed ways that a drug can have an antagonist effect.

4. How is it that "nonpharmacological factors" such as set and setting can influence drug effects, and why is it necessary to put the term "nonpharmacological factors" in quotes?

5. What similarities and differences between drugs can be grasped by studying dose-response curves?

REFERENCES

1. Barrett, J.E. Nonpharmacological factors determining the behavioral effects of drugs. In H.Y. Meltzer (Ed.) *Psychopharmacology: The third generation of progress*, New York: Raven Press, 1987.

2. Benet, L.Z., & Sheiner, L.B. Pharmacokinetics: The dynamics of drug absorption, distribution and elimination. In A. G. Gilman, L. S. Goodman, T. W. Rall, & F. Murad (Eds.) *The pharmacological basis of therapeutics* (7th ed.), New York: Macmillan, 1985.

3. Benson, H.,& Epstein, M.D. The placebo effect. *Journal of the American Medical Association*, 1975, 232, 1225-1227.

4. Blau, S. A guide to the use of psychotropic medications in children and adolescents. *Journal of Clinical Psychiatry*, 1978, 39, 766-772.

5. Critchlow, B. The powers of John Barleycorn: Beliefs about the effects of alcohol on social behavior. *American Psychologist*, 1986, 41, 751-764.

6. Deniker, P. Introduction of neuroleptic chemotherapy into psychiatry. In F.J. Ayd, & B. Blackwell (Eds.) *Discoveries in biological psychiatry*, Philadelphia: Lippincott, 1970.

7. Dworkin, S.I., & Smith, J.E. Behavioral contingencies involved in drug-induced neurotransmitter turnover changes. *NIDA Research Monograph*, 1986, 74, 90-105.

8. Falk, J.L., & Feingold, D.A. Environmental and cultural factors in the behavioral action of drugs. In H.Y. Meltzer (Ed.) *Psychopharmacology: The third generation of progress*, New York: Raven Press, 1987.

9. Hesp, B., & Resch. The medicinal chemist's approach to CNS drug discovery. In H.Y. Meltzer (Ed.) *Psychopharmacology: The third generation of progress*, New York: Raven Press, 1987.

10. Janowsky, D.S., Addario, D., & Risch, S.G. *Psychopharmacology case studies*. New York: Guilford Press, 1987.

11. Klaasen, C.D. Principles of toxicology. In A. G. Gilman, L. S. Goodman, T. W. Rall, & F. Murad (Eds.) *The pharmacological basis of therapeutics* (7th ed.), New York: Macmillan, 1985.

12. Langer, S.Z. Presynaptic regulation of monoaminergic neurons. In H.Y. Meltzer (Ed.) *Psychopharmacology: The third generation of progress*, New York: Raven Press, 1987.

13. Morley, J.E., Sterman, M.B., & Walsh, J.H. *Nutritional modulation of neural function*. New York: Academic Press, 1988.

14. Murad, F., & Gilman, A. G. Drug interactions. In A. G. Gilman, L. S. Goodman, T. W. Rall, & F. Murad (Eds.) *The pharmacological basis of therapeutics* (7th ed.), New York: Macmillan, 1985.

15. O'Connell, R.A. Psychological and social aspects of psychopharmacologic treatment. In F. Flach (Ed.) *Psychobiology and psychopharmacology*. New York: W.W. Norton, 1988.

16. Ross, E. M., & Gilman, A. G. Pharmacodynamics: Mechanisms of drug action and the relationship between drug concentration and effect. In A. G. Gilman, L. S. Goodman, T. W. Rall, & F. Murad (Eds.) *The pharmacological basis of therapeutics* (7th ed.), New York: Macmillan, 1985.

17. Ryall, R.W. *Mechanisms of drug action on the nervous system.* Cambridge, MA: Cambridge University Press, 1989.

18. *Sacks, O. *Awakenings.* New York: E.P. Dutton, 1983.

19. Schaffer, C.B., Donlon, P.T., & Schaffer, L.C. Drug combinations and interactions. In J.P. Tupin, R.I. Shader, & D.S. Harnett (Eds.) *Handbook of clinical psychopharmacology* (2nd ed.). Northvale, NJ: Jason Aronson, Inc., 1988.

20. Seeman, P. The membrane actions of anesthetics and tranquilizers. *Pharmacological Review*, 1972, 24, 583-655.

21. Stahl, S.M., Iversen, S.D., & Goodman, E.C. *Cognitive neurochemistry.* Oxford, England: Oxford Press, 1987.

22. Taylor, P. Anticholinesterase agents. In A. G. Gilman, L. S. Goodman, T. W. Rall, & F. Murad (Eds.) *The pharmacological basis of therapeutics* (7th ed.). New York: Macmillan, 1985.

23. Thompson, T.L., Moran, M.G., & Neis, A.S. Psychotropic drug use in the elderly: II. *New England Journal of Medicine*, 1983, 306, 194-199.

24. Veith, R.C. Depression in the elderly: Pharmacologic considerations in treatment. *Journal of the American Geriatric Society*, 1982, 30, 581-596.

25. Weiner, N., & Taylor, P. Neurohumoral transmission: The autonomic and somatic motor nervous systems. In A. G. Gilman, L. S. Goodman, T. W. Rall, & F. Murad (Eds.) *The pharmacological basis of therapeutics* (7th ed.). New York: Macmillan, 1985.

26. Werry, J.S. *Pediatric psychopharmacology: The use of behavior modifying drugs in children.* New York: Brunner/Mazel, 1980.

27. Wurtman, R.J., & Wurtman, J.J. *Food constituents affecting normal and abnormal behaviors.* New York: Raven Press, 1986.

28. Zinberg, N. E. *Drug, set and setting: The basis for controlled intoxicant use,* New Haven: Yale University Press, 1984.

* Introductory or intermediate reading

Chapter 5

TOLERANCE, SENSITIZATION, AND PHYSICAL DEPENDENCY

The purposes of this chapter are to:

1. Introduce the terms tolerance and sensitization, which describe a decrease or increase, respectively, in response to drug actions,

2. Discuss the special problems posed by the development of (a) differential tolerance, (b) tolerance to some aspects of a drug's actions with simultaneous sensitization to other aspects, and (c) cross tolerances and cross sensitizations,

3. Discuss controversies surrounding the concepts of physical dependence, withdrawal, addiction, psychological dependence, and compulsive use, and

4. Reveal the degree to which the severity of all the phenomena listed above can be powerfully influenced by factors under the control of the individual taking the drug.

TOLERANCE

The most widely recognized consequence of chronic drug use is the development of **tolerance**. Tolerance occurs because the body is attempting to maintain homeostasis in the face of chronic drug intake. Tolerance has occurred when chronic drug intake leads to a decreased response to the same dose administered repeatedly. Despite popular misconception, tolerance is not a tendency to increase dose, but instead an ability to withstand higher doses than could be tolerated before[41]. Thus, the phenomenon of tolerance in no way compels anyone to take more drug than before. Tolerance can,

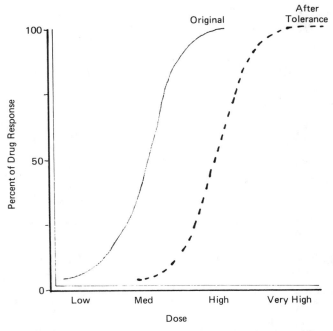

Figure 5.1. Tolerance as a rightward shift in the dose-response curve. Increases in drug dose are now required to obtain drug effects that could be obtained at lower doses prior to tolerance.

however, lead people who want a certain level of a specific drug action to decide that the best way to achieve it is through an increase in dose. For example, someone who takes a once-a-day prescribed pill to achieve sleep may find, after a few weeks or months, that two pills are now required to achieve the same amount of sleep. Tolerance is represented by a rightward shift in the dose-response curve (see Figure 5.1).

DIFFERENTIAL AND CROSS TOLERANCE

There is ample evidence that tolerance develops more rapidly to some aspects of a drug's actions than to others[24,28]. For example, researchers gave human volunteers an antianxiety agent for seven days (see Chapter 10). Although there was no tolerance to the subjective feelings of intoxication and relief of anxiety, there was tolerance to the influence of the drug on motor performance such as reaction time[1]. A more powerful demonstration of differential tolerance was offered by an experiment comparing drug-free volunteers to patients who had been taking an antianxiety agent for six months or more. When given a **challenge dose** of the drug at test, the patients revealed complete tolerance to the drug's effect on hormone levels, but only a partial tolerance to drug-induced sedation[29]. This **differential tolerance** can be exploited for medical purposes[6]. The most effective medicines are those in which chronic use leads to a tolerance to troublesome side effects,

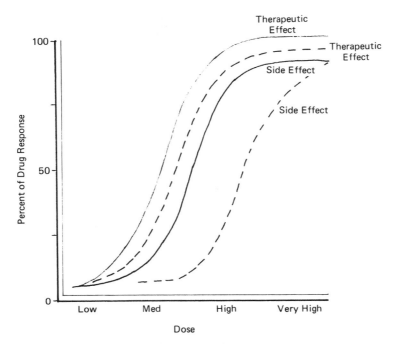

Figure 5.2. A dose-response curve revealing the positive effects of differential tolerance. Note that the more rapid development of tolerance to the side effect than to the therapeutic effect enables administration of doses that retain their therapeutic effect without inducing side effects.

without tolerance to the therapeutic effect of the drug. Figure 5.2 demonstrates this potential benefit of differential tolerance. Unfortunately, differential tolerance can also lead to negative consequences. This is most likely to occur when tolerance develops to the therapeutic effect of the drug but not to troublesome side effects (see Figure 5.3).

Further complications arise due to **cross tolerance**. Cross tolerance, a specific form of drug interaction, occurs when chronic consumption of one drug leads to the development of tolerance to specific actions of another drug. For instance, researchers found that volunteers given one antianxiety agent for seven days revealed tolerance when given, at test, a challenge dose of a different antianxiety agent[1]. That is, chronic consumption of the first drug led to a shift to the right in the dose-response curve for the second drug.

There are two important characteristics to cross tolerance. First, like regular tolerance, cross tolerance is usually not complete. **Differential cross tolerance** occurs when chronic consumption of one drug leads to variations in tolerance to the different aspects of a second drug's actions. Secondly, although cross tolerance is most often tested in drugs that have similar actions, cross tolerances can, and often do, occur between drugs that are superficially dissimilar[21].

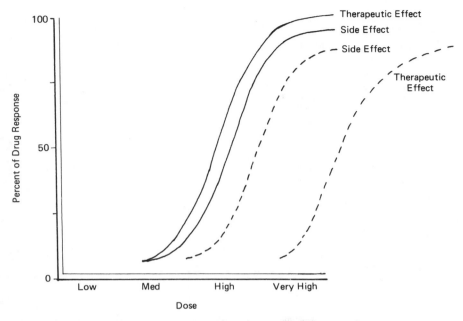

Figure 5.3. A dose-response curve revealing the negative effects of differential tolerance. Note that the more rapid development of tolerance to the therapeutic effect than to the side effect makes it difficult to administer any therapeutically effective dose without inducing significant side effects.

SENSITIZATION

Although most people have heard of tolerance, fewer are aware of the possibility of the opposite occurrence. When a drug is taken chronically, it is possible that the individual taking the drug may become more, rather than less, sensitive to particular actions of the drug. This increase in responsiveness is referred to as **sensitization**[13]. Sensitization shows itself as a shift in the dose-response curve to the left (see Figure 5.4).

As with tolerance, there are a variety of complicating factors that can make sensitization particularly troublesome. **Differential sensitization**, like differential tolerance, is the rule rather than the exception. Even worse, it is highly likely that a person taking a drug chronically will develop tolerance to some aspects of the drug and sensitization to other aspects. This is called **simultaneous tolerance/sensitization**. A person given a drug for a behavioral disorder may become tolerant to the beneficial effect of the drug while simultaneously developing a sensitization to some negative side effect. This can lead to a situation where the easy occurrence of these negative side effects makes it impossible to give the patient an effective therapeutic dose of the drug. Figure 5.5 demonstrates the effect of simultaneous tolerance/sensitization on dose-response curves.

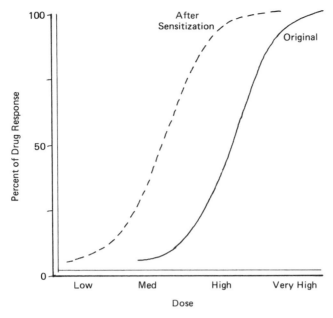

Figure 5.4. Sensitization as a leftward shift in the dose-response curve. Drug effects previously obtainable only at higher doses will now occur at lower doses.

Cross-sensitization may also occur. That is, individuals who chronically consume one drug may find that they are particularly sensitive to some action of a second drug, even though they may have never before taken that second drug. A patient who is taking medicine for some heart condition may be unpleasantly surprised to discover that a usually safe dose of a drug for a behavioral problem presents particular dangers in that cross sensitive individual.

MECHANISMS OF TOLERANCE AND SENSITIZATION

As mentioned above, both tolerance and sensitization can be viewed as particular examples of drug interactions (see Chapter 4). In these cases, though, the chronic consumption of one drug is interacting with the acute consequences of intake of the same (but sometimes a different) drug. There are, in general, three different categories of explanations of the mechanisms underlying the development of tolerance and sensitization[38].

Pharmacokinetic

The first category is **pharmacokinetic**[5]. A pharmacokinetic explanation emphasizes the effects of chronic drug intake on the absorption, distribution, or metabolism of the acute drug. For instance, chronic consumption of a drug may lead the body to attempt

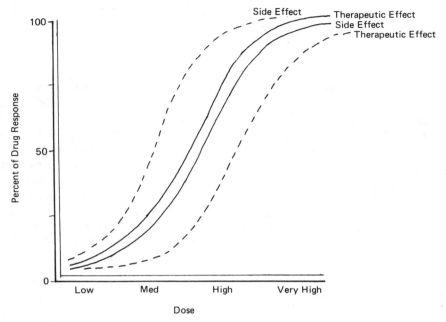

Figure 5.5. A dose-response curve revealing the extremely negative effects of simultaneous tolerance/sensitization. Note that the development of tolerance to the therapeutic effect, coupled with sensitization to the side effect, makes it impossible to administer any therapeutically effective dose without inducing maximal side effects.

to maintain homeostasis by increasing liver enzymes involved in metabolism of the drug. Thus, acute doses of the drug will be more rapidly metabolized, decreasing the amount of drug that gains access to the brain. This would shift the dose response curve to the right, indicating the occurrence of tolerance[18]. On the other hand, chronic consumption of a drug may lead to a **saturation** (complete filling) of blood-borne carrier proteins. Since none of the acute drug will then be bound to the carrier proteins, more of it can gain access to the brain. Thus, there will be a shift in the dose-response curve to the left, indicating the occurrence of sensitization. The influence of chronic consumption of one drug on the absorption, distribution, and metabolism of a different acute drug can explain cross tolerance and cross sensitization.

Pharmacodynamic

The second category of explanation for tolerance and/or sensitization is **pharmacodynamic**[25]. A pharmacodynamic explanation assumes that chronic intake of the drug has altered the synapse (see the discussion in Chapter 4 on the long-term effects of agonists and antagonists). For instance, chronic intake of a drug may lead to receptor supersensitivity (thus causing sensitization); it may also or instead lead to a decreased synthesis of neurotransmitter (thus causing tolerance). Since a drug can have an effect at many different synapses, pharmacodynamic explanations are especially useful when there is evidence of differential tolerance and/or sensitization or even simultaneous tolerance and sensitization.

Behavioral

The third category of explanation emphasizes a **behavioral** approach[23,33,34,35]. The behavioral approach notes that "the presence of tolerance is strongly related to crucial environmental variables"[11]. The behavioral explanation of tolerance emphasizes the fact that drugs can be viewed within the framework of Pavlovian conditioning[26]. A drug can be seen as an unconditioned stimulus (UCS) that, through interaction with receptors, induces unconditioned responses (UCR). One set of these unconditioned responses involves the beginning of pharmacokinetic and pharmacodynamic attempts to return the body to a pre-drug homeostasis. Environmental stimuli associated with the chronic administration of a drug become paired with the unconditioned attempts to maintain homeostasis. Thus, these environmental stimuli become conditioned stimuli (CS) that start these pharmacokinetic and pharmacodynamic processes even before the drug is taken (CR). When the acute drug consumption occurs in the

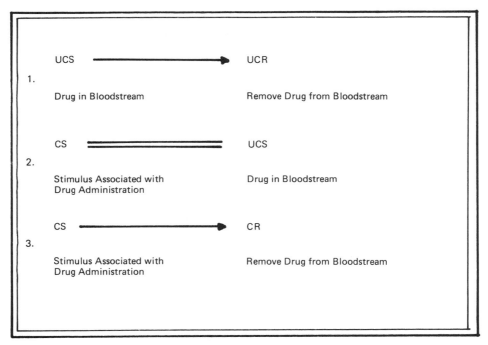

Figure 5.6. Pavlovian conditioning model of tolerance. Note how initially the presence of the drug in the bloodstream (UCS) leads to processes that remove the drug from the bloodstream (UCR). After repeated pairings of the presence of drug in the bloodstream with stimuli associated with administration of the drug (CS), the processes that remove the drug from the bloodstream begin with presentation of the stimuli usually associated with administration of the drug (CR). Tolerance is displayed because there is a lesser effect of drugs administered in the presence of the CS.

presence of the CS, the CS elicits the CR, thus reducing the effectiveness of the drug and shifting the dose-response curve to the right (see Figure 5.6). A Pavlovian model can also explain the occurrence of sensitization simply by assuming that the drug effect itself, rather than homeostatic consequences of the drug, is the UCR that eventually becomes the CR elicited by environmental stimuli[19]. Familiarity with the idea that most drugs have effects at more than one type of receptor (see Chapter 4) can help the understanding of how simultaneous tolerance/sensitization can occur. However, sophisticated learning theory must be applied in order to predict which drug effects will shift to the right, indicating tolerance, and which will shift to the left, indicating sensitization[8].

The behavioral explanation combines the influence of behavioral, pharmacodynamic, and pharmacokinetic mechanisms of tolerance and sensitization. Even better, behavioral explanations can account for the occurrence of tolerance and/or sensitization when drug administrations are so infrequent that the homeostatic pharmacokinetic or pharmacodynamic effects of each chronic drug administration fade away before they can have a direct effect on acute drug intake[3]. If the acute drug is given under the same environmental conditions as the chronic drug, the environment can act as a CS, thus causing tolerance. The occurrence of **environmental specificity of tolerance** is the most powerful evidence for the role of behavioral mechanisms in tolerance. Environmental specificity of tolerance is demonstrated when a person with tolerance to a drug in a setting associated with chronic drug intake reveals a lack of tolerance when tested in another environment. In one case, a patient given morphine for pain relief actually died from taking, in a novel environment, a dose that the patient had developed tolerance to as a result of chronic consumption in a stable environment[36]. Further experiments supported the role of behavioral mechanisms in tolerance, by providing evidence that the degree of tolerance is lawfully and predictably affected by the number of CS-UCS (environment-drug) pairings, the intensity of the UCS (drug dose), partial reinforcement (pairing only a few CS presentations with the UCS), and extinction of the CS (repeated presentation of the stimuli without the drug)[34]. Others add to this support by noting that the development of tolerance is influenced by such well-known conditioning phenomena as latent inhibition, conditioned inhibition, sensory preconditioning, overshadowing, and blocking[17].

None of the body's homeostatic adjustments or mechanisms for learning are without limit. Tolerance and sensitization therefore also have limits. In fact, patients on medication will likely find that after a period of tolerance and an increase in dose to attempt to counterbalance the tolerance, they are able to achieve the desired level of drug effect without any further increase in dose[6,41].

USER CONTROL OVER DEVELOPMENT OF TOLERANCE AND SENSITIZATION

It may appear that tolerance and sensitization to drug actions are things that simply happen to someone. However, a number of factors that influence the development of tolerance and sensitization are under the control of the person taking the drug.

The most obvious way to limit the development of tolerance, sensitization, cross tolerance, and cross sensitization is to **abstain** from drug consumption. The avoidance of consumption of any and all unnecessary drugs will insure that prescribed drugs will be effective (no tolerance) and safe (no sensitization). However, if someone must take medication because of some physical or behavioral disorder, it is still possible to exert some control over the development of tolerance and sensitization. The two most important factors under user control are **dose** and **frequency**. Smaller doses and infrequent consumption will lead to slower-developing and ultimately less tolerance and sensitization. On the other hand, larger doses and frequent consumption will lead to more rapid and more notable tolerance and sensitization. For instance, researchers found that the behavioral effects of an overdose of an antianxiety agent started to fade even before the drug was cleared from the body. The authors concluded that this extremely rapid tolerance revealed that the early effects of massive doses of a drug can induce tolerance to the later effects of that same drug administration[29]. Frequency refers to how often the drug is used and must include information about the time period between drug consumptions. With large gaps between drug consumptions, less tolerance or sensitization will occur[9]. However, it is important to remember the potential role of an environmental CS. For instance, humans displayed tolerance to some of the effects of an antianxiety drug even though the "chronic" doses of the drug were given at seven day intervals[12].

DEPENDENCY AND CROSS-DEPENDENCY

Another major problem of chronic use is the possibility that the individual taking the drug may become **physically dependent** upon the drug. It is assumed that physical dependency has occurred when a sudden halt of chronic drug consumption, or the administration of an antagonist to the chronically consumed drug, leads to a drug-specific set of physical symptoms. These **withdrawal symptoms** may be merely uncomfortable and annoying, or they may be life-threatening[20]. As specific drugs are discussed in future chapters, the drug's capacity to induce physical dependency will be discussed and the severity of withdrawal symptoms will be detailed.

Just as chronic consumption of one drug can lead to a cross tolerance or cross sensitization, drugs capable of inducing a physical dependency often induce a **cross dependency**. A cross dependency is demonstrated when an individual who is physically dependent upon one drug can have withdrawal symptoms eliminated through the administration of a second drug. Because of cross dependency, halting the intake of a drug with severe withdrawal symptoms can be made easier by substituting another drug with less severe withdrawal symptoms[30,32].

CESSATION PHENOMENA

Finding out whether a medicine causes physical dependency should be a simple matter of looking for withdrawal symptoms in chronic users who suddenly stop or are given an antagonist. However, there are a variety of types of **cessation phenomena**, or events that occur when drug use is halted. True withdrawal symptoms probably reflect the attempt of the body to maintain pharmacodynamic and pharmacokinetic homeostasis in the face of chronic drug consumption[5,25]. On the other hand, the sudden cessation of a chronically consumed medicine may result in **rebound**, an increase in the severity of the original disorder[14,22,24]. It can often be difficult to distinguish between true withdrawal symptoms and rebound, but careful attention to the distinction is important to the determination of whether a particular medicine can, or cannot, lead to physical dependency.

Finally, if a rewarding activity is engaged in on a regular basis, the sudden cessation of that behavior can lead to feelings of **frustration**[37]. Sudden cessation of chronically used medication can lead to symptoms of **frustrated nonreward** that include anxiety, discomfort, and a sense of longing (**craving**) for the drug. It can be difficult to distinguish true withdrawal symptoms from frustrated nonreward, thus complicating the difficulty in determining whether a particular medicine can, or cannot, lead to physical dependency.

Unfortunately, the confusion caused by the varieties of cessation phenomena are compounded by the fact that there is no real consensus within the scientific community regarding which drug cessation phenomena are true withdrawal symptoms, which are rebound, and which represent frustrated nonreward. Thus, a reading of the literature will reveal that reasonable scientists frequently disagree about whether a particular compound is, or is not, capable of causing physical dependency[27,31].

PHYSICAL DEPENDENCY VERSUS COMPULSIVE USE

Many non-scientists are less concerned with what they perceive as the technical question of whether a drug induces a physical dependency than with the fear that chronic use of a medicine will leave them "addicted" or "psychologically dependent"[7]. While these fears are not unfounded, some scientists feel that the terms used to describe the problem cause more confusion than necessary. In a text on pharmacology used in the education of most physicians in this country, it was stated that "the term addiction...has been used in so many ways that it can no longer be employed without further qualification or elaboration"[20]. Others have suggested that the idea of psychological dependency arose, not out of scientific necessity, but instead as an ideological tool to discourage the consumption of drugs that, while decidedly unhealthy, did not in fact cause a physical dependency[41].

It is difficult to disagree with the argument that there are diverse meanings of addiction and that the concept of psychological dependency has a questionable history. Nonetheless, both of these terms represent an attempt to label a real, although elusive and scientifically troublesome, set of consequences of chronic drug use. There is much evidence that, regardless of whether the drug can cause a physical dependency, behavioral factors insure that effective medication for behavioral disorders might sometimes induce **compulsive use**[15,16,27].

It has been stated that the two major behavioral factors are "the induction of pleasure by the drug and the avoidance of discomfort by its continued use"[25]. The "induction of pleasure" refers to the reinforcing effects of an exogenous compound[4] which are probably mediated by interaction with specific portions of the brain involved in identifying reinforcement provided by food, water, sex, heat, etc.[10]. The "avoidance of discomfort" refers to the phenomenon of **negative reinforcement**[37]. Negative reinforcement involves the *removal* of an *unpleasant* environmental stimulus. A behavior that generates negative reinforcement is likely to be repeated. Even if a medicine does not induce a pleasurable, positively reinforcing state, if it is an effective medicine it will remove the unpleasant aspects of the disorder it is prescribed to treat. Thus, effective medicine always acts as a negative reinforcer: The probability that the behavior of taking the medication the next time symptoms of the disorder reappear increases whenever the medication exerts its therapeutic action.

Since effective medicines, even those incapable of inducing positive reinforcement, will induce negative reinforcement, the sudden cessation of chronic intake will lead to frustrated nonreward. In addition, sudden cessation may, in some cases, lead to rebound and true withdrawal. Any one of these three types of cessation phenomena can usually be halted by intake of the medicine in question. This removal of the negative consequences of cessation provides negative reinforcement. The next time the individual stops taking the medicine, past experience with earlier attempts to halt will increase the probability that they will eliminate the feelings of drug cessation by a resumption of drug intake[34]. This can lead the compulsive user, whether or not physically dependent, to experience a subjective feeling of having "lost control" over drug intake. This is the state of "addiction" or "physical dependency" that many people fear[27].

A behavioral analysis reveals that physical dependency is not necessary for the development of compulsive use. Interestingly, physical dependency also does not insure that compulsive use will occur. Physical dependency is the inevitable result of a certain pattern of repeated intake of some specific drugs[20,41]. However, compulsive use arises because of the impact of positive and negative reinforcement. There are case histories of hospitalized individuals who were given reinforcing painkilling drugs in sufficient doses and patterns to induce physical dependency. When these individuals left the hospitals and thus halted their consumption of the painkilling drugs, they experienced true withdrawal symptoms. However, none of these individuals became compulsive users, since none of them experienced negative reinforcement by taking more painkillers to eliminate these withdrawal symptoms. Physically dependent individuals become compulsive users only if they (a) recognize the symptoms of withdrawal, (b) conclude that these symptoms are due to the cessation of chronic drug intake, and (c) experience negative reinforcement when they discover that intake of the drug will eliminate these symptoms[27].

USER CONTROL OVER DEVELOPMENT OF DEPENDENCY AND COMPULSIVE USE

Just as there are things that the chronic drug consumer can do to influence tolerance and sensitization, there are patterns of drug consumption that can decrease or increase the chances of physical dependency and compulsive use[41]. Naturally, abstinent individuals will not suffer withdrawal or the problems associated with compulsive use. However, physical and psychological difficulties may require the prescription of drugs that can induce a physical dependency or lead to compulsive use. Even if chronic drug use is necessary, steps may be taken to limit physical dependency and compulsive use. For instance, as with tolerance, smaller doses, infrequent consumption[2] and longer intervals between consumptions[40] will lead to less physical dependency than will larger doses, frequent consumption, and little gap between bouts of administration. Regardless of the degree of physical dependency, chronic drug use can be halted with relative ease, either through gradual reduction of dose[39] or pharmacological aids to cessation (see Chapter 12).

Compulsive use can also be limited by using small, infrequent doses with longer periods between drug consumptions[16]. In addition, controlling the development of compulsive use can employ the human faculty of reason to overcome the natural biological tendency to repeat things that provide pleasure or reduce unpleasant feelings. Those attempting to avoid compulsive use should not take prescribed medication for nonmedical purposes. They probably need to remind themselves with each legitimate prescribed intake that any pleasant effects of the drug are perhaps among the more serious side effects of that drug. They should also remind themselves, when they attempt to quit, that resuming drug intake will provide negative reinforcement. Finally, regardless of whether chronic consumption results in physical dependency or compulsive use (or both) individuals who question their strength in the face of the powerful physical forces underlying "addiction" will do well to remember the assertion that "people's values do not cease to operate in the face of physiological forces"[27]. Compulsive use may be a more powerful motivator than physical dependency, but it need not overcome the decision-making ability of an **autonomous** (independent and self-willed) human being.

CHAPTER SUMMARY

Chronic use of a drug may lead to tolerance (a shift in the dose-response curve to the right) or sensitization (a shift in the dose-response curve to the left). Each aspect of a drug's effects can undergo either tolerance or sensitization at different rates of speed than other aspects of the drug's effects (differential tolerance and/or differential sensitization). In addition, tolerance or sensitization to one or more aspects of a drug's effects can lead to tolerance or sensitization to the same, or different, aspects of another drug's effects (cross tolerance and/or cross sensitization). The development of tolerance and/or sensitization can be explained by reference to one or more of the following three mechanisms: pharmacokinetic, pharmacodynamic, or behavioral. The user of a drug has the potential to control the development of tolerance by abstaining from drug use, or by limiting the dose and frequency of drug intake.

Cessation of chronic use of a drug can lead to one or more of the following cessation phenomena: rebound, frustrated nonreward, and withdrawal symptoms. If the phenomena associated with cessation of a drug include withdrawal symptoms, it can be said that the drug caused a physical dependency. However, even drugs that don't cause withdrawal symptoms may lead to compulsive use. Compulsive use is motivated both by the positive reinforcement of the drug and by the negative reinforcement provided when a resumption of drug use eliminates cessation phenomena. As with tolerance, both physical dependence and compulsive use can best be avoided by abstaining from drug use. However, individuals who must take a drug chronically for medicinal purposes can limit the development of physical dependence and compulsive use by limiting dose and frequency of consumption.

REVIEW ESSAY QUESTIONS

1. Contrast tolerance and sensitization by (a) using language that a non-scientist could understand and (b) using graphs that reveal shifts in dose-response curves.

2. How do pharmacodynamic, pharmacokinetic, and behavioral theories of tolerance and sensitization differ in their ability to explain the occurrence of cross tolerance and cross sensitization?

3. What are the differences and similarities among the various phenomena that accompany the cessation of chronic drug use?

4. How can a medicine that does not provide positive reinforcement and is not capable of causing a physical dependency nonetheless be used compulsively?

5. What can people who must chronically consume prescribed medications do to decrease their chances of developing tolerance, sensitization, physical dependency, and compulsive use?

REFERENCES

1. Aranko, K., Mattila, M.J., & Seppala, T. Development of tolerance and cross-tolerance to the psychomotor actions of lorazepam and diazepam in man. *British Journal of Clinical Pharmacology*, 1983, 15, 545-552.

2. Ayd, F.R. Benzodiazepines: dependence and withdrawal. *Journal of the American Medical Association*, 1979, 242, 1401-1402.

3. *Barrett, J.E. Nonpharmacological factors determining the behavioral effects of drugs. In H.Y. Meltzer (Ed.) *Psychopharmacology: The third generation of progress*, New York: Raven Press, 1987.

4. Bigelow, G.E., Griffiths, R.R., Liebson, I., & Kaliszak, J.E. Double-blind evaluations of reinforcing and anorectic actions of weight control medications. *Archives of General Psychiatry*, 1980, 37, 1118-1123.

5. Busto, U., & Sellers, E. Pharmacokinetic determinants of drug abuse and dependence. A conceptual perspective. *Clinical pharmacokinetics*, 1986, 11, 144-153.

6. Colpaert, F.C. Can chronic pain be suppressed despite purported tolerance to narcotic analgesia? *Life Sciences*, 1979, 24, 1201-1210.

7. Council on Scientific Affairs. Drug abuse related to prescribing practices. *Journal of the American Medical Association*, 1982, 247, 864-866.

8. Eikelboom, R., & Stewart, J. Conditioning of drug-induced physiological responses. *Psychological Review*, 1982, 89, 507-528.

9. Emmett-Oglesby, M.W., & Taylor, K.E. Role of dose interval in the acquisition of tolerance to methylphenidate. *Neuropharmacology*, 1981, 20, 995-1002.

10. Engel, J., Oreland, L., Ingvar, D.H., Pernow, B., Roessner, S., & Pellborn, L.A. *Brain reward systems and abuse*. New York: Raven Press, 1985.

11. *Falk, J.L., & Feingold, D.A. Environmental and cultural factors in the behavioral action of drugs. In H.Y. Meltzer (Ed.) *Psychopharmacology: The third generation of progress*, New York: Raven Press, 1987.

12. File, S.E., & Lister, R.G. Does tolerance to lorazepam develop with once weekly dosing? *British Journal of Clinical Pharmacology*, 1983, 16, 645-650.

13. Fisher, S., Raskin, A., & Uhlenhuth, E.H. *Cocaine: Clinical and biobehavioral aspects*. New York: Oxford University Press, 1987.

14. Fontaine, R., Chouinard, G., & Annable, L. Rebound anxiety in anxious patients after abrupt withdrawal of benzodiazepine treatment. *American Journal of Psychiatry*, 1984, 141, 848-852.

15. Goldberg, S.R. The behavioral analysis of drug addiction. In S.D. Glick and J. Goldfarb (Eds.) *Behavioral pharmacology*, St. Louis: C.V. Mosby Company, 1976.

16. Goldberg, S.R., & Stolerman, I.P. *Behavioral analysis of drug dependence*. Orlando, FL: Academic Press, 1986.

17. Goudie, A.J., & Demellweek, C. Conditioning factors in drug tolerance. In S.R. Goldberg, & I.P. Stolerman (Eds.) *Behavioral analysis of drug dependence*, Orlando, FL: Academic Press, 1986.

18. Han, Y.H. Why do alcoholics require more anesthesia? *Anesthesiology*, 1969, 30, 341-342.

19. Hinson, R.E., & Poulos, C.X. Sensitization of the behavioral effects of cocaine: Modification by Pavlovian conditioning. *Pharmacology, Biochemistry and Behavior*, 1981, 15, 559-562.

20. Jaffe, J.H. Drug addiction and drug abuse. In A.S. Goodman, L.S. Goodman, T.W. Rall, & F. Murad (Eds.) *The pharmacological basis of therapeutics (7th ed.)*. New York: Macmillan, 1985.

21. Janowsky, D.S., Addario, D., & Risch, S.C. *Psychopharmacology case studies*. New York: Guilford Press, 1987.

22. Klein, H.E., Broucek, B., & Greil, W. Lithium withdrawal triggers psychotic states. *British Journal of Psychiatry*, 1981, 139, 255-256.

23. Krasnegor, N.A. *Behavioral tolerance: Research and treatment implications*. Washington, D.C.: U.S. Government Printing Office, 1978.

24. Lader, M. The psychopharmacology of addiction—Benzodiazepine tolerance and dependence. In M. Lader (Ed.) *The psychopharmacology of addiction*, Oxford: Oxford University Press, 1988.

25. Murphy, S.M., & Tyrer, P. The essence of benzodiazepine dependence. In M. Lader (Ed.) *The psychopharmacology of addiction*, Oxford: Oxford University Press, 1988.

26. Pavlov, I.P. *Conditioned reflexes (Translated by G.V. Anrep)*. London: Oxford University Press, 1927.

27. *Peele, S. *The meaning of addiction: Compulsive experience and its interpretation*. Lexington, MA: Lexington Books, 1985.

28. Petursson, H., & Lader, M.H. Benzodiazepine dependence. *British Journal of Addiction*, 1981, 76, 133-145.

29. Peturrson, H., & Lader, M. *Dependence on tranquilizers*. Oxford: Oxford University Press, 1984.

30. Rosenbloom, A. Emerging treatment options in the alcohol withdrawal syndrome. *Journal of Clinical Psychiatry*, 1988, 49, 28-31.

31. Russel, M.A.H. What is dependence? In M.A.H. Russell, D. Hawks, & M. MacCafferty (Eds.) *Drugs and drug dependence*, Westmead, England: Saxon House/Lexington Books, 1976.

32. Sellers, E.M., & Naranjo, C.A. New strategies for the treatment of alcohol withdrawal. *Psychopharmacology Bulletin*, 1986, 22, 88-92.

33. Shapiro, A.P., & Nathan P. Human tolerance to alcohol: The role of Pavlovian conditioning processes. *Psychopharmacology*, 1986, 88, 90-95.

34. Siegel, S. Classical conditioning, drug tolerance, and drug dependence. In Y. Israel, F.B. Glaser, H. Kalant, R.E. Popham, W. Schmidt, & R.G. Smart (Eds.) *Recent advances in alcohol and drug problems, Volume 7*, New York: Plenum Press, 1983.

35. Siegel, S. Drug anticipation and drug tolerance. In M. Lader (Ed.) *The psychopharmacology of addiction*, Oxford: Oxford University Press, 1988.

36. Siegel, S., & Ellsworth, D. Pavlovian conditioning and death from apparent overdose of medically prescribed morphine: A case report. *Bulletin of the Psychonomic Society*, 1986, 24, 278-280.

37. *Skinner, B.F. *About behaviorism.* New York: Alfred A. Knopf, 1974.

38. Tabakoff, B., Cornell, N., & Hoffman, P.L. Alcohol tolerance. *Annals of Emergency Medicine*, 1986, 15, 1005-1012.

39. Tyrer, P., Owen, R., & Dawling, S. Gradual withdrawal of diazepam after long-term therapy. *Lancet*, I, 1983, 1402-1406.

40. Tyrer, P., & Seivewright, N. Identification and management of benzodiazepine dependence. *Postgraduate Medical Journal*, 1984, 60, 41-46.

41. *Zinberg, N.E. *Drug, set and setting: The basis for controlled intoxicant use.* New Haven, CT: Yale University Press, 1984.

* Introductory or intermediate reading

Chapter 6

HISTORY, RESEARCH METHODOLOGY, AND CONTROVERSIES

The purposes of this chapter are to:

1. Provide a brief history of the physical treatment of behavioral disorders,

2. Present a discussion of the difficulties in evaluating the effectiveness of therapies for behavioral disorders,

3. Discuss the issue of whether behavioral disorders are stigmatizing labels, the result of psychological problems, or true mental illnesses arising from abnormal nervous systems, and

4. Examine the reasons for underuse and overuse of behavioral medicines by patients and physicians.

BRIEF HISTORY

Folk Medicine: Witchcraft and Shamanism

Long before the beginnings of the development of what can loosely be called medicine, people tried to cure behavioral disorders through treatment of the body. Witches and **shamans** (medicine "men," who as often as not were women) supplemented their chants and incantations with preparations made from local plants and minerals. People who believed that behavioral disorders were caused by possession by demons used **exorcism** (religious ceremonies), sometimes aided by beatings, burnings, and long dunks in water to try to make the body uncomfortable, thus driving the demons out. Still others proposed that behavioral disorders were caused by excesses of **vapors** (life-sustaining airs), blood, other fluids (**humors**), or bodily wastes. These theories logically led to such practices as **trephining** (the drilling of holes in the head to allow the vapors to escape), bleedings or the application of leeches, prolonged perspiration, and enemas[44]. Many of these practices were continued into the twentieth century, even in "enlightened" areas of the world[25].

Modern Behavioral Medicines

Significant progress in the drug treatment of behavioral disorders did not occur until the 1950s. During that decade, drugs that were effective in the treatment of severe behavioral disorders were developed. Drugs were used to treat the complete loss of contact with reality known as **psychosis**, to treat the severe sadness and melancholy known as **depression**, to treat the wild swings from an elated to depressed mood shown by people with **manic-depressive illness** or **bipolar affective disorder**, and to treat the poor attention span and excess of activity shown by those with **hyperactivity**[42]. The discovery that consuming small molecules could have specific beneficial effects upon people with the most severe behavioral problems led to attempts to cure other behavioral problems with drugs. Since the 1950s, drugs have been developed to treat free-floating fears (**anxiety**) and panic, to help people lose weight, and to help people quit taking drugs like alcohol and heroin[37].

EVALUATING THE EFFECTIVENESS OF BEHAVIORAL MEDICINES

When faced with the desperate problems posed by behavioral disorders, people of the past were likely to try desperate cures. Despite the advances of the present day, we might still resort to desperate attempts to cure behavioral disorders. The cautions raised by Elliot Valenstein in his book about psychosurgery[43] should be enough to insure demands that any treatment of behavioral disorder be proven to be safe and effective. In the U.S., the Food and Drug Administration assumes that all new drugs are both unsafe and ineffective, and requires that stringent proof be provided before the drug can be widely used in humans[29]. Providing proof that a behavioral medicine (or **psychopharmacotherapeutic**) is both safe and effective, though, presents a number of problems for the design and ethics of experiments with humans.

False Positives and False Negatives

There are two major errors that must be avoided when the effectiveness of a new drug for a behavioral disorder is investigated. First, it is important to avoid a **false positive**, where the drug is said to be effective despite the fact that it is not. False positives lead to dashed hopes and divert energy and attention from the development of drugs that actually are effective. Second, it is important to avoid **false negatives**, where the drug is said to be ineffective despite the fact that it actually works. False negatives prevent those who suffer from behavioral disorders from obtaining a beneficial treatment for their problem. Fortunately, a review of strategies for research of the effectiveness of drugs for behavioral disorders concluded that "the present methodology of clinical trials is such that it is impossible to conceive of an adequate study that would miss an effective drug or ascribe efficacy to an ineffective drug."[24] It is, therefore, important to study the characteristics that satisfy the conditions for an "adequate study."

Characteristics of an Adequate Study

An adequate study of the safety and effectiveness of a new drug for a behavioral disorder requires, at least, that care be taken in (a) the ethical selection and use of subjects, (b) the assigning of subjects to and creation of treatment groups, (c) the dispensing of the drug to subjects, (d) the measure of change in behavior, (e) the evaluation of basic pharmacology of the drug in humans (f) the experimenter's ability to detect side effects, and (g) the analysis of data[32,39].

Selection and ethical use of subjects. The use of humans in research on the effects of drugs on behavior disorders presents a host of ethical dilemmas[19,20]. Any human research requires that the subject provide **informed consent**[15]. That is, the subject must know about, understand, and agree to the consequences of participation in the experiment. Sometimes, though, individuals with behavioral disorders of thought and emotion have difficulty in truly understanding the world around them[12]. The study of behavioral disorders in children presents the possibility that potential research subjects may be too young to actually give their consent to participation[13,16]. All human research, especially that using subjects who may not be able to provide a true informed consent, must be approved by Institutional Review Boards consisting of members of the scientific and lay community who have no personal or professional stake in the proposed research[14].

Since humans are complex creatures, and there are many different types of behavioral disorders, similar symptoms may be shown by people with completely different behavioral disorders. Psychiatrists rely on the revised third edition of the Diagnostic and Statistical Manual of Mental Disorders (DSM-IIIR)[3] to enable them to say that one person suffers from problem X while another has the similar, yet importantly different, problem Z. Psychiatrists spend much time in developing and applying the **criteria for differential diagnosis** available to them in the DSM-IIIR. Nonetheless, it is at least logically possible that people with identical symptoms have different underlying problems (for example, swollen lymph glands may be the result of a cold or a symptom of AIDS). Thus, the failure of an experimental drug to treat absolutely every experimental subject may be due to a **heterogenous** (mixed) pool of subjects[6].

Assigning subjects to and creating treatment groups. Evaluation of the success of a drug treatment involves comparisons between **control** group(s) and **experimental** groups. Experimental groups consist of subjects that are given the investigated drug. Control groups consist of subjects that receive precisely the same handling as the experimental group, except that the "drugs" they are given are actually placebos (see Chapter 4). It is important to have a placebo-controlled group because such a large percentage of individuals with behavioral disorders respond to placebos[36]. In order for a drug to be considered effective, it must improve a greater percentage of subjects than the placebo. It is important to also insure that between-group differences at the end of the experiment are the result of the treatment, and not due instead to pre-experiment differences in age, socioeconomic status, severity of the illness, motivation to get well, etc. In order to insure that control and experimental groups are **homogenous** (unmixed), subjects must be **randomly assigned** to groups. That is, subjects must be put into the experimental or control group without any deliberate or accidental bias[9].

Random assignment of subjects to placebo or experimental groups presents a number of ethical questions. The evils of deceiving experimental subjects are somewhat reduced by clearly stating, in the informed consent form, that some subjects will be given the active investigational drug while others will get the placebo. However, as discussed above, it is questionable whether all subjects will actually understand the information provided in informed consent forms[38,40]. A much more serious question is whether it is ethically correct to withhold a potentially effective treatment from an experimental subject who might obtain relief from a disturbing behavioral disorder[7]. Of course, the entire purpose of the experiment is to find out whether the investigated drug is, in fact, safe and effective. The serious ethical problem of withholding treatment can be partially handled by insuring that all subjects gain access to any successful drug, after the experiment is completed. In some cases, it may be appropriate to use an **active placebo**. While the term may initially seem like an oxymoron, the use of an active placebo involves comparing the effects of the investigated drug to the effects of another drug, previously determined to be effective[19]. The use of an active placebo, though, changes the purpose of the experiment from determining whether the new drug works at all, to a new type of study that instead determines whether the new drug is better than what is already available.

Dispensing drugs to the subjects. It would, of course, render placebo control groups useless if subjects knew whether they were receiving the investigated drug or the placebo. Thus, well-designed experiments require that the subjects be **blind** to (or ignorant of) which group they are in. Thus, the placebo must be identical in size, shape, color, method of administration, etc., to the investigated drug. In addition, it is possible that the person providing the drug to the subject might somehow convey that a placebo, rather than active drug, is being given to that person. It is therefore best if the study is run **double-blind**. In a double-blind study, a third person keeps careful records so that the person dispensing the drug does not know whether any particular subject is given an active drug or placebo[39]. **Clinical trials** in which an experimental drug is administered by a physician to patients, fail to meet this important criterion for good experimental design, but can provide information about which drugs should be further investigated in better designed studies.

An improvement in the double-blind study involves a **cross-over design**. With this design subjects initially given the investigated drug for, as an example, three weeks are given a placebo for the next three weeks, with the cycle repeated as often as desired by the experimenter. Subjects initially given placebo for the first three weeks are given the investigated drug for the next three weeks, and so on. Figure 6.1 graphically

	WEEK 1	WEEK 2	WEEK 3
EXPERIMENTAL CONDITION	Group A	Group B	Group A
CONTROL CONDITION	Group B	Group A	Group B

Figure 6.1. A simple cross-over design. Note that all subjects serve, at different times, as experimental subjects and as control subjects.

represents the design of a cross-over study. If improvements and decrements in behavior closely follow double-blind changes in experimental drug versus placebo, respectively, then great confidence can be placed in the investigated drug. Some behavioral disorders occur in cycles, and may disappear without any type of treatment. The cross-over design eliminates concerns about these **spontaneous remissions.**

Measuring change in behavior. A variety of sophisticated tests are presently available for evaluating the effects of experimental drugs upon behavior[30]. However, it is often important to use interviews and questionnaires to elicit **self-reports** from experimental subjects. Using more than one person to assess changes in behavior measured by self-reports can help to limit the possibility of error and bias by particularly hard-nosed, or particularly lenient, evaluators[38]. Furthermore, a study can be designed so that it is run **triple-blind.** That is, careful records are kept by a fourth person so that the evaluator, along with the patient and drug-dispenser, is unaware of who was given an active drug and who was given a placebo[39].

Evaluating basic pharmacology in humans. Although the purpose of the study is to determine whether a drug is effective in treating a behavioral disorder, the study offers a number of opportunities to gain further knowledge. Whenever possible, clever experimenters will design a study to determine the best means of administration, the most appropriate dosing schedule based on evaluation of absorption and metabolism, the range of effective doses, the potential for interaction with other drugs, and the possibility of overdose[24].

Detecting side effects.   A special aspect of the study of the basic pharmacology of the drug is the ability to detect side effects. The two basic questions regarding side effects are (1) What side effects occur? and (2) How often do these side effects occur (that is, what is their **incidence**)?[17]. While these may seem like simple tasks, it is difficult to know what side effects to look for and even more difficult to prove that adverse events suffered by experimental subjects were actually caused by the experimental drug. Any observed troubles could have been caused by other medications that the subject was taking, a natural worsening of the original behavioral disorder, or even the onset of some other illness. The use of a cross-over design can help insure that the onset of drug effects is actually caused by the experimental drug.

Analyzing data.   The analysis of data from experiments is greatly aided by sophisticated computer programs. However, a major problem occurs when subjects drop out of the experiment[21]. Dropouts present little problem when they are caused by events, (such as moving away from the location of the study) that are likely to have an equal effect on experimental and control groups. However, complications arise when experimental subjects drop out because of the appearance of unpleasant side effects or control subjects drop out because lack of treatment allows their behavioral disorder to worsen so that they can no longer be consenting participants. Faulty analysis of data can destroy an otherwise well-designed study, so reports of experiments should always include information about the incidence of, reasons for, and statistical corrections for dropouts.

STIGMATIZING LABEL, PSYCHOLOGICAL DISORDER, OR MENTAL ILLNESS?

As science learns more about how the body determines the behavior of the individual, we can expect to be offered more drugs that can soften the harshness of life. Some thoughtful people have questioned the impact of these drugs upon our conceptions of freedom and responsibility[26]. It can be said that psychiatric diagnoses of behavioral disorders are (1) **stigmatizing labels**, (2) descriptions of a **psychological problem**, or (3) descriptions of a true **mental illness**. Those who see psychiatric diagnosis as stigmatizing labels emphasize the wide range of potential human behavior. They point out that what is completely acceptable at one time in one culture may be considered "crazy" or "abnormal" in another culture or time. Supporters of the stigmatizing label theory say that there is nothing physically wrong with the person who acts in an abnormal manner. The problem, if there is one, lies in a society that won't allow room for a wide range of behavior[33].

Those who see behavioral disorders as the result of psychological problems also deny that there is something physically wrong with the abnormally acting person. They do, however, concede that some humans do engage in behavior so bizarre and unusual that it can accurately be called abnormal. They say that it is not the nervous system that is in need of repair, but ways in which that nervous system is used[1,5]. Their point can be seen by comparing abnormal behavior to a bad television program. Bad television shows are not dealt with by repairing the television set. They are handled by changing channels or writing letters to network executives. Similarly, they say, bad behavior should not be fixed by altering the nervous system. It should instead be fixed by employing psycho-logical techniques to change the way in which that nervous system is used.

Tom Szasz and *The Myth of Mental Illness*

Perhaps the major proponent of the view that behavioral disorders are not proof of an abnormal nervous system is the psychiatrist Dr. Thomas Szasz, who wrote *The Myth of Mental Illness*[41]. Many people misunderstand Dr. Szasz's point, thinking that he denies that people have behavioral disorders. Quite the contrary, Dr. Szasz acknowledges that people do behave in inappropriate or troublesome ways. He even admits that there are physical disorders of the nervous system that can lead to abnormal behavior. What he greatly objects to is the unsupported assertion that *all* people who exhibit behavioral disorders do so because they have something wrong with their nervous system.

The Medicalization of Deviance

This myth has led to the **medicalization of deviance**, where behavior that would otherwise be well within the rights of free individuals is instead viewed as evidence of a medical disorder. By slapping a psychiatric diagnosis on someone who exhibits behavior that we don't like, we stigmatize that behavior as abnormal. Most often, it is also claimed that the behavior is beyond the control of the individual because it is the result of an abnormal nervous system. We now all chuckle when we hear of the quaint ideas of nineteenth-century medicine regarding masturbation as a major cause of insanity. We are shocked that the "disease" of masturbation was sometimes "cured" in females by the surgical removal of the clitoris[23,31]. Similarly, we are disturbed by the complicity of U.S. physicians who, before the Emancipation, "diagnosed" runaway slaves as having the disease of **drapetomania**, which caused them to flee the supposed comforts and security provided by their masters[10]. Drapetomania, as a "disease", was often cured by "treat-ments" including beatings and/or amputation of the feet. A major consequence of the medicalization of deviance is that it enables the **depoliticization** of deviant behavior and justifies a search for the causes and solutions of complex social problems (like slavery and changing sexual mores) on an individual basis. Most people could easily see the problem when the Soviet Union declared political dissenters mentally ill and confined them to mental hospitals. "This strategy served to neutralize the meaning of political protest and dissent, rendering it the ravings of a mad person."[10] Why, Dr. Szasz asks, don't we also employ the same skepticism when told that someone needs to be given medicine against their will in order to "cure" the physical problem said to underlay the "disease" of drug abuse?

The Abnormal Nervous System

The argument that abnormal behaviors do not necessarily reflect an abnormality of the nervous system must be taken seriously. Psychiatry and psychopharmacotherapeut-ics are powerful tools. These tools can be used to cure a sick person or instead to punish the unconventional person. No doubt, there are cases where people labeled as schizophrenic are instead merely strange or troublesome. Some people with anxiety may be better off being taught how to change their world to make it less fearsome rather than being given medicine to take away that fear.

However, it is possible that some, and maybe most, people with behavioral disorders have something physically wrong with their nervous system. The more we learn about the nervous system, the more obvious it is that minor changes in neurotransmitter activity or the number of receptors can have profound effects on behavior[2,11]. When behavioral problems arise from an abnormal nervous system, it can be said that this abnormality is truly an **illness**. In order to emphasize the fact that the primary symptoms are behavioral, these can justifiably be called **mental illnesses**. No amount of freedom to act in the abnormal manner and no amount of psychological intervention can be expected to enable a person with a defective nervous system to act in a normal way. Altering the nervous system to return it to a more normal condition may represent the best hope for getting a return of normal behavior[42].

The successes of psychopharmacotherapeutics provide strong evidence, but certainly not undeniable proof, that abnormal behavior frequently is the result of an abnormal nervous system. But there are a number of ways that drugs could change even behavior that is not the result of an abnormal nervous system[8]. It is possible that people "cured" by drugs may instead have all behavior suppressed to the point where they can't act either normally or abnormally. Even when the medicine affects only abnormal behavior, this abnormal behavior may be the result of psychological disorders. For example, alcohol will eliminate the anxious feelings one has the night before taking an exam for which one is insufficiently prepared. Does this mean that the anxiety caused by not studying stems from an abnormal nervous system that can be returned to normal by drinking a few beers? Few of the medicines discussed in this text actually cure the underlying disorder. When the medicine is stopped, the behavioral disorder frequently reappears[28]. However, this is true of insulin too, but it is still understood that insulin is a useful medicine for treating the disease of diabetes.

The Meaning of Effective Behavioral Medicines

This text takes the position that many behavioral disorders do in fact come from an abnormal nervous system. The fact that psychiatric labels and drugs can be used to oppress odd and eccentric individuals cannot, however, be ignored. In addition, the possibility that in certain cases there may be a perfectly normal nervous system underlying the most abnormal of behaviors cannot be easily dismissed. A thorough knowledge of the basic pharmacology, target effects, and side effects of the medications discussed in each chapter can enable rational decisions about whether the benefits of medication outweigh the risks. Only an intimate familiarity with specific instances of people engaging in abnormal behavior can allow conclusions that *in this particular case* society is dealing with a stigmatizing label, a psychological disorder, or a true mental illness. An old text warned about **therapeutic exclusiveness**, the dangerously rigid insistence that one and only one approach to behavioral disorders is effective[18]. Thus, even those who believe that behavioral disorders are merely stigmatizing labels or the result of psychological problems can benefit from learning about the use of psychopharmacotherapeutics.

UNDERUSE BY PATIENTS

Two major problems with psychopharmacotherapeutics are that some people may not take enough of the medication and others may take too much. When people do not take their medication in the right amount or on the right schedule, it is said that there has been a **lack of compliance**.

Side Effects

There are a number of reasons why someone might refuse to take their medication. Psychopharmacotherapeutics, like any other kinds of drugs, always have side effects. No matter whether they are labeled as major or minor, side effects can be bad enough that the person with the behavioral disorder may reduce the dose of, or even stop taking, their medication. The greater the concern about the occurrence of side effects, the more likely someone is to take less medicine than prescribed by the physician[4]. Since, as discussed in Chapter 4, drug effects are dose-dependent, failure to take the prescribed dose often leads to a treatment failure.

A major concern with side effects is the possibility that the individual will become dependent upon or "addicted" to their medication (see Chapter 5). The more a person believes that a particular medicine can "cause addiction," the more likely they are to avoid taking *any* of their prescribed medication[4].

Wounded Sense of Autonomy

Another reason for lack of compliance is that most people like to believe that they are normal, strong, and capable of handling life on its own terms. It is difficult to maintain this **sense of autonomy** or independence in the face of having to take a pill or pills, sometimes many times per day. Each time the pill is taken, there is a reminder that medicine has to be taken to control behavior that other people can apparently control without medication. People with behavioral disorders may fail to comply with treatment regimens because they think that not taking medication is proof of independence[35].

Symptom of Behavioral Disorder

Finally, it is possible that failure to take the medicine is a symptom of the problem that the medication is meant to relieve. Patients whose disorder causes them to be **paranoid** (so they fear that others are out to do them psychological or physical harm) may believe that their prescribed medication is the method by which their physician hopes to poison them. Alternatively, a depressed individual may fail to take their medication because of a feeling of hopelessness. They may feel that nothing, certainly not this little pill, can help them with their problem[35].

OVERUSE BY PATIENTS

While not taking as much medicine as prescribed can lead to treatment failure, the dose-dependent nature of drug effects makes it likely that taking more than the prescribed amount will result in an increased risk of side effects and toxicity. With some psychopharmacotherapeutics, there are side effects that make the drug reinforcing. This can result in people taking more of the drug than they are supposed to take, or to a continuation of drug intake long after the original disorder is gone. In addition, some people erroneously assume that if a little bit of medication makes them feel better, twice as much will make them feel twice as good, three times as much will make them feel three times as good, etc. Researchers have found that the less healthy someone felt, the more likely they were to take more than the prescribed dose of their medication[4].

UNDERUSE OR OVERUSE BY PHYSICIANS

Who Can Diagnose and Prescribe

At present, the only people who can prescribe psychopharmacotherapeutics are physicians. Psychiatrists are specialists in the use of these drugs and other physical treatments to handle behavioral disorders. Nonetheless, other physicians who have not been specially trained can also prescribe these medicines as part of their normal practice. Part of the objections raised by stigmatizing-label theorists involve assertions that physicians (psychiatrists in particular) are too willing to prescribe powerful medications with potentially dangerous side effects[26,33,41].

Psychiatric Calvinism and Underuse

On the other hand, supporters of the use of psychopharmacotherapeutics may accuse others of practicing **psychiatric calvinism**. Psychiatric calvinism is said to occur when a fear of psychopharmacotherapeutics or a desire to have people "tough it out" leads to a reluctance to use these drugs even though they may be the best treatment available. A particularly striking example of this is **opiophobia**, a physician's fear of giving people narcotics for even terminal cancer pain because of an inappropriate concern about physical dependency[34]. Although there are few well-designed studies investigating the role of narcotics in chronic pain, so-called "pain clinics" routinely require that individuals halt their medication in order to receive psychological therapies. Narcotics can impair thinking and interfere with psychological therapies, but arguments have been presented against this particular type of psychiatric calvinism by researchers who point out the impairments arising from persistent pain[22]. Other researchers have also noted that victims of other disorders sometimes suffer from a physician's unwillingness to seek a balance between the negative effects of psychopharmacotherapeutics and the negative effects of allowing a treatable disorder to continue[27].

It is likely that the arguments between those who support one or the other view of mental illness, and between those who advocate greater or lesser use of psychopharmacotherapeutics, will continue. Advocates of any position must admit that the incomplete state of present knowledge allows for rational persons to take alternate positions. Hopefully, though, the use of rigorously designed studies that reveal both the benefits and risks of psychopharmacotherapeutics will one day enable a consensus to emerge.

CHAPTER SUMMARY

Early treatments of behavioral disorders included a variety of physical "treatments" that may have caused more harm than benefit. To insure that drugs used to treat behavioral disorders are safe and effective, governments require well designed studies. Determining whether a particular study was well designed involves an analysis of: the selection and use of subjects, the assignment of subjects to experimental and control groups, the manner in which the drug was dispensed, the ways in which behavior was measured, the extent of interest in seeking information about basic pharmacology, the methods used to detect side effects, and the ways in which statistical analyses were used.

Individuals whose behavior leads to the application of a psychiatric diagnosis may be getting slapped with a stigmatizing label, provided with a description of their psychological problem, or given a name for a physical disorder underlying their mental illness. Only careful consideration of a particular case can reveal which of these three events is occurring in that instance. No conclusion about the "real nature" of the behavioral disorder necessarily excludes, or requires, the use of psychopharmacotherapeutics.

Some patients given medication for behavioral disorders will, for a variety of reasons, take either less or more than the prescribed amount of the drug. On the other hand, some physicians may be too eager to prescribe psychopharmacotherapeutics while others may be too reluctant. Well designed experiments aimed at determining the risks and benefits of psychopharmacotherapeutics will enable the education of patients and physicians, thus, it is hoped, insuring an appropriate use of these powerful exogenous compounds.

REVIEW ESSAY QUESTIONS

1. Name the eight characteristics of an adequate study of the effectiveness of a new drug for a behavioral disorder.

2. What is a false negative and what is a false positive? How does a single-blind study help prevent the occurrence of false positives and negatives? a double-blind study? a triple-blind study?

3. What is a cross-over design, and how can it help researchers deal with issues such as spontaneous remission, placebo effects, and the causes of side effects?

4. Could someone who viewed DSM-IIIR labels as (a) a description of a psychological problem or (b) the application of a stigmatizing label nonetheless advocate the use of psychopharmacotherapeutics? How? What special restrictions on drug therapy would likely arise from either outlook?

5. What are the similarities and differences between the reasons for people taking either too little or too much of their prescribed medication with the reasons for psychiatric calvinism and physician overuse of psychopharmacotherapeutics?

REFERENCES

1. Albee, G.W. Emerging concepts of mental illness and models of treatment: The psychological point of view. *American Journal of Psychiatry*, 1969, 125, 870-876.

2. Andreasen, N.C. Evaluation of brain imaging techniques in mental illness. *Annual Review of Medicine*, 1988, 39, 335-345.

3. APA (Work Group to Revise DSM-III of the American Psychiatric Association). *Diagnostic and Statistical Manual of Mental Disorders (3rd ed., rev.)*. Washington, D.C.: American Psychiatric Association, 1987.

4. Apsler, R., & Rothman, E. Correlates of compliance with psychoactive prescriptions. *Journal of Psychoactive Drugs*, 1984, 16, 193-199.

5. Ausubel, D.P. Personality disorder *is* disease. *American Psychologist*, 1961, 16, 69-74.

6. Ban, T.A., Guy, W., & Wilson, W.H. Research methodology and the pharmacotherapy of the chronic schizophrenias. *Psychopharmacology Bulletin*, 1986, 22, 36-41.

7. *Bok, S. The ethics of giving placebos. *Scientific American*, 1974, 231, 17-23.

8. Brown, T.R., Borden, K.A., & Clingerman, S.R. Pharmacotherapy in ADD adolescents with special attention to multimodality treatments. *Psychopharmacology Bulletin*, 1985, 21, 192-211.

9. Bulpitt, C.J. *Randomized controlled clinical trials*. The Hague, Netherlands: Martinus Nijhoff Publishers, 1983.

10. Conrad, P. The discovery of hyperkinesis: Notes on the medicalization of deviant behavior. In M.E. Kelleher, B.K. MacMurray, and T.M. Shapiro (Eds.) *Drugs and society: A critical reader*. Dubuque, Iowa: Kendall/Hunt, 1983.

11. Davis, J.M. Clinical utility of biochemical assays in psychiatry. *Annual Review of Medicine*, 1987, 38, 149-156.

12. *DHEW. Research involving those who are mentally infirm. *Report and Recommendations of National Commission for the Protection of Human Subjects of Biomedical and Behavioral Research, Vol. 43*, 1978a.

13. *DHEW. Research involving children. *Report and Recommendations of National Commission for the Protection of Human Subjects of Biomedical and Behavioral Research, Vol. 43*, 1978b.

14. *DHEW. Protection of human subjects: Institutional Review Board. *Report and Recommendations of National Commission for the Protection of Human Subjects of Biomedical and Behavioral Research, Vol. 43*, 1978c.

15. *DHHS. *Protection of human subjects: Informed consent*, 1981.

16. *DHHS. *Children involved as subjects in research: Additional protections*, 1983.

17. Fisher, S. Postmarketing surveillance of adverse drug reactions. In H.Y. Meltzer (Ed.) *Psychopharmacology: The third generation of progress*. New York: Raven Press, 1987.

18. Flach, F., & Regan, P. *Chemotherapy in emotional disorders*. New York: McGraw-Hill, 1960.

19. Gallant, D.M., & Eichelman, B. Ethical dilemmas in neuropsychopharmacologic research. In H.Y. Meltzer (Ed.) *Psychopharmacology: The third generation of progress*, New York: Raven Press, 1987.

20. Gallant, D.M., & Force, R. *Legal and ethical issues in human research and treatment*. New York: Spectrum Press, 1978.

21. Goldberg, S.C. Persistent flaws in the design and analysis of psychopharmacology research. In H.Y. Meltzer (Ed.) *Psychopharmacology: The third generation of progress*. New York: Raven Press, 1987.

22. *Halpern, L.M., & Robinson, J. Prescribing practices for pain in drug dependence: A lesson in ignorance. In B. Stimmel (Ed.) *Controversies in alcholism and substance abuse*. New York: Hayworth Press, 1986.

23. *Hare, E. H. Masturbatory insanity: The history of an idea. *Journal of Mental Science*, 1962, 108, 1-25.

24. Hollister, L.E. Strategies for research in clinical psychopharmacology. In H.Y. Meltzer (Ed.) *Psychopharmacology: The third generation of progress*. New York: Raven Press, 1987.

25. *Jiminez, M.A. *Changing faces of madness: Early American attitudes and treatment of the insane*. Cambridge, MA: University Press of New England, 1987.

26. *Johnstone, L. *Users and abusers of psychiatry: A critical look at traditional psychiatric practice*. New York: Routledge Press, 1989.

27. Keller, M.B. Undertreatment of depression. *Psychopharmacology Bulletin*, 1986, 24, 75-80.

28. Klerman, G.L. Future prospects for clinical psychopharmacology. In H.Y. Meltzer (Ed.) *Psychopharmacology: The third generation of progress*. New York: Raven Press, 1987.

29. Leber, P. FDA: The federal regulation of drug development. In H.Y. Meltzer (Ed.) *Psychopharmacology: The third generation of progress*. New York: Raven Press, 1987.

30. Levine, J., & Ban, T.A. Assessment methods in clinical trials. In H.Y. Meltzer (Ed.) *Psychopharmacology: The third generation of progress*. New York: Raven Press, 1987.

31. *McDonald, R. The frightful consequences of onanism: Notes on the history of a delusion. *Journal of the History of Ideas*, 1967, 28, 423-431.

32. Meinert, C.L. *Clinical trials*. New York: Oxford University Press, 1986.

33. *Miller, P. Critiques of psychiatry and critical sociologies of madness. In P. Miller & N. Rose (Eds.) *The power of psychiatry*, Cambridge, England: Polity Press, 1986.

34. *Morgan, J.P. American opiophobia: Customary underutilization of opioid analgesics. In B. Stimmel (Ed.) *Controversies in alcholism and substance abuse*. New York: Hayworth Press, 1986.

35. *O'Connell, R.A. Psychological and social aspects of pharmacological treatment. In *Psychobiology and psychopharmacology*, New York: W.W. Norton, 1988.

36. Prien, R.F. Methods and models for placebo use in pharmacotherapeutic trials. *Psychopharmacology Bulletin*, 1988, 24, 4-8.

37. *Rose, N. Psychiatry: The discipline of mental health. In P. Miller & N. Rose (Eds.) *The power of psychiatry*, Cambridge, England: Polity Press, 1986.

38. Spilker, B. Practical considerations in the clinical development of CNS drugs. In H.Y. Meltzer (Ed.) *Psychopharmacology: The third generation of progress*. New York: Raven Press, 1987.

39. Spriet, A, & Simon, P. *Methodology of clinical drug trials (trans. by R. Edelstein & M. Weintraub*. Karger Publishers, Basel, 1985.

40. Stanley, B. An integration of ethical and clinical considerations in the use of placebos. *Psychopharmacology Bulletin*, 1988, 24, 18-20.

41. *Szasz, T.S. *The myth of mental illlness: Foundations of a theory of personal conduct (Rev. ed.)*. New York: Harper & Row, 1974.

42. Trimble, M.R. *Biological psychiatry*. New York: Wiley, 1988.

43. *Valenstein, E.S. *Great and desperate cures*. New York: Basic Books, 1986.

44. *Zilboorg, G. & Henry, G.W. *A history of medical psychology*. New York: Norton, 1941.

* Introductory or intermediate reading

Chapter 7

SCHIZOPHRENIA

The purposes of this chapter are to:

1. Introduce you to the symptoms and characteristics of the psychosis schizo-phrenia,

2. Present information about the basic pharmacology, efficacy, interaction with endogenous systems, and suspected mechanism of action of antipsychotic drugs,

3. Place an emphasis on the nature and biochemical basis of the major and minor side effects of antipsychotic drugs, and

4. Discuss the selection and long-term use of antipsychotic drugs.

THE DISORDER

Basic Symptoms

Schizophrenia literally means "split mind," but the disorder is *not* characterized by a division of the personality into two or more parts. Schizophrenia is a chronic psychosis, characterized by a basic triad of symptoms. These include **hallucinations** (false sensations and perceptions), **delusions** (false beliefs), and **flat affect** (a restricted range of emotional feelings). Schizophrenia is a **recurrent disorder**, in which people may get better on their own only to later develop the disorder again. The happy situation where a disorder improves without treatment is called **spontaneous remission**. A spontaneous return of symptoms is called a **relapse**. Personal accounts of schizophrenia can be found in *These Are My Sisters* by Jefferson[21] and *The Eden Express* by Mark Vonnegut[50].

Table 7.1
DSM-IIIR Diagnostic Criteria for Schizophrenia (Summarized)

A. Presence of characteristic psychotic symptoms in the active phase: either (1), (2), or (3) for at least one week

(1) two of the following
   (a) delusions
   (b) prominent hallucinations
   (c) incoherence or marked loosening of associations
   (d) catatonic behavior
   (e) flat or grossly inappropriate affect

(2) bizarre delusions

(3) prominent hallucinations of a voice

B. During the course of the disturbance, functioning in such areas as work, social relations, and self-care is markedly below the highest level achieved before onset of the disturbance.

C. Schizoaffective disorder and mood disorder with psychotic features have been ruled out.

D. Continuous signs of the disturbance for at least six months.

E. It cannot be established that an organic factor initiated and maintained the disturbance.

Differential Diagnosis and the DSM-IIIR

Table 7.1 presents the DSM-IIIR criteria for diagnosis of schizophrenia. Individuals referred to psychiatrists because of their unusual behaviors must meet the specific criteria listed in Table 7.1 before they can be diagnosed as being schizophrenic. For our purposes, it will be enough to focus on the basic triad of symptoms. However, the symptoms of schizophrenia may occur in people with other behavioral disorders (some of which will be discussed in later chapters). People with such diverse disorders as mania, depression, organic brain damage, and drug-induced psychosis may sometimes be difficult to differentiate from those with schizophrenia. If someone is incorrectly diagnosed as schizophrenic, the medicine they are given for schizophrenia may worsen the disorder that they actually have.

Incidence and Subtypes

Schizophrenia occurs in approximately 1 out of every 100 people, and affects both sexes equally. One of the biggest problems in understanding and treating schizophrenia is that the term probably covers a number of different types of psychosis, each with its own unique biochemistry. In fact, in a study of the proper methodology for evaluating the effectiveness of different drug treatments for schizophrenia, the authors state that "one of the most important contributions for psychiatry...is the recognition that schizophrenia consists of a biologically heterogeneous population"[3]. Thus, it may even be best to refer to the disorder as the schizophrenias.

The number and variety of types of schizophrenia has undergone changes through the years. It is, however, enough to remember that if schizophrenia is a word that refers to more than one type of behavioral disorder, then there may be more than one cause. Surprisingly, one thing that has caused a decreased emphasis on the different forms of schizophrenia is the discovery that most of the subtypes seem to respond equally well to antischizophrenic (or **antipsychotic**) drugs[20].

Nervous System Abnormalities: The Dopamine Hypothesis

Support for the hypothesis that schizophrenia represents a true mental illness comes from a variety of sources. First, certain diseases of the nervous system of known causes, like untreated syphilis, are known to cause symptoms similar to schizophrenia[51]. Perhaps, it is argued, many of the present cases of schizophrenia are also caused by some as yet unknown disease process that similarly interferes with the normal function of the central nervous system. Second, evidence points to a genetic component in schizophrenia[33,39]. Third, there are specific anatomical abnormalities that occur much more frequently in schizophrenics than in the normal population. In particular, there is evidence that schizophrenics have **cortical atrophy** (shrinkage of the cortex) and enlarged cerebral ventricles[23,44]. Some of the evidence for anatomical abnormalities in schizophrenia is obtained from **postmortem** (after death) analysis of human brains[5]. Fortunately, a new technique named **PET** (Positron Emission Tomography) uses computers to enable visualization of the amount of energy used by discrete areas of brains in living human subjects. This technique has allowed researchers to show correlations between the severity of schizophrenia and alterations in brain anatomy[10].

Studies of the neuroanatomical abnormalities of schizophrenics are complex and often difficult to interpret. However, nearly all the neuroanatomical and neurochemical evidence points to the possibility that schizophrenia occurs because of an excess of activity of the mesolimbic dopamine neurotransmitter system. A review of Figure 2.4 will reveal the nervous system location of the mesolimbic and other important dopamine systems.

The **dopamine hypothesis**, the idea that the biochemical basis of schizophrenia is an excess activity of the mesolimbic dopamine system[31], receives additional strong support from two sources. First, chronic use of stimulant drugs (such as cocaine or amphetamine) that induce excess activity in the mesolimbic dopamine system can cause a drug-induced psychosis that is difficult to distinguish from schizophrenia (see Chapter 15 for a full discussion and citations). Second, the effectiveness of drugs typically used to treat schizophrenia, and stimulant-induced psychosis, is highly correlated with their ability to block dopamine receptors[19]. This second point will be discussed in more detail in a later section on the suspected mechanism of therapeutic action of drugs used to treat schizophrenia.

BASIC PHARMACOLOGY

Antipsychotic drugs are usually administered in pills, although they are also available in injectable form. There are a number of different biochemical types of antipsychotic drugs. There is an even greater number of generic and brand names. Table 7.2 provides you with a few examples of the biochemical types, generic names, and brand names of antipsychotic drugs[2,29]. Psychiatrists who prescribe antipsychotic drugs must know the subtle differences in basic pharmacology that exist among these drugs. A few generalities, though, should provide enough understanding of basic pharmacology to enable understanding of the use of these drugs as therapeutic tools.

Absorption of these drugs after oral administration tends to be unpredictable for any single individual and erratic when comparisons are made among different individuals. This can lead to great individual differences in what is an effective dose. Some people will absorb most of a given dose while others will excrete most of the dose before they can absorb any significant amount. Intramuscular injection can enable a bypass of this erratic absorption. All antipsychotics are highly bound to proteins circulating in the blood. The antipsychotics are highly lipophilic, so they tend to accumulate in the fatty areas of the body like the brain and lungs. The erratic absorption and binding to plasma proteins contribute to, but cannot explain all of, the slow onset of the therapeutic action of these drugs. The high affinity for lipids shown by antipsychotics means that they easily cross the placental barrier and affect the developing fetus.

Table 7.2
A Partial List of Antipsychotic Drugs

Chemical Name	Generic Name	Brand Name
Phenothiazine	Chlorpromazine Thioridazine Fluphenazine Trifluoperazine	Thorazine Mellaril Prolixin Stelazine
Thioxanthenes	Chlorprothixene Thiothixene	Taractan Navane
Butyrophenones	Haloperidol	Haldol
Dibenzoxazepines	Loxapine	Loxitane
Dihydroindolones	Molindone	Moban

Antipsychotic drugs are metabolized by liver enzymes. Most of the metabolites are inactive, but there are exceptions. The half-lives of antipsychotic drugs are extremely long, typically ranging from 20 to 40 hours. The high lipophilicity of antipsychotics means that they will remain in the brain for periods much longer than plasma half-lives. Metabolites are excreted mainly in the urine. It may take many steps to convert the original lipophilic drug into a metabolite that is hydrophilic enough to be excreted in the urine. Metabolites of some antipsychotics can be found in the urine months after the person has stopped taking the drug. The long half-life of these drugs and their, perhaps active, metabolites means that the offset of drug action is sometimes delayed for days or even weeks after a halt in drug use[2]. Table 7.3 provides a summary of these generalizations regarding the basic pharmacology of antipsychotic drugs.

Table 7.3
Basic Pharmacology of Antipsychotic Drugs

- Available in pill and injectable forms
- Erratic and unpredictable absorption after oral administration
- Highly bound to plasma proteins
- Slow onset of therapeutic effect
- Highly lipophilic, accumulate in brain and lungs
- Metabolized by liver enzymes
- Very long half-lives, some active metabolites
- Excreted in urine
- Metabolites may be found in urine for months after halt in use
- Slow offset of therapeutic and side effects

EFFECTS ON SYMPTOMS OF SCHIZOPHRENIA

Amelioration of Specific Symptoms

Each of the drugs listed in Table 7.2 has been found to reduce the basic triad of symptoms of schizophrenia in nearly 90% of subjects[27]. Despite the similar efficacy of all these drugs, they do differ greatly in potency[37]. A review of Figure 4.3 will reveal the different dose-response curves that can result when two drugs are equally efficacious, but one is more potent. For any particular antipsychotic used in a particular individual, there is a particular dose which will have the optimum therapeutic effect. As with all drugs, the effects of antipsychotics are dose-dependent, such that reducing the dose below this individually determined level can result in an increase in symptoms, while an increase in dose can result in an increase in side effects[35,49].

Delayed Therapeutic Onset

The effects of antipsychotics on the symptoms of schizophrenia do not occur rapidly. There is usually a four- to six-week delay before the maximal suppression of the entire triad of the symptoms of schizophrenia[11]. However, some of the symptoms of schizophrenia are reduced within the first week of treatment. One double-blind study involving 72 people with schizophrenia found improvement of some symptoms within one week of the beginning of treatment[38].

Antipsychotics do not permanently reverse the symptoms of schizophrenia. Instead, a person with schizophrenia must continue to take antipsychotic medication in order to have a continued reduction in the symptoms of the disorder[24].

INTERACTIONS WITH ENDOGENOUS SYSTEMS

Antipsychotic drugs interact with a large number of endogenous neurotransmitter and neuromodulator systems. Dopamine blockade occurs not only in the mesolimbic area but also in other areas, such as the basal ganglia, that also utilize dopamine as a neurotransmitter[34]. While dopamine blockade in the mesolimbic area is a desired action, the blockade of dopamine in the basal ganglia can lead to side effects such as severe movement disorders. Antipsychotics also block receptors for serotonin, epinephrine, acetylcholine, and histamine[34]. They thus have an effect on nearly all of the human body, including the autonomic and neuroendocrine systems[15]. The impact of antipsychotics on diverse neurotransmitter systems in different areas of the body suggests that these compounds are likely to have a wide variety of side effects to go along with their specific antipsychotic action.

SUSPECTED MECHANISM OF THERAPEUTIC ACTION

Since many of the antipsychotics cause sedation, it could be argued that antipsychotics do not have a specific antipsychotic effect, but are instead acting as "chemical straitjackets." That is, perhaps antipsychotics merely produce an individual who calmly and quietly suffers the delusions and hallucinations of the untreated underlying disorder of schizophrenia. However, an early study revealed that a wide variety of antipsychotics, regardless of how sedating they were, were effective in decreasing the symptoms of schizophrenia. This same study found that drugs like the barbiturates (see Chapter 16) induced severe sedation but had little effect on the specific symptoms of schizophrenia[27]. This suggests that it is not sedation, but a more specific action shared by all of the antipsychotics in Table 7.2, that is responsible for the therapeutic efficacy of these drugs.

Mesolimbic Dopamine Blockade

Despite the number of neurotransmitter systems and bodily organs influenced by the antipsychotics, evidence suggests that dopamine blockade in the mesolimbic area of the brain is responsible for the therapeutic effect of these drugs. In particular, it is believed that the blockade of a subset of dopamine receptors, D_2 receptors, in the mesolimbic area explains antipsychotic action[34]. There is evidence both for and against the hypothesis that dopamine blockade in the mesolimbic area is responsible for the therapeutic effect of antipsychotics.

Evidence for the role of dopamine blockade, rather than interaction with some other neurotransmitter system, was provided in a study that found that the effectiveness of any of the antipsychotic drugs was highly correlated with an ability to block D_2 receptors. The abilities of the drugs to block acetylcholine, serotonin, or norepinephrine receptors did not correlate with their effectiveness as antipsychotics[34]. Further support for the role of dopamine blockade was found by researchers who reflected upon the wildly differing potencies of the antipsychotics[42]. They studied a number of antipsychotics and determined the dose needed to cause blockade of mesolimbic dopamine neurons. They found a high correlation between therapeutic potency and dopamine blockade potency. That is, they demonstrated that drugs that suppressed the symptoms of schizophrenia when they were given at low doses also were capable of extensive blockade of mesolimbic dopamine neurons at low doses. Similarly, drugs that were not effective as antipsychotics unless they were given at high doses did not cause significant blockade of mesolimbic dopamine receptors unless they were given at high doses. Finally, PET scans have recently been used to provide a more direct confirmation of this correlation. Clinically effective doses of a wide variety of antipsychotic drugs were found to block a substantial number of D_2 dopamine receptors, while doses that were not clinically effective failed to block a significant number of D_2 dopamine receptors[13].

Opposing evidence. A major problem for the hypothesis that mesolimbic D_2 dopamine receptor blockade is the basis of the effectiveness of antipsychotic drugs is that dopamine blockade occurs at the very beginning of treatment with antipsychotic agents, while antipsychotic effectiveness is delayed. As mentioned above, maximal reduction of symptoms often doesn't occur until between four and six weeks after the beginning of therapy[11]. However, one study has found an early reduction of at least some of the symptoms of schizophrenia[38]. This suggests that the beginnings of the therapeutic effect does indeed correlate well with the beginnings of dopamine receptor blockade.

MINOR SIDE EFFECTS

The minor side effects of antipsychotic drugs include sedation, postural hypotension, anticholinergic effects, allergies, and endocrine effects. Anticholinergic effects include dry mouth, blurred vision, constipation, and inhibited urination. Allergies usually involve minor rashes, but may include extreme **photosensitivity** (a condition in which an individual easily sunburns)[20]. Endocrine effects include **amenorrhea**, or a halt in menstruation, and weight gain, part of which is caused by **edema** or retention of fluids. There may be **gynecomastia** (the development of breasts) and **galactorrhea** (the production of breast milk), even in males[15]. Deposits in the eye may reduce vision and even cause a change of eye color[40]. Tolerance develops to some side effects (particularly sedation). Many other side effects can be handled by directly treating the symptoms (chewing gum for dry mouth, exercise for weight gain). However, other side effects may require a reduction of dose, or, if they are sufficiently severe, a complete halt in antipsychotic treatment.

Many of the side effects of antipsychotic drugs can be explained on the basis of interaction with a number of different neurotransmitter systems. For example, postural hypotension is partly a result of anticholinergic blockade and partly a consequence of blockade of norepinephrine receptors on heart muscle. The anticholinergic effects, and perhaps sedation too, are due to blockade of acetylcholine receptors. Finally, blockade of dopamine, norepinephrine, and acetylcholine receptors in the brain influences the biochemistry and behavioral consequences of the hormones of the hypothalamus and pituitary[15]. The induction of endocrine side effects as a result of manipulation of the neurotransmitter systems of the brain reveals the hierarchical relationship between the brain and the endocrine system (see Chapter 2).

MAJOR SIDE EFFECTS

The major side effects of antipsychotics include motor problems that appear either early or late in treatment[7], and the neuroleptic malignant syndrome[25]. When antipsychotic drugs are given, the target effect is blockade of dopamine receptors in the mesolimbic system. However, there is also an inevitable blockade of dopamine receptors in the basal ganglia. This undesired blockade leads to the undesired motor problems. It is the occurrence of the movement disorders that sometimes causes people to refer to antipsychotics as **neuroleptics**. This word emphasizes side effects and does not describe the specific therapeutic action of these drugs.

Acute Dyskinesias

There are three types of **acute dyskinesias** (early appearing inappropriate motor movements) that may occur within one year of the beginning of treatment[8]. **Parkinsonism** is characterized by the symptoms of the neurological disorder of Parkinson's disease, including especially **rigidity** (or stiffness) and **bradykinesia** (severely reduced or limited movement). Parkinsonism is caused by the undesired blockade of dopamine receptors in the basal ganglia.

The **acute dystonias** are involuntary and inappropriate postures and muscle tones. They usually involve the face, tongue, lips, neck, arms, legs, and large muscles of the back. **Akathisia** is a compulsion to move that expresses itself in jitteriness and constant motion. Most people presently think that both acute dystonia and akathisia are the result of D_2 receptor supersensitivity. The undesired, but so far inevitable, chronic blockade of dopamine receptors in the basal ganglia leads them to be supersensitive. Blockade is not perfect however, since the antipsychotic and the neurotransmitter compete for the receptor. On those occasions when dopamine gains access to the supersensitive receptor, abnormal movements are generated[28]. Figure 7.1 depicts the development of supersensitivity due to chronic dopamine blockade and the competition between dopamine and antipsychotic drugs for these supersensitive receptors.

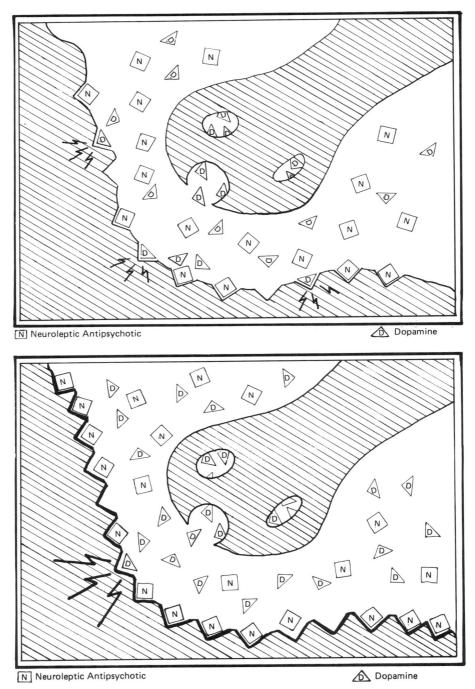

N Neuroleptic Antipsychotic   D Dopamine

N Neuroleptic Antipsychotic   D Dopamine

Figure 7.1. The competition between dopamine and antipsychotic drugs for receptors (upper figure). At most usual doses of antipsychotic drugs, it is likely that a few molecules of dopamine will interact with a supersensitive postsynaptic receptor. Such interaction will result in a larger than normal EPSP or IPSP (lower figure).

One solution to the acute dyskinesias is to reduce the dosage of the drug. Due to the long half-lives of antipsychotics, it may take weeks or even months for brain and blood levels of the drug to drop low enough to allow acute dyskinesias to disappear. Although the effect of antipsychotic drugs is dose-dependent[35], there is evidence that patients experiencing acute dystonias from antipsychotic treatment can undergo a reduction in dose without a return of psychotic symptoms. For example, in a study with patients with haloperidol-induced side effects of sedation and acute motor symptoms, a reduction in drug dose resulted in an elimination of side effects, but not therapeutic efficacy[49]. Figure 7.2 uses a dose-response curve to show how a reduction in dose of antipsychotics can lead to an elimination of side effects without eliminating therapeutic efficacy.

Tardive Dyskinesias

The **tardive dyskinesias** (or late-appearing movement disorders) may be similar in appearance to the acute dystonias. The tardive dyskinesias do not usually appear until after one year of treatment, and they are sometimes irreversible[41]. It appears that the amount of time on antipsychotics, rather than the doses given, is the most powerful determinant of whether or not tardive dyskinesias occur[2]. Fortunately, there is evidence that maintaining someone with tardive dyskinesia on a stable dose of antipsychotic will not result in a worsening of symptoms. For example, in a study of 33 people who had received up to 11 years of antipsychotic treatment, the authors stated that "the study of

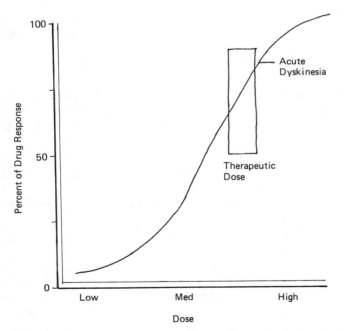

Figure 7.2.   A dose-responsive curve showing how a reduction in dose of antipsychotics can eliminate acute dyskinesias without eliminating efficacy.

long-term outcome of (tardive dyskinesia) indicates that this syndrome remains stable...in the majority of patients"[8].

If drug treatment is stopped when tardive dyskinesia first appears, symptoms might worsen as soon as the antipsychotics clear from the body. This is called **withdrawal-induced dyskinesias.** Fortunately, the tardive dyskinesias may reverse with time. One study revealed that 55% of people with tardive dyskinesia eventually showed improvement after medication was halted[22]. However, a different study found that it may take as long as five years after a halt in antipsychotic treatment for tardive motor symptoms to disappear entirely[26].

Just as it is hypothesized that acute dystonias and akathisia arise from receptor supersensitivity, it has been suggested that tardive dyskinesias also arise from dopamine receptor supersensitivity in the basal ganglia. When a molecule of dopamine successfully competes with the antipsychotic drug for the supersensitive receptor, an abnormal motor movement results. The worsening of symptoms upon suddenly stopping antipsychotic treatments occurs because supersensitive receptors are suddenly available for occupancy by dopamine. When dopamine does bind to these supersensitive receptors, an abnormal motor movement results. Figure 7.3 depicts the unblocking of supersensitive dopamine receptors as a consequence of stopping antipsychotic treatment in patients with tardive dyskinesias. If a halt in antipsychotic treatment leads to an eventual reversal of tardive dyskinesia, it is probably because homeostatic mechanisms have reduced the supersensitivity of these no-longer-blocked dopamine receptors.

There are a number of pharmacological treatments for tardive dyskinesia[30]. Attempts have been made to treat tardive dyskinesias with cholinergic agonists[14], norepinephrine antagonists like propranolol and clonidine[1,53], and even a dopamine agonist[32]. Unfortunately, the study of drug treatment of tardive dyskinesia is complicated by a number of factors. For example, 50% of people with tardive dyskinesia showed temporary improvement in their symptoms even when they were given a placebo[45]. Thus, a drug that reduces the symptoms of tardive dyskinesia in 50% of patients will generate false hopes that an effective treatment has been found. It is possible that the drug's "efficacy" is nothing more than the result of a temporary placebo effect. As a result of the discovery of the power of the placebo effect on tardive dyskinesia, researchers who reviewed the pharmacological treatment of tardive dyskinesias in the 1980s were forced to conclude that "those treatments that appeared promising at the end of the decade appear less promising now"[22].

Until a treatment is found, the best cure will remain prevention. Frequent checks for spontaneous remission can limit the development of tardive dyskinesias. Occasional **drug holidays**, during which antipsychotic drug treatments are temporarily withheld may retard or prevent the development of tardive dyskinesias[16]. Finally, the search continues for novel antipsychotics that do not block dopamine in the basal ganglia area[4]. For instance, the posterior pituitary hormone vasopressin was found, in a double-blind, placebo-controlled study, to have modest antipsychotic efficacy[18]. Since this drug does not block dopamine receptors in the basal ganglia, it is unlikely to induce tardive dyskinesia.

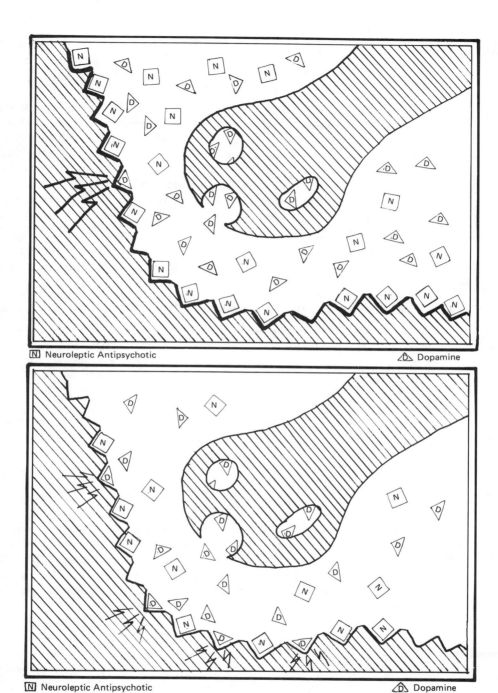

N Neuroleptic Antipsychotic   **D** Dopamine

N Neuroleptic Antipsychotic   **D** Dopamine

Figure 7.3. The effects of chronic antipsychotic treatment (upper figure) and drug holidays (lower figure) on mesolimbic dopamine receptors. Note that the use of drug holidays decreases the supersensitivity of postsynaptic receptors. Although the response of the postsynaptic receptor to interaction with dopamine is still greater than normal, the severity of tardive dyskinesia is reduced since the supersensivity of the receptor is not as great as that displayed by the receptors in Figure 7.1.

Neuroleptic Malignant Syndrome

The most dangerous side effect of the antipsychotics is the **malignant syndrome**[25]. The syndrome is a very severe form of Parkinsonism, with complete **catatonia** (inability to move), and the additional problems of unstable heart rate and blood pressure, high temperature, and stupor[6]. Death occurs in 10% of all people who suffer this side effect[43]. Even with an immediate halt in antipsychotic treatment, symptoms can last for more than a week as the drug is slowly eliminated from the body. There is some controversy about the importance and frequency of this problem[46]. However, researchers at a major psychiatric hospital looked at 500 individuals treated with neuroleptics and found that 1.4% of their patients developed the syndrome[36]. Table 7.4 lists the minor and major side effects of the antipsychotics.

Table 7.4
The Side Effects of Antipsychotic Drugs

Minor		Major
Sedation	Amenorrhea	Acute dyskinesias
Postural hypotension	Weight gain	Parkinsonism
Inhibited urination	Edema	Dystonias
Dry mouth	Gynecomastia	Akathisia
Blurred vision	Galactorrhea	Tardive dyskinesia
Constipation	Allergies	Malignant syndrome

TOXICITY

Aside from neuroleptic malignant syndrome or an allergic reaction, there is a large gap between the dose of antipsychotic that is needed to get a therapeutic effect and the dose that will cause other toxic effects. This large **therapeutic window** makes antipsychotics remarkably safe drugs, although, like most drugs, death from overdose is not unknown. However, the drugs are not reinforcing (in fact, most people find them aversive). This makes it unlikely that people will consume larger than prescribed doses[2].

WHICH ANTIPSYCHOTIC IS BEST?

Since each of the compounds listed in Table 7.1 is an effective antipsychotic drug, any of these compounds can be used in an attempt to treat schizophrenia. However, the drugs differ in therapeutic potency and in the likelihood of inducing different side effects[37]. Thus, if a person has in the past been effectively treated with few side effects, then the same dose of the same compound is likely to be effective and relatively free of side effects once again. A person who has never before received pharmacological treatment for schizophrenia might need to try a number of different antipsychotics to find the one with the best efficacy and least side effect[20].

In addition to drugs listed in Table 7.1, there are new antipsychotics being developed that may soon become generally available for the treatment of schizophrenia. Scientists are manipulating the physical characteristics of presently available antipsychotics in hopes of altering interactions with different types of receptors.   Hopefully, compounds with different patterns of receptor interaction will be less likely to induce the host of side effects associated with typical antipsychotics[4,16,19,47].

LONG-TERM MAINTENANCE

The Role of Psychotherapy

The social consequences of schizophrenia are usually devastating. Social isolation, loneliness, and institutionalization may compound the problems presented by the basic triad of symptoms. The person diagnosed as schizophrenic may require psychotherapy in order to deal with the social consequences of the original symptoms[48].

Side Effects

Side effects can be a problem in long-term maintenance with antipsychotics. Some of these do not appear until months, and perhaps years, after the start of drug therapy. Every attempt should be made to warn people about the side effects of the medication, particularly the possibility of the late-appearing side effects.

Tolerance and Dependency

Fortunately, tolerance develops to some of the minor side effects, although there is no evidence of tolerance to antipsychotic efficacy. This means that individuals can be maintained for a long time on a stable dose of antipsychotic.

Unlike many of the other drugs discussed in this book, the antipsychotics are not reinforcing in normal humans or animals. All too frequently, people are unwilling to take antipsychotic drugs. With good compliance, symptoms are likely to be suppressed and the person can lead a reasonably normal life outside of full-time institutions[24].

Compliance Problems

Some people would rather tolerate schizophrenia than suffer the side effects of treatment with antipsychotic drugs. In addition, some people with schizophrenia develop delusions that are **paranoid** in nature. They think that all kinds of people mean to do them harm. Considering the nature and severity of the side effects of antipsychotic drugs, it is easy to see how someone with a tendency towards paranoia might refuse to take this "poison."

The various reasons for noncompliance make it difficult to know what to do when someone whose symptoms are reduced nonetheless stops taking medication. Some argue that those diagnosed as schizophrenic are incapable of deciding for themselves whether or not they should take the medication. Persons who refuse oral medication may be given long-acting injectable forms of antipsychotics[52], although this method of administration presents significant ethical problems.

When to Stop Drug Treatment

Knowing when to stop medicine is difficult. Some people who are on antipsychotics may undergo a spontaneous remission of symptoms. Unfortunately, it is difficult to know if someone who has their symptoms suppressed by antipsychotics has undergone a spontaneous remission. There are two problems with the idea of scheduling occasional drug holidays in order to determine if a spontaneous remission has occurred. First, the lipid solubility of antipsychotics means that the drugs may affect behavior even a month or two after the halt in treatment. More importantly, just as chronic treatment with antipsychotics might lead to supersensitive dopamine receptors in the basal ganglia, it may also lead to a supersensitivity of dopamine receptors in the mesolimbic area. Persons chronically treated for schizophrenia may show a **supersensitivity psychosis** when chronic antipsychotic treatment is halted or the drug dosage is reduced[12]. That is, even before the drug is cleared from the body, dopamine gains the opportunity to bind to supersensitive mesolimbic receptors. This rapidly induces a psychosis that is worse than the patient had originally[17]. In a study of 224 outpatients with schizophrenia, drug holidays or reduction in dose led to a supersensitivity psychosis in 22% of the patients[9].

CHAPTER SUMMARY

Individuals with schizophrenia often suffer hallucinations, delusions, and flat affect. All antipsychotics listed in Table 7.2 are equally efficacious, but they differ greatly in potency. These drugs are highly lipophilic and are therefore usually administered orally and have a slow onset and offset of therapeutic effect. The effectiveness of antipsychotics in reducing the symptoms of schizophrenia is dose-dependent. The drugs interact with many different endogenous systems, but the most probable mechanism of therapeutic action is blockade of D_2 dopamine receptors in the mesolimbic area. Minor side effects include sedation, postural hypotension, anticholinergic effects, allergies, and endocrine effects. Major side effects include the acute dyskinesias, the potentially lethal neuroleptic malignant syndrome, and the potentially irreversible tardive dyskinesias. Tardive dyskinesias may be due to supersensitivity of chronically blocked dopamine receptors in the basal ganglia. Due to equal efficacy of the antipsychotic drugs, selection of a particular compound should be based on previous effectiveness or a search for the drug that has the optimum therapeutic effect with minimal side effects. Chronic treatment with antipsychotics is necessary due to the chronic nature of the disorder. Special attention should be paid to the possible occurrence of side effects, particularly the tardive dyskinesias. Compliance with antipsychotics is usually low. Knowing when to stop antipsychotic treatment is difficult, and it is complicated by the possible occurrence of supersensitivity psychosis.

REVIEW ESSAY QUESTIONS

1. What is the basic pharmacology of antipsychotic drugs, and what are the chemical and brand names of at least three of the drugs?

2. What evidence exists for and against the idea that the therapeutic effectiveness of antipsychotic drugs is due to the blockade of dopamine receptors in the mesolimbic area?

3. Use information about the effects of antipsychotics on neurotransmitter systems other than dopamine to explain some minor side effects.

4. What role does supersensitivity of dopamine receptors play in tardive dyskinesia and supersensitivity psychosis?

5. What are some important issues in the long-term use of antipsychotics in the treatment of schizophrenia?

REFERENCES

1. Adler, L., Angrist, B., Corwin, J., & Rotrosen, J. Noradrenergic mechanisms in akathisia: Treatment with propranolol and clonidine. *Psychopharmacology Bulletin*, 1987, 23, 21-25.
2. Baldessarini, R.J. Drugs and the treatment of psychiatric disorder. In A.G. Gilman, L.S. Goodman, T.W. Rall, & F. Murad (Eds.) *The pharmacological basis of therapeutics* (7th ed.). New York: Macmillan Publishing Company, 1985.
3. Ban, T.A., Guy, W., & Wilson, W.H. Research methodology and the pharmacotherapy of the chronic schizophrenias. *Psychopharmacology Bulletin*, 1986, 22, 36-41.
4. Borison, R.L., Shah, C., White, T.H., & Diamond, B.I. Atypical and typical neuroleptics and tardive dyskinesia. *Psychopharmacological Bulletin*, 1987, 23, 218-220.
5. Bracha, H.S., & Kleinman, J.E. Postmortem neurochemistry in schizophrenia. *The Psychiatric Clinics of North America*, 1986, 9, 133-142.
6. Caroff, S.N., & Mann, S.C. Neuroleptic malignant syndrome. *Psychopharmacology Bulletin*, 1988, 24, 25-29.
7. Casey, D.E. Tardive dyskinesia. In H.Y. Meltzer (Ed.) *Psychpharmacology: The third generation of progress*, New York: Raven Press, 1987.
8. Casey, D.E., Povlsen, U.J., Meidahl, B., & Gerlach, J. Neuroleptic-induced tardive dyskinesia and parkinsonism: Changes during several years of continuing treatment. *Psychopharmacology Bulletin*, 1986, 22, 250-253.
9. Chouinard, G., Annable, L., & Ross-Chouinard, A. Supersensitivity psychosis and tardive dyskinesia: A survey in schizophrenic outpatients. *Psychopharmacology Bulletin*, 1986, 22, 891-896.

10. Cohen, R.M., Semple, W.E., & Gross, M. Positron emission tomography. *The Psychiatric Clinics of North America*, 1986, <u>9</u>, 63-80.

11. Davis, J.M., & Garver, D.L. Neuroleptics: Clinical use in psychiatry. In L.L. Iversen, S.D. Iversen & S.H. Snyder (Eds.) *Handbook of psychopharmacology* (Vol. 10). New York: Plenum Press, 1978.

12. Diamond, B.I., & Borison, R.L. Basic and clinical studies of neuroleptic-induced supersensitivity psychosis and dyskinesia. *Psychopharmacological Bulletin*, 1986, <u>22</u>, 900-905.

13. Farde, L., Wiesel, F.A., Halldin, C., & Sedvall, G. Central D_2-dopamine receptor occupancy in schizophrenic patients treated with antipsychotic drugs. *Archives of General Psychiatry*, 1988, <u>45</u>, 71-76.

14. George, J., Pridmore, S., & Aldous, D. Double-blind controlled trial of deanol in tardive dyskinesia. *Australian and New Zealand Journal of Psychiatry*, 1981, <u>15</u>, 68-72.

15. Gunnet, J.W., & Moore, K.E. Neuroleptics and neuroendocrine function. *Annual Review of Pharmacology and Toxicology*, 1988, <u>28</u>, 347-366.

16. Hollister, L.E. Novel drug treatment of schizophrenia. *Psychopharmacology Bulletin*, 1987, <u>23</u>, 82-84.

17. Hunt, J.I., Singh, H., & Simpson, G.M. Neuroleptic-induced supersensitivity psychosis: Retrospective study of schizophrenic inpatients. *Journal of Clinical Psychiatry*, 1988, <u>49</u>, 258-261.

18. Iager, C., Kirch, D.G., Bigelow, L.B., & Karson, C.N. Treatment of schizophrenia with a vasopressin analogue. *American Journal of Psychiatry*, 1986, <u>143</u>, 375-377.

19. Iversen, L. L. Mechanism of action of antipsychotic drugs: Retrospect and prospect. In S.D. Iversen (Ed.) *Psychopharmacology: Recent advances and future prospects*. Oxford, England: Oxford University Press, 1985.

20. Janowsky, D.S., Addario, D., & Risch, S.C. *Psychopharmacology case studies* (2nd ed.). New York: The Guilford Press, 1987.

21. *Jefferson, L. *These are my sisters*. Tulsa, OK: Vickers Publishing Co., 1948.

22. Jeste, D.V., Lohr, J.B., Clark, K., & Wyatt, R.J. Pharmacological treatments of tardive dyskinesia in the 1980s. *Journal of Clinical Psychopharmacology*, 1988, <u>8</u>, 38S-48S.

23. Johnstone, Eve C. Structural changes in the brain in schizophrenia. In S.D. Iversen (Ed.) *Psychopharmacology: Recent advances and future prospects*. Oxford, England: Oxford University Press, 1985.

24. Kane, J.M., & Lieberman, J.A. Maintenance pharmacotherapy in schizophrenia. In H.Y. Meltzer (Ed.) *Psychopharmacology: The third generation of progress*, New York: Raven Press, 1987.

25. Kaufmann, C.A., & Wyatt, R.J. Neuroleptic malignant syndrome. In H.Y. Meltzer (Ed.) *Psychopharmacology: The third generation of progress*, New York: Raven Press, 1987.

26. Klawans, H.L., Tabner, C.M., & Barr, A. The reversibility of "permanent" tardive dyskinesia. *Clinical Neuropharmacology*, 1984, <u>7</u>, 153-159.

27. Klein, D.F., & Davis, J.M. *Diagnosis and drug treatment of psychiatric disorders*. Baltimore, MD: Williams & Wilkins, 1969.

28. Lake, C.R., Casey, D.E., McEvoy, J.P., Siris, S.G., Boyer, W.F., & Simpson, G. Anticholinergic prophylaxis in young adults treated with neuroleptic drugs. *Psychopharmacology Bulletin*, 1986, <u>22</u>, 981-984.

29. *Lawson, G.W., & Cooperrider, C.A. *Clinical psychopharmacology: A practical reference for nonmedical psychotherapists*. Rockville, MD: Aspen Publishers, 1988.

30. Lieberman, J., Lesser, M., Johns, C., Pollack, S., Saltz, B., & Kane, J. Pharmacologic studies of tardive dyskinesia. *Journal of Clinical Psychopharmacology*, 1988, <u>8</u>, 57S-63S.

31. Losonczy, M.F., Davidson, M., & Davis, K.L. The dopamine hypothesis of schizophrenia. In H.Y. Meltzer (Ed.) *Psychopharmacology: The third generation of progress*, New York: Raven Press, 1987.

32. Ludatscher, J.I. Stable remission of tardive dyskinesia by L-Dopa. *Journal of Clinical Psychopharmacology*, 1989, <u>9</u>, 39-41.

33. Murray, R.M., Reveley, A., & McGuffin, P. Genetic vulnerability to schizophrenia. *The Psychiatric Clinics of North America*, 1986, <u>9</u>, 3-16.

34. Peroutka, S.J., & Snyder, S.H. Relationship of neuroleptic drug effects at brain dopamine serotonin, alpha-adrenergic and histamine receptors to clinical potency. *American Journal of Psychiatry*, 1980, <u>137</u>, 1518-1522.

35. Perry, P.J., Pfohl, B.M., & Kelly, M.W. The relationship of haloperidol concentrations to therapeutic response. *Journal of Clinical Psychopharmacology*, 1988, <u>8</u>, 38-43.

36. Pope, H.G., Keck, P.E., & McElroy, S.L. Frequency and presentation of neuroleptic malignant syndrome in a large psychiatric hospital. *American Journal of Psychiatry*, 1986, <u>143</u>, 1227-1233.

37. Rifkin, A., & Siris, S. Drug treatment of acute schizophrenia. In H.Y. Meltzer (Ed.) *Psychopharmacology: The third generation of progress*, New York: Raven Press, 1987.

38. Rifkin, A., Doddi, S., Karajgi, B., Wachspress, M., & Boppana, V. Neuroleptic treatment and prediction of response. *Psychopharmacology Bulletin*, 1988, 24 169-171.

39. Rosenthal, D., Wender, P.H., Kety, S.S., Schulsinger, F., Welner, J., & Ostergaard, L. Schizophrenics' offspring reared in adoption homes. In D. Rosenthal & S.S. Kety (Eds.) *The transmission of schizophrenia*. London: Pergamon Press, 1968.

40. Satanove, A. Pigmentation due to phenothiazines in high and prolonged dosage. *Journal of the American Medical Association*, 1965, 191, 262.

41. Seeman, P. Tardive dyskinesia, dopamine receptors and neuroleptic damage to cell membranes. *Journal of Clinical Psychopharmacology*, 1988, 8, 3S-9S.

42. Seeman, P., & Lee, T. Antipsychotic drugs: Direct correlation between clinical potency and presynaptic action on dopamine neurons. *Science*, 1975, 188, 1217-1219.

43. Shalev, A., Hermesh, H., & Munitz, H. Mortality from neuroleptic malignant syndrome. *Journal of Clinical Psychiatry*, 1989, 50, 18-25.

44. Shelton, R.C., & Weinberger, D.R. Brain morphology in schizophrenia. In H.Y. Meltzer (Ed.) *Psychopharmacology: The third generation of progress*, New York: Raven Press, 1987.

45. Soni, S.D., Freeman, H.L., & Hussein, E.M. Oxypertine in tardive dyskinesia: An 8-week controlled study. *British Journal of Psychiatry*, 1984, 144, 48-52.

46. Sternberg, D.E. Neuroleptic malignant syndrome: The pendulum swings. *American Journal of Psychiatry*, 1986, 143, 1273-1275.

47. Tammings, C.A., & Gerlach, J. New neuroleptics and experimental antipsychotics in schizophrenia. In H.Y. Meltzer (Ed.) *Psychopharmacology: The third generation of progress*, New York: Raven Press, 1987.

48. Torrey, E.F. Management of chronic schizophrenic outpatients. *The Psychiatric Clinics of North America*, 1986, 9, 143-152.

49. van Putten, T., Marder, S.R., Mintz, J., & Poland, R.E. Haloperidol plasma levels and clinical response: A therapeutic window relationship. *Psychopharmacology Bulletin*, 1988, 24, 172-175.

50. *Vonnegut, M. *The eden express*. New York: Bantam Books, 1975.

51. *Williams, G. *The age of agony: The art of healing circa 1700—1800*. Chicago: Academy Chicago Publishers, 1986.

52. Yadalam, K.G., & Simpson, G.M. Changing from oral to depot fluphenazine. *Journal of Clinical Psychiatry*, 49, 1988, 346-348.

53. Yassa, R., Iskandar, H., & Nastase, C. Propranolol in the treatment of tardive akathisia: A report of two cases. *Journal of Clinical Psychopharmacology*, 1988, 8, 283-285.

* Introductory or intermediate reading

Chapter 8

DEPRESSION

The purposes of this chapter are to:

1. Introduce the symptoms and subtypes of depression and investigate the possible physical basis of unipolar major depression,

2. Present the basic pharmacology, interactions with endogenous systems, suspected mechanism of action, side effects, and toxic effects of tricyclic monoamine reuptake inhibitors used in the treatment of depression,

3. Briefly present the basic pharmacology, interactions with endogenous systems, suspected mechanism of action, side effects, and toxic effects of monoamine oxidase inhibitors (MAOIs) used in the treatment of depression,

4. Summarize the nature, efficacy, and side effects of new pharmacological treatments for depression, and

5. Discuss the selection of the appropriate antidepressant and the principles of sound long-term treatment of depression.

THE DISORDER

Incidence

Unipolar major depression is a disorder of **affect** (mood or emotion) that is likely to be experienced by 1 in 10 persons during their lifetime[69]. Although it is possible for an individual to have only one episode of major depression, a conservative estimate suggested that at least half of individuals who experience one episode will experience one recurrence or more during their lifetime[61].

Differential Diagnosis, Subtypes, and the DSM-IIIR

A variety of subtypes of affective disorder have been proposed and/or recognized, including bipolar affective disorder (manic-depression), depression with melancholia, depression with psychotic features, seasonal affective disorder, atypical depression, and dysthymic disorder[10,56,77]. Bipolar affective disorder will be discussed in Chapter 9. The actual existence of the varieties of depression, and the important possibility that they may be unique in their response to drug treatments[30], will be discussed within this chapter.

Table 8.1 presents the DSM-IIIR criteria for diagnosis of a unipolar major depression. This is the most frequently studied form of depression and is characterized by disturbances of sleep and appetite, decreased pleasure in otherwise rewarding activities, decreased ability to concentrate and pay attention, feelings of worthlessness, and possibly, suicidal thoughts[10]. The disorder is said to be **unipolar** because the aberration in mood goes in only one direction, unlike the bipolar disorder to be discussed in the next chapter. Unless otherwise stated, all of this chapter's references to "depression" may be assumed to be about unipolar major depression.

Table 8.1
DSM-IIIR Diagnostic Criteria for Depression (Summarized)

A. At least five of the following symptoms have been present during the same two-week period and represent a change from previous functioning: at least one of the symptoms is either (1) depressed mood, or (2) loss of interest or pleasure

(1) depressed mood most of the day, nearly every day

(2) markedly diminished interest or pleasure in all, or almost all, activities most of the day, nearly every day

(3) significant weight loss or weight gain when not dieting, or decrease in appetite nearly every day

(4) insomnia or hypersomnia nearly every day

(5) psychomotor agitation or retardation nearly every day

(6) fatigue or loss of energy nearly every day

(7) feelings of worthlessness or excessive or inappropriate guilt nearly every day

(8) diminished ability to think or concentrate, or indecisiveness, nearly every day

(9) recurrent thoughts of death, recurrent suicidal ideation without a specific plan, or a suicide attempt or a specific plan for committing suicide

B. (1) It cannnot be established that an organic factor initiated and maintained the disturbance
(2) the distrubance is not a normal reaction to the death of a loved one

C. At no time during the disturbance have there been delusions or hallucinations for as long as two weeks in the absence of prominent mood symptoms

D. Not superimposed on schizophrenia, etc.

Nervous System Abnormalities: The Monamine Deficiency Hypothesis

Much research has been driven by the **monoamine deficiency hypothesis of depression**. This hypothesis holds that depression is the result of shortages in the amount or activity of, at least, the two monoamine neurotransmitters, norepinephrine and serotonin[28,79]. Drugs and physical disorders that reduce monoamine activity consistently induce depression[77]. As noted in the previous chapter, the dopamine hyperactivity hypothesis of schizophrenia arose, in part, from the finding that effective antipsychotics were dopamine blockers. Similarly, the monoamine deficiency hypothesis of depression arose, in part, from the development of antidepressants, which were originally thought to be effective because they elevated levels of norepinephrine and serotonin[13]. Additional support for the monoamine deficiency hypothesis has been found in genetic studies[24] and studies that have found consistent deficiencies of serotonin in depressed individuals[13,14,46]. For instance, research has revealed that greater levels of depression are correlated with greater reductions in the levels of serotonin in discrete brain areas[12].

There are, however, problems for the monoamine deficiency hypothesis. A review of measures of levels of norepinephrine concluded that it was better to speak of "dysregulation" of the neurotransmitter, since different measures resulted in solid evidence of both increases and decreases in different depressed people subjected to different tests[80]. In addition, the evidence for the monoamine deficiency hypothesis is certainly no stronger than evidence that depression may be due to low levels of the hypothalamic thyroid releasing hormone[59], high levels of cortisol[84], or even an abnormality of endogenous opioids[5]. A complete theory of the physical basis of depression will need to specify the interactions of many different abberations in receptors, neurotransmitters, neuromodulators and receptors[29].

TRICYCLIC ANTIDEPRESSANTS FOR DEPRESSION

Basic Pharmacology

The tricyclic antidepressants are similar to the phenothiazine antipsychotics (see Chapter 7) in physical structure and pharmacological characteristics. They are available mainly as pills, although a few come as an oral liquid or as an injectable compound[2]. Table 8.2 lists the generic and brand names of many of the presently available tricyclic antidepressants. While there are subtle differences in basic pharmacology, some generalities exist. For example, all the drugs are highly lipophilic and therefore are rapidly absorbed when taken orally. They are highly (90%) bound to blood-borne carrier proteins[37]. Their lipophilicity insures that they are concentrated in fatty areas of the body, including the brain and lungs. They have long half-lives, ranging from 4 to 124 hours and can thus usually be given in once-nightly doses[76]. They are metabolized by liver enzymes, often to active metabolites, and excreted mainly in the urine. There are vast differences between individuals in the speed of the different steps of metabolism[76]. Table 8.3 summarizes the basic pharmacology of the tricyclic antidepressants.

Table 8.2
Common Tricyclic Antidepressants

Generic Name	Brand Name
Amitriptyline	Elavil, Endep
Desipramine	Norpramin, Pertofrane
Doxepin	Adapin, Sinequan
Imipramine	Tofranil, Janimine, Presamine, SK-Pramine
Nortriptyline	Aventyl, Pamelor
Protriptyline	Vivactil

Table 8.3
Basic Pharmacology of Tricyclic Antidepressants

Available mainly as pills
Highly lipophilic and easily absorbed orally
Highly bound to plasma protein
Accumulate in brain, lungs, etc.
Long half-lives
Metabolized by liver enzymes to active metabolites
Excreted in urine
Vast individual differences in metabolism

Effects on Symptoms of Depression

In the mid 1970s, a review of 93 placebo controlled studies of the effectiveness of the six tricyclics then available determined that 62 studies obtained positive, although delayed, results while only 31 failed to show a greater effect than placebo[49]. In a situation reminiscent of the criticisms of early work with antipsychotic drugs (see Chapter 7), the studies that failed to show an effect of the tricyclic were often complicated by the use of what are now known to be excessively small doses given for short periods of time[41,54,62].

Effectiveness in acute and chronic cases. When administered in the proper dose for an amount of time that takes into account their delayed effect, the tricyclics effectively remove the symptoms of an acute episode of depression in 70%-80% of treated subjects[86]. Furthermore, a double-blind, placebo controlled study found that imipramine was effective in chronic depression as well. While only 13% of placebo treated subjects showed improvement, 59% of the subjects treated with chronic imipramine revealed improvement in objective measures of depression severity and self-rated social and occupational functioning[36]. These well-designed studies demonstrate that the tricyclics provide an effective treatment for the symptoms of both acute and chronic depression.

Dose- and time-dependence. The importance of dose and duration of treatment on the effectiveness of the tricyclics' antidepressant effect has also been clearly demonstrated in well-designed studies. The dose-dependent effect of imipramine, for example, was demonstrated in a study that found 300 mg/day to be superior to 150 mg/day[81]. While the delayed effect means that reduction in the symptoms of depression usually takes two to three weeks, one study found that many patients did not obtain any benefit until the fifth or sixth week of treatment[64]. Depressed individuals given tricyclics should be warned about the delayed effects of these compounds, so that a failure to obtain immediate relief doesn't lead to a halt in drug intake.

Amelioration or cure of symptoms? Since the late 1950s, it has been assumed that tricyclics suppress the symptoms of depression without really curing whatever may be the underlying problem[58]. A number of studies have used a tricyclic to improve an acute depression, and then employed a double-blind procedure to substitute a placebo in half of the effectively treated subjects. For example, one study employing this technique revealed that 50% of the subjects given placebo instead of their usual dose of amitriptyline or imipramine suffered a return of the symptoms of depression[48]. This finding with amitriptyline was replicated in a more recent study[83], in which 69% of the subjects switched to placebo suffered a return of the symptoms of depression. Since the symptoms of depression return when medication is halted, it is likely that tricyclics do not cure the problem underlying depression. Just like insulin used in treating diabetes, tricyclics must be taken as long as the depression continues. Unlike diabetes, however, depression is a cyclic disorder that may disappear spontaneously. The section below on long-term treatment with tricyclics will discuss the complicated question of knowing when to stop tricyclic treatment.

Effects in non-depressed persons. It might be expected that a drug that could elevate the mood of depressed individuals would induce a stimulating or mood-elevating effect in normals. However, one reviewer[2] cited the 1958 experiment of Grunthal that found acute treatment with tricyclics caused normal subjects to feel light-headed, tired, "unhappy" and anxious, and to have a dry mouth, blurred vision, and unsteady gait. When these brave subjects continued, for the sake of Science, to ingest the tricyclic for several days, they found that they had an increase in all of the negative effects of acute treatment, plus a great deal of difficulty in concentrating and thinking. The negative effects of tricyclics in individuals who are not experiencing a unipolar major depression have been used to develop the hypothesis that tricyclics will not work in depressions that are **exogenous** (caused by negative external events such as death of a loved one or job loss rather than a biochemical abnormality)[53,67]. However, recent and well-designed studies have found that the tricyclics are, indeed, effective in treating exogenous depression[32]. The external events thought to cause the so-called exogenous depression can only effect behavior through an interaction with the central nervous system (see Chapters 1 and 2).

Tricyclics should be tried whenever the symptoms of depression include loss of interest in previously pleasurable activities and slowed thinking and movement, regardless of whether the presumed cause of the depression was "endogenous" or "exogenous"[32].

Interactions with Endogenous Systems

Because of the delayed onset of therapeutic effect, attention has focused on both the acute (within hours) and chronic (within weeks) effects of the tricyclics. The major effect of the tricyclics is to inhibit the reuptake of the monoamines, particularly norepinephrine and serotonin, with the degree of effect on norepinephrine vs. serotonin reuptake varying enormously between different tricyclics[21]. As noted in Chapter 4, blockade of monoamine reuptake leads to an increase in the amount of neurotransmitter available in the synaptic cleft. Figure 8.1 reveals how an inhibition of monoamine neurotransmitter reuptake causes an agonist action. In addition to blockade of reuptake, the acute effects of tricyclics also include an ability to block acetylcholine, histamine and epinephrine postsynaptic receptors, with the degree of blockade again varying enormously between different tricyclics[21].

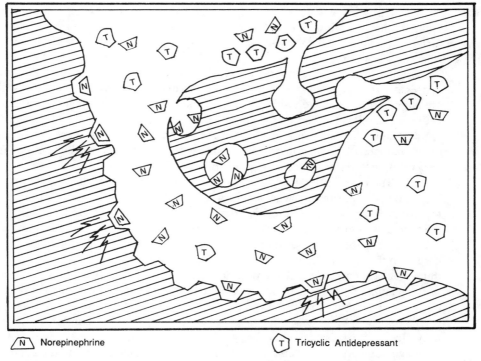

N Norepinephrine   T Tricyclic Antidepressant

Figure 8.1. Inhibition of neurotransmitter reuptake by tricyclic antidepressants causes an agonist action at a norepinephrine synapse. Note that the action of the tricyclic antidepressants prevents norepinephrine molecules from being removed from the synaptic cleft by the presynaptic neuron. There is therefore a larger than normal amount of norepinephrine in the cleft, leading to a larger than normal number of neurotransmitter-receptor interactions.

The acute effects of the tricyclics in turn lead to homeostatic changes during long-term therapy. For example, while blockade of monoamine reuptake continues, there is an increased sensitivity and/or number of acetylcholine and epinephrine receptors[21] as well as decreases (and some surprising increases) in the sensitivity of specific pre- and post-synaptic norepinephrine[80], and serotonin receptors[46]. Thus, both the acute and chronic effects of the tricyclics involve interaction with a variety of neurotransmitter receptors, particularly monoamine neurotransmitters.

Suspected Mechanism of Therapeutic Action

Evidence cited above for the monoamine deficiency hypothesis of depression has led some to suspect that it was the acute inhibition of reuptake of monoamines that reversed the biochemical disorder and removed the symptoms of depression. Some have even suggested that it is possible to speak of two depressive subtypes, some of whom suffer from low norepinephrine and thus benefit from those tricyclics that are predominantly norepinephrine reuptake inhibitors, and others who are deficient in serotonin and respond best to drugs that predominantly affect serotonin reuptake[42].

Opposing evidence. Two reviewers looked at the evidence that there are norepinephrine- vs. serotonin-deficient depressives who consistently respond differently to different tricyclics and concluded that "although the hypothesis of separate norepinephrine and serotonin depletions depressions is attractive, there is little support for it"[32]. Perhaps the strongest evidence against the idea of norepinephrine- vs. serotonin-deficient depressives comes from studies indicating that long-term treatment with tricyclics that are supposed to selectively inhibit the reuptake of serotonin leads to the production of active metabolites that inhibit the reuptake of norepinephrine[76]. It is, therefore, difficult to determine whether it was the effect of the parent compound on serotonin or the effect of active metabolites on norepinephrine that is responsible for the therapeutic effectiveness of these "serotonin selective" tricyclics.

There are at least two types of evidence against the idea that it is the acute inhibition of monoamines (whether specific to norepinephrine or not) that is responsible for the antidepressant actions of the tricyclics[28]. First, there is a great disparity between the time course of each effect. While the effect of the tricyclics on monoamine reuptake occurs within hours, the therapeutic effect doesn't occur for weeks. Second, unlike the case with the antipsychotics, where between-drug differences in ability to induce dopamine blockade correlate with therapeutic efficacy, there is no correlation between degree of monoamine reuptake and the therapeutic efficacy of tricyclic antidepressants. Once the acute monoamine reuptake hypothesis of tricyclic antidepressant action was rejected, researchers sought evidence for the hypothesis that it is the long-term effects of the tricyclics on various receptors that explains therapeutic efficacy. Reviewers of this evidence concluded that "all antidepressants produce changes in monoamine receptor sensitivity, and the time course of these changes is similar to the time course of therapeutic actions...what is not clear, however, is whether all antidepressants act uniformly on one type of receptor or on one neurotransmitter system"[28]. It appears that the therapeutic efficacy of tricyclic antidepressants, just like the cause(s) of depression[29], might be best explained by the drugs' interactions with receptors for many different neurotransmitters and neuromodulators, rather than just one type[82,85].

Side Effects

The tricyclic antidepressants have a number of troublesome and potentially serious side effects. For example, the anticholinergic effect arising from blockade of acetylcholine receptors can lead to dry mouth, blurred vision, and inhibited urination. In addition, central anticholinergic actions may lead to confusion and disorientation[77]. Blockade of peripheral epinephrine receptors can lead to **postural hypotension,** a fall in blood pressure when one's position is changed from sitting or lying down to standing. This can lead to fainting, falls, broken bones, heart attack, and even sudden death[26]. In a study with imipramine, it was found that 8% of the subjects had to stop treatment because of intolerable levels of postural hypotension[74]. Finally, the anticholinergic effects, perhaps combined with blockade of histamine receptors, can lead to sleepiness[77]. Rarely, tricyclics can induce tremor, sweating, and the eye disorder glaucoma[3]. Table 8.3 summarizes the side effects of the tricyclics.

Fortunately, tolerance will likely develop to the anticholinergic and antihistamine effects within a few weeks. If it is found that these side effects are intolerable, a tricyclic with little anticholinergic or antihistamine effect (for example, desipramine) can be substituted for one associated with more severe side effects (for example, amitriptyline). While there is no evidence of tolerance to postural hypotension[25] nortriptyline may be substituted in people who find other tricyclics to induce severe postural hypotension[74].

Table 8.3
Side Effects of the Tricyclics

Common	Occasional	Rare
Dry mouth	Confusion	Tremor
Blurred vision	Disorientation	Sweating
Inhibited urination		Glaucoma
Postural hypotension		
Sleepiness		

Toxicity

There is a relatively small window between the therapeutic and toxic doses of tricyclics. For example, the upper therapeutic range of imipramine is usually said to be at 300 mg per day[77] while severe intoxication occurs at about 1000 mg and death is likely at about 2000 mg[16]. Overdose with the tricyclics is life-threatening[19] and many physicians will not provide more than a seven-day supply of any antidepressant to an acutely depressed patient since the delay in therapeutic efficacy may result in a suicide attempt[51]. Early signs of excitement, restlessness, and seizures are quickly followed by coma, low blood pressure, low body temperature, and reduced breathing with strong signs of profound anticholinergic poisoning such as dry skin and flushed face. This coma may last for 24 to 72 hours, and is usually followed by anticholinergic-induced confusion and disorientation[51]. The most deadly toxic effects involve the heart and cardiovascular system, including the induction of lethal **arrhythmias** (heart beat irregularities) or a complete cessation of the heart's pumping action[26].

Most of the serious symptoms of overdose develop within two hours[38]. A study of 32 fatal overdoses determined that all the deaths occurred within 24 hours of ingestion[9], while another study determined that 70%-80% of those who died from tricyclic overdose didn't make it to the hospital alive[17]. Fortunately, improved treatments have meant that the majority of patients who make it to the hospital don't suffer major toxic side effects and recover without any long-term consequences[16]. Aggressive treatment of the anticholinergic symptoms by giving an acetylcholine agonist is usually effective and standard anticonvulsants can prevent seizures, but control of heart block and arrhythmias is complicated by the multiple actions of the tricyclics and their potential for interaction with emergency medications.

MONOAMINE OXIDASE INHIBITORS (MAOIs) FOR DEPRESSION

Basic Pharmacology

The monoamine oxidase inhibitors (MAOIs), initially developed for the treatment of tuberculosis, were the first type of antidepressants to be introduced into the U.S. market[15,35]. Table 8.4 lists the generic and brand names of the three most commonly used MAOIs. They are all available only in tablet form. Each is rapidly absorbed when taken orally with peak blood levels obtained within an hour or two[34]. They all irreversibly (and "suicidally") form a complex with the enzyme monoamine oxidase, perhaps accounting for the MAOIs short half-life of around two hours. There is no evidence that they bind to plasma proteins. They are metabolized by liver enzymes and are excreted in the urine

Table 8.4
Monoamine Oxidase Inhibitors

Generic Name	Brand Name
Isocarboxazid	Marplan
Phenelzine	Nardil
Tranylcypromine	Parnate

as inactive metabolites. They inhibit their own metabolism and blood levels build up over time[76]. Despite their short half-life, the irreversible inhibition of MAO results in longlasting biological effects that don't abate until new MAO is produced[72].

Effects on Symptoms of Depression

During the 1960s and early 1970s the MAOIs were considered to be both dangerous and ineffective against depression. For instance, one early study found that isocarboxazid was actually worse than placebo while phenelzine was no better than placebo[27]. This and other early studies finding MAOIs to be ineffective have been criticized as "slip-shod and poorly designed by today's standards"[78]. Early failures to find the MAOIs to be effective antidepressants may have been due to the use of inadequate doses that did not result in significant elevations in brain monoamines. In order to achieve an elevation of central nervous system monoamines, it is necessary to inhibit the activity of at least 75% of brain monoamine oxidase[23]. It was not until the mid-1970s that researchers used a measure of MAOI inhibition to determine that doses of MAOIs that induced 75% or greater inhibition of CNS monoamines were indeed effective against depression[66,68,73]. Literature reviews reveal that the efficacy of the MAOIs against depression has since been proven many times[34,50,70,72]. While all the MAOIs listed in Table 8.4 are effective antidepressants, tranylcypromine is the fastest acting. It exerts an almost immediate stimulating and antidepressant effect, while the other two MAOIs have a delayed stimulating and antidepressant action that may take from days to weeks[78].

Interaction with Endogenous Systems and Suspected Mechanism of Action

As their name implies, the MAOIs' main physical effect is an inhibition of the enzyme monoamine oxidase. Inhibition of this enzyme prevents the breakdown of a large number of neurotransmitters, particularly serotonin and to a somewhat lesser degree, norepinephrine and dopamine[72]. The delayed action of at least two of the MAOIs has resulted in a hypothesis that the delayed and long-term increase in the electrical activity of serotonin neurons is responsible for the therapeutic effect of the MAOIs[50]. Unfortunately, this hypothesis does not explain the rapid action of tranylcypromine, and it must be conceded that the mechanism of action of the MAOIs remains controversial.

Side Effects

The most dangerous side effects from the MAOIs arise from inhibition of MAO as well as other enzymes involved in the degradation of neurotransmitters, drugs, and foods. The breakdown of almost any compound that stimulates the sympathetic nervous system is inhibited by MAOIs, thus leading to a severe headache and life-threatening elevations in blood pressure and body temperature. This problem occurs not only with stimulant drugs like cocaine and phenylpropanolamine (which is contained in over-the-counter cold and diet preparations; see Chapter 15), but also with the amino acid **tyramine**, found in significant quantities in cheese, beer, red wine, liver, pickled herring, and certain other foods. The dangerous interaction of MAOIs with foods containing tyramine (the inaccurately named "cheese effect") was primarily responsible for the early reputation of MAOIs as unsafe drugs[78]. Fortunately, good patient education can enable avoidance of these foods, thus rendering the MAOIs remarkably safe. Even better, there is evidence that previously forbidden foods, including chocolate, sour cream, and yogurt, can be consumed in small quantities without any serious risk[44].

Additional side effects from MAOIs include postural hypotension, dry mouth, constipation, and weight gain[77]. Since the MAOIs exert a stimulating effect, they frequently cause insomnia. Over 90% of individuals who experience MAOI-induced insomnia can gain relief from standard prescribed sleep-inducing medications[52]. Thus, the side effects of MAOIs need not prevent their use as a treatment for depression.

Toxicity

While the side effects of MAOIs are less troublesome than once thought, overdose with the MAOIs causes a life-threatening emergency. The symptoms of overdose (agitation, hallucinations, abnormally strong reflexes, high body temperature, high blood pressure, and convulsions) reveal that the main problem is one of excess central nervous system stimulation. There is no antidote, and the best that can be done is to help the individual cope with the symptoms. Since the MAOIs listed in Table 8.4 are irreversible inhibitors of the enzyme, symptoms of overdose may last for at least a week, as the body synthesizes new MAO.

OTHER DRUG TREATMENTS FOR DEPRESSION

The side effects of the tricyclics, the potential for dangerous interaction with the MAOIs, the hazards of overdose, the failure of 20%-30% of depressed people to respond to pharmacological treatment, and the ability of chemists to make new drugs with a slightly different shape than the original compounds have all led to the development of a number of new compounds for the treatment of depression[6]. Some of these newer antidepressants represent variations in the structure of the tricyclics. For instance, **maprotiline** is similar in physical shape to the tricyclics, except that it has an additional ring structure, thus making it a four-ring molecule[38]. The basic pharmacology, efficacy, side effects, and toxicity of maprotiline are very similar to the other tricyclics, except that it is the most likely to induce seizures[3]. In a study of over 1,300 overdose cases with tricyclic and modified tricyclic drugs, it was found that maprotiline induced seizures in 12% of the cases, while only 3% of the overdoses involving standard tricyclics had seizures[87]. This finding suggests that maprotiline, while effective in removing the symptoms of depression, may not be sufficiently safe to justify its widespread use as an antidepressant.

Effective antidepressants have been found by focusing on drugs whose structure may differ greatly from the tricyclics, but nonetheless are capable of exerting an agonist action (particularly reuptake inhibition) at monoaminergic synapses. For example, **nomifensine** is a powerful inhibitor of the reuptake of dopamine and norepinephrine, but has little anticholinergic effect. The drug is more stimulating than the standard tricyclics, and is likely to induce insomnia and agitation. Also, about 10% of all patients have a high fever and flulike symptoms when they take the drug, and the manufacturer has withdrawn the drug from the worldwide market[77]. **Bupropion** primarily inhibits the reuptake of dopamine, and has no anticholinergic effect[57]. Like nomifensine, it induces insomnia and agitation, and like maprotiline, it may be associated with a high incidence of seizures[60]. **Trazadone** influences serotonin (although it is unclear whether it is a serotonin agonist or antagonist) with only a slight inhibition of norepinephrine reuptake and no anticholinergic effects[77]. While overdose on trazadone does not lead to convulsions, the therapeutic doses of the drug cause severe sedation and can even induce **priapism** (prolonged and painful erections)[87]. Finally, **fluoxetine** appears to be the most promising of a number of drugs that inhibit the reuptake of serotonin while having little effect on the reuptake of other monoamines and no anticholinergic effects[8,39]. Fluoxetine is an effective antidepressant even at very low doses that appears to be practically devoid of significant side effects[89,90]. It is likely that fluoxetine will be the only one of the four drugs discussed in this paragraph that will enjoy widespread popularity as a safe and effective alternative to standard tricyclics.

There are two types of monoamine oxidase. MAO-A (found mainly in the liver, gut, and brain) breaks down serotonin, norepinephrine, and a host of other monoamines, including tyramine, the amino acid that interacts with nonselective MAOIs to induce high blood pressure and temperature. MAO-B (found mainly in the liver and brain) breaks down many monoamines, including tyramine, but not serotonin and norepinephrine[31]. MAOIs that selectively inhibit the activity of MAO-A are effective antidepressants[91]. Unfortunately, since MAO-A is found in the gut where most of the tyramine found in foods is metabolized, selective MAO-A inhibitors are as capable of negative interaction with tyramine as the non-selective inhibitors listed in Table 8.4[1]. On the other hand, MAOIs that specifically inhibit the activity of MAO-B should not interact with tyramine, but the absence of inhibition of degradation of norepinephrine or serotonin should render them useless as antidepressants[91]. Despite this logic, a double-blind placebo controlled study revealed that the selective MAO-B inhibitor **selegiline** (also known as **deprenyl**) was an effective antidepressant[47]. Another double-blind placebo controlled study confirmed the antidepressant effect of deprenyl, and further found that neither interaction with tyramine nor any other side effect occurred at a level greater than that found with placebo[43]. These results suggest that the use of selective MAO-B inhibitors may one day replace the use of nonselective MAOIs.

LONG-TERM ANTIDEPRESSANT TREATMENT

The Role of Psychotherapy

The decision whether to treat depression with drugs alone or with psychotherapy can be aided by looking at research results. Well-designed studies have determined that the addition of psychotherapy to drug treatments doesn't prevent relapse, but psychotherapy does improve the functioning of the individual during and between episodes of depression[55]. In addition, the combination of therapies is more effective in reducing any single bout of depression than either one alone[20].

Which Antidepressant is Best?

There are a number of useful guidelines that can help patients and physicians in the decision as to which of the many different types of antidepressant drugs should be tried first. In a review of the pharmacology and efficacy of the newer antidepressants, it was noted that there is a "homogeneity of outcome (in the treatment of acute major depression)...despite differing biochemical mechanisms and behavioral profiles"[6]. Therefore, the decision to use a classical tricyclic, a MAOI or one of the newer compounds should be based upon (1) what drug and dose worked in any previous depression, (2) whether there is a health problem that requires the patient to take a medicine that may negatively interact with a specific antidepressant, (3) whether a drug with sedative properties is needed to calm agitated depression or a drug with stimulant properties is needed to energize a patient, and (4) a person's sensitivity to certain drug-specific side effects, particularly excessive CNS stimulation or anticholinergic action. If sedation is needed, then one of the tricyclics with greater anticholinergic and antihistamine action, such as amitriptyline, should be used. If stimulation is needed, then an MAOI or bupropion might be tried. The importance of side effects in specific individuals is most clearly seen when the tricyclics or MAOIs induce a "switch effect"[88] into severe mania when given to depressed individuals with bipolar affective disorder (see Chapter 9). Another example of the importance of side effects is provided by the cautions necessary in prescribing tricyclics to individuals with heart or blood circulation difficulties[18]. Safe and effective treatment with antidepressant drugs requires a thorough knowledge of characteristics of the patient, as well as the side effects of the different medications.

The variety of side effects of the newer antidepressants may render them, not safer, but only different. It has been claimed that particular types of antidepressants may be more effective for certain subtypes of depression[33,40,56]. There was for a time a general consensus that the MAOIs were superior to the tricyclic antidepressants in the treatment of **atypical depression**. Atypical depression is defined differently by different researchers[7,32,56] but it is generally agreed that it is a form of a depression that has, at least, the additional features of anxiety and phobias (see Chapter 10). There is some evidence for the argument that the MAOIs are better than the tricyclics in treating atypical depression[56]. For instance, one double-blind placebo controlled study found that the MAOI, phenelzine, but not the tricyclic imipramine, improved patients with atypical depression[40]. Another well designed study compared the effects of phenelzine versus the tricyclic amitriptyline in people with unipolar major depression versus people with atypical depression. Among the subjects with atypical depression, 100% showed improvement when given the MAOI, but only 60% showed improvement when given the tricyclic. Both drugs improved 79% of the subjects with unipolar major depression[33]. These experiments suggest that individuals with atypical depression should be prescribed MAOIs, rather than tricyclics. On the other hand, the choice of MAOIs versus tricyclics in individuals with unipolar major depression should be based on evidence of previous effectiveness in that person, the need for sedation versus stimulation, and a concern for heightened susceptibility to specific side effects.

It is important to note that the greater effectiveness of MAOIs than tricyclics in the treatment of atypical depression does not, by itself, prove that those who don't respond to tricyclics must have atypical depression that will respond to MAOIs. For example, the effects of tricyclics are dose-dependent and individuals differ greatly in their absorption and metabolism of the drugs. It could be argued that failures to respond positively to tricyclics occurred because inadequate doses were used. However, when researchers used blood levels of tricyclics to insure that adequate therapeutic doses were obtained despite individual differences in absorption and metabolism, they still found that around 20% of their subjects failed to respond to these elevated doses of tricyclics. In addition, when those subjects who failed to respond to the tricyclics were given MAOIs, they all showed improvement in their symptoms[75]. Similar, but less uniform findings were observed in another study in which patients who failed to respond to adequate doses of imipramine were switched, with a double-blind procedure, to the MAOI phenelzine. A total of 59% of the people who did not respond to imipramine improved when switched to phenelzine[45]. These experiments suggest that individuals who fail to respond to tricyclics may be aided by treatment with MAOIs, but this does not prove that all nonresponders are suffering from an atypical depression. There are, for example, a number of alternatives to MAOIs, especially fluoxetine, which can be tried in individuals who fail to respond to standard tricyclic treatment[86]. However, even with the wide range of choices available, there is still "an apparently irreducible residue of perhaps 20%-30% of patients who respond poorly or not at all to any of the available treatments for depression"[3].

Compliance Problems

Compliance problems with an antidepressant treatment regimen can come from several sources[11]. People may expect effects comparable to stimulant drugs and may halt their drug intake if their particular antidepressant proves to be sedating (of course, this is not a problem with the MAOIs). Others may not have received information from their physician about the delayed therapeutic action of many antidepressants, thus causing them to stop their intake before it can exert a beneficial effect. A prominent exponent of psychotherapy for depression noted that fear of addiction, a wounded sense of autonomy, and aversion to side effects can all result in poor compliance with potentially beneficial pharmacological treatments of depression[4].

Tolerance and Dependency

While the tricyclics are not themselves reinforcing, the MAOIs and some of the newer antidepressants may provide pleasurable feelings of stimulation. A physical dependency may develop to, at least, the tricyclic antidepressants with sudden cessation of chronic use leading to chills, muscle aches, a stuffy head, and a general feeling of illness[11].

As noted in the introduction to this chapter, at least half of individuals who experience one episode of depression will experience one or more reoccurrence during their lifetime[61]. Long-term therapy may be required for people who are known to have had previous episodes of depression or in people with chronic depression. The long-term efficacy of antidepressant treatments is only now beginning to be studied. The long-term efficacy of imipramine has been demonstrated in a double-blind placebo controlled study in which 59% of subjects given chronic imipramine demonstrated continued therapeutic effectiveness despite tolerance to adverse side effects[36]. Similarly, other experiments have demonstrated the long-term efficacy of other antidepressant drug treatments, for example, the MAOIs[71] and fluoxetine[22].

Drug Holidays

There is at present no place for drug holidays with standard antidepressant treatments due to the long t 1/2s of most of the drugs, their delayed therapeutic action, and the fact, noted above, that substitution of placebo for an effective antidepressant may lead to a return of symptoms[48,83]. However, when acute drug therapy is effective, it is difficult to know when to stop the treatment.

When to Stop Drug Treatment

Does an absence of symptoms mean that the underlying disorder has run its course, or is it simply that the drug is effectively suppressing the symptoms of a continuing disorder? Stopping an effective drug treatment might seem cruel given the problem of a return of the symptoms of depression. On the other hand, continuation of unnecessary treatment exposes the individual to the possibility of side effects, drug interactions, and possible physical dependence[61]. A usual practice has been to continue medication for 6-12 months after symptoms of depression have been controlled. The dose of the drug is then gradually reduced, with careful observation enabling an immediate return to drug treatment if symptoms should reappear[65].

In one study of halting drug treatment, a number of depressed individuals were treated with imipramine until their dose had been stable for two consecutive months and the individuals had returned to their previous level of functioning, as determined by psychiatrist opinion and objective tests. Half of the subjects were then subjected to a double-blind switch to placebo, while the remaining subjects continued to receive imipramine. The researchers found that only 5% of the subjects who continued on the tricyclic, compared to 38% of those switched to placebo, experienced a return of symptoms[62]. By examining the relationship between the number of weeks of successful treatment and return of symptoms in placebo treated subjects, the authors were able to determine that subjects who had been free of even mild symptoms of depression for 4 to 5 months were the least likely to relapse. This finding suggests that it may be better in many cases to try to discontinue effective drug treatment after a shorter period of time than the usual 6-12 month wait after a removal of symptoms.

CHAPTER SUMMARY

Both the tricyclics and MAOIs have demonstrated usefulness in the treatment of acute and/or chronic unipolar major depression. The tricyclics are highly lipophilic and are therefore available mainly as pills. The tricyclics tend to have long half-lives, although there are vast differences in the rates at which different people metabolize the different tricyclics. The dose-dependent antidepressant effect of the tricyclics is usually delayed for about two to three weeks after the onset of drug intake. The tricyclics are not positively reinforcing in individuals without depression. They most likely exert their therapeutic effect through some chronic effect on monoamine receptors, particularly those associated with norepinephrine and/or serotonin. The most common side effects of the tricyclics are related to their anticholinergic actions. The tricyclics have a small therapeutic window and are very toxic at overdose.

The MAOIs are effective when taken orally. They have a short half-life, but the duration of drug action is prolonged because of irreversible inhibition and the need to synthesize new MAO to halt the drug effect. In contrast to the tricyclics, the MAOIs have a relatively rapid therapeutic onset, although there may be a delay of days or even weeks. The mechanism of the MAOIs' antidepressant effect is controversial, but it is probably related to the effects of chronic monoamine oxidase inhibition upon monoamine receptors. The most important side effects include excess stimulation and a potentially powerful interaction with tyramine, an amino acid found in a number of common foods. Overdose with the MAOIs is serious and longlasting.

Safe and effective alternatives to the tricyclics and MAOIs include fluoxetine and the selective MAO-B inhibitors. For long-term use of any antidepressant medication, the addition of psychotherapy is likely to be helpful. All the antidepressants discussed appear to be equally efficacious. Therefore, selection of any particular drug should be based on what worked previously, whether stimulation or sedation is desired, and a careful avoidance of side effects to which an individual may be particularly sensitive. Careful diagnosis is required to insure that a depressed individual with bipolar affective disorder is not "switched" into mania by antidepressant treatment. While antidepressants appear to be effective regardless of any distinction between endogenous and exogenous depressions, it does appear that atypical depressions respond better to the MAOIs than to the tricyclics. Even when a variety of antidepressant drugs are tried at therapeutic doses, about 20% to 30% of depressed individuals will not respond to drug therapy.

Compliance with long-term therapy may be poor, particularly because of delays in therapeutic action and troublesome side effects. On the other hand, overuse may occur due to the stimulating and positively reinforcing effects of the MAOIs and some of the newer antidepressants. While there does not appear to be any use for drug holidays, after approximately a half year of effective treatment, the need for further drug treatment of depression should be evaluated.

REVIEW ESSAY QUESTIONS

1. What is the basic pharmacology of the tricyclic antidepressants, and how does their basic pharmacology influence treatment patterns?

2. How might the side effects of the tricyclic antidepressants result in poor compliance? What can be done to improve compliance?

3. What are the specific differences between the tricyclic antidepressants and the MAOIs in terms of (a) basic pharmacology, (b) effects on normal subjects, (c) side effects, and (d) efficacy in subtypes of depression?

4. What techniques have been used to create new antidepressants?

5. Why would a physician and patient choose one antidepressant over another? How does the physician know when to halt treatment?

REFERENCES

1. Baldessarini, R.J. Treatment of depression by altering monoamine metabolism: Precursors and metabolic inhibitors. *Psychopharmacology Bulletin*, 1984, 20, 224-239.
2. Baldessarini, R.J. Drugs and the treatment of psychiatric disorders. In A.G. Gilman, L.S. Goodman, T.W. Rall, & F. Murad (Eds.) *The pharmacological basis of therapeutics.* (7th ed.) New York: Macmillan Publishing Company, 1985.
3. Baldessarini, R.J. Update on recent advances in antidepressant pharmacology and pharmacotherapy. In F. Flach (Ed.) *Psychobiology and Psychopharmacology*, New York: W.W. Norton, 1988.
4. Beck, A.T., Rush, A.J., Shaw, B.F., & Emery, G. *Cognitive therapy of depression.* New York:Guilford Press, 1979.
5. Berger, P.A., & Nemeroff, C.B. Opioid peptides in affective disorders. In H.Y. Meltzer (Ed.) *Psychopharmacology: The third generation of progress*, New York: Raven Press, 1987.
6. Blackwell, B. Newer antidepressant drugs. In H.Y. Meltzer (Ed.) *Psychopharmacology: The third generation of progress*, New York: Raven Press, 1987.
7. Brotman, A.W., Falk, W.E., & Gelenberg, A.J. Pharmacologic treatment of acute depressive subtypes. In H.Y. Meltzer (Ed.) *Psychopharmacology: The third generation of progress*, New York: Raven Press, 1987.
8. Burrows, G.D., McIntyre, I.M., Judd, F.K., & Norman, T.R. Clinical effects of serotonin reuptake inhibitors in the treatment of depressive illness. *Journal of Clinical Psychiatry*, 1988, 49, 18-22.
9. Callaham, M., & Kassel, D. Epidemiology of fatal tricyclic antidepressant ingestion: Implications for management. *Annals of Emergency Medicine*, 1985, 14, 1-9.
10. Cooperrider, C.A. Depression and other mood disorders. In G.W. Lawson & C.A. Cooperrider (Eds.) *Clinical psychopharmacology: A practical reference for nonmedical psychotherapists.* Rockville, MD: Aspen Publishing, 1988a.
11. Cooperrider, C.A. Antidepressants. In G.W. Lawson & C.A. Cooperrider (Eds.) *Clinical psychopharmacology: A practical reference for nonmedical psychotherapists*, Rockville, MD: Aspen Publishing, 1988b.
12. Coppen, A.J., & Doogan, D.P. Serotonin and its place in the pathogenesis of depression. *Journal of Clinical Psychiatry*, 1988, 49, 4-11.
13. Coppen, A., & Wood, K. The biology of depressive illness: 5-HT and other matters. In S.D. Iversen (Ed.) *Psychopharmacology: Recent advances and future prospects.* Oxford, England: Oxford University Press, 1985.

14. Coppen, A., Turner, P., Rowsell, A.R., & Padgham, C. 5-hydroxytryptamine (5-HT) in the whole-blood of patients with depressive illness. *Post-graduate Medical Journal*, 1976, 52, 156-158.

15. Crane, G.E. Iproniazid (marsilid) phosphate: A therapeutic agent for mental disorders and debilitating diseases. *Psychiatric Research Reports*, 1957, 8, 142-152.

16. Crome, P. Antidepressant overdosage. *Drugs*, 1982, 23, 431-461.

17. Crome, P., & Newman, B. Fatal tricyclic antidepressant poisoning. *Journal of the Royal Society of Medicine*, 1979, 72, 649-653.

18. Davidson, J., & Wenger, T. When and how to use antidepressants in patients with cardiovascular disease. *Drug Therapy*, 1982, 12, 55.

19. U.S. Public Health Service, *Facts of life and death* (Publication #79-1222), Washington, D.C.: Government Printing Office, 1978.

20. Di Mascio, A., Weissman, M.M., Prusoff, B.A., Neu, C., Zwilling, M., & Klerman, G.L. Differential symptom reduction by drugs and psychotherapy in acute depression. *Archives of General Psychiatry*, 1979, 36, 1450-1456.

21. Enna, S.J., Malick, J.B., & Richelson, E. *Antidepressants: Neurochemical, behavioral and clinical perspectives.* New York: Raven Press, 1981.

22. Feighner, J.P., & Cohn, J.B. Double-blind comparative trials of fluoxetine and doxepin in geriatric patients with major depressive disorder. *Journal of Clinical Psychiatry*, 1985, 46, 20-25.

23. Ganrot, P.O., Rosengren, E., & Gottfries, C.G. Effects of iproniazid on monoamines and monoamine oxidase in human brain. *Experientia*, 1962, 18, 260-261.

24. Gershon, E.S., Berrettini, W., Nurnberger, J., & Goldin, L.R. In H.Y. Meltzer (Ed.) *Psychopharmacology: The third generation of progress*, New York: Raven Press, 1987.

25. Glassman, A.H., & Bigger, J.T., Giardina, E-G.V., Kantnor, S.J., Perel, J.M., & Davies, M. Clinical characteristics of imipramine-induced orthostatic hypotension. *Lancet*, 1979, 1, 468-471.

26. Glassman, A.H., Roose, S.P., Giardina, E-G.V., & Bigger, J.T. Cardiovascular effects of tricyclic antidepressants. In H.Y. Meltzer (Ed.) *Psychopharmacology: The third generation of progress*, New York: Raven Press, 1987.

27. Greenblatt, M., Grosser, G.H., & Wechsler, H. Differential response of hospitalized depressed patients to somatic therapy. *American Journal of Psychiatry*, 1964, 120, 935-943.

28. Heninger, G.R., & Charney, D.S. Mechanism of action of antidepressant treatments: Implications for the etiology and treatment of depressive disorders. In H.Y. Meltzer (Ed.) *Psychopharmacology: The third generation of progress*, New York: Raven Press, 1987.

29. Hsiao, J.K., Agren, H., & Bartke, J.J. Monoamine neurotransmitter interactions and the prediction of antidepressant response. *Archives of General Psychiatry*, 1987, 44, 1078-1083.

30. Insel, T.R.,& Murphy, D.L. Pharmacologic response and subgroups of patients with affective illness. In R.M. Post & J.C. Ballenger, (Eds.) *Neurobiology of mood disorders*. Baltimore, MD: William and Wilkins, 1984.

31. Johnston, J.P. Some observations upon a new inhibitor of monoamine oxidase in brain tissue. *Biochemical Pharmacology*, 1968, 17, 1285-1297.

32. Joyce, P.R., & Paykel, E.S. Predictors of drug response in depression. *Archives of General Psychiatry*, 1989, 46, 89-99.

33. Kayser, A., Robinson, D.S., Nies, A, & Howard, D. Response to phenelzine among depressed patients with features of hysteroid dysphoria. *American Journal of Psychiatry*, 1985, 142, 486-488.

34. Klein, D.F., & Quitkin, F.M. Problems with and promises of monoamine oxidase inhibitors. *Psychopharmacology Bulletin*, 1986, 22, 7-11.

35. Kline, N.S. Clinical experience with iproniazid (marsilid). *Journal of Clinical and Experimental Psychopharmacology*, 1958, 19, 72-78.

36. Kocsis, J.H., Frances, A.J., Voss, C., Mann, J., Mason, B.J., & Sweeney, J. Imipramine treatment for chronic depression. *Archives of General Psychiatry*, 1988, 45, 253-257.

37. Kragh-Sorenson, P., & Larsen, N.E. Factors influencing nortriptyline stead-state kinetics: Plasma and saliva levels. *Clinical Pharmacology and Therapeutics*, 1980, 28, 796-803.

38. Kulig, K. Management of poisoning associated with "newer" antidepressant agents. *Annals of Emergency Medicine*, 1986, 15, 1039-1045.

39. Leonard, B.E. Pharmacological effects of serotonin reuptake inhibitors. *Journal of Clinical Psychiatry*, 1988, 49, 12-17.

40. Liebowitz, M.R., Quitkin, F.M., Stewart, J.W., McGrath, P.J., Harrison, W., Rabkin, J.G., & Tricamo, E. Psychopharmacologic validation of atypical depression. *Journal of Clinical Psychiatry*, 1984, 45, 22-25.

41. Lydiard, R.R. Tricyclic-resistant depression: Treatment resistance or inadequate treatment. *Journal of Clinical Psychiatry*, 1985, 46, 412-417.

42. Maas, J.W. Clinical and biochemical heterogeneity of depressive disorders. *Annals of Internal Medicine*, 1978, 88, 556-563.

43. Mann, J.J., Aarons, S.F., Wilner, P.J., Kelip, J.G., Sweeney, J.A., Pearlstein, T., Frances, A.J., Kocsis, J.H., & Brown, R.P. A controlled study of the antidepressant efficacy and side effects of (-)-deprenyl: A selective monoamine oxidase inhibitor. *Archives of General Psychiatry*, 1989, 46, 45-50.

44. McCabe, B., & Tsuang, M.T. Dietary consideration in MAO inhibitor regimens. *Journal of Clinical Psychiatry*, 1982, 43, 178-181.

45. McGrath, P.J., Stewart, J.W., Harrison, W., & Quitkin, F.M. Treatment of tricyclic refractory depression with a monoamine oxidase inhibitor antidepressant. *Psychopharmacology Bulletin*, 1987, 23, 169-172.

46. Meltzer, H.Y., & Lowy, M.T. The serotonin hypothesis of depression. In H.Y. Meltzer (Ed.) *Psychopharmacology: The third generation of progress*, New York: Raven Press, 1987.

47. Mendlewicz, J., & Youdim, M.B.H. L-Deprenil, a selective monoamine oxidase type B inhibitor in the treatment of depression: A double-blind evaluation. *British Journal of Psychiatry*, 1983, 142, 508-511.

48. Mindham, R.H., Howland, C., & Shepherd, M. An evaluation of continuation therapy with tricyclic antidepressants in depressive illness. *Psychological Medicine*, 1973, 3, 5-17.

49. Morris, J.B., & Beck, A.T. The efficacy of antidepressant drugs. *Archives of General Psychiatry*, 1974, 30, 667-674.

50. Murphy, D.L., Aulakh, C.S., Garrick, N.A., & Sunderland, T. Monoamine oxidase inhibitors as antidepressants: Implications for the mechanism of action of antidepressants and the psychobiology of the affective disorders and some related disorders. In H.Y. Meltzer (Ed.) *Psychopharmacology: The third generation of progress*, New York: Raven Press, 1987.

51. Nicotra, M.B., Rivera, M., Pool, J.L., & Noall, M.W. Tricyclic antidepressant overdose: Clinical and pharmacological observations. *Clinical Toxicology*, 1981, 18, 599-613.

52. Nierenberg, A.A., & Keck, P.E. Management of monoamine oxidase inhibitor-associated insomnia with trazodone. *Journal of Clinical Psychopharmacology*, 1989, 9, 42-45.

53. Paykel, E.S. Depressive typologies and response to amitriptyline. *British Journal of Psychiatry*, 1972, 120, 147-156.

54. Paykel, E.S. How effective are antidepressants? In S.D. Iversen (Ed.) *Psychopharmacology: Recent advances and future prospects*. Oxford, England: Oxford University Press, 1985.

55. Paykel, E.S., DiMascio, A., Haskell, D., & Prusoff, B.A. Effects of maintenance amitriptyline and psychotherapy on symptoms of depression. *Psychological Medicine*, 1975, 5, 67-77.

56. Pies, R.W. Atypical depression. In J.P. Tupin, R.I. Shader, & D.S. Harnett (Eds.) *Handbook of clinical psychopharmacology* (2nd ed.). Northvale, NJ: Jason Aronson Inc., 1988.

57. Pinder, R.M. Antidepressant drugs of the future. In S.D. Iversen (Ed.) *Psychopharmacology: Recent advances and future prospects*. Oxford, England: Oxford University Press, 1985.

58. Post, R. Imipramine in depression. *British Medical Journal*, 1959, 2, 1252.

59. Prange, A.J., Garbutt, J.C., & Loosen, P.T. The hypothalamic-pituitary-thyroid axis in affective disorders. In H.Y. Meltzer (Ed.) *Psychopharmacology: The third generation of progress*, New York: Raven Press, 1987.

60. Preskorn, S.H., & Othmer, S.C. Bupropion: A monocyclic antidepressant. *Journal of Clinical Psychiatry Monograph*, 1984, 2, 23-26.

61. Prien, R.F. Long-term treatment of affective disorders. In H.Y. Meltzer (Ed.) *Psychopharmacology: The third generation of progress*, New York: Raven Press, 1987.

62. Prien, R.F., & Kupfer, D.J. Continuation drug therapy for major depressive episodes: How long should it be maintained? *American Journal of Psychiatry*, 1986, 143, 18-23.

63. Quitkin, F.M. The importance of dosage in prescribing antidepressants. *British Journal of Psychiatry*, 1985, 147, 593-597.

64. Quitkin, F.M., Rabkin, J.G., Ross, D., & McGrath, P.J. Duration of antidepressant drug treatment. *Archives of General Psychiatry*, 1984, 41, 238-245.

65. Quitkin, F., Rifkin, A., & Klein, D.H. Prophylaxis of affective disorders. *Archives of General Psychiatry*, 1976, 33, 337-341.

66. Raft, D., Davidson, J., Wasik, J., & Mattox, A. Relationship between response to phenelzine and MAO inhibition in a clinical trial of phenelzine, amitriptyline and placebo. *Neuropsychobiology*, 1981, 7, 122.

67. Raskin, A., & Crook, T.A. The endogenous-neurotic distinction as a predictor of response to antidepressant drugs. *Psychological Medicine*, 1976, 6, 59-70.

68. Ravaris, C.L., Nies, A., Robinson, D.S., Ives, J.O., Lamborn, K.R., & Korson, L. A multiple-dose controlled study of phenelzine in depression-anxiety states. *Archives of General Psychiatry*, 1976, 33, 347-350.

69. Robins, L.N., Helzer, J.E., Weissman, M.M., Orvaschel, H., Gruenberg, E., Burke, J.D., & Regier, D.A. Lifetime prevalence of specific psychiatric disorders in three sites. *Archives of General Psychiatry*, 1984, 41, 949-958.

70. Robinson, D.S. New perspectives on long-standing issues: The monoamine oxidase inhibitors. *Psychopharmacology Bulletin*, 1986, 22, 12-15.

71. Robinson, D.S., Kayser, A., Bennett, B., Devereaux, E., Lerfald, S., Albright, D., Laux, D., & Corcella, J. Maintenance phenelzine treatment of major depression: An interim report. *Psychopharmacology Bulletin*, 1986, 22, 553-557.

72. Robinson, D.S., & Kurtz, N.M. Monoamine oxidase inhibiting drugs: Pharmacologic and therapeutic issues. In H.Y. Meltzer (Ed.) *Psychopharmacology: The third generation of progress*, New York: Raven Press, 1987.

73. Robinson, D.S., Nies, A., Ravaris, C.L., & Lamborn, K.R. The monoamine oxidase inhibitor, phenelzine, in the treatment of depressive-anxiety states. *Archives of General Psychiatry*, 1973, 29, 407-413.

74. Roose, S.P., Glassman, A.H., Siris, S.G., Walsh, B.T., Bruno, R.L., & Wright, L.B. Comparison of imipramine- and nortriptyline-induced orthostatic hypotension: A meaningful difference. *Journal of Clinical Psychopharmacology*, 1981, 1, 316-319.

75. Roose, S.P., Glassman, A.H., Walsh, B.T., & Woodring, S. Tricyclic nonresponders: Phenomenology and treatment. *American Journal of Psychiatry*, 1986, 143, 345-348.

76. Rudorfer, M.V., & Potter, W.Z. Pharmacokinetics of antidepressants. In H.Y. Meltzer (Ed.) *Psychopharmacology: The third generation of progress*, New York: Raven Press, 1987.

77. Schatzberg, A.F. Depressive disorders. In J.P. Tupin, R.I. Shader, & D.S. Harnett (Eds.) *Handbook of clinical psychopharmacology* (2nd ed.). Northvale, NJ: Jason Aronson Inc., 1988.

78. Schiele, B.C. Discussion on the monoamine oxidase inhibitors. *Psychopharmacology Bulletin*, 1986, 22, 16-18.

79. Schildkraut, J.J. The catecholamine hypothesis of affective disorders: A review of supporting evidence. *American Journal of Psychiatry*, 1962, 122, 509-522.

80. Siever, L.J. Role of noradrenergic mechanisms in the etiology of the affective disorders. In H.Y. Meltzer (Ed.) *Psychopharmacology: The third generation of progress*, New York: Raven Press, 1987.

81. Simpson, G.M., Lees, J.H., Cuculic, Z., & Kellner, R. Two dosages of imipramine in hospitalized endogenous and neurotic depressives. *Archives of General Psychiatry*, 1976, 33, 1093-1102.

82. Staerke, K. Regulation of noradrenaline release by pre-synaptic receptor systems. *Review of Physiology, Biochemistry and Pharmacology*, 1977, 77, 1-124.

83. Stein, M.K., Rickels, K., & Weise, C.C. Maintenance therapy with amitriptyline: A controlled trial. *American Journal of Psychiatry*, 1980, 137, 370-371.

84. Stokes, P.E., & Sikes, C.R. Hypothalamic-pituitary-adrenal axis in affective disorders. In H.Y. Meltzer (Ed.) *Psychopharmacology: The third generation of progress*, New York: Raven Press, 1987.

85. Vetulani, J., Stawarz, R.J., Dingell, J.V., & Sulser, F. A possible common mechanism of action of antidepressant treatments. *Naunyn-Schmiedeberg's Archives of Pharmacology*, 1976, 293, 109-114.

86. Wager, S.G., & Klein, D.F. Drug therapy strategies for treatment-resistant depression. *Psychopharmacology Bulletin*, 1988, 24, 69-74.

87. Wedin, G.P., Oderda, G.M., Klein-Schwartz, W., & Gorman, R.L. Relative toxicity of cyclic antidepressants. *Annals of Emergency Medicine*, 1986, 15, 797-804.

88. Wehr, T.A., & Goodwin, F.K. Do antidepressants cause mania? *Psychopharmacology Bulletin*, 1987, 23, 61-65.

89. Wernicke, J.F., Dunlop, S.R., Dornseif, B.E., Bosomworth, J.C., & Humbert, M. Low-dose fluoxetine therapy for depression. *Psychopharmacology Bulletin*, 1988, 24, 183-188.

90. Wernicke, J.F., Dunlop, S.R., Dornseif, B.E., & Zerbe, R.L. Fixed-dose fluoxetine therapy for depression. *Psychopharmacology Bulletin*, 1987, 23, 164-168.

91. Youdim, M.B.H. Implications of MAO-A and MAO-B inhibition for antidepressant therapy. *Modern Problems in Pharmacopsychiatry*, 1983, 19, 63-74.

Chapter 9

MANIA

The purposes of this chapter are to:

1. Introduce the symptoms and characteristics of mania and bipolar affective disorder (BAD),

2. Present information about the basic pharmacology, efficacy, interactions with endogenous systems, suspected mechanism of action, and side effects of the most commonly used prophylactic antimanic drug, lithium,

3. Discuss the long-term use of lithium, and

4. Briefly cover the use of other drugs in the treatment of acute mania and bipolar affective disorder.

THE DISORDER

Basic Symptoms

Bipolar affective disorder (BAD) is sometimes better known as manic-depression. The disorder is characterized by alternating periods of depression (see Chapter 8), normalcy, and **mania**. To be diagnosed as having BAD, all that a person must experience is at least one episode of mania, although there is usually at least one (but usually more) episodes of depression. There is some evidence that individuals who have only mania, with no episodes of depression, may have a more severe disorder which is less likely to respond to treatment[27].

Differential Diagnosis and the DSM-IIIR

Table 9.1 presents the DSM-IIIR criteria for mania. Strict adherence to the use of DSM-IIIR criteria in the diagnosis of mania is important, since the acute disorder can be easily confused with schizophrenia, leading to the prescription of inappropriate medication[20,39]. Distinguishing mania from schizophrenia is complicated because approximately 30% of all individuals having a manic episode will experience hallucinations and/or delusions[13]. The major characteristic of mania is that the individual has, for a limited period, an inappropriately expansive or irritable mood.

Table 9.1
DSM-IIIR Diagnostic Criteria for Mania (Summarized)

A. A distinct period of abnormally and persistently elevated , expansive, or irritated mood.

B. During the period of mood disturbance, at least three of the following symptoms have persisted and have been present to a significant degree

    (1) inflated self-esteem or grandiosity

    (2) decreased need for sleep

    (3) more talkative than usual or pressure to keep talking

    (4) flight of ideas or subjective experience that thoughts are racing

    (5) distractibility

    (6) increase in goal-directed activity or psychomotor agitation

    (7) excessive involvement in pleasurable activities that have a high potential for painful consequences

C. Mood disturbance sufficiently severe to cause marked impairment in occupational functioning or in usual social activities or relationships with others, or to necessitate hospitalization to prevent harm to self or others.

D. At no time during the disturbance have there been delusions or hallucinations for as long as two weeks in the absence of prominent mood symptoms.

E. Not superimposed on schizophrenia, etc.

F. It cannot be established that an organic factor initiated and maintained the disturbance.

Incidence and Subtypes

BAD affects anywhere from 0 .4% to 1.2% of the general population and affects men and women to an equal degree[38]. Before the introduction of the **prophylactic** (or disease-preventing) drug lithium, an individual who had one episode of mania could expect, on average, about four additional episodes within the next ten years[14]. There are some unfortunate individuals who have **rapid-cycling** BAD. When left untreated, these individuals can experience four or more episodes of mania per year[29].

Nervous System Abnormalities

Genetics plays a powerful role in the occurrence of BAD[19]. The hypothesis that BAD is a true mental illness is supported by studies indicating that individuals showing symptoms of BAD have abnormal activity of and/or responsiveness to a number of neurotransmitters. For example, individuals with BAD have supersensitive serotonin receptors[31] and the occurrence of symptoms of BAD is correlated with abnormal release and/or metabolism of norepinephrine[41]. Finally, the mania experienced in BAD may be related to supersensitive dopamine receptors[25]. Many of the neurotransmitter abnormalities in BAD can be corrected by lithium[5].

BASIC PHARMACOLOGY OF LITHIUM

Lithium is one of the basic elements of chemistry. It is a positively charged ion that neurons treat similarly to sodium and potassium, other ions that are essential to neurotransmission[5]. Lithium, when given orally in the salt form, is rapidly absorbed. This is the only route of administration routinely used in humans. Peak concentrations in blood are obtained within one hour. A slow-release form of lithium which takes about four hours to reach peak concentrations in blood is available[10].

Lithium is not bound at all to plasma proteins, but is instead rapidly distributed in the fluids that surround all the cells of the body (**extracellular fluid**). Accumulation does occur in some parts of the body, such as muscle and bone, but the concentration of lithium in the brain is the same as that in extracellular fluids. Lithium is not metabolized, and about 95% of the parent compound can be recovered in the urine with the remainder being lost in saliva, sweat, and feces[10].

Since it is so similar to sodium, excretion of lithium can be powerfully influenced by the level of sodium in the body. Individuals who have high levels of sodium as a result of, for example, high levels of salt intake will excrete more than the usual amount of lithium. However, in individuals with low sodium levels (due, for example, to the use of urine-producing **diuretics** or to heavy perspiration), the body, in an attempt to retain sodium, will instead retain *substantial* amounts of lithium[21].

Lithium easily crosses the blood-brain and placental barriers, and has been associated with a 10% incidence of serious birth defects when given within the first trimester of pregnancy[18]. Table 9.2 summarizes the basic pharmacology of lithium.

Table 9.2
Basic Pharmacology of Lithium

- An element similar to sodium in size and electrical charge
- Most commonly given orally as a salt; available in slow-release form
- Rapidly absorbed orally with peak plasma levels at one hour
- Not bound to plasma proteins
- Widely distributed throughout extracellular spaces of body
- Not metabolized
- 95% of parent compound excreted in urine
- Low sodium levels lead to lithium retention
- Easily crosses blood-brain and placental barriers

EFFECTS OF LITHIUM ON SYMPTOMS OF BIPOLAR AFFECTIVE DISORDER (BAD)

Acute Depression

Most research has investigated the effects of lithium on acute mania and the prophylactic value of the drug. However, a psychiatrist may first see a patient with BAD when that person is suffering an episode of depression. Fortunately, the depression of an individual with BAD often responds to lithium[13]. In fact, lithium can be of value in the treatment of "unipolar" depressed individuals who do not respond to standard tricyclic antidepressant therapy. A double-blind, placebo-controlled study of individuals originally diagnosed as suffering unipolar depression that did not respond to tricyclic antidepressants found that nearly all of the 54 patients improved following treatment with lithium[23].

Acute Mania

Lithium is effective in controlling moderate mania. Antipsychotic drugs (see Chapter 7) are more effective for more severe mania, but have more side effects[36]. However, antipsychotics in acute mania are controversial[26], since they can induce depression in manic individuals[44] and there may be severe toxic consequences from combinations of antipsychotics and lithium[8,33]. Most disturbing of all is the possibility that the combination can lead to an increase in the incidence of the frequently fatal neuroleptic malignant syndrome[28,42].

Relapse

In 1985, a "consensus development panel" of the National Institute of Health and the National Institute of Mental Health concluded that lithium was *the* drug of choice for controlling and/or preventing the cyclic occurrence of BAD[9]. Double-blind, placebo-controlled studies have determined that lithium reduces the probability that individuals diagnosed with BAD will suffer a relapse of this recurrent disorder[15,16]. In one such study, only 25% of lithium-treated individuals suffered a relapse within two years while 61% of placebo-treated subjects had a relapse within that same two-year period[37]. Lithium is so effective that most psychiatrists who see, for the first time, a patient with BAD are seeing someone who is having a "first episode of mania or (is) relapsing because they are...non-compliant with lithium therapy"[13].

INTERACTIONS WITH ENDOGENOUS SYSTEMS

Effects of Neurotransmitters

Considering that lithium is so similar to sodium and that sodium is so important in all neurotransmission (see Chapter 1), it is not surprising that lithium affects a wide variety of neurotransmitters. Lithium enhances the activity of neurons containing serotonin or acetylcholine and reduces the activity of neurons containing dopamine or norepinephrine[4]. Lithium is unable to block supersensitivity induced in serotonin receptors, but is remarkably effective in blocking supersensitivity of dopamine receptors[5]. Lithium's interaction with a diverse set of endogenous systems complicates the determination of its mechanism of therapeutic action.

Effects on Second Messengers

A number of **second messengers** are used by neurons to convert the activation of postsynaptic receptors into alterations in the permeability of neuronal membranes. Lithium decreases the production of two of these second messengers, cyclic AMP and phosphoionositide[4,5]. Decreases in the production of second messengers can lead to either agonist or antagonist effects, depending upon whether the usual neurotransmitter-receptor interaction led to EPSPs or IPSPs. Since second messengers are involved in neurotransmission with nearly all endogenous systems, it may be that this particular effect of lithium can explain the drug's widespread impact upon a variety of endogenous systems.

SUSPECTED MECHANISM OF THERAPEUTIC ACTION

Observations of patients given lithium for acute mania may lead to the hypothesis that therapeutic effects occur simply because lithium was given at levels capable of inducing a **sedated** (or sleepy and groggy) state. In fact, a double-blind, placebo-controlled study determined that the sedating benzodiazepine, clonazepam, was indeed effective in treating acute mania. However, the degree of sedation did not correlate with therapeutic efficacy[7]; this suggests that something other than mere sedation was responsible for the therapeutic effect of lithium.

Although sedation is probably not the mechanism of action for lithium's effects on depression, mania, and BAD, there are a variety of plausible theories that take into account the effect(s) of lithium on various endogenous systems. The effectiveness of lithium against depression has been attributed to its action as a serotonin agonist[34] (see Chapter 8 for a discussion of the role of serotonin in depression). The effectiveness of lithium against mania and as a prophylactic against BAD are thought to arise from two additional mechanisms of action. Lithium blockade of dopamine receptor supersensitivity may, eliminate or prevent the more psychotic symptoms of mania (see the dopamine hypothesis of schizophrenia in Chapter 7). Inhibition of second messengers may prevent the excessive activity of a large number of different types of neurons, thus preventing a recurrence of manic symptoms[5]. In addition, it has been suggested that the inhibition of second messengers is strongest in more-active neurons[3]. For example, if hyperactive acetylcholine and norepinephrine neurons are most responsible for the manic state, this theory states, then lithium decreases the symptoms of mania because it reduces the hyperactivity of these neurons. Only more research will reveal whether the effects of lithium against the symptoms of depression, mania, and BAD must each be explained by reference to interaction(s) with different endogenous systems, or whether a single mechanism of action can explain the diverse therapeutic effectiveness of this drug.

SIDE EFFECTS

During the first 24 hours of lithium treatment, there is a loss of sodium and potassium in the urine, a return to normal excretion, and then a retention of sodium and water. The sodium and water retention usually disappear within a few days[45]. A particularly common yet rarely kidney-damaging[30] set of side effects from lithium are **polyuria** (frequent and large-volume urination) and **polydipsia** (frequent and excessive water intake)[45]. Tremor, which disappears during sleep, and weight gain are common side effects[30]. As with all drugs, some individuals are allergic to lithium and some will suffer skin rashes. Perhaps the most disturbing side effect of lithium is that it can, at therapeutic doses, induce convulsions in people with no history of any type of seizure disorder[1]. Less frequent side effects of lithium include blurred vision, ringing sounds in the ear (**tinnitus**), and a metallic taste in the mouth[44].

The simplest way to deal with lithium side effects is to reduce dose. Of course, care must be taken not to allow doses to go so low that therapeutic effect is lost[24]. Fortunately, tolerance does occur to sodium and water retention. Polydipsia and polyuria, while sometimes reaching annoying levels, do not represent a significant risk to health. These latter two side effects can be reduced by giving a once-daily dose[30], although this procedure may increase the risk of acute toxicity.

TOXICITY

Mild Toxicity: "Peak" Toxicity after Dose

The therapeutic window of lithium is small, and a mere doubling of blood levels can lead to mild toxicity. In fact, symptoms of mild toxicity can occur after each dose of lithium. Compliance with lithium regimens is improved when people are required to take as few daily doses as possible. However, with fewer doses per day, more drug must be taken with each dose. Figure 9.1 shows how the small therapeutic window of lithium can lead to mild **peak toxicity**. The symptoms of this mild toxicity include nausea, vomiting, abdominal pain, diarrhea, sedation, and fine tremor[22]. Peak toxicity from lithium is a powerful motivator for the development of methods of administration that will enable steady blood levels of lithium to be maintained (see Chapter 3). Short of the development of effective transdermal patches or subcutaneous pumps for lithium, the best way to minimize mild toxicity is for the person to take the lowest possible dose (without eliminating therapeutic efficacy) in the greatest possible number of divided doses (without making compliance too difficult)[40]. Avoiding peak toxicity by balancing these conflicting aims is a difficult task requiring good communication and close cooperation between physician and patient.

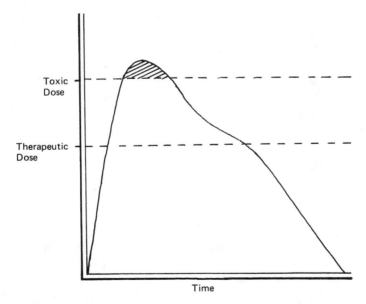

Figure 9.1. Lithium's small therapeutic window and dcse-onset mild toxicity. Note that in order to give lithium as few times a day as possible, it is necessary to give a dose that results in relatively high levels of the drug in the blood immediately after administration. Due to the small therapeutic window of lithium, this can easily lead to mild toxicity after each dose of the drug.

Toxicity from Overdose

Serious lithium toxicity occurs when lithium blood levels are between three and four times the therapeutic level. Serious lithium toxicity almost always occurs because of deliberate ingestion of large amounts of lithium during suicide attempts or because of sodium loss[40]. For example, dehydration leads to sodium loss and an attempt by the body to retain sodium. This leads to a disastrous retention of lithium as well. The symptoms of lithium toxicity include an intensification of the symptoms of mild toxicity, including intense nausea, severe vomiting and diarrhea, and agonizing stomach pain. Additional symptoms include mental confusion, a coarse tremor, coma, heartbeat irregularities, drastic reductions in blood pressure, and convulsions[22].

Treatment for Toxicity

There are three aspects to treating the severe toxicity of lithium[22]. First, if toxicity is due to overdose, care must be taken to insure that no more lithium is absorbed. The induction of vomiting may be unnecessary (since this is likely to be occurring anyway), but lithium may form hard-to-dissolve clumps in the intestinal system. These clumps can be retained even after vomiting and may eventually dissolve, causing unpredictable rises in blood concentration of lithium. Gastric lavage may aid the removal of these clumps of lithium. Second, whether caused by overdose or excessive retention of lithium, steps must be taken to increase excretion of the drug. It is often necessary to perform **hemodialysis** (cleansing of the blood by an artificial kidney) in order to insure that lithium is removed as rapidly as possible. Third, specific treatments can be applied to some symptoms of toxicity. In particular, standard anticonvulsants and stabilizers of heart rhythms should be given. The use of all three aspects of treatment may be necessary to save the life of a person suffering from severe lithium toxicity.

LONG-TERM USE OF LITHIUM

The Role of Psychotherapy

Approximately 25% of individuals who respond to lithium do not achieve a complete recovery[35]. It may be that these individuals would benefit from the addition of psychotherapy to their drug treatment program. A history of repetitive cycles of mania and depression can wreak havoc on an individual's capacity to cope with typical life events. Given the probability of peak toxicity, along with a wounded sense of autonomy, etc., compliance with lithium therapy is a problem. There is evidence that psychotherapy and group therapy can be useful in supporting compliance with drug-treatment regimens in mania and BAD[35].

Therapeutic Onset

The effects of lithium on depression and mania are fairly rapid[11], with effects noticed within three or four days and maximum effect achieved within one to two weeks[2]. The effects as a prophylactic against BAD are also usually rapid, but may take up to six months in some individuals[40]. However, like most psychopharmacotherapeutics, lithium is not a cure for the disorder it so effectively controls. Individuals with BAD who halt their lithium consumption are likely to have a recurrence of the symptoms of their disorder[12].

Importance of Plasma Levels vs. Dose

Most psychopharmacotherapeutics have a wide range between the effective and toxic doses. They can thus be administered in standard-size pills, so long as proper attention is paid to the weight of the treated individual. But the therapeutic window of lithium is quite small and special care must be taken to insure that individuals are receiving an adequate, yet not too large, dose. A common practice is to take blood samples from lithium-treated individuals and measure the amount of lithium in the individuals' blood. The unit of measure employed is mEq/l (or **milli-equivalents of lithium per liter of blood**).

The most effective treatment of acute mania is obtained when doses are given so that treated individuals have between 0 .8 and 1.0 mEq/l. Doses above 1.4 mEq/l are no more effective, but induce more severe side effects than the lower doses[10]. Mild toxicity occurs when lithium blood levels are between 1.5 and 2.5 mEq/l[22]. Severe toxicity occurs when blood levels of lithium are between 2.5 and 3.0 mEq/l. One percent of all cases where blood levels exceeded 3.0 mEq/l ended in death[21].

When used as a prophylactic against the recurrence of BAD, the most effective dose of lithium is between 0.6 and 0.8 mEq/l, which is lower than that needed for acute mania[10]. A study found that lowering the dosage of lithium to between 0.25 and 0.39 mEq/l removed the effectiveness of lithium in patients for whom the drug had previously been effective[24]. This experiment demonstrated that the use of lithium as a prophylactic against the recurrence of BAD is dose-dependent.

The small therapeutic window of lithium, the dangers of intoxication, and the effects of activity and diet on sodium levels requires that blood (actually, plasma) levels of lithium be monitored. During initial stages of treatment, lithium levels must be checked frequently, perhaps every few days. Once an individual is stabilized, lithium levels must be checked every six months, and even more frequently if there is a change in diet or activity level[40]. The levels of lithium in red blood cells are not influenced by recent consumption of lithium as much as are levels in the plasma of the blood. It has been suggested that examination of levels in red blood cells might be a more effective way of assuring compliance. When red blood cells rather than blood plasma is used, it eliminates the possibility that a patient could effectively hide his/her noncompliance by taking a single dose prior to testing[10].

Drug Interactions

The main concerns regarding drug interaction with lithium are those drugs that increase or decrease sodium and urine output. Depending upon their own individual mechanism of action, diuretics can have no effect or can raise or lower lithium blood levels. This can lead to toxicity or loss of therapeutic effectiveness, depending upon the specific diuretic. The psychomotor stimulant theophylline (see the Chapter 15 discussion of caffeine) can increase the amount of lithium lost in the urine. Theophylline is found mainly in teas and asthma medications, but also exists in varying amounts in coffee and chocolate. If there is a sudden increase in the consumption of theophylline, lithium excretion will be enhanced and therapeutic efficacy will be halted. If a regular consumer of theophylline decides to halt consumption, there can be a dangerous elevation of lithium levels and a serious chance of toxicity.

Compliance, Tolerance, and Dependency

Lithium's unpleasant side effects and the risk of peak toxicity often cause patients to fail to follow treatment regimens. Lithium is not a reinforcing drug, and abrupt cessation of drug treatment is usually followed, in a few days, by nothing more serious than restlessness and irritability[40]. The double-blind, placebo-controlled studies of the efficacy of prophylactic lithium mentioned above found no evidence of tolerance to the therapeutic effect of lithium. Thus, lithium can be given chronically as a prophylactic against BAD with no fear of physical dependency, compulsive use, or loss of therapeutic efficacy.

Drug Holidays and when to Stop Treatment

Since lithium is taken mainly as a prophylactic against a recurrent disorder, the questions of drug holidays and cessation of treatment often arise. While there is little reason for the "lithium holiday," there is also little risk in supervised attempts to halt the long-term use of lithium. Since the drug is so rapidly excreted, the treated individual and the physician will soon find out if absence of the drug leads to a return to psychiatric symptoms. A restart of drug therapy should bring a rapid return to normalcy. Starting and stopping lithium therapy should be particularly effective in those individuals whose cycles show a clear relationship to seasonal changes.

OTHER DRUGS FOR MANIA AND/OR BAD

While lithium is the drug of choice for mania and BAD, there have been a number of other experimentally evaluated drug treatments. As noted above, the benzodiazepine, clonazepam, was effective in treating acute mania[7]. This promising result has led to studies that are presently being conducted to determine if this, or other, benzodiazepines are equally effective in preventing the recurrent cycles of BAD[6].

Another drug found to be effective against acute mania is the anticonvulsant (and incidentally sedating) drug, carbamazepine[43]. In a review of the world literature on carbamazepine and acute mania/BAD, the author noted that the drug was effective in some 66% of rapid-cycling manics, as opposed to the 10%-15% success rate with this subgroup when given lithium[2]. Unfortunately, double-blind, placebo-controlled studies of the effectiveness of carbamazepine as a prophylaxis for the recurrent cycles of BAD have been contradictory. One study followed 83 BAD sufferers for three years and found that there was no difference between the efficacy of lithium and of carbamazepine[32]. However, another well-designed study found that the drug was effective in the short term, but that tolerance occurred to the therapeutic effect[17]. Further studies will be required to tell whether drugs that are effective against acute mania will be safe and effective prophylactics for the recurrence of BAD.

CHAPTER SUMMARY

Lithium effectively treats the symptoms of BAD, including acute mania, acute depression, and cycles of mania and depression. The drug is a basic element, given orally in salt form. It is distributed to all extracellular fluids and is not bound to plasma proteins nor concentrated in the brain. It is not metabolized, and 90% of the parent compound is found in the urine. Lithium interacts with a variety of endogenous systems, perhaps through reductions in the activity of second messengers. The effects of lithium on serotonin and second messengers are suspected to produce the therapeutic effect(s) of the drug. Side effects of lithium include polyuria, polydipsia, tremors, and weight gain. The fewer the daily doses of the drug, the greater the risk of peak toxicity. Severe toxicity at overdose requires gastric lavage, hemodialysis, and treatment for convulsions and heartbeat irregularities. Long-term use of lithium does not cure BAD, but does act as an effective prophylactic against recurrent cycles. It is important to monitor blood levels of the drug, with special attention paid to changes in sodium excretion due to alterations in diet or activity levels. In addition, drugs that can cause loss of sodium can lead to retention of lithium and an increased risk of toxicity. Lithium is not reinforcing in normals, and the side effects and risk of peak toxicity may lead to poor compliance in persons with BAD. Tolerance may occur to some of the side effects of chronic lithium therapy, but there is no evidence of tolerance to the therapeutic effectiveness of the drug. Other drugs that have been found to be effective against acute mania include specific benzodiazepines and anticonvulsants. The long-term effectiveness of these alternatives to lithium therapy remain controversial.

REVIEW ESSAY QUESTIONS

1. What is the basic pharmacology of lithium? What aspects of lithium pharmacology make it unique among the drugs studied so far?

2. Compare the effects of lithium on acute depression and acute mania and as a prophylaxis against the recurrent cycles of BAD.

3. Relate the way that lithium interacts with endogenous systems to its suspected therapeutic mechanisms of action against, in particular, the recurrent cycles of BAD.

4. Compare and contrast the causes and consequences of mild versus severe toxicity from lithium.

5. Present information about the long-term use of lithium, particularly regarding proper dose and the questions of physical dependency and compliance.

REFERENCES

1. Baldessarini, R.J. Drugs and the treatment of psychiatric disorders. In A.G. Gilman, L.S. Goodman, T.W. Rall, & F. Murad (Eds.) *The pharmacological basis of therapeutics* (7th ed.). New York: Macmillan, 1985.

2. Ballenger, J.C. The use of anticonvulsants in manic-depressive illness. *Journal of Clinical Psychiatry*, 1988, 49, 21-26.

3. Berridge, M.J. Inositol triphosphate and diacylglycerol as second messengers. *Biochemical Journal*, 1984, 220, 345-360.

4. Bloom, F.E., Baetge, G., Deyo, S., Ettenberg, A., Koda, L., Magisretti, P.J., Shoemaker, W.J., & Staunton, D.A. Chemical and physiological aspects of the actions of lithium and antidepressant drugs. *Neuropharmacology*, 1983, 22, 359-365.

5. Bunney, W.E., & Garland-Bunney, L. Mechanisms of action of lithium in affective illness: Basic and clinical implications. In H.Y. Meltzer (Ed.) *Psychopharmacology: The third generation of progress*. New York: Raven Press, 1987.

6. Chouinard, G. The use of benzodiazepines in the treatment of manic-depressive illness. *Journal of Clinical Psychiatry*, 1988, 49, 15-19.

7. Chouinard, G., Young, S.N., & Annable, L. Antimanic effect of clonazepam. *Biological Psychiatry*, 1983, 18, 451-466.

8. Cohen, W.J., & Cohen, N.H. Lithium carbonate, haloperidol and irreversible brain damage. *Journal of the American Medical Association*, 1974, 230, 1283-1287.

9. Consensus Development Panel. Mood disorders: Pharmacological prevention of recurrence. *American Journal of Psychiatry*, 1985, 142, 469-476.

10. Cooper, T.B. Pharmacokinetics of lithium. In H.Y. Meltzer (Ed.) *Psychopharmacology: The third generation of progress*. New York: Raven Press, 1987.

11. Davis, J.M. Overview: Maintenance therapy in psychiatry. II. Affective disorders. *American Journal of Psychiatry*, 1976, 133, 1-13.

12. *Dunner , D. L. Mania. In J.P. Tupin, R.I. Shader, & D.S. Harnett (Eds.) *Handbook of clinical psychopharmacology* (2nd ed.). Northvale, NJ: Jason Aronson, 1988.

13. Dunner, D.L., & Clayton, P.J. Drug treatment of bipolar disorder. In H.Y. Meltzer (Ed.) *Psychopharmacology: The third generation of progress*. New York: Raven Press, 1987.

14. Dunner, D.L., Murphy, D., Stallone, F., & Fieve, R.R. Episode frequency prior to lithium treatment in bipolar manic depressive patients. *Comprehensive Psychiatry*, 1979, 20, 511-515.

15. Dunner, D.L., Stallone, F., & Fieve, R.R. Prophylaxis with lithium carbonate: An update. *Archives of General Psychiatry*, 1982, 39, 1344-1345.

16. Fieve, R.R., Kumbaraci, T., & Dunner, D.L. Lithium prophylaxis of depression in bipolar I, bipolar II and unipolar patients. *American Journal of Psychiatry*, 1976, 133, 925-929.

17. Frankenburg, F.R., Tohen, M., & Cohen, B.M. Long-term response to carbamazepine: A retrospective study. *Journal of Clinical Psychopharmacology*, 1988, 8, 130-132.

18. Gelenberg, A.J. Lithium efficacy and adverse effects. *Journal of Clinical Psychiatry*, 1988, 49, 8-9.

19. Gershon, E.S., Berrettini, W., Nurnberger, J., & Goldin, L.R. Genetics of affective illness. In H.Y. Meltzer (Ed.) *Psychopharmacology: The third generation of progress*. New York: Raven Press, 1987.

20. Goodwin, D.W., Alderson, P., & Rosenthal, R. Clinical significance of hallucinations in psychiatric disorders. *Archives of General Psychiatry*, 1971, 24, 76-80.

21. Goodwin, J.M., Janowsky, D.S., & El-Yousef, M.K. The use of lithium in clinical psychiatry. *Psychiatric Annals*, 1973, 3, 78-99.

22. Groleau, G., Barish, R., Tso, E., Whye, D., & Browne, B. Lithium intoxication: Manifestations and management. *American Journal of Emergency Medicine*, 1987, 5, 527-532.

23. Heninger, G.R., Charney, D.S., & Sternberg, D.E. Lithium carbonate augmentation of antidepressant treatment. *Archives of General Psychiatry*, 1983, 40, 1335-1342.

24. Hullin, R.P. Minimum serium lithium levels for effective prophylaxis. In F.N. Johnson (Ed.) *Handbook of lithium therapy*. Lancaster, England: MTP Press, 1980.

25. Jimerson, D.C. Role of dopamine mechanisms in the affective disorders. In H.Y. Meltzer (Ed.) *Psychopharmacology: The third generation of progress*. New York: Raven Press, 1987.

26. Kane, J.M. The role of neuroleptics in manic-depressive illness. *Journal of Clinical Psychiatry*, 1987, 49, 12-14.

27. Keller, M.B. The course of manic-depressive illness. *Journal of Clinical Psychiatry*, 1988, 49, 4-6.

28. Levenson, J.L. Neuroleptic malignant syndrome. *American Journal of Psychiatry*, 1985, 142, 1137-1145.

29. McElroy, S.L., Keck, P.E., Pope, H.G., & Hudson, J.I. Valproate in the treatment of rapid-cycling bipolar disorder. *Journal of Clinical Psychopharmacology*, 1988, 8, 275-279.

30. Mellerup, E.T., Plenge, P., & Rafaelsen, O.J. Renal and other controversial adverse effects of lithium. In H.Y. Meltzer (Ed.) *Psychopharmacology: The third generation of progress*. New York: Raven Press, 1987.

31. Meltzer, H.Y. Serotonergic function in the affective disorders: The effect of antidepressants and lithium on the 5-hydroxytryptophan-induced increase in serum cortisol. *Annals of the New York Academy of Sciences*, 1984, 430, 115-137.

32. Placidi, G.F., Lenzi, A., & Lazzerini, F. The comparative efficacy and safety of carbamazepine versus lithium: A randomized double-blind 3-year trial in 83 patients. *Journal of Clinical Psychiatry*, 1986, 47, 490-494.

33. Prakash, R., Lelwala, S., & Ban, T.A. Neurotoxicity with combined administration of lithium and a neuroleptic. *Comprehensive Psychiatry*, 1982, 23, 567-571.

34. Price, L.H., Charney, D.S., Delgado, P.L., & Heninger, G.R. Neuroendocrine and behavioral responses to intravenous tryptophan in affective disorder. *Archives of General Psychiatry*, 1989, 46, 13-19.

35. Prien, R.F. Long-term treatment of affective disorders. In H.Y. Meltzer (Ed.) *Psychopharmacology: The third generation of progress*. New York: Raven Press, 1987.

36. Prien, R.F., Caffey, E.M., & Kleett, C.J. Comparison of lithium carbonate and chlorpromazine in the treatment of mania: Report of the Veterans Administration and National Institute of Mental Health collaborative study group. *Archives of General Psychiatry*, 1972, 26, 146-153.

37. Prien, R.F., Caffey, E.M., & Kleett, C.J. Factors associated with lithium responses in the prophylactic treatment of bipolar manic-depressive illness. *Archives of General Psychiatry*, 1974, 31, 189-192.

38. Rosenbaum, J.F. The course and treatment of manic-depressive illness: An update. *Journal of Clinical Psychiatry*, 1988, 49, 3.

39. Rosenthal, N.E., Rosenthal, L.N., Stallone, F., Dunner, D.L., & Fieve, R.R. Toward the validation of RDC schizoaffective disorder. *Archives of General Psychology*, 1980, 37, 804-810.

40. *Schou, M. Practical problems of lithium maintenance treatment. In D. Kemali, & G. Racagni (Eds.) *Chronic treatments in neuropsychiatry*. New York: Raven Press, 1985.

41. Siever, L.J. Role of noradrenergic mechanisms in the etiology of the affective disorders. In H.Y. Meltzer (Ed.) *Psychopharmacology: The third generation of progress*. New York: Raven Press, 1987.

42. Spring, G., & Frankel, M. New data on lithium and haloperidol incompatibility. *American Journal of Psychiatry*, 1981, 138, 818-821.

43. Stomgren, L.S., & Boller, S. Carbamazepine in treatment and prophylaxis of manic-depressive disorder. *Psychiatric Developments*, 1985, 4, 349-367.

44. Thrasher, D, & Lawson, G.W. Lithium. In G.W. Lawson, & C.A. Cooperrider (Eds.) *Clinical psycho-pharmacology: A practical reference for nonmedical psychotherapists.* Rockville, MD: Aspen Publishers, 1988.
45. Vestergaard, P., Amdisen, A., & Schou, M. Clinically significant side effects of lithium treatment. A survey of 232 patients in long-term treatment. *Acta Psychiatrica Scandinavica*, 1980, 62, 193-200.

* Introductory or intermediate reading

Chapter 10

GENERALIZED ANXIETY DISORDER

The purposes of this chapter are to:

1. Discuss the differential diagnosis of the varieties of anxiety, with a particular emphasis upon the symptoms and possible physical basis of generalized anxiety disorder (GAD),

2. Present an in-depth discussion of the psychopharmacology and use of benzodiazepine compounds as antianxiety agents, and

3. Briefly discuss the use of nonbenzodiazepine antianxiety agents.

———————————

THE DISORDER

Differential Diagnosis and the DSM-IIIR

Advances in the treatment of anxiety have been greatly aided by the use of differential diagnosis and the DSM-IIIR[6,14]. There are specific criteria for distinguishing between different varieties of anxiety, including generalized anxiety disorder (GAD), simple phobia, social phobia, obsessive-compulsive disorder, posttraumatic stress disorder, panic disorder, and agoraphobia without history of panic disorder. The need to find effective treatment for the varieties of anxiety was demonstrated in a house-to-house survey involving almost 10,000 persons. The survey revealed that 8.3% of the adult population of the U.S. experienced symptoms of one or the other anxiety disorder during the previous six months[66]. Unfortunately, this same survey found that only 23% of individuals suffering from abnormal anxiety received any treatment.

There have been successful attempts to provide pharmacological treatments for each variety of anxiety[2,13,30,33,37,49,50,53,54]. This chapter, however, focuses on benzodiazepines and pharmacological treatment of GAD, the most common and thoroughly studied variety of anxiety. Table 10.1 presents the DSM-IIIR criteria for the diagnosis of GAD.

Table 10.1
DSM-IIIR Diagnostic Criteria
for Generalized Anxiety Disorder (Summarized)

A. Unrealistic or excessive anxiety and worry about two or more life circumstances...for a period of six months or longer.

B. The focus of the anxiety and worry in A is unrelated to...having a panic attack, being embarrassed in public, being contaminated, or gaining weight.

C. The disturbance does not occur only during the course of a mood disorder or a psychotic disorder.

D. At least 6 of the following 18 symptoms are often present when anxious
  - *Motor tension*...trembling, twitching or feeling shaky: muscle tension, aches, or soreness: restlessness: easy fatigability

  - *Autonomic hyperactivity*...shortness of breath or smothering sensations: palpitations or accelerated heart rate: sweating, or cold clammy hands: dry mouth: dizziness or lightheadedness: nausea, diarrhea, or other abdominal distress: flushes (hot flashes) or chills: frequent urination: trouble swallowing or "lump in throat"

  - *Vigilance and scanning*...feeling keyed up or on edge: exaggerated startle response: difficulty concentrating or "mind going blank" because of anxiety: trouble falling or staying asleep: irritability

E. It cannot be established that an organic factor initiated and maintained the disturbance.

Nervous System Abnormalities in GAD

As with other behavioral problems, there are those who assert that individuals suffering from GAD have a true mental illness caused by nervous system abnormalities[29,55]. Anxiety, when appropriately activated to optimum intensity, is a useful characteristic for humans existing in a hostile environment that includes predators, toxins, germs, bad weather, and limited food and water. Individuals suffering from GAD may have inherited an exaggerated and inappropriate degree of responsiveness to the dangers of life in a hostile world. In support of this idea, drugs that antagonize receptors associated with the amino acid neurotransmitter GABA (see Chapter 1) induce symptoms of GAD in normal volunteers[9]. This, and other data about the pharmacological induction of anxiety[8,24] suggest that "anxiety might result from a deficit in GABA receptor function, or in the activity of selected GABAergic neurons"[11].

BENZODIAZEPINE TREATMENT OF GAD

At present, the main drug for the treatment of GAD is one or the other of the class of Valium-like drugs known as the **benzodiazepines**[17,20,63]. Nearly 10% of the adult population of the U.S. takes a benzodiazepine at least once per year, and approximately 1.6% of the total population has taken benzodiazepines for at least a year's duration[44].

Basic Pharmacology

All of the benzodiazepines are available in oral form, but only a few are available as injectable drugs[1]. Table 10.2 presents the generic and trade names of some of the more common benzodiazepine compounds. While diazepam is absorbed rapidly, with peak concentrations in blood obtained as soon as 15 minutes after oral administration, the remainder of the benzodiazepines are absorbed more slowly and may take hours to reach peak blood concentrations. They are all moderately to highly lipid soluble, except for midazolam, which has been called "the first water-soluble benzodiazepine"[32]. All the benzodiazepines, except for alprazolam, are very highly (85% to 95%) bound to plasma proteins; the remainder of the drug is distributed rapidly and fairly evenly throughout the rest of the body. Although they easily cross the blood-brain and placental barriers, the possibility of teratogenicity is controversial. All of the benzodiazepines are metabolized by liver enzymes and excreted mainly in urine, but only some become converted to active metabolites. There is no evidence that long-term use of the benzodiazepines induces a more rapid metabolism[18]. While the t 1/2s of the different benzodiazepines differ greatly, the actual duration of action depends upon whether or not active metabolites are created[19]. Since undesirable degrees of sedation can occur at only twice the dose needed for antianxiety effects, drugs with short half-lives but active metabolites may build up in an individual who takes doses at what would, without active metabolites, be appropriately short intervals[47]. Figure 10.1 compares the effect of dosing interval on the potential accumulation of two different benzodiazepines with equivalent half-lives where only one compound is converted to an active metabolite. Table 10.3 summarizes the basic pharmacology of the benzodiazepines.

Table 10.2
A Selected List of Benzodiazepines

Generic	Trade
Alprazolam	Xanax
Chlordiazepoxide	Librium
Diazepam	Valium
Lorazepam	Ativan
Midazolam	Versed, Dormicum
Oxazepam	Serax
Triazolam	Halcion

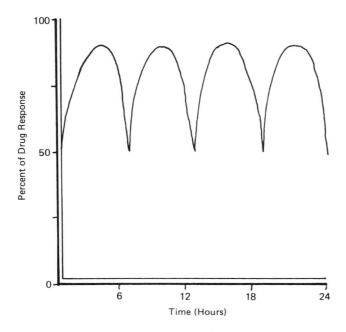

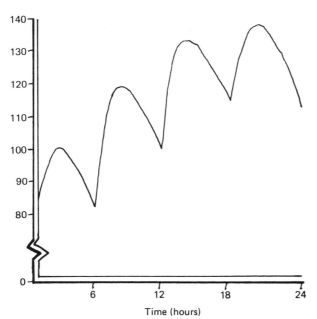

Figure 10.1. Effect of dosing interval on the accumulation of benzodiazepines with equivalent half-lives, only one converted to an active metabolite. Note how a dosing interval that enables safe administration of the drug that is not converted to an active metabolite nonetheless results in excessive drug effects from the drug which is converted to an active metabolite.

Table 10.3
Basic Pharmacology of the Benzodiazepines

- All available in oral form, some as injectables
- Moderately to highly lipid soluble
- Variable absorption, fastest absorbed in 15 minutes
- Usually very highly bound to plasma proteins
- Rapid and fairly even distribution in body after protein binding
- Metabolized by liver enzymes
- Some create active metabolites
- Variable half-lives
- Excreted in urine

Effects on Symptoms of GAD

Although the benzodiazepines differ greatly in potency, they are all equally effective in treating the symptoms of GAD. Many different double-blind, placebo-controlled studies have demonstrated the ability of each benzodiazepine to reduce the specific physical and psychological symptoms of anxiety. Of course, the differences in basic pharmacology lead to "clinical differences ...in the time course of onset, intensity and duration of clinical activity"[19]. For example, double-blind comparison of lorazepam and clorazepate (a benzodiazepine not found in Table 10.2) revealed that both caused a rapid (within one week) reduction in subjective feelings of anxiety[62]. However, the effective dose of clorazepate averaged around 25 mg/day while the effective dose of lorazepam averaged around 2.7 mg/day. A person who is switched from one benzodiazepine to another should be told that increases or decreases in the dose of one drug over the other are influenced more by the relative potency of the drugs than by alterations in the severity of the anxiety disorder.

Like most of the presently available treatments for behavioral disorders, the benzodiazepines do not "cure" anxiety. Anxiety is likely to occur in unpredictable cycles, and a halt in medication may well lead to a return of the original symptoms[59]. Furthermore, approximately 40% of the patients who did respond to benzodiazepines did not show a complete elimination of all their symptoms[57]. This finding suggests that even those who find benzodiazepines useful in the treatment of their anxiety might require additional treatment, perhaps in the form of psychotherapy. On the other hand, it is possible that a complete elimination or "cure" of anxiety would have unfortunate consequences. It is likely that all humans experience temporary bouts of anxiety that are unpleasant, yet not of sufficient intensity or duration to qualify as symptoms of GAD. It has been noted that anxiety is "both an emotion and an essential drive" and it is "predominantly concerned with choice and uncertainty"[70]. Unfortunately, since they reduce the symptoms of anxiety rather than cure the disorder, benzodiazepines will reduce the minor anxieties that people apparently require to motivate themselves to perform necessary tasks. In addition, double-blind, placebo-controlled studies have revealed that normal humans find the effects of benzodiazepines to be reinforcing and pleasant[22]. This contrasts greatly with the experience of normal subjects to the effects of tricyclic antidepressants (see Chapter 8) or antipsychotics (see Chapter 7), and has led to a problem of benzodiazepine abuse among the general population[23].

Interactions with Endogenous Systems

The frontal lobes and various "limbic" structures associated with emotion in the human central nervous system contain specific receptors that benzodiazepine molecules bind to with great **affinity** (ease and intensity)[28,46]. The endogenous substance intended for binding to these receptors has yet to be discovered. However, a few facts about these receptors are known. Benzodiazepine receptors are part of a larger "complex" which includes receptors for the "inhibitory" neurotransmitter GABA[11]. Although there is some evidence that there may be some binding of benzodiazepines to the actual GABA receptor, the drugs do not themselves induce postsynaptic potentials. Benzodiazepines instead exert a modulation of the IPSPs induced by GABA in the postsynaptic neuron (see Chapter 1). That is, when benzodiazepines bind to their own receptor in the receptor complex, they increase the effect of any GABA that may bind to GABA receptors. This effect is enhanced because the binding of benzodiazepines to their receptor changes the structure of the whole complex, making it more likely that a GABA molecule will bind to a GABA receptor[4]. Figure 10.2 reveals the effects of benzodiazepines upon the receptor complex. The main result of this neuromodulation of GABA neurons is an increase in the ability of chloride to cross the postsynaptic membrane and induce hyperpolarizations associated with IPSPs. This leads to a reduction in the electrical activity of specific brain areas involved in emotion[40].

Suspected Mechanism of Action: Neuromodulation of GABA

A consensus is emerging that the mechanism of action of the antianxiety effect of the benzodiazepines involves benzodiazepine-receptor mediated neuromodulation, specifically enhancement, of GABA activity[4,40]. This neuromodulation enhances the inhibitory effects of GABA neurotransmission on presumably "anxiety-generating" information passing back and forth from the limbic areas of the brain to the frontal lobes of the cortex. The best evidence for this hypothesis is that, once differences in lipid-solubility (and hence, absorption, distribution, and metabolism) are taken into account, the antianxiety potency of a particular benzodiazepine is highly correlated with the ability to bind to benzodiazepine receptors and modulate GABA neurotransmission[28].

Additional support for this hypothesis of the mechanism of action of the benzodiazepines arises from findings that drugs that block benzodiazepine receptors can induce anxiety and, furthermore, that this antagonist-induced anxiety can be blocked with

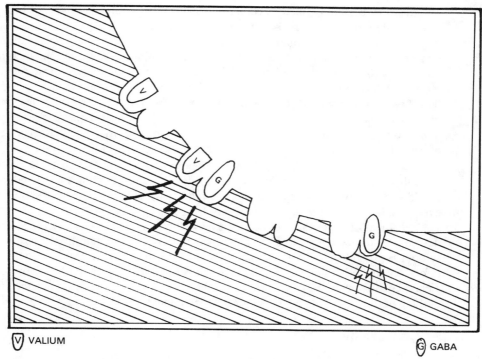

V VALIUM   G GABA

Figure 10.2. Effects of the benzodiazepine Valium upon the GABA receptor complex. The binding of a benzodiazepine to the receptor complex (a) enables GABA molecules to bind more easily by changing the shape of that portion of the receptor that interacts with GABA and (b) increases the strength of the response of the postsynaptic neuron to GABA-receptor interactions.

the administration of benzodiazepines[8]. However, there are arguments against the idea that benzodiazepines exert their antianxiety effect via modulation of endogenous systems involving GABA. For example, other drugs that do not block the benzodiazepine receptor, such as the stimulant drug caffeine[3], induce anxiety in normal volunteers, and they also induce anxiety at lower doses in people with a history of GAD. Even worse for the theory, drugs that are GABA agonists, and should thus mimic the effects of activation of benzodiazepine receptors, are not as effective as the benzodiazepines in reducing the symptoms of anxiety[41]. These data suggest that, while neuromodulation of GABA plays an important role, interaction with benzodiazepine receptors that are part of the GABA receptor complex does not entirely explain the antianxiety effect of the benzodiazepines.

Side Effects

Sedation (sleepiness and impairment of thought and memory) can occur at the onset of therapy, but it is likely to be the only significant reported side effect[21,61]. Sedation can lead to impaired acquisition of new memories and impaired driving performance[67].

Tolerance to sedation usually occurs, and it usually occurs rapidly[35]. When lack of tolerance does occur, it might be because, as mentioned above, benzodiazepines may have long half-lives, active metabolites, and a small therapeutic window, with sedation occurring at only twice the recommended dose. Thus, failure to observe tolerance to acute doses could be the result of a buildup of blood levels into the sedative dose range.

Additional, but much more rare, side effects include skin rash, nausea, headache, light-headedness, impairment of sexual performance, menstrual irregularities, or a paradoxical increase in anxiety[1]. Anecdotal reports of a loss of control over aggressive impulses were not strongly supported by double-blind experimental studies nor analysis of the incidence of adverse drug effects . Less than 1% of individuals given benzodiazepines show loss of control over aggression, a level that "may be no different from that found in patients treated with a placebo"[7]. Furthermore, there is nothing that would enable physicians or researchers to predict which subjects would show more, or even less, hostility subsequent to intake of benzodiazepines.

In most cases, side effects can be reduced by either waiting for tolerance to develop, or by reducing the dose of the benzodiazepine and administering the drug as seldom as possible[59]. Of course, reduction in dose may lead to a reduction in therapeutic effect. On the other hand, intermittent administration may allow for between-dose drug clearance to occur to a degree that allows effective treatment without a side effect inducing buildup of drugs with long t 1/2s and/or active metabolites.

Toxicity

Despite the small window between therapeutic dose and sedative dose, "the striking advantage of (benzodiazepines) is the remarkable margin of safety" between the therapeutic dose and the toxic dose[1]. In fact, an expert on handling poisoning and drug overdose argued that there is no single case where it can be unequivocally proven that benzodiazepine overdose alone, rather than in combination with alcohol, other drugs, or in the face of severe illness, was responsible for any deaths[39]. This researcher noted that of the 51,236 cases of benzodiazepine overdose, there were only 66 fatalities, most involving the simultaneous ingestion of alcohol or some other sedative drug. Unless complicated by the ingestion of some other compound, the treatment of overdose involves concerns about decreased respiration and heart function[38].

Long-Term Use of Benzodiazepines

The role of psychotherapy. In a study of 119 long-term users of benzodiazepines, it was found that many people required intensive psychiatric and social support in order to deal with their anxiety and other related behavioral problems[60].

Intermittency vs. continuous treatment. An earlier report from the same laboratory concluded that most people given benzodiazepines should be given the drug for short periods with the drug offered on an intermittent rather than continuous basis[58]. However, there are certain individuals who would benefit from long-term, continuous, treatment, in particular those with chronic (more than 12 months long) GAD[59] or those with chronic physical diseases that induce uncomfortable levels of anxiety[26].

Tolerance. It has been noted that therapy should be aimed at "not only the reduction of symptoms and the return to more appropriate social functioning, but also the improvement of the patient's quality of life"[59]. Similarly, "a drug treatment may be excellent at relieving the symptoms of anxiety but lead to marked impairment of functioning through its adverse effects"[68]. Fortunately, rapid tolerance occurs to the side effects associated with excess sedation while there is little evidence of tolerance to the therapeutic effect of the drugs[34,67]. For example, a double-blind study was conducted in which people who were chronically consuming one of five different benzodiazepines were told to abstain from medication immediately prior to a laboratory visit. During the laboratory visit, they were given their usual dose of the drug. Tolerance to sedation was revealed when none of the subjects demonstrated any effect of the acute dose upon memory or motor skills[42]. Furthermore, despite an average of 58 months of chronic benzodiazepine therapy, all subjects obtained an acute antianxiety effect from the acute administration of their usual drug and dose. Because of this differential tolerance, patients are likely to be compliant with prescribed treatment regimens and thus receive substantial benefit from long-term treatment with benzodiazepines[60,71].

Compliance. Although the benzodiazepines are effective when given chronically, there has been much concern about the possibility that people may take too much, rather than too little, of prescribed benzodiazepines. For instance, there have been demonstrations of abuse of benzodiazepines by both anxious and normal individuals[23]. Some studies, however, find that anxious individuals are unlikely to abuse benzodiazepines. For example, a study involving 71 patients with either anxiety alone or anxiety plus depression found that only those suffering anxiety plus depression were likely to take their medication in greater than prescribed doses[15]. It has been suggested that the abuse of benzodiazepines by non-anxious individuals has led to psychiatric calvinism which "may be depriving many anxious patients of appropriate treatment"[71].

Dependency. Part of the concern about the potential abuse of benzodiazepines arises from their potential to cause physical dependence. For example, patients experienced drug-induced impairment of performance at work and at home and suffered withdrawal symptoms when they halted their alprazolam use[31]. Caution must be exercised, however, in evaluating the meaning of drug-cessation phenomena (see Chapter 5). Sudden cessation of chronic benzodiazepine intake can lead to rebound anxiety, which may lead to an unnecessary continuation of drug therapy[61]. For example, in a double-blind experiment 62 anxious patients were given four weeks of therapy with clorazepate or lorazepam. Two-thirds of each drug group was abruptly, and blindly, switched to placebo for the following two weeks, while the remaining one-third of each group kept taking their medication. The long t 1/2s of the drugs resulted in 70% of the patients experiencing a therapeutic benefit through the two weeks of placebo treatment. However, the remaining subjects experienced a drug cessation rebound of anxiety to levels worse than when drug treatment was started[62]. Since lorazepam had the shorter half-life of the two drugs, patients using that drug showed the most intense and earliest rebound. This result suggested that gradual, rather than abrupt, withdrawal would limit rebound anxiety. In a direct, double-blind test of this hypothesis, four weeks of chronic benzodiazepine therapy was followed by a gradual placebo substitution over a three-week period or by an abrupt placebo substitution. Abrupt substitution resulted in significant rebound anxiety, while gradual substitution merely resulted in a slow return to pretreatment levels of anxiety[12]. These results suggest that "withdrawal" from sudden cessation of benzodiazepine therapy (and the induction of negative reinforcement when drug administration begins anew) can be avoided by either gradual cessation or the use of a benzodiazepine with a long t 1/2.

It has been known since the early 1960s that subjects engaging in high-dose chronic use of benzodiazepines experience true withdrawal symptoms when placebo is blindly and abruptly substituted for the high dose of the chronically consumed drug. Symptoms of withdrawal may include seizures and a **paranoid psychosis** involving fears of being followed and persecuted[27]. Controversy exists over whether even low-dose, therapeutically determined, chronic use of a benzodiazepine can lead to physical dependency if the drug is used long enough[35,48,70]. Even though the title of one paper asserted that the authors were conducting an evaluation of the "risk of withdrawal," they concluded that their findings revealed no significant withdrawal symptoms other than rebound anxiety[61]. Another study found that between 30%-40% of chronic benzodiazepine-using subjects experienced "withdrawal" when they were merely told that a placebo had been substituted for the active drug[69]. This finding means that anecdotal self-reports of withdrawal in chronic users must be greeted with great skepticism. Further research with greater emphasis upon varieties of drug cessation phenomena will be needed before scientists can agree whether therapeutic doses of benzodiazepines can cause a true physical dependency[35].

Drug holidays. Some authors assert that physical dependence upon benzodiazepines is not a significant clinical problem[43]. However, there is a possibility of physical dependence from long-term use of even therapeutic doses, and there is a certainty of dependence from chronic use of high doses. This suggests that people who must consume benzodiazepines on a chronic basis should attempt frequent, physician-controlled drug holidays. Such holidays will enable the physician to tell if continued drug use is the result of an attempt to avoid withdrawal, in which case the drug should be gradually withdrawn, or instead a real attempt to treat continuing symptoms of anxiety[59]. The possibility of long half-lives and active metabolites requires that drug holidays be of several weeks' duration.

When to stop treatment. The facts emphasize the value of "chronic intermittent therapy"[59] where frequent bouts of a drug-free condition enable avoidance of dependency plus an excellent opportunity to evaluate the appropriateness of a halt to all drug therapy. If a person does show signs of physical dependence when halting chronic intermittent benzodiazepine use, he or she should be told (a) that it may be severe but nonetheless of limited duration, (b) that a gradual withdrawal can be set up so that their own symptoms control the speed of tapering of the dose, and (c) that the substitution of a benzodiazepine with a long half-life and/or active metabolites may be helpful if they have been on a drug with a short half-life[52].

NONBENZODIAZEPINE TREATMENT OF GAD

There have been two approaches to finding treatment for GAD that avoids the problems of early sedation and the possibilities of physical dependence and withdrawal. The first has been to modify the chemical structure of the benzodiazepines so that tney will still induce antianxiety effects but lose the unwanted side effects. Unfortunately, attempts so far have resulted in **partial agonists** that demonstrate decreased side effects but, unfortunately, also decreased ability to act as antianxiety agents[45]. The second, and so far more successful, approach has been to "abandon the benzodiazepine structure altogether"[72]. This has led, for example, to investigations comparing the efficacy of tricyclics and MAOIs (see Chapter 8) to the more standard benzodiazepine treatments of GAD. One double-blind study found that alprazolam and the tricyclic imipramine both reduced the symptoms of GAD in a depression-free subject population within one week of treatment. However, the drugs were found to effect different aspects of GAD, with the benzodiazepine reducing physical symptoms such as muscular tension, and imipramine reducing the psychological symptoms such as worry[25]. A greater amount of clinical research has focused on the nonbenzodiazepine drug, buspirone. While buspirone is as effective as benzodiazepines in reducing the symptoms of GAD[16], the drug does not cause sedation[51], has no anticonvulsant properties[10], does not bind to benzodiazepine receptors[56], and is not reinforcing in humans who have a history of sedative abuse[5]. Furthermore, buspirone does not induce physical dependency or result in withdrawal symptoms. For example, in one study, subjects treated for six months with buspirone or the long-acting benzodiazepine clorazepate were blindly and abruptly switched to placebo. Subjects treated with clorazepate showed a clear rebound effect, while those given buspirone did not[64]. Another study comparing buspirone to placebo found no evidence of rebound or withdrawal, or evidence of tolerance to the antianxiety effect, after 12 months of continuous treatment[36]. This same study revealed that buspirone did not show cross-tolerance with benzodiazepines, and did nothing to alleviate the symptoms of sudden cessation of benzodiazepine use. A study employing a blind shift from a chronically consumed benzodiazepine to buspirone found that prior treatment with the benzodiazepine reduced the effectiveness of buspirone[65]. This may have occurred because buspirone's lack of cross-tolerance meant it could not alleviate the rebound anxiety associated with benzodiazepine cessation. On the other hand, prior benzodiazepine treatment may in some way alter the nervous system of the patient so that buspirone actually becomes less effective. Further research involving a longer time interval between benzodiazepine cessation and the onset of buspirone therapy should resolve this important problem. Nonetheless, it appears that buspirone can reduce the symptoms of anxiety without inducing many of the troublesome side effects of the benzodiazepines.

CHAPTER SUMMARY

There are various types of anxiety, with the variant referred to as generalized anxiety disorder (GAD) most commonly treated with benzodiazepines. Most benzodiazepines are given orally, are absorbed slowly, and have moderate to high lipid solubility. The benzodiazepines differ greatly in terms of half-lives, and some are converted to active metabolites. Despite differences in potency and rapidity of onset, all the benzodiazepines are equally efficacious in suppressing, but not curing, the symptoms of GAD. Benzodiazepines bind to receptors that form a part of the GABA receptor complex. They probably exert their antianxiety effect by enhancing the inhibitory effect of GABA. The major side effect of the benzodiazepines is sedation. The drugs are not, by themselves, very toxic. There is even some question as to whether an overdose with benzodiazepines alone can induce death. The drugs should usually be administered as chronic intermittent therapy. There is tolerance to the side effect of sedation, but no evidence of tolerance to the therapeutic effect of chronic use. Although they are reinforcing in normal individuals, the benzodiazepines are not likely to be abused by most individuals with GAD. Chronic use of high doses can lead to physical dependency. Sudden cessation or placebo substitution can result in rebound anxiety as well as withdrawal symptoms including convulsions and a paranoid psychosis. The development of tolerance following chronic use of therapeutic doses is controversial. The use of chronic intermittent therapy will decrease the probability of physical dependency and will provide multiple opportunities to assess the value of continued pharmacological treatment. Modifications of the benzodiazepine structure have led to partial agonists with limited efficacy. However, the non-benzodiazepine buspirone is an effective antianxiety agent, even though it does not effect the GABA receptor, does not induce physical dependency, and is not reinforcing.

REVIEW ESSAY QUESTIONS

1. What are the generic and trade names of at least four of the benzodiazepines listed in Table 10.2?

2. What is the basic pharmacology of the benzodiazepines? What is the importance of long t 1/2s and the possibility of active metabolites?

3. Provide evidence both for and against the hypothesis that the antianxiety effects of the benzodiazepines are the result of neuromodulation of GABA neurons.

4. Can the therapeutic use of benzodiazepines lead to physical dependency?

5. What advantages does buspirone have over benzodiazepine antianxiety agents?

REFERENCES

1. Baldessarini, R.J. Drugs and the treatment of psychiatric disorders. In A.G. Gilman, L.S. Goodman, T.W. Rall, & F. Murad (Eds.) *The pharmacological basis of therapeutics* (7th ed.). New York: Macmillan Publishing Company, 1985.

2. Benkelfat, C., Murphy, D.L., Zohar, J., Hill, J.L., Grover, G., & Insel, T.R. Clomipramine in obsessive-compulsive disorder: Further evidence for a serotonergic mechanism of action. *Archives of General Psychiatry*, 1989, 46, 23-28.

3. Boulenger, J.P., & Uhde, T.W. Caffeine consumption and anxiety: Preliminary results of a survey comparing patients with anxiety disorders and normal controls. *Psychopharmacology Bulletin*, 1982, 18, 53-57.

4. Bowery, N.G. *Actions and Interactions of GABA and Benzodiazepines*. New York: Raven Press, 1984.

5. Cole, J.O., Orzack, M.H., & Beake, B. Assessment of the abuse liability of buspirone in recreational sedative users. *Journal of Clinical Psychiatry*, 1982, 43, 69-75.

6. Cooperrider, C. Anxiety disorders. In *Clinical psychopharmacology: A practical reference for nonmedical psychotherapists*. Rockville, MD: Aspen Publishers, 1988.

7. Dietch, J.T., & Jennings, R.K. Aggressive dyscontrol in patients treated with benzodiazepines. *Journal of Clinical Psychiatry*, 1988, 49, 184-188.

8. Dorow, R. Anxiety and its generation by pharmacological means. In S.D. Iversen (Ed.) *Psychopharmacology: Recent advances and future prospects*, Oxford, England: Oxford University Press, 1985.

9. Dorow, R., Horowski, R., Paschelka, G., Amin, M., & Braestrup, C. Severe anxiety induced by FG 1742, a beta-carboline ligand for benzodiazepine receptors. *Lancet*, 1983, 8341, 98-99.

10. Eison, M.S., & Temple, D.S. Buspirone: Review of its pharmacology and current perspectives on its mechanism of action. *The American Journal of Medicine*, 1986, 80, 1-9.

11. Enna, S.J., & Moehler, H. GABA receptors and their association with benzodiazepine recognition sites. In H.Y. Meltzer (Ed.) *Psychopharmacology: The third generation of progress*. New York: Raven Press, 1987.

12. Fontaine, R., Chouinard, G., & Annable, L. Rebound anxiety in anxious patients after abrupt withdrawal of benzodiazepine treatment. *American Journal of Psychiatry*, 1984, 141, 848-852.

13. Friedman, M.J. Toward rational pharmacotherapy for posttraumatic stress disorder: An interim report. *The American Journal of Psychiatry*, 1988, 145, 281-285.

14. Gallant, D.M. Clinical indications for antianxiety agents. In F. Flach (Ed.) *Psychobiology and psychopharmacology*. New York: W.W. Norton & Co., 1988.

15. Garvey, M.J., & Tollefson, G.D. Prevalence of misuse of prescribed benzodiazepines in patients with primary anxiety disorder or major depression. *American Journal of Psychiatry*, 1986, 143, 1601-1603.

16. Goldberg, H.L., & Finnerty, R. Comparison of buspirone in two separate studies. *Journal of Clinical Psychiatry*, 1982, 43, 87-91.

17. Greenblatt, D.J., & Shader, R.I. *Benzodiazepines in clinical practice*. New York: Raven Press, 1974.

18. Greenblatt, D.J., & Shader, R.I. Long-term administration of benzodiazepines: Pharmacokinetic versus pharmacodynamic tolerance. *Psychopharmacology Bulletin*, 1986, 22, 416-423.

19. Greenblatt, D.J., & Shader, R.I. Pharmacokinetics of antianxiety agents. In H.Y. Meltzer (Ed.) *Psychopharmacology: The third generation of progress*. New York: Raven Press, 1987.

20. Greenblatt, D.J., Shader, R.I., & Abernethy, D.R. Current status of benzodiazepines (second of two parts). *New England Journal of Medicine*, 1983, 309, 410-416.

21. Greenblatt, D.J., Shader, R.I., Divoll, M., & Harmatz, J.S. Adverse reactions to triazolam, flurazepam, and placebo in controlled clinical trials. *Journal of Clinical Psychiatry*, 1984, 45, 192-195.

22. Griffiths, R.R., & Roache, J.D. Abuse liability of benzodiazepines: A review of human studies evaluating subjective and/or reinforcing effects. In D.E. Smith & D.R. Wesson (Eds.) *The benzodiazepines: Current standards for medical practice*, Lancaster, PA: MTP Press, 1985.

23. Griffiths, R.R., & Sannerud, C.A. Abuse of and dependence on benzodiazepines and other anxiolytic/sedative drugs. In H.Y. Meltzer (Ed.) *Psychopharmacology: The third generation of progress*. New York: Raven Press, 1987.

24. Guttmacher, L.B., Murphy, D.L., & Insel, T.R. Pharmacologic models of anxiety. *Comparative Psychiatry*, 1983, 24, 312-326.

25. Hoehn-Saric, Macleod, & Zimmerli. Differential effects of alprazolam and imipramine in generalized anxiety disorder: Somatic versus psychic symptoms. *Journal of Clinical Psychiatry*, 1988, 49, 293-301.

26. Hollister, L.E., Conley, F.K., Britt, R.H., & Shuer, L. Long-term use of diazepam. *Journal of the American Medical Association*, 1981, 246, 1568-1570.

27. Hollister, L.E., Motzenbecker, F.P., & Degan, R.O. Withdrawal reactions from chlordiazepoxide ("Librium"). *Psychopharmacologica*, 1961, 2, 63-68.

28. Hommer, D.W., Skolnick, P., & Paul, S.M. The benzodiazepine/GABA receptor complex and anxiety. In H.Y. Meltzer (Ed.) *Psychopharmacology: The third generation of progress*. New York: Raven Press, 1987.

29. Jefferson, J.W. Biologic systems and their relationship to anxiety: A summary. In G. Winokur & W. Coryell (Eds.) *Biologic systems: Their relationship to anxiety*, Philadelphia: W.B. Saunders Company, 1988.

30. Johnston, D.G., Troyer, I.E., & Whitsett, S.F. Clomipramine treatment of agoraphobic women. *Archives of General Psychiatry*, 1988, 45, 453-459.

31. Jurgens, S.M., & Morse, R.M. Alprazolam dependence in seven patients. *American Journal of Psychiatry*, 1988, 145, 625-627.

32. Kanto, J.H. Midazolam: The first water-soluble benzodiazepine. *Pharmacotherapy*, 1985, 5, 138-155.

33. Kasvikis, Y., & Marks, I.M. Clomipramine in obsessive-compulsive ritualizers treated with exposure therapy: Relations between dose, plasma levels, outcome and side effects. *Psychopharmacology*, 1988, 95, 113-118.

34. Lader, M. Long-term anxiolytic therapy: The issue of drug withdrawal. *Journal of Clinical Psychiatry*, 1987, 48, 12-16.

35. Lader, M. The psychopharmacology of addiction—Benzodiazepine tolerance and dependence. In M. Lader (Ed.) *The psychopharmacology of addiction*. Oxford, England: Oxford University Press, 1988.

36. Lader, M., & Olajide, D. A comparison of buspirone and placebo in relieving benzodiazepine withdrawal symptoms. *Journal of Clinical Psychopharmacology*, 1987, 7, 11-15.

37. Liebowitz, M.R., Gorman, J., Fyer, A., Campeas, R., Levin, A., Davies, S., & Klein, D.F. Psychopharmacological treatment of social phobia. *Psychopharmacology Bulletin*, 1985, 21, 610-614.

38. Litovitz, T. Benzodiazepines. In L.M. Haddad & J.F. Winchester (Eds.) *Clinical management of poisoning and drug overdose*, Philadelphia: W.B. Saunders, 1983.

39. Litovitz, T. Fatal benzodiazepine toxicity? A reply. *American Journal of Emergency*, 1987, 5, 472.

40. Lloyd, K.G., & Morselli, P.L. Psychopharmacology of GABAergic drugs. In H.Y. Meltzer (Ed.) *Psychopharmacology: The third generation of progress*. New York: Raven Press, 1987.

41. Lloyd, K.G., Morselli, P.L., Depoortere, H., Fournier, V., Zivkovic, B., Scatton, B., Broekkamp, C.L.E., Worms, P., & Bartholini, G. The potential use of GABA agonists in psychiatric disorders: Evidence from studies with progabide in animal models and clinical trials. *Pharmacology, Biochemistry and Behavior*, 1983, 18, 957-966.

42. Lucki, I., & Rickels, K. The behavioral effects of benzodiazepines following long-term use. *Psychopharmacology Bulletin*, 1986, 22, 424-433.

43. Marks, J. *The benzodiazepines: Use, overuse, misuse and abuse*. MTP Press, Lancaster, Eng.: 1978.

44. Mellinger, G.D., & Balter, M.B. Prevalence and patterns of use of psychotherapeutic drugs: Results from a 1979 national survey of American adults. In G. Tognoni, C. Bellantuono, & M. Lader (Eds.) *Epidemiological impact of psychotropic drugs*. New York: Elsevier Press, 1981.

45. Merz, W.A. Partial benzodiazepine agonists: Initial results in man. *Clinical Neuropharmacology*, 1984, 7, 672-673.

46. Moehler, H., & Okada, T. Benzodiazepine receptor: Demonstration in the central nervous system. *Science*, 1977, 198, 849-851.

47. Morselli, P.L. Psychotropic drugs. In P.L. Morselli (Ed.) *Drug disposition during development*. New York: Spectrum Publications, 1977.

48. Murphy, S.M., & Tyrer, P. The essence of benzodiazepine dependence. In M. Lader (Ed.) *The psychopharmacology of addiction*. Oxford, England: Oxford University Press, 1988.

49. Navissakalian, M., & Perel. J. Imipramine in the treatment of agoraphobia: Dose-response relationships. *American Journal of Psychiatry*, 1985, 142, 1032-1036.

50. Navissakalian, M., & Perel. J. Imipramine dose-response relationship in panic disorder with agoraphobia. *Archives of General Psychiatry*, 1989, 46, 127-131.

51. Newton, R.E., Marunycz, J.D., Alderdice, M.T., & Napoliello, M.J. Review of the side-effect profile of buspirone. *American Journal of Medicine*, 1986, 80, 17-21.

52. Noyes, R., Garbey, M.J., Cook, B.L., & Perry, P.J. Benzodiazepine withdrawal: A review of the evidence. *Journal of Clinical Psychiatry*, 1988, 49, 382-389.

53. Pyke, R.E., & Kraus, M. Alprazolam in the treatment of panic attack patients with and without major depression. *Journal of Clinical Psychiatry*, 1988, 49, 66-68.

54. Reich, J., & Yates, W. A pilot study of treatment of social phobia with alprazolam. *American Journal of Psychiatry*, 1988, 145, 590-594.

55. Reiman, E.M. The quest to establish the neural substrates of anxiety. In G. Winokur & W. Coryell (Eds.) *Biologic systems: Their relationship to anxiety*. Philadelphia: W.B. Saunders Company, 1988.

56. Riblet, L.A., Taylor, D.P., Eison, M.S., & Stanton, H.C. Pharmacology and neurochemistry of buspirone. *Journal of Clinical Psychiatry*, 1982, 43, 11-16.

57. Rickels, K. Use of antianxiety agents in anxious outpatients. *Psychopharmacology*, 1978, 58, 1-17.

58. Rickels, K. Alprazolam in the management of anxiety. In M.H. Lader & H.C. Davies (Eds.) *Drug treatment of neurotic disorders—focus on alprazolam*. Edinburgh, Scotland: Churchill Livingstone, 1985.

59. Rickels, K. Antianxiety therapy: Potential value of long-term treatment. *Journal of Clinical Psychiatry*, 1987, 48, 7-11.

60. Rickels, K., Case, W.G., Downing, R.W., & Wiknokur, A. Indications and contraindications for chronic anxiolytic treatment: Is there tolerance to the anxiolytic effect. In D. Kemali & G. Racagni (Eds.) *Chronic treatments in neuropsychiatry*. New York: Raven Press, 1985.

61. Rickels, K., Case, W.G., Schweizer, E.E., Swenson, C., & Fridman, R.B. Low-dose dependence in chronic benzodiazepine users: A preliminary report on 119 patients. *Psychopharmacology Bulletin*, 1986, 22, 407-415.

62. Rickels, K., Fox, I.L., Greenblatt, D.J., Sandler, K.R., & Schless, A. Clorazepate and lorazepam: Clinical improvement and rebound anxiety. *American Journal of Psychiatry*, 1988, 145, 312-317.

63. Rickels, K., & Schweizer, E.E. Current pharmacotherapy of anxiety and panic. In H.Y. Meltzer (Ed.) *Psychopharmacology: The third generation of progress*. New York: Raven Press, 1987.

64. Rickels, K., Schweizer, E., Csanalosi, I., Case, W.G., & Chung, H. Long-term treatment of anxiety and risk of withdrawal: Prospective comparison of clorazepate and buspirone. *Archives of General Psychiatry*, 1988, 45, 444-450.

65. Schweizer, E., Rickels, K., & Lucki, I. Resistance to the anti-anxiety effect of buspirone in patients with a history of benzodiazepine use. *New England Journal of Medicine*, 1986, 314, 719-720.

66. Shapiro, S., Skinner, E.A., Kessler, L.G., Von Kroff, M., & German, P.S. Utilization of health and mental health services—Three epidemiologic catchment area sites. *Archives of General Psychiatry*, 1984, 41, 971-978.

67. Taylor, J.L., & Tinklenberg, J.R. Cognitive impairment and benzodiazepines. In H.Y. Meltzer (Ed.) *Psychopharmacology: The third generation of progress*. New York: Raven Press, 1987.

68. Tyrer, P. Prospects in treating anxiety. In S.D. Iversen (Ed.) *Psychopharmacology: Recent advances and future prospects*. Oxford, England: Oxford University Press, 1985.

69. Tyrer, P., Owen, R., & Dawling. S. Gradual withdrawal of diazepam after long-term therapy. *Lancet*, 1983, 1, 1402-1406.

70. Tyrer, P., & Seivewright, N. Identification and management of benzodiazepine dependence. *Postgraduate Medical Journal*, 1984, 60, 41-46.

71. Uhlenhuth, E.H., DeWit, H., Balter, M.B., Johanson, C.E., & Mellinger, G.D. Risks and benefits of long-term benzodiazepine use. *Journal of Clinical Psychopharmacology*, 1988, 8, 161-167.

72. VanderMaelen, C.P., Taylor, D.P., Gehlbach, G., & Eison, M.S. Nonbenzodiazepine anxiolytics: Insights into possible mechanisms of action. *Psychopharmacology Bulletin*, 1986, 22, 807-812.

Chapter 11

ATTENTION DEFICIT DISORDER

The purposes of this chapter are to:

1. Introduce the symptoms, nomenclature, and characteristics of attention defcit disorder (ADD), with or without hyperactivity,

2. Present information about the biochemical and treatment aspects of the typical stimulant anti-ADD drug, methylphenidate (Ritalin), and

3. Briefly discuss the use of other drugs in the treatment of ADD.

THE DISORDER

Basic Symptoms

Although the main problems vary with age, individuals with Attention Deficit Disorder (ADD), experience a basic triad of symptoms that occur throughout life. These include (1) **inappropriate restlessness**, (2) **attentional difficulties**, and (3) **impulsivity**[67]. Inappropriate restlessness is often noted by parents or teachers as a tendency to be "always on the go." Attentional difficulties are revealed by an inability to focus on a single task for any length of time or by being easily bored by school and other structured activities. Impulsivity can show itself as a tendency to say or do whatever comes to mind without concern for the consequences[69].

Differential Diagnosis and the DSM-IIIR

As in previous chapters, the specific DSM-IIIR criteria for the diagnosis of ADD have been provided (see Table 11.1). The disorder has gone by many other names, including, but not limited to, maturational lag, hyperkinetic reaction, perceptual-motor problems, and minimal brain dysfunction[69].

148

Table 11.1
DSM-IIIR Diagnostic Criteria for Attention-Deficit Hyperactivity Disorder (summarized)

A. A disturbance of at least six months during which at least eight of the following are present:

    (1) often fidgets with hands or feet or squirms in seat

    (2) has difficulty remaining seated when required to do so

    (3) is easily distracted by extraneous stimuli

    (4) has difficulty awaiting turn in games or group situations

    (5) often blurts out answers to questions before they have been completed

    (6) has difficulty following through on instructions from others

    (7) has difficulty sustaining attention in tasks or play activities

    (8) often shifts from one uncompleted activity to another

    (9) has difficulty playing quietly

    (10) often talks excessively

    (11) often interrupts or intrudes on others

    (12) often does not seem to listen to what is being said to him or her

    (13) often loses things necessary for tasks or activities at school or at home

    (14) often engages in physically dangerous activities without considering the possible consequences

B. Onset before the age of seven.

C. Does not meet the criteria for a pervasive developmental disorder.

ADD is the most common behavioral disorder diagnosed in children, occurring in from 3%-10% of all children[70]. Boys are three to four times as likely as girls to be diagnosed as having ADD[58]. It used to be thought that ADD was a disorder of childhood that would be outgrown by the time a child reached adolescence[65]. For example, in the early 1980s the majority of physicians stopped giving their ADD patients medication either before or sometime during adolescence[66]. By the late 1980s, authors were able to state "contrary to previous belief, the disturbances associated with the syndrome of attention deficit disorder (ADD) do not disappear in adolescence"[40]. Anywhere from one-third to two-thirds of children with ADD will continue to suffer one or more of the symptoms of ADD into adolescence and adulthood[24,26,43].

As with every other behavioral disorder, it can often be difficult to tell ADD from similar problems. Similar symptoms may occur in individuals with conduct disorders or mania. Although ADD is often treated with stimulants, high doses of the same drugs, usually taken for recreational purposes (see Chapter 15), can cause the basic triad of symptoms[4].

People with ADD are often incorrectly viewed as spitefully unwilling to improve their behavior. A childhood sufferer said, "I did not know how to slow down"[67]. A man who was not diagnosed as having ADD until he was an adult says that the attention deficit is "a very egalitarian kind of disability: the trash collector in the alley demands as much attention as the boss on the phone"[77].

Nervous System Abnormalities in ADD

Since the disorder is so often diagnosed in children, lay people and psychiatrists have been particularly concerned with the question of whether the diagnosis of ADD is a stigmatizing label, a disorder with psychosocial causes, or a true mental illness[14,60]. Those who view ADD as a true mental illness point to evidence that there are abnormal levels of specific neurotransmitters, particularly norepinephrine[41,78], and problems with the frontal lobes in people diagnosed with ADD[30,57]. Studies of autonomic nervous system function (see Chapter 2) and analysis of the electrical activity of the brain of children with ADD have not, however, found any consistent differences from normal children[61]. In addition, measures of either central or peripheral nervous system levels of norepinephrine and/or its metabolites have also failed to find consistent differences between normal children and those with ADD[78].

Advocates of pharmacological therapy are likely to appreciate the problems associated with giving powerful medications to children and they likely acknowledge the possible effectiveness of behavioral therapies. Nonetheless, they argue, there are individuals with ADD whose symptoms cannot be controlled by changes in the environment or the application of behavioral techniques teaching self-control. Advocates of pharmacological therapy for ADD note that carefully monitored drug treatment can help persons with ADD to control their own behavior. They can then obtain the full benefit of behavioral therapies and less restrictive environments[12,34,35,63].

BASIC PHARMACOLOGY OF METHYLPHENIDATE

The drugs of choice for the treatment of ADD with or without hyperactivity include methylphenidate (Ritalin), amphetamine (Dexedrine) and pemoline (Cylert). Most people treated for ADD are given methylphenidate[55], a drug with a chemical structure similar to the originally used treatment drug, amphetamine[39]. Methylphenidate is available in 5, 10, and 20 mg pills, as well as a sustained release pill[73]. Orally consumed methylphenidate is quickly absorbed into the bloodstream and poorly bound to plasma proteins. This results in a rapid onset of the therapeutic effect of the drug and a greater concentration in the brain than in plasma[48]. Despite the common practice of telling people to take the drug before meals, there is no evidence that food affects the absorption of an oral dose[11]. Special enzymes called **esterases** metabolize most of an oral dose of methylphenidate into an inactive metabolite in the gut and as it circulates within the bloodstream[11]. Methylphenidate has a half-life of two to four hours. This means that the offset of drug action is nearly as rapid and abrupt as its onset. Eighty percent of the administered dose can be found in the urine as an inactive metabolite[21]. Table 11.2 summarizes the data on the basic pharmacology of methylphenidate.

Table 11.2
The Basic Pharmacology of Methylphenidate

- Available in pills; various doses and sustained release
- Oral doses rapidly absorbed
- Absorption not inhibited by food
- Poorly bound to plasma proteins
- Rapid therapeutic onset
- Metabolized by esterases in gut and blood
- Half-life of two to four hours
- Rapid offset of drug action
- 80% found as inactive metabolite in urine

EFFECTS ON SYMPTOMS OF ADD AND HYPERACTIVITY

Amelioration of Symptoms

Methylphenidate effectively and immediately controls the basic triad of symptoms of ADD[71]. For example, placebo-controlled crossover studies have revealed that, compared to when they are being given placebo, methylphenidate-treated children require less direction and control and comply better with commands from their mother[5], require less control from and initiate fewer contacts with teachers[72], and perform better on certain cognitive tasks[9]. Great concern about the specificity of the action of methylphenidate was aroused by a study which found that the best dose for controlling the behavior of children with ADD induced a decrement in learning[62]. More sophisticated testing, however, has revealed that doses that improve behavior in a child also induce increases in school performance[18]. The positive effect of methylphenidate on any particular task is very dependent upon the nature of that task, and improvements in the performance on some tasks is small while improvements on other tasks is great[17]. This fact must be remembered when evaluating studies that use a single measure of learning or memory and claim that anywhere from 30%-40% of children with ADD fail to respond to methylphenidate[45,64]. It is possible that all the children in the study benefited in some way from the drug treatment, but that the single task evaluated was not sensitive to this improvement. The diversity of symptoms of ADD requires that well-designed studies of the effectiveness of methylphenidate treatment include evaluation of a diverse set of behaviors.

As with all drugs for behavioral disorders, different people respond best to different doses of methylphenidate. Usually, improved behavior and school performance can be obtained by giving between 0.5 and 1.5 mg/kg per day[19]. In some individuals, it may be necessary to give even larger amounts. Individual differences in absorption and metabolism can result in a small, lightweight person requiring substantially more drug than a taller, heavier person.

"Paradoxical Effect"

Original work showing a calming effect of methylphenidate on hyperactive children appeared paradoxical. How could a stimulant drug that increased activity in normal people, it was asked, result in a decrease in the activity of these hyperactive children? The answer offered was that the paradoxical response of hyperactive children was caused by an abnormal nervous system. When the child outgrew the disorder, it was claimed, they would then respond to stimulants as would anyone else[29]. It is now believed that the dose-response curves of normals and hyperactives to stimulants are similar and that both depend upon the subject's previous levels of activity. At high doses, normals and those with ADD show increases in activity. However, normal children, hyperactive children, normal adults, and adults with ADD all show decreased restlessness, increased attention, and decreased impulsivity when given the smaller doses of methylphenidate that are used in therapy[49].

Rate-Dependent Effects

Part of the explanation for the apparent paradoxical effect can be found through reference to the **rate dependent** effects of stimulants. Both animal and human studies revealed that subjects who were exhibiting low rates of behavior displayed an increase in behavior when given stimulants, while those who were already exhibiting high rates of behavior displayed a decrease in behavior[15,16]. Thus, the effect of the stimulant drug was dependent upon the rate of pre-drug behavior. A study with a double-blind, placebo-controlled, crossover design revealed that high levels of pre-drug behavior in children with ADD led to methylphenidate-induced reductions in behavior, while low levels of pre-drug behavior led to methylphenidate-induced increases in behavior[50].

Part of the reason for suggesting that there was a "paradoxical effect" of methylphenidate in ADD children can be found in the discredited idea that children with ADD would outgrow their disorder in adolescence and the drug's calming effect would be replaced by a stimulating one[24,26,40]. A follow-up study of 63 drug-free adults with ADD, some of whom had been given previous stimulant therapy for childhood ADD, revealed that about half of them had, in fact, spontaneously recovered from their disorder. However, the remaining half continued to show symptoms of ADD into adulthood[68]. Thus, while methylphenidate can control the symptoms of ADD, it is not a cure[31].

Effectiveness in Adolescents and Adults

Fortunately for those who suffer symptoms into adulthood, adolescent and adult subjects continue to receive a positive therapeutic effect from methylphenidate treatment. For example, a double-blind, placebo-controlled study showed that adolescents and their parents both reported beneficial effects of methylphenidate treatment[40]. In addition, a review of studies with varying quality of design determined that about 60% of adults with symptoms of ADD responded favorably to methylphenidate and other standard treatments of childhood ADD[71]. An accessible analysis of the usefulness of methylphenidate and other stimulant treatments for ADD throughout the lifespan can be found in Wender[69].

INTERACTION WITH ENDOGENOUS SYSTEMS

Methylphenidate is a stimulant drug (see Chapter 15) that can be characterized as **sympathomimetic** because it induces, among other effects, an activation of the sympathetic nervous system (see Chapter 2). Both the stimulation of the central nervous system and the sympathomimetic effect of methylphenidate arise from its ability to act as a **monoamine** agonist. That is, methylphenidate acts as an agonist at synapses that use epinephrine, norepinephrine, dopamine, and serotonin. It does this by a variety of mechanisms, including facilitated release, decreased reuptake, inhibition of enzymatic degradation by **monoamine oxidase** (or **MAO**), and possibly by direct postsynaptic stimulation[19]. Figure 11.1 reveals the four possible ways that methylphenidate can act as an agonist at a monoaminergic synapse, in this case, one involving norepinephrine.

R) Ritalin   N \ Norepinephrine

Figure 11.1. Four ways that methylphenidate can have agonist action at a norepinephrine synapse. Methylphenidate (labeled as R, for Ritalin): (a) binds to postsynaptic norepinephrine receptors, (b) inhibits reuptake of norepinephrine, (c) prevents the reuptake of norepinephrine by the presynaptic neuron, and (d) prevents the metabolism of norepinephrine by enzymes in the synaptic cleft.

SUSPECTED MECHANISM OF ACTION

Monoamine Agonist Effect

Much controversy exists about the mechanism of methylphenidate's anti-ADD action. Those who believed in ADD as a true mental illness caused by a physical abnormality often assumed that methylphenidate acted to specifically reverse the proposed underlying abnormality. An early theory held that the methylphenidate norepinephrine-agonist effect reversed a lowered level of arousal arising from impaired activity of norepinephrine in the reticular activating system[56]. As noted above, though, careful analysis of the electrical activity of the brains of children with ADD revealed no obvious abnormality of the reticular activating system[61]. Other theories have also emphasized the agonist influence of methylphenidate on norepinephrine, but not necessarily just in the RAS[41]. These types of theories have been hampered by the inconsistencies in attempts to show noradrenergic, or other monoaminergic, abnormalities in children with ADD[78].

General Stimulant Effect

One theorist who investigated the evidence regarding the neuropharmacological basis of anti-ADD drug action determined that the similar rate-dependent effects of methylphenidate on normal and ADD populations "argues against the possibility of a specific drug interaction with an organic disturbance in hyperactivity"[61]. She suggested that it was instead the stimulant action of the drug, mediated by its general action as a monoamine agonist, that reduced the symptoms of ADD by decreasing the high levels of behavior exhibited by hyperactives. This theory of generalized stimulation presents a clear alternative to the idea that methylphenidate alters some specific central nervous system pathology involving specific neurotransmitters.

The effectiveness of other drugs in combating ADD can be used to help decide whether methylphenidate's effects are due to generalized stimulation or to a specific effect on a particular neurotransmitter. Unfortunately, some effective anti-ADD drugs, such as amphetamine, pemoline, and the MAOIs (see Chapter 8) mimic both the specific monoaminergic agonist and general stimulating effects of methylphenidate[78]. Because of these parallels, the effectiveness of these drugs cannot reveal which of the two theories is correct. There are, however, some drugs that cause stimulation without directly affecting the same monoamines as methylphenidate and other drugs that are not stimulating even though they do affect the same monoamines as methylphenidate. For example, the stimulating drug caffeine (see Chapter 15) fails to exhibit any reliable anti-ADD effect[2], while the non-stimulating norepinephrine agonist tricyclic antidepressants (see Chapter 8) do have an anti-ADD action[22,23]. This information supports the position that it is not stimulation per se, but monoaminergic agonist action, that is responsible for the anti-ADD effects of methylphenidate.

SIDE EFFECTS

The fact that methylphenidate is a stimulant drug so often given to children has caused intense concern about the severity and duration of side effects[62]. A review of 29 studies that reported on methylphenidate side effects in children revealed that the most common side effects are insomnia and decreased appetite, followed by irritability, weight loss, headache, and abdominal pain[4]. Adolescents treated with methylphenidate report similar side effects, particularly decreased appetite and insomnia[40]. Since it is a sympathomimetic, methylphenidate also causes increased heart rate and blood pressure that may be particularly pronounced during exercise[1]. Occasional side effects include a generalized bad mood (**dysphoria**), dizziness, nausea, nightmares, dry mouth, and constipation[19]. Rare side effects include **tics** (involuntary muscle movement, usually involving the hands and/or face), allergic reactions, particularly rashes[19], and the possibility of a drug-induced psychosis[46]. Table 11.3 summarizes the side effects of methylphenidate.

Table 11.3
Side Effects of Methylphenidate

Common	Occasional	Rare
Insomnia	Dizziness	Tics
Decreased Appetite	Nausea	Allergies
Weight loss	Nightmares	Psychosis
Abdominal pain	Dry mouth	
Headache	Constipation	
Increased blood pressure	Dysphoria	
Increased heart rate		

Considerable concern was generated by reports that methylphenidate could induce a suppression of height and weight gain[52,53,54]. However, more careful analysis has revealed that this is a temporary phenomenon that lasts for only a year or two. Rebound gains in height and weight after this first year result in no significant differences in the height and weight in adulthood of children treated with methylphenidate[51].

Fortunately, tolerance develops to insomnia, decreased appetite, headache, abdominal pain and height and weight loss[19]. It may, however, be necessary to reduce the dose of methylphenidate or even to halt methylphenidate treatment in order to deal with allergic reactions to the drug. There is no evidence of tolerance to, nor evidence of physical damage from, elevations in heart rate and blood pressure[1]. Since the onset and offset of methylphenidate action is so rapid, insomnia can be prevented by insuring that the drug is administered only in the morning and early afternoon[69]. Sensitization (see Chapter 5) may occur to methylphenidate-induced psychosis, necessitating the use of a non-stimulating drug, such as the tricyclic antidepressants[46]. Chronic methylphenidate use, therefore, provides an excellent example of differential tolerance and simultaneous tolerance/sensitization (see Chapter 5).

TOXICITY

The toxic effects of methylphenidate are shared with other stimulants (see Chapter 15). There is a likely toxic interaction with other stimulants, including sympathomimetics frequently included in cold medicines. At toxic doses, methylphenidate can cause paranoia, combativeness, repetitive and purposeless movements, dangerously high blood pressure, burst cerebral blood vessels, convulsions, and death. Although there is no antidote to methylphenidate overdose, the drug is rapidly cleared from the body[21] and most symptoms of overdose can be treated symptomatically.

LONG-TERM USE OF METHYLPHENIDATE

The Role of Psychotherapy

There are strong supporters of the necessity of psychotherapy of one form or another as an addition to methylphenidate therapy[3,7]. However, a review of well-designed studies investigating the effects of such combined therapy found no consistent evidence that combined therapy displayed significant advantages over therapy with methylphenidate alone[39].

However, it may be that what is needed to increase the effectiveness of methylphenidate therapy is not general psychotherapy but specific treatments aimed at improving compliance[8].

Compliance

Compliance with treatment programs involving chronic methylphenidate may be as low as 40%[20,38,59]. Part of the problem may be a parental concern about ADD being a psychological, rather than physical, problem, with methylphenidate providing an artificial and temporary solution. Children may experience a wounded sense of autonomy, or may simply dislike being made to feel "different," especially if bad behavior leads unthinking adults to ask, "Have you taken your medicine?"[69]. In addition, side effects may lead to a reluctance to take methylphenidate as prescribed. Fortunately, tolerance develops to most side effects, and the remainder can usually be handled by reducing dose.

Tolerance and Dependency

Reviewers have asserted that tolerance develops to only the side effects, but not the therapeutic effects, of methylphenidate[25,47]. However, various experiments have found that tolerance can occur to the anti-ADD effect[74,75,76]. For example, one study used a single-blind, placebo-controlled procedure to study subjects given six months of treatment with twice-daily methylphenidate given at three therapeutic doses. There was a dose-dependent tolerance to the therapeutic effect of the drug, indicated by a return of hyperactive symptoms in subjects who chronically received the highest, and most effective, acute dose[76]. This suggests that it may be necessary to increase the dose of methylphenidate at various times during chronic therapy. Unfortunately, the possibility of differential tolerance and sensitization to drug-induced psychosis makes this a less than perfect solution to the problem of tolerance to therapeutic effectiveness.

One researcher has stated that "there is no evidence that stopping (methylphenidate) results in symptoms of withdrawal"[47]. In addition, controversy exists over whether any stimulant, including methylphenidate, can induce a true physical dependency (see Chapter 15). As noted above, the main problem with compliance is underuse, rather than overuse or abuse. Nonetheless, there has been concern that by providing medication to children with behavioral problems, there might be an inadvertent lesson that the solution to all difficulties is to be found in pharmacology[37,44]. There is, in fact, a single report in the literature of a child diagnosed with ADD who abused methylphenidate[27]. However, one well-designed study found no differences in the patterns of illicit drug use between methylphenidate-treated adolescents and normal controls[33]. Similarly, other studies have found that the duration of stimulant treatment did not influence drug abuse rates in adolescents[42] or adults[32]. In fact, one study found that ADD sufferers who failed to receive methylphenidate therapy were at the greatest risk of drug (particularly stimulant) abuse at adolescence. The authors suggested that stimulant abuse in untreated ADD subjects may have reflected an attempt to self-medicate the unpleasant symptoms of their untreated disorder[26].

Drug Holidays

Since the onset and offset of the effects of methylphenidate are so rapid, it is possible to have frequent drug holidays. Drug holidays are particularly appropriate for children whose routine allows for weekends and summers off from the demands of formal schooling, thus enabling an easier toleration of the symptoms of untreated ADD.

When to Stop Treatment

Knowing when to stop medication is difficult. When it was thought that all children with ADD would outgrow their "paradoxical" response to stimulant treatment, it seemed that all that was needed was to wait for the drug to begin to act in a "normal" way (that is, to stimulate rather than to counteract ADD). When the drug caused an increase rather than a decrease in hyperactivity, the person had outgrown the disorder. However, as mentioned above, one-third to two-thirds of childhood sufferers of ADD continue to display some symptoms into adulthood. These individuals may require medication for the rest of their lives. Nonetheless, some children will stop showing symptoms of ADD once they reach adolescence. Instead of hoping for a halt of the "paradoxical effect" of the stimulant, frequent drug holidays can be used to reveal if a child is no longer in need of methylphenidate treatment. If the child is not fortunate enough to remain free of symptoms, rapid elimination of the renewed symptoms will occur when the child is put back on the previously effective dose of medication[4].

OTHER DRUGS USED TO TREAT ADD

Some attempt has been made to treat the symptoms of ADD with "tranquilizers." Antipsychotic drugs do work in some individuals, but they are less effective than stimulants in most cases[69], and have the potential to induce tardive dyskinesia and other movement disorders (see Chapter 7).

In a review of nine studies investigating the effects of the stimulant drug caffeine (contained in coffee, soft drinks, and headache medicines; see Chapter 15) on the behavior of children with ADD, the author concluded that "the clinical results with caffeine are, on the whole, negative"[39]. For example, one study that directly compared methylphenidate and caffeine found that caffeine caused significant side effects with no positive therapeutic effect[2]. On the other hand, two other stimulant drugs, namely amphetamine and pemoline, have been successfully used to treat ADD.   Both share most of the properties of methylphenidate. Important differences from methylphenidate, however, may result in these drugs being a better, or worse, form of treatment in certain individuals. In 1937, amphetamine became the first stimulant to be used in the treatment of ADD[6], and it remains an effective, yet less often used, means of controlling the symptoms of ADD[28].   However, amphetamine is a drug that is frequently taken for recreational purposes by the normal population. It is more likely to elicit comments from pharmacists, teachers and others about "speed" or "drugs"[19]. Such comments need to be met with calm, yet forceful, statements regarding the usual lack of abuse of medication by people with ADD[32,33,42].

A double-blind comparison of pemoline, methylphenidate, and placebo revealed that pemoline was more effective than placebo, but not quite as effective as methylphenidate[13].   Pemoline has a significantly longer half-life than either methylphenidate or amphetamine. Thus, the drug can be given once daily, making it easier for people to remember when they need to take their medication[21]. However, this longer half-life also means that people taking pemoline may be more likely to be bothered by side effects such as insomnia. In a double-blind, placebo-controlled study demonstrating the effectiveness of pemoline in adults with ADD, some subjects found that even half of the smallest pemoline tablet available induced agitation, headaches, stomachaches, and insomnia[71]. Since tolerance developed to these side effects, all of these subjects were gradually able to increase the dose of pemoline until a reduction of the symptoms of ADD was obtained. The authors of this experiment noted the importance of taking repeated tests of liver function, since unlike methylphenidate and amphetamine, pemoline may cause abnormalities in liver enzymes in 2%-3% of treated individuals[71].

Other new treatments for ADD that may become more prominent as additional experimental support of their efficacy is obtained includes the use of drugs that have an agonist effect on monoamines, including tricyclic antidepressants or MAOIs (see Chapter 8) or clonidine (see Chapter 12). For example, a double-blind, placebo-controlled study found that the newer antidepressant, bupropion, was effective in treating the symptoms of ADD[10]. The authors found that bupropion did not have the cardiovascular side effects of the typical tricyclic antidepressants nor the usual effects of stimulants on height and weight. A double-blind, placebo-controlled study revealed that clonidine improved the symptoms of ADD, although the drug did induce a dose-dependent increase in sleepiness that faded after three weeks of continuous treatment[36]. It is likely that further understanding of the mechanism of action of standard stimulant therapy for ADD will result in the testing and discovery of more drugs with specific anti-ADD actions and few side effects.

CHAPTER SUMMARY

ADD, whether diagnosed in children, adolescents, or adults, is most often treated with the psychomotor stimulant methylphenidate. The drug is quickly absorbed, and the onset of the anti-ADD action after oral administration is rapid. It is converted to an inactive metabolite by esterases in the gut and bloodstream. Methylphenidate has a short half-life, so the offset of drug action is also rapid. Differences in the rate of absorption and metabolism may require widely different doses in different individuals. While it may appear paradoxical to give a stimulant to a person who may show signs of hyperactivity, research with controls and those with ADD have determined that the effects of methylphenidate are rate-dependent (that is, the effect of the drug is dependent upon pre-drug activity levels). Methylphenidate is a monoamine agonist and a sympathomimetic. Controversy exists over whether the mechanism of anti-ADD action results from a generalized stimulation or a specific monoamine agonist action. The most common side effects of methylphenidate treatment include insomnia, decreased appetite, irritability, weight loss, headache, abdominal pain, increased heart rate, and elevated blood pressure. Tolerance develops to the therapeutic action and most of the side effects, excluding increased heart rate, and elevated blood pressure. Compliance with treatment regimens is low, but can be aided by effective psychotherapy. Careful timing of drug administration and individualized dose selection can limit difficulties caused by insomnia, but can decrease compliance. There is no evidence of physical dependence following chronic methylphenidate therapy, and no evidence of increased drug abuse. Frequent drug holidays are possible because of the rapid onset and offset of anti-ADD action. Rapid onset and offset of drug effect also enables efficient determination of the need for continued medication. A number of other drugs have been investigated for anti-ADD action. The antipsychotics and the psychomotor stimulant caffeine have been found to be ineffective in treating the symptoms of ADD. However, tricyclic antidepressants, MAOIs, clonidine, d-amphetamine, pemoline, and bupropion have each been shown to have an anti-ADD effect. Pemoline is not as effective as methylphenidate. The longer half-life of pemoline enables once-a-day administration, but the drug causes more severe side effects than methylphenidate.

REVIEW ESSAY QUESTIONS

1. What are the basic symptoms of ADD? Is it correct to call ADD a childhood central nervous system disorder?

2. What is the basic pharmacology of methylphenidate, and how does this influence the timing of administration?

3. What is the "paradoxical effect" of methylphenidate, and what is the mechanism of the drug's action?

4. List the side effects of methylphenidate therapy for ADD. Why does overuse of the medication rarely occur, and why is compliance so often poor?

5. What are the similarities and differences between methylphenidate and two other drugs less frequently used in drug treatment of ADD?

REFERENCES

1. Aman, M.G., & Werry, J.S. Ritalin in children: Effects on cardiorespiratory function on exertion. *International Journal of Mental Health*, 1975, 4, 119-131.

2. Arnold, L.E., Christopher, I., & Huestis, R. Methylphenidate vs. dextroamphetamine vs. caffeine in minimal brain dysfunction. *Archives of General Psychiatry*, 1978, 35, 463-473.

3. Ayllon, T., Layman, D., & Kandel, H. A behavioral-educational alternative to drug control of hyperactive children. *Journal of Applied Behavioral Analysis*, 1975, 8, 137-146.

4. Barkley, R.A. *Hyperactive children: A handbook for diagnosis and treatment.* New York: Guilford Press, 1981.

5. Barkley, R.A., Karlsson, J., Pollard, S., & Murphy, J.V. Developmental changes in the mother-child interactions of hyperactive boys: Effects of two doses of Ritalin. *Journal of Child Psychology and Psychiatry*, 1985, 26, 705-715.

6. Bradley, C. The behavior of children receiving benzedrine. *American Journal of Psychiatry*, 1937, 94, 577-586.

7. Brown, R.T., Borden, K.A., & Clingerman, S.R. Pharmacotherapy in ADD adolescents with special attention to multimodality treatments. *Psychopharmacology Bulletin*, 1985a, 21, 192-211.

8. Brown, R.T., Borden, K.A., & Clingerman, S.R. Adherence to methylphenidate therapy in a pediatric population: A preliminary investigation. *Psychopharmacology Bulletin*, 1985b, 21, 28-36.

9. Brown, R.T., & Sleator, E.K. Ritalin in hyperactive children: Differences in dose effects on impulsive behavior. *Pediatrics*, 1979, 64, 408-410.

10. Casta, C.D., Pleasants, D.Z., & Fleet, J.V.W. A double-blind trial of bupropion in children with attention deficit disorder. *Psychopharmacology Bulletin*, 1987, 23, 120-122.

11. Chan, Y.M., Swanson, J.M., Soldin, S.S., Thiessen, J.J., Macleod, S.M., & Logan, W. Methylphenidate hydrochloride given with or before breakfast. II. Effects of plasma concentrations of methylphenidate and ritinalic acid. *Pediatrics*, 1983, 72, 56-59.

12. Christensen, D.E., & Sprague, R.L. Reduction of hyperactive behavior by conditioning procedures alone and combined with methylphenidate (Ritalin). *Behavior Research and Therapy*, 1973, 11, 331-334.

13. Conners, C.K., & Taylor, E. Pemoline, methylphenidate and placebo in children with minimal brain dysfunction. *Archives of General Psychiatry*, 1980, 37, 922-930.

14. Conrad, P. The discovery of hyperkinesis: Notes on the medicalization of deviant behavior. In M.E. Kelleher, B.K. MacMurray, & T.M. Shapiro (Eds.) *Drugs and society: A critical reader*. Dubuque, Iowa: Kendall/Hunt, 1983.

15. Dews, P.B. Rate-dependency hypothesis. *Science*, 1977, 198, 1182.

16. Dews, P.B., & Morse, W.H. Some observations on an operant in human subjects and its modification by dextroamphetamine. *Journal of the Experimental Analysis of Behavior*, 1958, 1, 359-364.

17. Douglas, V.I., Barr, R.G., Amin, K., O'Neill, M.E., & Britton, B.G. Dosage effects and individual responsivity to methylphenidate in attention deficit disorder. *Journal of Child Psychology and Psychiatry*, 1988, 29, 453-475.

18. Douglas, V.I., Barr, R.G., O'Neill, M.E., & Britton, B.G. Short-term effects of methylphenidate on the cognitive, learning and academic performance of children with Attention Deficit Disorder in the laboratory and the classroom. *Journal of Child Psychology and Psychiatry*, 1986, 27, 191-211.

19. Dulcan, M.K. The psychopharmacologic treatment of children and adolescents with Attention Deficit Disorder. *Psychiatric Annals*, 1985, 15, 69-86.

20. Firestone, P. Factors associated with children's adherence to stimulant medication. *American Journal of Orthopsychiatry*, 1982, 52, 447-457.

21. Franz, D.N. Central nervous system stimulants. In A.G. Goodman, L.S. Goodman, T.W. Rall, & F. Murad (Eds.) *The Pharmacological basis of therapeutics* (7th ed.). New York: Macmillan Publishing Company, 1985.

22. Garfinkel, B.D., Wender, P.H., Sloman, L., & O'Neil, I. Tricyclic antidepressants and methylphenidate treatment of attention deficit disorder in children. *Journal of the American Academy of Child Psychiatry*, 1983, 22, 343-348.

23. Gastfriend, D.R., Biederman, J., & Jellinek, M.S. Desipramine in the treatment of adolescents with attention deficit disorder. *American Journal of Psychiatry*, 1984, 14, 906-908.

24. Gauthier, M. Stimulant medications in adults with attention deficit disorder. *Canadian Journal of Psychiatry*, 1984, 29, 435-439.

25. Gittelman, R. Experimental and clinical studies of stimulant use in hyperactive children with other behavioral disorders. In I. Creese, (Ed.) *Neurochemical, behavioral and clinical perspectives*, New York: Raven Press, 205-226, 1983.

26. Gittelman, R., Mannuzza, S., Shenker, R., & Bonagura, N. Hyperactive boys almost grown up: I. Psychiatric status. *Archives of General Psychiatry*, 1985, 42, 937-947.

27. Goyer, P.F., Davis, G.C., & Rapoport, J.L. Abuse of prescribed stimulant medication by a 13-year-old hyperactive boy. *Journal of the American Academy of Child Psychiatry*, 1979, 18, 1170-1178.

28. Grinspoon, L., & Singer, S.B. Amphetamines in the treatment of hyperkinetic children. *Harvard Educational Review*, 1973, 43, 515-555.

29. Gross, M.D., & Wilson, N.C. *Minimal Brain Dysfunction*. New York: Brunner & Mazel, 1974.

30. Hartsough, C.S., & Lambert, N.M. Medical factors in hyperactive and normal children: Prenatal, developmental and health history findings. *American Journal of Orthopsychiatry*, 1985, 55, 190-201.

31. Hechtman, L. Adolescent outcome of hyperactive children treated with stimulants in childhood: A review. *Psychopharmacology Bulletin*, 1985, 21, 178-191.

32. Hechtman, L., Weiss, G., & Perlman, T. Hyperactives as young adults: Past and current substance abuse and antisocial behavior. *American Journal of Orthopsychiatry*, 1984, 54, 415-425.

33. Henker, B., Whalen, C.K., Bugenthal, D.B., & Barker, C. Licit and illicit drug use patterns in stimulant treated children and their peers. In K. Gadow, & J. Loffey (Eds.) *Psychosocial aspects of drug treatment for hyperactivity*, Boulder Colorado: Westview Press, 1981.

34. Hinshaw, S.P., Henker, B., & Whalen, C.K. Cognitive-behavioral and pharmacologic interventions of hyperactive boys: Comparative and combined effects. *Journal of Consulting and Clinical Psychology*, 1984, 52, 739-749.

35. Horn, W.F., Chatoor, I., & Conners, C.K. Additive effects of dexidrine and self-control training. *Behavior Modification*, 1983, 7, 383-402.

36. Hunt, R.D., Minderaa, R.B., & Cohen, D.J. The therapeutic effect of clonidine in attention deficit disorder with hyperactivity: A comparison with placebo and methylphenidate. *Psychopharmacology Bulletin*, 1986, 22, 229-236.

37. Jessor, R., & Jessor, S. *Problem behavior and psychosocial development: A longitudinal study of youth.* New York: Academic Press, 1977.

38. Kaufman, R.E., Smith-Wright, D., & Reese, C.A. Medication compliance in hyperactive children. *Pediatric Pharmacology*, 1981, 1, 231-237.

39. Klein, R.G. Pharmacology of childhood hyperactivity: An update. In H.Y. Meltzer (Ed.) *Psychopharmacology: A Third generation of progress.* New York: Raven Press, 1987.

40. Klorman, R., Coons, H.W., Brumaghim, J.T., Borgstedt, A.D., & Fitzpatrick, P. Stimulant treatment for adolescents with attention deficit disorder. *Psychopharmacology Bulletin*, 1988, 24, 88-92.

41. Kornetsky, C. The psychopharmacology of the immature organism. *Psychopharmacologia*, 1970, 17, 105-136.

42. Kramer, J., & Loney, J. Childhood hyperactivity and substance abuse: A review of the literature. In K. Gadow, & I. Bialer (Ed.) *Advances in learning and behavioral disabilities* (Vol. 1), Greenwich, CT: JAI Press, 1982.

43. Lambert, N.M., Hartsough, C.S., Sassone, D., & Sandoval, J. Persistence of hyperactivity symptoms from childhood to adolescence and associated outcomes. *American Journal of Orthopsychiatry*, 1987, 57, 22-32.

44. Loney, J. Hyperkinesis comes of age: What do we know and where should we go. *American Journal of Orthopsychiatry*, 1980, 50, 28-42.

45. Loney, J. Predicting stimulant drug response among hyperactive children. *Psychiatric Annals*, 1986, 16, 16-19.

46. Lucas, A.R., & Weiss, M. Ritalin hallucinosis. *Journal of the American Medical Association*, 1971, 217, 1079-1081.

47. McDaniel, K.D. Pharmacologic treatment of psychiatric and neurodevelopmental disorders in children and adolescents (Part 1). *Clinical Pediatrics*, 1986, 25, 65-71.

48. Patrick, K.S., Mueller, R.A., Gualtieri, T., & Breese, G.R. Pharmacokinetics and actions of methylphenidate. In H.Y. Meltzer (Ed.) *Psychopharmacology: A third generation of progress.* New York: Raven Press, 1987.

49. Rapoport, J.L., Buchsbaum, M.S., & Weingartner, H. Dextroamphetamine: Cognitive and behavioral effects in normal and hyperactive boys and normal adult males. *Archives of General Psychiatry*, 1980, 37, 933-943.

50. Rapport, M.D., & DuPaul, G.J. Ritalin: Rate-dependent effects on hyperactivity. *Psychopharmacology Bulletin*, 1986, 22, 223-228.

51. Roche, A.F., Lipman, R.S., Overall, J.E., & Hung, W. The effects of stimulant medication on the growth of hyperkinetic children. *Pediatrics*, 1979, 63, 847-850.

52. Safer, R.P., & Allen, D.J. Factors influencing the suppressant effect of two stimulant drugs on the growth of hyperactive children. *Pediatrics*, 1973, 51, 660-667.

53. Safer, R.P., & Allen, D.J. Side effects from long-term use of stimulants in children. In R. Gittelman-Klein (Ed.) *Recent advances in child psychopharmacology*, New York: International Arts and Science Press, 1975.

54. Safer, R.P., Allen, D.J., & Barr, E. Depression of growth in hyperactive children on stimulant drugs. *New England Journal of Medicine*, 1972, 287, 217-220.

55. Safer, R.P., & Krager, M.D. Trends in medication treatment of hyperactive school children. *Clinical Pediatrics*, 1983, 22, 500-504.

56. Satterfield, J.H., & Dawson, M.E. Electrodermal correlates of hyperactivity in children. *Psychophysiology*, 1971, 8, 191-197.

57. Shaywitz, S.E., Cohen, D.J., & Shaywitz, B.A. The biochemical basis of minimal brain dysfunction. *Journal of Pediatrics*, 1978, 92, 179-187.

58. Shaywitz, S.E., & Shaywitz, B.A. Diagnosis and management of attention deficit disorder: A pediatric perspective. *Pediatric Clinics of North America*, 1984, 31, 429-457.

59. Sleator, E.K., Ullmann, R.K., & Von Neumann, A. How do hyperactive children feel about taking stimulants and will they tell the doctor? *Clinical Pediatrics*, 1982, 21, 474-479.

60. Small, L. *The minimal brain dysfunctions: Diagnosis and treatment.* New York: The Free Press, 1982.

61. Solanto, M.V. Neuropharmacological basis of stimulant drug action in attention deficit disorder with hyperactivity: A review and synthesis. *Psychological Bulletin*, 1984, 95, 387-409.

62. Sprague, R.L., & Sleator, E.K. What is the proper dose of stimulant drugs in children? In R. Gittelman-Klein (Ed.) *Recent advances in child psychopharmacology*, New York: International Arts and Science Press, 1975.

63. Uhlenhuth, E.H., Lipman, R.S., & Covi, L. Combined pharmacotherapy and psychotherapy: Controlled studies. *Journal of Nervous and Mental Disorders*, 1969, 148, 52-64.

64. Ullmann, R.K., & Sleator, E.K. Responders, non-responders and placebo responders among children with Attention Deficit Disorder: Importance of a blinded placebo evaluation. *Clinical Pediatrics*, 1986, 25, 594-599.

65. Varley, C.K. A review of studies of drug treatment efficacy for attention deficit disorder with hyperactivity in adolescents. *Psychopharmacology Bulletin*, 1985, 21, 216-221.

66. Weiss, G. Controversial issues of the pharmacotherapy of the hyperactive child. *Canadian Journal of Psychiatry*, 1981, 26, 385-392.

67. Weiss, G., & Hechtman, L.T. *Hyperactive children grown up: Empirical findings and theoretical considerations.* New York: Guilford Press, 1986.

68. Weiss, G., Hechtman, L., Milroy, T., & Perlman, T. Psychiatric status of hyperactives as adults: A controlled prospective 15-year follow-up of 63 hyperactive children. *Journal of the American Academy of Child Psychiatry*, 1985, 24, 211-220.

69. *Wender, P.H. *The hyperactive child, adolescent, and adult: Attention deficit disorder through the lifespan.* New York: Oxford University Press, 1987.

70. Wender, P.H. Attention deficit disorder residual type (ADD-RT) or adult hyperactivity. In J.P. Tupin, R.I. Shader, & D.S. Harnett (Eds.) *Handbook of clinical psychopharmacology* (2nd ed.). Northvale, NJ: Jason Aronson, 1988.

71. Wender, P.H., Wood, D.R., & Reimherr, F.W. Pharmacological treatment of attention deficit disorder, residual type (ADD,RT) "minimal brain dysfunction,""hyperactivity" in adults. *Psychopharmacology Bulletin*, 1985, 21, 222-231.

72. Whalen, C.K., Henker, B., & Dotemoto, S. Methylphenidate and hyperactivity: Effects on teacher behavior. *Science*, 1980, 208, 1280-1282.

73. Whitehouse, D., Shah, U., & Palmer, F.B. Comparison of sustained release and standard methylphenidate in the treatment of minimal brain dysfunction. *Journal of Clinical Psychiatry*, 1980, 41, 283-285.

74. Winsberg, B.G., Bialer, I., Kupietz, S.S., Botti, E., & Balka, E.B. Home vs. hospital care of children with behavioral disorders: A controlled investigation. *Archives of General Psychiatry*, 1980, 37, 413-418.

75. Winsberg, B.G., Kupietz, S.S., Sverd, J., Hungund, B.J., & Young, N.L. Ritalin oral dose plasma concentrations and behavioral response in children. *Psychopharmacology*, 1982, 7, 81-84.

76. Winsberg, B., Matinsky, S., Kupietz, S., & Richardson, E. Is there dose-dependent tolerance associated with chronic methylphenidate therapy in hyperactive children: Oral dose and plasma considerations. *Psychopharmacology Bulletin*, 1987, 23, 107-110.

77. *Wolkenberg, F. Out of darkness. *New York Times Sunday Magazine*, October 11, 1987, pp. 1-7.

78. Zametkin, A.J., & Rapoport, J.L. Noradrenergic hypothesis of attention deficit disorder with hyperactivity: A critical review. In H.Y. Meltzer (Ed.) *Psychopharmacology: A third generation of progress.* New York: Raven Press, 1987.

* Introductory or intermediate reading

Chapter 12

DRUG ABUSE

The purposes of this chapter are to:

1. Reveal that no outlook on the question of whether drug abuse is a true mental illness, psychological disorder, or stigmatizing label must necessarily exclude the use of pharmacological agents in the treatment of drug abuse,

2. Discuss the different techniques by which pharmacological agents can be used to aid reduction or cessation of drug abuse. Particular emphasis will be placed on considering the importance of psychological variables in the maintenance of drug abuse, and

3. Provide information about the basic pharmacology, appropriateness, and effectiveness of currently used pharmacological aids in the reduction and/or cessation of heroin, alcohol, cocaine, and nicotine abuse.

THE DISORDER

Stigmatizing Label, Psychological Problem, or Mental Illness?

Discussions of the use of pharmacological aids to drug cessation are greatly helped by placing chronic drug use within the context of other behavioral disorders. It is important to know whether identifying someone as a drug abuser is the application of a stigmatizing label, a description of a psychological disorder, and/or a diagnosis of a true mental illness. As with the other behavioral problems discussed in previous chapters, approaches to treatment are likely to differ vastly depending on which of these three views one supports. However, none of the three viewpoints necessarily rejects the use of pharmacological aids to helping individuals halt or reduce their drug consumption. Table 12.1 presents the DSM-IIIR criteria for substance dependence.

Table 12.1
DSM-IIIR Diagnostic Criteria
for Substance Dependence (Summarized)

A. At least three of the following:

(1) substance often taken in larger amounts or over a longer period than the person intended

(2) persistent desire or one or more unsuccessful efforts to cut down or control sub stance use

(3) a great deal of time spent in activities necessary to get the substance, taking the substance, or recovering from its effects

(4) frequent intoxication or withdrawal symptoms when expected to fulfill major role obligations at work, school, or home, or when substance use is physically hazardous

(5) important social, occupational, or recreational activities given up or reduced be-cause of substance use

(6) continued substance use despite knowledge of having a persistent or recurrent social, psychological or physical problem that is caused or exacerbated by use of the substance

(7) marked tolerance

NOTE: The following items may not apply to cannabis, hallucinogens, or phencyclidine (PCP)

(8) characteristic withdrawal symptoms

(9) substance often taken to relieve or avoid withdrawal symptoms

B. Some symptoms of the disturbance have persisted for at least one month, or have occurred repeatedly over a longer period of time

---

The use of pharmacological aids to drug cessation is probably most strongly supported by those who view drug abuse as a disease or true mental illness. Those who view drug abuse as a psychological disorder may tend to emphasize the importance of positive and negative reinforcement in the maintenance of chronic drug use. However, those who share this view are not always opposed to pharmacological aids to drug cessation. A major point of this chapter is that pharmacological aids to drug cessation can be used in a psychologically sound manner to influence the positive and negative reinforcement provided by drug consumption.

Finally, there are those who suggest that calling someone a "drug abuser" is nothing more than the application of a stigmatizing label. Stigmatizing-label theorists are likely to hold that drug use represents the free choice of autonomous individuals. They argue that a claim of mental illness or psychological disorder is merely an attempt to justify the use of **coercion** (threats of physical violence, jail terms, or civil fines) to force individuals to conform to the drug-taking habits of the majority. It is important to recognize that stigmatizing-label theorists neither encourage drug use nor deny the negative physical and psychological consequences of chronic drug use. Even though they abhor the application of the label "drug abuser," supporters of the stigmatizing label theory need not oppose pharmacological treatment of **ego-dystonic drug use**, a situation where the user decides that drug use is a problem. Just as stigmatizing-label theorists view the choice to use drugs as an individual decision, they view the choice of treatments for drug use, including the use of pharmacological aids, as yet another individual decision.

Risks of Pharmacological Treatment

While no position on the true nature of drug abuse precludes the use of pharmacological aids to drug cessation, holders of any position can spot easily recognizable risks. Obvious risks of pharmacological treatments for drug abuse include interactions with the patient's preferred drug(s) of abuse or even the development of abusive self-administration of the drug intended as a treatment[90]. Another risk of pharmacological treatment is that it may lead the drug abuser to ignore individual responsibility, turning instead to a search for a "magic drug to cure their addiction for them"[67]. Finally, the goals of the patient and physician may be pitted against those of the legal system. The goal of the physician and patient will be to employ whatever methods are available, including but not limited to abstinence, to enable a reduction in the harm occurring to the patient as a result of drug consumption. The legal system may instead demand specific treatment programs or complete abstinence from entire categories of compounds[72,105]. A thorough understanding of the strengths and shortcomings of various treatments of drug abuse may enable a balance between the concerns of those who care for the individual drug abuser and those who wish to protect society as a whole from the consequences of individual drug abuse[67].

VARIETIES OF TECHNIQUES TO AID CESSATION OR REDUCTION OF DRUG USE

Table 12.2 provides a summary of the five different ways that pharmacological treatments have been employed to help individuals reduce or halt their drug consumption. Specific examples involving heroin, alcohol, nicotine, and cocaine will be used to demonstrate the pharmacological and behavioral logic underlying the use of each of these techniques. However, a review of Chapter 5 will provide reminders of the importance of behavioral variables in the development of physical dependency and compulsive use of any type of psychoactive compound. There are three important facts to remember. First, all of the drugs that individuals abuse provide positive reinforcement, which increases the probability that drug consumption will be repeated. Second, physically dependent and/or compulsive users will experience negative physical and psychological symptoms upon drug cessation or a reduction in dose. Resumption of drug consumption removes these unpleasant experiences, thus providing negative reinforcement. This negative reinforcement increases the probability that the negative consequences of future attempts to halt or reduce drug use will again be halted by a resumption of drug intake. Third, people, places, or things that are associated with previous experiences of drug-induced positive or negative reinforcement can become **discriminative stimuli** that cue the individual to consume drugs again. The presence of these discriminative stimuli may induce feelings of **craving** (an intense desire for the drug), frustration or even rebound and withdrawal phenomena in individuals who have been drug free for long periods of time[39,89,103].

Table 12.2
Ways in which Pharmacological Compounds Can Aid Drug Cessation

---

1. Substitute for "safer" intoxication and/or avoid withdrawal
2. Suppress symptoms of drug cessation
3. Block drug effects
4. Punish drug consumption
5. Treat underlying disorder

The presence of discriminative stimuli can easily lead to **slips**, where the previously abstinent user indulges in drug consumption or a controlled user indulges in a bout of uncontrolled use. The psychologically sound use of certain pharmacological agents can help prevent a slip from turning into a full-blown **relapse**. A relapse occurs when an individual who has successfully halted or reduced drug use returns to a pretreatment level of drug abuse. As revealed below, pharmacological compounds can sometimes be as useful in preventing the occurrence of a relapse as they are in aiding the initial cessation or reduction in use.

Technique 1

Substitution can involve two possible variations. In mere **maintenance,** individuals abusing one drug are given another pharmacological agent or the drug of abuse in a different form. This is done on the assumption that consumption of the treatment drug is less harmful to the individual or society. Sometimes, the treatment drug is substituted so that the individual will not undergo life-threatening withdrawal symptoms from sudden cessation of the drug of abuse. If the drug is truly being used to **avoid withdrawal**, the treatment drug also induces a physical cross-dependency. However, the characteristics of the treatment drug are selected so that withdrawal is less difficult and/or dangerous[52]. Confusion over whether a particular drug of abuse is capable of causing a true physical dependency can make it difficult to tell which variation of Technique 1 is being used. For example, methadone and antianxiety agents are used both as maintenance drugs and to prevent withdrawal from heroin and alcohol, respectively. However, the controversy surrounding whether stimulants can induce a true physical dependency (see

Chapter 15) can confuse the logic underlying the use of methylphenidate and nicotine-containing chewing gum in the treatment of cocaine and nicotine abuse, respectively.

Technique 2

The suppression of the symptoms of drug cessation depends upon determining the neurochemical basis of the unpleasant physical and psychological symptoms associated with drug cessation. This technique can often aid the well-motivated individual to rapidly halt abusive drug intake, but additional treatment may be necessary to enable continued abstinence. The drug clonidine, to be discussed in detail below, is an excellent example of a pharmacological agent that may suppress the symptoms of cessation of a variety of drugs, particularly heroin and alcohol.

Technique 3

The blocking of drug effects will enable the extinction of discriminative stimuli influencing drug abuse. So long as the blocking agent is in effect, future self-administrations of the drug of abuse will be devoid of reinforcing effect. This technique is most effective when used after the successful cessation of drug use with Technique 2. The drug naltrexone, used to treat heroin abuse, is an example of a pharmacological treatment that blocks the effects of the drug of abuse. This technique contrasts most strongly with substitution, in that no consideration is given to the individual's desire for positively reinforcing drug effects.

Technique 4

The punishing of drug consumption attempts to go farther than mere extinction of discriminative stimuli. This technique seeks to set up an **aversion** to, a dislike or distaste for, the drug of abuse by arranging things so that consumption of the drug of abuse leads to negative rather than positive consequences. The drug antabuse, used to treat alcohol abuse, is an example of this technique.

Technique 5

Treating the underlying disorder assumes that, in some cases at least, drug abuse is motivated by an attempt to **self-medicate** a behavioral disorder such as depression, mania, psychosis, anxiety, or hyperactivity. If a pharmacological agent that has been found to effectively treat the symptoms of the presumed disorder is available, the argument goes, the individual will easily be able to halt intake of the abused drug. The administration of antidepressants to individuals who abuse stimulants, on the assumption that they abuse the stimulants in order to treat the symptoms of their depression, is an example of the use of Technique 5.

An understanding of the pharmacological treatment of drug abuse is made difficult by the fact that some treatments can be used in a variety of ways. When determining whether a particular drug is effective in treating a specific form of drug abuse, it is sometimes as important to know the technique being used as it is to understand the basic pharmacology of the treatment drug.

TREATMENT OF HEROIN ABUSE

Heroin belongs to the group of drugs known as the opioids, all of which are depressants capable of inducing physical dependency (see Chapter 16). There are four general types of pharmacological aids that have been used to enable cessation or reduced use of heroin and other opioid drugs. These compounds include general psychopharmacotherapeutics, as well as specific drugs such as methadone, naltrexone, and clonidine.

Psychopharmacotherapeutics

Some opiate abusers have been found to suffer from depression, mania, anxiety, and psychosis[39]. The administration of the appropriate psychopharmacotherapeutic is suggested by the idea that opioid abuse is motivated by an attempt to self-medicate these underlying disorders (Technique 5). It is generally agreed that antipsychotic drugs, lithium, and tricyclic antidepressants can help aid reduction or cessation in opioid abusers suffering from schizophrenia, mania, or depression, respectively. However, the abuse potential of antianxiety agents and MAO inhibitors limits their usefulness in opioid abusers[39].

Methadone

Methadone is a positively reinforcing, longlasting, opioid drug capable of preventing the symptoms of withdrawal from other opioid drugs[8]. It is the most widely used form of drug treatment for heroin abuse[82]. Methadone is used as a maintenance drug that enables users of heroin to avoid withdrawal. Methadone given once a day can substitute for "the four-hour cycle of euphoria and withdrawal that characterize heroin use"[105]. The reinforcing effect of methadone was demonstrated when researchers found that subjects who were on a steady low dose of methadone nonetheless experienced a decrease in heart rate and pupil diameter, an increase in skin temperature, and subjective euphoria when given moderate to high doses of methadone[66]. This experiment suggests that methadone is being used both to prevent withdrawal and as a "safer" form of intoxication.

The goal of substitution is rehabilitation of the user of illicit drugs, not abstinence. Since abstinence is not the goal of substitution, special attention must be paid to individual differences in the dose of methadone required to enable a reduction in the use of illicit opioids. Some states and clinics place strict upper limits upon daily methadone doses and then, "when a patient continues to supplement methadone with illicit heroin, the ineffectiveness of methadone is confirmed in the mind of state regulators"[105]. There is experimental support for the hypothesis that increased doses of methadone will reduce illicit opioid use. One study examined outpatient subjects who were on a maintenance dose of 30 mg methadone per day but nonetheless delivered 80% of their urine samples with evidence of consumption of illicit opioids. Half the subjects were given a blind doubling of their methadone dose while the remaining subjects were maintained upon their usual dose. Those subjects given increased doses of methadone, but not those maintained on the usual 30 mg/day dose, revealed an 18% decrease in urine samples with evidence of illicit opioid use[92]. The results of this experiment suggest that a continued desire for the positive reinforcement provided by dose-dependent opioid intoxication influences the degree of illicit drug use by opioid abusers in methadone treatment programs. While this experiment investigated the effects of blind increases in methadone upon illicit opioid use, research cited below also reveals that reductions in methadone dose lead to an increase in illicit opioid use by opioid abusers in methadone treatment programs.

A strong argument can be made for evaluating the effectiveness of methadone by determining the positive impact upon the individual's life and his or her role in society[105]. For example, it has been noted that there have been hundreds of thousands of patients receiving methadone and that there is ample evidence of decreases in criminality, reductions in opioid use, and improvements in general health[86]. Sometimes, though, the effectiveness of methadone is evaluated not by whether it enables reduction in the use of illicit opioids or a return to a healthier and more productive lifestyle. The effectiveness of methadone is sometimes instead evaluated by whether or not individuals abstain from all opioids after withdrawal from methadone programs. Critics of the effectiveness of methadone treatment point to an experiment that demonstrated that methadone treatment does not cure the opioid abuser. Among patients demonstrating remarkably low use of illicit opioids during methadone treatment, 60% of their urine samples revealed a return to the use of illicit opioids after a gradual (and blind) reduction of their methadone dose to zero[91]. While this is a distressing outcome, it must be remembered that many psychopharmacotherapeutics (such as the antipsychotics and lithium, for example) are effective only so long as drug administration continues. Dismissal of the utility of methadone as a treatment because it does not "cure" heroin abuse is similar to rejecting the utility of the birth control pill because many women become pregnant after they quit taking the medication[68].

Naltrexone

Naltrexone, a long-acting opioid receptor antagonist, is devoid of reinforcing properties. Receptors blocked by naltrexone cannot simultaneously be occupied by opioid agonists such as heroin. Naltrexone is lipid soluble and is effective when taken orally. It is rapidly absorbed into the bloodstream, with peak concentrations occurring after one to two hours. It is metabolized by liver enzymes, and excreted in the urine. Although naltrexone has a half-life in the blood of only 10 hours, it can be taken once daily because it is converted to an active metabolite with a longer half-life[13,50]. Table 12.3 summarizes the basic pharmacology of naltrexone.

Table 12.3
The Basic Pharmacology of Naltrexone

- Opioid receptor antagonist
- Lipid soluble and effective orally
- Rapidly absorbed with peak blood levels after 1 to 2 hours
- Metabolized by liver enzymes
- Excreted in urine
- Half-life of 10 hours
- Converted to active metabolite with longer half-life
- Duration of action of 24 hours

Two classic experiments demonstrated that the repeated pairings of discriminative stimuli with the reinforcing effects of heroin could enable these stimuli to induce physiological changes that led to craving. Male heroin users, drug-free for one week, responded with physiological changes and cravings when viewing slides of drug-related, but not neutral, stimuli[94]. In another study, videotapes of heroin-related activities, but not neutral activities, induced physiological changes that led to a craving for heroin[87]. Since naltrexone blocks opiate receptors, it blocks the reinforcing effects of heroin consumption. In fact, a sustained-release preparation of naltrexone successfully blocked the effects of opioid drugs in heroin-dependent individuals for a period of one month[10]. The theory behind the psychologically sound use of naltrexone notes that discriminative stimuli that cue cravings for heroin should lose their effectiveness each time that heroin is consumed in their presence, but reinforcing consequences do not follow. In a double-blind study, fully one-half of the naltrexone-treated heroin abusers self-administered heroin at least once during a three-month period during which they were otherwise virtually opioid-free[56]. Presumably, such trial self-administrations were not reinforcing, since a study revealed evidence of illicit opioid use in only 3% of the urine samples of a group of 160 heroin-dependent individuals given naltrexone[97]. These results suggest that naltrexone-induced blockade of the reinforcing effects of heroin can reduce the power of discriminative stimuli that act as cues for heroin intake.

Unfortunately, there are three problems with the use of naltrexone. The physically dependent heroin user will undergo a severe and abrupt antagonist-induced withdrawal when given naltrexone[13]. This means that naltrexone cannot normally be used until the individual has been abstinent for a specific period of time, usually about 7 days for heroin and about 21 days for methadone[36]. Another problem with naltrexone is that the binding and blocking of opioid receptors is not permanent. Naltrexone and heroin **compete** for receptors, and relative success is determined by the ever-changing number of molecules of each drug in the area of the receptor. By taking a greater than usual dose of heroin, a naltrexone-treated person can flood the synaptic cleft with heroin molecules. When there are more heroin molecules than naltrexone molecules, a reinforcing effect of heroin will be achieved. The over-eager abuser may, however, **overshoot**, taking a dose that greatly exceeds the amount necessary to successfully compete with naltrexone for opioid receptors. When this happens, the individual is at risk of overdose. This problem can be best dealt with by giving naltrexone only to those individuals who volunteer for treatment, indicating strong motivation to alter their ego-dystonic opioid use[36]. When care is taken to avoid naltrexone-induced withdrawal and attempts to overshoot, "naltrexone appears to be a very safe drug" with stomach irritation and mild elevations in blood pressure being the most common side effects[13]. Unfortunately, the third problem with naltrexone is that compliance with the treatment program is low. One study found that only 5% of all heroin users are willing to comply with treatment programs involving naltrexone[45]. The relatively greater compliance with methadone versus naltrexone treatment reveals, once again, the importance of the reinforcing effect of opioids in the behavior of the opioid abuser.

Clonidine

There are presynaptic autoreceptors on the cell bodies of norepinephrine neurons that enable feedback control of norepinephrine release. The drug clonidine, commonly used to control high blood pressure, is an agonist for these receptors. Clonidine can mimic the action of norepinephrine at these receptors, resulting in a decrease in the release of norepinephrine. Thus, clonidine results in an antagonist effect at the norepinephrine synapse, specifically because of its agonist effect at the autoreceptor[39,43]. Figure 12.1 is a pictorial representation of the action of clonidine on norepinephrine neurons.

The basic pharmacology of clonidine is well known, since it has been used for some time as a treatment for high blood pressure[79]. The oral form of the drug is rapidly absorbed, with peak plasma concentrations achieved within one to three hours. The half-life of the compound is approximately nine hours. The drug is very lipid soluble and thus concentrates in the brain, lungs, and other fatty areas of the body. It is metabolized by liver enzymes and none of the metabolites are active. About one-half of the parent compound is found in the urine. Table 12.4 summarizes the basic pharmacology of clonidine.

Even when gradually withdrawn from heroin, individuals are likely to experience some withdrawal symptoms[44]. There is ample evidence that some of the symptoms of drug cessation occur because of hyperactivity of norepinephrine neurons[39,40,102]. The ability of clonidine to decrease the activity of norepinephrine neurons suggested that it was capable of reducing the symptoms of heroin withdrawal (Technique 2). Double-blind studies have revealed that clonidine is effective in reducing, but not totally eliminating, the symptoms of withdrawal from methadone[78] and heroin[41]. The hypothesis that clonidine exerts its therapeutic effect because it is a norepinephrine autoreceptor agonist is supported by evidence revealing the effectiveness of other drugs that are also autoreceptor agonists[39].

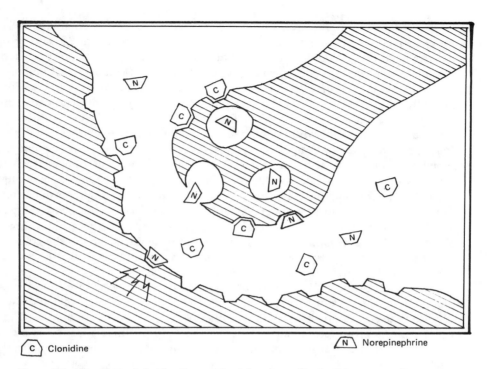

C Clonidine   N Norepinephrine

Figure 12.1. The effects of clonidine at a norepinephrine neuron. By stimulating presynaptic receptors that reduce the number of norepinephrine molecules localized in and released from the synaptic vesicles, clonidine results in the availability of fewer norepinephrine molecules to stimulate postsynaptic receptors. The net result of clonidines's autoreceptor agonist activity is thus a norepinephrine antagonist action.

Table 12.4
Basic Pharmacology of Clonidine

- A norepinephrine autoreceptor agonist, hence a norepinephrine antagonist
- Rapidly absorbed when taken orally
- Peak plasma concentrations at 1 to 3 hours
- Very lipid soluble
- Plasma half-life of 9 hours
- Metabolized by liver enzymes
- No active metabolites
- One-half of parent compound found in urine

More recent research revealed the effectiveness of a combined treatment program involving clonidine and naltrexone. The relapse rate at 30 days in opioid abusers undergoing clonidine-aided withdrawal was found to be significantly reduced in subjects who were given post-withdrawal naltrexone[73]. Presumably, clonidine made the acute symptoms of withdrawal easier to tolerate while relapse prevention was aided by naltrexone's ability to help extinguish the strength of discriminative stimuli that provided cues for heroin use. Even more interesting is the possibility that simultaneous treatment with naltrexone and clonidine may enable opioid dependent individuals to undergo a rapid, antagonist-induced withdrawal. In one study, combined clonidine and naltrexone enabled methadone-dependent subjects to be completely withdrawn in 4-5 days rather than the usual 21 days[9]. Researchers in the same laboratory later found that clonidine suppressed many of the symptoms of naltrexone-induced withdrawal in heroin-dependent individuals. The combined treatment enabled 86% of the subjects to complete an abrupt withdrawal from heroin[60]. Improved ability to tolerate withdrawal should prevent the readministration of the abused drug in order to halt the symptoms of withdrawal. This would then lead to a reduction in the probability of negative reinforcement.

In all of the studies with clonidine, there were reports of postural hypotension. However, careful evaluation of blood pressure revealed that the doses of clonidine used did not lead to dangerous lowering of blood pressure[9]. The only other consistently reported side effect was sedation. Since sedation is a distinct possibility, it is useful for someone to supervise transportation from the treatment site[60].

Summary of Drug Treatment of Heroin Abuse

The abuse of heroin by individuals who suffer the symptoms of schizophrenia, mania, and depression will often be reduced by the use of standard psychopharmacotherapeutics. Methadone treatment leads to reduced heroin use and a positive impact upon the heroin abuser's life and role in society. It should be recognized that the goal of methadone treatment is rehabilitation, not abstinence, and that motivation for continued participation in treatment involves avoidance of withdrawal *and* the positive reinforcement provided by methadone. Naltrexone can be useful in preventing the reinforcing effects of heroin, thus providing an individual who desires abstinence with an ability to decrease the power of discriminative stimuli that can act as cues for heroin consumption. However, naltrexone can induce an intense withdrawal, consumption of a large amount of heroin can overcome the blockade of reinforcing effects, and compliance with naltrexone treatment is low. Clonidine can reduce the intensity of heroin withdrawal, thus enabling individuals to avoid the negative reinforcement that would occur when intense withdrawal symptoms were used to justify a readministration of heroin. The combined use of naltrexone and clonidine can enable a rapid withdrawal from heroin.

Treatment Of Alcohol Abuse

Alcohol is a depressant capable of causing a physical dependency (see Chapter 16). A variety of pharmacological aids have been investigated for their effectiveness in helping alcohol abusers reduce or halt their consumption of alcohol[24]. This section will discuss the use of lithium, serotonin agonist antidepressants, antianxiety agents, and alcohol-sensitizing agents such as disulfiram (Antabuse).

Lithium and Antidepressants

A variety of studies have demonstrated that lithium and antidepressants that inhibit the reuptake of serotonin can promote abstinence in alcohol abusers[88]. For example, in a double-blind, placebo-controlled study, subjects who maintained a therapeutic blood level of lithium (see Chapter 9) achieved a 67% abstinence rate, while placebo-treated subjects showed an abstinence rate of only 7%[26]. In a double-blind study with the serotonin agonist antidepressant zimelidine (see Chapter 8) the drug enabled 50% of subjects to achieve abstinence from alcohol while a remaining 35% significantly reduced their alcohol consumption[61].

If it is hypothesized that some alcohol abusers suffer from mania and/or depression, it might be easy to conclude that lithium and antidepressants are being used consistent with Technique 5 to treat the psychological disorder presumed to motivate alcohol abuse. However, experiments with a double-blind design have revealed that whether subjects suffered an affective disorder or not did not influence the aiding of abstinence in people treated with lithium[26,55]. Furthermore, another study found zimelidine to be effective even though researchers specifically selected non-depressed alcohol abusers for their subjects. In addition, "zimelidine's effect on (alcohol) intake occurred in less than 2 weeks, indicating a rapid onset and offset of effect, in contrast to the usual 2- to 3-week delay required to observe the clinical effects of most antidepressant drugs"[61]. These findings suggest that these drugs are influencing alcohol consumption through an as-yet undetermined interaction with the effect of alcohol on brain neurotransmitters[88], rather than suppressing alcohol consumption as a symptom of mania or depression. This suggests that the use of standard psychopharmacotherapeutics in the treatment of alcohol abuse differs greatly from the use of standard psychopharmacotherapeutics in the treatment of heroin abuse.

Antianxiety Agents

Severe alcohol withdrawal can lead to death in 5% to 10% of all cases[77]. The goals of pharmacological treatment of alcohol withdrawal include relief of subjective symptoms and the prevention of seizures[85]. Clonidine[3] and the norepinephrine autoreceptor agonist lofexidine[16] have both been found to reduce the subjective effects of alcohol withdrawal. Unfortunately, both animal and human studies suggest that clonidine and lofexidine might actually increase the probability of seizures[5,6]. While standard anticonvulsant drugs can be effective in achieving the twin goals of drug therapy for alcohol withdrawal[64], their use is limited by the possibility of severe respiratory depression and other toxic effects[85].

Antianxiety agents have been repeatedly demonstrated to be safe and effective in decreasing the subjective symptoms and seizures of alcohol withdrawal[77,85] and are therefore used consistent with Technique 2 to suppress the symptoms of cessation of alcohol abuse. As revealed in Chapter 10, antianxiety agents do not carry a great risk of inducing lethal respiratory depression. However, the use of benzodiazapines to treat alcohol withdrawal is not completely risk-free. Antianxiety agents are themselves likely to be abused by alcohol abusers[11]. Although there is, compared to anticonvulsant drugs, a greatly decreased likelihood of severe respiratory depression, the benzodiazapines can induce a powerful sedation. This may necessitate prolonged bed rest that can interfere with communication between the patient and the physician, and can even lead to the development of complications including pneumonia and **embolisms** (blood clots)[77].

Fortunately, there are a wide number of benzodiazapines available, each with its own pharmacological properties. Hospitalized alcohol-dependent patients were randomly assigned to groups receiving either diazepam (Valium) or lorazepam, an antianxiety agent free of active metabolites that might increase sedation and interfere with therapy. The researchers found that Valium did not interfere with cognitive abilities, including memory, to a greater degree than lorazepam and that Valium enabled a more comfortable withdrawal. The general effectiveness of antianxiety agents was supported by the finding that both drugs prevented the occurrence of seizures and reduced the subjective discomforts of withdrawal[75]. Despite these findings, however, some physicians nonetheless prefer the use of lorazepam because the lack of active metabolites enables the administration of large doses, which may be necessary in severe withdrawal[77].

Antabuse

Antabuse is used to punish alcohol consumption (Technique 4). The drug was accidentally discovered when people working in rubber factories found that industrial work with the compound made after-hours consumption of alcohol a decidedly unpleasant experience[104]. The metabolism of alcohol involves the production of **acetaldehyde**. The body uses the enzyme **aldehyde dehydrogenase** to quickly convert this toxic product into a harmless acetate which is further metabolized into carbon dioxide and water. Antabuse prevents the breakdown of acetaldehyde by permanently changing the chemical structure of aldehyde dehydrogenase (see Figure 12.2).

Antabuse is a highly lipid soluble and is rapidly absorbed when taken orally. However, only small amounts of the compound are found in the bloodstream, because enzymes in the blood rapidly convert it into an active metabolite. Further metabolism into an inactive compound occurs in the liver, followed by excretion in urine. Despite the high lipid solubility of the compound, it has a short half-life because of its conversion by blood enzymes. However, the effects of Antabuse are relatively longlasting (from 6

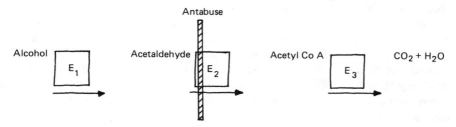

Figure 12.2. The effect of antabuse on the metabolism of alcohol. By preventing the complete metabolism of alcohol, antabuse causes a buildup of the toxic metabolite acetaldehyde.

to 14 days). This occurs because Antabuse permanently inhibits the activity of aldehyde dehydrogenase. As a result, the effects of Antabuse do not disappear when someone stops taking the medicine. Instead, the effects do not disappear until the body is able to create new aldehyde dehydrogenase[71,74]. Table 12.5 summarizes the basic pharmacology of Antabuse.

If an alcohol abuser has a sincere desire to stop drinking, the individual can take Antabuse once each morning. When a person taking Antabuse consumes alcohol, he or she will experience, within 5 to 10 minutes, a host of horrible feelings and physical symptoms known as the **acetaldehyde syndrome.** The face becomes hot, and then flushes a bright red. A throbbing headache precedes nausea, vomiting, chest pain, breathing problems, dizziness, weakness, blurred vision, and confusion. The typical syndrome will last from 30 minutes to several hours. An antabuse-treated person may foolishly decide to rapidly consume a large amount of alcohol, in the hopes of having a few moments of intense intoxication prior to the onset of the aldehyde syndrome. This can enhance the severity of the syndrome and may cause fatal respiratory and circulatory problems. The intensity and duration of the acetaldehyde syndrome depend upon (1) the dose of antabuse, (2) the time since the last dose of antabuse, and (3) the dose of alcohol

Table 12.5
The Basic Pharmacology of Antabuse

- Highly lipid soluble
- Rapidly absorbed when taken orally
- Quickly converted to active metabolite by blood enzymes
- Further metabolized in liver and excreted in urine
- Short half-life due to metabolism by blood enzymes
- Long duration of action due to permanent inactivation of the enzyme aldehyde dehydrogenase

consumed. Other unknown factors must also influence the intensity and duration of the acetaldehyde syndrome, since it is "difficult to predict the severity...within an individual, from one drinking session to the next"[71]. However, there is powerful evidence that the primary determinant of the acetaldehyde syndrome is antabuse inhibition of the metabolism of acetaldehyde. When the syndrome was deliberately induced by giving an alcohol challenge to human volunteers who had earlier taken antabuse, a drug that prevented the conversion of alcohol to acetaldehyde (see Figure 12.2) prevented the occurrence of the acetaldehyde syndrome[62].

The combined effects of the acetaldehyde syndrome make alcohol consumption remarkably unpleasant. Thus, a previously reinforcing activity is now punished. However, the early practice of demonstrating, in a clinical setting, the effects of antabuse plus alcohol on the individual alcohol abuser have been stopped because of the danger of the syndrome. An informed consent form which provides a graphic description of the syndrome now substitutes for the trial in the clinic[1].

Unfortunately, despite 40 years of the use of this compound, its effectiveness is highly questionable, since early studies of antabuse's effectiveness were seriously flawed[1,2,88]. A recent series of large, double-blind studies found antabuse to be no more effective than placebos in promoting abstinence among alcohol abusers[27,28].

One possible reason for the clinical ineffectiveness of antabuse is the fact that compliance with therapy is remarkably low. A study found that only 20% of outpatients on antabuse were likely to continue with the program for one year[76]. It is unlikely that people drop out of treatment due to the side effects of antabuse, since mild sedation and a metallic or garlicky taste are the only common side effects, and tolerance occurs rapidly[1]. It is more likely that individuals stop consuming antabuse because the acetaldehyde syndrome can be as easily prevented by halting antabuse consumption as it can be by halting alcohol consumption. The poor compliance with antabuse treatment, designed to punish the consumption of alcohol, should not be surprising given the poor compliance with naltrexone treatment, which only blocks the reinforcing effects of heroin. An additional reason for poor compliance with antabuse treatment may be a wounded sense of autonomy (see Chapter 6) arising from a feeling that use of antabuse is a "crutch" that will deny the individual personal credit for halting alcohol consumption. In discussing the fear of antabuse as a "crutch," one researcher pointed out the anomaly of "men and women who have used alcohol as a 'crutch' for years (who) appear paradoxically fastidious about this one"[1].

Summary of Drug Treatment of Alcohol Abuse

Lithium and serotonin agonist tricyclics can help reduce alcohol consumption even in individuals not suffering from mania or depression. Antianxiety agents are the preferred drug for suppression of the symptoms of alcohol withdrawal, since clonidine can increase the probability of seizures and standard anticonvulsants can induce severe respiratory depression. Problems include the fear that antianxiety agents may be abused by alcohol abusers in treatment and that antianxiety agents may induce sedation that could interfere with psychotherapy. Antabuse punishes the consumption of alcohol by allowing the buildup of toxic acetaldehyde. Research does not indicate that antabuse is an effective treatment, perhaps because compliance with treatment regimens is low.

TREATMENT OF NICOTINE ABUSE

Nicotine is a stimulant drug available through consumption by any means of self-administration, but usually consumed via inhalation or chewing of tobacco (Chapter 15). Regardless of the position taken over the controversy of whether nicotine induces a true physical dependency (see Chapter 15), the use of drugs to aid the reduction and/or cessation of nicotine abuse can be supported. First, even if nicotine is not capable of causing a physical dependency, it is often used compulsively in a manner that causes devastating physical and psychological harm[100]. Second, the abrupt cessation of compulsive nicotine use leads to uncomfortable and persistent negative physical and psychological consequences[48]. Since these effects can be eliminated by a resumption of nicotine intake, compulsive users often experience the same subjective feeling of loss of control as do people who consume drugs unarguably capable of inducing a physical dependency. Thus, it can be predicted that, when used in a psychologically sound way, medicines can aid the cessation of nicotine abuse, regardless of the presence or absence of physical dependency[12]. Nonetheless, it should be remembered that approximately 95% of all tobacco smokers who quit manage to do so on their own, without any psychological or pharmacological therapy[46,49].

Experiments on the cessation of nicotine abuse have evaluated the effectiveness of three of the techniques listed in Table 12.2. The effectiveness of Technique 2 has been reviewed[84] and demonstrated in double-blind placebo controlled studies of oral clonidine[38] and clonidine delivered via a transdermal patch[70]. Reviews of preliminary experiments on the effects of a nicotine antagonist on cigarette smoking have provided suggestions of the effectiveness of Technique 3[52,93]. However, the use of nicotine-containing chewing gum consistent with Technique 1 is the most thoroughly investigated and most commonly employed pharmacological aid to smoking reduction or cessation[52].

Nicotine-Containing Chewing Gum

The provision of nicotine in some form should enable the halt of cigarette smoking without the discomforts of drug cessation, regardless of whether these discomforts result from true withdrawal, rebound phenomena or frustrated nonreward. Support for this statement has been found in numerous studies which indicate that cigarette smoking can be decreased by nicotine administered orally in a capsule[51], intravenously[63], or intranasally[53]. However, nicotine-containing chewing gum offers the best substitute for tobacco smoke. It has been noted that "release of the nicotine from the gum requires active and proper chewing and swallowing patterns: this level of safety engineering has yet to be achieved with any other marketed or publicly tested form of nicotine replacement"[52].

Nicotine-containing chewing gum contains either 2 mg or 4 mg of nicotine. Depending upon the rate and intensity of chewing, about 90% of the nicotine in the gum is released during the first 30 minutes. The gum is specially prepared to insure the best absorption through the linings of the mouth, but the absorption is still slow. Peak plasma levels occur a full 15 to 30 minutes after chewing has begun. Thus, delivery of nicotine to the brain is substantially slower than with cigarette smoking[54]. Metabolism and excretion of nicotine is reviewed in Chapter 15.

A double-blind, placebo-controlled study determined that the physical and psychological symptoms of cessation of cigarette smoking could be reversed by nicotine-containing chewing gum[80]. Another double-blind, placebo-controlled study found that nicotine-containing chewing gum enabled 48% of the 60 subjects to successfully quit smoking at six months (compared to 20% in the placebo group). At the end of one year, 30% of the treated subjects had remained abstinent, while only 20% of the placebo-treated subjects were abstinent[81]. Further well-designed experiments have compared the effects of gum containing different doses of nicotine[99] and the importance of psychological counseling and/or self-help manuals as adjuncts to the gum[47]. The latter experiment is particularly important because of the role of psychological factors in tobacco smoking. In a review of the literature, it was noted that, while nicotine-containing gum is effective by itself, its effectiveness is increased when "used in conjunction with an appropriate ancillary treatment program"[52].

As with all treatments for drug abuse, determinations of success depend, in part, upon how success is defined. Some researchers define the gum as a failure after looking at the number of subjects who remained abstinent after removal of the gum[23]. This situation is analogous to evaluating methadone by the number of heroin-abstinent users remaining after the withdrawal of methadone, except that continued consumption of cigarettes is not presently illegal. It is possible for chronic heavy smokers to reduce, for long periods of time, their consumption of cigarettes[37]. The health benefits of such reduction, while inferior to complete abstinence, are well documented[100]. While there are methodological problems that do not allow experimenters to equate reductions in number of cigarettes with a true reduction in levels of inhaled nicotine, simple technologies can approximate blood levels of nicotine by examining smoker's saliva[12]. There is a need for studies to include reduction in self-administered nicotine as a criterion for the success of nicotine-containing gum. In addition, if the gum is to be used as a maintenance therapy, studies need to be conducted to compare the long-term consequences of such a drug delivery system with smoking and or chewing tobacco[52].

Summary of Drug Treatment of Nicotine Abuse

Regardless of whether nicotine induces a true physical dependency, pharmacological treatments can aid the cessation of nicotine abuse. There is evidence that pharmacological techniques can suppress the intensity of symptoms of drug cessation and that blockade of the reinforcing effects of nicotine by an antagonist may aid cessation.

However, substitution of nicotine-containing chewing gum for inhaled cigarette smoke is the most common and thoroughly studied form of drug treatment for nicotine abuse. Nicotine contained in chewing gum, while absorbed more slowly than inhaled nicotine, leads to a dose-dependent reduction in cigarette smoking and increased rates of abstinence from cigarettes. The effectiveness of nicotine-containing chewing gum is enhanced when it is combined with psychological treatment programs. Studies need to be conducted to determine whether nicotine-containing chewing gum is indeed a "safe" substitute for inhaled nicotine.

TREATMENT OF COCAINE ABUSE

Cocaine, like nicotine, is a stimulant drug that can be taken by any means of administration. Usually, cocaine is insufflated, injected, or inhaled as free-base "crack" (see Chapter 15). The controversy over the capacity of cocaine to induce a true physical dependency is even more intense than that regarding nicotine. Positive versus negative answers to the question of cocaine dependence result in vastly different treatment approaches. For example, some advocate a treatment program that recognizes cocaine abuse "as an addictive disease requiring total abstinence from all mood-altering chemicals"[101]. Other researchers recognize that "cocaine abuse, like any other excess, can sometimes be controlled without treatment"[32], but also acknowledge the basic psychopharmacological fact that "the nervous system's usual response to persistent neurochemical perturbation is compensatory adaptation...chronic high-dose use (of cocaine) may generate sustained neurophysiological modification"[31]. Thus, even those who do not support the hypothesis that cocaine causes a true physical dependency can nonetheless support the use of pharmacological aids to cocaine use reduction or cessation.

Although there is no analogue to the use of antabuse in alcohol abuse, each of the remaining techniques of Table 12.2 have been applied to cocaine abuse. However, differences of opinion about the motivations for cocaine abuse have led different investigators to conclude that the same drugs are being used for different reasons. Despite these controversies, pharmacological treatments have been found to be effective in approximately 80% of experimental subjects[31]. In addition, the use of pharmacological aids, compared to psychotherapy without pharmacological treatment, has resulted in twice as many cocaine abusers remaining in treatment[30]. A wide variety of pharmacological aids have shown promise in the treatment of cocaine abuse. This section will examine the treatment of cocaine abuse by lithium, methylphenidate, tricyclic antidepressants, and dopamine agonists.

Lithium

Lithium (see Chapter 9) is an effective treatment for cocaine-induced psychosis[83]. Two case studies reported that lithium blocked cocaine-induced euphoria in humans[14,65]. However, when researchers investigated the effect of lithium on cocaine use, they found that three subjects with bipolar affective disorder halted their cocaine use while three other subjects who did not have an affective disorder continued their cocaine abuse. Neither group of subjects reported that the drug blocked cocaine-induced euphoria[30]. A more recent double-blind, placebo-controlled study also found lithium to be ineffective in influencing cocaine use in subjects without psychological disorders[33]. These results suggest that lithium be used only in cocaine abusers who suffer bipolar affective disorder[31]. The use of this standard psychopharmacotherapeutic is therefore more comparable to the use of psychopharmacotherapeutics in the treatment of heroin abuse than to the use of such drugs in the treatment of alcohol abuse.

Methylphenidate

A number of studies have found that the reinforcing stimulant drug methylphenidate (see Chapter 11) is effective in reducing cocaine use in individuals diagnosed as having ADD[30,57,58]. These results suggested that methylphenidate can be used consistent with Technique 5. On the other hand, methylphenidate is a reinforcing stimulant drug and thus may be used as a "safer" (and legal) maintenance substitute (Technique 1). Methylphenidate may also be able to block the euphoria-inducing effects of cocaine through cross-tolerance (Technique 3) or may be able to "smooth out the dysphoria between cocaine highs and during withdrawal" (Technique 2)[25]. A single open-trial experiment using cocaine abusers who showed no symptoms of ADD found that methylphenidate decreased cocaine craving during the first week. Unfortunately, this effect faded, and was replaced by a situation where methylphenidate induced greater cravings as the reinforcing effects of the drug cued a desire for the more intense effects of cocaine[30]. These results suggest that methylphenidate should only be used in cocaine abusers who suffer ADD[31]. Again, the use of a standard psychopharmacotherapeutic in cocaine abuse is more comparable to the use of these drugs in heroin abuse than to drug treatment of alcohol abuse.

Tricyclic Antidepressants

A number of open trials suggested that tricyclic antidepressants (see Chapter 8) decreased cocaine craving and promoted abstinence[4,7,30,96]. When researchers excluded depressed subjects from their open trial, they still found decreased cocaine craving and use[30]. The first double-blind, placebo-controlled study of antidepressants and cocaine abuse failed to find any effect of desipramine upon cocaine cravings or rates of abstinence[98]. However, this study has been criticized for using too low a dose over too short a period of time[29]. A more recent study using larger doses in subjects without depression found that desipramine enabled 59% of cocaine abusers to be abstinent for three to four weeks, while only 17% of placebo-treated subjects remained abstinent for a similar length of time[33]. Similarly, another double-blind study revealed that desipramine, compared to placebo, resulted in decreased cocaine craving and decreased number of days with cocaine use in a subject population free of depression, schizophrenia, and other forms of psychopathology[69]. These results suggest that tricyclic antidepressants may be useful in the treatment of the general population of cocaine abusers. This conclusion is reminiscent of conclusions regarding the effectiveness of lithium and serotonin agonist tricyclics in the treatment of the general population of alcohol abusers.

The available information makes it difficult to determine which of the techniques listed in Table 12.2 is being used when tricyclic antidepressants treat cocaine abuse. Evidence of effectiveness in non-depressed subjects[30,33,69] suggests that antidepressants are capable of doing more than simply treating a depression which may underlie cocaine abuse (Technique 5)[34]. Antidepressants may be acting through Technique 3, since there is evidence that antidepressants can block some of the effects of cocaine[29,31]. However, desipramine has been shown to block the **hypersomnolence** (or excessive sleepiness) which occurs at cocaine cessation[4]. This result suggests that antidepressants may also be effective because they can suppress the symptoms of cocaine cessation (Technique 2), including, perhaps, cessation-induced depression[15]. Further research will be required to determine which technique is being utilized in the effective treatment of cocaine abuse by tricyclic antidepressants.

Dopaminergic Agonists

Some investigators have theorized that long-term cocaine use leads to supersensitive dopamine receptors that induce cravings for cocaine when cocaine use is suddenly halted[17,18,42]. This led directly to the idea that stimulation of these receptors with dopamine agonists could desensitize these receptors, leading to an eventual reduction of craving (Technique 2). Preliminary open trials have suggested that precursors to dopamine, including l-tyrosine and l-dopa, the direct dopamine agonist bromocriptine, and the indirect dopamine agonist amantadine can reduce cocaine craving and use[19,20,22,29]. Two double-blind, placebo-controlled studies found that bromocriptine reversed cocaine craving[21,35]. When researchers compared bromocriptine and amantadine in a double-blind study, they found amantadine to be more effective with fewer side effects[95]. These results suggest that the use of dopamine agonists may present a pharmacologically sound way to treat the psychological consequences of the neurochemical impact of chronic cocaine use.

Summary Of Drug Treatment Of Cocaine Abuse

Pharmacological treatment of cocaine abuse can be effective and can increase the number of cocaine abusers who remain in treatment. Lithium and methylphenidate are effective in reducing the abuse of cocaine by individuals who suffer from bipolar affective disorder and attention deficit disorder, respectively. On the other hand, tricyclic antidepressants can lead to a reduction of cocaine craving and increased abstinence even in cocaine abusers who do not show signs of depression. It is difficult to tell which technique is being used when the tricyclics successfully treat cocaine abuse. It is likely that the tricyclics are doing more than treating an underlying depression. However, it is unclear whether the tricyclics are blocking the reinforcing effects of cocaine or suppressing the symptoms of drug cessation, or both. Dopamine agonists have been found to decrease cocaine craving and abuse, perhaps by treating the negative physical and psychological consequences caused by chronic cocaine use.

CHAPTER SUMMARY

There are five ways in which pharmacological compounds can be used to aid a reduction or cessation of drug abuse. These include substitution, suppression of symptoms of cessation, blockade of drug effects, punishment of drug consumption, and treatment of underlying disorder(s). It is not always clear, however, which technique is being used when a treatment is found to aid the reduction or cessation of drug abuse. Standard psychopharmacotherapeutics can be of use when they provide treatment for a behavioral disorder suffered by a drug abuser. In addition, lithium and serotonin agonist tricyclics can reduce alcohol consumption in alcohol abusers without mania or depression, and tricyclic antidepressants can reduce cocaine consumption in cocaine abusers without depression. The mechanism by which these agents suppress alcohol or cocaine consumption are controversial. Antianxiety agents are effective in suppressing the symptoms of alcohol cessation. The technique of substitution is used when methadone treatment is provided to heroin abusers and when nicotine-containing chewing gum is provided to nicotine abusers. Clonidine has been found to effectively suppress the symptoms of cessation of a variety of forms of drug abuse. Naltrexone blocks the effects of heroin, thus reducing the power of discriminative stimuli that act as cues for heroin consumption. Antabuse punishes the consumption of alcohol. Compliance with treatment regimens involving either naltrexone or antabuse tends to be low.

REVIEW ESSAY QUESTIONS.

1. Discuss the five techniques of using pharmacological aids to help the reduction and/or cessation of drug abuse. Pay particular attention to those that show the importance of psychological variables.

2. Compare and contrast the uses of methadone, naltrexone, and clonidine in aiding heroin reduction or cessation.

3. Compare and contrast the use of antabuse in alcohol abuse with the use of naltrexone in heroin abuse.

4. Discuss the differences and similarities between nicotine-containing chewing gum in nicotine abuse and methadone or clonidine in heroin abuse.

5. Explain why it is difficult to tell which technique(s) are being used when methylphenidate or the tricyclic antidepressants are used in cocaine abuse.

REFERENCES

1. Banys, P. The clinical use of disulfiram (Antabuse): A review. *Journal of Psychoactive Drugs*, 1988, 20, 243-260.

2. Barnes, H.N. The use of disulfiram. In H.N. Barnes, M.D. Aronson, & T.L. Delvanco (Eds.) *Alcoholism: A guide for the primary care physician*. New York: Springer-Verlag, 1987.

3. Baumgartner, G.R., & Rowen R.C. Clonidine vs. chlordiazepoxide in the management of acute alcohol withdrawal syndrome. *Archives of Internal Medicine*, 1987, 147, 1223-1226.

4. Baxter, L.R. Desipramine in the treatment of hypersomnolence following abrupt cocaine cessation. *American Journal of Psychiatry*, 1983, 140, 1525-1526.

5. Blum, K., Briggs, A.H., & DeLallo, L. Clonidine enhancement of ethanol withdrawal in mice. *Substance and Alcohol Action and Misuse*, 1983, 4, 59-63.

6. Borkqvist, S.E. Clonidine in alcohol withdrawal. *Acta Psychiatrica Scandinavia*, 1975, 52, 256-263.

7. Brotman, A.W., Witkie, S.M., Gelenberg, A.J., Falk, W.E., Wojcik, J., & Leahy, L. An open trial of maprotiline for the treatment of cocaine abuse: A pilot study. *Journal of Clinical Psychopharmacology*, 1988, 8, 125-127.

8. Callahan, E.J., Long, M.A., Pecsok, E.H., & Simone, S. Opiate addiction. In T.D. Nirenberg, & S.A. Maisto (Eds.) *Developments in the assessment and treatment of addictive behaviors*. Norwood, NJ: Ablex Publishing, 1987.

9. Charney, D.S., Heninger, G.R., & Klever, H.D. The combined use of clonidine and naltrexone as a rapid, safe and effective treatment of abrupt withdrawal from methadone. *American Journal of Psychiatry*, 1986, 143, 831-837.

10. Chiang, C.N., Kishimoto, A., Barnett, G., & Hollister, L.E. Implantable narcotic antagonists: A possible new treatment for narcotic addiction. *Psychopharmacology Bulletin*, 1985, 3, 672-675.

11. Ciraulo, D.A., Barnhill, J.G., Greenblatt, D.J., Shader, R.I., Ciraulo, A.M., Tarmey, M.F., Molloy, M.A., & Foti, M.E. Abuse liability and clinical pharmacokinetics of alprazolam in alcoholic men. *Journal of Clinical Psychiatry*, 1988, 49, 333-337.

12. Colletti, G., Payne, T.J., & Rizzo, A.A. Treatment of cigarette smoking. In T.D. Nirenberg, & S.A. Maisto (Eds.) *Developments in the assessment and treatment of addictive behaviors*. Ablex Publishing Co., Norwood, NJ, 1987.

13. Crabtree, B.L. Review of naltrexone, a long-acting opiate antagonist. *Clinical Pharmacy*, 1984, 3, 273-280.

14. Cronson, A.J., & Flemenbaum, A. Antagonism of cocaine highs by lithium. *American Journal of Psychiatry*, 1978, 135, 856-857.

15. *Crowley, T.J. Clinical issues in cocaine abuse. In S. Fisher, A. Raskin, & E.H. Uhlenhuth (Eds.) *Cocaine: Clinical and biobehavioral aspects*. New York: Oxford University Press, 1987.

16. Cushman, P., Lerner, W., & Cramer, C. Adrenergic agonist therapy in alcohol withdrawal states in man. *Psychopharmacology Bulletin*, 1985, 21, 651-656.

17. Dackis, C.A., & Gold, M.S. Bromocriptine as a treatment of cocaine abuse. *Lancet*, 1985a, 1, 1151-1152.

18. Dackis, C.A., & Gold, M.S. New concepts in cocaine addiction: The dopamine hypothesis. *Neuroscience and Biobehavioral Reviews*, 1985b, 9, 469-477.

19. Dackis, C.A., Gold, M.S., & Pottash, A.L.C. Central stimulant abuse: Neurochemistry and pharmacotherapy. In M.S. Gold, M. Galanter, & B. Stimmel (Eds.) *Cocaine: Pharmacology, addiction and therapy*. New York: Haworth Press, 1987.

20. Dackis, C.A., Gold, M.S., Davis, R.K., & Sweeney, D.R. Bromocriptine treatment for cocaine abuse: The dopamine depletion hypothesis. *International Journal of Psychiatric Medicine*, 1985, 15, 125-135.

21. Dackis, C.A., Gold, M.S., Sweeney, D.R., Byron, J.P., & Climko, R. Single-dose bromocriptine reverses cocaine craving. *Psychiatric Research*, 1987, 20, 261-264.

22. *Daigle, R.D., Clark, H.W., & Landry, M.J. A primer on neurotransmitters and cocaine. *Journal of Psychoactive Drugs*, 1988, 20, 283-295.

23. DeWitt, H., & Camic, P.M. Behavioral and pharmacological treatment of cigarette smoking: End of treatment comparisons. *Addictive Behaviors*, 1986, 11, 331-335.

24. Edwards, G., & Littleton J. *Pharmacological treatments for alcoholism*. New York: Methuen, 1984.

25. Esteroff, T.W., & Gold, M.S. Medical and psychiatric complications of cocaine abuse with possible points of pharmacological treatment. In B. Stimmel (Ed.) *Controversies in alcoholism and substance abuse*. New York: Haworth Press, 1986.

26. Fawcett, J., Clark, D.C., Aageson, C.A., Pisani, V.D., Tilkin, J.M., Sellers, D., McGuire, M., & Gibbons, R.D. A double-blind, placebo-controlled trial of lithium carbonate therapy for alcoholism. *Archives of General Psychiatry*, 1987, 44, 248-256.

27. Fuller, R.K. A critical analysis of the efficacy and toxicity of the alcohol sensitizing drugs. In G. Edwards, & J. Littleton (Eds.) *Pharmacological treatments for alcoholism*, London: Croom Helm, London, 1984.

28. Fuller, R.K., Branchey, L., Brightwell, D.R., Derman, R.M., Emrick, C.D., Iber, F.L., James, K.E., Lacoursiere, R.B., Lee, K.K., Lowenstam, I., Maany, I., Neiderhiser, R.T., Nocks, J.J., & Shaw, S. Disulfiram treatment of alcoholism: a Veterans Administration cooperative study. *Journal of the American Medical Association*, 1986, 256, 1449-1455.

29. Gawin, F.H. Chronic neuropharmacology of cocaine: Progress in pharmacotherapy. *Journal of Clinical Psychiatry*, 1988, 49, 11-16.

30. Gawin, F.H., & Kleber, H.D. Cocaine abuse treatment: Open pilot trial with desipramine and lithium carbonate. *Archives of General Psychiatry*, 1984, 41, 903-909.

31. Gawin, F.H., & Kleber, H.D. Pharmacological treatments of cocaine abuse. *Substance Abuse*, 1986, 9, 573-583.

32.*Gawin, F.H., & Kleber, H.D. Issues in cocaine-abuse treatment research. In S. Fisher, A. Raskin, & E.H. Uhlenhuth (Eds.) *Cocaine: Clinical and biobehavioral aspects*. New York: Oxford University Press, 1987.

33. Gawin, F.H., Kleber, H.D., Byck, R., Rounsaville, B.J., Kosten, T.R., Jatlow, P.I., & Morgan C. Desipramine facilitation of initial cocaine abstinence. *Archives of General Psychiatry*, 1989, 46, 117-121.

34. Giannini, A.J., Malone, D.A., & Giannini, J.C. Treatment of depression in chronic cocaine and phencyclidine abuse with desipramine. *Journal of Clinical Pharmacology*, 1986, 26, 211-224.

35. Giannini, A.J., Baumbartel, P., & DiMarzio, L.R. Bromocriptine therapy in cocaine withdrawal. *Journal of Clinical Pharmacology*, 1987, 27, 267-270.

36.*Ginzburg, H.M. Naltrexone: Its clinical utility. In B. Stimmel (Ed.) *Controversies in alcoholism and substance abuse*. New York: Haworth Press, 1986.

37. Glasgow, R.E., Klesges, R.C., & Vasey, M.W. Controlled smoking and chronic smokers: An extension and replication. *Addictive Behaviors*, 1983, 8, 143-150.

38. Glassman, A.H., Stetner, F., Walsh, T., Raizman, P.S., Fleiss, J.L., Cooper, T.B., & Covey, L.S. Heavy smokers, smoking cessation, and clonidine. *Journal of the American Medical Association*, 1988, 243, 2863-2866.

39. Gold, M.S., Dackis, C.A., Pottash, A.L.C., & Lydiard, R.B. Narcotic addiction. In M.S. Gold, R.B. Lydiard, & J.S. Carman (Eds.) *Advances in psychopharmacology: Predicting and improving treatment response*. Boca Raton, FL: CRC Press, 1984.

40. Gold, M.S., Pottash, A.L.C., & Extein, I. Clonidine: Inpatient studies from 1978 to 1981. *Journal of Clinical Psychiatry*, 1982, 43, 35-38.

41. Gold, M.S., Redmond, D.E., & Kleber, H.D. Noradrenergic hyperactivity in opiate withdrawal supported by clonidine reversal of opiate withdrawal. *American Journal of Psychiatry*, 1979, 136, 100-106.

42. Gold, M.S., Washton, A.M. & Dackis, C.A. Cocaine abuse: Neurochemistry, phenomenology and treatment. In N.J. Kozel, & E.H. Adams (Eds.) *Cocaine use in America: Epidemiologic and clinical perspectives*. (NIDA Research Monograph Series No. 61), Rockville, MD: NIDA, 1985.

43. Gossop, M. Clonidine and the treatment of opiate withdrawal syndrome. *Drug and Alcohol Dependence*, 1988, 21, 253-259.

44. Gossop, M., Bradley, B., & Phillips, G.T. An investigation of withdrawal symptoms shown by opiate addicts during and subsequent to a 21-day in-patient methadone detoxification procedure. *Addictive Behaviors*, 1987, 12, 1-6.

45. Greenstein, R.A., Evans, B.D., & McLellan, A.T. Predictors of favorable outcome following naltrexone treatment. *Drug and Alcohol Dependence*, 1983, 12, 173-180.

46. Griffiths, R.R., Bigelow, G.E., & Liebson, L. Facilitation of human tobacco self-administration by ethanol: A behavioral analysis. *Journal of the Experimental Analysis of Behavior*, 1976, 25, 279-292.

47. Harackiewicz, J.M., Blair, L.W., Sansone, C., Epstein, J.A., & Stuchell, R.N. Nicotine gum and self-help manuals in smoking cessation: An evaluation in a medical context. *Addictive Behaviors*, 1988, 13, 319-330.

48. Hughes, J.R., Gust, S.W., & Pechacek, T.F. Prevalence of tobacco dependence and withdrawal. *American Journal of Psychiatry*, 1987, 144, 205-208.

49. Jaffe, J.H. Pharmacological agents in treatment of drug dependence. In H.Y. Meltzer (Ed.) *Psychopharmacology: The third generation of progress.* New York: Raven Press, 1987.

50. Jaffe, J.H., & Martin, W.R. Opioid analgesics and antagonists. In A.G. Gilman, L.S. Goodman, T.W. Rall, & F. Murad (Eds.) *The pharmacological basis of therapeutics, (7th ed.).* New York: Macmillan Publishing Company, 1985.

51. Jarvik, M.E., Glick, S.D., & Nakamura, R.K. Inhibition of cigarette smoking by orally administered nicotine. *Clinical Pharmacology and Therapeutics*, 1970, 11, 574-576.

52. Jarvik, M.E., & Henningfield, J.E. Pharmacological treatment of tobacco dependence. *Pharmacology, Biochemistry and Behavior*, 1988, 30, 279-294.

53. Jarvis, M.J., Hajek, P., Russell, M.A.H., West, R.J., & Feyerabend, C. Nasal nicotine solution as an aid to cigarette withdrawal: A pilot clinical trial. *British Journal of Addiction*, 1987, 82, 983-988.

54. Jones, R.T. Tobacco dependence. In H.Y. Meltzer (Ed.) *Psychopharmacology: The third generation of progress.* New York: Raven Press, 1987.

55. Judd, L.L., & Huey, L.Y. Lithium antagonizes ethanol intoxication in alcoholics. *American Journal of Psychiatry*, 1984, 141, 1517-1521.

56. Judson, B.A., Carney, T.M., & Goldstein, A. Naltrexone treatment of heroin addiction: Efficacy and safety in a double-blind dosage comparison. *Drug and Alcohol Dependence*, 1981, 7, 325-346.

57. Khantzian, E.J., Gawin, F.H., & Kleber, H.D. Methylphenidate (Ritalin) treatment of cocaine dependence: A preliminary report. *Journal of Substance Abuse Treatment*, 1984, 1, 107-112.

58. Khantzian, E.J. Extreme case of cocaine dependence and marked improvement with methylphenidate treatment. *American Journal of Psychiatry*, 1983, 140, 784-785.

59. *Kleber, H.D. The use of psychotropic drugs in the treatment of compulsive opiate abusers: The rationale for their use. In B. Stimmel (Ed.) *Controversies in alcoholism and substance abuse.* New York: Haworth Press, 1986.

60. Kleber, H.D., Topazian, M., Gaspari, J., Riordan, C.E., & Kosten, T. Clonidine and naltrexone in the outpatient treatment of heroin withdrawal. *American Journal of Drug and Alcohol Abuse*, 1987, 13, 1-17.

61. Lawrin, M.O., Naranjo, C.A., & Sellers, E.M. Identification and testing of new drugs for modulating alcohol consumption. *Psychopharmacology Bulletin*, 1986, 22, 1020-1025.

62. Lindros, K.O., Stowall, A., Pikkarainen, P., & Salaspuro, M. The disulfiram (Antabuse)-alcohol reaction in male alcoholics: Its effecient management by 4-methylpyrazole. *Alcoholism*, 1981, 5, 528-530.

63. Lucchesi, B.R., Schuster, C.R., & Emley, G.S. The role of nicotine as a determinant of cigarette smoking frequency in man with observations of certain cardiovascular effects associated with the tobacco alkaloid. *Clinical Pharmacology and Therapeutics*, 1967, 8, 789-796.

64. Malcolm, R., Ballenger, J.C., Sturgis, E.T., & Anton, R. Double-blind controlled trial comparing carbamazepine to oxazepam treatment of alcohol withdrawal. *American Journal of Psychiatry*, 1989, 146, 617-620.

65. Mandell, A.J., & Knapp, S. Neurobiological antagonism of cocaine by lithium. In E.H. Ellinwood & M. M. Kilbey (Eds.) *Cocaine and other stimulants.* New York: Plenum Press, 1976.

66. McCaul, M.E., Bigelow, G.E., Stitzer, M.L., & Liebson, I. Short-term effects of oral methadone in methadone maintenance subjects. *Clinical Pharmacology and Therapeutics*, 1982, 31, 753-761.

67. Mitchenson, M., Hartnoll, R., & Lewis, R. Opioids. In S.D. Iversen (Ed.) *Psychopharmacology: Recent advances and future prospects.* Oxford, England: Oxford University Press, 1985.

68. Newman, R.G. Methadone treatment: Defining and evaluating success. *New England Journal of Medicine*, 1987, 317, 447-450.

69. O'Brien, C.P., Childress, A.R., Arndt, I.O., McLellan, A.T., Woody, G.E., & Maany, I. Pharmacological and behavioral treatments of cocaine dependence: Controlled studies. *Journal of Clinical Psychiatry*, 1988, 49, 17-22.

70. Ornish, S.A., Zisook, S., & McAdams, L.A. Effects of transdermal clonidine treatment on withdrawal symptoms associated with smoking cessation. *Archives of Internal Medicine*, 1988, 148, 2027-2031.

71. Peachey, J.E., Brien, J.F., Roach, C.A., & Loomis, C.W. A comparative review of the pharmacological and toxicological properties of disulfiram and calcium carbimide. *Journal of Clinical Psychopharmacology*, 1981, 1, 21-26.

72. *Peele, S. Can alcoholism and other drug addiction problems be treated away or is the current treatment binge doing more harm than good? *Journal of Psychoactive Drugs*, 1988, 20, 375-383.

73. Rawson, R.A., Washton, A.M., Resnick, R.B., & Tennant, F.S. Clonidine hydrochloride detoxification from methadone treatment: The value of naltrexone aftercare. *Advances in Alcohol and Substance Abuse*, 1984, 3, 41-49.

74. Ritchie, J.M. The aliphatic alcohols. In A.G. Gilman, L.S. Goodman, T.W. Rall, & F. Murad (Eds.) *The pharmacological basis of therapeutics, (7th ed.).* New York: Macmillan Publishing Company, 1985.

75. Ritson, B., & Chick, J. Comparison of two benzodiazepines in the treatment of alcohol withdrawal: Effects on symptoms and cognitive recovery. *Drugs and Alcohol Dependence*, 1986, 18, 329-334.

76. Rosenberg, C.M. Drug maintenance in the outpatient treatment of chronic alcoholism. *Archives of General Psychiatry*, 1974, 30, 373-377.

77. Rosenbloom, A. Emerging treatment options in the alcohol withdrawal syndrome. *Journal of Clinical Psychiatry*, 1988, 49, 28-31.

78. Rounsaville, B.J., Kosten, T., & Kleber, H. Success and failure at outpatient opioid detoxification: Evaluating the process of clonidine- and methadone-assisted withdrawal. *The Journal of Nervous and Mental Disease*, 1985, 173, 103-110.

79. Rudd, P., & Blaschke, T.F. Antihypertensive agents and the drug therapy of hypertension. In A.G. Gilman, L.S. Goodman, T.W. Rall, & F. Murad (Eds.) *The pharmacological basis of therapeutics, (7th ed.).* New York: Macmillan, 1985.

80. Schneider, N.G., Jarvik, M.E., & Forsyth, A.B. Nicotine vs. placebo gum in the alleviation of withdrawal during smoking cessation. *Addictive Behaviors*, 1984, 9, 149-156.

81. Schneider, N.G., Jarvik, M.E., Forsythe, A.B., Read, L.L., Elliott, M.L., & Schweiger, A. Nicotine gum in smoking cessation: A placebo-controlled, double-blind trial. *Addictive Behaviors*, 1983, 8, 253-261.

82. Schuster, C.R. Implications of laboratory research for the treatment of drug dependence. In S.R. Goldbert & I.P. Stolerman (Eds.) *Behavioral analysis of drug dependence.* Orlando, FL: Academic Press, 1986.

83. Scott, M.E., & Mullaly, R.W. Lithium therapy for cocaine-induced psychosis: A clinical perspective. *Southern Medical Journal*, 1981, 74, 1475-1477.

84. Sees, K.L., & Clark, H.W. Use of clonidine in nicotine withdrawal. *Journal of Psychoactive Drugs*, 1988, 20, 263-268.

85. Sellers, E.M., & Naranjo, C.A. New strategies for the treatment of alcohol withdrawal. *Psychopharmacology Bulletin*, 1986, 22, 88-92.

86. Senay, E.C. Methadone maintenance treatment. *International Journal of the Addictions*, 1985, 20, 803-821.

87. Sideroff, S.I., & Jarvik, M.E. Conditioned responses to a video-tape showing heroin related stimuli. *International Journal of the Addictions*, 1980, 74, 251-265.

88. Sinclair, J.D. The feasibility of effective psychopharmacological treatments for alcoholism. *British Journal of Addiction*, 1987, 82, 1213-1223.

89. Stewart, J. Conditioned and unconditioned drug effects in relapse to opiate and stimulant drug self-administration. *Progress in Neuropsychopharmacology and Biological Psychiatry*, 1983, 7, 591-597.

90. *Stimmel, B. Prescribing psychotropic agents in opiate dependency: The need for caution. In B. Stimmel (Ed.) *Controversies in alcoholism and substance abuse.* New York: Haworth Press, 1986.

91. Stitzer, M.L., McCaul, M.E., Bigelow, G.E., & Liebson, I. Treatment outcome in methadone detoxification: Relationship to initial levels of illicit opiate use. *Drug and Alcohol Dependence*, 1983, 12, 259-267.

92. Stitzer, M.L., McCaul, M.E., Bigelow, G.E., & Liebson, I.A. Chronic opiate use during methadone detoxification: Effects of a dose increase treatment. *Drug and Alcohol Dependence*, 1984, 14, 37-44.

93. Stolerman, I.P. Could nicotine antagonists be used in smoking cessation? *British Journal of Addiction*, 1986, 81, 47-53.

94. Teasdale, J.D. Conditioned abstinence in narcotic addicts. *International Journal of the Addictions*, 1973, 8, 273-293.

95. Tennant, F.S., & Sagherian, A.A. Double-blind comparison of amantadine and bromocriptine for ambulatory withdrawal from cocaine dependence. *Archives of Internal Medicine*, 1987, 147, 109-112.

96. Tennant, F.S., & Rawson, R.A. Cocaine and amphetamine dependence treated with desipramine. In L.S. Harris (Ed.) *Problems of drug dependence, 1982* (NIDA Research Monograph Series No. 43). Washington, D.C.: U.S. Government Printing Office,1983.

97. Tennant, F.S., Rawson, R.A., Cohen, A.J., & Mann, A. Clinical experience with naltrexone in suburban opioid addicts. *Journal of Clinical Psychiatry*, 1984, 45, 42-45.

98. Tennant, F.S., & Tarver, A.L. Double-blind comparison of desipramine and placebo in withdrawal from cocaine dependence *(National Institute on Drug Abuse Research Monograph Series No. 55)*, 1984.

99. Tonnesen, P., Fryd, V., Hansen, M., Helsted, J., Gunnersen, A.B., Forchammer, H., & Stockner, M. Two and four mg nicotine chewing gum and group counseling in smoking cessation: An open, randomized, controlled trial with a 22 month follow-up. *Addictive Behaviors*, 1988, 13, 17-27.

100. *U.S. Department of Health and Human Services. *Tobacco and Health.* Washington, D.C.: U.S. Government Printing Office, 1987.

101. Washton, A.M. Preventing relapse to cocaine. *Journal of Clinical Psychiatry*, 1988, 49, 34-38.

102. Washton, A.M., & Resnick, R.B. Outpatient opiate detoxification with clonidine. *Journal of Clinical Psychiatry*, 1982, 43, 39-41.

103. Wickler, A. Dynamics of drug dependence: Implications of a conditioning theory for research and treatment. *Archives of General Psychiatry*, 1973, 28, 611-616.

104. Williams, E.E. Effects of alcohol on workers with carbon disulfide. *Journal of the American Medical Association*, 1937, 109, 1472-1473.

105. *Zweben, J.E., & Sorensen, J.L. Misunderstandings about methadone. *Journal of Psychoactive Drugs*, 1988, 20, 275-281.

*Introductory or intermediate reading

Chapter 13

MOTIVATIONS FOR USE AND PRIMARY DANGERS

The purposes of this chapter are to:

1. Investigate the wide range of theories that attempt to explain the motivation(s) for the initiation and/or continuation of drug use and abuse,

2. Discuss the main dangers of acute doses of abusable drugs, including drug interactions, behavioral toxicity, organ toxicity, and overdose, and

3. Discuss the main dangers of chronic consumption of abusable drugs, including tolerance/sensitization, compulsive use, physical dependency, brain and other organ damage, violence, and psychosis.

PROBLEMS IN DEVELOPING SCIENTIFIC THEORIES OF DRUG USE AND ABUSE

An Emotion-Charged Issue

The issues of drug use and drug abuse arouse intense emotions. Previous chapters dealing with the dose-dependent effects of psychopharmacotherapeutics revealed that drugs that effect behavior can have profound, and sometimes disastrous, consequences. Psychopharmacotherapeutics, even when taken within the confines of a physician-prescribed regimen, can result in behavioral and physical side effects, overdose, tolerance/sensitization, physical dependency, and compulsive use[77]. Despite these problems these drugs are generally viewed positively, as medicines taken to help individuals with behavioral disorders. **Abusable** (sometimes called **recreational**) **drugs** are compounds, legal or illegal, that people consume voluntarily because they desire some of the psychological, and sometimes physical, consequences of ingestion. Those who abhor the use of drugs for recreational purposes wonder why anyone would take the risks of side effects, overdose, physical dependency, and the like without the promised benefit of "curing a disorder." Why, the public asks, would people take the risk of recreational use of illegal drugs? What is the **motivation**, the reason or purpose, of taking illegal drugs? Part of the problem with the above question is the focus on the motivation for use of illegal drugs. The better question is, why do people take abusable drugs of any sort, whether legal or illegal? One reviewer has noted that "concern about illegal drug use is both laudable and justified...(but) sadly, the degree of emphasis on responding to illegal drug use and misuse is out of proportion in relation to current responses to the far, far bigger problems linked to tobacco and alcohol"[56].

The emotion surrounding the entire issue of drug use and abuse leads to legalistic or moralistic, rather than scientific, views of the topic. In an editorial in the prestigious *New England Journal of Medicine,* a theorist bemoans the fact that advances in theory have been hampered by definitions of the problem "based more on legislative fiat and judicial rulings than on pharmacological or clinical evidence"[52]. Another author noted that the ascendancy of a particular theoretical viewpoint may reflect the consequences of political power struggles, rendering them "a social rather than a scientific or medical accomplishment"[61]. Concerns about the implications of inappropriate emotionality surrounding the issues of drug use and drug abuse are succinctly stated by Szasz[70] and Satinder[59].

Lack of Agreement in the Scientific Community

Even when the issues of drug use and drug abuse are viewed dispassionately, scientists find it difficult to agree on any particular theory. The philosopher of science Thomas Kuhn has investigated the various stages in the development of any particular field of science[41]. It has been noted that theories on drug use and abuse are in what Kuhn referred to as a "preparadigmatic" stage, where there is little agreement about what the problem really is and hence even less agreement about any explanation of the problem[64]. The complexity of human motivation for any behavior is a part of the reason for this lack of agreement. For example, the behavior of drug intake itself can serve a number of functions at different times in different individuals[53]. One researcher has noted some people smoke cigarettes because they find them stimulating, others because they find them relaxing, and others smoke them for either stimulation or relaxation, depending upon circumstances[75].

Changeability in Motivators for Drug Use

Another reason for lack of theoretical agreements about drug use and abuse is that the motivations for drug use probably change as a person becomes older, takes on different social roles, and experiences different degrees of involvement with drug use. A person may desire certain drugs when they are young because they find any behavior of which their parents disapprove to be stimulating and exciting, then partake of different drugs when they are gainfully employed adults because they desire after-work relaxation, and finally consume yet another new set of drugs when retired due to boredom and feelings of worthlessness[53]. A study of the development of serious drug abuse in young people in New York showed that the motivation(s) for drug taking varied greatly over time even within any single individual[33]. Dr. Ronald Siegel emphasized possible changes in motivations for drug use and determined that there were five categories that specify different degrees of involvement with recreational drugs[65]. Table 13.1 lists these five categories, and presents the characteristic pattern of intake likely to be shown by a person at each level.

Table 13.1
Degrees of Involvement with Recreational Drugs

1. *Experimental use.* Short-term, non-patterned trials, with varying intensity but limited maximum lifetime frequency. Motivated by curiosity and desire for reinforcing experience.
2. *Social-recreational use.* Most common pattern. Drug experience shared with friends or acquaintances. More frequent than experimental use.
3. *Circumstantial-situational use.* Task-specific use, self-limited and variable in pattern, frequency, and intensity. Drug is used to achieve a specific drug effect (enhanced mood or performance) considered desirable for specific circumstances. May be more or less frequent than social-recreational.
4. *Intensified use.* Long-term use of at least once a day. Motivated by desire to achieve some desired level of performance or relief from problem or stress.
5. *Compulsive use.* High-frequency and high-intensity use of long duration. Use cannot be discontinued without psychological discomfort. Preoccupation with drug and drug-seeking behaviors. Motivated by desire to obtain persistent euphoria or to avoid discomfort of cessation.

Various Levels of Drug Use

Any adequate theory must explain the motivations for each of the various levels of involvement with drugs, not just the last two levels, which were discussed in the previous chapter. Unfortunately, scientists are hampered from developing a theory with sufficient complexity because of an erroneous impression among legislators, policymakers and the public that a single theoretical explanation will suffice since any involvement with abusable (particularly illegal) drugs must inevitably lead to compulsive use. One researcher complained that "the trivialization of research findings by the popular press and some political figures can contribute to an attitude that minimizes the complexity of the problem"[47]. Two others noted that for some "drug use, certainly any use of an illegal drug, has been traditionally considered as equivalent to drug abuse"[46]. These researchers noted two specific examples where this conceptual confusion has made it difficult to correctly interpret data obtained from experiments[15,66]. The attitude that equates drug use with drug abuse did not disappear in the early 1970s. For example, a federal government task force report on drug abuse in 1986 went so far as to recommend that federal funds be denied to any group or person that utilized the phrase "recreational drug use" when discussing presently illicit drugs[57]. This dogmatism is particularly disheartening in the context of calls from as far back as the mid-1960s for scientists to consider the possibility that those things responsible for drug use might be different from those responsible for drug abuse[11]. More recently, a scientist/editorialist asked the rhetorical question, "Has the time come to reject the long-held assumption that alcoholism develops in only a small minority of drinkers, whereas addiction is an almost universal consequence of repeated exposure to opiates?"[52]

The data suggest that this question must be answered affirmatively. The classification scheme in Table 13.1 was developed to describe the use of cocaine, and there were cocaine users in each category, some moving to more involvement with the drug, but others moving towards less involvement. In addition, identical results were found when researchers looked at users of LSD, marijuana, and heroin, despite the fact that the last drug is unarguably capable of inducing a physical dependency[83]. Other researchers have demonstrated that more than one-third of those who used marijuana and nearly one-half of those who used cocaine in their mid twenties completely stopped using the drugs by their thirties[34]. Any adequate theory of drug use and drug abuse must take into account that "for almost all substances...many more individuals have experienced the effects and not developed addictive patterns than have become habitual users...in fact, many people who experiment with drugs discontinue their use after an initial experience"[44]. As noted in Chapters 5 and 12, compulsive use and physical dependency are neither inevitable nor untreatable consequences of using drugs that can influence behavior. Theorists have often noted the importance of taking into account various degrees of involvement with drug use especially when developing programs and policies aimed at preventing the onset of drug use, preventing progression to more intense degrees of involvement, or treating those who engage in drug abuse[46,83].

THEORIES OF DRUG USE AND ABUSE

Commonalities in the use of different drugs, by different people, in different places and times[8] have motivated the search for a single grand theory of drug abuse. However, given the complexity of recreational drug use and drug abuse, it is unlikely that any "single theory or set of principles can be expected to organize all or even most features"[44]. At the beginning of the 1980s, the National Institute on Drug Abuse published a monograph in which the editors presented a grand total of 43 *selected* theories of drug use and abuse written by a total of over 50 different authors[43]. Little winnowing of this list occurred over the next decade, as evidenced by the diversity of viewpoints presented in the May 1988 issue of the *Journal of Abnormal Psychology*, devoted to "Models of Addiction" (emphasis added). Despite the vast disparity in theories, there are enough similarities to make it is possible to provide some organization to the various theories of drug use and abuse. Understanding of theories can be aided by classifying them as ones that emphasize (a) the personality of the user, (b) social and cultural factors, (c) basic learning processes, (d) neurobiology, or (e) combinations of the previous four.

Personality

An earlier statement by Sigmund Freud, who said "only the addiction prone become addicted"[23] encompasses the idea that there is some defect in the personality of the individual drug user that renders that person more likely to enter into a self-destructive involvement with drugs, and perhaps other activities such as gambling and uncondoned sexual behavior. Studies of drug abuse in twins and studies of family history reveal that there is most likely an influence of genetics on drug abuse[10,63]. Some researchers have focused on individual differences in the inheritance of "temperament"[71]. Others have hypothesized that what drug abusers suffer is a specific personality defect that causes them to be "thrill seekers" who search for excitement wherever they may find it, including in the subjective effects of drugs[84]. Still other theorists have proposed that an individual drug abuser's intensity of involvement and choice of drug may be motivated by an attempt to "self-medicate" a specific DSM-IIIR behavioral disorder[36,49,82]. For example, excessive cocaine intake in some individuals has been explained by the finding that they have been attempting to decrease their symptoms of an undiagnosed ADD[14] (see Chapter 11) or an undiagnosed depression[25] (see Chapter 8). Opioid use may reflect an attempt to self-medicate depression[40]. The excessive use of alcohol by some individuals has been suggested to arise from an attempt to self-medicate anxiety[78]. Even the excessive intake of chocolate was found to be most likely in people with undiagnosed depression[62].

Despite the intuitive appeal of the self-medication hypothesis, it is impossible to tell whether excessive drug intake is the result of, or a cause of, the behavioral disorder or personality defect[46,51]. One review investigated a number of studies where individuals with personality abberations were identified and then followed throughout life to see if drug abuse would occur. The reviewers concluded that there was no evidence for a type of personality disorder that inevitably led to drug abuse, rather than some other behavioral abnormality such as delinquency or violence[46].

Social and Cultural Factors

There are theorists who emphasize the role of social and cultural factors in the occurrence of drug abuse. They note the "100 centuries of romance with psychoactive substances"[79], culturally determined definitions of what is a drug, what is drug use, and what is drug abuse[22] and societal differences in the encouragement and discouragement of specific drugs and specific patterns of drug consumption[17,44,59,70,83]. One author who emphasized social and cultural factors stressed that "compulsive chemical use was no less subject to self-control and cognitive and social influences than was any other strongly felt urge"[55].

Learning

Theorists who emphasize the role of learning in the development of abusive patterns of drug use stress the stimulus properties of drugs, especially their ability to act as discriminative and reinforcing stimuli[2,12,16,76]. Chapter 12 reveals the importance of theoretical consideration of the positive and negative reinforcement provided by drugs necessary for the effective use of pharmacological aids to reduction or cessation of drug use. Learning theorists differ from personality theorists in that learning theory implies that there is a mechanism which could, when appropriately engaged, result in drug abuse in anyone, rather than just in "addiction prone" individuals[28,72,73]. For example, there is a phenomenon, discovered during studies of the effect of reinforcement schedules upon animals, that has proven important to learning theorists of drug abuse. Studies were conducted in which animals were forced to wait for long intervals before performance of the desired behavior would be reinforced (for instance, a bar press by a rat was reinforced only if there had been a 60-second delay since the last bar press). This resulted in the animals engaging in remarkably high levels of experimentally unnecessary behaviors while the animal waited. These interim activities were referred to as "schedule-induced" or "adjunctive behavior"[19,20]. Research results have since indicated that people forced to wait a long time between reinforcing activities may also engage in a variety of excessive "adjunctive behaviors," including the consumption of drugs[58]. This finding may have relevance to the phenomenon of drug abuse. For example, people who experience long delays between reinforcement, including sports figures or students given occasional exams, may engage in adjunctive behaviors leading to "persistent and problematic excesses, including drug abuse"[21].

Neurobiology

Many theorists focus on neurobiology and the pharmacology of the drug to explain the phenomenon of drug abuse[27,42]. Theorists who emphasize pharmacology are likely to emphasize the existence of receptors in the central nervous system for exogenous drugs[1] and the search for the physical mechanisms underlying the reinforcement provided by drugs[18,45]. This type of theorizing has led to the idea that drugs are rewarding because they stimulate neurons that usually inform the central nervous system of the performance of behaviors that lead to the obtainment of natural rewards such as food, sex, and warmth[7,38,68,80,81]. The emphasis upon neurobiology is different from personality theories, but similar to learning theories, in that the neurobiological approach emphasizes that all individuals who share a common nervous system share a common susceptibility to drug abuse.

Combined Approaches

While the various theories have so far been presented in isolation, it must be noted that most theorists hold that the complexity of the phenomenon requires that personality, social and cultural factors, learning, and neurobiology all be taken into account when explaining drug use and abuse. Personality theorists recognize the importance of social and cultural factors. For example, two personality theorists acknowledged that "it is likely…that a person who compulsively uses drugs in one society would not do so in another" and conceded that "it is more likely that there are several ways to arrive at…compulsive drug use"[46]. Behavioral theorists recognize the importance of neurobiology as a powerful influence upon the stimulus properties that people learn drugs possess[5,69]. A social theorist recognized the importance of what he called the biological tradition for his social approach to drug abuse and argued that early aspects of drug use are influenced by social forces while more intensive involvement most likely involves neurobiological phenomena[53]. Two biological theorists recognized that people with depression may be influenced by factors discovered by learning theorists as the depressed individual learns that the pharmacological effects of cocaine suppress their symptoms[25]. Similarly, others with a neurobiological view are likely to appreciate the importance of learning theory[38,80,81] and those with a behavioral view are likely to appreciate the importance of understanding neurobiology[67,76].

The most ambitious attempt to synthesize all the various approaches was represented in a book which advanced what the authors referred to as the "biopsychosocial theory of substance abuse"[24]. This theory emphasizes analysis of how the various factors make their relative contributions to the use and abuse of different drugs by different people under different schedules of reinforcement at different times and in different cultures. This synthesizing approach may one day enable the development of a single grand theory that explains all the diverse phenomena associated with drug use and abuse.

Summary of Theories of Motivation for Drug Use

A number of factors have hampered the search for a theory or theories about drug use and abuse. The intense emotion aroused by the issue has resulted in an underemphasis upon questions about presently legal drugs, insufficient concern about differential factors influencing drug use versus drug abuse, and inadequate investigation of variations in motivation at different ages under different circumstances. Theories of drug abuse are in a preparadigmatic stage, where there is little agreement about the nature of the problem and even less agreement about any explanation of the problem. Theories of drug use and abuse may be classified as placing an emphasis upon (a) the personality of the user, (b) social and cultural factors, (c) basic learning processes, (d) neurobiology, or (e) combinations of the previous four. These categories are not mutually exclusive, and it is perhaps the synthesis of all the above approaches that will one day provide a single grand theory that can explain all the various aspects of drug use and abuse.

No matter what the theory of drug use and abuse, theorists tend to agree that their own motivation for even bothering to theorize is the negative consequences that can arise from the acute or chronic effects of the drugs[37]. Even those who emphasize the role of social and cultural factors to the point of denying the importance of pharmacology in determining the consequences of drug ingestion are unlikely to deny that there are particular dangers arising from human intake of behaviorally active drugs.

PRIMARY DANGERS OF ACUTE USE

Drug Interactions.

As discussed in Chapter 4, the consequences of drug interaction can range from uncomfortable to lethal[50]. Individuals contemplating the use of any psychoactive drug should be concerned about the possibility of interaction with other substances. The list of other substances that need to be checked include medicines of all sorts, legal and illegal recreational drugs, foods, and environmental substances[60].

Behavioral Toxicity

A second primary danger of acute use of any abusable drug is **behavioral toxicity**. This is an indulgence in behavior so remarkably careless and stupid that self-injury occurs. Drugs may be consumed in order to achieve reinforcing effects, but they also have profound effects upon other aspects of behavior and emotion. Someone feeling euphoric and powerful may act on the mistaken assumption that they possess some unusual powers or cannot be harmed. Someone feeling suspicious and paranoid may act on these feelings, engaging in behavior ranging from self-induced isolation to armed search for imagined tormentors. Like most drug effects, the occurrence of behavioral toxicity is dose-dependent. That is, while behavioral toxicity can occur at even low doses, it is more frequent and more extreme at high doses[9,31].

Organ Toxicity

Behavioral toxicity might be explainable as the result of a toxic effect on the organs most responsible for behavior, especially the brain. However, acute intake can also lead to damage to the liver, kidneys, lungs, heart, and any other organs of the body. Toxic effects on bodily organs may wear off once the drug is metabolized and excreted. Unfortunately, toxic effects may also be permanent[26]. They may occasionally be lethal[37].

Overdose

The fourth danger of acute use of abusable drugs is **overdose**. Consumers of legal drugs may take an overdose because they forget how much they have consumed or they have been encouraged by ignorant peers to prove their capacity for excessive use. Consumers of illicit drugs can be influenced by both of these factors. In addition, consumers of illicit drugs may overdose because they are nearly always unaware of the dose or purity of what they are consuming[30]. Finally, overdose may occur because of a drug interaction that enhances the effect of the drug, shifting the dose response curve to the left.

No matter what the reason for overdose, the consequences are usually devastating. Both behavioral and organ toxicity are likely to occur[54]. Drug overdose is a medical emergency that requires immediate intervention, including an analysis of bodily fluids to insure correct identification of all drugs consumed[35]. There is no drug that does not have overdose at the far right of the dose-response curve. Even excessive water intake can be lethal[74]. Thus, the question "Can acute use of this drug reach overdose?" must always be answered affirmatively. However, the more important question is, How large (or small) is the gap between recreational dose and lethal overdose? Each psychopharmacotherapeutic has a unique therapeutic window that expresses the range between its therapeutic dose and toxic dose. Discussions of abusable drugs should include information that enables calculation of a **recreational window**, the range between the usual recreational dose and toxic dose.

Summary of Primary Dangers of Acute Use

The primary dangers of acute drug use include the possibility of drug interactions, behavioral toxicity, organ toxicity, and overdose. While focus on drug interactions most often involves a concern only with other "drugs," foods and environmental contaminants may also interact with ingested compounds. Behavioral and organ toxicity are both dose-dependent phenomena whose consequences can range from trivial to lethal. Overdose, at the far right of the dose-response curve of any drug, is a medical emergency. Different drugs have different size recreational windows, defined as the range between the recreational dose and the dose which results in toxicity.

PRIMARY DANGERS OF CHRONIC USE

Tolerance and Sensitization

As discussed in Chapter 5, chronic intake of any drug is likely to result in different degrees of tolerance and sensitization to various aspects of the drug effect. The attempts of the body to maintain homeostasis in the face of chronic drug ingestion means that the question "Does chronic consumption of this drug lead to tolerance and/or sensitization?" must always be answered affirmatively. However, the more important question is, "Which responses to the drug are shifted to the right on dose-response curves, and which are shifted to the left?" Once answered, this question must be followed with, "How rapid are these shifts? and What user-controlled factors influence these shifts?"

Chronic consumption of an abusable drug may lead to tolerance to the reinforcing effect of the drug. This might, but need not inevitably, result in an increase in dose in an attempt to once again achieve the reinforcing effect (see Chapter 5). If an individual chooses to take an increased dose, he or she is more likely to experience troublesome side effects and toxicities. This is especially likely if tolerance develops more slowly to these drug effects than to the target effect of reinforcement. If chronic consumption leads instead or also to sensitization, dangerous and potentially lethal side effects may occur with previously safe doses. In the most dangerous circumstances, the combined effects of tolerance and sensitization can lead to a progressive closing of the recreational window.

Finally, cross-tolerances and cross-sensitizations may occur. Those who chronically consume abusable drugs may find that cross-tolerances render other drugs, whether taken recreationally or as medicine, completely ineffective. They may also find that cross-sensitizations have converted previously safe compounds into inducers of behavioral and organic toxicities.

Compulsive Use and Physical Dependency

Learning and neurobiological theorists of drug use and abuse demonstrated that all drugs that are taken recreationally are by definition reinforcing, and might, but need not inevitably, lead to compulsive use[80]. Therefore, the question "Can this recreational drug lead to compulsive use?" must always be answered affirmatively. It is a grievous error to assume that only illegal drugs can cause compulsive use, especially in the context of a society with alcoholics, three-pack-a-day cigarette smokers and those who drink 10 or more cups of strong coffee every day.

Some, but by no means all, drugs used recreationally can result in a physical dependency. Despite the assertions of those who emphasize social and cultural factors[55], it is legitimate to ask, "Is this recreational drug capable of causing a physical dependency?" It is, however, important to avoid using evidence of compulsive use as "evidence" for physical dependency. It is also important not to assume that only illegal drugs can cause physical dependency[55]. Finally, as noted above, people can stop and have stopped, taking psychopharmacotherapeutics to which they are physically dependent. Similarly, people can stop and have stopped, taking abusable drugs to which they are physically dependent. However, some people find drug cessation to be incredibly difficult and require the support of psychological and perhaps pharmacological aids (see Chapter 12).

Brain and Other Organ Damage

Since acute administration can cause toxic effects upon the brain and other bodily organs, it is no surprise that chronic consumption also can result in damage to bodily organs, including the brain[38,48]. Sometimes, the chronic damage is the predictable summation of a series of acute damages. At other times, chronic damage arises from a series of **subclinical insults**. Subclinical insults are acute toxicities that are not noticeable at the time of acute intake. However, they may accumulate over time, until they appear as consequences of chronic drug use[4].

Statements that a drug causes "brain damage" must be carefully evaluated. Remember that "correlation doesn't equal causation." Is it possible that the differences between the brains of drug users and of "normal subjects" existed before drug use? Are these physical differences perhaps the result of pharmacological treatments for drug use? Are these physical differences the result of head injuries resulting from falling down during intoxicated states[32]? Can observed physical differences fully account for behavioral differences? Do physical differences in the absence of behavioral differences mean that the damage is irrelevant, or is the damage merely subclinical at present[11]? Could behavioral differences be a result of intoxication from the last dose of a lipid soluble drug with a long half-life and active metabolites?

Violence and/or Psychosis

Like other questions about abusable drugs, the question "Does this drug cause violence?" is difficult to answer. If the question is, "Will this drug inevitably lead even the most mild-mannered person to commit unprovoked acts of violence?" then it must be answered in the negative. A negative answer must be given because the influences of set and setting make it impossible to assert that a particular psychological effect of chronic drug use is *inevitable*[22,83]. However, it is legitimate to ask, "Are people under the influence of this drug more likely to commit violence than when they are not under the influence?" This question removes the problem of inevitability. The question also acknowledges that you have to take into account the **baseline**, or pre-drug, level of violence.

Trying to determine whether a drug causes people to act violently is difficult because most information is obtained from retrospective studies. Press reports of violent behavior by people who chronically consume a drug cannot be used as evidence that the drug causes violence. It may be that these people are violent even without the drug in their system. Perhaps they take the drug because it removes inhibitions and enables them to express their violent feelings. On the other hand, controlled experiments may be difficult to conduct in an ethical manner. It may be that violent behavior can only be induced by doses that are sufficient to cause organ damage or other behavioral toxicities.

Even more difficult to determine is the question of whether a drug can make people "crazy"[3,6,29]. First, people are notoriously imprecise in their use of the term "crazy." If the question is, "Can this drug cause people to act in a bizarre way, or to experience unusual emotions?"; then it must be answered affirmatively. All abusable drugs can induce unusual emotions and, sometimes, behaviors. If the question is, "Can acute doses of this drug cause behavioral toxicities?"; the answer must also be affirmative. Any substance, including water, might induce behavioral toxicities, especially when taken at high doses that cause damage to bodily organs including the brain[74].

The real question about drug-induced psychosis should be, "Can chronic consumption of recreational doses of this drug lead to an **insidious** and long-lasting behavioral disorder?" An insidious disorder is one that is at first imperceptible and then develops gradually. An abrupt onset of a drug-induced behavioral disorder probably reflects acute intoxication and/or behavioral toxicity. A short-term psychosis may reflect a prolonged intoxication, rather than a brain altered by chronic drug consumption.

Abrupt onset and/or short-term psychosis are serious problems worthy of great concern. These conditions may lead to self-injury or violent behavior. However, there is no consequence of chronic drug use, other than death, that concerns the drug user and the general public more than the possibility of drug-induced psychosis. Psychopharmacologists would do well to ponder the design of ethical and methodologically sound experiments that could determine the influences of drug, dose of drug, frequency, intermittency, set and setting on the probability of drug-induced psychosis.

Summary of Primary Dangers of Chronic Use

The primary dangers of chronic use include tolerance/sensitization, compulsive use and physical dependency, brain and other organ damage, and violence and/or psychosis. It is important to determine the direction, degree, and rate at which chronic drug use causes different aspects of the drug's effects to shift on dose-response curves. Compulsive drug use may, but need not inevitably, arise from chronic use of any abusable drug. However, there are only some compounds whose chronic use presents a risk of physical dependency. Brain and other organ damage may arise as the result of the cumulative effects of a series of subclinical insults. Special care must be taken when evaluating statements that chronic consumption of a drug caused brain or other organ damage, since alternative explanations of the damage may be available. Similarly, assertions that a drug can cause violence and/or psychosis must be carefully evaluated, since the determinants of these behaviors are varied and complex, and experiments involving drug-induced violence and/or psychosis are fraught with ethical difficulties.

CHAPTER SUMMARY

Theories of drug use and abuse are in a preparadigmatic stage, but may be classified as placing an emphasis upon (a) the personality of the user, (b) social and cultural factors, (c) basic learning processes, (d) neurobiology, or (e) combinations of these four. The primary dangers of acute drug use include the possibility of drug interactions, behavioral toxicity, organ toxicity, and overdose. The primary dangers of chronic use include tolerance/sensitization, compulsive use, physical dependency, brain and other organ damage, violence and psychosis.

REVIEW ESSAY QUESTIONS

1. List and discuss the theoretical importance of Siegel's five degrees of involvement with recreational drugs.

2. What problems make it difficult for scientists to develop a comprehensive theory of drug use and abuse?

3. What are the similarities and differences between the learning and neurobiological theories of drug abuse? Can the two be reconciled, or will they always be in opposition to each other?

4. What four items constitute the primary dangers of acute abusable drug use?

5. What are the primary dangers of chronic use of abusable drugs?

REFERENCES

1. Barbaccia, M.L., Costa, E. and Guidotti, A. Endogenous ligands for high-affinity recognition sites of psychotropic drugs. *Annual Review of Pharmacology and Toxicology*, 1988, 28, 451-476.
2. Barrett, J.E., & Witkin, J.M. The role of behavioral and pharmacological history in determining the effects of abused drugs. In S.R. Goldberg, & I.P. Stolerman (Eds.) *Behavioral analysis of drug dependence*, Orlando, FL: Academic Press, 1986.
3. Baruk, C.E. Early experiments leading to the chemical concept of psychosis. In M. Rinkel, & H.C.B. Denber (Eds.) *Chemical concepts of psychosis*, London: Peter Owen Limited, 1958.
4. *Becker, J.T., & Kaplan, R.F. Neurophysiological and neuropsychological concomitants of brain dysfunction in alcoholics. In R.E. Meyer (Ed.) *Psychopathology and addictive disorders*. New York: Guilford Press, 1986.

5. *Bejerot, N. Addiction: Clinical and theoretical considerations. In J. Engel, L. Oreland, D.H. Ingvar, B. Pernow, S. Roessner, & L.A. Pellborn (Eds.) *Brain reward systems and abuse*, New York: Raven Press, 1987.

6. Bowers, M.B. The role of drugs in the production of schizophreniform psychoses and related disorders. In H.Y. Meltzer, *Psychopharmacology: The third generation of progress*, New York: Raven Press, 1987.

7. Bozarth, M.A. Ventral tegmental reward system. In J. Engel, L. Oreland, D.H. Ingvar, B. Pernow, S. Roessner, & L.A. Pellborn (Eds.) *Brain reward systems and abuse*, New York: Raven Press, 1987.

8. Brady, J.V. Common mechanisms in substance abuse. In T. Thompson, & C.E. Johanson (Eds.) *Behavioral pharmacology of human drug dependence. (NIDA Research Monograph 37)*. Rockville, MD: U.S. Department of Health and Human Services, 1981.

9. Burns, R.S., & Lerner, S.E. Perspectives: Acute phencyclidine intoxication. *Clinical Toxicology*, 1976, 9, 477-501.

10. Cadoret, R., Troughton, E., O'Borman, T., & Heywood, E. An adoption study of genetic and environmental factors in drug abuse. *Archives of General Psychiatry*, 1986, 43, 1131-1136.

11. *Chein, I., Gerard, D.L., Lee, R.S., & Rosenfeld, E. *The road to H*. New York: Basic Books, 1964.

12. Childress, A.R., McLellan, A.T., & O'Brien, C.P. Role of conditioning factors in the development of drug dependence. In S.M. Mirin (Ed.) *Substance abuse*, Philadelphia: W.B. Saunders Co., 1986.

13. *Cipra, B.A. Neurotoxicity creates regulatory dilemma. *Science*, 1989, 243, 29-31.

14. Cocores, J.A., Patel, M.D., Gold, M.S., & Pottash, A.C. Cocaine abuse, attention deficit disorder and bipolar disorder. *The Journal of Nervous and Mental Disease*, 1987, 175, 431-432.

15. Cohen, M., & Klein, D. Drug abuse in a young psychiatric population. *American Journal of Orthopsychiatry*, 1970, 40, 448-455.

16. Colpaert, F.C. Drug discrimination: Behavioral, pharmacological and molecular mechanisms of discriminative drug effects. In S.R. Goldberg & I.P. Stolerman (Eds.) *Behavioral analysis of drug dependence*, Orlando, FL: Academic Press, 1986.

17. DeRios, M.D., & Smith, D.E. Drug use and abuse in cross-cultural perspective. In J.E. Mezzich & C.E. Berganza (Eds.) *Culture and psychopathology*, New York: Columbia University Press, 1984.

18. Engel, J., Oreland, L., Ingvar, D.H., Pernow, B., Roessner, S., & Pellborn, L.A. *Brain reward systems and abuse*. New York: Raven Press, 1987.

19. Falk, J.L. Conditions producing psychogenic polydipsia in animals. *Annals of the New York Academy of Sciences*, 1969, 157, 569-593.

20. Falk, J.L. The nature and determinants of adjunctive behavior. In R.M. Gilbert & J.D. Keehn (Eds.) *Schedule effects: Drugs, drinking and aggression*, Toronto, Canada: University of Toronto Press, 1972.

21. Falk, J.L. The place of adjunctive behavior in drug abuse research. In T. Thompson & C.E. Johanson (Eds.) *Behavioral pharmacology of human drug dependence. (NIDA Research Monograph 37)*. Rockville, MD: U.S. Department of Health and Human Services, 1981.

22. Falk, J.L., & Feingold, D.A. Environmental and cultural factors in the behavioral actions of drugs. In H.Y. Meltzer, *Psychopharmacology: The third generation of progress*, New York: Raven Press, 1987.

23. Freud, S. *Three essays on the theory of sexuality (Standard ed., Vol. 7)*. London: Hogarth Press, 1953.

24. *Galizio, M., & Maisto, S.A. *Determinants of substance abuse: Biological, psychological and environmental factors*. New York: Plenum Press, 1985.

25. Gawin, F.H., & Kleber, H.D. Abstinence symptomatology and psychiatric diagnosis in cocaine abusers. *Archives of General Psychiatry*, 1986, 43, 107-113.

26. Goldstein, D.B. Effect of alcohol on cellular membranes. *Annals of Emergency Medicine*, 1986, 15, 1013-1018.

27. Goldstein, A. *Molecular and cellular aspects of the drug addictions*. Berlin: Springer-Verlag, 1989.

28. Henningfield, J.E., Lukas, S.E., & Bigelow, G.E. Human studies of drugs as reinforcers. In S.R. Goldberg & I.P. Stolerman (Eds.) *Behavioral analysis of drug dependence*. Orlando, FL: Academic Press, 1986.

29. Hollister, L.E. Psychotomimetic drugs in man. In L.L. Iversen, S.D. Iversen, & S. H. Snyder (Eds.) *Handbook of psychopharmacology (Vol. 11)*. New York: Plenum Press, 1978.

30. Insley, B.M., Grufferman, S., & Ayliffe, H.E. Thallium poisoning in cocaine abusers. *American Journal of Emergency Medicine*, 1988, 4, 545-548.

31. Jehle, D., & Cottington, E. Effect of alcohol consumption on outcome of pedestrian victims. *Annals of Emergency Medicine*, 1988, 17, 953-956.

32. Jones, R.T. Clinical and behavioral considerations in emission tomography study design. In S. I. Szara (Ed.) *Neurobiology of behavioral control in drug abuse. (NIDA Research Monograph 74)*. Rockville, MD: U.S. Department of Health and Human Services, 1986.

33. Kandel, D.B., & Faust, R. Sequence and changes in patterns of adolescent drug use. *Archives of General Psychiatry*, 1975, 32, 929-932.

34. Kandel, D.B., & Raveis, V.H. Cessation of illicit drug use in young adulthood. *Archives of General Psychiatry*. 1989, 143, 109-116.

35. Kellerman, A.L., Fihn, S.D., LoGerfo, J.P., & Copass, M.K. Impact of drug screening in suspected overdose. *Annals of Emergency Medicine*, 1987, 16, 1206-1216.

36. *Khantzian, E.J. The self-medication hypothesis of addictive disorders; Focus on heroin and cocaine dependence. *American Journal of Psychiatry*, 1985, 142, 1259-1264.

37. Klaasen, C.D. Principles of toxicology. In A.G. Gilman, L.S. Goodman, T.W. Rall, & F. Murad (Eds.) *The pharmacological basis of therapeutics (7th ed.)*, New York: Macmillan Publishing Co., 1985.

38. Koob, G.F., Vaccarino, F., Amalric, M., & Bloom, F.E. Positive reinforcement properties of drugs: Search for neural substrates. In J. Engel, L. Oreland, D.H. Ingvar, B. Pernow, S. Roessner, & L.A. Pellborn (Eds.) *Brain reward systems and abuse*, New York: Raven Press, 1987.

39. *Kornbluth, A.B. Multiple drug abuse involving nonopiate, nonalcoholic substances: II. Physical damage, long-term psychological effects and treatment approaches and success. *The International Journal of the Addictions*, 1981, 16, 527-540.

40. Kosten, T.R., & Rounsaville, B.J. Psychopathology in opioid addicts. In S.M. Mirin (Ed.) *Substance abuse*, Philadelphia: W.B. Saunders Co., 1986.

41. Kuhn, T.S. *The structure of scientific revolutions (2nd ed.)*. Chicago: University of Chicago Press, 1970.

42. Lader, M. *The psychopharmacology of addiction*. Oxford, England: Oxford University Press, 1988.

43. *Lettieri, D.J., Sayers, M., & Pearson, H.W. (Eds.) *Theories on drug abuse*. Rockville, MD: National Institute on Drug Abuse, 1980.

44. Levinson, P.K. An analysis of commonalities in substance abuse and habitual behavior. In T. Thompson & C.E. Johanson (Eds.) *Behavioral pharmacology of human drug dependence (NIDA Research Monograph 37)*, Rockville MD: U.S. Department of Health and Human Services, 1981.

45. Liebman, J.M., & Cooper, S.J. *The neuropharmacological basis of reward*. Oxford, England: Clarendon Press, 1989.

46. Long, J.V.F., & Scherl, D.J. Developmental antecedents of compulsive drug use: A report on the literature. *Journal of Psychoactive Drugs*, 1984, 16, 169-182.

47. *Meyer, R.E. Who can say no to illicit drug use? *Archives of General Psychiatry*, 1989, 46, 189-190.

48. Miller, L. Neuropsychological assessment of substance abusers: Review and recommendations. *Journal of Substance Abuse Treatment*, 1985, 2, 5-17.

49. Mirin, S.M., & Weiss, R.D. Affective illness in substance abusers. In S.M. Mirin (Ed.) *Substance abuse*, Philadelphia: W.B. Saunders Co., 1986.

50. Murad, F., & Gilman, A.G. Drug interactions. In A.G. Gilman, L.S. Goodman, T.W. Rall, & F. Murad (Eds.) *The pharmacological basis of therapeutics (7th ed.)*. New York: Macmillan, 1985.

51. Nathan, P.E. The addictive personality is the behavior of the addict. *Journal of Counseling and Clinical Psychology*, 1988, 56, 183-188.

52. Newman, R.G. The need to redefine "addiction." *New England Journal of Medicine*, 1983, 308, 1096-1098.

53. Orford, J. Psychopharmacology and social psychology: Complementary or contradictory. In M. Lader (Ed.) *The psychopharmacology of addiction*, Oxford, England: Oxford University Press, 1988.

54. Osborn, H. Medical management of toxic overdosage of behavior-modifying drugs. In F. Flach (Ed.) *Psychobiology and psychopharmacology*, New York: W.W. Norton, 1988.

55. *Peele, S. *The meaning of addiction*. Lexington, MA: Lexington Books, 1985.

56. *Plant, M. Let's come out of the closet. *British Journal of Addiction*, 1986, 81, 447-449.

57. *President's Commission on Organized Crime. *America's habit: Drug abuse, drug trafficking and organized crime*. Washington, D.C.: U.S. Government Printing Office, 1986.

58. Sanger, D.J. Drug taking as adjunctive behavior. In S.R. Goldberg & I.P. Stolerman (Eds.) *Behavioral analysis of drug dependence*, Orlando, FL: Academic Press, 1986.

59. *Satinder, K.P. *Drug use: Criminal, sick or cultural?* Roslyn Heights, NY: Libra Publishers, 1980.

60. Schaffer, C.B., Donlon, P.T., Schaffer, L.C. Drug combinations and interactions. In J.P. Tupin, R.I. Shader, & D.S. Harnett (Eds.) *Handbook of clinical psychopharmacology (2nd ed.).* Northvale, NJ: Jason Aronson, Inc., 1988.

61. *Schneider, J.W. Deviant drinking as disease: Alcoholism as a social accomplishment. In M.E. Kelleher, B.K. MacMurray, & T.M. Shapiro (Eds.) *Drugs and society: A critical reader,* Dubuque, IA: Kendall/Hunt, 1983.

62. Schuman, M., Gitlin, M.J., & Fairbanks, L. Sweets, chocolates, and atypical depressive traits. *Journal of Nervous and Mental Disease,* 1987, 175, 491-495.

63. Searles, J.S. The role of genetics in the pathogenesis of alcoholism. *Journal of Abnormal Psychology,* 1988, 97, 153-167.

64. *Shaffer, H. *Myths and realities: A book about drug issue.* Boston: Zucker, 1977.

65. Siegel, R.K. Changing patterns of cocaine use: Longitudinal observations, consequences, and treatment. In J. Grabowski (Ed.) *Cocaine: Pharmacology, effects and treatment of abuse. (NIDA Research Monograph 50).* Rockville, MD: U.S. Department of Health and Human Services, 1984.

66. Smart, R.G., & Fejer, D. Drug use among adolescents and their parents. *Journal of Abnormal Psychology,* 1972, 79, 153-160.

67. Spealman, R.D., & Goldberg, S.R. Drug self-administration by laboratory animals: Control by schedules of reinforcement. *Annual Review of Pharmacology and Toxicology,* 1978, 18, 313-319.

68. Stein, L., & Belluzzi, J.D. Reward transmitters and drugs of abuse. In J. Engel, L. Oreland, D.H. Ingvar, B. Pernow, S. Roessner, & L.A. Pellborn (Eds.) *Brain reward systems and abuse,* New York: Raven Press, 1987.

69. Stolerman, I.P., & Goldberg, S.R. Introduction: Brief history and scope of behavioral approaches to dependence. In S.R. Goldberg & I.P. Stolerman (Eds.) *Behavioral analysis of drug dependence,* Orlando, FL: Academic Press, 1986.

70. *Szasz, T.S. *Ceremonial chemistry: The ritual persecution of drugs, addicts, and pushers (Rev.Ed.).* Holmes Beach, FL: Learning Publications, 1985.

71. Tarter, R.E. Are there inherited behavioral traits that predispose to substance abuse? *Journal of Counseling and Clinical Psychology,* 1988, 56, 189-196.

72. Thompson, T. Behavioral mechanisms and loci of drug dependence: An overview. In T. Thompson & C.E. Johanson (Eds.) *Behavioral pharmacology of human drug dependence (NIDA Research Monograph 37),* Rockville, MD: U.S. Department of Health and Human Services, 1981.

73. Thompson, T., & Johanson, C.E. *Behavioral pharmacology of human drug dependence. (NIDA Research Monograph 37).* Rockville, MD: U.S. Department of Health and Human Services, 1981.

74. Viewig, W.V.R., David, J.J., Rowe, W.T., Wampler, G.J., Burns, W.J., & Spradlin, W.W. Death from self-induced water intoxication among patients with schizophrenic disorders. *Journal of Nervous and Mental Disease,* 1985, 173, 161-165.

75. Warburton, D.M. The puzzle of nicotine use. In M. Lader (Ed.) *The psychopharmacology of addiction,* Oxford, England: Oxford University Press, 1988.

76. Weiner, H. Contributions of reinforcement schedule histories to our understanding of drug effects in human subjects. In T. Thompson & C.E. Johanson (Eds.) *Behavioral pharmacology of human drug dependence (NIDA Research Monograph 37),* Rockville, MD: U.S. Department of Health and Human Services, 1981.

77. Weiss, K.J., & Greenfield, D.P. In S.M. Mirin (Ed.) *Substance abuse,* Philadelphia, PA: W.B. Saunders Co., 1986.

78. Weissman, M. Anxiety and alcoholism. *Journal of Clinical Psychiatry,* 1988, 49, 117-119.

79. *Westermeyer, J. The pursuit of intoxication: Our 100 century-old romance with psychoactive substances. *American Journal of Drug and Alcohol Abuse,* 1988, 14, 175-187.

80. Wise, R.A. The neurobiology of craving: Implications for the understanding and treatment of addiction. *Journal of Abnormal Psychology,* 1988, 97, 118-132.

81. Wise, R.A. The brain and reward. In J.M. Liebman & S.J. Cooper (Eds.) *The neuropharmacological basis of reward,* Oxford, England: Clarendon Press, 1989.

82. Woody, G.E., McLellan, T., O'Brien, C.P., & Luborsky, L. Personality factors in methadone self-administration by heroin addicts. In T. Thompson & C.E. Johanson (Eds.) *Behavioral pharmacology of human*

drug dependence (NIDA Research Monograph 37). Rockville, MD: U.S. Department of Health and Human Services, 1981.

83. *Zinberg, N.E. *Drug, set and setting: The basis for controlled intoxicant use*. New Haven: Yale University Press, 1984.

84. Zuckerman, M. Biological connection between sensation seeking and drug abuse. In J. Engel, L. Oreland, D.H. Ingvar, B. Pernow, S. Roessner, & L.A. Pellborn (Eds.) *Brain reward systems and abuse*, New York: Raven Press, 1987.

*Introductory or intermediate reading

Chapter 14

RESEARCH METHODOLOGY
AND A SYSTEM
OF CATEGORIZATION

The purposes of this chapter are to:

1. Introduce the advantages and disadvantages of retrospective and prospective studies of drug use and abuse,

2. Briefly describe and criticize drug categorizations based on legal status, and

3. Present a system of categorization that emphasizes the full dose-response curve of abusable drugs and creates categories for stimulants, depressants, hallucinogens, and phencyclinoids.

RESEARCH METHODOLOGY

The study of the effects of abusable drugs in humans is burdened by a host of problems in ethics and experimental design. There are two general types of studies that may be conducted, namely, **retrospective studies** and **prospective studies**. Retrospective studies involve a "looking backward" at people who have been consuming drugs. Prospective studies involve giving drugs to people under controlled experimental conditions and then studying the consequences. Both of these techniques have advantages and disadvantages.

Retrospective Studies

There are literally millions of users of most abusable drugs, legal and illegal. Why not, the question is asked, simply study these people to determine the short-term and long-term consequences of the use of the full range of abusable drugs? Retrospective studies can be placed into three categories: (1) case histories and case series, (2) analyses of trends, and (3) case-control and case cohort studies[42].

Case histories and case series. In case histories, there is a report that a person with a history of a certain kind of drug use showed up at a physician's office or emergency setting with a certain medical problem. Case series are single reports that tell the related stories of a number of case histories, where subjects have either the same drug use history or the same problem. In the simplest instance of analysis of trends, there is a retrospective look at the changes over time in the incidence of a particular type of drug use and the changes over time in the incidence in a particular type of medical problem. In case cohort studies, people with and people without a particular drug use history are compared to see the relative incidence of the development of the medical problem. On the other hand, in case-control studies, people with and people without a medical problem are compared in a search for similar drug use histories.

Case studies tell nothing about whether or not drug use actually was responsible for the observed physical disorder. That is, it may be impossible to tell if the drug effect will always occur whenever anybody uses the drug in the same manner as described in the case history, since the patient in the report may have been part of a subpopulation that was uniquely susceptible to the disorder. In addition, it is inappropriate to rely on the accuracy of the patient's report of the presumably precipitating drug use. Users of either legal or illegal drugs may underreport their use, out of embarrassment at having acted in a potentially self-destructive way[3] or because they are unable to accurately recall the frequency, intermittency, and length of their drug use. In addition, users of illegal drugs are unlikely to know the actual dose and purity of the drugs they obtained from street dealers, and they may use or abuse a number of different drugs[36].

Analysis of trends. Analysis of trends can be used to disprove a causal relationship when the incidence of drug use does not correlate with the incidence of a particular medical problem. For instance, the idea that "lookalike" stimulants caused certain negative consequences because they contained amphetamine was discounted when a study revealed that the percentages of problems increased over time even as the content of amphetamine in the preparations decreased[30]. However, it is impossible for an analysis of trends to prove that it was the drug use, and not some other unstudied variable, that was responsible for the medical problem. Simply put, **correlation does not equal causation.** The numbers of drowning and amount of ice cream eaten on any particular summer day are highly correlated. This does not prove that eating ice cream causes drowning any more than it proves that drowning causes the eating of ice cream. Similarly, no matter how many times a researcher documents that when drug use goes up, the incidence of a problem goes up and vice versa, it can never be asserted with any certainty that there is not some other variable (poor nutrition, maternal drug use, cultural factors, a different drug, etc.) that is responsible for each of them going up together, and coming down together. For example, analysis of trends revealed that moderate alcohol use was associated with a lowered rate of heart disease and sudden death[20]. Mere retrospective analysis of trends, however, cannot reveal whether alcohol actually protects from heart disease, or if instead relaxed, compared to tense, individuals are more likely to have less heart disease and are more likely to allow themselves recreational alcohol intoxication.

Although they can't establish causality, analyses of trends can make use of a number of well established data systems. Four particular data systems are of great importance to retrospective studies of drug use and abuse[21]. The Annual High School Senior Survey has employed standardized procedures to measure the drug use patterns of between 16,000 and 18,000 high school seniors in every year since 1975. The National Household Survey on Drug Abuse has been run every two or three years since 1971 and has asked detailed questions about the drug use of all household members aged 12 and over. The Drug Abuse Warning Network (DAWN) collects data on characteristics of drug-related emergency room visits. Finally, the Client Oriented Data Acquisition Process (CODAP) collects data on the characteristics of physician treatment of any drug-related problem. Cautions about the use of survey data in drug abuse research have been expressed[4]. However, techniques have been developed that can be used to assess the usefulness of survey data[3].

Case control and case cohort studies. The final forms of retrospective study, case-control and case cohort studies, allow for greater control over the determination of causal relationships between drug use and medical problems. Subjects in experimental and control groups can be selected and matched to insure similarities in education, economic background, and other demographic characteristics. While it may be difficult to find a group of subjects who used only one drug and not others[36], it is possible to also match subjects for the use of other drugs. The importance of using control groups was revealed in a "cohort" study of daily marijuana use among adults[16]. The vast amount of data collected about the psychological and physical experiences of these daily marijuana users was impossible to accurately interpret, since there was no control group to reveal the incidence of similar problems in individuals who abstain from all drugs and/or daily consumed some drug other than marijuana. On the other hand, a different study was able to provide evidence for a genetic component to the development of alcoholism by the use of a true cohort design. This study revealed that a greater number of sons of alcoholics, as compared to a matched control group consisting of sons of nonalcoholics, developed problems with alcohol abuse[38].

Pharmacoepidemiology

All of these retrospective techniques have been developed from the techniques used in **epidemiology**, the study of the incidence and causes of the spread of diseases. The use of these techniques to study drug effects is referred to as **pharmacoepidemiology**[42].

While the individual shortcoming of each technique is discussed briefly above, it is important to point out a major problem with the use of pharmacoepidemiology. As noted in earlier chapters, reasonable people disagree whether behavioral disorders, particularly drug use and abuse, are the actual result of a disease. While it may be argued that pharmacoepidemiology studies drug use and abuse only *as if* it were a disease, it is easy for this use of metaphor to be seen by some as proof that drug use is, in fact, a disease. For example, two pharmacoepidemiologists acknowledged that critics had a point in insisting that since drug abuse was a self-imposed condition, it was outside the area of concern of epidemiologists, who were after all trained to study infectious diseases. These researchers provided an adequate rebuttal to this by pointing out that "drug abusers demonstrate patterns of behavior that can be measured, incidence curves that can be drawn, rates of prevalence that can be computed, attack rates can be calculated, risk factors can be identified, etiologies and consequences can be determined, and prevention programs can be implemented"[21]. Unfortunately, the authors go beyond this use of epidemiological technique when they approvingly quote a different author who "made a strong case that heroin addiction was a communicable disease in the classical sense, with the drug itself being the infectious agent, the host and reservoir being man, and the drug-using peer as the vector"[21]. This represents an example of how the appropriate application of technique can lead to an inappropriate confusion of metaphor and reality.

Even when the temptation to equate the use of epidemiological techniques with proof that drug use is a disease is resisted, the advantages of retrospective techniques must be viewed within the context of their disadvantages. None of the techniques will be of much use if a drug is rarely used or if the consequence of the drug use is extremely rare[42].

Prospective Studies

Since each of the techniques of retrospective study has major problems, researchers in the field of drug use and abuse have turned to the use of the same techniques as have been employed by psychiatric researchers to study the effects of psychopharmacotherapeutics (see Chapter 6). It has been noted that "experimental laboratory studies provide the most scientifically rigorous context in which to study human drug self-administration"[17]. Well-designed studies of the effects of drugs on human volunteers must have random assignment of subjects to control and experimental groups, blind designs, and accurate measurement and analysis of data[6].

Ethics. The ethical problems associated with prospective studies of drug use and abuse are, if anything, more complex than those associated with the study of psychopharmacotherapeutics. One researcher noted that his early work involving the administration of marijuana to volunteers was criticized on the grounds that he may have been exposing his subjects to the dangers of low-dose marijuana use[52]. Obviously, even greater ethical concern must be directed toward studies that aim to determine the effects on humans of high or chronic doses of potentially harmful drugs. However, there are ethical problems in *not* doing research on the effects of high or chronic doses of drugs[31], including a failure to identify "side effects" that may prove useful for the pharmacological treatment of other behavioral disorders.

One ethicist has suggested that subjects in experiments with abusable drugs should always be allowed to grant their informed consent to the experiment. If the dangers and potential benefits of the experiment are clearly explained to the individual, it was argued, then any negative consequences would not be unethical injury by the researcher, but the result of the informed decision of the research subject[49]. Furthermore, the ethical problems of experimentation can be somewhat decreased by having a trained team of physicians, skilled in drug abuse emergencies, as part of the experimental team. Of course, experiments are designed to find out new facts. Even experienced physicians may be unable to deal with newly discovered negative consequences arising from experiments involving acute, or especially chronic, administration of new drugs.

Methods of administration. There are two basic ways that the effects of abusable drugs can be studied prospectively in humans. The drugs can be given to the subject at times and doses determined by the experimenter, or the subject may be allowed to **self-administer** the drug within the constraints of the experimental design. Experimenter-controlled drug administrations have been found to be useful for studies of human abilities in drug discrimination[10] and the effects of classical conditioning on opiate withdrawal[32]. In addition, administration of fixed doses at fixed times has enabled determination of the effects of different routes of administration[46] and the distribution, metabolism and elimination of low, medium, and high doses of the same drug[5]. Finally, evaluation of the subjective effects of experimenter-controlled drug administrations can enable evaluations of whether specific doses (usually "recommended doses") of a drug are found reinforcing by humans[29].

The fact that animals will self-administer many, but not all, of the drugs abused by humans outside the laboratory[51] has led to evaluations of the self-administration of drugs by humans in the laboratory. Studies of "recommended doses" ignores the possibility that a drug may be reinforcing at doses well above the "recommended dose"[27]. Perhaps the earliest study of human self-administration was conducted in 1952, when a person with a history of morphine dependence was studied as he was given access to needles, syringes, and a variety of drugs[48]. Although there were early critics of the use of human subjects in behavioral research[41], this work was continued by researchers who investigated alcohol self-administration in chronic alcoholics[26]. By the early 1980s, the National Institute on Drug Abuse published a monograph that revealed the sound design and innovative techniques that had been used during the past decade and a half in studying human self-administration of abusable drugs[44]. A review of the field a few years later noted approvingly that studies had been conducted with self-administration involving oral, intravenous, and inhalation routes, in settings ranging from test chambers to home environments, and with behavioral designs involving positive reinforcement, negative reinforcement, and a variety of responses[17]. In addition, the review noted, subjects have sometimes been allowed to self-administer the drug only at certain times; at other times have been given continuous access; and in some circumstances must choose between two different drugs or different doses of the same drug. Finally, self-administration studies have also been used to evaluate the physical consequences (heart rate, blood pressure, brain electrical activity, etc.) of reinforcing self-administrations of drugs[13,14].

Selection of subjects.   Three types of subjects could be used for self-administration experiments: drug-naive subjects, drug-experienced subjects, or drug-dependent
subjects[17]. Chapter 4 revealed that every single administration of a psychoactive drug
may have profound effects on the same or other psychoactive drugs taken later. The best
subjects would therefore appear to be those who have never taken any psychoactive drug.
Where are people who have never tasted even alcohol, soft-drinks, or chocolate to be
found? How likely is it that such a drug-free person would be willing to take powerful
and potentially dangerous psychoactive drugs in the laboratory? And how meaningful
will the results of such experiments be to the general population that so frequently
consumes legal and illegal drugs? If drug-experienced subjects are used, then decisions
must be made about the allowance of which drugs, what degree of involvement, and over
what period of time[36]. Finally, the use of drug-dependent subjects presents great ethical
difficulties and also insures that results may not be applicable to a member of a general
population who has not yet developed a physical dependency. Since each class of subjects
will present particular disadvantages, the best knowledge of drug self-administration is
acquired by a comprehensive analysis of data obtained from all three types of subjects.

Summary of Research Methodology

The effects of abusable drugs can be evaluated with either retrospective or
prospective studies. Each type of study has particular advantages and disadvantages.
Some retrospective techniques make it difficult to establish causality, but they all take
advantage of the existence of individuals from the general population who have used, or
are using, abusable drugs. Prospective studies allow a much greater degree of control
over the variables likely to influence a drug response. Drug administration can be
controlled either by the experimenter or by the subject. Well designed prospective studies
involving a variety of types of subjects can provide information about causal relationships
between drug intake and specific physical and psychological effects. Ethical concerns
about prospective studies require the use of subjects who provide informed consent.

CATEGORIES OF DRUGS

There are a wide variety of naturally occurring and synthetic compounds that can
influence behavior. It would be difficult to talk about "animals" without making distinctions between mammals and insects, or even poodles and St. Bernards, and it would be
equally difficult to talk about "drugs" without making some distinctions among them.
The organization of this book is itself a testimony to the need for categorization of
psychopharmacological agents. That is, behaviorally active drugs have been split into
two general categories: psychopharmacotherapeutics and abusable drugs. Within each of
these classes, there remains a great diversity of drugs. However, there are ways to
highlight similarities without losing track of significant differences.
        The way that drugs are categorized has a profound effect upon which differences
and similarities are stressed and which are ignored. This section will examine two ways
in which drugs can be categorized. One emphasizes the present legal status of a drug,

and uses that legal status in an attempt to gain scientific understanding[35]. The second method categorizes drugs based on the full dose-response curve for that drug. Each of these methods of categorization has advantages and presents some problems.

Categorization by Legal Status

A simplistic distinction between psychopharmacotherapeutics and abusable drugs will quickly prove inadequate. Psychopharmacotherapeutics are drugs that are legally restricted so they may be prescribed only by physicians, dispensed only by pharmacists, and possessed only by patients. Anything else, this simple logic decides, is an abusable recreational drug. Unfortunately, this doesn't take into account the diversity of legal categories that exist. Nor does it take into account the fact that some psychopharmacotherapeutics, specifically MAOIs, antianxiety agents, methylphenidate, and many of the drugs used to treat drug abuse, can be taken for the specific purpose of getting pleasurable, reinforcing drug actions[11].

Categorization by legal status involves more than a simple division into "either medicine or illegal drug." The legal status of any particular drug is very much dependent upon time and place[2,50]. In addition, there are a variety of ways, short of a complete prohibition of manufacture, sale, and possession, in which a society can express its disapproval of self-administration of abusable drugs. Some drugs (such as caffeine-containing products) may not be regulated at all, others may be available over the counter (**OTC**), and still others may be available only to people above a certain age. Compounds placed into the OTC and age-based regulated categories, for example, are recognized as compounds about which rational adults can make informed decisions. Although different societies ban different drugs[43], nearly every society holds that there are certain drugs that are so seductive and dangerous that even rational adults must be protected from their perceived allure. In the U.S., for example, certain substances are placed within the Federal Schedule of Controlled Substances[12]. Illicit possession of a controlled substance may, depending upon the society, be punished by a fine, or a prison term, or by physical violence up to and including a death sentence.

The legal status of drugs is the result of **proscriptive** laws that detail what is permissible and what is not. Confusion arises when these proscriptive laws are mistaken for **descriptive laws**, descriptions of a set of facts regarding drugs. It has been noted that "drug policy has been very uninformed by medical knowledge and has been very much motored by a prosecutorial perspective"[37]. The history of placing drugs into the most restricted legal categories is replete with hysterical exaggerations and outright distortions of the known facts[7,8,9,15]. There are thus some aspects of the drug laws that are glaringly inconsistent with what is known of psychopharmacology. For example, in the U.S., cocaine is erroneously classified as a Schedule II narcotic rather than a Schedule II non-narcotic drug[39]. In addition, marijuana is classified as a Schedule I drug, one without any medical benefit, even though it is, in fact, known to have a wide variety of medicinal uses[18,25] (see Chapter 17).

It has been noted that "the question of what…society is willing to pay for the regulation of the use of any intoxicant must be raised and answered" and that part of the answer was that "regulations that attempt to limit risks have their own social costs"[52]. There are a variety of costs that are of great importance to students of behaviorally active drugs. The first cost of prohibition of certain compounds is that those with the least sanctions are likely to be viewed by the public as "safe." This erroneous conclusion arises despite the importance of such pharmacological variables as dose, method of administration, set and setting and the host of other variables that influence the nature and intensity of a drug effect[9] (see Chapter 4). In a discussion of attempts at control of the abuse of alcohol, a researcher noted that "it is evident that when a drug is popular and is defended by powerful vested interests the health lobby is a relatively weak force"[34]. A second cost of drug regulations is that a moderate, and even abusive, user of presently illicit compounds must fear being forced to choose "either to be branded as a criminal or to submit to 'treatment'", a process which "ties the therapeutic process to criminal justice (and) has bastardized and denigrated a significant aspect of the mental health system"[52]. A third cost of regulation is that legitimate concern about the negative physical and psychological consequences of the use of behaviorally active compounds may express itself through epidemiological metaphors ("drug plague") and militaristic terminology. There have been a number of calls for a "War on Drugs" since the first announcement by Richard Nixon on June 17, 1971[19]. Inappropriate use of such metaphors and terminology can lead to a trampling of civil rights[2]. For example, the American Management Association expressed concern about the inappropriate use of urine testing for drug use[1]. Significantly, there have been calls in the U.S. to use the military for domestic enforcement of drug laws[22] and the U.S. government has frequently used its own military to destroy fields of marijuana and cocaine in foreign countries[28]. Finally, society in general pays a price for the treatment of individuals who consume drugs that are not under government regulation regarding purity, truth in advertising, etc., and for the violent black market that surrounds the trade in illegal drugs.

Perhaps the most destructive aspect of the call for a "War on Drugs" is the tendency to view the scientific pronouncements of those with an alternative viewpoint as a "surrender" to nefarious evil[19]. Those who research and theorize about the effects of drugs may feel pressured to distort their findings in order to satisfy political leaders who insist on a unitary viewpoint[40]. In the context of a discussion of the relative dangers of licit versus illicit drugs, one writer felt it necessary to encourage his colleagues in Great Britain to "be forthright in drawing attention to the real world implications of the evidence before their own eyes"[34]. When Norman Zinberg performed his early studies on the effects of marijuana, he was warned by a senior partner in the law firm representing Harvard Medical School that if his research should find out marijuana was not harmful "our findings could be morally damaging because they would remove the barrier of fear that deterred drug use." Dr. Zinberg noted also that "those presenting the information that not all drug use is misuse, thus contravening formal social policy, run the...risk that their work will be interpreted and publicized as condoning use"[52]. It must be pointed out, however, that even the context of a "War on Drugs" has not prevented the expression of unconventional views regarding drug use and abuse[2,33,43,45,47,50,52].

Categorization Based on Full Dose-Response Curves

When full dose-response curves are done for all psychoactive compounds, similar curves are obtained for compounds cutting across legal categories. If legal status is ignored, a number of large charts can be generated, each with full dose-response curves for those drugs that have similar effects at each of their own low, medium, and high doses. Differences in potency may result in one drug being to the left or right of some other drug on the chart. However, when one chart is compared to another the differences in potency within the chart should pale in comparison to the differences between the charts. Between-chart comparisons will reveal differences in efficacy.

Within-category differences. There are a number of reasons why two drugs within the same category might appear to be wildly different. Differences in the basic pharmacology of two abusable drugs might result in one being rapidly absorbed when taken orally and being metabolized to an active metabolite while the other drug undergoes first-pass metabolism to an inactive metabolite and is therefore only effective when injected. Different drugs within the same class can exert their similar effects despite interaction with different neurotransmitter and neuromodulator systems in diverse parts of the nervous system. These differences in basic pharmacology and site and mechanism of action can lead to widely disparate side effects, symptoms, treatment of overdose, chronic effects, and drug interactions. A thorough knowledge of any category of abusable drugs requires an understanding of these important differences as well as a firm grasp of why they must nonetheless be categorized together. A focus upon the entire range of doses at which drugs can affect behavior avoids confusing differences in efficacy with differences in potency.

Categories discovered and defined. Use of full dose-response curves results in a system of categorization of abusable drugs that involves division into **stimulants** (Chapter 15), **depressants** (Chapter 16), and **hallucinogens** (Chapter 17). The category of stimulants includes, but is not limited to, methylphenidate, caffeine, other methyl xanthines, nicotine, amphetamine, cocaine, strychnine, and some industrial and household products. Stimulants are drugs that induce wakefulness, increased attention, increased heart rate, and elevated blood pressure at low doses. At medium doses, stimulants cause insomnia, anxiety, repetitive motor movements (**stereotypies**), fever, tremor, and dangerous elevation of blood pressure and heart rate. At high doses, they cause paranoia, confusion, convulsions, stroke, high fever, heart attack, and death.

The category of depressants includes alcohol, tranquilizers, antihistamines, some household and industrial products, and opioid drugs like heroin, morphine, and codeine. Depressants are drugs that decrease inhibitions and motor coordination at low doses. At medium doses, depressants cause sleepiness, great loss of coordination, a depression of breathing rate, and loss of pain sensations. At high doses, they cause anesthesia, failure to breathe, coma, convulsions, and death.

The category of hallucinogens includes marijuana, LSD, psilocybin, Jimpson weed, DMT, and a host of other compounds. Hallucinogens are drugs that have, at low doses, relatively limited physical effects and cause slight distortions of perception. At medium doses, they can cause hallucinations and delusions and may stimulate the sympathetic nervous system. At high doses, they cause a loss of contact with reality, profound hallucinations and delusions, and perhaps sympathetic nervous system overstimulation. Figure 14.1 (A, B, and C) provides three charts that present the dose-response curves for a typical drug from the psychopharmacological classes of stimulants, depressants, and hallucinogens, respectively.

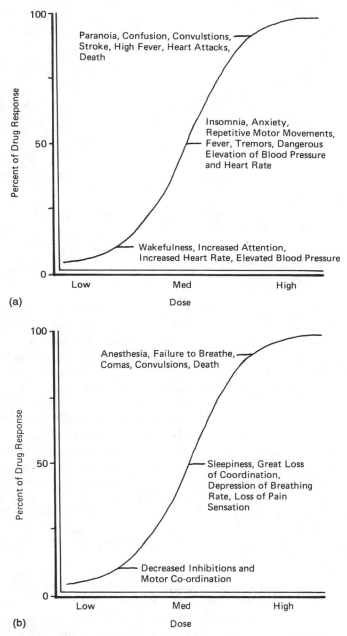

(a)

(b)

Figure 14.1 A, B, and C. Full dose-response curves for stimulants, depressants, and hallucinogens, respectively.

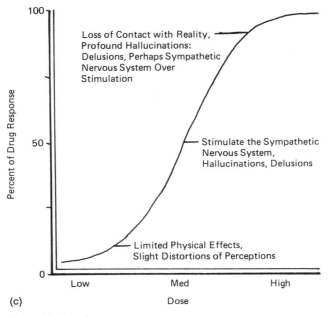

(c)

Figure 14.1 (cont.)

Synthetic drugs. While the three-part system may have been adequate previously, technology has led to the development of synthetic drugs that are abused for recreational purposes and yet will not fit into the stimulant-depressant-hallucinogen system. Full dose-response curves for phencyclidine (PCP, angeldust) reveal that the drug is similar to a hallucinogen at low, medium, and high doses. In addition, though, the drug also has powerful stimulant effects at low and medium doses and remarkable depressant effects at medium and high doses[24]. Attempts to employ full dose-response curves to categorize PCP as a stimulant, depressant, or hallucinogen will be stymied by the unique overlap of drug effects over the full range of behaviorally active doses. Thus, the unique psychopharmacology of PCP makes it necessary to create another category for the system of abusable drug classification. The great number of synthetic compounds that are chemically and behaviorally similar to PCP are called **phencyclinoids**[23], just as drugs that are chemically similar to opium are frequently referred to as opioids. Chapter 18 will discuss the details of this fourth category of abusable drugs. In the future, it may be necessary to create even more categories as technological advances result in the creation of new drugs that similarly defy categorization into a simple stimulant-depressant-hallucinogen system[31].

Summary of Categorization of Drugs

This book itself is a testimony to the usefulness of categorizing drugs, in that it is divided into one section that deals with psychopharmacotherapeutics and another that deals with abusable drugs. However, any method of categorization presents difficulties. Categorizing drugs by legal status can lead to confusion between descriptive and proscriptive laws. Legal categorization of drugs can lead to overestimations of the safety of legal drugs, a confusion of treatment and punishment, inappropriate use of epidemiological and military metaphors, suppression of science, and the creation of a black market. By focusing on the full dose-response curves of drugs, differences in efficacy and potency will be clarified. Abusable drugs can be divided into three general categories: stimulants, depressants, and hallucinogens. The creation of "designer drugs" requires the creation of another category, the phencyclinoids, and may one day require the creation of even more categories.

CHAPTER SUMMARY

The physical and psychological consequences of acute and chronic drug use can be investigated with either retrospective or prospective studies. Each of these presents certain advantages, yet each suffers from specific disadvantages. Categorization of exogenous compounds is necessary yet difficult. Categorization by legal status leads to a host of difficulties. On the other hand, employing full dose-response curves enables the creation of useful categories and allows for the development of new categories to keep up with technological advances in drug design.

REVIEW ESSAY QUESTIONS

1. In what different ways can retrospective studies of abusable drug use be conducted, and what are the advantages and disadvantages of each?

2. What are the ethical problems, design difficulties, and practical advantages of prospective human self-administration studies?

3. Why it is important to categorize psychoactive drugs in general and abusable drugs in particular?

4. Can the proscriptive laws of the legal system aid the development or understanding of the descriptive laws of psychopharmacology? Give specific examples to support your answer.

5. Describe how full dose-response curves can be used to develop a system of categorization for abusable drugs. What are the similarities and differences in the effects of low, medium, and high doses of a stimulant versus a depressant versus a hallucinogen?

REFERENCES

1. *American Management Association. *Drug abuse: The workplace issues: An executive summary.* New York: American Management Association, 1987.

2. *Bakalar, J.B., & Grinspoon, L. *Drug control in a free society.* Cambridge, England: Cambridge U. Press, 1984.

3. Barnea, Z., Rahav, G., & Teichman, M. The reliability and consistency of self-reports on substance use in a longitudinal study. *British Journal of Addiction*, 1987, 82, 891-898.

4. *Barnes, D.M. Drugs: Running the numbers. *Science*, 1988, 240, 1729-1731.

5. Barnett, G., Hawks, R., & Resnick, R. Cocaine pharmacokinetics in humans. *Journal of Ethnopharmacology*, 1981, 3, 353-366.

6. Bigelow, G.E., Griffiths, R.R., Liebson, I.A., & Kaliszak, J.E. Double-blind evaluation of reinforcing and anorectic actions of weight control medications. *Archives of General Psychiatry*, 1980, 37, 1118-1123.

7. *Bonnie, R.J., & Whitebread, C.H. *The marihuana conviction: A history of marihuana prohibition in the United States.* Charlottesville, VA: University Press of Virginia, 1974.

8. *Brecher, E.M. Drug laws and drug law enforcement: A review and evaluation based on 111 years of experience. In B. Segal (Ed.) *Perspectives on drug use in the United States*, New York: Haworth Press, 1986.

9. *Byck, R. Cocaine use and research: Three histories. In S. Fisher, A. Raskin, & E.H. Uhlenhuth (Eds.) *Cocaine: Clinical and biobehavioral aspects.* New York: Oxford University Press, 1987.

10. Colpaert, F.C. Drug discrimination: Behavioral, pharmacological, and molecular mechanisms of discriminative drug effects. In S.R. Goldberg & I.P. Stolerman (Eds.) *Behavioral analysis of drug dependence*, Orlando, FL: Academic Press, 1986.

11. Council on Scientific Affairs. Drug abuse related to prescribing practices. *Journal of the American Medical Association*, 1982, 247, 864-866.

12. Drug Enforcement Administration. *Physicians manual: An informational outline of the Controlled Substances Act of 1970.* Washington, D.C.: DEA, Department of Justice, 1985.

13. Fischman, M.W. Behavioral pharmacology of cocaine. *Journal of Clinical Psychiatry*, 1988, 49, 7-10.

14. Fischman, M.W., Schuster, C.R., & Resnekov, L. Cardiovascular and subjective effects of intravenous cocaine administration in humans. *Archives of General Psychiatry*, 1976, 33, 983-989.

15. *Helmer, J. Blacks and cocaine. In M.E. Kelleher, B.K. MacMurray, & T.M. Shapiro (Eds.) *Drugs and society: A critical reader.* Dubuque, IA: Kendall/Hunt Publishing Co., 1983.

16. *Hendin, H., Haas, A.P., Singer, P., Ellner, M., & Ulman, R. *Living high: Daily marijuana use among adults.* New York: Human Sciences Press, 1987.

17. Heningfield, J.E., Lukas, S.E., & Bigelow, G.E. Human studies of drugs as reinforcers. In S.R. Goldberg & I.P. Stolerman (Eds.) *Behavioral analysis of drug dependence*, Orlando, FL: Academic Press, 1986.

18. Hollister, L.E. Health aspects of Cannabis. *Psychopharmacological Review*, 1986, 38, 1-22.

19. *Jaffe, J.H. Footnotes in the evolution of the American national response: Some little known aspects of the first American Strategy for Drug Abuse and Drug Traffic Prevention. The Inaugural Thomas Okey Memorial Lecture. *British Journal of Addiction*, 1987, 82, 587-600.

20. Klatsky, A.L., Friedman, G.D., & Siegelaub, A.B. Alcohol use, myocardial infarction, sudden cardiac death and hypertension. *Alcoholism in Clinical and Experimental Research*, 1979, 3, 33-39.

21. Kozel, N.J., & Adams, E.H. Epidemiology of drug abuse: An overview. *Science*, 1986, 234, 970-974.

22. *Marshall, E. A war on drugs with real troops? *Science*, 1988, 241, 13-15.

23. Mattia, A., Leccese, A.P., Marquis, K.L., El-Fakahany, E.E., & Moreton, J.E. Electroencephalographic (EEG), psychopharmacological, and receptor-binding profiles of "phencyclinoids". In D.H. Clouet (Ed.) *Phencyclidine: An update (NIDA Research Monograph 64).* Rockville, MD: U.S. Department of Health and Human Services, 1986.

24. McCarron, M.M. Phencyclidine intoxication. In D.H. Clouet (Ed.) *Phencyclidine: An update (NIDA Research Monograph 64).* Rockville, MD: U.S. Department of Health and Human Services, 1986.

25. Mechoulam, R. *Cannabinoids as therapeutic agents.* Boca Raton, FL: CRC Press, 1986.

26. Mendelson, J.H., & Mello, N.K. Experimental analysis of drinking behavior of chronic alcoholics. *Annals of the New York Academy of Science*, 1966, 133, 828.

27. Miller, L.G. Phenylpropanolamine: A controversy unresolved. *Journal of Clinical Psychopharmacology*, 1989, 9, 1-3.

28. *Morales, E. *Cocaine: White gold rush in Peru.* Tucson, AZ: U. of Arizona Press, 1989.

29. Morgan, J.P., Funderburk, F.R., Blackburn, G.L., & Noble, R. A subjective profile of phenylpropanolamine: Absence of stimulant or euphorigenic effects at recommended dose levels. *Journal of Clinical Psychopharmacology*, 1989, 9, 33-38.

30. Morgan, J.P., Wesson, D.R., Puder, K.S., & Smith, D.E. Duplicitous drugs: The history and recent status of look-alike drugs. *Journal of Psychoactive Drugs*, 1987, 19, 21-31.

31. *Nichols, D.E. Discovery of psychoactive drugs: Has it ended? *Journal of Psychoactive Drugs*, 1987, 19, 33-37.

32. O'Brien, C.P., Ehrman, R.N., & Ternes, J.W. Classical conditioning in human opioid dependence. In S.R. Goldberg & I.P. Stolerman (Eds.) *Behavioral analysis of drug dependence*, Orlando, FL: Academic Press, 1986.

33. *Peele, S. *The meaning of addiction: Compulsive experience and its interpretation.* Lexington MA: Lexington, Books, 1985.

34. *Plant, M. Let's come out of the closet. *British Journal of Addiction*, 1986, 81, 447-449.

35. *President's Commission on Organized Crime. *America's habit: Drug abuse, drug trafficking and organized crime.* Washington, D.C.: U.S. Government Printing Office, 1986.

36. Rainone, G.A., Deren, S., Kleinman, P.H., & Wish, E.D. Heavy marijuana users not in treatment: The continuing search for the "pure" marijuana user. *Journal of Psychoactive Drugs*, 1987, 19, 353-359.

37. *Richards, D.A.J. Symposium proceedings: Roundtable discussion of "The War on Drugs: In Search of a Breakthrough". *Nova Law Review*, 1987, 11, 939-1024.

38. Schuckit, M.A. Studies of populations at high risk for alcoholism. *Psychiatric Development*, 1985, 3, 31-63.

39. Schultz, C.B. Statutory classification of cocaine as a narcotic: An illogical anachronism. *American Journal of Law and Medicine*, 1983, 9, 225-245.

40. *Shaffer, H. Academic freedom and the development of science. *Psychology of Addictive Behaviors*, 1987, 1, 62-69.

41. Sidman, M. *Tactics of scientific research.* New York: Basic Books, 1960.

42. Strom, B.L. The promise of pharmacoepidemiology. *Annual Review of Pharmacology and Toxicology*, 1987, 27, 71-86.

43. *Szasz, T.S. *Ceremonial chemistry: The ritual persecution of drugs, addicts, and pushers (Rev.ed.).* Holmes Beach, FL: Learning Publications, 1985.

44. Thompson, T., & Johanson, C.E. *Behavioral pharmacology of human drug dependence: (NIDA Research Monograph 37).* Rockville, MD: Dept. of Health and Human Services, 1981.

45. *Trebach, A.S. *Why we are losing the great drug war: And radical proposals that could make America safe again.* New York: Macmillan, New York, 1987.

46. Van Dyke, C., Jatlow, P., & Ungerer, J. Oral cocaine: Plasma concentrations and central effects. *Science*, 1978, 200, 211-213.

47. *Weil, A., & Rosen, W. *Chocolate to morphine: Understanding mind-active drugs.* Boston: Houghton, Mifflin 1986.

48. Wikler, A. A psychodynamic study of a patient during self-regulated readdiction to morphine. *Psychiatric Quarterly*, 1952, 26, 270-293.

49. Wikler, D. The central ethical problem in human experimentation and three solutions. *Clinical Research*, 1978, 26, 380-383.

50. *Wisotsky, S. *Breaking the impasse in the war on drugs.* New York: Greenwood Press, 1986.

51. Woods, J.H. Some thoughts on the relations between animal and human drug-taking. *Progress in Neuropsychopharmacology and Biological Psychiatry*, 1983, 7, 577-584.

52. *Zinberg, N.E. *Drug, set and setting: The basis for controlled intoxicant use.* New Haven: Yale University Press, 1984.

*Introductory or intermediate reading

Chapter 15

STIMULANTS

The purposes of this chapter are to:

1. Identify the commonalities of and discover the differences between the wide variety of stimulant drugs,

2. Compare the basic pharmacology, and sites and mechanisms of action, of a few representative stimulant drugs, including cocaine, caffeine, nicotine, and strychnine,

3. Present the acute pharmacological and behavioral side effects of low and medium doses of representative stimulant drugs, with a special emphasis on within-class differences,

4. Reveal commonalities in stimulant overdose, with a special emphasis on selected within-class differences in the nature and treatment of overdose, and

5. Discuss the pharmacological and behavioral effects of chronic stimulant use, including drug interactions, brain and other organ damage, tolerance and sensitization, cross-tolerance and cross-sensitization, physical dependency, compulsive use, and stimulant-induced violence and/or psychosis.

COMMONALITIES AND DIFFERENCES

Partial List of Stimulants

Table 15.1 presents a partial list of the more common compounds, both licit and illicit, that are considered to be stimulant drugs. The term "stimulant" describes those behaviorally active drugs with a certain pattern of effects at low, medium, and high doses.

There are differences in physical characteristics that provide each drug with some unique behavioral and pharmacological effects.

The Full Dose-Response Curve Revisited

For the purpose of categorizing abusable drugs, it is appropriate to, at least initially, stress the similarities that separate stimulants from other drugs. Particularly important are these three facts: (1) people consume these drugs because they enjoy the increased alertness, decreased fatigue and improved mood induced by low and medium doses[50,51], (2) all stimulants increase temperature, blood pressure and heart rate[6,37], and (3) all these drugs induce a similar pattern of physical and behavioral effects at the far right of their individual dose-response curves[9,39].

Table 15.1
A Partial List of Common Stimulant Drugs

Cocaine   Amphetamine   Methylphenidate   Strychnine

Methyl Xanthines (Caffeine, Theophylline, Theobromine)   Khat

Phenylpropanolamine   Physostigmine   Ephedrine

Time- and Place-Dependent Differences

Once it is clear that all these drugs can be categorized together, it becomes possible to investigate the differences among, rather than the similarities of, the stimulants listed in Table 15.1 It is, however, sometimes difficult to identify true within-class differences that arise because of differences in physical structure, basic pharmacology, and sites and mechanisms of action. This difficulty occurs because some of the easiest to observe differences between stimulants occur because of culturally determined variations in (1) the most commonly used dose of each drug, (2) the most commonly used method of administration, and (3) general cultural acceptability. For example, some writers assert the need to create a special subcategory for "convulsant stimulants"[30]. This category usually includes the drugs strychnine and physostigmine. These drugs are rarely taken by humans for their stimulant effects, but they are frequently used in the laboratory to enable the study of potentially anticonvulsant drugs. They induce convulsions at relatively low doses, especially when compared to a drug like caffeine. However, if strychnine and physostigmine are given at low doses (for those particular drugs), the same gross behavioral and physical effects arising from all other stimulants given at low doses can be observed. Additionally, when any of the other stimulant drugs listed in Table 15.1 are given at what is, for that drug, a high dose, convulsions will occur. It is thus incorrect to categorize only some stimulants as "convulsants."

It is unlikely that anyone other than a scientist more interested in strychnine's chemical structure and/or interaction with endogenous receptors and neurotransmitters would be bothered by the drug's inclusion in Table 15.1. However, the typical coffee or soft drink consumer is often confused, distressed, and annoyed to hear that their preferred, and completely legal, drug belongs in the same psychopharmacological class as the vilified and illegal drug, cocaine. Cocaine, the argument goes, produces a powerful stimulant effect, while coffee is a much more mild stimulant. While cocaine is a more potent stimulant than caffeine, the argument that it is a more powerful stimulant ignores similarities in efficacy. Differences in efficacy are obscured by the fact that, in developed countries, cocaine is usually insufflated, injected, or inhaled in a relatively pure form at high doses. On the other hand, the caffeine in coffee is taken orally at low doses in very dilute form. Understanding true within-class differences requires that scientists ignore apparent within-class differences that arise from culturally determined practices that vary from time to time and from place to place.

True Within-Class Differences

True within-class differences can be discovered by focusing on differences in the physical characteristics of the different compounds. The basic pharmacology of chemicals with different physical characteristics is likely to differ in important ways. Compounds with different physical characteristics are, in addition, almost certain to affect behavior through interaction with different endogenous molecules and receptors, perhaps even in different parts of the nervous system. For example, all stimulants are sometimes referred to as **sympathomimetic**[17,44] in order to emphasize their stimulation of the sympathetic nervous system. However, only some of these drugs directly stimulate the sympathetic nervous system. Others depend upon stimulation of the central nervous system to indirectly stimulate the sympathetic nervous system.

Differences in basic pharmacology and sites and mechanism of action can also lead to variations in potency, the rate and nature of the development of tolerance and/or sensitization, acute side effects, symptoms and treatment of overdoses, potential drug interactions, and the physical effects of chronic use. For example, even though amphetamine and methylphenidate "cause similar behavioral and symptomatic effects" they do so through "distinct mechanisms of potential clinical relevance"[35]. Study of differences in basic pharmacology and the sites and mechanisms of action can enable understanding of the nature and reasons for differences between different stimulant drugs.

Rather than discuss the basic pharmacology, as well as sites and mechanisms of action, of each and every drug listed in Table 15.1, this chapter emphasizes those that best reveal how differences in basic pharmacology and sites and mechanism of action can explain true within-class differences: cocaine, caffeine, nicotine, and strychnine. (Specifics about the stimulant methylphenidate, or Ritalin, can be obtained from Chapter 11.) A thorough study of the similaritins and differences of these four compounds will prepare the more advanced student to independently learn about the remaining stimulants listed in Table 15.1.

Summary of Commonalities and Differences

All the stimulants listed in Table 15.1 have certain commonalities at their individually determined low, medium, and high doses. The low and medium doses provide physical and psychological effects that are reinforcing, there are dose-dependent elevations in temperature, blood pressure and heart rate, and there are common physical and behavioral effects at overdose. Differences in potency are, however, often obscured by culturally determined differences in the usually employed dose, method of administration, etc. There are important within-class differences between the stimulants, each of which can be best understood by first gaining a thorough knowledge of the basic pharmacology of representative stimulant drugs.

BASIC PHARMACOLOGY

Cocaine

Cocaine can be administered by any of the methods discussed in Chapter 3. Cocaine can be taken orally, either by swallowing saliva mixed with chewed leaves of the plant **erythroxylone coca,** or by swallowing a pure form of powdered cocaine. The drug can be inserted anally or vaginally, and can be applied directly to the nasal mucosa (insufflation). It can be dissolved in water or saline and injected under the skin, intramuscularly, or intravenously. Finally, when properly prepared, the drug can be heated and inhaled (as **crack**). Preparation of crack requires converting **cocaine hydro-chloride** (the salt form of the drug) into a **free base**. It is a common misconception to believe that crack cocaine will necessarily be purer than cocaine obtained as a salt. However, many of the adulterants typically found in illicit cocaine will "**base out,**" meaning that these adulterants can also be converted into their base form, thus contaminating the free base cocaine[13].

Cocaine may be rapidly administered via intravenous injection or inhalation. In addition, cocaine is rapidly absorbed when applied to any mucus membrane, including those in the nose, vagina, anus, and gastrointestinal system. After absorption, the drug is then rapidly distributed to all parts of the body, with no significant binding to plasma proteins. The drug easily crosses the blood-brain barrier and the placental barrier[46].

In humans, the drug is metabolized primarily by enzymes in the bloodstream. Metabolites and small amounts of the parent compound are excreted in the urine. The half-life of cocaine in the blood is about one hour. The duration of the desired effects may be as short as a few minutes when the drug is smoked or injected, approximately 20 minutes when insufflated, and perhaps as long as an hour when taken orally. Table 15.2 summarizes the basic pharmacology of cocaine[46].

Table 15.2
The Basic Pharmacology of Cocaine

- Can be taken by any method of administration
- Rapidly absorbed, with rapid onset of drug effects
- Widely distributed
- Easily crosses blood-brain and placental barriers
- Metabolized by enzymes in blood
- Excreted in urine
- Little of parent compound found in urine
- Plasma half-life of about 1 hour
- Duration from a few to 60 minutes, dependent upon method of administration

Caffeine

Caffeine shares a basic pharmacology with a group of drugs called the **methyl xanthines**, which includes **theophylline** (found primarily in tea) and **theobromine** (found primarily in chocolate). All three are products of plants that were originally indigenous to the New World. Caffeine is readily absorbed when taken orally or rectally. Although it is difficult to get caffeine into solution unless it is in a very hot liquid, the drug can, and sometimes is, injected. Of course, the onset of drug action is much faster with injection than when caffeine is taken orally. Once absorbed, the drug is widely distributed, easily crossing the blood-brain and placental barriers. Some binding occurs to plasma protein. Caffeine is metabolized by liver enzymes. These inactive metabolites, and only a small portion of the original drug, are then excreted in the urine. The half-life of caffeine is between three and seven hours. However, the half-life of caffeine is shortened considerably in individuals who consume nicotine. Table 15.3 summarizes the basic pharmacology of caffeine[44].

Table 15.3
The Basic Pharmacology of Caffeine

- Usually taken orally, but can be injected or taken anally
- Widely distributed, with some binding to plasma proteins
- Easily crosses blood-brain and placental barriers
- Metabolized by liver enzymes
- Excreted in urine
- Very little parent compound found in urine
- Plasma half-life of 3 to 7 hours
- Half-life decreased by nicotine

Nicotine

Nicotine is obtained from the plant **nicotiana tabacum**. Like cocaine, nicotine can be taken by almost any method of administration. It can be inhaled, insufflated, absorbed from the anus, vagina, or the **buccal membrane** (between cheek and gum), injected, or taken orally. Nicotine is poorly absorbed from the stomach, due to the presence of strong digestive acids, but is easily absorbed from the small intestines. Thus, oral administration of nicotine is slower than the oral administration of most drugs. Once absorbed, the drug is widely distributed, easily crossing the blood-brain and placental barriers. The majority of the metabolism of nicotine occurs in the liver, but some metabolism occurs in the kidney and, especially if the drug was inhaled, the lungs. The metabolites of nicotine, and up to 20% of the original compound, are excreted in the urine. Significant amounts of nicotine are excreted in breast milk. The half-life of inhaled nicotine is about two hours, but this is shortened in interaction with caffeine. Table 15.4 summarizes the basic pharmacology of nicotine[57].

Table 15.4
The Basic Pharmacology of Nicotine

- Can be taken by any method of administration
- Usually inhaled or absorbed buccally
- Poorly absorbed from the stomach, but absorbed from small intestines
- Widely distributed
- Easily crosses blood-brain and placental barriers
- Metabolized mainly by liver enzymes, but also by enzymes in lung and kidney
- Plasma half-life of about 2 hours
- Half-life decreased by caffeine

Strychnine

Strychnine is obtained from the seeds of the plant **Strychnos nox-vomica**. It can be taken by any method of administration, but is usually taken orally or by injection. It is rapidly absorbed and widely distributed throughout the body. It is metabolized by liver enzymes and excreted mainly in urine. About 20% of the parent compound can be found in the urine. It has such a short plasma half-life that nearly all the parent compound is metabolized or excreted within a 12-hour period. Table 15.5 summarizes the basic pharmacology of strychnine[17].

Table 15.5
The Basic Pharmacology of Strychnine

- Usually taken orally or by injection
- Rapidly absorbed and widely distributed
- Metabolized by liver enzymes
- Excreted in urine
- Twenty percent of parent compound found in urine
- Short plasma half-life

Summary of Basic Pharmacology of Stimulants

All of the stimulant drugs may be administered in a variety of ways, but culturally determined factors have led to differences in the most commonly employed methods of administration. Each of the four drugs is widely distributed throughout the body, with caffeine being the only one that shows any degree of binding to plasma proteins. Caffeine, strychnine, and nicotine are all metabolized by liver enzymes, but nicotine is also metabolized by enzymes in the lung and kidney. Cocaine, on the other hand, is metabolized mainly by enzymes in the blood. All four stimulants have short half-lives, with caffeine having a longer half-life than the remaining three drugs. Strychnine is the only one of the four stimulants that is found to any significant degree as the parent compound in urine.

SITES AND MECHANISMS OF STIMULANT ACTION

Cocaine, caffeine, nicotine, and strychnine are all stimulants despite the fact that they interact with different neurotransmitters in different parts of the central and peripheral nervous system. Future research may reveal that the commonalities between these drugs arise from a common effect on some group of neurotransmitters (probably monoamines like dopamine, norepinephrine, and serotonin) farther "down the line" of divergent neuronal communication. At present, though, more is known about differences in interaction with neurotransmitters and receptors in different parts of the brain and body.

Cocaine

Figure 15.1 shows the synaptic mechanisms of the action of cocaine. The most powerful effect of cocaine is its action as a potent inhibitor of reuptake of monoamine neurotransmitters, especially norepinephrine and dopamine, but including serotonin as well[10]. Cocaine is, therefore, an agonist at monoaminergic synapses. This agonist effect is enhanced by a lesser ability to facilitate release of neurotransmitter and to bind directly

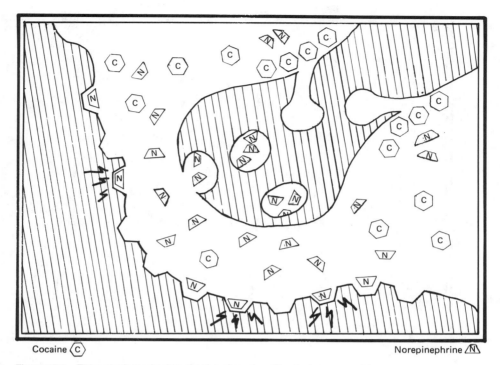

Cocaine Ⓒ   Norepinephrine ⎰N⎱

Figure 15.1. The synaptic mechanism of action of cocaine. Cocaine has an agonist effect because it inhibits the reuptake of norepinephrine. This leads to a larger than normal amount of norepinephrine in the cleft, leading to a larger than normal number of norepinephrine-receptor interactions.

to postsynaptic receptors[40]. Studies using PET provided evidence that these areas of the nervous system are indeed influenced by acute and chronic cocaine administration[4]. In addition to the monoamine agonist action, cocaine is also a local anesthetic. By blocking the action potential at nodes of Ranvier (see Chapter 1), cocaine can prevent the action potential from making its way down to the terminal button. When applied to a neuron connected to, for example, a pain receptor, cocaine prevents the release of neurotransmitter onto the next neuron in the pain pathway.

Caffeine

Figure 15.2 shows the synaptic mechanism of action of caffeine. Recent research suggests that caffeine's stimulant effect occurs because it is a direct antagonist of **adenosine** receptors[5,54]. Adenosine is an inhibitory neurotransmitter, with receptors located on the membranes of diverse neuronal and non-neuronal cells. As explained in Chapter 4, an antagonist of an inhibitory neurotransmitter increases the probability that the postsynaptic neuron will reach threshold and have an action potential. Just as the multiplication of two negative numbers results in a positive number, caffeine's antagonism of the inhibitory effect of adenosine leads to a stimulant effect on the central nervous system.

Caffeine ⟨C⟩   Adenosine ⟨A⟩

Figure 15.2. The synaptic mechanism of action of caffeine. Caffeine has an antagonist effect because it blocks postsynaptic adenosine receptors.

Nicotine

Figure 15.3 shows, in schematic form, the synaptic mechanism of action of nicotine. Nicotine is a direct agonist at many postsynaptic acetylcholine receptors[1,47]. Acetylcholine receptors responsive to nicotine are found in the central nervous system, in the ganglia of both the sympathetic and parasympathetic nervous system, in the target organs reached by the parasympathetic nervous system, and in **striated muscle** (muscle that is predominantly involved in voluntary movement).

Strychnine

Figure 15.4 shows the synaptic mechanism of action for strychnine. Like caffeine, strychnine owes its stimulant effect to a direct antagonist effect at receptors for an inhibitory neurotransmitter. In the case of strychnine, the relevant neurotransmitter is **glycine**[17]. Glycine is an amino acid that is obtained from the breakdown of consumed proteins. Glycine and glycine receptors are found mainly in the spinal cord, but also in

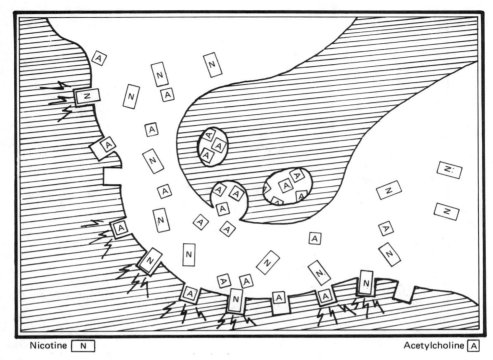

Nicotine [N]   Acetylcholine [A]

Figure 15.3. The synaptic mechanism of action of nicotine. Nicotine has an agonist effect because it acts as a direct agonist that interacts with postsynaptic acetylcholine receptors. Nicotine thus results in the presynaptic acetylcholine neuron having a greater than normal effect on the postsynaptic neuron.

the brainstem and thalamus. However, strychnine apparently has no direct interaction with glycine in the brain. The stimulant action of strychnine is instead due to a removal of the **tonic inhibition** (a steady, long-term, and exquisitely balanced limitation of excitation) normally exerted by spinal cord glycine neurons on the remainder of the central nervous system.

Summary of Sites and Mechanisms of Stimulant Action

Cocaine is a monoaminergic agonist that is particularly effective in inhibiting the reuptake of dopamine, norepinephrine, and serotonin. Cocaine has, in addition, local anesthetic properties. Nicotine is a direct agonist at many postsynaptic acetylcholine receptors. Caffeine is an antagonist at adenosine receptors, and strychnine acts as an antagonist at spinal cord receptors for glycine. The stimulant action of caffeine and strychnine results from the blockade of receptors involved in reduction of nervous system stimulation.

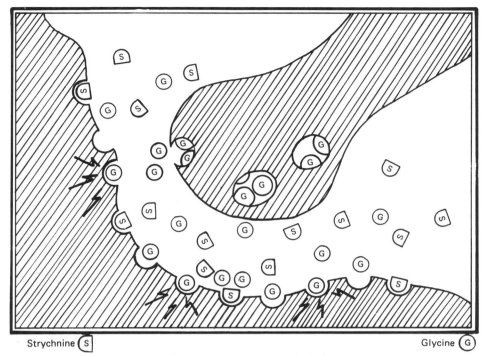

Strychnine Ⓢ   Glycine Ⓖ

Figure 15.4. The synaptic mechanism of action of strychnine. Strychnine has an antagonist effect because it blocks postsynaptic glycine receptors.

ACUTE SIDE EFFECTS AT LOW AND MEDIUM DOSES

While the preceding paragraphs emphasize differences, it is important to stress again that the commonalities of the four drugs justify classifying them together as stimulants. Since they are all members of the same psychopharmacological class, they are likely to share common side effects at their individually defined low and medium doses. That is, low doses of any stimulant will lead to elevated blood pressure and heart rate. At medium doses, they will all cause even greater elevations in blood pressure and heart rate, an onset of fever, tremors and stereotypies, and the occurrence of psychological side effects including insomnia and anxiety. Some of these effects can be explained by the common stimulation of the central nervous system. Since the nervous system is arranged in a hierarchical manner (see Chapter 2), all stimulants are, to a greater or lesser degree, sympathomimetic. That is, central nervous system stimulation leads to enhanced activity in all "lower" parts of the nervous system, especially in the sympathetic nervous system.

Despite these similarities, the common stimulant action of each drug is mediated via unique basic pharmacologies and interactions with different neurotransmitters and receptors in diverse parts of the body. This suggests that any one or more of the four drugs may induce some unique side effects. Study of the nature and mechanism of side effects of these various drugs can enhance the understanding of how interaction with endogenous neurotransmitters and receptors can lead to both common and unique stimulant drug effects.

Cocaine

The side effects of cocaine arise from four sources. These include (1) agonist action leading to central nervous system stimulation, (2) agonist action on organs stimulated by neurons of the sympathetic nervous system, (3) agonist action on receptors on heart muscle, and (4) local anesthetic action, particularly upon heart muscle. The simultaneous effects of these four mechanisms can lead to some confusing, but temporary, decreases in heart rate and blood pressure. However, the balance of the multiple effects of cocaine insures that the predominant effect of increased heart rate and blood pressure can occur even at low doses. This explains the potency of cocaine in inducing negative cardiovascular consequences[32].

Multiple mechanisms can also explain the increases in temperature caused by cocaine. All stimulants have an effect on central heat-regulating centers, and all increase temperature through increasing muscle activity and inducing a centrally mediated constriction of blood vessels resulting in decreased heat loss. Cocaine is a particularly potent inducer of fever because it also acts as an agonist at receptors that cause vasoconstriction, thus enhancing the centrally mediated constriction of blood vessels[46].

Cocaine is unique among the four stimulants being emphasized because it has local anesthetic action[46]. Although this property was discovered early[13] and exploited extensively in medicine, the potency of cocaine in inducing cardiovascular side effects limits the drug's usefulness as a local anesthetic. Nonetheless, cocaine is the only one of the four stimulants being emphasized that will induce numbness when applied to mucosal areas.

Caffeine

The cardiovascular effects of caffeine are most likely due to the generalized disinhibition of the central nervous system that comes from inhibition of adenosine receptors. Centrally mediated release of catecholamine from the adrenal glands and sympathetic nerve endings can explain the effects of caffeine on temperature, heart rate, and blood pressure.

Caffeine is unique among the four stimulants studied in that it causes a relaxation of most smooth muscle. Methyl xanthines related to caffeine are sometimes used in asthmatics, who occasionally need medicine to relax their constricted bronchial tubes[44].

Consumers of caffeine in the form of coffee or soft drinks may notice an increase in urgency and amount of urination. They often incorrectly assume that this can all be explained by noting that they have taken in increased amounts of liquid in order to self-administer their drug. However, caffeine has a powerful **diuretic** effect, meaning that it leads to the loss of even more fluids than were consumed to get the drug[14,55].

Finally, caffeine increases the secretion of a number of glands, especially those in the stomach and small intestines. Caffeine-induced release of stomach acids and digestive enzymes in the absence of food can lead to significant stomach upset[14].

Nicotine

The typical stimulant side effects of nicotine can be explained as the consequences of central nervous system stimulation. However, nicotine also stimulates acetylcholine receptors involved in the activity of both the sympathetic and parasympathetic nervous systems (See Figure 2.1). All autonomic neurons that finally connect with target organs have their own activity controlled by acetylcholine receptors on their dendrites. As a result, nicotine stimulates both branches of the autonomic nervous system. In addition, parasympathetic neurons release acetylcholine onto their target organs. However, nicotine does not act as an agonist at these receptors, since these acetylcholine receptors are instead sensitive to a different agonist called **muscarine**[38].

The sympathetic and parasympathetic branches of the autonomic nervous system interact via reciprocal inhibition, yet both are stimulated by nicotine. The stronger and more prolonged effect of stimulation of the sympathetic branch, combined with direct central actions, results in nicotine-induced increases in blood pressure and heart rate. On the other hand, parasympathetic stimulation can lead to increased bowel muscle tone, and perhaps diarrhea, particularly after medium doses[57].

Finally, while tremor from other stimulants is mediated by central nervous system stimulation, nicotine also induces tremor from direct stimulation of acetylcholine receptors on muscle. This combined effect accounts for the ability of nicotine to induce tremors at remarkably low doses.

Strychnine

All of the central and peripheral effects of strychnine are mediated by disinhibition of the central nervous system. There is no direct effect of the drug on the heart, the gastrointestinal system or skeletal muscle[17].

Summary of Acute Side Effects at Low and Medium Doses

Most of the side effects of all four of the stimulant drugs can be explained as a result of stimulation of the central nervous system. However, there are between-drug differences in the ability to induce certain side effects at low doses and/or the production of unique side effects. Cocaine has multiple actions on heart muscle and is thus able to induce negative cardiovascular effects even at low doses. While all four stimulants increase temperature through central nervous system stimulation, cocaine is a potent inducer of fever because it acts as an agonist at receptors that control vasoconstriction. In addition, cocaine is the only one of the four stimulants that can exert a local anesthetic action. Caffeine is unique in that it is able to relax smooth muscle, directly stimulates secretions in the gastrointestinal system, and has a powerful diuretic effect. Nicotine stimulates the autonomic nervous system directly, as well as indirectly through stimulation of the central nervous system. In addition, nicotine is particularly potent in inducing tremors, because it is a direct agonist for acetylcholine receptors on muscle. All of the effects of strychnine can be attributed directly to its disinhibition of the central nervous system.

OVERDOSE

Among the factors used in classifying drugs is the existence of commonalities at the far right of the dose response curve. Of course, the extreme far right of the dose-response curve of all drugs results in severe toxicities, but the different classes of drugs can be identified by the unique set of circumstances surrounding overdose. With all of the stimulants listed in Table 15.1, overdose results in paranoia, confusion, high fever, strokes, heart palpitations, heart attacks, convulsions, and finally, death. Death usually occurs from heart failure or a halt in breathing following prolonged convulsions[39,41].

It is important to remember that the dose consumed, with its strong influence on final levels of the drug in the blood and central nervous system, is the most relevant factor in overdose. Method of drug administration, on the other hand, influences mainly the rapidity of onset of symptoms of overdose. For instance, there are reported cases of cocaine insufflation leading to such high levels of blood pressure that brain blood vessels burst, leading to stroke[34]. While symptoms take longer to develop, even vaginal application of cocaine can lead to overdose and death[15].

Most of the toxic effects of stimulants are the result of central nervous system overstimulation or centrally-mediated overstimulation of the sympathetic nervous system. Overdose with any stimulant drug is a medical emergency requiring immediate attention. If the drug was taken orally, vomiting can be induced or **gastric lavage** ("stomach pumping") may be used to limit absorption. A thorough knowledge of the chemistry of distribution and excretion can sometimes enable the use of techniques to rapidly eliminate the drug from the body. If an antagonist is available, drug effects can be rapidly halted, as the antagonist successfully competes for occupancy of receptors. Sometimes, however, the only available treatment for overdose is **symptomatic**, where the consequences or symptoms, rather than the causes, of overstimulation is dealt with. The body may be cooled to avoid the consequences of high fever. Antipsychotics may be given to deal with psychological symptoms. Muscle relaxants or anticonvulsants often help reduce the number or intensity of seizures. Certain medicines (such as propranolol, see Chapter 10) can reduce the effects of overdose on heart and blood pressure[45].

Differential Symptoms and Treatment

Despite all these similarities, the differences in basic pharmacology and sites and mechanism of action of cocaine, caffeine, nicotine, and strychnine result in some unique symptoms and treatments of overdose for each of these drugs.

Cocaine. Since cocaine is a monoaminergic agonist, many of the consequences of overdose of the drug can be controlled by administration of antagonists for the monoamines. For example, the antipsychotic drugs, which block dopamine receptors, often control many of the physical as well as psychological effects of cocaine overdose. Since one of the side effects of antipsychotics is the lowering of seizure threshold, some physicians have been reluctant to use them in cocaine overdose[20]. However, more recent data suggests that the overall benefits of antipsychotics more than balance the danger of seizure induction[8].

However, not all of the symptoms of cocaine overdose are due to an agonist action at dopamine synapses. Of particular concern with cocaine is the direct effect of the drug on the heart. At toxic doses, the anesthetic action of the drug may slow or halt heart rate. On the other hand, the anesthetic action may interact with the direct agonist effect on monoaminergic receptors on the heart to cause wildly fluctuating increases and decreases in heart rate. A study of emergency room cases of cocaine overdose revealed that, next to adverse psychological effects, the chief complaint of patients was chest pain, a well-known symptom of impending heart attack[11]. Blockers of beta-adrenergic receptors, like propranolol, are typically used to deal with the rapid heart beat caused by most stimulants. However, these drugs are not recommended for use in cocaine overdose, since receptor blockade may add to the slowing of heart rate caused by the anesthetic action of cocaine[45].

Caffeine. Although coffee and soft-drink consumption is widespread, and overdose is unusual[44], scientists have been aware since the late 1800s of the negative consequences of consumption of large doses of caffeine[48]. Since caffeine is an adenosine antagonist, it might be thought that treatment of overdose would routinely involve the administration of adenosine. However, it is instead much more likely that overdose with caffeine would be treated symptomatically. That is, the consequences of central nervous system overstimulation are dealt with by administering antipsychotics, medicines to affect blood pressure and heart rate, and anticonvulsants.

Nicotine. Overdose with nicotine can be treated symptomatically, although there are some peculiarities that have to be kept in mind. At low and medium doses, sympathetic stimulation predominates and there is an increase in blood pressure. At high doses, parasympathetic stimulation may predominate, leading to a fall in blood pressure. It is therefore very important to carefully monitor the blood pressure of a victim of nicotine overdose, to make sure that drug treatment of overdose symptoms doesn't make matters worse[57].

Of course, many of the symptoms of nicotine overdose can be controlled by administering a drug that antagonizes acetylcholine receptors. Unfortunately, acetylcholine antagonists are very potent substances with their own side effects and toxicities. Effective treatment of nicotine overdose would mean giving just enough of the antagonist to insure that receptors were being neither overstimulated by nicotine, nor understimulated as a result of receptor blockade. However, the limitations of present day technology and the chaos of the emergency room make such a fine balance difficult to achieve.

Strychnine. Treatment of strychnine overdose mainly involves the administration of anticonvulsant drugs. The mechanism by which strychnine induces stimulant actions, namely antagonism of inhibitory glycine receptors, results in unique motor seizures. With the other stimulants, both the muscles that work with gravity, and those that work against gravity, are stimulated. This leads to an alternating pulling in and throwing out of, for example, the arms and legs. Strychnine's action is mediated at the spinal cord, and this leads to a powerful contraction of all voluntary muscles, including those in the back, the face and those associated with breathing. Thus, strychnine convulsions can lead to the back of the head touching the back of the heels[17]. Prolonged contraction of muscles in the chest and throat lead to a halt in breathing. If strychnine convulsions are not immediately brought under control by anticonvulsants, they can cause broken bones and a complete paralysis of breathing.

Summary of Overdose

Overdose on any of the four stimulants can result in death, usually from heart failure or a post-convulsion halt in breathing. Stimulant overdose is usually treated symptomatically by the administration of anticonvulsants, antipsychotics, and medications to lower blood pressure, heart rate and temperature. Specific characteristics of each drug results in some differences in the treatment of overdose by the different stimulants. Pharmacological blockade of cocaine-induced rapid heartbeat is complicated by the periodic decreases in heart rate arising from cocaine's local anesthetic effect on the heart. Similarly, treatment of nicotine overdose is complicated by a potential interaction between treatment-induced decreases in blood pressure and periodic decreases in blood pressure caused by nicotine itself. Use of an acetylcholine antagonist in treatment of nicotine overdose is complicated by the toxicities of these treatments. Finally, strychnine overdose leads to peculiar and powerful convulsions that require immediate and vigorous administration of anticonvulsant drugs.

INTERACTIONS

No matter what the mechanism of action, stimulant drugs lead to central and sympathetic nervous system stimulation. Obviously, consumption of more than one drug from within this single psychopharmacological class can be dangerous. In addition, since all stimulants share certain effects on the body and behavior, there are certain drugs that will interact with all stimulants. It is particularly important to remember that many commonly employed beverages and OTC drugs contain stimulant drugs.

Differences in basic pharmacology, as well as sites and mechanism of action, also mean that certain of these stimulants will have particularly dangerous interactions with drugs that will have little or no interaction with other stimulants. For example, some nonstimulant compounds bind to plasma proteins. They will interact with stimulants that also bind to plasma proteins, but may have no effect on other stimulants. Understanding the details of all possible interactions would require a thorough knowledge of the basic pharmacology and sites and mechanisms of action of all possible nonstimulant drugs, medicines, foodstuffs, environmental toxins, etc. The important guiding principles are that interaction is a two-way street and that a wide variety of things can interact with drugs taken for recreational purposes. Compounds interacting with stimulants may result in a reduction of stimulation, or they may instead lead to a disastrous increase in some or all of the effects of the stimulant. An individual who has developed tolerance to the stimulant effects of caffeine may discover, for example, that caffeine's enhancement of the metabolism of nicotine reduces the stimulant effect of nicotine consumed with a cup of coffee. An individual with sinus difficulties who consumes a recommended dose of an OTC product containing phenylpropanolamine might suffer seizures from an otherwise "safe" dose of cocaine. Of equal importance, recreationally used stimulants may decrease the effectiveness of important medicines, or may instead result in toxicity from a previously safe dose of medicine. While drug use is no more common in individuals treated for ADD with methylphenidate than it is in the normal population, a methylphenidate-treated individual may suffer a drug-induced psychosis from the consumption of caffeine and/or nicotine. Recreational users need to keep in mind that drug interactions may represent the most dangerous of all the consequences of abusable drug use.

CHRONIC EFFECTS

It is difficult to make accurate comparisons of the physical and behavioral effects of chronic consumption of cocaine vs. caffeine vs. nicotine vs. strychnine. Differences in basic pharmacology, and more importantly, sites and mechanisms of action, suggest that there will likely be very different effects on specific neurotransmitter systems in different parts of the body. Unfortunately, there are vastly different, culturally determined, differences in the most likely dose, method of administration, and pattern of consumption of each of these drugs. Cocaine may be taken once a month for ten years as a three-week-long run of once-every-four-hours intravenous injection of high doses. Caffeine may be consumed as weak coffee, twice daily for ten years. Nicotine may be inhaled, suspended in cancer-causing tars, over 400 times per day for those same ten years. Obviously, more than basic pharmacology and sites and mechanisms of action are responsible for the differences in the physical and psychological consequences of chronic consumption of different stimulants.

It is, however, possible to make some generalizations about the chronic effects of stimulant drugs. Sometimes, it can be safely proposed, all of the stimulants listed in Table 15.1 are capable of inducing some common chronic effects. In other cases, only certain drugs have been investigated, and it is unclear whether the chronic effect arises from something specific to that drug or is instead an effect shared by all stimulants. Clearly, research must be conducted to determine which chronic effects of stimulants are shared by all members of this class, and which arise from true within-class differences. In the meantime, it is instructive to examine the consequences that are likely to occur with chronic consumption of nearly any stimulant drug.

Brain and Other Organ Damage

While the physical consequences of chronic stimulant intake are sensitive to method of administration, dose, frequency, etc., two main consequences are likely to occur from consumption of any stimulant. First, since it appears that central nervous system stimulation, however initiated, is mediated by central monoamines, chronic use of stimulants could lead to any of the usual consequences of prolonged agonist action (see

Chapter 4): a depletion of monoamine neurotransmitters, decreased sensitivity to receptor stimulation, or cell death.

The second likely consequence of chronic use of any stimulant is a negative effect on the cardiovascular system. All stimulants exert a direct or indirect effect on the sympathetic nervous system. Chronic consumption of drugs that induce elevations in heart rate and blood pressure at medium and high doses may lead to chronic hypertension and heart rhythm abnormalities.

Tolerance and Sensitization

Depending on the host of factors detailed in Chapter 5, either tolerance or sensitization may occur to the effects of stimulant drugs. Culturally dependent factors interact with differences in basic pharmacology, and sites and mechanisms of action, to make it difficult to specify true within-class differences in the nature, and rates of development, of tolerance and sensitization. It is perhaps more appropriate to focus on the commonalities within this class, leaving a discussion of true within-class differences to a time when appropriate studies have been conducted.

The main commonality is that of differential tolerance. In particular, tolerance occurs rapidly to the reinforcing effects of most stimulants. While tolerance also rapidly occurs to the acute increases in heart rate, tolerance to the effects on blood pressure may be nonexistent. For instance, healthy adult volunteers were given the opportunity to self-administer 96 mg of intranasal cocaine at 35-minute intervals. There was some evidence of acute tolerance, in that heart rate and self-report of the subjective rewarding effect of the cocaine either reached **asymptote** (a maximum point) or increased only gradually. On the other hand, blood pressure steadily increased to the point where the session had to be stopped[16].

Perhaps the most distressing effect of chronic stimulant consumption is the development of sensitization to convulsions and psychiatric difficulties[43,52]. For example, an individual may chronically consume a particular dose of cocaine, only to find that sensitization has converted this previously subconvulsant dose into one capable of causing convulsions. Researchers have warned that "repeated administrations of a given dose of cocaine without resulting seizures would in no way assure the continued safety of this drug even for that given individual and even assuming equal purity of the drug used"[42]. Despite the perception of safety generated by their widespread use at low doses, sensitization may occur to the convulsant and unpleasant psychiatric effects of chronic caffeine and nicotine.

Cross-Tolerance and Cross-Sensitization

Chronic consumption of one stimulant can lead to cross-tolerance and cross-sensitization. For instance, tolerance to certain effects of caffeine induces a cross-tolerance to the same effects of methylphenidate[26]. This suggests that an adult coffee drinker finally diagnosed as having ADD without hyperactivity may require a particularly large dose of methylphenidate in order to get a therapeutic effect. On the other hand, the chronic amphetamine user may find that an otherwise "safe" cup of coffee may, as a result of cross-sensitization, result in a drug-induced psychosis[2].

Physical Dependency/Compulsive Use

As discussed in Chapter 5, the question of whether a drug induces a physical dependency is quite different from the question of whether it can lead to compulsive use. The most important question is whether drug cessation phenomena include true withdrawal symptoms, along with rebound effects and frustrated nonreward. An increase in public concern with the health consequences of caffeine consumption, cigarette smoking, and the increase in use of "crack" cocaine has stimulated a new look at whether these drugs produce "addiction." Unfortunately, little attention is paid to the lack of precision of this term. Some scientists go so far as to say that the distinctions between physical dependency and compulsive use have no bearing upon the search for the physical basis of drug use[31]. Even worse, some go so far as to assert that previous claims that stimulants don't cause physical dependency promoted "the misconception that cocaine was a "safe" recreational drug"[40]. It is, of course, possible to point to many negative physical and psychological consequences of cocaine use even as assertions of physical dependency are questioned.

Those who investigate the possibility that stimulants can produce a physical dependency have additionally confused the argument by asserting that all drug cessation phenomena, including rebound and frustrated nonreward, are symptoms of "withdrawal." It is easy to find instances of otherwise well-designed studies where all drug cessation phenomena are used as evidence of "withdrawal" and the existence of physical dependence. For example, in a review of 37 clinical reports of caffeine use, phenomena such as fatigue, headache, impaired psychomotor performance, anxiety, and craving were included among a list of "withdrawal" symptoms[22]. In one study, nine male heavy coffee drinkers were given a double-blind substitution of caffeine-free coffee for caffeine-containing coffee. The experiment clearly showed that there were drug cessation phenomena, but these were again limited to fatigue, headache, and impaired psychomotor performance[23]. An analysis of experiments of cessation of cocaine and nicotine reveals that conceptual confusion regarding drug cessation and "withdrawal" have influenced assertions that these compounds are capable of inducing physical dependency[3,27]. Supporters of the hypothesis that stimulants cause physical dependency must remember that anxiety and craving are symptoms of frustrated nonreward, and all likely to occur when any preferred activity is halted. Even fatigue, headache, and impaired psychomotor performance may be rebound phenomena occurring upon sudden cessation of a stimulant, like caffeine, that can relieve headaches in abstainers.

Powerful evidence for the existence of a true physical dependency to stimulants would be provided by the induction of an antagonist-precipitated withdrawal (see Chapter 5). A researcher reviewed the evidence regarding the effects of the nicotine receptor antagonist mecamylamine on the physical and psychological consequences of nicotine use. Despite the fact that mecamylamine blocked the behavioral and physical effects of nicotine obtained from tobacco smoke, there was no induction of cessation phenomena in confirmed cigarette smokers[56]. The authors of an article on the pharmacological treatment of tobacco dependence noted the absence of antagonist-induced withdrawal in cigarette smokers, but did not discuss the importance of this finding to their ideas about "tobacco dependence"[29].

Fortunately, some researchers are beginning to recognize these important distinctions. For example, two researchers were recently careful to distinguish between the enduring symptoms of cocaine cessation and those associated with sudden cessation of an acute binge of cocaine intake. They recommended that the term withdrawal be "dispensed with altogether due to conceptual confusion with dissimilar 'withdrawal' in alcohol, barbiturate or opiate abuse"[19].

The question of whether stimulants induce a physical dependency is, of course, an important one that can be settled by careful research on the nature and causes of the consequences of cessation of chronic stimulant use. At present, though, it must be admitted that reasonable people can disagree about the ability of stimulants to induce a physical dependency. In a discussion of the scope of the problem of cocaine abuse, a scientist stated that "one can debate about the extent to which physiological dependency occurs, but the issue is really of little consequence since the overwhelming problem is the degree of psychological dependency and craving"[21]. Like all reinforcing drugs, stimulants are capable of inducing compulsive use. The negative consequences of acute cessation of stimulant use are quickly and effectively relieved when drug consumption is restarted. This negative reinforcement, combined with the positive effects of stimulants on mood and performance, can easily lead to frequent use and a subjective feeling of loss of control. Nonetheless, the intensity of the subjective feelings associated with stimulant abstinence and craving must not be confused with evidence for physical dependency.

Stimulant-Induced Violence and/or Psychosis

Perhaps the most interesting consequence of chronic stimulant use is the possibility that it can alter the brain so that symptoms of psychosis occur in the user. Nearly any drug can cause such an effect acutely, especially as brain and other organ damage occurs when doses taken are towards the far right of the dose response curve. However, there is evidence that chronic use of even small doses of cocaine[43], amphetamine[7,49], and methylphenidate[28] can eventually have a **psychotomimetic** (or psychosis mimicking) effect that may result in many of the symptoms of paranoid schizophrenia. That is, a chronic stimulant user may gradually develop hallucinations and vague suspicions that can turn into true delusions.

If the delusions happen to be paranoid in nature, the chronic user may resort to violence in order to "get them before they get me." Subjects given an IV "loading" of either 40 or 80 mg of cocaine followed by a four-hour continuous IV infusion of more cocaine developed suspicious, guarded, and paranoid behavior[53]. Although stimulants can induce paranoia, it is not necessary for a person to be suffering a drug-induced psychosis in order to engage in violence. The central and sympathetic nervous system stimulation arising from acute doses of stimulants may result in agitation and confusion that can lead to violence. Of course, the temptation to label all violent acts by people using stimulants as "stimulant-induced violence" must be resisted. Correlation (violence correlated with stimulant use) does not imply causation, particularly when the illicit status of some stimulants makes it more likely that it is a third factor, namely the opportunity to amass large sums of tax-free money, that can explain "drug-related violence." In addition, current claims that a particular compound "causes violence" must be viewed within a historical context in which prejudices against minorities have sometimes been vented through hostilities towards culturally determined drug preferences. There is, for example, a history of links between exaggerations of the effects of cocaine (and other stimulants) and the oppression of African Americans in the U.S.[25].

A number of objections can be raised to the assertion that stimulants induce psychosis. Some suggest that social and political factors, rather than the physical characteristics of stimulants, lead to the application of the pejorative label of psychoto-mimetic. However, stimulant-induced psychosis occurred in individuals who were taking cocaine and amphetamine when these were legal drugs[7]. Similarly, stimulant-induced psychosis occurs today in those who are taking prescription stimulants, and hence have nothing to fear from the law[24]. On the other hand, the idea that stimulant-induced psychosis is nothing more than a case of applying a stigmatizing label to unwanted or offensive behaviors can be supported by references to difficulties in determining whether chronic use leads to true psychosis (and in that case, which psychosis?), or instead to anxiety, panic or some other less severe psychological problem[36,42]. However, individuals who once suffered the symptoms of schizophrenia but no longer do, report that chronic low-dose consumption of stimulants leads to a return of the specific symptoms of their schizophrenia. In fact, a review of 36 studies revealed that 40% of patients with schizophrenia developed a drug-induced psychosis from stimulant doses that would not induce psychosis in the normal population[33].

A disturbing question arises from a discussion of stimulant-induced psychosis. Is it possible that nicotine, caffeine, and other legal stimulants are capable of inducing psychosis? Historians have reported the concerns of a late 1800s government official concerning "the prevalence of the so-called coca cola fiend"[25]. There is certainly some evidence that chronic users of licit stimulants occasionally suffer drug-induced psycho-sis[24], and the negative effects of caffeine on the psychological health of normal and psychiatric populations is well documented[12,18,55]. As mentioned above, there is evidence of a cross-sensitization where acute caffeine can induce "psychosis" in animals given chronic amphetamine[2]. On the other hand, there are literally millions of coffee drinkers and cigarette smokers who have no evidence of psychosis. Is there something about the physical characteristics of nicotine and caffeine that render them devoid of psychotomimetic potential? Or is the fact that these drugs are typically consumed at very low doses responsible for a failure to see many cases of full-blown stimulant-induced psychosis? Further research is needed to determine whether apparent differences between the stimulants in their ability to induce psychosis are the result of time- and place-dependent cultural variables or are instead true within-class differences.

Summary of Chronic Effects

Chronic consumption of low or medium doses of any stimulant may lead to decreases in endogenous substances, chronic hypertension, heartbeat irregularities, differential tolerance, and sensitization to convulsions and psychological difficulties. While it is clear that chronic stimulant use may lead to compulsive use, it is difficult to determine whether physical dependency occurs. Caution must be employed in evaluating experiments that characterize all cessation phenomena as "withdrawal" symptoms that indicate the existence of physical dependency. Chronic use of stimulants may lead to violent behavior, although ethical difficulties in experimentation, malicious exaggerations, and failures to appreciate the fact that correlation doesn't equal causation have clouded the issue. Similarly, ethical and logical difficulties have hampered investigations of whether the stimulants can induce psychosis. Most research about stimulant-induced psychosis has focused on the presently illicit stimulants, leaving unanswered the disturbing question of whether widely used drugs like nicotine and caffeine may be able to induce psychosis.

CHAPTER SUMMARY

Determinations of similarities and differences among the stimulants is hampered by differences in culturally determined factors such as typically consumed dose, method of administration, etc. Nonetheless, certain commonalities can be emphasized even as specific peculiarities are recognized. For instance, all four of the stimulants discussed are rapidly absorbed by any method of administration, are widely distributed throughout the body, and have short half-lives. They all increase central nervous system stimulation and are all sympathomimetic, yet each of the compounds discussed has unique sites and mechanisms of action. In addition, cocaine is particularly potent as an inducer of heart problems and fever, while nicotine is particularly potent in inducing tremors. The diuretic and smooth-muscle relaxing effects of caffeine and the local anesthetic action of cocaine are unique side effects that can be exploited for medical purposes. Overdose with any of the four compounds is life-threatening, although heartbeat irregularities from cocaine, blood pressure fluctuations from nicotine, and the unique nature of strychnine-induced convulsions all complicate the usual symptomatic treatment of stimulant overdose. The four stimulants discussed can interact with a wide variety of other drugs. Chronic consumption of any stimulant can lead to a number of physical problems, some of which are made worse by tolerance and/or sensitization. Compulsive use may result from chronic use, but the existence of physical dependency is controversial. Violence and/or psychosis may also arise from chronic use, but ethical concerns and conceptual problems regarding design of experiments and interpretation of data make it difficult to establish a direct causal link between stimulant use and instances of violence and/or psychosis.

REVIEW ESSAY QUESTIONS

1. Provide two of your own examples showing how culturally defined differences in dose, frequency, and method of administration of stimulants can lead to incorrect conclusions about differences between stimulants.

2. Construct a table that enables rapid comparison of the specifics of the basic pharmacology of cocaine, caffeine, nicotine, and strychnine.

3. Construct a table that enables rapid comparison of the specifics of the site(s) and mechanism(s) of action of cocaine, caffeine, nicotine, and strychnine.

4. For each of the four emphasized drugs, list at least two unique facts about acute side effects at low or medium doses or the symptoms and treatment of overdose. Explain these within-class differences by reference to differences in basic pharmacology and/or sites and mechanisms of action.

5. Provide evidence for and against the ideas that chronic stimulant use can (1) lead to physical dependency, or (2) cause violence/psychosis.

REFERENCES

1. Abood, L.G., Reynolds, D.T., Booth, H., & Bidlack, J.M. Sites and mechanisms of nicotine's action in the brain. *Neuroscience and Biobehavioral Reviews*, 1981, 5, 479-486.
2. Ando, K., Hironka, N., & Yanagita, T. Psychotic manifestations in amphetamine abuse-Experimental study on the mechanism of psychotic recurrence. *Psychopharmacology Bulletin*, 1986, 22, 763-767.
3. *ASPET (American Society for Pharmacology and Experimental Therapeutics) & CPDD (Committee on Problems of Drug Dependence). Scientific perspectives on cocaine abuse. *The Pharmacologist*, 1987, 29, 20-27.
4. Baxter, L.R., Schwartz, J.M., Phelps, M.E., Mazziotta, J.C., Barrio, J., Rawson, R.A., Engel, J., Guze, B.H., Selin, C., & Sumida, R. Localization of neurochemical effects of cocaine and other stimulants in the human brain. *Journal of Clinical Psychiatry*, 1988, 49, 23-26.
5. Boulenger, J.P., Butts-Lamb, P., & Padgett, W. Subclasses of adenosine receptors in the central nervous system: Interaction with caffeine and related methylxanthines. *Cell and Molecular Neurobiology*, 1983, 3, 69-80.
6. Chait, L.D., & Johanson, C.E. Discriminative stimulus effects of caffeine and benzphetamine in amphetamine-trained volunteers. *Psychopharmacology*, 1988, 96, 302-308.
7. Connel, P.H. *Amphetamine psychosis*. London: Oxford University Press, 1958.
8. Crowley, T.J. Clinical issues in cocaine abuse. In S. Fisher, A. Raskin, & U.H. Uhlenhuth (Eds.) *Cocaine: Clinical and biobehavioral aspects*. New York: Oxford University Press, 1987.
9. Curatolo, P.W., & Robertson, D. The health consequences of caffeine. *Annals of Internal Medicine*, 1983, 98, 641-653.
10. *Daigle, R.D., Clark, H.W., & Landry, M.J. A primer on neurotransmitters and cocaine. *Journal of Psychoactive Drugs*, 1988, 20, 283-295.
11. Derlet, R.W., & Albertson, T.E. Emergency department presentation of cocaine intoxication. *Annals of Emergency Medicine*, 1989, 18, 182-186.
12. Dews, P.B. Behavioral effects of caffeine. In P.B. Dews (Ed.) *Caffeine: Perspectives from recent research*. Berlin: Springer-Verlag, 1984.

13. *Erickson, P.G., Adlaf, E.M., Murray, G.F., & Smart, R.G. *The steel drug: Cocaine in perspective.* Lexington, MA: Lexington Books, 1987.

14. Ernster, V.L. Epidemiologic studies of caffeine and human health. In G.A. Spiller (Ed.) *The methylxanthine beverages and foods: Chemistry, consumption and health effects.* New York: Liss, 1984.

15. Ettinger, T.B., & Stine, R.J. Sudden death temporally related to vaginal cocaine abuse. *American Journal of Emergency Medicine,* 1989, 7, 129-130.

16. Foltin, R.W., Fischman, M.W., Pedroso, J.J., & Pearlson, G.D. Repeated intranasal cocaine administration: Lack of tolerance to pressor effects. *Drug and Alcohol Dependence,* 1988, 22, 169-177.

17. Franz, D.N. Central nervous system stimulants: Strychnine, picrotoxin, pentylenetetrazol, and miscellaneous agents. In A.G. Gilman, L.S. Goodman, T.W. Rall, & F. Murad (Eds.) *The pharmacological basis of therapeutics (7th Ed.),* New York: Macmillan, 1985.

18. Furlong, F.W. Possible psychiatric significance of excessive coffee consumption. *Canadian Psychiatric Association Journal,* 1975, 20, 577-583.

19. Gawin, F.H., & Kleber, H.D. Abstinence symptomatology and psychiatric diagnosis in cocaine abusers. *Archives of General Psychiatry,* 1986, 43, 107-113.

20. Gay, G.R. Clinical management of acute and chronic cocaine poisoning. *Annals of Emergency Medicine,* 1982, 11, 562-572.

21. Gottheil, E. Cocaine abuse and dependence: The scope of the problem. In M.S. Gold, M. Galanter, & B. Stimmel (Eds.) *Cocaine pharmacology: Addiction and therapy.* New York: Hayworth Press, 1987.

22. Griffiths, R.R., & Woodson, P.P. Caffeine physical dependence: A review of human and laboratory animal studies. *Psychopharmacology,* 1988, 94, 437-451.

23. Griffiths, R.R., Bigelow, G.E., & Liebson, I.A. Human coffee drinking: Reinforcing and physical dependence producing effects of caffeine. *Journal of Pharmacology and Experimental Therapeutics,* 1986, 239, 416-425.

24. Havey, R.J. Over-the-counter and iatrogenically induced psychoses: A review of the literature. *Journal of the American Osteopathic Association,* 1984, 83, 412-418.

25. *Helmer, J. Blacks and cocaine. In M.E. Kelleher, B.K. Mac Murray, & T.M. Shapiro (Eds.) *Drugs and society: A critical reader,* Dubuque, Iowa: Kendall/Hunt, 1983.

26. Holtzman, S.G. Discriminative stimulus effects of caffeine: Tolerance and cross-tolerance with methylphenidate. *Life Sciences,* 1987, 40, 381-389.

27. Hughes, J.R., Gust, S.W., & Pechacek, T.F. Prevalence of tobacco dependence and withdrawal. *American Journal of Psychiatry,* 1987, 144, 205-208.

28. Janowsky, D., El-Yousef, M.K., & Davis, J.M. The elicitation of psychotic symptomatology by methylphenidate. In J.O. Cole, A.M. Freedman, & A.J. Friedhoff (Eds.) *Psychopathology and psychopharmacology.* Baltimore: Johns Hopkins University Press, 1973.

29. Jarvik, M.E., & Henningfield, J.E. Pharmacological treatment of tobacco dependence. *Pharmacology, Biochemistry and Behavior,* 1988, 30, 279-294.

30. *Julien, R.M. *A primer of drug action (4th Ed.).* New York: W.H. Freeman, & Co., 1985.

31. Koob, G.F., & Bloom, F.E. Cellular and molecular mechanisms of drug dependence. *Science,* 1988, 242, 715-723.

32. Kossowsky, W.A., & Lyon, A.F. Cocaine and acute myocardial infarction: A probable connection. *Chest,* 1984, 86, 729-731.

33. Lieberman, J.A., Kane, J.M., & Alvir, J. Provocative tests with psychostimulant drugs in schizophrenia. *Psychopharmacology,* 1987, 91, 415-433.

34. Litchenfeld, P.J., Ruben, D.B., & Feldman, R.S. Subarachnoid hemorrhage precipitated by cocaine snorting. *Archives of Neurology, 1984,* 41, 223-224.

35. Little, K.Y. Amphetamine, but not methylphenidate, predicts antidepressant efficacy. *Journal of Clinical Psychopharmacology,* 1988, 8, 177-183.

36. Louie, A.K., Lannon, R.A., & Ketter, T.A. Treatment of cocaine-induced panic disorder. *American Journal of Psychiatry,* 1989, 146, 40-44.

37. Nencini, P., Ahmed, A.M., & Elmi, A.S. Subjective effects of khat chewing in humans. *Drug and Alcohol Dependence,* 1986, 18, 97-105.

38. Netter, F.H. *The CIBA collection of medical illustrations: Nervous system anatomy and physiology.* West Caldwell, NJ: CIBA Pharmaceutical Co., 1986.

39. Olson, K.R., & Benowitz, N.L. Life-threatening cocaine intoxication. *Problems in Critical Care*, 1987, 1, 95-105.

40. Ondrusek, G. Cocaine. In G.W. Lawson & C.A. Cooperrider (Eds.) *Clinical Psychopharmacology: A practical reference for nonmedical psychotherapists.* Rockville, MD: Aspen Publishers, 1988.

41. Pollin, W. The danger of cocaine. *Journal of the American Medical Association*, 1985, 254, 98.

42. Post, R.M., Weiss, S.R.B., Pert, A., & Uhde, T.W. Chronic cocaine administration: Sensitization and kindling effects. In S. Fisher, A. Raskin, & U.H. Uhlenhuth (Eds.) *Cocaine: Clinical and biobehavioral aspects.* New York: Oxford University Press, 1987.

43. Post, R.M., & Kopanda, R.T. Cocaine, kindling and psychosis. *American Journal of Psychiatry*, 1976, 133, 627-634.

44. Rall, T.W. Central nervous system stimulants (continued): The methylxanthines. In A.G. Gilman, L.S. Goodman, T.W. Rall, & F. Murad (Eds.) *The pharmacological basis of therapeutics (7th Ed.)*, New York: Macmillan, 1985.

45. Rappolt, R.T., Gay, G.R., & Inaba, D.S. Propranolol: A specific antagonist to cocaine. *Clinical Toxicology*, 1977, 10, 265-271.

46. Ritchie, J.M., & Greene, N.M. Local anesthetics. In A.G. Gilman, L.S. Goodman, T.W. Rall, & F. Murad (Eds.) *The Pharmacological basis of therapeutics (7th Ed.)*, New York: Macmillan, 1985.

47. Rosecrans, J.A., & Meltzer, L.T. Central sites and mechanisms of action of nicotine. *Neuroscience and Biobehavioral Review*, 1981, 5, 497-501.

48. Rugh, J.T. Profound toxic effects from the drinking of large amounts of strong coffee. *Medical and Surgical Reports*, 1896, 75, 549-550.

49. Sato, M. Acute exacerbation of methamphetamine psychosis and lasting dopaminergic supersensitivity-A clinical survey. *Psychopharmacology Bulletin*, 1986, 22, 751-756.

50. Schuman, M., Gitlin, M.J., & Fairbanks, L. Sweets, chocolate and atypical depressive traits. *The Journal of Nervous and Mental Disease*, 1987, 175, 491-495.

51. Seecof, R., & Tennant, F.S. Subjective perceptions to the intravenous "rush" of heroin and cocaine in opioid addicts. *American Journal of Drug and Alcohol Abuse*, 1986, 12, 79-87.

52. Segal, D.S., & Kuczenski, R. Behavioral and neurochemical characteristics of stimulant-induced augmentation. *Psychopharmacology Bulletin*, 1987, 23, 417-424.

53. Sherer, M.A., Kumor, K.M., Cone, E.J., & Jaffe, J.H. Suspiciousness induced by four-hour intravenous infusions of cocaine. *Archives of General Psychiatry*, 1988, 45, 673-677.

54. Snyder, S.H. Adenosine as a mediator of the behavioral effects of xanthines. In P.B. Dews (Ed.) *Caffeine: Perspectives from recent research.* Berlin: Springer-Verlag, 1984.

55. Stephenson, P.E. Physiologic and psychotropic effects of caffeine on man. *Journal of the American Dietetic Association*, 1977, 71, 240-247.

56. Stolerman, I.P. Could nicotine antagonists be used in smoking cessation? *British Journal of Addiction*, 1986, 81, 47-53.

57. Taylor, P. Ganglionic stimulating and blocking agents. In A.G. Gilman, L.S. Goodman, T.W. Rall, & F. Murad (Eds.) *The pharmacological basis of therapeutics (7th Ed.)*, New York: Macmillan, 1985.

* Introductory or intermediate reading

Chapter 16

DEPRESSANTS

The purposes of this chapter are to:

1. Identify the commonalities of and discover the differences among the wide variety of depressant drugs,

2. Compare the basic pharmacology, and sites and mechanisms of action, of a few representative depressant drugs, including ethyl alcohol, the opioid drugs heroin and morphine, and a representative barbiturate, pentobarbital,

3. Present the acute pharmacological and behavioral side effects of low and medium doses of representative depressant drugs, with an emphasis on within-class differences,

4. Reveal commonalities in depressant overdose, with an emphasis on selected within-class differences in the nature and treatment of overdose, and

5. Discuss the pharmacological and behavioral effects of chronic depressant use, including drug interactions, physical dependency and compulsive use, tolerance and cross-tolerance, and brain and other organ damage.

COMMONALITIES AND DIFFERENCES

Characteristics of Depressants

Table 16.1 presents a partial list of the more common compounds, both licit and illicit, that are considered to be depressant drugs. The term "depressant" describes this group because, despite important differences, they share equally important commonali-

Table 16.1
A Partial List of Common Depressant Drugs

Opioids (heroin, morphine, codeine, meperidine)

Barbiturates (phenobarbital, secobarbital, pentobarbital)

Antihistamines (diphenhydramine)

Organic Solvents (ethyl alcohol, carbon tetrachloride, ether, benzene, toluene, methanol, propylene glycol)

Meprobamate Chloral Hydrate Methaqualone
Ethclorvynol Glutethimide Paraldehyde

---

ties. The three main commonalities are that (1) people consume them because they enjoy the improved mood and decreased inhibitions they experience when the drugs are taken at low doses[30,41,52]; (2) all depressants affect judgment, impair motor coordination, and have antianxiety effects at low doses, while inducing sedation at medium doses (hence, they are often referred to as **sedatives** or **hypnotics**)[52] and (3) all these drugs induce a similar pattern of decreased respiration, the possibility of convulsions and death at the far right of their individual dose-response curves[108]. As with stimulants, it is sometimes difficult to identify true within-class differences because of culturally determined variations in the most common method of administration, the typical dose employed, and general cultural acceptability. For example, people who engage in recreational consumption of alcohol or take antihistamines for sinus problems may be surprised and annoyed at comparisons between their drug and the presently illegal and vilified drug heroin. However, all depressant drugs share important commonalities, especially the three cited above.

Subcategories

In addition to the commonalities that justify placing these apparently disparate drugs in the same class, there are sets of drugs within the category that have so much in common with each other that it is possible to create subcategories of depressants.

In particular, the drugs heroin, morphine, codeine, meperidine, and a large number of others are all the natural product (or synthetic variations) of compounds obtained from the poppy plant. All these drugs appear to interact with the various receptors for specific endogenous opium-like compounds and so are referred to as **opioids.** Phenobarbital, pentobarbital, and secobarbital are very closely related in their chemical structure, and can be referred to as **barbiturates**. Diphenhydramine is one of many different drugs that are antagonists at receptors for histamine and are therefore called **antihistamines**. Toluene and benzene are just two of a large number of organic solvents found in paint, glue, lighter fluid, typewriter correction fluid, etc. All of these are **organic solvents**. Although most of the concern about organic solvents arises from involuntary exposures of workers, there are those who deliberately inhale, swallow, or otherwise ingest these substances in order to experience their depressant effects[41]. The drug **ethyl alcohol** is an organic solvent, and thus the consequences of chronic alcohol consumption are as devastating as those associated with chronic exposure to related organic solvents[41].

When a drug does not easily fit into one of these subcategories (meprobamate through paraldehyde in Table 16.1, for example), they are often categorized together as **non-barbiturate depressants**.

True Within-Class Differences

While it is important to appreciate why these different subcategories of depressants can be formed, it is also important to appreciate that important differences exist between the various drugs within each subcategory. This is especially true of the organic solvents and non-barbiturate depressants.

It would be difficult to discuss the basic pharmacology, as well as sites and mechanisms of action, of each and every drug in Table 16.1. The remainder of this chapter focuses on **ethyl alcohol** or **ethanol**, the prototypical opioids **heroin** and **morphine,** and the prototypical barbiturate drug called **pentobarbital**.

Summary of Commonalities and Differences

There are commonalities among all the depressant drugs listed in Table 16.1. This includes the improved mood and decreased inhibitions that motivate the consumption of low doses, antianxiety effects at low doses and sedation at medium doses, and decreased respiration as well as convulsions and death at overdose. Within-class differences may be obscured by culturally determined variations in most commonly employed dose, method of administration, etc. However, some within-class differences are so clear that it is necessary to create subcategories of depressant drugs, including opioids, barbiturates, antihistamines, organic solvents, and non-barbiturate depressants.

BASIC PHARMACOLOGY

Ethyl Alcohol

Alcohol is one of the excretory products of yeast given access to sugar in the presence of water[62]. The consumption of ethyl alcohol (also known as ethanol) is usually accomplished through oral consumption, although the drug can be injected, taken as an enema, or vaporized and inhaled into the lungs[98]. It is rapidly absorbed from the stomach, small intestines, and colon. Individual differences in the rate of absorption, and the presence or absence of food or other material in the stomach, means that while intoxicating effects are usually noticeable within a half hour, full absorption may take from two to six hours[56]. Ethyl alcohol is extremely hydrophilic (it is 30 times more soluble in water than in fat) and is widely distributed throughout the body with no binding to blood-borne carrier proteins[18]. It easily crosses both the blood-brain and placental barriers[70]. Under usual circumstances, 98% of orally consumed alcohol is metabolized by liver enzymes into carbon dioxide and water (see Figure 12.2 for the metabolism of ethanol). Alcohol is unique among the drugs studied in this text in that the rate of metabolism is not influenced by the acute concentration of the drug. It takes about three hours to metabolize one ounce of ethanol, and raising the dose of alcohol neither hastens nor slows metabolism. What is not metabolized is excreted in the urine[46]. Table 16.2 summarizes the basic pharmacology of alcohol.

Table 16.2
The Basic Pharmacology of Ethyl Alcohol

- Usually taken orally, but can be absorbed in colon or lungs or injected
- Rapidly absorbed and widely distributed
- Easily crosses blood-brain and placental barriers
- Over 90% is metabolized by liver enzymes to carbon dioxide and water
- Metabolism not influenced by acute concentration
- Three hours are required to metabolize one ounce of ethanol
- Extremely small amount of parent compound excreted in urine

Morphine

The drug **opium** is obtained from the juices of the poppy plant, *Papaver somniferum*. There are at least 20 distinct compounds in opium, and in 1806 a pure substance capable of inducing sleep and relieving pain was isolated and named morphine, after Morpheus, the Greek god of dreams[90]. There are more than a dozen compounds (completely natural, semisynthetic or totally synthetic) that have been developed since that time. One that many people have heard of is the drug **heroin**. Heroin is a semisynthetic form of morphine that has been altered in order to increase its lipid solubility. Thus, it more easily crosses the blood-brain barrier and is therefore three to four times more powerful than morphine. However, the first step in the metabolism of heroin is to strip it of the synthetic additions, resulting once again in morphine[51].

Morphine, like most of the opioid drugs, is rapidly absorbed from the gut, and thus can be given orally but for reasons discussed below is usually not. Many opioids can also be absorbed from the nasal mucosa after insufflation, and they can be inhaled as smoke into the lungs. Of course, they can also be injected either subcutaneously, intramuscularly, or, most commonly, intravenously. Many opioids, including morphine, undergo **first-pass metabolism** (see Chapter 3). That is, when taken orally, they are broken down by liver enzymes immediately after they enter the bloodstream and before they can have any kind of behavioral or physical effect[87]. For instance, an experiment with patients with cancer pain revealed first-pass metabolism of oral morphine that breaks down between 51% to 85% of an oral dose before it can have any effect on pain[104]. Injection, insufflation, or inhalation bypasses this first-pass metabolism.

Once absorbed into the bloodstream, about one-third of the dose of morphine is bound to blood-borne plasma proteins. Since it is less lipid soluble than other opioids such as heroin, **codeine**, and methadone, morphine crosses the blood-brain barrier at a relatively slow rate and does not tend to accumulate in the body[94]. Morphine is rapidly metabolized by enzymes in the liver, and has a half-life of about three hours in healthy young adults[95]. About 90% of any given dose of morphine is excreted within 24 hours in the urine, with the remaining 10% found in the feces. Since the drug is so rapidly metabolized, there is very little of the parent compound found in either urine or feces[51]. Table 16.3 summarizes the basic pharmacology of morphine.

Table 16.3
Basic Pharmacology of Morphine

- Can be taken orally, by injection, or through insufflation or inhalation
- Undergoes significant first-pass metabolism when given orally
- Approximately 1/3 of any given dose is bound to blood proteins
- Crosses the blood-brain barrier slowly and does not accumulate in the body
- Rapidly metabolized in the liver: Half-life of about 3 hours
- Excreted mainly in urine as metabolite
- About 10% of metabolites found in feces

Pentobarbital

Pentobarbital is one of many barbiturate depressants. Most of the differences among barbiturates can be accounted for by their differences in lipid solubility, which influences the rapidity of onset of drug effects, duration of action, the potential for toxic buildup, etc.[43]. Pentobarbital, which is moderately lipophilic when compared to all other barbiturates, is rapidly absorbed when taken orally. Intravenous injection is sometimes used during emergencies, but intramuscular injection is not employed because of irritation at the site of injection. How well a barbiturate binds to plasma proteins is directly related to its degree of lipid solubility. Pentobarbital is widely distributed throughout the body, and easily crosses the blood-brain and placental barriers. Like most other barbiturates, pentobarbital is metabolized in the liver to an inactive compound and excreted mainly in the urine. However, some other barbiturates are also metabolized to a small degree by enzymes in the kidney and the brain[15]. The half-lives of the barbiturates vary from 8 to 120 hours. Predictably, the moderately lipid soluble drug pentobarbital has, for a barbiturate, a moderate half-life of 15 to 48 hours. The long half-lives of most barbiturates insures that use of these agents as once nightly sedatives will lead to a carryover of drug effects to the next day, a potential for toxic buildup unless the dose is adjusted, and an increased probability of physical dependency[43]. Table 16.4 summarizes the basic pharmacology of pentobarbital.

Table 16.4
Basic Pharmacology of Pentobarbital

- Rapidly absorbed when taken orally
- Moderately bound to plasma proteins
- Widely distributed throughout body
- Easily crosses blood-brain and placental barriers
- Metabolized in liver to inactive metabolite
- Excreted mainly in urine
- Half-life of 15-48 hours insures carryover and toxic buildup

Summary of Basic Pharmacology

Each of the three depressants can be administered in a variety of ways, but morphine undergoes significant first-pass metabolism when taken orally. Morphine and pentobarbital tend to be moderately bound to plasma proteins, while there is no evidence of ethyl alcohol binding to plasma proteins. Morphine crosses the blood-brain barrier slowly, while ethyl alcohol and pentobarbital easily cross this barrier. The metabolism of ethyl alcohol, unlike the metabolism of most other drugs, is not affected by acute concentration of the drug. Each of the three drugs is metabolized by liver enzymes, although the metabolism of pentobarbital is much slower than the metabolism of the other two drugs, and pentobarbital therefore has a greater potential for carryover and toxic buildup. Each of the three depressant drugs is excreted mainly in the urine as an inactive metabolite, although 10% of morphine metabolites are excreted in feces and an extremely small amount of ethyl alcohol can be found in urine.

SITES AND MECHANISMS OF ACTION

Ethyl Alcohol

There are a number of fruitful approaches to investigations about the sites and mechanisms of action of the intoxicating and physical dependency-inducing effects of ethanol. Some researchers, particularly impressed with the fact that a metabolic product of alcohol interacts with endogenous opiate receptors, have hypothesized that interaction with this endogenous opiate system is responsible for the depressant effects of alcohol[122,124,126]. Other researchers have been equally impressed with the fact that physical dependency upon ethyl alcohol involves a cross-dependency with benzodiazepine anti-anxiety agents (see Chapter 10) and barbiturate depressants. These researchers emphasize the possibility that all three drugs might exert their mechanism of action through interaction with the GABA-benzodiazepine receptor complex[12,114,120]. In addition, there are those who focus on the effects of ethanol on other neurotransmitters and neuromodulators, including especially the posterior pituitary hormone vasopressin[7,48,103]. Finally, there are those who suggest that it is not alcohol at all, but the metabolite acetaldehyde that is responsible for intoxication, dependency and effects on various peptides and neurotransmitters[115].

A most fruitful approach has been developed by those who recognized that ethanol had specific effects on certain neurotransmitter systems, but that many of these specific effects occurred without interaction with a specific "alcohol receptor"[123]. Some theorists have been particularly critical of those whose theories (that alcohol exerts its effect via interaction with the GABA-benzodiazepine receptor complex) are based on data obtained from studies that employ a concentration of alcohol many times above the lethal, let alone intoxicating, dose of the drug[72]. These theorists suggest that the binding to the GABA-benzodiazepine complex that occurs at exceptionally high doses of ethyl alcohol may not even occur when the drug is administered at the usually employed recreational doses. When more relevant doses are used, a variety of experimental results suggests that alcohol disrupts neuronal membranes in all parts of the nervous system[107] (see Figure 16.1). For example, the ability of various types of alcohols to induce intoxication is highly correlated with their individual abilities to disrupt neuronal membranes[67,80]. In addition, genetic differences in sensitivity to alcohol reflect the ease with which ethanol can disrupt the neuronal membranes of that subject under study[31].

A consensus is developing in support of the theory that ethyl alcohol exerts a particularly strong disrupting effect around particular areas of the neuronal membrane, including especially those areas surrounding receptors[119,123]. It is, therefore, possible that the generalized disruption of neuronal membranes caused by ethyl alcohol may be the single mechanism responsible for the diverse changes in neurotransmitter and neuromodulator activity induced by ethanol[65]. This possibility is supported by an experiment that investigated why a benzodiazepine antagonist was able to block the intoxicating effects of ethyl alcohol[119]. It may at first appear that this receptor-mediated blockade of intoxication would provide evidence for intoxication arising from a binding of ethyl alcohol to the benzodiazepine receptor. However, it was found instead that blockade of

Figure 16.1. Alcohol has an antagonist action because it disrupts the membrane of the postsynaptic neuron. Note that alcohol is particularly destructive to the area of the membrane that surrounds the postsynaptic receptors.

intoxication was dependent upon the antagonist's ability to block the flow of chloride ions across the alcohol-disrupted neuronal membrane. This experiment provided strong evidence that the consequences of disruption of the neuronal membrane, and not interaction with some particular receptor, is responsible for the intoxicating effect of ethyl alcohol. If this theory is true, it means that the intoxicating effect of even small doses of ethanol are necessarily accompanied by neuronal death, thus explaining the uniquely severe brain damage and psychological problems arising from chronic ethanol consumption[8,9,39,84].

Morphine

There is, in the bodies of mammals, including humans, "a highly organized anatomical system for control of pain transmission"[6] that utilizes endogenous opioid hormones to modulate pain under conditions of stress, injury, electrical brain stimulation, acupuncture and when drugs such as morphine are administered[1]. These same endogenous opioid hormones and their receptors have also been implicated in social relationships[10] and a variety of behavioral disorders involving inappropriate thought processes and emotions[110,127]. In humans, these endogenous opioids and their receptors can be found in the hypothalamus, various midbrain structures, and the spinal cord[45].

Two of the most exciting pharmacological discoveries of this century have been (1) the identification of a variety of receptors for endogenous opioids[66,74], and (2) experimental results indicating that different aspects of exogenous opioids, such as

○ Opioid   M Morphine

Figure 16.2.   The synaptic mechanism of action of morphine. Morphine has an agonist
effect because it acts as a direct agonist that interacts with postsynaptic opioid receptors.
Morphine thus results in the presynaptic opioid neuron having a greater than normal effect
on the postsynaptic neuron.

morphine, are mediated by interaction with different receptors[66,129]. There is, at least, a
"mu receptor" that mediates pain reduction, euphoria, respiratory depression, and possibly physical dependency and is found above the spinal cord in areas such as the midbrain
and brainstem, a "kappa receptor" which mediates analgesia and increased urine flow and
is mainly in the spinal cord, and perhaps even a "beta receptor"[129] and a "delta receptor"[66].
Exogenous opioids can have effects at one or more of these different receptors[88]. In
addition, the effects that these exogenous drugs will exert depends upon the degree to
which they interact with these different receptors. That is, some drugs bind very strongly
to a particular type of receptor and are thus referred to as "strong agonists." Others are
much less potent and are referred to as "partial agonists." Finally, those that bind to the
receptors but don't exert any effect are, predictably, referred to as "antagonists." A drug that
is a strong agonist at one receptor may be an antagonist at another, and this is called a "mixed
agonist-antagonist"[75]. These mixed agonist-antagonists are of great interest because they
offer the possibility of being effective pain relievers without the induction of opioid/sedative
side effects such as respiratory depression and physical dependency[37,97,100].

      Morphine is generally recognized to be a mu receptor agonist[75] and thus its ability
to reduce pain, decrease respiration, induce euphoria, and cause physical dependency are
thought to result from its agonist action at this receptor (see Figure 16.2). There is

powerful evidence against the idea that morphine is an agonist at the kappa receptor. For example, kappa receptor antagonists had no effect on dogs given chronic morphine[27], while mu receptor antagonists similar to naloxone and naltrexone[16] induced a severe antagonist-induced withdrawal (see Chapter 5). In addition to interaction with mu receptors, there is evidence that morphine causes the release of the neurotransmitter **histamine**[51].

Evidence that interaction with endogenous opioid receptors is responsible for the reinforcing effects of heroin and morphine comes from a number of sources. As mentioned in Chapter 12, the mu receptor agonist methadone can substitute for heroin and morphine[136], and naltrexone, which antagonizes at least mu receptors, blocks the reinforcing effect of heroin and morphine[16]. There is also laboratory support for the hypothesis that opioid receptors mediate the reinforcing effects of exogenous opioids. The mixed agonist-antagonist **buprenorphine** decreased the amount of self-administered heroin injections taken by subjects in the laboratory[82]. Another experiment gave experienced opioid users a choice as to whether their experimental responses would lead to cash or heroin. When subjects were pretreated with naltrexone, response rates stayed basically the same, but subjects chose money over intravenous heroin[83]. These experiments reveal that blockade of opioid receptors removes the reinforcing effect of heroin, thus suggesting that the reinforcing effect of the opioids are, in fact, mediated by interaction with these endogenous opioid receptors.

Pentobarbital

A variety of evidence points to the probability that pentobarbital and other barbiturates exert their effects through interaction with the benzodiazepine/GABA receptor complex (see Chapter 10). Barbiturates given at low doses can have an antianxiety effect and, more importantly, barbiturates and the benzodiazepines reveal cross-tolerance and cross-dependency[114]. However, despite this appealing logic, early work demonstrated that the barbiturates do not compete with benzodiazepines for the benzodiazepine receptor portion of the receptor complex[14]. More recent work, though, has shown that pentobarbital binds to a separate aspect of the receptor complex and enhances the effect of bindings of endogenous, or exogenous, benzodiazepines[114]. Thus, it is generally accepted that barbiturates exert both their antianxiety and sedative effects through agonist action at a portion of the GABA receptor complex[69]. Support for this theory is provided by experiments revealing that the reticular activating system (see Chapter 2) has a large number of such GABA receptor complexes, and demonstrations that the reticular activating system is also "exquisitely sensitive" to the barbiturates[43].

Summary of Sites and Mechanisms of Action

Ethyl alcohol influences a wide number of endogenous systems, most probably because it disrupts neuronal membranes, particularly in areas surrounding receptors. Therefore, the mechanism of depressant action of ethyl alcohol leads to uniquely severe consequences of chronic consumption. The depressant effects of morphine are most likely mediated through interaction with the "mu" endogenous opioid receptor. Pentobarbital probably induces depressant effects though interaction with a portion of the benzodiazepine-GABA receptor complex, particularly in the reticular activating system.

ACUTE SIDE EFFECTS AT LOW AND MEDIUM DOSES

Of course, all the depressants induce certain common effects on the body and on behavior, including improved mood, decreased inhibitions, impaired judgment, impaired motor coordination and antianxiety effects at low doses, and sedation at medium doses. In addition, cessation of acute depressant effects is often followed by a "hangover" that includes headache, fatigue, nausea, dizziness and tremors[102]. While these appear to be the result of rebound overactivity in the previously depressed sympathetic nervous system, the failure of propranolol to block the symptoms of alcohol-induced hangover even as it effectively blocked sympathetic activity calls this simplistic explanation into question[11].

Ethyl Alcohol

While a lack of coordination that makes driving and perhaps even walking[53] unsafe will occur when alcohol represents 0.05%-0.15% of the blood, blood alcohol levels of 0.15%-0.20% will result in obvious intoxication[62]. While alcohol affects specific portions of all neuronal membranes, animal studies reveal that the reticular activating system is particularly sensitive[47]. The inhibition of the activity of the reticular activating system is probably responsible for the impaired attention and judgment, inappropriate emotional and behavioral responses, uncoordination, slurred speech, prolonged reaction time, and perhaps even the euphoria caused by low and medium dose of ethanol. The immediate effects of alcohol on the heart and blood are minor, but they do cause a dilation of those vessels closest to the surface, thus inducing a feeling of warm and flushed skin. In addition to this dilation, even a single drink of alcohol can cause a constriction of certain blood vessels in the brain, leading to a reduced level of oxygen availability[2,3]. Low and moderate doses induce sweating, which, when combined with the dilation of skin vessels, can easily lead to a great degree of heat loss even as the intoxicated individual feels warm[98]. On the positive side, ethanol does decrease "bad" types of fat circulating in the blood as it increases the levels of "good" fat[42].

Depending on a variety of circumstances, low to moderate doses of alcohol may increase or decrease respiration rate. However, the acid secretions of the stomach are greatly increased by alcohol consumption, which can lead to stomach upset, vomiting, and ulcers. The probability of ulcers is increased because any dose of alcohol irritates and inflames the stomach lining[29]. Alcohol increases the output of urine more than what could be calculated from adding in the excess fluid consumed with the drug, probably because of an inhibition of the production and release of the antidiuretic hormone, vasopressin[7,48]. Finally, the acute effects of low and moderate doses of ethanol have no negative effects on the liver, although they do cause an accumulation of fat that, if prolonged, can lead to the death of liver cells[20].

As discussed in Chapter 4, nonpharmacological factors, especially set and setting, can have a great influence upon the effects of drugs, especially at low and medium doses. For example, it is clear that the setting in which alcohol is consumed has a profound effect on whether it leads to an antianxiety (or anti-"stress") effect or instead an increase in anxiety or "stress"[32]. It has even been argued that the pharmacology of low-dose alcohol consumption could not explain its effect on interactions between people, since these effects were so different in different cultures[68]. It must be accepted that the pharmacological effects of alcohol are influenced by set and setting[71], especially since some of the effects of alcohol are demonstrated by people who are given placebo liquids that smell and taste like alcohol[61,73]. However, researchers who emphasize the effect of set and setting have nonetheless had to concede that low and medium doses of ethanol have clearcut pharmacological effects, especially on motor coordination[17,18].

The effects of alcohol on sexual behavior offers perhaps the most powerful demonstration of the interaction of pharmacology and expectancy in determining the effects of alcohol. Early authors attributed the perceived increase in sexual desire following alcohol consumption to the pharmacologically mediated depression of activity in "higher" areas of the brain that normally maintained more socially acceptable behavior[35,89]. This enabled alcohol to develop an undeserved reputation as an **aphrodisiac** (enhancer of sexual desire and performance). Unfortunately, as was recognized by Shakespeare, alcohol "provokes the desire, but it takes away the performance" (from Macbeth, Act II, Scene 3). This poetic statement has been supported by studies using objective measures of physical changes in the genitalia of both men and women. These studies determined that ethyl alcohol does indeed decrease sexual performance in both sexes[132].

Morphine

While there is a widespread myth that consumption of opioids, particularly intravenous injection of heroin or morphine, is universally pleasurable, it has been known for some time that the first few experiences with intravenous morphine are usually accompanied by vomiting[49]. Vomiting is a result of direct stimulation of that area of the brain responsible for detecting the introduction of toxins into the bloodstream (see Chapter 3). It should be noted, however, that tolerance develops fairly rapidly to this side effect, and the reinforcing effects of intravenous morphine and heroin[106] are sufficiently strong that most users "don't mind vomiting behind smack"[30].

Like all depressants, morphine causes low body temperature, reduced blood pressure, and respiratory depression. In addition, like alcohol, morphine causes dilation of the blood vessels in the skin, thus leading to a flushed and warm face and neck[51]. As a mu receptor agonist, morphine induces a number of side effects that render it, and other like opioids, unique among the depressant drugs. For example, the drug causes constriction of the pupils (**meiosis**) until they are mere pinpoints, a suppression of the cough reflex, and **catalepsy** (severe bodily rigidity)[96]. The release of histamine is partially responsible for the decreased blood pressure, and seems to be the main cause of generalized itching and sweating, as well as one of a number of causes of irritation and inflammation at injection sites. There is evidence that morphine-induced itching may be due to some direct interaction with a type of opioid receptor, since even opioids that don't release histamine can induce widespread itching[105]. Finally, morphine and similar opioids have profound effects on the stomach and small and large intestines. Their main effect is to decrease the secretion of acids into the stomach and decrease the contractions of the intestines. This can lead to the side effect of constipation. However, decreased intestinal contractions have also been viewed as a target effect. Opioids have been used for centuries as the most common treatment for diarrhea[51].

Perhaps the most useful aspect of opioids is their ability to diminish pain even at low doses. Other depressants induce analgesia as a result of widespread and nonspecific inhibition of the brain's ability to receive and process the full spectrum of sensory stimulation, including pain. Thus, alcohol, for example, is effective against pain only when it is taken at doses that cause sedation and impaired performance, emotional control, and thinking abilities. However, any opioid, including morphine, that is at least a partial agonist at either mu or kappa receptors has profound pain-relieving abilities at doses that have little effect on a person's ability to hear, feel, see, or sense nonpainful stimuli[37,100].

Pentobarbital

The behavioral effects of acute ingestion of low or moderate doses of pentobarbital are indistinguishable from those occurring with ethanol. Thus, intoxication induces poor judgment, impaired motor performance, memory difficulties, impaired respiration, etc. However, since the basic pharmacology, mechanism of action, and preparations for self-administration of alcohol and the barbiturates differ, there are differences in acute side effects. Unlike ethyl alcohol, pentobarbital does not cause peripheral vasodilation or central nervous system blood vessel constriction. There is no direct effect on stomach secretions, so there is less probability of the development of ulcers or impairment of the absorption of vitamins. Finally, rather than increasing urine output as alcohol does, pentobarbital and other barbiturates lead to a net reduction in urine output[43].

Summary of Acute Side Effects at Low and Medium Doses

While there are commonalities in the motivations for low- and medium-dose consumption of depressants, there are important differences among the three representative compounds. For instance, ethyl alcohol induces vasodilation and sweating, which can lead to significant heat loss. In addition, ethyl alcohol increases the acid secretions of the stomach and induces fat accumulation in the liver. Initial experiences with intravenous morphine often result in vomiting. Like ethyl alcohol, morphine lowers body temperature and breathing rates. Morphine additionally causes meiosis, a suppression of the cough reflex, catalepsy, and a decrease in the acid secretions and activity of the digestive organs. Unlike ethyl alcohol and pentobarbital, morphine is an effective analgesic even at low doses. Pentobarbital differs from alcohol in that it does not cause vasodilation nor does it increase stomach secretions. While ethyl alcohol increases urine output, pentobarbital decreases urine output.

OVERDOSE

Overdose with any depressant drug represents a life-threatening emergency. Both behavioral abnormalities and physical difficulties, including especially respiratory depression, must be expected and treated symptomatically no matter what the depressant used. However, the treatment of overdose depends greatly upon the drug employed. For example, the rapid absorption of alcohol means that emptying the stomach of its contents through gastric lavage will probably be ineffective unless the drug has been consumed very recently. Since alcohol is so freely soluble in water, the use of an artificial kidney to **dialyze** or cleanse the blood can be very helpful in causing a rapid reduction in the symptoms of acute alcohol overdose[98]. On the other hand, overdose of orally consumed barbiturates or antihistamines might be helped by gastric lavage, since the pills dissolve gradually in the stomach[108]. Barbiturates may be removed by dialysis, but overdose with the antihistamine drug diphenhydramine will not be aided by dialysis, since the lipid solubility of the drug insures that little of it will be found in the blood[26]. An additional problem is caused by the anticholinergic action of most antihistamines. It has long been known that overdose with antihistamines often leads to an **anticholinergic crisis**, which includes excitement, tremor, hyperactivity, high fever, and seizures. The acetylcholine agonist **physostigmine** can immediately reverse the symptoms of an antihistamine-caused anticholinergic crisis. However, this dangerous treatment should be reserved only for those overdose patients who are suffering heartbeat irregularities or convulsions[54].

Morphine overdose, like other depressants, can cause life-threatening respiratory depression. Fortunately, naloxone and naltrexone are specific antagonists for the mu receptor and can induce an immediate reversal of the effects of morphine overdose[16,77,93]. Equally fortunate, meosis is an effect that is unique to the opioid depressants, and can enable diagnosis of opioid overdose (and the need for an antagonist) in a comatose or uncommunicative individual. There is, however, no specific antidote to the effects of overdose from alcohol or the barbiturates. Previous attempts to treat alcohol and barbiturate overdose by administering central nervous system stimulants, based on a pharmacologically naive confusion of the meaning of "antagonist" with the meaning of "antidote," resulted in death rates as high as 40%. Continuous monitoring of a patient's blood, heart, and lung activities has resulted in a reduction of mortality rate to less than 2%[43].

Summary of Overdose

While overdose with any depressant represents a life-threatening emergency, treatment depends upon which drug is consumed. The symptoms of morphine overdose can be rapidly reversed by naloxone or naltrexone. While rapid absorption of the ethyl alcohol limits the usefulness of gastric lavage, alcohol overdose may be treated with kidney dialysis. Gastric lavage can be of use in removing barbiturates taken as pills. Treatment of antihistamine overdose is complicated by anticholinergic crisis. Careful monitoring of heart and lung function can increase the number of individuals who survive depressant overdose. Stimulant medications should not be used in any form of depressant overdose.

INTERACTIONS

All of the depressants interact with one another to produce dangerous degrees of sedation and respiratory depression. The widespread use of alcohol and OTC preparations containing antihistamines result in frequent cases of dangerous interactions. Of equal importance, though, is the fact that specific drugs can interact with specific depressants. For example, methylphenidate and the MAOIs can each increase the respiratory depressant effects of the barbiturates[43]. MAOIs, tricyclic antidepressants, and the phenothiazine antipsychotics can greatly intensify the sedative and respiratory depressant effects of the opioids[51]. The painkilling and sedative effects of morphine are, for unknown reasons, particularly enhanced by even small doses of amphetamine[22]. The weak opioid agonist **pentazocine** is rendered particularly reinforcing when it is taken intravenously in combination with the antihistamine **tripelennamine**[40]. The common use of the analgesic drug aspirin to deal with "hangovers" is ill advised, since aspirin can contribute to the stomach irritation arising from alcohol consumption[98].

A wide variety of drugs can be influenced by the effects of acute and chronic consumption of depressants upon liver enzymes. For example, part of the reason for the interaction between barbiturates and alcohol was that each competed for the same enzymes in the liver[98]. Consumption of alcohol plus barbiturates can lead to an overwhelming amount of material for the enzymes to break down. On the other hand, chronic consumption of almost any depressant that is metabolized by liver enzymes can lead to a homeostatic increase in the activity of the enzyme that breaks it down. Thus, someone who has recently halted a long period of alcohol consumption may find that they need a large dose of, for example, a barbiturate prescribed as a sedative.

CHRONIC EFFECTS

Chronic intake of any of the depressant drugs (excluding, perhaps, the antihistamines) leads to the possibility of truly astonishing degrees of tolerance[121] and physical dependence[65]. Chronic use of a depressant like alcohol may, because of cross-tolerance, lead to a need for a greater amount of anesthetic prior to any required surgery[36]. Physical dependence can, depending upon the drug, lead to life-threatening withdrawal symptoms. However, there are some unique aspects of the chronic use of each of the specific depressants detailed in this chapter. Nonetheless, it is important to remember that most people who abuse one type of depressant also use other depressants (and likely nicotine, caffeine, marijuana, etc.) and significant degrees of cross-tolerance and cross-dependency occur within the general category of depressant drugs[60,81].

Ethyl Alcohol

The chronic consumption of ethanol causes so many health problems that treatment of alcohol-related problems consumes 12% of the U.S. health budget[81]. Deaths from a variety of problems, especially cancer of the mouth, throat, liver, and lung, are much more common in individuals who consume six or more drinks daily than in individuals who abstain from alcohol[58]. Surveys of individuals showing up at hospitals for treatment of chronic alcohol consumption reveal that over 70% of them had a significant medical problem, including diseases of the liver, gall bladder, pancreas, and circulatory and respiratory systems[84,85]. The liver is particularly affected by chronic alcohol consumption. The acute accumulation of fat that comes from acute alcohol consumption may eventually lead to cell death and **cirrhosis** of the liver[64]. An additional organ that is especially effected by chronic alcohol consumption is the skin. Long-term alcohol consumption is associated with **acne rosacea** (the "glowing red" cheeks and nose of W.C. Fields are a well known example), bruises, and visible damage to peripheral nerves[98]. The long list of negative consequences of chronic ethanol consumption arises, in part, because the drug is an organic solvent obtained from the excrement of single-celled organisms. When alcohol is not available, individuals may turn to other organic solvents, including ether[5].

The negative acute effects of alcohol on sexual performance are made worse by chronic consumption[132]. In particular, chronic ingestion of alcohol by men leads to impotence, sterility, and **feminization** characterized by a wasting away of the testicles and the development of breasts. There is evidence that feminization, mediated by damage to the liver, is irreversible in those males with atrophied testicles[125]. While there have been few studies on the effects of chronic alcohol ingestion in women, it is known that female alcohol abusers have various disorders, particularly menstrual abnormalities that are associated with infertility and a high risk of spontaneous abortions[38]. Alcohol easily crosses the placental barrier and is a known cause of birth defects, including the Fetal Alcohol Syndrome. This syndrome is characterized by mental retardation, growth retardation, and physical abnormalities. It is estimated that alcohol consumption causes birth defects in about 3 out of 1,000 births[81].

In addition to this lengthy list of negative effects, there are particular abnormalities of brain and behavior. These include **Korsakoff's syndrome** (a disorder characterized primarily by an inability to recall old memories or, more impressively, form new ones), **Wernicke's syndrome** (characterized by loss of contact with reality plus articulate speech utterly free of meaningful content), and **polyneuritis** (destruction of central and peripheral nerves causing weakness, tingling sensations, etc.)[8]. Evidence of damage to cerebral neurons is provided by reduced autopsy brain weights of alcohol-abusing, compared to normal, subjects[39] and clearcut demonstrations of brain atrophy obtained from **CAT scans** in 33% to 95% of alcohol abusers[9]. Although much emphasis has been placed on **avitaminosis** (lack of consumption or absorption of vitamins), "there is growing evidence that the action of alcohol is neurotoxic in itself, without accompanying avitaminosis"[41]. Since the nervous system itself is often the target of this neurotoxic effect[55], there may be recovery after a cessation of alcohol abuse, but in other cases brain damage causes permanent deficits in behavior[24,25]. Even worse, there is evidence that 50%-70% of all alcohol abusers have problems with memory, motor performance, coordination, and emotion even in the absence of any demonstrable damage to central or peripheral nervous system neurons[19,131].

Depending upon the severity of the physical dependency to alcohol, withdrawal may be either somewhere between mild and moderate, or severe. Mild to moderate withdrawal can normally be treated on an outpatient basis. However, the symptoms of severe withdrawal, which include about one full week of confusion, difficulty in sustaining attention, disorientation, hallucinations, autonomic hyperactivity, hyperventilation, collapse of the cardiovascular system, fever, and seizures, represent a life-threatening emergency that must be treated in a hospital[50].

Morphine

Older users of heroin and morphine have a mortality two to three times higher than the normal population, while younger users are likely to have a death rate 20 times higher than normal[111]. However, the thousands of individuals maintained on high doses of oral methadone have experienced no direct injurious effects[59]. Despite the clear lack of any physical brain damage from chronic opioid use, it might be possible that subtle consequences of long-term ingestion could induce psychological or performance problems. However, extensive testing of individuals who had long been physically dependent upon various opioids has revealed that there were no differences between the drug users and control groups[21,101]. These findings contrast greatly with the devastation observed in individuals who chronically abuse alcohol. It appears that the majority of deaths from morphine and heroin can be attributed to overdose (which might be more likely due to the lack of quality control over the sale of illicit drugs), homicide (perhaps brought about by association with the criminal underworld), suicide, and infections[111].

The worst dangers from chronic morphine or heroin use occur in those who administer the drug by injection, particularly intravenous injection. Distressingly, chronic heroin users in England who have access to free and pure heroin from physicians nonetheless suffered increased mortality because of infections arising from poor hygiene and the sharing of needles[111]. Of course, most people are presently aware of the possibility that the sharing of needles might result in infection by the deadly AIDS virus. Finally, the illicit nature of opioids in the U.S., combined with advances of technology, have enabled the introduction of a variety of **designer drugs**[109]. Minor manipulations of the structure of various opioids renders them (at least for now) outside the system of legal categorization. Unfortunately, these drugs may be many times more potent than what the chronic user is used to, and consumption may lead to overdose[135].

Differential tolerance develops to the various effects of morphine and other opioids. It has been noted that "even users highly tolerant to respiratory-depressant effects continue to exhibit some degree of meosis and complain of constipation" while "experience with thousands of patients maintained on methadone for periods of several years suggests that, while constipation is a continuing problem, substantial sedation and apathy are easily managed by reductions in dosage"[50]. Despite the myth that physically dependent heroin or morphine users get no pleasure from their drug intake, individuals with a great degree of tolerance to other effects of heroin nonetheless reported experiencing a brief period of euphoria after intravenous self-administration in an experimental laboratory[78]. This finding was confirmed in later experiments, which determined that although chronic users allowed to self-administer heroin in the laboratory developed significant tolerance to the reinforcing effects within one to two weeks, they still experienced an intensely pleasurable feeling for 30 to 60 minutes after each intravenous injection[86].

Popular misconceptions about opioids are held so passionately that scientists have felt it necessary to state that "perhaps the most common misconception about heroin is that after one trial a user is addicted for life"[63]. A review of Chapter 5 will reveal that physical dependence upon any drug requires low intermittency of multiple administrations of appropriately large doses. Even though early studies have found that a high percentage of those who experiment with heroin and morphine become physically dependent[99], these studies may have been confounded by their focus on disadvantaged minorities. Research has clearly demonstrated that a substantial percentage of opioid users are neither physically dependent nor, for that matter, compulsive users[134].

However, if someone does become physically dependent upon an opioid drug, they will experience withdrawal symptoms when they halt or reduce their use below some specific level or when they are given a drug that antagonizes the opioid receptor stimulated by their chronically used opioid. For example, a variety of studies involving different animals indicate that animals physically dependent upon mu agonists go into antagonist-induced withdrawal when given mu, but not kappa, antagonists while the opposite is true for animals physically dependent upon kappa agonists[133]. In addition, studies of what physically dependent opioid users do when their preferred drug is unavailable find that they take advantage of receptor-specific cross-dependency by obtaining and consuming a drug that is an agonist at the same receptor as their preferred opioid[79].

In a discussion of misconceptions about heroin (and other opioids), two scientists noted that "the addict undergoing withdrawal without medication is always portrayed as being in excruciating pain"[63]. However, the intensity of withdrawal depends upon the swiftness of the reduction in number of opioid receptors receiving agonist stimulation. Thus, antagonist-induced withdrawal induces the most rapid and severe symptoms[28]. Withdrawal symptoms from sudden cessation depend upon the intensity of physical dependency (itself determined by dose, frequency, intermittency, etc.) and the nature, particularly the lipid solubility, half-life, metabolism, and strength of binding to opioid receptors, of the chronically consumed drug. For example, withdrawal symptoms from the more lipid soluble drug heroin begin within 6 hours of the last intravenous self-administration, while withdrawal doesn't begin until 24 hours after the most recent intake of morphine[63]. A similar influence of lipid solubility upon withdrawal severity is seen with other opioids. For example, sudden cessation of the very lipid soluble opioid **meperidine** leads to withdrawal symptoms within 3 hours while withdrawal symptoms may not appear until 48 hours after the last dose of the slowly metabolized opioid, methadone. In general, more rapid onsets of withdrawal led to more severe, but shorter-lasting, symptoms[50].

Regardless of the onset and intensity of opioid withdrawal, it is likely that the individual going through opioid withdrawal will experience a number of symptoms, all dependent upon the time since last administration. Early symptoms include typical psychological distress associated with rebound and frustrated nonreward phenomena, including anxiety, restlessness, irritability, and drug craving. Later, symptoms of true withdrawal occur, including yawning, perspiration, **lacrimation** (teary eyes), and **rhinorrhea** (a runny nose). More severe symptoms which may appear even later include anorexia, vomiting, abdominal cramps, bone pains, tremor, weakness, insomnia, and **piloerection** ("goose bumps," which are responsible for the phrase "cold turkey"). While morphine withdrawal, for example, will usually be completed within 7 to 10 days, there is some evidence of abnormal physical and psychological conditions that may persist for many weeks[76].

Unlike alcohol or barbiturate withdrawal, it is very rare for opioid withdrawal to lead to convulsions, collapse of the circulatory system and death[28]. However, opioid withdrawal is unpleasant. Not surprisingly, experimental results reveal that the strength of self-reports of craving for opioids was directly dependent upon the intensity of other symptoms of cessation, which were themselves dependent upon the time since the last opioid consumption[130]. Furthermore, when intravenous users are denied the opportunity to inject their drug of choice, they do not simply acquiesce to this involuntary cessation. They are likely to instead resort to a different form of administration with the same or a different drug. For example, intravenous heroin users smoked opium when heroin was not available[128]. One research project found that some of their subjects who took oral **hydromorphine** (or **Dilaudid**) began their use of the drug during periods when intravenous heroin was temporarily unavailable[79].

Pentobarbital

Like other depressants, the barbiturates induce a dose-dependent reinforcing effect in humans. Subjects who had to ride a stationary bicycle in order to obtain an injection of pentobarbital rode the bike for longer periods of time when offered 90 mg/injection than when offered 30 mg/injection. Subjects offered placebo injections eventually stopped riding the bicycle altogether[33]. A review of studies comparing the reinforcing effects of benzodiazepines and various barbiturates, revealed that the barbiturates were generally more reinforcing than the benzodiazepines and that pentobarbital was preferred over other barbiturates, particularly phenobarbital[34].

Chronic consumption of pentobarbital or other barbiturates may lead to profound difficulties with memory. In particular, there are deficits in both short-term and long-term memory even during unintoxicated conditions. This phenomenon occurs earlier during chronic use than do the memory problems associated with alcohol. Fortunately, cessation of barbiturate use usually leads to a full recovery[116].

The reinforcing properties of the barbiturates and their previously mentioned long half-lives makes it probable that chronic consumption will lead to tolerance and/or physical dependency. Barbiturate-induced enhancement of sleep undergoes a 50% reduction within two weeks of regular nightly intake[43]. In addition, as with alcohol and the opioids, differential tolerance occurs so that the therapeutic or recreational window closes as tolerance to the reinforcing effect occurs at a faster rate than does tolerance to respiratory depression.

When taken regularly at prescribed sleep-inducing doses, the barbiturates can induce a physical dependency[117]. Physical dependency is, of course, even more likely if larger doses are consumed. Barbiturate withdrawal is similar in appearance to alcohol withdrawal. Since, as with alcohol, sudden withdrawal from pentobarbital or other barbiturates can lead to seizures and death[23], barbiturate withdrawal should be attempted only under medical supervision. As with opioid withdrawal, the severity of symptoms is directly related to the speed with which the chronically consumed drug is removed from the body. Thus, the long-acting barbiturate phenobarbital may be administered to individuals undergoing withdrawal from a shorter-acting barbiturate. Gradual reductions in phenobarbital dose will lead to a decrease in the intensity, but a lengthening of duration, of withdrawal symptoms[118]. When the chronically consumed drug is pentobarbital, untreated withdrawal will likely end within eight days, unless death intervenes earlier[50].

Summary of Chronic Effects

Evaluation of the consequences of chronic consumption of specific depressants is complicated by the fact that most individuals who use one depressant consume other depressants as well as drugs outside this category. However, chronic consumption of nearly any depressant drug can lead to great degrees of differential tolerance and to compulsive use and/or physical dependency. However, physical dependency to depressants, including the opioids, is powerfully influenced by the dose of the drug and the pattern of drug administration. While opioid withdrawal rarely results in death, withdrawal symptoms from sudden cessation of alcohol or the barbiturates can be lethal. The severity and duration of withdrawal symptoms from the opioids and the barbiturates are strongly influenced by the lipid solubility of the chronically consumed drug.

Chronic alcohol consumption is associated with a variety of severe consequences. These include increased mortality, increased risk of a number of types of cancer, impotence, menstrual abnormalities, spontaneous abortions, and birth defects including Fetal Alcohol Syndrome. In addition, chronic alcohol consumption can lead to severe neurological and behavioral problems, including Korsakoff's syndrome, Wernicke's syndrome, and polyneuritis. In contrast, chronic morphine use is not associated with any direct injurious effects on bodily organs nor with psychological or performance impairments. The increased mortality of opioid users compared to drug-abstinent individuals arise primarily from involvement with an illicit drug trade and the peculiar risks of intravenous injection. The long half-lives of most barbiturates increases the probability of the development of differential tolerance and/or physical dependency. Chronic consumption of barbiturates leads to deficits in memory that appear more swiftly than similar deficits induced by alcohol. However, unlike the permanent memory deficits that can be induced by alcohol, memory deficits decrease after a cessation of chronic barbiturate use.

CHAPTER SUMMARY

Within-class differences among the depressants require the creation of subcategories of depressants, including opioids, barbiturates, antihistamines, organic solvents, and non-barbiturate depressants. All depressants can be administered in a variety of ways, although some opioids undergo first-pass metabolism and thus are not administered orally. Depressants are usually metabolized by liver enzymes to inactive metabolites found mainly in urine. While opioids and barbiturates bind to specific receptors, the mechanism of action of ethyl alcohol involves a disruption of neuronal membranes.

Despite many similarities, ethyl alcohol, morphine, and pentobarbital induce remarkably different side effects at low and medium doses. Overdose with morphine can be treated by an antagonist, but overdose with other depressants must, at present, be treated symptomatically. Overdose with alcohol or barbiturates can lead to death from impairment of respiration and/or heart functioning. Compulsive use, differential tolerance, and physical dependency can arise from chronic use of the depressants. Chronic alcohol use is associated with a wide variety of severe physical and psychological consequences. Chronic opioid use is not associated with any direct organ damage, although intravenous administration and dangers arising from the illicit status of opioids cause specific complications. Chronic barbiturate use may lead to early, yet reversible, memory deficits.

REVIEW ESSAY QUESTIONS

1. What commonalities exist among all depressants, and what subcategories of depressants can be developed?

2. What differences exist among the basic pharmacologies of ethanol, morphine, and pentobarbital? How do these differences affect method of administration?

3. What is the mechanism of the intoxicating action of ethanol? of morphine? of pentobarbital?

4. What unique aspects of the characteristics and/or treatment of overdose enable differentiation among ethanol, morphine, and pentobarbital overdose?

5. How do the consequences of chronic use differ among ethanol, morphine, and pentobarbital?

REFERENCES

1. Adams, M.L., Brase, D.A., Welch, S.P., & Dewey, W.L. The role of endogenous peptides in the action of opioid analgesics. *Annals of Emergency Medicine*, 1986, 15, 1030-1035.
2. Altura, B.M., & Altura, B.T. Microvascular and vascular smooth muscle actions of ethanol, acetaldehyde and acetate. *Federation Proceedings*, 1982, 41, 2447-2451.

3. Altura, B.M., & Altura, B.T. Alcohol, the cerebral circulation and strokes. *Alcohol*, 1984, 1, 325-331.

4. Amit, Z., Sutherland, E.A., Gill, K.,, & Ogren, S.O. Zimelidine: A review of its effects on ethanol consumption. *Neuroscience and Biobehavioral Review*, 1984, 8, 35-54.

5. Barnes, G.E. Solvent abuse: A review. *International Journal of the Addictions*, 1979, 14, 1-26.

6. Basbaum, A.I., & Fields, H.L. Endogenous pain control mechanisms: Review and hypothesis. *Annals of Neurology*, 1978, 4, 451-462.

7. Beard, J.D., & Sargent, W.Q. Water and electrolyte metabolism following ethanol intake and during acute withdrawal from ethanol. In E. Majchrowicz & E.P. Noble (Eds.) *Biochemistry and pharmacology of ethanol, (Vol. 2)*, New York: Plenum Press, 1979.

8. Becker, J.T., & Kaplan, R.F. Neurophysiological and neuropsychological concomitants of brain dysfunction in alcoholics. In R.E. Meyer (Ed.) *Psychopathology and Addictive Disorders*. New York: Guilford Press, 1986.

9. Begleiter, H., Porjesz, B., & Tenner, M. Neuroradiological and neuropsychological evidence of brain deficits in chronic alcoholics. *Acta Psychiatrica Scandinavica*, 1980, 62, 3-13.

10. Benton, D. The role of opiate mechanisms in social relationships. In M. Lader (Ed.) *The psychopharmacology of addiction*, Oxford, England: Oxford University Press, 1988.

11. Bogin, R.M., Nostrant, T.T., & Young, M.J. Propranolol for the treatment of the alcoholic hangover. *American Journal of Drug and Alcohol Abuse*, 1986, 12, 279-284.

12. Boisse, N.N., & Okamoto, M. Ethanol as a sedative hypnotic: Comparison with barbiturate and non-barbiturate hypnotics. In H. Rigter, & J.C. Crabbe (Eds.) *Alcohol tolerance and dependence*. Amsterdam: Elsevier North Holland Biomedical Press, 1981.

13. Borg, S., Liljeberg, P., & Mossberg, D. Alcohol consumption, dependence, and central norepinephrine metabolism in humans. In M. Lader (Ed.) *The psychopharmacology of addiction*, Oxford, England: Oxford University Press, 1988.

14. Braestrup, C., Albrechtsen, R., & Squire, R.F. High density of benzodiazepine receptors in human cortical areas. *Nature*, 1977, 266, 732-734.

15. Breimer, D.D. Clinical pharmacokinetics of hypnotics. *Clinical Pharmacokinetics*, 1977, 2, 93-109.

16. Crabtree, B.L. Review of naltrexone, a long-acting opiate antagonist. *Clinical Pharmacy*, 1984, 3, 273-280.

17. *Critchlow, B. The powers of John Barleycorn: Beliefs about the effects of alcohol on social behavior. *American Psychologist*, 1986, 41, 751-764.

18. Curson, D. Alcohol. In S.D. Iversen (Ed.) *Psychopharmacology: Recent advances and future prospects*, Oxford, England: Oxford University Press, 1985.

19. Eckardt, M.J., & Martin, P.R. Clinical assessment of cognition in alcoholism. *Alcoholism: Clinical and Experimental Research*, 1986, 10, 123-127.

20. Feinman, L., & Lieber, C.S. Liver disease in alcoholism. In B. Kissin, & H. Begleiter (Eds.) *The biology of alcoholism, (Vol. 3: Clinical Pathology)* New York: Plenum Press, 1974.

21. Fields, S., & Fullerton, J. Influence of heroin addiction on neuropsychological functioning. *Journal of Consulting and Clinical Psychology*, 1975, 43, 114.

22. Forrest, W.H., Brown, B.W., Brown, C.R., Defalque, R., Gold, M., Gordon, H.E., James, K.E., Katz, J., Mahler, D.L., Schroff, P., & Teutsch, G. Dextroamphetamine with morphine for the treatment of postoperative pain. *New England Journal of Medicine*, 1977, 296, 712-715.

23. Fraser, H.F., Shaver, M.R., & Maxwell, E.S. Fatal termination of barbiturate abstinence syndrome in man. *Journal of Pharmacology and Experimental Therapeutics*, 1952, 106, 387.

24. Gallant, D.M. Psychiatric aspects of alcohol intoxication, withdrawal and organic brain syndromes. In J. Solomon (Ed.) *Alcoholism and clinical psychiatry*, New York: Plenum Press, 1982.

25. Gallant, D.M. Treatment of organic mental disorders. In American Psychiatric Association (Eds.) *Treatment of psychiatric disorders: A task force report of the American Psychiatric Association*, Washington, D.C.: American Psychiatric Association, 1989.

26. Gary, N.E., & Tresnewsky, O. Clinical aspects of drug intoxication: Barbiturates and a potpourri of other sedatives, hypnotics and tranquilizers. *Heart and Lung*, 1983, 12, 122-127.

27. Gilbert, P.E., & Martin, W.R. The effects of morphine- and nalorphine-like drugs in the nondependent, morphine-dependent and cyclazocine-dependent chronic spinal dog. *Journal of Pharmacology and Experimental Therapeutics*, 1976, 198, 66-82.

28. Ginzburg, H.M. Naltrexone: Its clinical utility. In B. Stimmel (Ed.) *Controversies in alcoholism and substance abuse*, New York: The Hayworth Press, 1986.

29. Glass, G.B.J., Slomiany, B.L., & Slomiany, A. Biochemical and pathological derangements of the gastrointestinal tract following acute and chronic digestion of ethanol. In E. Majchrowicz & E.P. Noble (Eds.) *Biochemistry and pharmacology of ethanol*, New York: Plenum Press, 1979.

30. Goldstein, A. Heroin addiction and the role of methadone in its treatment. *Archives of General Psychiatry*, 1972, 26, 291-297.

31. Goldstein, D.B. Effect of alcohol on cellular membranes. *Annals of Emergency Medicine*, 1986, 15, 1013-1018.

32. Gottheil, E., Druley, K.A., Pashko, S., & Weinstein, S.P. *Stress and Addiction*. New York: Brunner/Mazel, 1987.

33. Griffiths, R.R., Bigelow, G.E., & Leibson, I. Human sedative self-administration: Double-blind comparison of pentobarbital, diazepam, chlorpromazine and placebo. *Journal of Pharmacology and Experimental Therapeutics*, 1979, 210, 301-310.

34. Griffiths, R.R., & Sannerud, C.A. Abuse of and dependence on benzodiazepines and other anxiolytic/sedative drugs. In H.Y. Meltzer (Ed.) *Psychopharmacology: The third generation of progress*, New York: Raven Press, 1987.

35. *Haggard, H.W., & Jellinek, E.M. *Alcohol explored*. New York: Doubleday, 1942.

36. Han, Y.H. Why do alcoholics require more anesthesia? *Anesthesiology*, 1969, 30, 341-342.

37. Hanks, G.W. The clinical usefulness of agonist-antagonist opioid analgesics in chronic pain. *Drug and Alcohol Dependence*, 1987, 20, 339-346.

38. Harlap, S., & Shiono, P.H. Alcohol, smoking and incidence of spontaneous abortions in the first and second trimester. *Lancet*, 1980, 2, 173-176.

39. Harper, C.G., & Blumbergs, P.C. Brain weights in alcoholics. *Journal of Neurology, Neurosurgery and Psychiatry*, 1983, 45, 838-840.

40. Harris, L.S. Pharmacological characteristics of agonist-antagonist analgesics. *Drugs and Alcohol Dependence*, 1987, 20, 293-301.

41. Hartman, D.E. *Neuropsychological toxicology: identification and assessment of human neurotoxic syndromes*. New York: Pergamon Press, 1988.

42. Hartung, G.H., Foreyt, J.P., Mitchell, R.E., Mitchell, J.E., Reeves, R.S., & Gottom, A.M. Effect of alcohol intake on high-density lipoprotein in runners and inactive men. *Journal of the American Medical Association*, 1983, 249, 747-750.

43. Harvey, S.C. Hypnotics and sedatives. In A.G. Gilman, L.S. Goodman, T.W. Rall, & F. Murad (Eds.) *The pharmacological basis of therapeutics: (7th Ed.)*, New York: Macmillan, 1985.

44. Hawley, R.J., Major, L.F., Schulman, E.A., & Lake, C.R. CSF levels of norepinephrine during alcohol withdrawal. *Archives of Neurology*, 1981, 38, 289-292.

45. Herz, A., Hollt, V., Przewlocki, R., Osborne, H., Gramsch, C., & Duka, T. Functional aspects of endorphins. *Progress in Biochemical Pharmacology*, 1980, 16, 11-21.

46. Higgins, J.J. Control of ethanol oxidation and its interaction with other metabolic systems. In E. Majchrowicz & E.P. Noble (Eds.) *Biochemistry and pharmacology of ethanol*, New York: Plenum Press, 1979.

47. Himwich, H.E., & Callison, D.A. The effects of alcohol on evoked potentials of various parts of the central nervous system of the cat. In B. Kissin & H. Begleiter (Eds.) *The biology of alcoholism, (Vol. 2: Physiology and Behavior)*. New York: Plenum Press, 1972.

48. Hoffman, P.L., Melchoir, C.L., & Tabakoff, B. Vasopressin maintenance of ethanol tolerance requires intact brain noradrenergic systems. *Life Sciences*, 1983, 32, 1065-1071.

49. Isbell, H., & White, W.M. Clinical characteristics of addiction. *American Journal of Medicine*, 1953, 14, 558-565.

50. Jaffe, J.H. Drug addiction and drug abuse. In A.G. Gilman, L.S. Goodman, T.W. Rall, & F. Murad (Eds.) *The pharmacological basis of therapeutics: (7th Ed.)*. New York: Macmillan, 1985.

51. Jaffe, J.H., & Martin, W.R. Opioid analgesics and antagonists. In A.G. Gilman, L.S. Goodman, T.W. Rall, & F. Murad (Eds.) *The pharmacological basis of therapeutics: (7th Ed.)*. New York: Macmillan, 1985.

52. Jasinski, D.R. Assessment of the abuse potentiality of morphine-like drugs (methods used in man). In W.R. Martin (Ed.) *Handbook of experimental pharmacology*, New York: Springer-Verlag, 1977.

53. Jehle, D., & Cottington, E. Effect of alcohol consumption on outcome of pedestrian victims. *Annals of Emergency Medicine*, 1988, 17, 953-956.

54. Jones, J., Dougherty, J., & Cannon, L. Diphenhydramine-induced toxic psychosis. *American Journal of Emergency Medicine*, 1986, 4, 369-371.

55. Juntunen, J. Alcoholism in occupational neurology: Diagnostic difficulties with special reference to the neurological syndromes caused by exposure to organic solvents. *Acta Neurologica Scandinavica*, 1982, 66, 89-108.

56. Kalant, H. Absorption, diffusion, distribution and elimination of ethanol: Effects on biological membranes. In B. Kissin, & H. Begleiter (Eds.) *The biology of alcoholism (Vol. 1: Biochemistry)*. New York: Plenum Press, 1971.

57. Kalant, H. Interactions of ethanol and neuropeptides. In C.A. Naranjo & E.M. Sellers (Eds.) *Research advances in new psychopharmacological treatments for alcoholism*, Amsterdam: Elsevier Science Publishers, 1985.

58. Klatsky, A.L., Friedman, G.D., & Siegelaub, A.B. Alcohol and mortality: A ten-year Kaiser-Permanente experience. *Annals of Internal Medicine*, 1981, 95, 139-145.

59. Kreek, M.J. Health consequences associated with the use of methadone. In J.R. Cooper, F. Altman, B.S. Brown, & D. Czechowicz (Eds.) *Research on the Treatment of Narcotic Addiction: State of the Art*, Washington, D.C.: U.S. Govt. Printing Office, 1983.

60. Kreek, M.J. Multiple drug abuse patterns and medical consequences. In H.Y. Meltzer (Ed.) *Psychopharmacology: The third generation of progress*, New York: Raven Press, 1987.

61. Lang, A. Drinking and disinhibition: Contributions from psychological research. In R. Room, & G. Collins (Eds.) *Alcohol and disinhibition: Nature and meaning of the link*, Washington, D.C.: U.S. Government Printing Office, 1983.

62. *Lawson, G.W. Alcohol. In G.W. Lawson, & C.A. Cooperrider (Eds.) *Clinical Psychopharmacology: A practical reference for nonmedical psychotherapists*, Rockville, MD: Aspen Publishers, 1988.

63. *Lewis, G.R., & Lawson, G.W. Heroin. In G.W. Lawson & C.A. Cooperrider (Eds.) *Clinical psychopharmacology: A practical reference for nonmedical psychotherapists*, Rockville, MD: Aspen Publishers, 1988.

64. Lieber, C.S. Pathogenesis and early diagnosis of alcoholic liver injury. *New England Journal of Medicine*, 1978, 298, 888-893.

65. Littleton, J., Harper, J., Hudspith, M., Pagonis, C., Dolin, S., & Little, H. Adaptation in neuronal CA^2_+-channels may cause alcohol physical dependence. In M. Lader (Ed.) *The psychopharmacology of addiction*, Oxford, England: Oxford University Press, 1988.

66. Lord, J.A.H., Waterfield, A.A., & Hughes, J. Endogenous opioid peptides: Multiple agonists and receptors. *Nature*, 1977, 267, 495-499.

67. Lyon, R.C., McComb, J.A., & Schreurs, J. A relationship between alcohol intoxication and the disordering of brain membranes by a series of short-chain alcohols. *Journal of Pharmacology and Experimental Therapeutics*, 1981, 218, 669-675.

68. MacAndrew, C., & Edgerton, R.B. *Drunken comportment: A social explanation*. Chicago: Aldine, 1981.

69. Macdonald, R.L., & McLean, M.J. Cellular bases of barbiturate and phenytoin anticonvulsant drug action. *Epilepsia*, 1982, 23, S7-S18.

70. Madden, J.S. *Alcohol and drug dependence*. Bristol, England: John Wright, 1979.

71. Maisto, S.A., Connors, G.J., & Sachs, P.R. Expectation as a mediator in alcohol intoxication: A reference level model. *Cognitive Therapy and Research*, 1981, 5, 1-18.

72. Majchrowicz, E. Biologic properties of ethanol and the biphasic nature of the ethanol withdrawal syndrome. In M.M. Gross (Ed.) *Alcohol intoxication and withdrawal-IIb: Studies in alcohol dependence*, New York: Plenum Press, 1977.

73. Marlatt, G.A., & Rohsenow, D. Cognitive processes in alcohol use: Expectancy and the balanced placebo design. In N.K. Mello (Ed.) *Advances in substance abuse: Behavioral and biological research*. Greenwich, CT: JAI Press, 1980.

74. Martin, W.R. Opioid antagonists. *Pharmacological Review*, 1967, 19, 463-521.

75. Martin, W.R. Clinical evidence for different narcotic receptors and relevance for the clinician. *Annals of Emergency Medicine*, 1986, 15, 1026-1029.

76. Martin, W.R., Jasinski, D.R., Haertzen, C.A., Kay, D.C., Jones, B.E., Mansky, P.A., & Carpenter, R.W. Methadone--A reevaluation. *Archives of General Psychiatry*, 1973, 28, 286-295.

77. Martin, W.R., Jasinski, D.R., & Mansky, P.P. Naltrexone: An antagonist for the treatment of heroin dependence. *Archives of General Psychiatry*, 1973, 28, 784-791.

78. McAuliffe, W.E., & Gordon, R.A. A test of Lindesmith's theory of addiction: The frequency of euphoria among long-term addicts. *American Journal of Sociology*, 1974, 79, 795-840.

79. McBride, D.C., McCoy, C.B., Rivers, J.E., & Lincoln, C.A. Dilaudid use: Trends and characteristics of users. *Chemical Dependencies: Behavioral and Biomedical Issues*, 1980, 4, 85-100.

80. McCreery, M.J., & Hunt, W.A. Physico-chemical correlates of alcohol intoxication. *Neuropharmacology*, 1978, 17, 451-461.

81. Mello, N.K. Alcohol abuse and alcoholism: 1978-1987. In H.Y. Meltzer (Ed.) *Psychopharmacology: The third generation of progress*, New York: Raven Press, 1987.

82. Mello, N.K., Mendelson, J.H., & Kuehnle, J.C. Buprenorphine effects on human heroin self-administration: An operant analysis. *Journal of Pharmacology and Experimental Therapeutics*, 1982, 223, 30-39.

83. Mello, N.K., Mendelson, J.H., Sellers, M.L., & Kuehnle, J.C. Effects of heroin self-administration on cigarette smoking. *Psychopharmacology*, 1980, 67, 45-52.

84. Mendelson, J.H., Babor, T.F., Mello, N.K., & Pratt, H. Alcoholism and prevalence of medical and psychiatric disorders. *Journal of Studies on Alcohol*, 1986, 47, 361-366.

85. Mendelson, J.H., Miller, D., Mello, N.K., & Pratt, H. Hospital treatment of alcoholism: A profile of middle income Americans. *Alcoholism: Clinical and Experimental Research*, 1982, 67, 377-383.

86. Meyer, R.E., & Mirin, S.M. *The heroin stimulus: Implications for a theory of addiction*. New York: Plenum Press, 1979.

87. Misra, A.L. Metabolism of opiates. In M.L. Adler, L. Manara, & R. Samanin (Eds.) *Factors affecting the action of narcotics*, New York: Raven Press, 1978.

88. Mitchelson, M., Hartnoll, R., & Lewis, R. Opioids. In S.D. Iversen (Ed.) *Psychopharmacology: Recent advances and future prospects*, Oxford, England: Oxford University Press, 1985.

89. Muehlberger, C.W. Medicolegal aspects of alcohol intoxication. *Michigan State Bar Journal*, 1956, 35, 38-42.

90. Musto, D.F. *The American disease*. Hartford, CT: Yale University Press, 1973.

91. Naranjo, C.A., Sellers, E.M., & Lawrin, M.O. Modulation of ethanol intake by serotonin uptake inhibitors. *Journal of Clinical Psychiatry*, 1986, 47, 16-22.

92. Naranjo, C.A., Sellers, E.M., Sullivan, J.T., Woodley, D.V., Kadlec, K., & Sykora, K. Serotonin uptake inhibitors (SUI) consistently moderate ethanol intake (EI) in humans: Citalopram (C) effects. *Clinical Pharmacology and Therapeutics*, 1986, 39, 215.

93. O'Brien, C.P., Greenstein, R., & Mintz, J. Clinical experience with naltrexone. *American Journal of Drug and Alcohol Abuse*, 1975, 2, 365-377.

94. Oldendorf, W.H., Hyman, S., Braun, L., & Oldendorf, S.Z. Blood-brain barrier penetration of morphine, codeine, heroin and methadone after carotid injection. *Science*, 1972, 178, 984-986.

95. Owen, J.A., Sitar, D.S., Berger, L., Brownell, L., Duke, P.C., & Mitenko, P.A. Age-related morphine kinetics. *Clinical Pharmacology and Therapeutics*, 1983, 34, 364-368.

96. Pasternak, G.W. Opioid receptors. In H.Y. Meltzer (Ed.) *Psychopharmacology: The third generation of progress*, New York: Raven Press, 1987.

97. Peachey, J.E. Clinical observations of agonist-antagonist analgesic dependence. *Drug and Alcohol Dependence*, 1987, 20, 347-365.

98. Ritchie, J.M. The aliphatic alcohols. In A.G. Gilman, L.S. Goodman, T.W. Rall, & F. Murad (Eds.) *The pharmacological basis of therapeutics: (7th Ed.)*. New York: Macmillan, 1985.

99. Robins, L.N., & Murphy, G.E. Drug use in a normal population of young Negro men. *American Journal of Public Health*, 1967, 570, 1580-1596.

100. Rosow, C.E. The clinical usefulness of agonist-antagonist analgesics in acute pain. *Drug and Alcohol Dependence*, 1987, 20, 329-337.

101. Rounsaville, B.J., Jones, C., Novelly, R.A., & Kleber, H. Neuropsychological functioning in opiate addicts. *Journal of Nervous and Mental Disease*, 1982, 170, 209-216.

102. *Royal College of Physicians. *Alcohol: Our favorite drug*. London: Tavistock Publications, 1986.

103. Ruwe, W.D., Flemons, W.W., Veale, W.L., & Pittman, Q.J. The role of arginine vasopressin in alcohol dependence and withdrawal. *Peptides*, 1985, 6, 1043-1049.

104. Sawe, J., Dahlstrom, B. Paalzow, L., & Rane, A. Morphine kinetics in cancer patients. *Clinical Pharmacology and Therapeutics*, 1981, 30, 629-635.

105. Scott, P.V., & Fischer, H.B.J. Intraspinal opiates and itching: A new relief? *British Journal of Medicine*, 1982, 284, 1015-1016.

106. Secoff, R., & Tennant, F.S. Subjective perceptions to the intravenous "rush" of heroin and cocaine in opioid addicts. *American Journal of Drug and Alcohol Abuse*, 1986, 12, 79-87.

107. Seeman, P. The membrane actions of anesthetics and tranquilizers. *Pharmacological Review*, 1972, 24, 583-655.

108. Seymour, R.B., Gorton, J.G., & Smith, D.E. The client with a substance abuse problem. In J.G. Gorton, & R. Partridge (Eds.) *Practice and management of psychiatric emergency care*. St. Louis: CV Mosby Co., 1982.

109. Shafer, J. Designer drugs. *Science*, 1985, 85, 60-67.

110. Shah, N.S., & Donald, A.G. *Endorphins and opiate antagonists in psychiatric research: Clinical implications*. New York: Plenum Press, 1982.

111. Simpson, D.D., Joe, G.W., & Bracy, S.A. Six-year follow-up of opioid addicts after admission to treatment. *Archives of General Psychiatry*, 1982, 39, 1318-1326.

112. Sjoquist, B., Borg, B., & Kvande, H. Catecholamine derived compounds in urine and cerebrospinal fluid from alcoholics during and after long-standing intoxication. *Substance and Alcohol Actions and Misuse*, 1981, 2, 63-72.

113. Skolnick, P., Moncada, V., Barker, J.L., & Paul. S.M. Pentobarbital: Dual actions to increase brain benzodiazepine receptor affinity. *Science*, 1981, 211, 1448-1450.

114. Skolnick, P., & Paul, S.M. Benzodiazepine receptors in the central nervous system. *International Review of Neurobiology*, 1982, 23, 103-140.

115. Smith, B.R., Amit, Z., Aragon, C.M.G., & Socaransky, S.M. Neurobiological correlates of ethanol self-administration: The role of acetaldehyde. In C.A. Naranjo & E.M. Sellers (Eds.) *Research advances in new psychopharmacological treatments for alcoholism*, Amsterdam: Elsevier Science Publishers, 1985.

116. Smith, D.E., Landry, M.J., & Wesson, D.R. Barbiturate, sedative, hypnotic agents. In American Psychiatric Association (Eds.) *Treatment of psychiatric disorders: A task force report of the American Psychiatric Association*, Washington, D.C.: American Psychiatric Association, 1989.

117. Smith, D.E., Milkman, H.B., & Sunderwith, S.G. Addictive disease: Concept and controversy. In H.B. Milkman & H.J. Shaffer (Eds.) *The addictions: Multidisciplinary perspectives and treatment*. Lexington, MA: D.C. Heath and Co., 1985.

118. Smith, D.E., & Wesson, D.R. Benzodiazepine dependency syndrome. *Journal of Psychoactive Drugs*, 1983, 15, 85-95.

119. Suzdak, P.D., Glowa, J.R., Crawley, J.N., Schwartz, R.D., Skolnick, P., & Paul, S.M. A selective imidazobenzodiazepine antagonist of ethanol in the rat. *Science*, 1986, 234, 1243-1247.

120. Suzdak, P.D., & Paul, S.M. Ethanol stimulates GABA receptor-mediated Cl- ion flux in vitro: Possible relationship to the anxiolytic and intoxicating actions of alcohol. *Psychopharmacology Bulletin*, 1987, 23, 445-451.

121. Tabakoff, B., Cornell, N., & Hoffman, P.L. Alcohol tolerance. *Annals of Emergency Medicine*, 1986, 15, 1005-1012.

122. Tabakoff, B., & Hoffman, P.L. Alcohol interactions with brain opiate receptors. *Life Science*, 1983, 32, 197-204.

123. Tabakoff, B., & Hoffman, P.L. Biochemical pharmacology of alcohol. In H.Y. Meltzer (Ed.) *Psychopharmacology: The third generation of progress*, New York: Raven Press, 1987.

124. Trachtenberg, M.C., & Blum, K. Alcohol and opioid peptides: Neuropharmacological rationale for physical craving of alcohol. *American Journal of Drug and Alcohol Abuse*, 1987, 13, 365-372.

125. VanThiel, D.H., Gavaler, J.S., & Sanghvi, A. Recovery of sexual function in abstinent alcoholic men. *Gastroenterology*, 1983, 84, 677-682.

126. Vereby, K., & Blum, K. Alcohol euphoria: Possible mediation via endorphinergic mechanisms. *Journal of Psychedelic Drugs*, 1979, 11, 305-311.

127. Vereby, K., Volavka, J., & Clouet, D. Endorphins in psychiatry. *Archives of General Psychiatry*, 1978, 35, 877-888.

128. Way, E.L. The narcotics situation in Hong Kong. In *Bulletin: Drug Addiction and Narcotics*. Washington, D.C.: NAS-NRC, 1964.

129. Way, E.L. Sites and mechanisms of basic narcotic receptor function based on current research. *Annals of Emergency Medicine*, 1986, <u>15</u>, 1021-1025.

130. Wikler, A. Neurophysiological and neuropsychiatric aspects of opioid dependence. In W.R. Martin & H. Isbell (Eds.) *Drug addiction and the U.S. Public Health Service*. Washington, D.C.: U.S. Govt. Printing Office, 1978.

131. Wilkinson, D.A., & Carlen, P.L. Relation of neuropsychological test performance in alcoholics to brain morphology measured by computed tomography. In H. Begleiter (Ed.) *Biological effects of alcoholism*, New York: Plenum Press, 1980.

132. Wilson, G.T. Alcohol and human sexual behavior. *Behavior Research and Therapy*, 1977, <u>15</u>, 239-252.

133. Woods, J.H., & Winger, G. Opioids, receptors and abuse liability. In H.Y. Meltzer (Ed.) *Psychopharmacology: The third generation of progress*, New York: Raven Press, 1987.

134. *Zinberg, N.E. Nonaddictive opiate use. In R.L. Dupont, A. Goldstein, & J. O'Donnel (Eds.) *Handbook on drug abuse*, Washington, D.C.: U.S. Govt. Printing Office, 1979.

135. Ziporyn, T. A growing industry and menace: Makeshift laboratory's designer drugs. *Journal of the American Medical Association*, 1986, <u>256</u>, 3061-3063.

136. *Zweben, J.E., & Sorensen, J.L. Misunderstandings about methadone. *Journal of Psychoactive Drugs*, 1988, <u>20</u>, 275-281.

*Introductory or intermediate reading

Chapter 17

HALLUCINOGENS

The purposes of this chapter are to:

1. Identify the commonalities of and differences among the hallucinogens,

2. Compare the basic pharmacology, and sites and mechanisms of action, of a few representative hallucinogens, including marijuana, LSD, and MDMA (Ecstasy),

3. Present the acute pharmacological and behavioral side effects of low and medium doses of representative hallucinogenic drugs, with an emphasis on within-class differences, and

4. Briefly cover hallucinogen overdose and discuss the controversies surrounding the pharmacological and behavioral effects of chronic hallucinogen use.

COMMONALITIES AND DIFFERENCES

Despite the erroneous view that the use of hallucinogenic drugs is a phenomenon of the turbulent 1960s, a variety of evidence demonstrates that "primitive" cultures have been using mescaline, hallucinogenic mushrooms, and marijuana for centuries[36,50,102]. Despite some important differences at overdose, the hallucinogens can be categorized together because they induce similar behavioral and physiological effects at their individually determined low and medium doses. At low and medium doses that do not induce significant toxic effects, they induce dose-dependent "states of alternate perception, thought and feeling that are not experienced otherwise except in dreams or at times of religious exaltation"[69]. Thus, compounds obtained from the belladonna or related plants, such as **atropine** and **scopolamine**, are often considered to not be hallucinogens, since their hallucinogenic effects occur only at doses where there are widespread toxic effects that induce an **anticholinergic delirium**[33,165]. A partial list of the compounds included in this category is displayed in Table 17.1. Observers of the chemical structure of the various hallucinogens have noted that many of the compounds could be placed into subcategories dependent upon whether they were predominantly norepinephrine-like or predominantly serotonin-like[67,126].

Table 17.1
A Partial List of Hallucinogens

Marijuana Amanita muscaria

Serotonin-like
LSD   Harmine   Psilocybin   Psilocin   Bufotenine   DMT

Norepinephrine-like
Mescaline   DOM(STP)   MDA   MDMA   TMA   Myristicin   Elemicin

The Labeling Problem

While the term "hallucinogen" will be used in this text to label this class of drugs, the term does present a number of difficulties. Most importantly, true **hallucinations** (the perception of events that have not actually occurred) are not always a significant aspect of consumption of the drugs placed into this category[13,79]. Additionally, a variety of prescription and over-the-counter compounds may induce hallucinations in some individuals even at low chronic doses[53], and toxic reactions that occur at the right of the dose-response curve of any drug may induce hallucinations[136]. Unfortunately, other proposed labels, rather than providing a more accurate description, tend to instead reflect the enthusiasm or antagonism that the individual proposing the label holds toward this class of drugs. For example, those who viewed these drugs as "mind-expanding" or "growth-enhancing" revealed their positive bias when they labeled the compounds "psychedelic"[66,83]. Those who deplore the use of these compounds reveal their negative bias by suggesting that the compounds be labeled as "psychotomimetics"[12]. However, the ability of the compounds in Table 17.1 to induce a true psychosis remains controversial and scientists acknowledge that a variety of compounds not found in Table 17.1 may also be psychotomimetic[29,53,62].

As in previous chapters on stimulants and depressants, the evaluation of true within-class differences among the hallucinogens is hampered by differences in the most commonly employed dose of each drug and the most commonly used method of administration. It would be beyond the scope of the present text to discuss each and every compound in Table 17.1. Instead, emphasis will be placed on the following representative hallucinogens: marijuana, LSD, and MDMA (more commonly known as "ecstasy")[37].

Summary of Commonalities and Differences

The compounds listed in Table 17.1 exhibit within-class differences that are sometimes obscured by culturally determined variations in dose, method of administration, and other factors. However, they all have in common the capability of inducing alterations in thought, perception, and mood, even at low or medium doses that are free of acute toxic effects. Despite the fact that they are not always taken at doses sufficient to induce hallucinations, there is a general consensus that the term "hallucinogen" provides the least biased label for drugs in this category.

BASIC PHARMACOLOGY

Marijuana

There are at least 60 compounds in the common hemp plant, **cannabis sativa**, that are unique to that plant. These compounds are referred to as **cannabinoids**. The most potent of the three major cannabinoids are **delta**^{9}- and delta ^{8}-tetrahydrocannabinol (THC). Of the remaining two major cannabinoids, **cannabinol** has only one-tenth of the activity of THC in humans, while **cannabidiol** seems to be devoid of psychoactive effects in humans[123]. Research about "marijuana" may involve inhalation of marijuana smoke, oral administration of an extract of some or all of the cannabinoids, or even intravenous injection of a single type of cannabinoid. When used illicitly, leaves and flowers of the plant are usually smoked, but oral administration is not uncommon. THC is extremely lipid soluble, and when it is administered intravenously, it produces a nearly immediate state of intoxication. Similarly, smoking marijuana also leads to a nearly immediate state of intoxication, with peak blood levels of the drug obtained within three minutes. When consumed orally, peak blood levels are not obtained for about 30-90 minutes[116]. Once absorbed, THC is highly bound to plasma proteins. Since THC is so lipid soluble, the drug tends to be stored in fatty areas of the body, with the greatest concentrations being in liver, heart and lung. Within 30 minutes of smoking, levels in the lipid-rich brain are three to six times higher than those found in the blood. This suggests that the drug easily crosses the blood-brain barrier[21]. The high lipid solubility of THC enables easy crossing of the placental barrier and results in THC concentrations in mother's milk that are much higher than levels in maternal blood[120].

Analysis of the metabolism of marijuana is complicated by a number of factors. First, there are a great number of potentially relevant constituents of the plant, each of which must be studied separately[4]. Secondly, there may be differences between active and passive inhalers of marijuana smoke[122], chronic versus first-time users[44,115], and between light and heavy chronic users[116]. Third, there are vast differences in metabolism between the drug when taken orally versus the drug when inhaled or injected. In particular, orally consumed marijuana undergoes significant first-pass metabolism, such that by the time the drug has gone from intestines through the liver and into the bloodstream, only 10% to 20% of the original psychoactive ingredients remains[21]. Finally, the half-life of THC in the blood is a matter of minutes since it and the other active ingredients of marijuana are rapidly converted to both active and inactive metabolites by the liver[52]. Blood levels then decrease very slowly as the lipophilic drug is slowly released from fatty areas of the body, and then this newly released drug is rapidly metabolized by the liver. Due to this slow release from fatty tissue, marijuana's **biological half-life** (the time it takes for half of the drug to leave the body, rather than to simply be removed from the bloodstream) is somewhere between 25 and 30 hours[32].

Very little of the original compound is excreted unchanged from the body. Within five days, about 90% of an original dose of THC will be found to have been excreted as metabolite. The majority of these metabolites are found in the feces, with only about 20% found in the urine[52]. The basic pharmacology of marijuana is summarized in Table 17.2.

Table 17.2
Basic Pharmacology of Marijuana

- Obtained from common hemp plant, cannabis sativa
- Crude marijuana contains many active and inactive ingredients
- Is usually smoked, but can be taken orally or injected
- Extremely lipid soluble with rapid onset of effects
- Easily crosses blood-brain and placental barriers
- Stored in lipid soluble areas of the body
- Highly bound to plasma proteins
- Extensively metabolized by liver enzymes to active and inactive metabolites
- Complex metabolism: blood half-life much shorter than biological half-life
- Majority of metabolites excreted in feces, only 20% in urine

LSD

LSD (LySergic acid Diethylamide) was created by Albert Hofmann at Sandoz Laboratories as he searched for a new cure for sinus problems. He discovered the psychological properties of the compound on April 16, 1943, when he accidentally, through contact or inhalation, received a small dose of the drug[59,132]. LSD is a clear, colorless, odorless liquid that can be prepared in a variety of ways and administered by a variety of methods. Since it is highly lipid soluble, the drug is rapidly absorbed when consumed orally. It is rarely injected, except in laboratory settings. However administered, LSD easily passes the blood-brain and placental barriers. Physical effects occur rapidly, while subjectively noticeable psychological events begin from 30 to 60 minutes after oral ingestion. The highest concentrations of the drug after consumption are found in the liver and kidneys, while only a small fraction of the administered drug is found in the brain[68]. LSD is metabolized by liver enzymes and the majority of its behaviorally inactive metabolites are found in the feces. Estimates of the half-life of LSD in human plasma range from three hours[46] to eight hours[3]. The acute psychological effects of LSD consumption last from eight to ten hours[43]. Table 17.3 summarizes the basic pharmacology of LSD.

Table 17.3
Basic Pharmacology of LSD

- Tasteless, colorless, odorless liquid available in many preparations
- Rapidly absorbed when taken orally
- Easily crosses blood-brain and placental barriers
- Rapid physical effects with psychological effects delayed for 30 to 60 minutes
- Metabolized by liver enzymes to inactive metabolites
- Metabolites found mainly in feces
- Half-life ranging from 3 to 8 hours
- Acute psychological effects last from 8 to 10 hours

MDMA

MDMA (3,4-MethyleneDioxyMethAmphetamine), and the related compound MDA, are structurally similar to both amphetamine and mescaline. As a result, both MDMA and MDA are sympathomimetic and often considered as a member of a subset of hallucinogens sometimes referred to as the "stimulant-hallucinogens"[8]. MDMA is usually taken in pill form, although it is sometimes insufflated and, even more rarely, injected. The normal effective dose is between 100 and 150 mg[147]. The drug is moderately lipid soluble, with peak blood levels being reached within two hours of oral administration. Psychoactive effects normally begin within half an hour of oral ingestion and continue for approximately six hours, with maximal effects at two hours after oral ingestion[69]. MDMA is metabolized by liver enzymes to the psychoactive metabolite, MDA. The majority of the parent drug is excreted unchanged in the urine. The half-life of MDMA in humans is poorly studied, but has been estimated at about 7 1/2 hours[6]. Table 17.4 summarizes the basic pharmacology of MDMA.

Table 17.4
Basic Pharmacology of MDMA

- Usually taken in pill form, but can be insufflated or injected
- Moderately lipid soluble
- Onset of drug effects within half-hour of oral ingestion
- Metabolized by liver enzymes to psychoactive MDA
- Majority of parent drug found unchanged in urine
- Half-life of about 7 1/2 hours
- Psychoactive effects continue for approximately 6 hours

Summary of Basic Pharmacology

LSD, MDA, and MDMA are synthetic compounds, while crude marijuana comes from the common hemp plant and contains many active and inactive ingredients. LSD is usually consumed orally, MDMA is taken orally, insufflated, or injected, and marijuana is usually smoked or consumed orally. Both marijuana and LSD are highly lipid soluble and easily cross blood-brain and placental barriers, while MDMA is only moderately lipid soluble. Physical effects of marijuana and LSD are rapid, while the psychological effects of LSD and MDMA tend to be delayed. Of the three hallucinogens, marijuana is the only one whose ingredients show significant binding to plasma proteins and tend to be stored in lipid soluble areas of the body. The various components of marijuana have a complex metabolism to many active and inactive metabolites. These are excreted mainly in feces but also in urine. LSD is metabolized to inactive metabolites found mainly in feces, while the majority of MDMA is excreted as the parent compound in urine.

SITES AND MECHANISM OF ACTION

Marijuana

There is evidence that the cannabinoids may exert their effects through interactions with neuronal membranes, through influencing second messengers involved in neurotransmission, through alterations in the synthesis of the hormone **prostaglandin**, and through interaction with specific receptors for a variety of neurotransmitters, steroids, opioids, and cannabinoids[30,94]. However, most research has focused on the still unresolved question of whether marijuana's mechanism of action is disruption of the neuronal membrane or instead an interaction with specific cannabinoid receptors. A proposed resolution of this dilemma suggests that the central nervous system depressant effects of marijuana are due to disruption of neuronal membranes, while those hallucinogenic and other characteristics unique to marijuana are due to interaction with specific cannabinoid receptors[93,95]. However, this resolution may be underestimating the role of specific cannabinoid receptors in the depressant effects of marijuana.

While the location and function of specific cannabinoid receptors in human brain are only beginning to be elucidated, increases in knowledge about these receptors have already led to a number of benefits, including increased understanding about how to manipulate the structure of cannabinoids to create compounds that induce only specific aspects of marijuana ingestion[93]. Perhaps the most exciting aspect of the identification of cannabinoid receptors is the possibility of the development of an antagonist[95]. Development of an antagonist can be expected to provide vast amounts of new information about the role of specific cannabinoid binding sites in the mechanism of action of marijuana.

LSD

There is some evidence that the mechanism of action of LSD is through interaction with receptors for a number of different neurotransmitters. Nonetheless, many researchers concur with the assertion that "however the data are marshalled, the evidence is overwhelming of a linkage of LSD to serotonin systems"[45]. The effects of LSD may be due to the strong postsynaptic agonist effect on serotonin neurons. In a study of the effects of a variety of hallucinogens in human cortex, LSD was the most powerfully attracted to serotonin receptors in human brain[126]. Even more specifically, other researchers have found a very high ($r=0.97$) positive correlation between the hallucinogenic capacity of a variety of drugs and their ability to bind to a subpopulation of serotonin receptors referred to as **5-HT$_2$** receptors. Interestingly, LSD was both the most powerful hallucinogen and the drug that bound most strongly to the 5-HT$_2$ receptors[138]. Figure 17.1 shows the effect of LSD as a serotonin postsynaptic receptor agonist.

MDMA

Although MDMA was first developed, but never marketed, as a diet pill in 1914[147], little is known about its mechanism of action. There was little scientific concern about the compound until prohibitionist attitudes were fueled by the drug's "discovery" by the general population in the mid-1980s[124]. Since MDMA is best considered a "stimulant-hallucinogen"[8], it is not surprising that studies have found that the drug may act by enhancing the release of presynaptic dopamine and by interaction with serotonin, particularly 5-HT$_2$ receptors[143]. More recently, it has been suggested that the effects of MDMA on the two different neurotransmitter systems are time-dependent. That is, in rats, MDMA interacted with serotonin receptors, but had no effect on dopamine, at 20 minutes post-injection. By 90 minutes after injection, there was a clear effect on dopamine receptors[144]. Further research will be required to determine the precise site and mechanism of action of MDMA in humans.

L > LSD   S > Serotonin

Figure 17.1.   The synaptic mechanism of action of LSD. LSD has an agonist effect because it acts as a direct agonist that interacts with postsynaptic serotonin receptors. LSD thus results in the presynaptic serotonin neuron having a greater than normal effect on the postsynaptic neuron.

Summary of Sites and Mechanisms of Action

The active ingredients in marijuana may induce some of their effects through disruption of neuronal membranes, although there is mounting evidence of the importance of interaction with endogenous THC receptors. LSD most probably exerts its hallucinogenic effect(s) as a result of a postsynaptic agonist action at $5HT_2$ receptors. The mechanism of action of MDMA in humans is unclear, although data from animals suggests a role for a time-dependent enhancement of presynaptic dopamine release followed by a postsynaptic agonist action at $5HT_2$ receptors.

ACUTE SIDE EFFECTS AT LOW AND MEDIUM DOSES

There are, of course, a variety of physical and, in particular, psychological effects common to all the hallucinogens. However, differences in common methods of administration, basic pharmacology, and sites and mechanism of action result in significant differences in the acute side effects experienced at low and medium doses of marijuana, LSD, and MDMA.

Marijuana

At low doses, setting can have a profound impact upon the behavioral consequences of marijuana, while at higher doses, setting has less of an impact[15]. Like all drugs,
the acute effects of marijuana are dose-dependent. After subjects were trained to contrast
the reinforcing effects of marijuana cigarettes containing 2.7% THC versus 0.0% THC
(placebo), they were asked to evaluate cigarettes with intermediate levels of THC. These
trained subjects rated cigarettes with 0.9% THC as being placebo cigarettes while they
rated cigarettes with 1.4% THC as clearly containing marijuana[18]. Even stronger evidence for the dose-dependent effects of marijuana was demonstrated in a comparison of
the subjective "high" versus plasma levels of THC in humans given the drug orally, by
injection, or in marijuana smoke[115]. This study found that variations in the intensity of
the subjective "high" and a number of physical responses correlated well with variations
in the plasma levels of the drug. The common misconception that a marijuana smoker
must be either "straight" or "stoned" is challenged by this laboratory evidence of
dose-dependent variations in subjective "high."

The question of whether present-day marijuana is more potent than that employed by users in the past is a controversial issue[105]. Concerns that individuals smoking
today's "more powerful" marijuana are inadvertently exposing themselves to unexpect-
edly high levels of THC could be minimized by laboratory evidence demonstrating that
more potent marijuana leads to a dose-dependent decrease in acute marijuana consumption. There have been contradictory reports from laboratory research on whether individuals who smoke marijuana of various potencies are able to **titrate** their dose to regulate
their state of intoxication. Some studies show that people smoke less of higher potency
marijuana than weaker potency marijuana[121], while others fail to find evidence that
smokers adjust their intake of marijuana to account for variations in THC content[169]. Only
widespread evaluation of the potency of illicitly available marijuana and further studies
of smoker's ability to titrate dose will provide an accurate answer to the question of
whether consumption of presently available marijuana is more dangerous than was
consumption of marijuana available in the past[105].

A wide range of well-designed studies have determined that the acute effects of
low and medium dose marijuana intoxication include profound effects on sensory and
perceptual processes (especially time distortion), and cognitive function (especially
short-term memory)[62,104,119]. Not surprisingly, these often sought-after effects may, in
some individuals, induce a state of acute panic or severe anxiety[2]. One study found that
individuals who suffer from the form of anxiety associated with acute panic (see Chapter
10) were more likely than control subjects to experience anxiety and panic after marijuana
smoking[154].

There are a number of physical side effects of acute marijuana consumption,
including a dose-dependent reduction in the temperature of the body[22,30]. Since smoking
marijuana involves the inhalation of hot gases, there is acute irritation to the mouth, air
passageways, and lungs. Subjects being trained to discriminate between placebo and
THC-containing marijuana cigarettes noted that the active cigarettes were even more
"harsh" than the placebo cigarettes, which consisted of marijuana from which all active
cannabinoids had been removed[18]. The negative respiratory consequences of chronic

marijuana consumption will be discussed below, although it should be noted that a positive effect of acute THC consumption is a dilation of the bronchial tubes[129].

Consumption of marijuana also cut in half the intraocular pressure in the eyes of 9 of 11 subjects. This reduction began 30 minutes after smoking and continued for four to five hours[55]. Reddening of the conjunctival area of the eye and increases in pulse rate have been found to correlate closely with both plasma levels of THC and the subjective experience of intoxication[5]. Research with 10 healthy males revealed that ingestion of a moderate-dose (1.8% THC) marijuana cigarette led to an average increase of 18 heartbeats per minute[14]. Part of this effect is due to a direct stimulation of heart rate observable even after oral administration[62], but part also comes from the fact that smoking marijuana leads to inhalation of significant amounts of carbon monoxide that decrease the oxygen-carrying capacity of red blood cells[156].

LSD

The most remarkable fact about LSD is the incredible potency of the compound compared to the other hallucinogens. For example, the average dose of LSD is 100 to 500 micrograms, while the average dose of mescaline is 100-500 milligrams and the average dose of psilocybin or psilocin is 10 to 50 milligrams[152].

While present restrictive laws make it difficult to conduct prospective research with LSD, much laboratory experimentation occurred during the 1950s and early 1960s. A major advantage of this research is that it was conducted when the general population's state of knowledge regarding the hallucinogens was practically nonexistent. Since the influence of set and setting have such a profound effect on a subject's reaction to LSD[127], these early studies offer the advantage of data obtained from subjects with few expectations about the physical or psychological effects of LSD.

The initial examination of the time course of the psychological effects of LSD in normal human volunteers was conducted in the mid-1950s[139]. This work was later replicated and expanded in a single-blind, placebo-controlled study that revealed the similar time course of the effects of LSD on a wide range of physical variables and psychological measures covering cognition, perception, affect, and self-image[88].

The acute psychological effects of low to moderate doses of LSD can be grouped into "psychic symptoms" such as changes in mood, distorted time sense, dreamlike feelings, and visual hallucinations, "perceptual symptoms" such as alterations in the perception of shapes and colors, a perceived increase in the sense of hearing, and **synesthesia** (a crossing over of sensory input such that colors are "felt" and sounds are "seen")[29]. Early studies of the time course of these psychological effects revealed that they tend to wax and wane simultaneously in an unpredictable pattern[88,139]. The effects of LSD are dose-dependent, with increases in the intensity of physical and psychological effects correlating with increases in dose. Evidence for the dose-dependent effects of LSD was obtained when research demonstrated that performance on simple arithmetic tests was most impaired when blood levels of the drug were maximal, with performance improving as blood levels dropped[3].

The early experimental studies of LSD also revealed that, even in laboratory settings with carefully selected subjects, unpleasant psychological effects occurred, sometimes after only a single administration, sometimes after many previous positive experiences. Later evaluations of a great number of such studies revealed that these unpleasant psychological effects included troublesome visual and/or auditory hallucinations, anxiety, panic, severe depression, suicidal thoughts, or extreme confusion[161]. When illicit LSD of unknown potency and purity is consumed under uncontrolled settings by self-selected individuals who may, or may not, be psychologically unstable, the "bad trips" sometimes observed in the laboratory might lead to an acute "psychosis" that sometimes required hospitalization[12]. The rapid alterations in perception and affect may be particularly upsetting to the consumer of illicit LSD[31], although it must be remembered that others find these effects reinforcing.

Physical symptoms of LSD consumed at low or medium doses tend to be minimal, since by definition hallucinogens induce their psychological effects at doses that are not acutely toxic to the brain or rest of the body[69]. However, the sympathomimetic effect of LSD is clear in that the usually consumed doses induce markedly dilated pupils, heightened reflexes, increased muscle tension, mildly increased temperature, and variable effects on salivation, blood pressure, heart rate, and respiration[43,60]. In addition, laboratory studies have found an unpredictable and variable instance of minor physical complaints including dizziness, weakness, nausea, drowsiness, blurred vision and tingling in the extremities[92,139].

MDMA

The 1986 statement that "there have been no controlled studies designed to assess the subjective effects of MDMA in humans"[77] is an unfortunate truth. However, an evaluation of the structurally similar compound, MDA, revealed that it induces an experience similar to, but significantly less potent than, that caused by LSD. In addition, the "stimulant" action of the compound, while perhaps enhancing the probability that the experience will be subjectively perceived as pleasurable, also increases the probability of stimulant-like side effects including increased blood pressure and heart rate, anxiety, muscle rigidity, and tremor[160]. Placebo-controlled and triple-blind studies of the potential psychiatric therapeutic effectiveness of MDMA will be required to evaluate anecdotal reports which may be biased by the enthusiasm of both therapist and patient.

Summary of Acute Side Effects
at Low and Medium Doses

The acute behavioral and physical side effects of marijuana, LSD, and MDMA are all dose-dependent and, to greater or lesser degrees, time-dependent. The sought after psychological effects of any of these hallucinogens can sometimes be so excessive that they lead to acute states of anxiety and/or panic. The physical side effects of LSD are limited to a sympathomimetic action, while MDMA shares the central and peripheral nervous system side effects of the stimulants discussed in Chapter 15. Marijuana consumption leads to a reddening of the conjunctiva, an increase in heart rate, a decrease in body temperature, and a decrease in intraocular pressure. While marijuana smoke irritates the respiratory system, THC itself induces a relaxation of the bronchial tubes.

OVERDOSE

Although there have been questionable reports of deaths from excess intake of marijuana[110], it appears that there are no fatal cases of marijuana overdose in humans that can be directly attributed to the biological effects of the drug. Animal studies of the toxicity of marijuana and THC indicate that the recreational window between the commonly employed recreational dose and the lethal dose is forty-fold[125]. Animal fatalities are usually due to respiratory depression, perhaps complicated by a severe drop in body temperature[118]. In a comparison of alcohol and marijuana, it was noted that the great lipid solubility of marijuana made it "almost impossible to absorb a fatal dose of marijuana sufficiently rapidly...via the lungs in smoke before the onset of coma"[159]. It is much more likely that overdose on marijuana will lead to psychological disturbances, ranging from anxiety, to paranoia, to a toxic delirium including an acute psychosis[62]. The negative psychological effects of acute marijuana overdose are best dealt with by calm reassurance, or the timely administration of antianxiety agents[80].

A reviewer has noted that "in man, deaths attributed to the *direct* effects of LSD are unknown, although fatal accidents and suicides during states of LSD intoxication have occurred"[69]. When studied in animals, death from LSD overdose occurs at widely varying doses depending upon the animal species studied and whether the drug was administered orally or by injection[92]. It has been suggested that the toxic dose of LSD in humans is approximately 0.2 mg/kg[58]. One researcher noted the extremely high safety margin of a drug that can induce effects at doses as low as 10 to 15 micrograms and yet is known to not be fatal even at doses hundreds of times higher[23]. Individuals showing up at emergency rooms as cases of "LSD overdose" are more likely suffering from an acute adverse reaction. They may be treated with antianxiety agents and calm reassurance ("talking down")[71].

It has been noted that while death following consumption of MDMA is rare, it has occurred, particularly in individuals with heart disease[34]. As is so often the case with illicit drugs, it is possible to find cases where death was associated with the use of MDMA or MDA, but it is more difficult to assert a causal relationship between drug ingestion and death. For example, a report on overdose with MDA was difficult to interpret because the patients had been taking other drugs, particularly amphetamine and secobarbital, prior to their intake of MDA[131]. The consequences of overdose with MDMA or MDA must be treated symptomatically, since they are similar to those seen with overdose of stimulants (see Chapter 15) and include stroke, heartbeat irregularities, convulsions, etc.[34].

Summary of Overdose

It is difficult to find cases of death in humans from the direct physical consequences of overdose with marijuana or LSD since each of these drugs has a large recreational window. While the immediate cause of death in cases of MDMA or MDA overdose in humans may be difficult to interpret, the stimulant action of these drugs can render overdose lethal. Treatment of marijuana or LSD overdose is most often directed at negative psychological consequences, which may be treated by calm reassurance or antianxiety agents. Treatment of MDMA overdose should be directed towards the symptoms of stimulant overdose.

CHRONIC EFFECTS

There are a number of factors that make it difficult to group together the chronic effects of the three characteristic hallucinogens under study in this chapter. First, the patterns of chronic use of the hallucinogens differ widely. For example, marijuana consumption ranges from occasional use to compulsive patterns of daily consumption of large amounts of the drug[107]. On the other hand, consumption of LSD and MDMA tend to follow a pattern of single intakes separated by weeks or months[124]. While there have been and probably continue to be individuals who consume LSD more frequently over long periods of time, even these individuals rarely take the drug more than once every two weeks[69]. In a ten-year follow-up of the medical uses of LSD, researchers found that even with illicit use "compulsive patterns of LSD use rarely develop"[98]. Second, LSD and MDMA are usually taken orally, while marijuana is most often smoked. Finally, the widespread use of MDMA is a fairly recent phenomenon, while the longer history of use of LSD and, particularly, of marijuana, has led to a great deal of information about the various long-term consequences of these latter two drugs. Thus, this section focuses upon the extensive literature which examined the putative chronic effects of marijuana and LSD, and then concludes with a brief discussion of the possibility of brain damage from chronic MDMA use.

Marijuana

As with all drugs, the chronic effects of marijuana are dependent upon the method of administration, dose, frequency and intermittency of administration, and the concurrent use of other drugs. Experiments regarding drug interactions showed that while alcohol does not increase the subjective level of intoxication of marijuana, marijuana does increase the intoxication obtained from alcohol[90]. Other researchers found that the simultaneous use of both marijuana and cocaine increases the heart rate of experimental subjects significantly more than either drug alone[42].

Reverse tolerance. Early reports suggested that marijuana was unique among drugs in that there was a sensitization to the reinforcing effects of the drug[164]. However, experimental and anecdotal evidence of this "reverse tolerance" in regular marijuana users has been questioned on a number of grounds. First, heavy users of marijuana smoke more efficiently. One study found that frequent smokers extract 23% of the THC in marijuana while infrequent smokers obtain only 10% of the THC[87]. Second, the vast majority of experimental studies have, in fact, demonstrated the occurrence of tolerance to the reinforcing and other effects of marijuana, both in animals[30] and humans[56,75,114]. One study employing double-blind conditions gave male subjects 5 to 21 days of from 10-30 mg of oral THC every three or four hours. At the end of the chronic administration of THC, subjects were abruptly switched, again under double-blind conditions, to placebo. At various times after the placebo substitution, active THC was again administered, either intravenously or through inhalation, under double-blind conditions so that the researchers could evaluate the effect of the chronic treatment upon the acute response. A variety of evidence clearly demonstrated the existence of tolerance. This evidence included a 50% reduction in intoxication from a 30 mg oral dose of THC after only five days of 10 mg/day of oral THC, and a virtual disappearance of many of the physical consequences of each dose during chronic intake after, at most, 10 days of chronic consumption[76]. This experimental evidence of tolerance to the reinforcing effects of marijuana suggests that "reverse tolerance" probably results from increases in dose obtained by efficient and experienced marijuana smokers.

Physical dependency. The potential for chronic use of marijuana to result in physical dependency remains controversial. A reviewer of animal studies concluded that clear evidence of dependence had yet to be produced, since experiments differed as to whether the cessation phenomena could be reversed by a renewal of marijuana intake[30]. Laboratory demonstrations of dependence in humans have noted that an abrupt halt in consumption of THC led to irritability, sleep disturbances, decreased appetite, nausea, vomiting, diarrhea, sweating, salivation and tremors[39]. The study on tolerance to THC in humans discussed above found similar symptoms when subjects were switched to placebo, and furthermore found that these symptoms could be reduced for two to three hours by the consumption of a marijuana cigarette[76]. These laboratory demonstrations have been criticized, however, for employing doses and drug regimens that greatly exceed the usual pattern of illicit use of marijuana[62].

Toxicity. The long biological half-life of marijuana has fueled concern that the persistence of the drug in the body for long periods of time "might lead to serious physical toxicity or overt and subtle psychological changes"[27]. There have been demonstrations that the effects of marijuana persist, at least until the day after smoking marijuana, inducing effects on mood[19] and impairments in the performance of complex tasks such as piloting an airplane[170]. However, consideration of the slow release of THC from lipid-rich areas of the body and the subsequent rapid metabolism of this recently released THC suggests that "the apprehension about accumulation of THC from repeated use is based on evidence indicating only the accumulation of drug that is either in inactive form to begin with or is rendered inactive before reaching the circulation in any pharmacologically active amount"[62].

Effects on the brain. There is evidence that chronic consumption of marijuana may have negative effects upon the brain. For example, studies in rats have found that "aginglike" changes in the brain might be accelerated by chronic marijuana administration[82]. In addition, studies in humans have demonstrated changes in the electrical activity of the brain as a result of chronic marijuana use[153]. However, regional cerebral blood flow, a measure of the level of activity of discrete areas of the brain, was not different in chronic marijuana users compared to control subjects[96]. Studies have been inconsistent in providing evidence of cognitive deficits in chronic marijuana users. Some studies have found that chronic marijuana use does impair short-term memory and a variety of mental operations[16,17]. Other studies, also involving complex and varied tests of cognitive function, have failed to find evidence of cognitive impairment[49,134], even in users of remarkably high doses who have consumed marijuana on a regular basis for many years[142].

Other physical effects. Concern has been expressed regarding the negative effects of chronic marijuana use upon the respiratory, cardiovascular, reproductive and immune system. There is substantial evidence that the dilation of the bronchial tubes induced by acute marijuana consumption does not protect against damage to the respiratory system[155]. In addition, there is evidence of precancerous changes in the lungs of chronic marijuana smokers[40], despite the fact that "as yet, it is far easier to find pulmonary cripples from the abuse of tobacco than it is to find any evidence of clinically important pulmonary insufficiency from smoking of cannabis"[62]. Chronic use of marijuana does not induce a nicotine-cigarette-like chronic decrease in the oxygen carrying capacity of red blood cells, perhaps because of the long time interval between smoking sessions and the associated acute elevations in carbon monoxide[156]. While early studies suggested that marijuana may cause chromosomal damage, recent prospective studies have found no differences in the number of chromosomal breaks in controls versus subjects given chronic (in one case up to 72 days) administrations of marijuana[97,113]. Finally, evidence of damage to the immune system from chronic marijuana consumption is contradictory. Critics have pointed out that studies indicating impairment of the immune system have used test-tube assays involving extremely large doses of marijuana and that there is no compelling clinical evidence of impaired immunity in chronic marijuana smokers[63].

Therapeutic potential. The diverse psychological and physical effects of marijuana have led to investigations of the therapeutic potential of the drug. There is a long history of the use of marijuana as medicine for a variety of disorders[102,135], and a number of reviews of the potential of marijuana as medicine have been published[62,84,93,103]. These reviews evaluated the accumulating evidence suggesting a use for marijuana as an analgesic, anticonvulsant, antinausea agent, sleeping aid, muscle relaxant, and treatment for asthma and the eye disease of **glaucoma.**

Psychological effects. Alterations in the physical structure of THC and other behaviorally active cannabinoids may result in therapeutic drugs devoid of negative psychological effects[93]. However, there is, at present, concern that chronic use of marijuana, whether illicit or prescribed, may have negative psychological consequences. One concern has been with the so-called **amotivational syndrome.** Early clinical reports suggested that chronic use of marijuana led to reduced work and a loss of the interest and motivation that makes daily life possible[100,149]. It has been suggested that clinical reports of amotivational syndrome could arise solely in chronic users of marijuana who already lacked conventional degrees of motivation even prior to their use of marijuana[57]. Recent retrospective research supporting the idea of the amotivational syndrome[54] has been hampered by logical difficulties regarding distinctions between correlation and causation[158], and methodological difficulties, including the absence of appropriate controls and use of individuals who consume drugs other than marijuana. Prospective experiments involving evaluation of the effort put into various types of work by subjects before and after exposure to chronic marijuana use have not supported the idea that marijuana causes an amotivational syndrome[41,106,117].

Scientific interest in the possibility that marijuana can induce a "model psychosis" extends at least to the 1845 classic of J.J. Moreau, *Hashish and Mental Illness.*

Experiments have revealed that marijuana can increase the severity of symptoms displayed by schizophrenics, but it has been suggested that this effect may be the result of interference with the effectiveness of antipsychotic drugs[111]. Research on the ability of marijuana to induce a psychosis has otherwise not been as extensive as that conducted with LSD (see below). Reviews reveal that methodologically unsound retrospective reports abound[29,74]. There are many alternative explanations for observed correlations between marijuana and psychosis, including the possibilities that only individuals who were already psychotic or had a tendency to develop psychosis experience this negative effect of chronic marijuana use[47]. One prospective study that examined the issue gave psychiatric evaluations to 100 chronic marijuana users and 50 non-using controls. All the control subjects and 97 of the chronic marijuana using subjects were evaluated after a six- to seven-year interval during which marijuana users continued their usual pattern of consumption. There was no significant increase in the incidence of psychiatric conditions, including psychosis, among the marijuana smoking, as compared to the control, groups[166].

LSD

A wide variety of chronic effects of LSD have been proposed, including brain damage, chromosomal damage, **flashbacks** (where, despite the absence of additional drug intake, the LSD-induced state returns after a period of normalcy has passed since the original experience)[167], alterations in personality (both positive and negative), and a drug-induced psychosis[13]. Perhaps due to the usually sporadic pattern of intake, there is no published evidence of humans who have become physically dependent on LSD[69]. An early study demonstrated that tolerance to the psychological effects of LSD develop, and dissipate, extremely rapidly, such that a typically effective dose had no psychological effect if the same dose of LSD had been taken in the last 24 hours[137]. An early researcher noted that the study of tolerance to LSD was hampered by the fact that few of the experimental subjects wished to take the drug multiple times[137].

Brain damage. Concern about brain damage and cognitive deficits from chronic LSD use appears to be unfounded. For example, a study of subjects with an average number of 75 experiences with illicit LSD employed an elaborate battery of tests of memory, verbal skills, motor skills, etc., and found no significant impairment[99]. Another study employing subjects with an average of 30 experiences with illicit LSD similarly found no significant differences between this group and a control group of carefully matched subjects[168]. A review of the literature in 1984 concluded that "the most carefully performed studies to date do not...support the contention that frequent LSD use is associated with permanent brain damage"[152].

Chromosomal damage. Another apparently unfounded fear about chronic LSD use involves the possibility of damage to the chromosomes necessary for successful replication of the human species. Studies demonstrating the negative effects of LSD on the chromosomes of mice are of limited use. These studies used doses 25 to 1,000 times that typically employed by humans and made no attempt to link the chromosomal abnormalities to the production of abnormal offspring[148]. Significantly, a subsequent study involving a dose of LSD 100 times that usually employed by humans failed to replicate the early studies and found no effect of LSD on the chromosomes of mice[70]. Studies have found evidence that test tube cultures of human cells suffered chromosomal damage after the addition of LSD[72,78]. However, one of these studies[78] also determined that aspirin induced chromosomal abnormalities in numbers identical to that caused by LSD. Retrospective studies of the correlation of chronic LSD use and instances of chromosomal abnormalities have been decidedly mixed, with some studies showing a greater incidence in LSD users and others showing LSD users to be indistinguishable from matched controls. Of course, retrospective studies are hampered by a number of methodological difficulties, including especially the possibility that chronic users of illicit LSD may indulge in a variety of drugs and may suffer from a variety of health problems associated with lifestyle. Prospective studies are hampered by a host of ethical problems, but two studies have looked at the chromosomes of subjects both before and after a single ingestion of LSD and neither found any evidence of chromosomal abnormalities[26,157]. One prospective study did find some evidence of chromosomal damage after LSD use, but the number of subjects was so small that the authors did not attempt to demonstrate the statistical significance of their data[65]. Although the evidence for chromosomal damage from LSD is slight, the ability of the drug to cross the placental barrier suggests that it may nonetheless be a potential teratogen[72].

Flashbacks. While a number of theories have been presented to account for LSD-induced flashbacks[152], the amount of empirical evidence about flashbacks is small. There is some data to suggest that, while flashbacks have been reported in subjects who have used LSD only once[146,151], greater numbers of experiences with LSD lead to a greater probability of flashbacks[109]. In addition, it has been suggested that individuals who experienced an unpleasant acute reaction to LSD are more susceptible to flashback than those who had a predominantly positive experience[64]. When considering flashbacks, it is important to remember that the data show "only that a spontaneous experience, subjectively described as LSD-like, followed the use of the drug--not that it was *caused* by such use"[98]. A prime example of an erroneous assertion of a causal relationship between LSD use and flashback is found in a case report in which a subject's ingestion of delirium-producing doses of the anticholinergic agents in belladonna was seen as merely being "associated with" what was, the authors asserted, a case of LSD-induced flashback[150].

Therapeutic potential. The profound effects of LSD on behavior have suggested to some that the compound may have use as a therapeutic drug. Experiments and case studies have suggested that LSD may be of use in the treatment of a wide variety of disorders[86], including alcoholism[20,73,91], opiate addiction[141], obsessive-compulsive disorder[85], and the pain and emotional anguish of terminal cancer patients[81]. There is controversy over whether the present lack of interest in the therapeutic use of LSD is the result of restrictive legislation regarding research[28,51,108,112], or a consensus that the potential dangers of the drug, combined with limited evidence of efficacy, has simply led to a decreased interest among researchers[69]. What is certain is that the absence of research on this topic leaves unanswered the early question of whether any potential positive therapeutic benefits of LSD arises from a specific action of the drug or instead is the result of a nonspecific aspect of the complex LSD-experience[112,133].

Psychosis. Case report studies of prolonged psychosis in users of illicit LSD[1,162,163], and similar events sometimes happening to laboratory subjects who ingested LSD, led researchers to investigate the psychotomimetic potential of LSD. It is important to remember that the possibility of chronic psychosis differs substantially from the equally controversial and important question of whether the acute LSD reaction is a good "model" for spontaneously occurring psychosis[10]. The general consensus is that while there are significant differences between *typical* examples of acute responses to LSD and *typical* examples of spontaneously occurring psychosis, "individual features of the drug reaction are remarkably similar to some of the experiences of the more acute schizophrenic psychoses"[29]. However, researchers and the public have been more concerned with the possibility that chronic use of LSD over long periods may induce a chronic psychosis, even in the absence of future drug intake[48].

As noted in earlier chapters, it is difficult to obtain useful and ethical experimental evidence on whether a drug can induce a prolonged psychosis. Evaluation of the data regarding the possible induction of a long-term psychosis from chronic LSD use is hampered by the illicit and officially reviled nature of the drug and the context of a subculture that extols the use of LSD as a means to an "alternate reality." Nonetheless, both retrospective and prospective techniques have been used to investigate the psychotomimetic potential of LSD. There have been a number of retrospective studies revealing the occasional occurrence of prolonged psychosis when LSD was given to subjects, sometimes psychotic individuals[38], in hopes of obtaining some psychotherapeutic benefit[24]. However, these studies are difficult to interpret, because (1) pre-LSD data on the subjects was not provided, (2) it is possible that the drug may unmask or worsen, rather than create, prolonged psychological disturbances[61], and (3) other studies have revealed positive outcomes of LSD therapy where there were no reported instances of chronic psychosis[140]. There is even one report where disturbed individuals given placebo required more follow-up therapy than individuals given LSD[145]. Even data indicating the occurrence of prolonged psychosis after LSD ingestion in normal human volunteers has been questioned since there is evidence that paid volunteers for studies involving hallucinogens had a high rate of personality disturbances[35]. Thus, even in the case of presumptively "normal" volunteers, it may be that cases of prolonged psychosis following LSD ingestion are the result of an unmasking, rather than a creation, of a psychosis.

Although there are numerous case reports of psychosis following consumption of illicit LSD, the question of whether LSD induced or unmasked a preexisting psychological disorder is impossible to answer. All these case studies of illicit LSD use are hampered by the usual problems of uncertainties about the purity, dose, and frequency of drug intake. However, there is some evidence that individuals experiencing prolonged psychosis from chronic LSD ingestion may have consumed the drug in an attempt to self-medicate an existing psychological disorder, only to find out that the drug worsened, rather than helped, their problem[11]. For example, one study reported that 34.2% of individuals suffering acute or prolonged psychotic reactions subsequent to LSD use had preexisting psychological problems[89].

While the literature on prolonged psychosis following chronic LSD ingestion is fraught with ethical and interpretive difficulties, it is possible to concur with two reviewers who stated that "although it is evident that persons may develop serious psychological disturbances after taking LSD, a causal relation between the two events is most difficult to determine"[101]. Evidence of a greater incidence of prolonged psychosis in individuals with psychological disturbances[89] should give pause to those who would consume illicit LSD in an attempt at self-medication, particularly if there is a history of psychiatric disturbances among their close relatives[7].

MDMA

Initial studies demonstrated that MDA selectively destroys serotonin nerve terminals in rats[130], and that chronic MDMA administration led to depleted serotonin levels in rats and guinea pigs[25]. Subsequent research found that the destruction of serotonin nerve terminals by chronic MDMA in rats is dependent upon the dose of the drug and the number of administrations, that it can be blocked by simultaneously giving a serotonin reuptake inhibitor, and that there were toxic effects of the drug in rats and guinea pigs, but not mice[9]. There is, at present, little information about whether chronic MDMA use leads to destruction of serotonin neurons in the brains of humans. However, one study has compared chronic MDMA users (average use of five years with an average administration of around twice a month) with healthy normal controls[128]. Subjects were given infusions of the precursor for serotonin, l-tryptophan, and alterations in mood and fluctuations in the levels of the hormone **prolactin** were measured. Under most circumstances, the failure to find statistically significant differences between experimental and control groups would make interpretation of data difficult. However, in this study, the authors nonetheless stated that the blunted, but not statistically significant, response of the chronic MDMA users to intravenous l-tryptophan provided "suggestive evidence of altered (serotonin) function in MDMA users" although they did acknowledge that "more definitive studies clearly are needed"[128].

Summary of Chronic Effects

The relatively frequent use of marijuana, compared to the usual pattern of infrequent use of LSD or MDMA, and the shortage of information about chronic MDMA use, makes it difficult to identify common consequences of chronic hallucinogen intake. There is animal data, and a bit of human data, suggesting that chronic MDMA use may have a lethal effect upon serotonin neurons. Laboratory experiments have demonstrated tolerance to many of the consequences of marijuana use, including its reinforcing effect. Anecdotal reports of "sensitization" to the reinforcing effect of marijuana probably reflect the influence of experience on the efficiency of consumption. Tolerance to LSD is extreme and rapid, and apparently just as rapidly reversed by a period of abstinence.

Physical dependence does not develop after chronic LSD use and only weak evidence supports the possibility that physical dependence may develop after chronic marijuana use. Despite a long half-life and great lipid solubility, there is little evidence for prolonged (greater than 24 hours) intoxication from marijuana. There is no evidence of brain damage or permanent cognitive deficits subsequent to chronic LSD use. Experiments regarding brain damage or permanent cognitive deficits from chronic marijuana use have provided contradictory results. Marijuana has a host of potential therapeutic actions, while the medicinal potential of LSD is more questionable and limited to use as a psychiatric medicine. LSD does not cause chromosome damage, although the ability to cross the placental barrier renders it a suspected teratogen. Marijuana also does not cause chromosome damage. Chronic marijuana smoking is harmful to the respiratory system, but experimental evidence of damage to the immune system is not supported by evidence of immune impairment in chronic marijuana consumers. Acute LSD intoxication may be similar to acute psychosis, and both LSD and marijuana can worsen the symptoms of a pre-existing psychological disorder. The ability of either chronic marijuana or LSD to induce psychosis in presumptively normal individuals is questionable. In addition, there is no laboratory support for the notion of a marijuana-induced amotivational syndrome.

CHAPTER SUMMARY

Differences in pattern of intake make it difficult to detect similarities among the hallucinogens. Of the three hallucinogens discussed, marijuana is the only one stored for significant periods of time in lipid rich areas of the body. Both LSD and marijuana are converted to metabolites prior to excretion mainly in the feces, while MDMA is excreted as the parent compound in urine. Marijuana most probably acts through interaction with an endogenous THC receptor, LSD is a $5HT_2$ postsynaptic receptor agonist, and MDMA acts as a dopamine and serotonin agonist. MDMA shares the side effects of stimulant drugs, LSD is sympathomimetic, and marijuana induces a reddening of the conjunctiva, a decrease in body temperature, intraocular pressure, an increase in heart rate, and an irritation of the respiratory system accompanied by bronchial relaxation. The desired psychological effects at low and medium doses of any of the three hallucinogens may occur at undesirably excessive levels, leading to acute panic or anxiety. Overdose with marijuana or LSD is unlikely to be a life-threatening emergency, while MDMA overdose may well be lethal. Chronic MDMA use may destroy serotonin neurons. Neither marijuana nor LSD causes chromosomal damage. There is no evidence for brain damage or permanent cognitive deficits in chronic LSD users, nor is there evidence of an impaired immune system or risk of amotivational system in chronic marijuana smokers. Chronic marijuana smoking does cause damage to the respiratory system. Physical dependence probably does not occur to either LSD or marijuana. Neither drug appears to be capable of inducing psychosis in normal individuals. However, unpleasant states may occur in normal individuals and adverse psychological reactions to chronic use are of increased probability in individuals with preexisting psychological difficulties.

REVIEW ESSAY QUESTIONS

1. Provide two examples of how culturally defined differences in usual dose and method of administration can lead to incorrect conclusions about differences among hallucinogens.

2. Construct a table that compares the basic pharmacology of marijuana, LSD, and MDMA.

3. Contrast the putative mechanisms of action of marijuana, LSD, and MDMA.

4. Discuss the chronic effects of marijuana, with a special emphasis upon those effects unique to smoked marijuana versus those that occur regardless of how the drug is consumed.

5. Discuss the possibility of brain and/or chromosomal damage from chronic use of LSD and MDMA.

REFERENCES

1. Abraham. H.D. L-5-hydroxytryptophan for LSD-induced psychosis. *American Journal of Psychiatry*, 1983, 140, 456-458.
2. Abruzzi, W. Drug-induced psychosis. *International Journal of Addiction*, 1977, 12, 183-193.
3. Aghajanian, G., & Bing, O. Persistence of lysergic acid diethylamide in the plasma of human subjects. *Clinical Pharmacology and Therapeutics*, 1964, 5, 611-614.
4. Agurell, S., Gillespie, H., Halldin, M., Hollister, L.E., Johansson, E., Lindgren, J.E., Ohlsson, A., Szirmai, M., & Widman, M.A. Review of recent studies on the pharmacokinetics and metabolism of delta^1 tetrahydrocannabinol, cannabidiol, and cannabinol in man. In D.J. Harvey (Ed.) *Marijuana '84*, Oxford, England: IRL Press, 1985.
5. Allen, T. Tetrahydrocannabinol and chemotherapy. *New England Journal of Medicine*, 1976, 294, 168.
6. Alrazi, J., & Verebey, K. MDMA biological disposition in man: MDA is a biotransformation product. *NIDA Research Monograph*, 1988, 90, 34.
7. Anastasopoulos, G., & Photiades, H. Effects of LSD-25 on relatives of schizophrenic patients. *Journal of Mental Science*, 1962, 108, 95-98.
8. Anthony, J.C., & Trinkoff, A.M. Epidemiologic issues pertinent to international regulation of 28 stimulant-hallucinogen drugs. *Drug and Alcohol Dependence*, 1986, 17, 193-211.
9. Battaglia, G., Yeh, S.Y., & De Souza, E.B. MDMA-induced neurotoxicity: Parameters of degeneration and the recovery of brain serotonin neurons. *Pharmacology, Biochemistry and Behavior*, 1988, 29, 269-274.
10. Bercel, N.A., Travis, L.E., Olinger, L.B., & Dreikurs, E. Model psychoses induced by LSD-25 in normals. *Archives of Neurological Psychiatry*, 1956, 75, 588-611.
11. Blumenfield, M., & Glickman, L. Ten months experience with LSD users admitted to a country psychiatric receiving hospital. *New York State Journal of Medicine*, 1967, 67, 1849-1853.
12. Bowers, M.B. Acute psychosis induced by psychotomimetic drug abuse: I. Clinical findings. *Archives of General Psychiatry*, 1972, 27, 437-440.
13. Brown, R.T., & Braden, N.J. Hallucinogens. *Pediatric Clinics of North America*, 1987, 34, 341-347.
14. Capriotti, R.M., Foltin, R.W., Brady, J.V., & Fischman, M.W. Effects of marijuana on the task-elicited physiological response. *Drugs and Alcohol Dependence*, 1988, 21, 183-187.
15. Carlin, A.S., Bakker, C.B., Halpern, L., & Post, R.D. Social facilitation of marijuana intoxication. *Journal of Abnormal Psychology*, 1972, 80, 132-140.
16. Carlin, A.S., & Trupin, E. The effects of long-term chronic cannabis use on neuropsychological functioning. *International Journal of the Addictions*, 1977, 12, 617-624.
17. Casswell, S., & Marks, D.F. Cannabis and temporal disintegration in experienced and naive subjects. *Science*, 1973, 179, 803-805.

18. Chait, L.D., Evans, S.M., Grant, K.A., Kamien, J.B., Johanson, C.E., & Schuster, C.R. Discriminative stimulus and subjective effects of smoked marijuana in humans. *Psychopharmacology*, 1988, 94, 206-212.

19. Chait, L.D., Fischman, M.W., & Schuster, C.R. "Hangover" effects the morning after marijuana smoking. *Drug and Alcohol Dependence*, 1985, 15, 229-238.

20. Chwelos, N., Blewett, D.B., Smith, C.W., & Hoffer, A. The use of LSD in the treatment of alcoholism. *Quarterly Journal of Studies on Alcoholism*, 1959, 20, 577-590.

21. Chiang, C.N., & Rapaka, R.S. Pharmacokinetics and disposition of cannabinoids. *National Institute of Drug Abuse Research Monograph Series*, 1987, 79, 173-188.

22. Clark W.G. Changes in body temperature after adminstration of antipyretics, LSD, delta 9-THC and related agents: II. *Neuroscience and Biobehavioral Reviews*, 1987, 11, 35-96.

23. Cohen, S. The hallucinogens and the inhalants. *Psychiatric Clinics of North America*, 1984, 7, 681-688.

24. Cohen, S., & Ditman, K.S. Prolonged adverse reactions to lysergic acid diethylamide. *Archives of General Psychiatry*, 1963, 8, 475-480.

25. Commins, D.L., Vosmer, G., Virus, R.M., Wolverton, C.R., Schuster, C.R., & Seiden, L.S. Biochemical and histological evidence that methylenedioxymethamphetamine (MDMA) is toxic to neurons in the rat brain. *Journal of Pharmacology and Experimental Therapeutics*, 1987, 241, 338-345.

26. Corey, M.J., Andrews, J.C., & McLeod, M.J. Chromosome studies on patients (in vivo) and cells (in vitro) treated with lysergic acid diethylamide. *New England Journal of Medicine*, 1970, 282, 939-943.

27. Dackis, C.A., Pottash, A.L.C., & Gold, M.S. Is there "reverse tolerance" to marijuana?: Dr. Dackis, and associates reply. *American Journal of Psychiatry*, 1983, 140, 656.

28. Dahlberg, C.C., Mechanek, R., & Feldstein, S. LSD research: The impact of lay publicity. *American Journal of Psychiatry*, 1968, 125, 685-689.

29. Davison, K. Drug-induced psychoses and their relationship to schizophrenia. In D. Kemali, G. Bartholini, & D. Richter (Eds.) *Schizophrenia Today*, Oxford, England: Pergamon Press, 1976.

30. Dewey, W.L. Cannabinoid pharmacology. *Pharmacological Review*, 1986, 38, 151-178.

31. Dewhurst, K., & Hatrick, J.A. Differential diagnosis and treatment of LSD-induced psychoses. *Practitioner*, 1972, 209, 327-332.

32. DiGregorio, G.J., & Sterling, G.H. Marijuana pharmacology and urine testing. *American Family Physician*, 1987, 35, 209-212.

33. Dilsaver, S.C. Antimuscarinic agents as substances of abuse: A review. *Journal of Clinical Psychopharmacology*, 1988, 8, 14-22.

34. Dowling, G.P., McDonough, & Bost, R.O. "Eve" and "Ecstasy": A report of 5 deaths associated with the use of MDEA and MDMA. *Journal of the American Medical Association*, 1987, 257, 1615-1617.

35. Esecover, H., Malitz, S., & Wilkins, B. Clinical profiles of paid normal subjects volunteering for hallucinogen drug studies. *American Journal of Psychiatry*, 1961, 117, 910-915.

36. Falk, J.L., & Feingold, D.A. Environmental and cultural factors in the behavioral action of drugs. In H.Y. Meltzer (Ed.) *Psychopharmacology: The third generation of progress.* New York: Raven Press, 1987.

37. Farrell, M. Ecstasy and the oxygen of publicity. *British Journal of Addiction*, 1989, 84, 943.

38. Fink, M., Simeon, J., Haque, W., & Itil, T. Prolonged adverse reactions to LSD in psychotics. *Archives of General Psychiatry*, 1966, 15, 209-213.

39. Fink, M., Volavka, J., Panayiotopoulos, C., & Stefanis, C. Quantitative EEG studies of marijuana, delta-9-THC, and hashish in man. In M. Braude & S. Szara (Eds.) *Pharmacology of marijuana.* New York: Raven Press, 1976.

40. Fligiel, S.E.G., Vankat, H., Gong, H., & Tashkin, D.P. Bronchial pathology in chronic marijuana smokers: A light and electron microscopic study. *Journal of Psychoactive Drugs*, 1988, 20, 33-42.

41. Foltin, R., Fischman, M., & Brady, J. Interactions between social behavior and smoked marijuana. *NIDA Research Monograph*, 1988, 81, 47-51.

42. Foltin, R.W., Fischman, M.W., Pedroso, J.J., & Pearlson, G.D. Marijuana and cocaine interactions in humans: cardiovascular consequences. *Pharmacology, Biochemistry and Behavior*, 1987, 28, 459-464.

43. Forrer, G.R., & Goldner, R.D. Experimental physiological studies with lysergic acid diethylamide (LSD-25). *Archives of Neurology and Psychiatry*, 1951, 65, 581-588.

44. Fraser, H.S., Dotson, O.Y., Loward, L., Grell, G.A., & Knight, F. Drug metabolizing capacity in Jamaican cigarette and marijuana smokers and non-smokers. *Western Indian Medical Journal*, 1983, 32, 207-211.

45. Freedman, D.X. Psychotomimetic drugs and brain biogenic amines. *American Journal of Psychiatry*, 1963, 119, 843-850.

46. Freedman, D.X. The psychopharmacology of hallucinogenic agents. *Annual Review of Medicine*, 1969, 20, 409-418.

47. Ghodse, A.H. Cannabis psychosis. *British Journal of the Addictions*, 1986, 81, 473-478.

48. Glass, G.S., & Bowers, M.B. Chronic psychosis associated with long-term psychotomimetic drug abuse. *Archives of General Psychiatry*, 1970, 23, 97-103.

49. Grant, I., Rochford, J., Fleming, T., & Strunkard, H. A neuropsychological assessment of the effects of moderate marihuana use. *Journal of Nervous and Mental Disease*, 1973, 156, 278-280.

50. Grinspoon, L., & Bakalar, J.B. Can drugs be used to enhance the psychotherapeutic process? *American Journal of Psychotherapy*, 1986, 40, 393-404.

51. Grinspoon, L., & Bakalar, J.B. *Psychedelic drugs reconsidered.* New York: Basic Books, 1979.

52. Halldin, M.M., Widman, M.V., Bahr, C., Lindgren, J.E., & Martin, B.R. Identification of in vitro metabolites of delta^1-tetrahydrocannabinol formed by human livers. *Drug Metabolism and Disposition*, 1982, 10, 297-301.

53. Havey, R.J. Over-the-counter and iatrogenically induced psychoses: A review of the literature. *The Journal of the American Osteopathic Association*, 1984, 83, 412-418.

54. Hendin, H., Haas, A.P., Singer, P., Ellner, M., & Ulman, R. *Living high: Daily marijuana use among adults.* New York: Human Sciences Press, 1987.

55. Hepler, R.S., & Frank, I.M. Marijuana smoking and intraocular pressure. *Journal of the American Medical Association*, 1971, 217, 1392-1394.

56. Herning, R.I., Jones, R.T., & Peltzman, D.J. Changes in human event related potentials with prolonged delta-9-tetrahydrocannabinol use. *Electroencephalography and Clinical Neurophysiology*, 1979, 47, 556-570.

57. Hochman, J.S., & Brill, N.Q. Chronic marijuana use and psychosocial adaptation. *American Journal of Psychiatry*, 1973, 130, 132-140.

58. Hoffer, A. D-Lysergic diethylamide (LDS): A review of its present status. *Clinical Pharmacology and Therapeutics*, 1965, 6, 183-204.

59. Hofmann, A. *LSD: My problem child.* Los Angeles: J.P. Tarcher, 1983.

60. Hollister, L.E. *Chemical psychoses.* Springfield, IL: Charles C. Thomas, 1968.

61. Hollister, L.E. Psychotomimetic drugs in man. In L.L. Iversen, S.D. Iversen, & S.H. Snyder (Eds.) *Handbook of psychopharmacology (Vol. 11: Stimulants).* New York: Plenum Press, 1978.

62. Hollister, L.E. Health aspects of cannabis. *Pharmacological Reviews*, 1986, 38, 1-20.

63. Hollister, L.E. Marijuana and immunity. *Journal of Psychoactive Drugs*, 1988, 20, 3-8.

64. Holsten, F. Flashbacks: A personal follow-up. *Archives Psychiatry and Nervenkranken*, 1976, 222, 293-304.

65. Hungerford, D.A., Taylor, K.M., & Shagass, C. Cytogenic effects of LSD-25 therapy in man. *Journal of the American Medical Association*, 1968, 206, 2287-2291.

66. Huxley, A. *Doors of perception.* New York: Harper & Row, 1954.

67. Jacobs, B.L. *Hallucinogens: Neurochemical, behavioral and clinical perspectives.* New York: Raven Press, 1984.

68. Jacobsen, R. The clinical pharmacology of the hallucinogens. *Clinical Pharmacology and Therapeutics*, 1963, 4, 480-503.

69. Jaffe, J.H. Drug addiction and drug abuse. In A.G. Gilman, L.S. Goodman, T.W. Rall, & F. Murad (Eds.) *The pharmacological basis of therapeutics (7th ed.).* New York: Macmillan, 1985.

70. Jagiello, G., & Polani, P.E. Mouse germ cells and LSD-25. *Cytogenetics*, 1969, 8, 136-147.

71. Janowsky, D.S., Addario, D., & Risch, S.C. *Psychopharmacology case studies.* New York: Guilford Press, 1987.

72. Jarvik, I.F., & Kato, T. Is lysergide a teratogen? *Lancet*, 1968, 1, 250.

73. Johnson, F.G. LSD in the treatment of alcoholism. *American Journal of Psychiatry*, 1969, 126, 481-487.

74. Jones, R.T. Drug models of schizophrenia--Cannabis. In J.O. Cole, A.M. Freedman, & A.J. Friedhoff (Eds.) *Psychopathology and psychopharmacology.* Baltimore, MD: Johns Hopkins University Press, 1986.

75. Jones, R.T., Benowitz, N.L., & Bachman, J. Clinical studies of cannabis tolerance and dependence. *Annals of the New York Academy of Scientists*, 1976, 282, 221-239.

76. Jones, R.T., Benowitz, N.L., & Herning, R.I. Clinical relevance of cannabis tolerance and dependence. *Journal of Clinical Pharmacology*, 1981, 21, 143S-152S.

77. Kamien, J.B., Johanson, C.E., Schuster, C.R., & Wolverton, W.L. The effects of methylenedioxymethamphetamine and methylenedioxyamphetamine in monkeys trained to discriminate amphetamine from saline. *Drug and Alcohol Dependence*, 1986, 18, 139-147.

78. Kato, T., & Jarvik, I.F. LSD-25 and genetic damage. *Diseases of the Nervous System*, 1969, 30, 42-46.

79. Kety, S.S. The hypothetical relationships between amines and mental illness: a critical synthesis. In H.E. Himwich, S.S. Kety, & J.R. Smythies (Eds.) *Amines and schizophrenia*. Oxford, England: Pergamon Press, 1967.

80. Khantzian, E.J., & McKenna, G.J. Acute toxic and withdrawal reactions associated with drug use and abuse. *Annals of Internal Medicine*, 1979, 90, 361-373.

81. Kurland, A.A. LSD in the supportive care of the terminally ill cancer patient. *Journal of Psychoactive Drugs*, 1985, 17, 279-290.

82. Landfield, P.W. Delta-9-tetrahydrocannabinol-dependent alterations in brain structure. *NIDA Research Monograph*, 1987, 78, 143-157.

83. Leary, T. The religious experience: Its production and interpretation. *Psychedelic Review*, 1964, 1, 324-346.

84. Lemberger, L. Potential therapeutic usefulness of marijuana. *Annual Review of Pharmacology and Toxicology*, 1980, 20, 151-172.

85. Leonard, H.L., & Rapoport, J.L. Relief of obsessive-compulsive symptoms by LSD and psilocin. *American Journal of Psychiatry*, 1987, 144, 1239-1240.

86. Lewis, D.J., & Sloane, R.B. Therapy with LSD. *Journal of Clinical and Experimental Psychopathology*, 1958, 19, 19-27.

87. Lindgren, J.E., Ohlsson, A., Agurell, S., Hollister, L.E., & Gillespie, H. Clinical effect and plasma level of delta-9-tetrahydrocannabinol (delta-9-THC) in heavy and light users of cannabis. *Psychopharmacology*, 1980, 74, 208-212.

88. Linton, H.B., & Lang, R.J. Subjective reactions to Lysergic Acid Diethylamide (LSD-25). *Archives of General Psychiatry*, 1962, 6, 352-368.

89. Louria, D.B. LSD--perhaps a boon, nonmedically a danger. *Medical Tribune*, 1967, 8, 18-19.

90. Lucas, S., Mendelson, J., Henry, J., Amass, L., & Budson, A. Ethanol effects on marijuana-induced intoxication and electroencephalographic activity. *NIDA Research Monograph*, 1988, 90, 62.

91. Ludwig, A., Levine, J., & Stark, L. A clinical study of LSD treatment in alcoholism. *American Journal of Psychiatry*, 1969, 126, 59-69.

92. Mace, A. LSD. *Clinical Toxicology*, 1979, 15, 219-224.

93. Makriyannis, A., & Rapaka, R.S. The medicinal chemistry of cannabinoids: An overview. *NIDA Research Monograph*, 1987, 79, 204-210.

94. Martin, B.R. Cellular effects of cannabinoids. *Pharmacological Review*, 1986, 38, 45-74.

95. Martin, B.R., Compton, D.R., Little, P.J., Martin, T.J., & Beardsley, P.M. Pharmacological evaluation of agonistic and antagonistic activity of cannabinoids. *NIDA Research Monograph*, 1987, 79, 108-122.

96. Mathew, R.J., Tant, S., & Burger, C. Regional cerebral blood flow in marijuana smokers. *British Journal of Addictions*, 1986, 81, 567-571.

97. Matsuyama, S.S., Jarvik, L.F., Fu, T.K., & Yen, F.S. Chromosomal studies before and after supervised marijuana smoking. In M. Braude & S. Szara (Eds.) *Pharmacology of Marijuana*. New York: Raven Press, 1976.

98. McGlothlin, W.H., & Arnold, D.O. LSD-revisited: A ten-year follow-up of medical LSD use. *Archives of General Psychiatry*, 1971, 24, 35-49.

99. McGlothlin, W., Arnold, D., & Freedman, D.X. Organicity measures following repeated LSD ingestion. *Archives of General Psychiatry*, 1969, 21, 704-709.

100. McGlothin, W.H., & West, L.J. The marijuana problem: An overview. *American Journal of Psychiatry*, 1968, 125, 1126-1134.

101. McWilliams, S.A., & Tuttle, R.J. Long-term psychological effects of LSD. *Psychological Bulletin*, 1973, 79, 341-351.

102. Mechoulam, R. The pharmacohistory of Cannabis Sativa. In R. Mechoulam (Ed.) *Cannabinoids as Therapeutic Agents*. Boca Raton, FL: CRC Press, 1986a.

103. Mechoulam, R. *Cannabinoids as therapeutic agents.* Boca Raton, FL: CRC Press, 1986b.

104. Mendelson, J.H. Marijuana. In H.Y. Meltzer (Ed.) *Psychopharmacology: The third generation of progress.* New York: Raven Press, 1987.

105. Mikuriya, T.H., & Aldrich, M.R. Cannabis 1988: Old drug, new dangers--The potency question. *Journal of Psychoactive Drugs*, 1988, 20, 47-56.

106. Miles, G.C., Congreve, G.R.S., Gibbins, R.J., Marshman, J.A., Devenyi, P., & Hicks, R.C. An experimental study of the effects of daily cannabis smoking on behavior patterns. *Acta Pharmacologica et Toxicologia*, 1974, 34, 1-44.

107. Milman, R.B., & Sbriglio, R. Patterns of use and psychopathology in chronic marijuana users. *Substance Abuse*, 1986, 9, 533-545.

108. Mogar, R.E. Current status and future trends in psychedelic research. *Journal of Humanistic Psychology*, 1965, 4, 147-166.

109. Naditch, M., & Fenwick, S. LSD flashbacks and ego functioning. *Journal of Abnormal Psychology*, 1977, 86, 352-359.

110. Nahas, G.G. *The deceptive weed.* New York: Raven Press, 1973.

111. Negrette, J.C., & Knapp, W.P. The effects of cannabis use on the clinical condition of schizophrenics. *NIDA Research Monograph*, 1986, 67, 321-327.

112. Neill, J.R. "More than medical significance": LSD and American psychiatry, 1953-1966. *Journal of Psychoactive Drugs*, 1987, 19, 39-45.

113. Nichols, W.W., Miller, R.C., Heneen, W., Bradt, C., Hollister, L., & Kanter, S. Cytogenetic studies on human subjects receiving marijuana and delta-9-tetrahydrocannabinol. *Mutagen Research*, 1974, 26, 413-417.

114. Nowlan, R., & Cohen S. Tolerance to marijuana. Heart rate and subjective "high." *Clinical Pharmacology and Therapeutics*, 1977, 22, 550-556.

115. Ohlsson, A., Lindgren, J.E., Andersson, S., Agurell, S., Gillespie, H., & Hollister, L.E. Single dose kinetics of cannabidiol in man. In S. Agurell, W.L. Dewey, & R. Willette (Eds.) *The cannabinoids: Chemical, pharmacologic and therapeutic aspects.* New York: Academic Press, 1984.

116. Ohlsson, A., Lindgren, J.E., Wahlen, A., Agurell, S., Hollister, L.E., & Gillespie, H.K. Single dose kinetics of deuterium labelled delta^1-tetrahydrocannabinol in heavy and light cannabis users. *Biomedical Mass Spectrometry*, 1982, 9, 6-10.

117. Page, J.B., Fletcher, J., & True, W.R. Psychosociocultural perspectives on chronic cannabis use: The Costa Rican follow-up. *Journal of Psychoactive Drugs*, 1988, 20, 57-66.

118. Paton, W.D.M. Pharmacology of marijuana. *Annual Review of Pharmacology*, 1975, 15, 191-220.

119. Paton, W.D.M., & Pertwee, R.G. The actions of cannabis in man. In R. Mechoulam (Ed.) *Marijuana: Chemistry, pharmacology, metabolism and clinical effects.* New York: Academic Press, 1973.

120. Perez-Reyes, M. Presence of delta-9-tetrahydrocannabinol in human milk. *New England Journal of Medicine*, 1982, 307, 819-820.

121. Perez-Reyes, M., DiGuiseppi, S., Davis, K.H., Schnidler, V.H., & Cook, C.E. Comparison of effects of marihuana cigarettes of three different potencies. *Clinical Pharmacology and Therapeutics*, 1982, 31, 617-624.

122. Perez-Reyes, M., DiGuiseppi, S., Mason, A.P., & Davis, K.H. Passive inhalation of marijuana smoke and urinary excretion of cannabinoids. *Clinical Pharmacology and Therapeutics*, 1983, 34, 36-41.

123. Perez-Reyes, M., Timmons, M.C., Davis, K.H., & Wall, M.E. A comparison of the pharmacological activity in man of intravenously administered delta^9-tetrahydrocannabinol, cannabinol, and cannabidiol. *Experientia*, 1973, 29, 1368-1369.

124. Peroutka, S.J. Incidence of recreational use of 3,4-methylenedioxymethamphetamine (MDMA, "ecstasy") on an undergraduate campus. *New England Journal of Medicine*, 1987, 317, 1524-1543.

125. Phillips, R.N., Turk, R.F., & Forney, R.R. Acute toxicology of delta^9-THC in rats and mice. *Proceedings of the Society for Experimental Biology*, 1971, 136, 260-263.

126. Pierce, P.A., & Peroutka, S.J. Hallucinogenic drug interactions with neurotransmitter receptor binding sites in human cortex. *Psychopharmacology*, 1989, 97, 118-122.

127. Pollard, J.C., Uhr, L., & Stern, E. *Drugs and phantasy: The effects of LSD, psilocybin and sernyl on college students.* Boston: Little, Brown, 1965.

128. Price, L.H., Ricaurte, G.A., Krystal, J.H., & Henninger, G. Neuroendocrine and mood responses to intravenous l-tryptophan in 3,4-methylenedioxymethamphetamine users. *Archives of General Psychiatry*, 1989, 46, 20-22.

129. Renaud, A., & Cornmier, Y. Acute effects of marijuana smoking on maximal exercise performance. *Medical Science in Sports and Exercise*, 1986, <u>18</u>, 685-690.

130. Ricaurte, G., Bryan, G., Strauss, L., Seiden, L.K., & Schuster, C. Hallucinogenic amphetamine selectively destroys brain serotonin nerve terminals. *Science*, 1986, <u>229</u>, 986-988.

131. Richard, K.C., & Bergstedt, H.H. Near fatal reaction to ingestion of the hallucinogenic drug MDA. *Journal of the American Medical Association*, 1971, <u>218</u>, 1826-1827.

132. Rinkel, M. The psychological aspects of the LSD psychosis. In M. Rinkel, & H.C.B. Denber (Eds.) *Chemical concepts of psychosis*. London: Peter Owen Limited, 1958.

133. Robinson, J.T., Daview, L.S., Sack, E.L.N.S., & Morrissey, J.D. A controlled trial of abreaction with lysergic acid diethylamine (LSD-25). *British Journal of Psychiatry*, 1963, <u>109</u>, 46-53.

134. Rochford, J., Grant, I., & LaVigne, G. Medical students and drugs: Neuropsychological and use pattern considerations. *International Journal of the Addictions*, 1977, <u>12</u>, 1057-1065.

135. Roffman, R.A. *Marijuana as medicine*. Seattle: Madrona Publications, 1982.

136. Ross, E.M., & Gilman, A.G. Pharmacodynamics: Mechanisms of drug action and the relationship between drug concentration and effect. In A.G. Gilman, L.S. Goodman, T.W. Rall, & F. Murad (Eds.) *The pharmacological basis of therapeutics, (7th ed.)*. New York: Macmillan, 1985.

137. Rothlin, E. Lysergic acid diethylamide and related substances. *Annals of the New York Academy of Sciences*, 1957, <u>66</u>, 668-676.

138. Sadzot, B., Baraban, J.M., Glennon, R.A., Lyon, R.A., Leonhardt, S., Jan, C-R, & Titeler, M. Hallucinogenic drug interactions at human brain 5-HT$_2$ receptors: Implications for treating LSD-induced hallucinogenesis. *Psychopharmacology*, 1989, <u>98</u>, 495-499.

139. Salvatore, S., & Hyde, R. Progression of effects of lysergic acid diethylamide. *AMA Archives of Neurological Psychiatry*, 1956, <u>76</u>, 50-59.

140. Savage, C., Fadiman, J., Mogar, R., & Allen, M.H. The effects of psychedelic (LSD) therapy on values, personality, and behavior. *International Journal of Neuropsychiatry*, 1966, <u>2</u>, 241-254.

141. Savage, C., & McCabe, O.L. Residential psychedelic (LSD) therapy for the narcotic addict. *Archives of General Psychiatry*, 1973, <u>28</u>, 808-814.

142. Schaeffer, J., Andrysiak, T., & Ungerleider, J.T. Cognition and long-term use of ganja (Cannabis). *Science*, 1981, <u>213</u>, 465-466.

143. Schecter, M. Discriminative profile of MDMA. *Pharmacology, Biochemistry and Behavior*, 1986, <u>24</u>, 1533-1536.

144. Schecter, M. Serotonergic-dopaminergic mediation of 3,4-methylenedioxymethamphetamine (MDMA, "Ecstasy"). *Pharmacology, Biochemistry and Behavior*, 1989, <u>31</u>, 817-824.

145. Shagass, C., & Bittle, R.M. Therapeutic effects of LSD: A follow-up study. *Journal of Nervous and Mental Disease*, 1967, <u>144</u>, 471-478.

146. Shick, J., & Smith, D. Analysis of the LSD flashback. *Journal of Psychedelic Drugs*, 1970, <u>3</u>, 13-19.

147. Shulgin, A.T. The background and chemistry of MDMA. *Journal of Psychoactive Drugs*, 1986, <u>18</u>, 291-304.

148. Skakkeback, N.E., Philip, J., & Rafaelsen, O.J. LSD in mice: Abnormalities in meiotic chromosomes. *Science*, 1968, <u>160</u>, 1246-1248.

149. Smith, D.E. Acute and chronic toxicity of marijuana. *Journal of Psychedelic Drugs*, 1968, <u>2</u>, 37-47.

150. Smith, J.A., Walters, G., & Johnston, D. LSD "flashback" as a cause of diagnostic error. *Postgraduate Medical Journal*, 1980, <u>56</u>, 421-422.

151. Stanton, M., & Bardoni, A. Drug flashbacks: Reported frequency in a military population. *American Journal of Psychiatry*, 1972, <u>129</u>, 751-755.

152. Strassman, R.J. Adverse reactions to psychedelic drugs: A review of the literature. *Journal of Nervous and Mental Disease*, 1984, <u>172</u>, 577-595.

153. Struve, F., & Straumanis, J. Topographic mapping of quantitative EEG variables in chronic heavy marijuana (THC) users. *NIDA Research Monograph*, 1988, <u>90</u>, 61.

154. Szuster, R.R., Pontius, E.B., & Campos, P.E. Marijuana sensitivity and panic anxiety. *Journal of Clinical Psychiatry*, 1988, <u>49</u>, 427-429.

155. Tashkin, D.P., Simmons, M., & Clark, V. Effect of habitual smoking of marijuana alone and with tobacco on nonspecific airways hyperreactivity. *Journal of Psychoactive Drugs*, 1988, <u>20</u>, 21-26.

156. Tashkin, D.P., Wu, T-C., & Djahed, B. Acute and chronic effects of marijuana smoking compared with to-bacco smoking on blood carboxyhemoglobin levels. *Journal of Psychoactive Drugs*, 1988, 20, 27-32.

157. Tijo, J.H., Pahnke, W.N., & Kurland, A.A. LSD and chromosomes: A controlled experiment. *Journal of the American Medical Association*, 1969, 210, 849-856.

158. Triesman, D. Logical problems in contemporary cannabis research. *The International Journal of the Addictions*, 1973, 8, 667-682.

159. Truitt, E.B. Marijuana vs. alcohol: A pharmacologic comparison. *Advances in Experimental Medicine and Biology*, 1975, 56, 291-309.

160. Turek, I.S., Soskin, R.A., & Kurland, A.A. Methylenedioxyamphetamine (MDA) subjective effects. *Journal of Psychoactive Drugs*, 1974, 69, 7-13.

161. Ungerleider, J.T., & Fisher, D.D. The problems of LSD[25] and emotional disorder. *California Medicine*, 1967, 106, 49-55.

162. Ungerleider, J.T., Fischer, D.D., & Fuller, M. The dangers of LSD: Analysis of seven months experience in a university hospital's psychiatric service. *Journal of the American Medical Association*, 1966, 197, 389-392.

163. Ungerleider, J.T., Fisher, D.D., Goldsmith, S.R., Fuller, M., & Forgy, E.A. A statistical survey of adverse reactions to LSD in Los Angeles County. *American Journal of Psychiatry*, 1968, 125, 352-357.

164. Weil, A.T., Zinberg, N.E., & Nelsen, J.M. Clinical psychological effects of marijuana in man. *Science*, 162, 1968, 1234-1242.

165. Weiner, N. Atropine, scopolamine, and related antimuscarinic drugs. In A.G. Gilman, L.S. Goodman, T.W. Rall, & F. Murad (Eds.) *The pharmacological basis of therapeutics, (7th ed.).* New York: Macmillan, 1985.

166. Weller, R.A., & Halikas, J.A. Marijuana use and psychiatric illness: A follow-up study. *American Journal of Psychiatry*, 1985, 142, 848-850.

167. Wesson, D., & Smith, D. An analysis of psychedelic drug flashbacks. *American Journal of Drug and Alcohol Abuse*, 1976, 3, 425-438.

168. Wright, M., & Hogan, T.P. Repeated LSD ingestion and performance on neuropsychological tests. *Journal of Nervous and Mental Disease*, 1972, 154, 432-438.

169. Wu, T.-C., Tashkin, D.P., Rose, J.E., & Djahed, B. Influence of marijuana potency and amount of cigarette consumed on marijuana smoking patterns. *Journal of Psychoactive Drugs*, 1988, 20, 43-46.

170. Yesavage, J.A., Leirer, V.O., Denari, M., & Hollister, L.E. Carry-over effects of marijuana intoxication on aircraft pilot performance: A preliminary report. *American Journal of Psychiatry*, 1985, 142, 1325-1329.

Chapter 18

PHENCYCLINOIDS

The purposes of this chapter are to:

1. Introduce the chemical diversity and basic pharmacology of the phencyclinoids,

2. Discuss the sites and mechanisms of action responsible for the diverse effects of the phencyclinoids,

3. Describe the pharmacological and behavioral side effects of low and medium doses of the phencyclinoids,

4. Present the symptoms and possible treatments for phencyclinoid overdose, and

5. Discuss the consequences of chronic phencyclinoid use, including tolerance and sensitization, physical dependency and/or compulsive use, violence and/or psychosis, and the potential for brain or other organ damage.

BRIEF HISTORY

Phencyclidine (PCP) is a completely synthetic drug that was first developed by Parke-Davis Laboratories as the anesthetic Sernyl. It offered significant advantages over other available barbiturate and opioid anesthetics, including especially that anesthetic doses of PCP did not induce respiratory depression or dangerous decreases in blood pressure and heart rate[14,29,35]. The tendency for anesthetized patients to keep their eyes open and yet seem somehow "disconnected" from their environment led scientists to consider the drug as representing a new class of drugs, which they referred to as "dissociative anesthetics"[17]. Despite the advantages of PCP as an anesthetic, it unfortunately led to a **post-anesthetic delirium**, which caused many patients to wake up in a confused, agitated, manic, or psychotic condition[21,47]. Early studies of the effects of PCP on normal human volunteers confirmed the tendency of high doses of the drug to induce unpleasant and bizarre psychological states[7,19,42,55,63]. The use of PCP as an anesthetic in humans was halted, although the drug was reintroduced as an animal anesthetic (under the trade name, Sernylan) in 1967. However, even this use of the drug was stopped in 1978, and PCP was placed under Schedule II of the U.S. Government's Schedule of Controlled Substances[44].

In spite of, or perhaps because of, the profound psychological consequences of acute PCP intoxication, the drug achieved a short burst of popularity as an illicit drug during the late 1960s. The drug was available primarily in pill form, making it difficult for users to control the effects of this powerful drug. PCP developed a reputation during the late 1960s for being capable of inducing bizarre and violent behavior. An article in the popular magazine *Rolling Stone* noted that widespread use in the Haight-Ashbury area of San Francisco in 1967 lead to a situation where "people named Strawberry were going around punching people named Wildflower"[9]. The drug's popularity waned, only to be followed by a sudden resurgence during the middle of the 1970s[44]. Part of this increase in use occurred because the drug became available as a powder and as a liquid dipped onto cigarettes. Administration of these preparations made it possible for users to **titrate** (or achieve relatively precise drug effects through control of dose)[74]. During the early 1980s, before media and government attention focused on "crack" cocaine, there were those who asserted that the cheap and easily manufactured PCP was becoming as popular as marijuana[28,48,54,68].

CHEMICAL DIVERSITY

There are at least sixty different compounds that are behaviorally-active **structural analogues** (chemical variations) of PCP (**phencyclidine** or "angel dust"). Figure 18.1 presents the chemical structure of PCP and a few of the more common analogues. The PCP molecule and the structural analogues are referred to collectively as the **phencyclinoids**[45]. As mentioned above, PCP and some of its chemical variants are Schedule II drugs. Others of the chemical variants have been placed in the most restrictive category as Schedule I drugs. There are some known analogues that have not yet been placed on the Schedule of Controlled Substances. The drug **ketamine** is the only phencyclinoid that is still used in humans for medical purposes. Ketamine is thought to be less likely to induce post-anesthetic delirium, although there is little laboratory data to support the idea that it differs qualitatively from PCP[72].

Despite the differences in chemical structure of the phencyclinoids in Figure 18.1, each of these compounds shares all, or nearly all, of the behavioral effects of the original PCP molecule. Differences exist mainly in the overall potency of the analogues. Sometimes, an analogue that is otherwise very similar to PCP in terms of most dose-response relationships, will nonetheless induce toxic or other behavioral effects at remark-

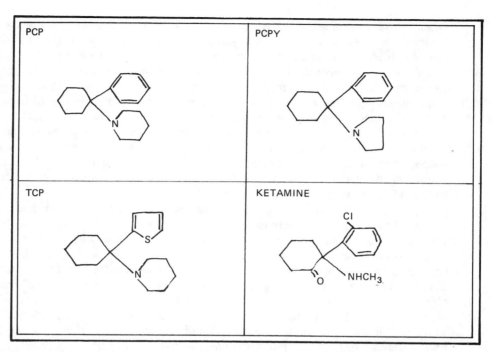

Figure 18.1. The chemical structure of PCP and a few related analogues, including PCPY, TCP, and Ketamine.

ably low doses[45]. Amateur chemists in illicit laboratories are constantly creating new phencyclinoids and other **designer drugs**[36]. When lay people tinker with the chemical structure of a drug they often find that their manipulations have removed the reinforcing or other sought-after behavioral effects of the drug. Sometimes, however, powerful analogues result from these manipulations[66]. In one study, somewhere between one-third and one-half of all analyzed samples of illicitly obtained "PCP" contained phencyclinoids other than PCP[40]. Clearly, consumers of illicit PCP are at serious risk of unknowingly consuming compounds with potencies, and maybe other characteristics, that far exceed expectations developed as a result of previous experiences with PCP.

BASIC PHARMACOLOGY

The phencyclinoids are tasteless, odorless, colorless drugs that can be produced in pills, powders, and liquids of any color or consistency. They are effective by any means of administration, although they are usually smoked (sprinkled on marijuana or via a tobacco cigarette dipped in liquid phencyclinoid), snorted, or injected.

Phencyclinoids are extremely lipid soluble. They are thus easily absorbed when taken orally and they concentrate in lipid-rich areas of the body, including the brain.

When smoked, the onset of behavioral effects occurs within two to five minutes while obvious intoxication lasts for four to six hours[8]. Accumulation of the lipid soluble compounds may mean that a state of normalcy might not be obtained until weeks after chronic use[46]. In one of the few studies conducted with PCP in humans since the early 1960s, about 65% of orally or intravenously administered PCP was bound to blood-borne carrier proteins and only 16% of the parent compound was found in urine, the primary means by which the drug and its metabolites leave the body[16]. Parent phencyclinoids are metabolized by liver enzymes. It may take a couple of steps for the parent compound to be made sufficiently hydrophilic to enable its excretion in the urine[2]. Some of the metabolic products are behaviorally active. The half-lives of the phencyclinoids are notoriously difficult to determine, but they can be as long as 72 hours. Metabolites may be found in urine long after a halt in drug use[27,32].

The most interesting pharmacological fact about the phencyclinoids is a consequence of their being extremely lipophilic and therefore concentrating in areas like the brain and lungs. After administration, levels of the drug in the blood and in lipid rich areas eventually reach an equilibrium. As blood levels are reduced by metabolism and excretion, lipid soluble areas release their stored phencyclidine into the bloodstream. This **recirculated** drug can now gain access to those brain areas that induce a behavioral effect. Intoxication from phencyclinoids can therefore follow a cyclic pattern. That is, after the initial intoxication, there is a period of no behavioral effect, followed by an additional intoxication, without the consumption of further drug. This cycle may repeat itself a number of times. While some phencyclinoid users find this a convenient and economical way to achieve multiple intoxications, recirculation can induce intoxication and side effects at erratic and unpredictable intervals[21]. Table 18.1 summarizes the basic pharmacology of the phencyclinoids.

Table 18.1
Basic Pharmacology of the Phencyclinoids

- Tasteless, odorless, colorless drug available in many forms
- Rapid absorption after any method of administration
- Highly lipophilic, accumulates in brain and lungs
- Moderately high binding to plasma proteins
- Metabolized by liver enzymes
- Very long half-lives, some active metabolites
- Excreted in urine
- Metabolites found in urine long after halt in use
- Recirculation can lead to cycles of intoxication

SITES AND MECHANISMS OF ACTION

The unique psychopharmacological status of the phencyclinoids arises, in part, from the diverse biochemical effects of these drugs. They influence nearly every known neurotransmitter or neuromodulator[1,33,52]. For example, PCP acts as an acetylcholine antagonist by inhibiting the activity of enzymes that synthesize the neurotransmitter[43] and by preventing the binding of acetylcholine to postsynaptic receptors[23,37]. PCP has presynaptic effects at norepinephrine and dopamine neurons, including a facilitation of release and blockade of reuptake[34,51]. The drug also acts as an direct agonist at serotonin receptors[49,65].

In addition to these diverse effects on various neurotransmitters, their have been numerous studies that have identified specific binding sites for PCP in rat brains[30,70,76] and in human brains[12], particularly in the cerebral cortex and the hippocampus[6]. Phencyclinoids bind to these PCP receptors and to sigma opioid receptors[6]. Early opinions that these "PCP receptors" were instead the previously discovered sigma opioid receptors have been discounted by the creation of specific drugs that bind to either only the PCP receptor or only the kappa receptor[15,33,53,69].

Although the specific mechanism(s) of action for the behavioral effects of phencyclinoids have not yet been determined, there are three specific research endeavors that have arisen from the discovery of PCP receptors. First, it has been determined that the PCP receptors are actually part of a receptor complex that contains receptors for a variety of **excitatory amino acid neurotransmitters**[39]. Amino acids are the basic building blocks of proteins, and excitatory amino acid neurotransmitters (which include **glutamate, aspartate** and **NMDA**) are small molecules that bind to postsynaptic receptors and induce EPSPs (see Chapter 1). When PCP binds to its portion of the receptor complex, it exerts an antagonist effect through neuromodulation of the consequences of binding of glutamate, aspartate, or NMDA to their own portion of the receptor[56]. Second, the discovery of PCP receptors has led to a search for the endogenous substance for these receptors[6,57,58,75] in hopes that these endogenous substances will reveal something about the physical basis of various forms of psychosis, particularly schizophrenia[11,20]. Finally, the discovery of a specific receptor for PCP has fueled the search for an antagonist that will block these receptors and the behavioral effects of PCP[50,59,61,71].

ACUTE SIDE EFFECTS AT LOW AND MEDIUM DOSES

Different authors may define low and medium doses differently, and consumption of a phencyclinoid with a potency greater or lesser than that of PCP will obviously lead to drug effects at very different doses. However, it is safe to say that in a 160 lb human in good health, the effects of low doses of PCP occur when 0 to 5 mg of active drug are consumed, while medium-dose effects occur when between 5 and 15 mg are consumed[54,74].

Since the phencyclinoids have such diverse and widespread effects on neurotransmitters and neuromodulators, it is not surprising that ingestion of intoxicating low or medium doses induce a wide variety of acute side effects[4]. The phencyclinoids are said to be taken for their "euphoric effects, pseudo-hallucinogenic potential, ability to decrease inhibitions, and ability to instill feelings of power and to eliminate pain"[74]. However, in a preview of a text devoted to summarizing the results of studies conducted up to and during the mid-1970s, the editors noted that one study found that only 1 of 12 users experienced the pleasant psychological state of "euphoria." In fact, the majority of phencyclinoid users reported negative effects including perceptual disturbances, restlessness, disorientation and anxiety while one quarter of the users reported paranoia, irritability, and mental confusion[54]. Two studies in 1959 examined the psychological effects of a moderate dose of PCP on normal human volunteers and discovered a number of "psychopathological effects" including distorted body image, lack of distinction between self and nonself stimuli, intellectual impairment, emotionally charged memories of personal experiences, and a sense of isolation[42,63].

       Along with the possibility of unpleasant or behaviorally disruptive psychological states, the effects of low and medium doses of phencyclinoids on diverse receptors induce a wide-ranging set of physical side effects. Low doses induce a blank stare, bizarre repetitive eye movements known as **nystagmus** (which can be either vertical or horizontal), numbness in the hands and feet, increased sweating, **hypersalivation** (drooling), increased blood pressure, increased reflexes, slurred speech, and ataxia. Moderate doses induce muscle rigidity, even greater increases in blood pressure and reflexes, a **rotary nystagmus** (where the eyes make uncontrollable circling motions that can easily lead to nausea and vomiting), analgesia, stereotypic motor movements, **amnesia** (a forgetting of experiences during the intoxicated state) and an unresponsive stare sometimes referred to as an **eyes open coma**[22,32,74].

OVERDOSE

When more than 15 mg of PCP is consumed, the user will likely experience an overdose. Early discussions of the emergency management of PCP overdose suggested that there were three stages of overdose[60]. Present knowledge suggests that the first two proposed categories instead reflect the negative physical and psychological consequences of low- and medium-dose intoxication. However, the Stage III category of "heavy overdose" accurately describes the life-threatening potential of acute consumption of large doses of the phencyclinoids. Individuals in the Stage III category will likely enter into a prolonged coma. Researchers examined 18 cases of emergency room visits for PCP intoxication, and found that 61% of the patients were completely unresponsive to even the most painful of stimuli[8]. This fact is not surprising given the initial development of this drug as an anesthetic. The unresponsive state (plus other behavioral and physical characteristics of phencyclinoid intake) **wax and wane**[60]. That is, the symptoms of overdose may spontaneously disappear when PCP in the bloodstream is stored in fatty areas of the body. However, these stores may later be once again released into the bloodstream, leading to another life-threatening experience. These **cycles of intoxication** may occur repeatedly throughout a two- or three-week period, depending upon the initial dose of phencyclinoid.

Convulsions, almost always preceded by tremors, twitching, and bizarre body postures, can lead to potentially lethal constant seizures (**status epilepticus**)[8]. Death may also occur due to the elevated body temperature and blood pressure leading to burst brain blood vessels and stroke or heartbeat arrhythmias leading to cardiac arrest. In addition, extremely high doses may induce a respiratory depression (comparable to that seen in depressant overdose) which can itself be life threatening[60], although some authors suggest that respiratory depression is unlikely except when the phencyclinoid overdose is taken in combination with alcohol or some other depressant drug[74]. Since there is at present no clinically useful antidote for phencyclinoids, treatment of severe overdose is usually aimed at preventing the person from hurting themselves or others, symptomatic treatment of the more dangerous consequences of overdose, and attempts to hasten the removal of the drug from the patient's body[54]. Preventing dangerous behavior may be difficult, especially since restraint may result in a breakdown of the fibers of excessively tensed muscles. This can lead to **rhamdomyolisis** where the muscle particles circulating in the bloodstream do permanent damage to the kidneys and/or liver[38]. Unfortunately, the alternative of trying to calm the overdose victim by verbal reassurance is also usually ineffective, due to distortion of sensory input, the probability of the patient being in an unresponsive coma, and the chance that even mild verbal stimuli may set off severe convulsions or agitated behavior[32,74]. Therefore, it is usually recommend that the overdose victim who does not require symptomatic treatment be placed in isolation and observed for self-destructive behavior[54].

For symptomatic treatment, "hypersalivation may require suction, respiratory depression may require artificial ventilation and fever may require external cooling"[32]. Convulsions normally respond to standard anticonvulsants and high blood pressure normally responds to standard antihypertensives. Controversy exists over the best way to hasten the removal of the drug from the body of the overdosed individual. Some recommend **gastric lavage** (stomach pumping) and the use of drugs to make the urine more acid so phencyclinoid excretion will be enhanced[54]. Others suggest that cranberry juice, rather than medication, may acidify the urine and enhance excretion to an appropriate degree[60]. Since, as noted above, even calm verbal stimulation may lead to convulsions, the induction of vomiting by chemical or mechanical means is not a useful alternative for gastric lavage, which may itself lead to convulsions[54]. There is a general consensus that the rapid distribution of phencyclinoids to fatty areas of the body means that artificial dialysis of the blood is ineffective in treating overdose.

Treating any degree of phencyclinoid overdose is complicated by the fact that the diverse effects of the drug enable it to mimic the consequences of ingestion of stimulants, depressants, and/or hallucinogens. However, careful consideration of the entire spectrum of behavioral and physical effects can enable the appropriate diagnosis of PCP overdose. While agitated or bizarre behavior can be induced by stimulants, hallucinogens, and the phencyclinoids, only phencyclinoid users are likely to also show nystagmus, ataxia, and an absence of dilated pupils. When a patient is in a coma, it may be difficult to tell whether the problem is caused by phencyclinoids or a depressant overdose. Fortunately, diagnosis is made easier by the fact that victims of phencyclinoid overdose, but not of depressant overdose, have high blood pressure and exaggerated reflexes, even if they are suffering from decreases in breathing rate[8,18].

CHRONIC EFFECTS

Tolerance and Sensitization

Little research has been conducted regarding the ability of phencyclinoids to induce tolerance or sensitization and even less on the question of whether they induce cross-tolerance or cross-sensitization. Tolerance to the behavioral effects of phencyclinoids in animals has been clearly, and repeatedly, demonstrated[4]. However, while anecdotal reports suggest that tolerance occurs in humans as well[32], experimental evidence for the development of tolerance in humans is incomplete[13,74]. Despite the lack of experimental investigation, it seems reasonable to assume that since sensitization occurs to the convulsant and psychosis-inducing effects of stimulants (see Chapter 15), sensitization may occur to these same effects when they are induced by phencyclinoid consumption. More research will be needed to determine if chronic phencyclinoid consumption induces cross-tolerance to the respiratory depressant effects of depressants or cross-sensitization to the convulsant and psychosis-inducing effects of stimulants.

Physical Dependency/Compulsive Use

The widespread use of phencyclinoids despite their reputation for inducing unpleasant psychological and physical symptoms suggests that individuals may use the drugs compulsively. One study found that 72% of the subjects reporting negative consequences from PCP ingestion continued to use the drug anyway[24]. The question of whether phencyclinoids can induce physical dependency remains controversial. In the early 1980s, a reviewer stated that the evidence for the occurrence of physical dependency from chronic phencyclinoid use is incomplete[13]. However, a number of experiments have indicated that abrupt withdrawal after chronic high dose ingestion of PCP by monkeys or rats led to disruptions of behavior, **bruxism** (teeth grinding), diarrhea, tremor, and perhaps even convulsions. All of these symptoms were immediately suppressed by the administration of phencyclinoids[4,5]. The general absence of reports of withdrawal symptoms in users of illicitly obtained phencyclinoids may be due to unwitting consumption of low doses due to impurities. On the other hand, the absence of withdrawal symptoms in humans may arise from the fact that drugs with long half-lives (such as PCP or certain opioids discussed in Chapter 16) are eliminated so slowly from the body that abrupt cessation of chronic use nonetheless leads to a gradual, and virtually unnoticeable, withdrawal.

Violence and/or Psychosis

As mentioned at the beginning of this chapter, the early use of PCP as an anesthetic was halted because otherwise normal patients awoke from anesthesia with bizarre and/or agitated behavior[29,35]. When given to normal human volunteers in laboratories, PCP often induced a brief psychotic state which resembled spontaneously occurring schizophrenia[3,19,42,63]. Although there are grave ethical concerns surrounding the experiments, there was some early research in which the ability of PCP to induce psychosis was investigated by administration of the drug to hospitalized schizophrenics[42,63]. All schizophrenic patients displayed a worsening of symptoms of their disorder, including "an intensification of the thought disorder, together with the stimulation of considerable affect...(with each patient becoming) generally more assertive, hostile and unmanageable" for periods that lasted between four and six weeks[22]. In a study of PCP overdose, it was noted that overdose victims may display psychotic behavior that can easily be misdiagnosed as schizophrenia[54]. All this evidence, combined with sensational news reports of the bizarre behavior sometimes engaged in by chronic users of phencyclinoids, has led to consideration of whether the drugs are capable of inducing psychosis, or more particularly, schizophrenia, in individuals who would, without chronic use, not suffer from the disorder[26]. If phencyclinoids did induce schizophrenia in otherwise normal individuals, study of the drug might lead to the development of new theories of schizophrenia and, perhaps, novel treatments. Some authors go so far as to state that the phencyclinoids "may provide the best available drug model for schizophrenia"[68], while others more cautiously state that "phencyclidine...psychosis is patently not schizophrenia...(since) phencyclidine clearly does not reproduce in normal subjects exactly the signs or symptoms of this complex disease"[22]. It has been suggested that at least some cases of PCP-induced psychosis may be better mimics of mania than schizophrenia[62].

Of course, retrospective studies of individuals revealing psychotic or schizophrenic behaviors after chronic phencyclinoid use are plagued by difficulties in obtaining accurate information about doses consumed and patterns of administration of these illicit drugs. Despite the evidence from early experiments with normal volunteers, some authors assert that the drug may simply unmask psychosis in individuals who had a preexisting tendency towards severe behavioral disorder[54]. However, determination of whether or not phencyclinoids induce or merely unmask psychosis only becomes more difficult when authors who otherwise provide documentation for claims of negative consequences of phencyclinoid use resort to undocumented assertions that "individuals with no history of pre-existing psychosis have experienced a PCP-precipitated episode after a single administration of the drug"[74].

The question of whether chronic phencyclinoid use leads to violence is intertwined with the question of whether it is capable of inducing psychosis or schizophrenia. Authors who write on the management of phencyclinoid overdose caution that the psychological and physical effects of the drugs may result in individuals who are a danger to themselves and to others[54]. The lay press often reports in lurid detail the violent behavior of some phencyclinoid users and there have been letters to the editor of medical journals about "violence and PCP abuse"[73], articles devoted to "violence associated with phencyclidine abuse"[25] or "phencyclidine, criminal behavior and the defense of diminished capacity"[67], and, finally, books investigating the phencyclinoids as part of a more general study of the *Psychopharmacology of Aggression*[64]. As usual, retrospective studies are plagued with difficulties regarding the possibility that individuals may have had preexisting tendencies towards violence and the probability that drugs other than the phencyclinoids have been deliberately consumed within a pattern of multiple drug abuse or accidentally as a result of contamination of illicitly obtained preparations[18,40]. Despite their bad reputation, it is difficult at present to assert with any degree of certainty that phencyclinoids can, in fact, induce violent behavior in otherwise peaceful individuals. One researcher who conducts research with animals stated that "the bulk of evidence (from animal studies) indicates that PCP decreases aggression at most doses under most conditions"[4]. This same researcher suggested that the evidence of a correlation between PCP use and violence in human drug abusers is not due to a "profound direct effect of PCP on aggressive behaviors (but is instead) more likely a complex interaction of the propensity of the individuals attracted to PCP use with the conditions of its use"[4].

Brain and Other Organ Damage

Information provided above revealed that acute phencyclinoid overdose may lead to damage of the muscles, liver, kidneys, circulatory system and brain. Experimental determinations about whether the illicit phencyclinoids are capable of inducing brain or other organ damage are hampered by the usual concerns about the ethics of giving dangerous doses to normal volunteers and the shortcomings of retrospective studies. For example, indications that chronic users of PCP suffer more severe behavioral disorders than users of other illicit drugs[41] may be due to either prolonged intoxication with this lipid soluble drug or instead to psychological disorders that existed prior to chronic phencyclinoid use. There are a host of physical problems associated with chronic phencyclinoid use, including anorexia, insomnia, constipation, urinary hesitancy, memory impairment and speech problems[74]. It is, however, difficult to tell which of these problems arise directly from phencyclinoid use, and which are instead due to poor personal care and/or pre-existing difficulties. Sophisticated neuropsychological tests of chronic PCP users have similarly revealed evidence of significant brain damage, including low IQ, poor fine motor coordination and motivational deficits[10,40]. However, at least one reviewer has concluded that these studies were poorly designed and did not allow the definite conclusion that PCP use caused, rather than was merely correlated with, the observed indicators of brain damage[31].

CHAPTER SUMMARY

PCP was originally developed as an anesthetic. Its popularity has waxed and waned, but there are presently a number of structural variants, collectively referred to as "phencyclinoids," that are available as illicit drugs. The phencyclinoids are tasteless, odorless, and colorless, and can be administered in a variety of ways. They all tend to be extremely lipid soluble, and thus have longlasting effects. Recirculation of phencyclinoids stored in lipids can lead to cycles of intoxication. PCP affects a wide range of endogenous systems, perhaps through interaction with an endogenous PCP receptor. The multiple pharmacological effects of PCP lead to a diverse set of psychological and physical consequences at low and medium doses. Overdose can lead to death due to prolonged convulsions, stroke, or heartbeat irregularities. Treatment of overdose is symptomatic, due to the absence of an effective antagonist. There is some evidence of tolerance to certain aspects of PCP intoxication, and there is reason to suspect that there might be sensitization to convulsions and psychological difficulties. Compulsive use has been observed, even in individuals who regularly report the occurrence of unpleasant psychological and physical effects. Evidence that physical dependency can develop after chronic phencyclinoid use is inconclusive. Acute and chronic PCP use has been correlated with violent and/or psychotic behavior, but ethical problems and difficulties in designing and interpreting experiments make it difficult to assert that there is a causal relationship between chronic phencyclinoid use and violence and/or psychosis. While phencyclinoid overdose causes damage to a host of bodily organs, further research is needed to confirm early indications that chronic phencyclinoid use can induce brain damage.

REVIEW ESSAY QUESTIONS

1. Use dose-response curves to demonstrate how structural analogues of the original PCP molecule can induce some of PCP's effects at low doses while other effects occur only at higher doses.

2. Reconcile the idea that there are specific PCP receptors in the human brain with the idea that PCP affects a wide number of neurotransmitters.

3. How might the diverse pharmacological effects of the phencyclinoids explain the specific side effects of low and medium dose intoxication?

4. Explain the characteristic symptoms of phencyclinoid overdose and discuss difficulties in treatment.

5. Provide evidence for and against the ideas that chronic phencyclinoid use can lead to violence and/or psychosis.

REFERENCES

1. Albuquerque, E.X., Aguayo, L., Swanson, K.L., Idriss, M., & Warnick, J.E. Multiple interactions of phencyclidine at central and peripheral sites. In E.F. Domino, & J.-M. Kamenka (Eds.) *Sigma and Phencyclidine-like compounds as molecular probes in biology*, Ann Arbor, MI: NPP Books, 1988.

2. Aniline, O., & Pitts, F.N. Phencyclidine (PCP): A review and perspective. *CRC Critical Reviews in Toxicology*, 1982, 10, 145-177.

3. Bakker, C.B., & Amini, F.B. Observations on the psychotomimetic effects of Serynl. *Comparative Psychiatry*, 1961, 2, 269-280.

4. Balster, R.L. The behavioral pharmacology of phencyclidine. In H.Y. Meltzer (Ed.) *Psychopharmacology: The third generation of progress*. New York: Raven Press, 1987.

5. Balster, R.L., & Woolverton, W.H. Tolerance and dependence to phencyclidine. In E.F. Domino (Ed.) *PCP (Phencyclidine): Historical and current perspectives*, Ann Arbor, MI: NPP Books, 1981.

6. Barbaccia, M.L., Costa, E., & Guidotti, A. Endogenous ligands for high-affinity recognition sites of psychotropic drugs. *Annual Review of Pharmacology and Toxicology*, 1988, 28, 451-476.

7. Beach, H.E., Davies, V.M., & Morgenstern, F.S. Preliminary investigations of the effects of sernyl upon cognitive and sensory processes. *Journal of Mental Science*, 1961, 108, 509-513.

8. Burns, R.S., & Lerner, S.E. Perspectives: Acute phencyclidine intoxication. *Clinical Toxicology*, 1976, 9, 477-502.

9. *Cahill, T. Moonwalk serenade. *Rolling Stone*, July 13, 1978.

10. Carlin, A.S., Grant, K., Adams, K.M., & Reed, R. Is phencyclidine (PCP) abuse associated with organic brain impairment? *American Journal of Drug and Alcohol Abuse*, 1979, 6, 273-281.

11. Castellani, S., & Bupp, S.J. Molecular mechanisms in phencyclidine-induced psychosis and its treatment. In E.F. Domino, & J.-M. Kamenka (Eds.) *Sigma and Phencyclidine-like compounds as molecular probes in biology*, Ann Arbor, MI: NPP Books, 1988.

12. Chicheportiche, R., Agid, Y., Chaudieu, I., Gusdinar, T., Javoy-Agid, F., Journot, L., Kamenka, J.-M., & Vignon, J. The multiple binding sites of [³H] PCP and [³H] TCP in the rat and human CNS. In E.F. Domino, & J.-M. Kamenka (Eds.) *Sigma and Phencyclidine-like compounds as molecular probes in biology*, Ann Arbor, MI: NPP Books, 1988.

13. *Cohen, S. *The substance abuse problem*. New York: Hayworth Press, 1981.

14. Collins, V.J., Gorospe, C.A., & Rovenstine, E.A. Intravenous nonbarbiturate, nonnarcotic analgesics: Preliminary studies. I. Cyclohexylamines. *Anesthesiology and Analgesia*, 1960, 39, 302-306.

15. Contreras, P.C., Contreras, M.L., Compton, R.P., & O'Donohue, T.L. Biochemical and behavioral characterization of PCP and sigma receptors. In E.F. Domino & J.-M. Kamenka (Eds.) *Sigma and Phencyclidine-like compounds as molecular probes in biology*, Ann Arbor, MI: NPP Books, 1988.

16. Cook, C.E., Brine, D.R., Jeffcoat, A.R., Hill, J.M., Wall, M.E., Perez-Reyes, M., & Di Guiseppi, S.R. Phencyclidine disposition after intravenous and oral doses. *Clinical Pharmacology and Therapeutics*, 1982, 31, 625-634.

17. Corssen, G., & Domino, E.F. Dissociative anesthesia: Further pharmacologic studies and first clinical experience with the phencyclidine derivative CI-581. *Anesthesia and Analgesia*, 1966, 45, 29-40.

18. Daghestani, A.N. & Schnoll, S.H. Phencyclidine abuse and dependence. In T.B. Karasu (Ed.) *Treatment of psychiatric disorders (Vol.2)*. Washington, D.C.: APA, 1989.

19. Davies, B.M., & Beach, H.R. The effect of 1-arcyclohexylamine (Sernyl) on twelve normal volunteers. *Journal of Mental Science*, 1960, 106, 912-924.

20. DiMaggio, D.A., Contreras, P.C., & O'Donohue, T.L. Biological and chemical characterization of the endopsychosins: Distinct ligands for PCP and sigma sites. In E.F. Domino & J.-M. Kamenka (Eds.) *Sigma and Phencyclidine-like compounds as molecular probes in biology*. Ann Arbor, MI: NPP Books, 1988.

21. Domino, E.F. Neurobiology of phencyclidine (Sernyl): A drug with an unusual spectrum of pharmacological activity. *International Review of Neurobiology*, 1964, 6, 303-347.

22. Domino, E.F., & Luby, E.D. Abnormal mental states induced by phencyclidine as a model of schizophrenia. In J.O. Cole, A.M. Freedman, & A.J. Friedhoff (Eds.) *Psychopathology and psychopharmacology*. Baltimore, MD: Johns Hopkins U. Press, 1973.

23. Eldefrawi, M.E., Eldefrawi, A.T., Aronstam, R.S., Warnick, S.E., & Albuquerque, E.X. [³H]Phencyclidine: A probe for the ionic channel of the nicotinic receptor. *Proceedings of the National Academy of Sciences, 1980, 77*, 7458-7462.

24. Fauman, M.A., & Fauman, B.G. The psychiatric aspects of chronic phencyclidine (PCP) abuse: A study of phencyclidine users. In R.C. Petersen & R.C. Stillman (Eds.) *Phencyclidine (PCP) abuse: An appraisal*. Rockville, MD: NIDA, 1978.

25. Fauman, M.A., & Fauman, B.J. Violence associated with phencyclidine abuse. *American Journal of Psychiatry*, 1979, 136, 1584-1586.

26. Fauman, M.A., & Fauman, B.G. Chronic phencyclidine (PCP) abuse: A psychiatric perspective. In E.F. Domino (Ed.) *PCP (Phencyclidine): Historical and current perspectives*. Ann Arbor, MI: NPP Books, 1981.

27. Gole, D.J., Pirat, J.-L., & Domino, E.F. New aspects of phencyclidine (PCP) metabolism. In E.F. Domino & J.-M. Kamenka (Eds.) *Sigma and Phencyclidine-like compounds as molecular probes in biology*. Ann Arbor, MI: NPP Books, 1988.

28. Graeven, D.B. Patterns of phencyclidine use. In R.C. Petersen & R.C. Stillman (Eds.) *Phencyclidine (PCP) abuse: An appraisal*. Rockville, MD: NIDA, 1978.

29. Greifenstein, F.E., Yoshitake, J., Devault, M. et al. A study of l-aryl cyclo hexyl amine for anesthesia. *Anesthesia and Analgesia*, 1958, 37, 283-294.

30. Hampton, R.Y., Medzihradsky, F., Woods, J.H., & Dahlstrom, P.J. Stereospecific binding of ³H-phencyclidine in rat brain membranes. *Life Science*, 1982, 30, 2147-2154.

31. Hartman, D.E. *Neuropsychological toxicology: Identification and assessment of human neurotoxic syndromes*. New York: Pergamon Press, 1988.

32. Jaffe, J.H. Drug addiction and drug abuse. In A.G. Gilman, L.S. Goodman, T.W. Rall, & F. Murad (Eds.) *The pharmacological basis of therapeutics, (7th Ed.)*. New York: Macmillan, 1985.

33. Johnson, K.M. Neurochemistry and neurophysiology of phencyclidine. In H.Y. Meltzer (Ed.) *Psychopharmacology: The third generation of progress*. New York: Raven Press, 1987.

34. Johnson, K.M., Vicroy, T.W., Leventer, S.M., & Mok., L.S. Phencyclidine: Effects on striatal dopaminergic and cholinergic systems. In J.-M. Kamenka, E.F. Domino, & P. Geneste (Eds.) *Phencyclidine and related arylcyclohexylamines: Present and future applications*. Ann Arbor, MI: NPP Books, 1983.

35. Johnstone, M. The use of Sernyl in clinical anesthesia. *Anaesthetist*, 1960, 9, 114.

36. *Kirsch, M. M. *Designer drugs*. Minneapolis, MI: Compcare Publications, 1986.

37. Kloog, Y., Gabrielevitz, A., Kalier, A., Balderman, D., & Sokolovsky, M. Functional evidence for a second binding site of nicotinic antagonists using phencyclidine derivatives. *Biochemical Pharmacology*, 1979, 28, 1447-1450.

38. Lahmeyer, H.W., & Stock, P.G. Phencyclidine intoxication, physical restraint, and acute renal failure: Case report. *Journal of Clinical Psychiatry*, 1983, 44, 184-185.

39. Lehmann, J., & Wood, P.L. Interactions between the NMDA-type receptor complex and PCP recognition sites. In E.F. Domino & J.-M. Kamenka (Eds.) *Sigma and Phencyclidine-like compounds as molecular probes in biology*. Ann Arbor, MI: NPP Books, 1988.

40. Lewis, J.E., & Hordan, R.B. Neuropsychological assessment of phencyclidine abusers. In D.H. Clouet (Ed.) *Phencyclidine: An update*, Washington, D.C.: Dept. of Health and Human Services, NIDA, 1986.

41. *Linder, R., Lerner, S., & Burns, R. *PCP: The devil's dust*. Belmont, CA: Wadsworth, 1981.

42. Luby, E.D., Cohen, B.D., Rosenbaum, G., Gottlieb, J.S., & Kelly, R. Study of a new schizophrenicomimetic drug-Sernyl. *Archives of Neurological Psychiatry*, 1959, 81, 363-369.

43. Maayani, S., Weinstein, A., Ben-Zvi, N., Cohen, S., & Sokolovsky, M. Psychotomimetics as anticholinergic agents. I. 1-Cyclohexylpiperidine derivatives: Anticholinesterase activity and antagonistic activity to acetylcholine. *Biochemical Pharmacology*, 1974, 23, 1263-1281.

44. Maddox, V.H. The historical development of phencyclidine. In E.F. Domino (Ed.) *PCP (Phencyclidine): Historical and current perspectives*. Ann Arbor, MI: NPP Books, 1981.

45. Mattia, A., Leccese, A.P., Marquis, K.L., El-Fakahany, E.E., & Moreton, J.E. Pharmacologic profile of Phencyclidine (PCP) and PCP analogues: Electroencephalographic, Behavioral, and Receptor Binding Studies. In L.S. Harris (Ed.) *Problems of drug dependence*. Rockville, MD: NIDA, 1986.

46. McAdams, M., Linder, R., Lerner, S., & Burns, R. *Phencyclidine abuse manual*. Los Angeles: University of California Extension, 1980.

47. McCarthy, D.A., Chen G., & Kaump, D.H. General anesthetic and other pharmacological properties of 2-(o-chlorophenyl)-2-methylaminocyclohexanone HCL (CI-581). *Journal of New Drugs*, 1965, Jan-Feb, 21-22.

48. Micik, S. PCP update. *Western Journal of Medicine*, 1980, 132, 62-63.

49. Nabeshima, T., Ishikawa, K., Yamaguchi, K., Furukawa, H., & Kameyama, T. Property of phencyclidine as a 5-HT$_2$ receptor agonist. In E.F. Domino & J.-M. Kamenka (Eds.) *Sigma and Phencyclidine-like compounds as molecular probes in biology*. Ann Arbor, MI: NPP Books, 1988.

50. Ornstein, P.L., Zimmerman, D.M., Leander, J.D., Mendelsohn, L., Reel, J.K., & Evrard, D.A. The search for a phencyclidine (PCP) antagonist: PCP-like effects of a series of substituted dioxolanes related to dexoxadrol. In E.F. Domino & J.-M. Kamenka (Eds.) *Sigma and Phencyclidine-like compounds as molecular probes in biology*. Ann Arbor, MI: NPP Books, 1988.

51. Palmer, M.R., Bickford, P.C., Hoffer, B.J., & Freedman, R. Electrophysiological evidence for presynaptic actions of phencyclidine on noradrenergic transmission in rat cerebellum and hippocampus. In J.-M. Kamenka, E.F. Domino, & P. Geneste (Eds.) *Phencyclidine and related arylcyclohexylamines: Present and future applications*. Ann Arbor, MI: NPP Books, 1983.

52. Palmer, M.R., Wang, Y., Hoffer, B.J., & Freedman, R. Mechanisms of PCP action in the central nervous system. In J. Engel, L. Oreland, D.H. Ingvar, B. Pernow, S. Roessner, & L.A. Pellborn (Eds.) *Brain reward systems and abuse*. New York: Raven Press, 1987.

53. Paterson, S.J. The in vitro pharmacology of selective opioid ligands. In M.Lader (Ed.) *The psychopharmacology of addiction*. Oxford, England: Oxford University Press, 1988.

54. Petersen, R.C., & Stillman, R.C. Phencyclidine: An overview. In R.C. Petersen & R.C. Stillman (Eds.) *Phencyclidine (PCP) abuse: An appraisal*. Rockville, MD: NIDA, 1978.

55. Pollard, J.C., Uhr, L., & Stern, E. *Drugs and phantasy: The effects of LSD, psilocybin and Sernyl on college students.* Boston: Little Brown, 1965.

56. Pullan, L.M., Roufa, D.G., Monahan, J.B., Contreras, P.C., & O'Donohue, T.L. Interactions between phencyclidine and N-methyl-D-aspartate receptors: Behavioral, cellular and biochemical evidence. In E.F. Domino & J.-M. Kamenka (Eds.) *Sigma and Phencyclidine-like compounds as molecular probes in biology.* Ann Arbor, MI: NPP Books, 1988.

57. Quiron, R., DiMaggio, D.A., French, E.D., Contreras, P.C., Shiloach, J., Pert, C.B., Everist, H., Pert, A., & O'Donohue, T.L. Evidence for an endogenous peptide ligand for the phencyclidine receptor. *Peptides,* 1984, 5, 967-974.

58. Quiron, R., O'Donohue, T.L., Everist, H., Pert A., & Pert, C.B. Phencyclidine receptors and possible existence of an endogenous ligand. In J.-M. Kamenka, E.F. Domino, & P. Geneste (Eds.) *Phencyclidine and Related arylcyclohexylamines: Present and future applications.* Ann Arbor, MI: NPP Books, 1983.

59. Rafferty, M.F., Mattson, M., Jacobson, A.E., & Rice, K.C. A specific acylating agent for the [^{3}H]phencyclidine receptors in rat brain. *Federation of European Biochemical Society Letter,* 1985, 181, 318-322.

60. Rappolt, R.T., Gay, G.R., & Farris, R.D. Emergency management of acute phencyclidine ("PCP") intoxication. *Veterinary and Human Toxicology,* 1979, 21, 92-99.

61. Reel, J.K., Leander, J.D., Mendelsohn, L.G., Schoepp, D.D., Ornstein, P.L., Evrard, D.A., Hermann, R.B., & Zimmerman, D.M. The search for a PCP antagonist: Synthesis and characterization of novel arylcyclohexylamine derivatives. In E.F. Domino & J.-M. Kamenka (Eds.) *Sigma and Phencyclidine-like compounds as molecular probes in biology.* Ann Arbor, MI: NPP Books, 1988.

62. Rosen, A. Case report: Symptomatic mania and phencyclidine abuse. *American Journal of Psychiatry,* 1979, 136, 118-119.

63. Rosenbaum, G., Cohen, B.D., Luby, E.D., Gottlieb, J.S., & Yelen, D. Comparison of Serynl with other drugs. *Archives of General Psychiatry,* 1959, 1, 651-656.

64. Sandler, J.N. *Psychopharmacology of aggression.* New York: Raven Press, 1979.

65. Sani, J.-M., Christophe de Lamotte, F., Fayolle, C., & Fillion, G. Interactions of phencyclidine and two derivatives with serotonergic receptors. In E.F. Domino & J.-M. Kamenka (Eds.) *Sigma and Phencyclidine-like compounds as molecular probes in biology.* Ann Arbor, MI: NPP Books, 1988.

66. Schnoll, S.H. Street PCP scene: Issues on synthesis and contamination. *Journal of Psychedelic Drugs,* 1980, 12, 229-233.

67. Siegel, R.K. Phencyclidine, criminal behavior and the defense of diminished capacity. In R.C. Petersen & R.C. Stillman (Eds.) *Phencyclidine (PCP) abuse: An appraisal.* Rockville, MD: NIDA, 1978.

68. *Snyder, S.H. Phencyclidine. *Nature,* 1980, 285, 355-356.

69. Tam, S.W., Steinfels, G.F., & Cook, L. Biochemical and behavioral aspects of sigma and phencyclidine receptors: Similarities and differences. In E.F. Domino & J.-M. Kamenka (Eds.) *Sigma and Phencyclidine-like compounds as molecular probes in biology.* Ann Arbor, MI: NPP Books, 1988.

70. Vincent, J.-P., Kartalovski, B., Geneste, P., Kamenka, J.-M., & Lazdunski, M. Interaction of phencyclidine ("angel dust") with a specific receptor in rat brain membranes. *Proceedings of the National Academy of Scientists, USA,* 1979, 79, 4678-4682.

71. Wang, Y., Palmer, M., Freedman, R., Hoffer, B., Mattson, M., Lessor, R.A., Rafferty, M.F., Rice, K.C., & Jacobson, A.E. Electrophysiological and biochemical study of the antagonism of PCP action by metaphit in rat cerebellar Purkinje cells. *Proceedings of the National Academy of Scientists, USA,* 1986, 83, 2724-2727.

72. Winters, W.D., Ferrer, A.T., & Guzman-Flores, C. The cataleptic state induced by ketamine: A review of the neuropharmacology of anesthesia. *Neuropharmacology,* 1972, 11, 303-315.

73. Wright, H.H. Violence and PCP abuse. *American Journal of Psychiatry,* 1980, 137, 752-753.

74. Young, T., Lawson, G.W., & Gacono, C.B. Phencyclidine: A clinical review. In G.W. Lawson & C.A. Cooperrider (Eds.) *Clinical psychopharmacology: A practical reference for nonmedical psychotherapists.* Rockville, MD: Aspen Publishers, 1988.

75. Zhang, A.Z., Mitchell, K.N., Cook, L., & Tam, S.W. Human endogenous brain ligands for sigma and phencyclidine receptors. In E.F. Domino & J.-M. Kamenka (Eds.) *Sigma and Phencyclidine-like compounds as molecular probes in biology.* Ann Arbor, MI: NPP Books, 1988.

76. Zukin, S.R., & Zukin, S.R. Specific [^{3}H]phencyclidine binding in rat central nervous system. *Proceedings of the National Academy of Scientists, USA,* 1979, 76, 5372-5376.

* Introductory or intermediate reading

AUTHOR INDEX

Aageson, C. A., 175
Aarons, S. F., 109
Abermethy, D. R., 135
Abood, L. G., 228
Abraham, H. D., 289
Abruzzi, W., 280
Adams, E. H., 209
Adams, K. M., 308
Adams, N. L., 252
Addario, D., 25, 45, 54, 82, 86, 93, 283
Adlaf, E. M., 223, 231
Adler, L., 90
Adler, N. T., 19
Aghajanian, G., 281
Agid, Y., 303
Agren, H., 100, 104
Aguayo, L., 303
Agurell, S., 274, 275, 284
Ahmed, A. M., 221
Albee, G. W., 72
Albertson, T. E., 234
Albrechtsen, R., 254
Albright, D., 112
Albuquerque, E. X., 303
Alderice, M. T., 143
Alderson, P., 120
Aldous, D., 90
Aldrich, M. R., 280
Allen, D. J., 155
Allen, M. H., 289
Allen, T., 281
Alrazi, J., 276
Altura, B. M., 255
Altura, B. T., 255
Alvir, J., 240
Amalric, M., 195, 196, 199
Aman, M. G., 155
Amass, L., 284
Amdisen, A., 124
American Management Association, 213
Amini, F. B., 306
Amin, K., 151
Amin, M., 134

Amit, Z., 251, 266
Anastasopoulos, G., 290
Ando, K., 238, 240
Andresen, N. C., 74
Andrews, J. C., 288
Andrysiak, T., 285
Angrist, B., 90
Aniline, O., 302
Annable, L., 61, 94, 128, 142
Anthony, J. C., 276, 278
Anton, R., 176
APA (Work Group to Revise DSM-III of the American Psychiatric Association), 69
Apsler, R., 75, 76
Aragon, C. M. G., 251
Aranko, K., 53, 54
Arndt, I. O., 83, 182
Arnold, D. O., 284, 288
Arnold, L. E., 154, 158
Aronstam, R. S., 303
ASPET (American Society for Pharmacology and Experimental Therapeutics), 238
Aulakh, C. S., 107
Ausubel, D. P., 72
Ayd, F. R., 63
Ayliffe, H. E., 197
Ayllon, T., 156

Babor, T. F., 252, 260
Bachman, J., 284
Baetge, G., 123
Bahr, C., 275, 288
Bakalar, J. B., 212, 213, 272, 288
Bakker, C. B., 280, 306
Balderman, D., 303
Baldessarini, R. J., 83, 84, 89, 92, 102, 105, 108, 111, 124, 135, 140
Balka, E. B., 156
Ballenger, J. C., 129, 176
Balster, R. L., 306, 308

Balter, M. B., 135, 141
Bamea, Z., 207, 208
Bames, H. N., 178
Ban, T. A., 69, 71, 82, 122
Banys, P., 178
Baraban, J. M., 278
Barbaccia, M. L., 201, 303
Barchas, J. D., 8
Bardoni, A., 288
Barish, R., 125, 126, 127
Barker, C., 157, 158
Barker, J. L., 270
Barkley, R. A., 149, 151, 155, 157
Barnes, D. M., 208
Barnes, G. E., 260
Barnett, G., 171, 210
Barnhill, J. G., 176
Barr, A., 90
Barr, E., 155
Barrett, J. E., 44, 45, 59, 194
Barrio, J., 227
Barr, R. G., 151
Bartke, J. J., 100, 104
Baruk, C. E., 200
Basbaum, A. I., 252
Battaglia, G., 290
Baumbartel, P., 183
Baumgartner, G. R., 175
Baxter, L. R., 182, 183, 227
Beach, H. E., 300
Beach, H. R., 300, 306
Beake, B., 143
Beard, J. D., 251, 255
Beardsley, P. M., 278
Beck, A. T., 101, 111
Becker, J. T., 199, 252, 260
Begleiter, H., 252, 260
Bejerot, N., 195
Belluzzi, J. D., 195
Benet, L. Z., 29, 31, 44
Benkelfat, C., 134
Bennett, B., 112
Benowitz, N. L., 221, 233, 284, 285

313

Benson, H., 46
Benton, D., 266
Ben-Zvi, N., 303
Bercel, N. A., 289
Berger, L., 249
Berger, P. A., 100
Bergstedt, H. H., 283
Berrettini, W., 100, 121
Berridge, M. J., 124
Bialer, I., 156
Bickford, P. C., 303
Bidlack, J. M., 228
Biederman, J., 154
Bigelow, G. E., 61, 169, 170, 179, 195, 209, 210, 211, 238, 263
Bigelow, L. B., 90
Bigger, J. T., 105, 106
Bing, O., 281
Bittle, R. M., 289
Blackburn, G. L., 210
Blackwell, B., 108, 110
Blair, L. W., 180
Blaschke, T. F., 172
Blau, S., 44
Blewett, D. B., 288
Bloom, F. E., 9, 18, 123, 195, 196, 199, 238
Blumbergs, P. C., 252, 260
Blumenfield, M., 290
Blum, K., 176, 251
Boer, G. J., 21
Bogin, R. M., 255
Boiler, S., 129
Boisse, N. N., 251
Bok, S., 70
Bonagura, N., 149, 152, 157
Bonnie, R. J., 212
Booth, H., 228
Boppana, V., 85, 86
Borden, K. A., 74, 156
Borg, B., 270
Borg, S., 266
Borgstedt, A. D., 149, 152, 153, 155, 156
Borison, R. L., 90, 93, 94
Borkqvist, S. E., 176
Bosomworth, J. C., 109
Bost, R. O., 283
Botti, E., 156
Boulenger, J. P., 139, 227
Bourne, P. D., 30
Bowers, M. B., 200, 273, 282, 289
Bowery, N. G., 138
Boyer, W. F., 87
Bozarth, M. A., 195
Bracha, H. S., 82
Bracy, S. A., 261
Braden, N. J., 273, 287
Bradley, B., 172, 174

Bradley, C., 158
Bradt, C., 296
Brady, J. V., 193, 281
Braestrup, C., 134, 254
Branchey, L., 178
Brase, D. A., 252
Braude, M. C., 31
Braum, L., 249
Brecher, E. M., 212
Breese, G. R., 150
Breimer, D. D., 250
Brien, J. F., 177, 178
Briggs, A. H., 176
Brightwell, D. R., 178
Brill, N. Q., 286
Brine, D. R., 302
Britton, B. G., 151
Britt, R. H., 141
Brotman, A. W., 110, 182
Broucek, B., 61
Brown, B. W., 259
Brown, C. R., 259
Browne, B., 125, 126, 127
Brownell, L., 249
Brown, L. B., 28
Brown, R. P., 109
Brown, R. T., 151, 156, 273, 287
Brownstein, M. J., 19
Brown, T. R., 74
Brumaghim, J. T., 149, 152, 153, 155, 156
Bruno, R. L., 105
Bryan, G., 290
Buchsbaum, M. S., 152
Budson, A., 284
Bugenthal, D. B., 157, 158
Bulpitt, C. J., 70
Bunney, W. E., 121, 123, 124
Bupp, S. J., 310
Burger, C., 285
Burke, J. D., 98
Burns, R., 302, 308
Burns, R. S., 197, 302, 304, 305
Burrows, G. D., 109
Busto, U., 56, 61
Butts-Lamb, P., 227
Byck, R., 182, 183, 212, 213
Byron, J. P., 183

Cadoret, R., 194
Caffey, E. M., 122, 123
Cahill, T., 300
Callaham, M., 106
Callahan, E. J., 169
Callison, D. A., 255
Camic, P. M., 180
Campeas, R., 134
Campos, P. E., 280
Cannon, L., 258

Capriotti, R. M., 281
Carlen, P. L., 260
Carlin, A. S., 280, 285, 308
Carney, T. M., 171
Caroff, S. N., 92
Carpenter, R. W., 263
Cartmill, M., 18
Case, W. G., 139, 140, 141, 142, 143
Casey, D. E., 87, 90
Casswell, S., 285
Casta, C. D., 158
Castellani, S., 310
Catterall, W. A., 6
Chait, L. D., 221, 280, 285
Chamey, D. S., 100, 104
Chan, Y. M., 150
Charney, D. S., 122, 124, 174
Chatoor, I., 150
Chaudieu, I., 303
Chein, I., 193, 199
Chen, G., 300
Chiang, C. N., 171, 274, 275
Chicheportiche, R., 303
Chick, J., 176
Childress, A. R., 83, 182, 194
Chouinard, G., 61, 94, 128, 142
Christensen, D. E., 150
Christopher, I., 154, 158
Chung, H., 143
Chwelos, N., 288
Cipra, B. A., 202
Ciraulo, A. M., 176
Ciraulo, D. A., 176
Clark, D. C., 175
Clark, H. W., 179, 183, 226
Clark, K., 90
Clark, V., 286
Clark, W. G., 280
Clayton, P. J., 120, 122, 123
Climko, R., 183
Clingerman, S. R., 74, 156
Clouet, D., 252
Cocores, J. A., 194
Cohen, A. J., 171
Cohen, B. D., 300, 304, 306, 307
Cohen, B. M., 129
Cohen, D. J., 150, 159
Cohen, M., 192
Cohen, N. H., 122
Cohen, R. M., 82
Cohen, S., 283, 284, 289, 303, 306, 310
Cohen, W. J., 122
Cohn, J. B., 112
Cole, J. O., 143
Colletti, G., 179, 180
Collins, V. J., 299

Colpaert, F. C., 53, 59, 194, 210
Commier, Y., 281
Commins, D. L., 290
Compton, D. R., 278
Compton, R. P., 303
Cone, E. J., 239
Congreve, G. R. S., 286
Conley, F. K., 141
Conlon, P. T., 45
Connel, P. H., 239, 240
Connors, C. K., 150, 158
Connors, G. J., 256
Conn, P. M., 18
Conrad, P., 73, 150
Consensus Development Panel, 123
Contreras, M. L., 299
Contreras, P. C., 303, 310
Cook, B. L., 143
Cook, C. E., 280, 302
Cook, L., 303
Coons, H. W., 149, 152, 153, 155, 156
Cooperrider, C., 133
Cooperrider, C. A., 83, 99, 111
Cooper, S. J., 195
Cooper, T. B., 121, 127, 179
Copass, M. K., 197
Coppen, A., 100
Coppen, A. J., 100
Corcella, J., 112
Corey, M. J., 288
Cornell, N., 56, 259
Corospe, C. A., 299
Corssen, G., 310
Corwin, J., 90
Costa, E., 201, 303
Cottington, E., 197, 255
Council on Scientific Affairs, 61, 212
Covey, L. S., 179
Covi, L., 150
Coyle, J. J., 16
CPDD (Committee on Problems of Drug Dependence), 238
Crabtree, B. L., 170, 171, 172, 254, 258
Cramer, C., 175
Crane, G. E., 106
Crawley, J. N., 251
Critchlow, B., 45, 256
Crome, P., 105, 106
Cronson, A. J., 181
Crook, T. A., 102
Crowley, T. J., 183, 233
Csanalosi, I., 143
Cuculic, Z., 102
Cuff, G., 25, 29
Curatolo, P. W., 221
Curson, D., 248, 256

Cushman, P., 175

Dackis, C. A., **167, 169, 172, 174,** 183, 285
Daghestani, A. N., 305, 308
Dahlberg, C. C., 288
Dahlstrom, B., 249
Dahlstrom, P. J., 303
Daigle, R. D., 183, 226
Davault, M., 299, 306
David, J. J., 197, 200
Davidson, J., 107, 110
Davidson, M., 82
Davies, B. M., 300, 306
Davies, M., 105
Davies, S., 134
Davies, V. M., 300
Daview, L. S., 289
Davis, G. C., 157
Davis, J. M., 74, 84, 85, 86, 127, 239
Davis, K. H., 274, 275, 280
Davis, K. L., 82
Davis, R. K., 183
Davison, K., 273, 281, 287, 289
Dawling, S., 56, 63, 142
Dawson, M. E., 154
DeArmond, S. J., 16
Defalque, R., 259
Degan, R. O., 142
DeLallo, L., 176
de Lamontte, F. C., 312
Delgado, P. L., 124
Demellweek, C., 59
Denari, M., 285
Deniker, P., 41
Deren, S., 207, 208, 209
DeRios, M. D., 194
Derlet, R. W., 234
Derman, R. M., 178
De Souza, E. B., 290
Devenyi, P., 286
Devereaux, E., 112
Dewey, M. M., 16
Dewey, W. L., 252, 277, 280, 284, 285
Dewhurst, K., 282
DeWitt, H., 141, 180
Dews, P. B., 152, 240
Deyo, S., 123
DHEW, 69
DHHS, 69
Diamond, B. I., 90, 93, 94
Dietch, J. T., 140
DiGregorio, G. J., 275
DiGuiseppi, S. R., 275, 280, 302
Dilsaver, S. C., 273
DiMaggio, D. A., 303, 310
DiMarzio, L. R., 183

DiMascio, A., 110
Dingell, J. V., 105
Ditman, K. S., 289
Divoli, M., 139
Djahed, B., 276, 280, 281, 286
Doddi, S., 85, 86
Dolin, S., 251, 259
Domino, E. F., 300, 302, 304, 307, 310
Donald, A. G., 252
Donlon, P. T., 196
Donovan, B. T., 21
Doogan, D. P., 100
Dornseif, B. E., 109
Dorow, R., 134, 139
Dotemoto, S., 151
Dotson, O. Y., 275
Dougherty, J., 258
Douglas, V. I., 151
Dowling, G. P., 283
Downing, R. W., 140, 141
Dreikurs, E., 289
Drug Enforcement Administration, 212
Druley, K. A., 256
Duka, T., 252
Duke, P. C., 249
Dulcan, M. K., 152, 153, 155, 158
Dunlop, S. R., 109
Dunner, D. L., 120, 121, 122, 123, 127
DuPaul, G. J., 152
Dworkin, S. I., 45

Eckardt, M. J., **260**
Edgerton, R. B., 256
Edwards, G., 175
Ehrman, R. N., 210
Eichelman, B., 69, 70
Eikelboom, R., 59
Eison, M. S., 143
Eldefrawi, A. T., 303
Eldefrawi, M. E., 303
El-Fakahany, E. E., 216, 300, 301
Elliott, G. R., 8
Elliott, M. L., 180
Ellner, M., 208, 286
Ellsworth, D., 59
Elmi, A. S., 221
El-Yousef, M. K., 121, 127, 239
Emery, G., 111
Emley, G. S., 179
Emmett-Oglesby, M. W., **68**
Emna, S. J., 103, 104
Emrick, C. D., 178
Emster, V. L., 231

Engel, J., 62, 195, 227
Enna, S. J., 134, 138
Epstein, C., 180
Epstein, M. D., 46
Erickson, P. G., 223, 231
Esecover, H., 289
Esteroff, T. W., 182
Ettenberg, A., 123
Ettinger, T. B., 233
Evans, B. D., 172
Evans, S. M., 280
Everist, H., 303
Evrard, D. A., 303
Extein, I., 172, 174

Fadiman, J., 289
Fairbanks, L., 194, 221
Falk, J. L., 46, 58, 194, 195, 199, 272
Falk, W. E., 110, 182
Farde, L., 86
Farfinkel, B. D., 154
Farrell, M., 274
Farris, R. D., 304, 305
Fauman, B. G., 307
Fauman, B. J., 307
Fauman, M. A., 306, 307
Faust, R., 192
Fawcett, J., 175
Fayolle, C., 312
Feighner, J. P., 112
Feingold, D. A., 46, 58, 194, 199, 272
Feinman, L., 256
Feirtag, M., 14
Fejer, D., 192
Feldman, R. S., 233
Feldstein, S., 288
Fenstermacher, J. D., 5
Fenwick, S., 288
Ferrer, A. T., 300
Feyerabend, C., 179
Fields, H. L., 252
Fields, S., 261
Fieve, R. R., 120, 121, 123
Fihn, S. D., 197
File, S. E., 60
Fillion, G., 312
Fink, M., 285, 289
Finnerty, R., 143
Firestone, P., 156
Fischer, D. D., 298
Fischer, H. B. J., 257
Fischman, M., 286
Fischman, M. W., 210, 237, 281, 285
Fisher, D. D., 282, 289
Fisher, S., 55, 72

Fitzpatrick, P., 149, 152, 153, 155, 156
Flach, F., 74
Fleet, J. V. W., 158
Fleiss, J. L., 179
Flemenbaum, A., 181
Fleming, T., 285
Flemons, W. W., 251
Fletcher, J., 286
Fligiel, S. E. G., 286
Foltin, R., 286
Foltin, R. W., 237, 281
Fomey, R. R., 283
Fontaine, R., 61, 142
Force, R., 69
Foreyt, J. P., 255
Forgy, E. A., 289
Forrer, G. R., 276, 282
Forrest, W. H., 259
Forsyth, A. B., 180
Foti, M. E., 176
Fox, I. L., 139, 141, 142
Frances, A. J., 102, 109, 112
Frankel, M., 122
Frankenburg, F. R., 129
Frank, I. M., 281
Franz, D. N., 150, 156, 158, 222, 225, 228, 232, 235
Fraser, H. S., 275
Freedman, D. X., 276, 278
Freedman, R., 303
Freeman, H. L., 90
French, E. D., 303
Freud, S., 194
Fridman, R. B., 139, 141, 142
Friedman, G. D., 208, 260
Friedman, M. J., 134
Fryd, V., 180
Fuller, M., 289, 298
Fuller, R. K., 178
Fullerton, J., 261
Funderburk, F. R., 210
Furlong, F. W., 240
Furukawa, H., 311
Fusco, M. M., 16
Fu, T. K., 286
Fyer, A., 134

Gabrielevitz, A., 303
Gacono, C. B., 300, 303, 304, 305, 306, 307, 308
Galizio, M., 196
Gallant, D. M., 69, 70, 133, 260
Galssman, A. H., 105
Ganong, W. F., 25
Ganrot, P. O., 107
Garbey, M. J., 143
Garbutt, J. C., 100

Garland-Bunney, L., 121, 123, 124
Garrick, N. A., 107
Garver, D. L., 85, 86
Garvey, M. J., 141
Gary, N. E., 258
Gash, D. M., 21
Gaspari, J., 174
Gastfriend, D. R., 154
Gauthier, M., 149, 152
Gavaler, J. S., 260
Gawin, F. H., 181, 182, 183, 194, 196, 239
Gay, G. R., 233, 234, 304, 305
Gehibach, G., 143
Gelenberg, A. J., 110, 121, 182
Geneste, P., 303
George, J., 90
Gerard, D. L., 193, 199
Gerlsch, J., 87, 90, 93
German, P. S., 133
Gershon, E. S., 100, 121
Getz, A. L., 5
Ghodse, A. H., 287
Giannini, A. J., 183
Giannini, J. C., 183
Giardina, E.-G. V., 105, 106
Gibbins, R. J., 286
Gibbons, R. D., 175
Gilbert, P. E., 254
Gillespie, H., 275, 284
Gillespie, H. K., 274, 275
Gill, K., 266
Gilman, A. G., 37, 44, 45, 47, 196, 273
Ginzburg, H. M., 171, 172, 262, 263
Gitlin, M. J., 194, 221
Gittelman, R., 149, 152, 156, 157
Glasglow, R. E., 180
Glass, G. B. J., 255
Glass, G. S., 289
Glassman, A. H., 105, 106, 111, 179
Glennon, R. A., 278
Glickman, L., 290
Glick, S. D., 179
Glowa, J. R., 251
Goldberg, H. L., 143
Goldberg, S. C., 72
Goldberg, S. R., 61, 63, 195, 196
Goldin, L. R., 100, 121
Gold, M., 259
Gold, M. S., 167, 169, 172, 174, 182, 183, 194, 285
Goldner, R. D., 276, 282
Goldsmith, S. R., 289

Goldstein, A., 171, 195, 246, 256
Goldstein, D. B., 197, 251
Goldstein, G. W., 5
Gole, D. J., 302
Gong, H., 286
Goodie, A. J., 59
Goodman, E. C., 45
Goodwin, D. W., 120
Goodwin, F. K., 110
Goodwin, J. M., 121, 127
Gordon, H. E., 259
Gordon, R. A., 262
Gorman, J., 134
Gorman, R. L., 108, 109
Gorton, J. G., 246, 258
Gossop, M., 172, 174
Gottfries, C. G., 107
Gottheil, E., 239, 256
Gottlieb, J. S., 300, 304, 306, 307
Gottom, A. M., 255
Goyer, P. F., 157
Graeven, D. B., 300
Gramsch, C., 252
Grant, I., 285
Grant, K., 308
Grant, K. A., 280
Greenblatt, D. J., 135, 137, 139,
    141, 142, 176
Greenblatt, M., 107
Greene, N. M., 223, 234
Greenfield, D. P., 190
Greenstein, R., 258
Greenstein, R. A., 172
Greifenstein, F. E., 299, 306
Greil, W., 61
Grell, G. A., 275
Griffiths, R. R., 61, 138, 179, 209,
    238, 263
Grinspoon, L., 158, 212, 213, 272,
    288
Groleau, G., 125, 126, 127
Grosser, G. H., 107
Gross, M., 82
Gross, M. D., 152
Grover, G., 134
Gruenberg, E., 98
Grufferman, S., 197
Grumbach, M. M., 8
Gualtieri, T., 150
Guidotti, A., 201, 303
Gunnet, J. W., 85, 86, 87
Gusdinar, T., 303
Gust, S. W., 179, 238
Guttmacher, L. B., 134
Guy, W., 69, 82
Guze, B. H., 227
Guzman-Flores, C., 300

Haas, A. P., 208, 286

Hadley, M. E., 21
Haertzen, C. A., 263
Haggard, H. W., 256
Hajek, P., 179
Halbrecht, J. D., 21
Halikas, J. A., 287
Halldin, C., 86
Halldin, M., 275
Halldin, M. M., 275, 288
Halpern, L., 280
Halpern, L. M., 76
Hampton, R. Y., 303
Hanks, G. W., 253, 257
Hansen, M., 180
Han, Y. H., 57, 259
Haque, W., 289
Harackiewicz, J. M., 180
Hare, E. H., 73
Harlap, S., 260
Harmatz, J. S., 139
Harper, C. G., 252, 260
Harper, J., 251, 259
Harris, L. S., 259
Harrison, W., 110, 111
Hartman, D. E., 246, 247, 260, 308
Hartnoll, R., 166, 253
Hartsough, C. S., 149, 150
Hartung, G. H., 255
Harvey, S. C., 249, 250, 254, 257,
    258, 259, 263
Haskell, D., 110
Hatrick, J. A., 282
Havey, R. J., 240, 273
Hawks, R., 210
Hawley, R. J., 267
Haywood, E., 194
Hechtman, L., 152, 157, 158
Hechtman, L. T., 148, 150
Helmer, J., 212, 240
Helsted, J., 180
Helzer, J. E., 98
Heming, R. I., 284, 285
Hendin, H., 208, 286
Heneen, W., 296
Henker, B., 150, 151, 157, 158
Henninger, G., 290
Henninger, G. R., 100, 104, 122,
    124, 174
Henningfield, J. E., 167, 179, 180,
    195, 209, 210, 211, 239
Henry, G. W., 68
Henry, J., 284
Hepler, R. S., 281
Hermann, R. B., 303
Hermesh, H., 92
Herz, A., 252
Hesp, B., 37
Hicks, R. C., 286
Higgins, J. J., 248
Hille, B., 7

Hill, J. L., 134
Hill, J. M., 302
Himwich, H. E., 255
Hinshaw, S. P., 150
Hinson, R. E., 59
Hironka, N., 238, 240
Hochman, J. S., 286
Hoehn-Saric, 143
Hoffer, A., 283, 288
Hoffer, B., 303
Hoffer, B. J., 303
Hoffman, P. L., 56, 251, 255,
    259
Hofmann, A., 276
Hogan, T. P., 287
Holit, V., 252
Hollister, L., 296
Hollister, L. E., 69, 71, 90, 93,
    141, 142, 171, 200, 212,
    273, 274, 275, 280, 281,
    282, 283, 284, 286, 289
Holsten, F., 288
Holtzman, S. G., 237
Hommer, D. W., 138
Hordan, R. B., 301, 308
Horning, M. G., 31
Horn, W. F., 150
Horowski, R., 134
Howard, D., 110
Howland, C., 102, 112
Hsiao, J. K., 100, 104
Hudson, J. I., 121
Hudspith, M., 251, 259
Huestis, R., 154, 158
Huey, L. Y., 175
Hughes, J., 252, 253
Hughes, J. C., 18
Hughes, J. R., 179, 238
Hullin, R. P., 124, 127
Humbert, M., 109
Hungerford, D. A., 288
Hungund, B. J., 156
Hung, W., 155
Hunt, J. I., 94
Hunt, R. D., 159
Hunt, W. A., 251
Hussein, E. M., 90
Huxley, A., 273
Hyde, R., 281, 282
Hylander, W. L., 18
Hyman, S., 249

Iager, C., 90
Iber, F. L., 178
Idriss, M., 303
Inaba, D. S., 233, 234
Ingvar, D. H., 62, 195
Insel, T. R., 99, 134
Insley, B. M., 197

Isbell, H., 256
Ishikawa, K., 311
Iskandar, H., 90
Itil, T., 289
Iversen, L. L., 83, 93
Iversen, S. D., 45
Ives, J. O., 107

Jacobs, B. L., 273
Jacobson, A. E., 303
Jacobson, R., 276
Jaffe, J. H., 60, 61, 62, 170, 179, 213, 239, 248, 249, 254, 257, 259, 261, 262, 264, 272, 282, 283, 284, 287, 289, 302, 304, 305
Jagiello, G., 288
James, K. E., 178, 259
Jan, C.-R., 278
Janowsky, D. S., 25, 45, 54, 82, 86, 93, 121, 127, 283
Janowsky, J. R., 239
Jarvik, I. F., 288
Jarvik, L. F., 286
Jarvik, M. E., 167, 171, 179, 180, 239
Jarvis, M. J., 179
Jasinski, D. R., 246, 258, 263
Jatlow, P., 210
Jatlow, P. I., 182, 183
Javoy-Agid, F., 303
Jeffcoat, A. R., 302
Jefferson, J. W., 134
Jefferson, L., 80
Jehle, D., 197, 255
Jellinek, E. M., 256
Jellinek, M. S., 154
Jennings, R. K., 140
Jessor, R., 157
Jessor, S., 157
Jeste, D. V., 90
Jimerson, D. C., 121
Jiminez, M. A., 68
Joe, G. W., 261
Johanson, C. E., 195, 210, 221, 280, 282
Johansson, E., 275
Johns, C., 90
Johnson, C. E., 141
Johnson, F. G., 288
Johnson, K. M., 303
Johnston, D., 288
Johnston, D. G., 134
Johnstone, Eve C., 82
Johnstone, L., 72, 76
Johnstone, M., 299, 306
Johnston, J. P., 109
Jones, B. E., 263
Jones, C., 261
Jones, J., 255

Jones, R. T., 180, 199, 284, 285, 287
Journot, L., 303
Joyce, P. R., 102, 103, 104, 110
Judd, F. K., 109
Judd, L. L., 175
Judson, B. A., 171
Julien, R. M., 221
Juntunen, J., 260
Jurgens, S. M., 141

Kadlec, K., 269
Kalant, H., 248, 268
Kalier, A., 303
Kaliszak, J. E., 61, 209
Kalivas, P. W., 18
Kalst, J. W., 14
Kamenka, J.-M., 303
Kameyama, T., 311
Kamien, J. B., 280, 282
Kandel, D. B., 192, 193
Kandel, H., 156
Kane, J., 90
Kane, J. M., 85, 93, 122, 240
Kanter, S., 296
Kantnor, S. J., 105
Kanto, J. H., 135
Kaplan, R. F., 199, 252, 260
Karajgi, B., 85, 86
Karlsson, J., 151
Karson, C. N., 90
Kartalovski, B., 303
Kassel, D., 106
Kasvikis, Y., 134
Kato, T., 288
Katz, J., 259
Kaufman, C. A., 87, 92
Kaufman, R. E., 156
Kaump, D. H., 300
Kay, D. C., 263
Kayser, A., 110, 112
Keck, P. E., 92, 108, 121
Kelip, J. G., 109
Keller, J. M., 119
Kellerman, A. L., 197
Keller, M. B., 76
Kellner, R., 102
Kelly, M. W., 84, 89
Kelly, R., 300, 304, 306, 307
Kessler, L. G., 133
Ketter, T. A., 240
Kety, S. S., 82, 273
Khantzian, E. J., 182, 194, 283
Kirch, D. G., 90
Kirsch, M. M., 301
Kishimoto, A., 171
Klaasen, C. D., 43, 196, 197
Klatsky, A. L., 208, 260
Klawans, H. L., 90
Kleber, H., 172, 174, 261

Kleber, H. D., 169, 172, 174, 181, 182, 183, 194, 196, 239
Kleett, C. J., 122, 123
Klein, D., 192
Klein, D. F., 84, 85, 101, 106, 107, 111, 134
Klein, D. H., 112
Klein, H. E., 61
Kleinman, J. E., 82
Kleinman, P. H., 207, 208, 211
Klein, R. G., 150, 156, 158
Klein-Schwartz, W., 108, 109
Klerman, G. L., 74, 110
Klesges, R. C., 180
Klever, H. D., 174
Kligman, A. M., 28
Kline, N. S., 106
Kloog, Y., 303
Klorman, R., 149, 152, 153, 155, 156
Knapp, S., 181
Knapp, W. P., 287
Knight, F., 275
Kocsis, J. H., 109, 112
Kocsis, J. S., 102
Koda, L., 123
Kolb, B., 17, 22
Koob, G. F., 195, 196, 199, 238
Kopanda, R. T., 237, 239
Kormetsky, C., 150, 154
Kornbluth, A. B., 203
Korson, L., 107
Kossowsky, W. A., 231
Kosten, T., 172, 174
Kosten, T. R., 182, 183, 194
Kozel, N. J., 209
Krager, M. D., 150
Kragh-Sorenson, P., 100
Kramer, J., 157, 158
Krasnegor, N. A., 58
Kraus, M., 134
Kreek, M. J., 259, 261
Krieger, D. T., 8, 18, 19
Krulich, L., 18
Krystal, J. H., 290
Kuczenski, R., 237
Kuehnle, J. C., 254
Kuhn, T. S., 191
Kulig, K., 106, 108
Kumbaraci, T., 123
Kumor, K. M., 239
Kupfer, D. J., 101, 112
Kupietz, S., 156, 157
Kupietz, S. S., 156
Kurland, A. A., 282, 288
Kurtz, N. M., 107
Kvande, H., 270

LaBella, F., 8, 21
Lacoursiere, R. B., 178
Lader, M., 53, 60, 134, 140, 141, 142, 143, 195
Lader, M. H., 53
Lahmeyer, H. W., 305
Lake, C. R., 87, 267
Lal, H., 8, 21
Lambert, N. M., 149, 150
Lamborn, K. R., 107
Landfield, P. W., 285
Landry, M. J., 183, 226, 263
Lane, J., 8, 21
Lang, A., 256
Langer, R., 28
Langer, S. Z., 41
Lang, R. J., 281
Lannon, R. A., 240
Larsen, N. E., 100
Lauz, D., 112
LaVigne, G., 285
Lawrin, M. O., 175, 269
Lawson, G. W., 83, 122, 124, 247, 255, 262, 300, 303, 304, 305, 306, 307, 308
Layman, D., 156
Lazdunski, M., 303
Lazzerini, F., 129
Leahy, L., 182
Leander, J. D., 303
Leary, T., 273
Leber, P., 29, 68
Leccese, A. P., 216, 300, 301
Lee, J. H., 102
Lee, K. K., 178
Lee, R. S., 193, 199
Lee, T., 86
Lehmann, J., 303
Leibson, I., 263
Leirer, V. O., 285
Lelwala, S., 122
Lemberger, L., 25, 29, 286
Lenzi, A., 129
Leonard, B. E., 109
Leonard, H. L., 288
Leonhardt, S., 278
Lerfald, S., 112
Lerner, S., 302, 308
Lerner, S. E., 197, 302, 304, 305
Lerner, W., 175
Lesser, M., 90
Lessor, R. A., 303
Lettieri, D. J., 193
Leventer, S., M., 303
Leverson, J. L., 122
Levin, A., 134
Levine, J., 71, 288
Levinson, P. K., 193, 194
Levy, R., 30
Lewis, D. J., 288

Lewis, G. R., 262
Lewis, J. E., 301, 308
Lewis, R., 166, 253
Lieber, C. S., 256, 260
Lieberman, J., 90
Lieberman, J. A., 85, 93, 240
Liebman, J. M., 195
Liebowitz, M. R., 110, 134
Liebson, I., 61, 169, 170, 179
Liebson, I. A., 170, 209, 238
Liljeberg, P., 266
Lincoln, C. A., 262, 263
Linder, R., 302, 308
Lindgren, J. E., 274, 275, 284, 288
Lindros, K. O., 178
Linton, H. B., 281
Lipman, R. S., 150, 155
Lister, R. G., 60
Litchenfeld, P. J., 233
Litovitz, T., 140
Little, H., 251, 259
Little, K. Y., 222
Little, P. J., 278
Littleton, J., 175, 251, 259
Lloyd, K. G., 138, 139
Logan, W., 150
LoGerfo, J. P., 197
Lohr, J. B., 90
Loney, J., 151, 157, 158
Long, J. V. F., 192, 193, 194, 195
Long, M. A., 169
Loomis, C. W., 177, 178
Loosen, P. T., 100
Lord, J. A. H., 252, 253
Losonczy, M. F., 82
Louie, A. K., 240
Louria, D. B., 290
Loward, L., 275
Lowenstam, I., 178
Lowry, M. T., 100, 104
Luborsky, L., 194
Lucas, A. R., 155
Lucas, S., 284
Lucchesi, B. R., 179
Lucki, I., 141, 143
Ludatscher, J. I.
Ludwig, A., 288
Lukas, S. E., 195, 209, 210, 211
Lydiard, R. B., 167, 169, 172, 174
Lydiard, R. R., 101
Lyon, A. F., 231
Lyon, R. A., 278
Lyon, R. C., 251

Maany, I., 178, 182, 183
Maas, J. W., 104
Maayani, S., 303
McAdams, L. A., 179

McAdams, M., 302
MacAndrew, C., 256
McAuliffe, W. E., 262
McBride, D. C., 262, 263
McCabe, B., 108
McCabe, O. L., 288
McCarron, M. M., 216
McCarthy, D. A., 300
McCaul, M. E., 169, 170
McComb, J. A., 251
McCoy, C. B., 262, 263
McCreery, M. J., 251
McDaniel, K. D., 156, 157
McDonald, R., 73
Macdonald, R. L., 254
McDonough, 283
Mace, A., 282, 283
McElroy, S. L., 92, 121
McEvoy, J. P., 87
McEwen, B. S., 21
McGlothlin, W. H., 284, 287, 288
McGrath, P. J., 102, 110, 111
McGuffin, P., 82
McGuire, M., 175
MacIntosh, F. C., 16
McIntrye, I. M., 109
McKenna, G. J., 283
McLean, M. J., 254
McLellan, A. T., 83, 172, 182, 194
McLellan, T., 194
McLeod, M. J., 288
Macleod, S. M., 143, 150
McWilliams, S. A., 290
Madden, J. S., 248
Maddox, V. H., 300
Magisretti, P. J., 123
Mahler, D. L., 259
Maisto, S. A., 196, 256
Majchrowicz, E., 251
Major, L. F., 267
Makriyannis, A., 278, 286
Malcolm, R., 176
Malick, J. B., 103, 104
Malitz, S., 289
Malone, D. A., 183
Mandell, A. J., 181
Mann, A., 171
Mann, J., 102, 112
Mann, J. J., 109
Mann, S. C., 92
Mannuzza, S., 149, 152, 157
Mansky, P. A., 263
Mansky, P. P., 258
Marder, S. R., 84, 89
Marks, D. F., 285
Marks, J., 142
Marks, L. M., 134
Marlett, G. A., 256

Marquis, K. L., 216, 300, 301
Marshall, E., 213
Marshman, J. A., 286
Martin, B. R., 275, 277, 278, 288
Martin, J. B., 19
Martin, P. R., 260
Martin, T. J., 278
Martin, W. R., 170, 248, 249, 252, 253, 254, 256, 257, 258, 259, 263
Marunycz, J. D., 143
Mason, A. P., 275
Mason, B. J., 102, 112
Mathew, R. J., 285
Matinsky, S, 156, 157
Matsuyama, S. S., 286
Mattia, A., 216
Mattila, M. J., 53, 54
Mattis, A., 300, 301
Mattox, A., 107
Mattson, M., 303
Maxwell, E. S., 259
Mazziotta, J. C., 227
Mechanek, R., 288
Mechoulam, R., 212, 272, 286
Medzihradsky, F., 303
Meidahl, B., 87, 90
Meinert, C. L., 69
Melchoir, C. L., 251, 255
Mellerup, E. T., 124
Mellinger, G. D., 135, 141
Mello, N. K., 210, 252, 254, 259, 260
Meltzer, H. Y., 100, 104, 121
Meltzer, L. T., 228
Mendelsohn, L., 303
Mendelsohn, L. G., 303
Mendelson, J., 284
Mendelson, J. H., 210, 252, 254, 260, 280
Mendlewicz, J., 109
Merz, W. A., 143
Meyer, R. E., 192, 262
Micik, S., 300
Mikuriya, T. H., 280
Miles, G. C., 286
Milkman, H. B., 264
Miller, D., 260
Miller, L., 199
Miller, L. G., 210
Miller, P., 72, 76
Miller, R. C., 296
Milman, R. B., 284
Milroy, T., 152
Minderaa, R. B., 159
Mindham, R. H., 102, 112
Mintz, J., 84, 89, 258
Mirim, S. M., 194, 262
Misra, A. L., 249

Mitchell, J. E., 255
Mitchell, J. R., 31
Mitchell, K. N., 303
Mitchell, R. E., 255
Mitchelson, M., 253
Mitchenson, M., 166
Mitenko, P. A., 249
Moehler, H., 134, 138
Mogar, R., 289
Mogar, R. E., 288
Mok, L. S., 303
Molloy, M. A., 176
Monahan, J. B., 303
Moncada, V., 270
Moore, K. E., 85, 86, 87
Morales, E., 213
Moran, M. G., 45
Moreton, J. E., 216, 300, 301
Morgan, C., 182, 183
Morgan, J. P., 76, 207, 210
Morgenstern, F. S., 300
Morley, J. E., 39
Morre, R. Y., 18
Morris, J. B., 101
Morrissey, J. D., 289
Morselli, P. L., 135, 138, 139
Morse, R. M., 141
Morse, W. H., 152
Mossberg, D., 266
Motzenbecker, F. P., 142
Muehlberger, C. W., 256
Mueller, R. A., 150
Mullaly, R. W., 181
Munitz, H., 92
Murad, F., 45, 196
Murphy, D., 121
Murphy, D. L., 99, 107, 134
Murphy, G. E., 262
Murphy, J. V., 151
Murphy, S. M., 57, 61, 142
Murray, G. F., 223, 231
Murray, R. M., 82
Musto, D. F., 248

Nabeshima, T., 311
Naditch, M., 288
Nahas, G. G., 283
Nakamura, R. K., 179
Napoliello, M. J., 143
Naranjo, C. A., 60, 175, 176, 269
Nastase, C., 90
Nathan, P., 58, 61
Nathan, P. E., 194
Nauta, W. J. H., 14
Navissakalian, M., 134
Negrett, J. C., 287
Negro-Vilar, A., 18
Neiderhiser, R. T., 178
Neill, J. R., 288, 289

Neis, A. S., 45
Nelsen, J. M., 284
Nemeroff, C. B., 18, 100
Nencini, P., 221
Netter, F. H., 13, 18, 232
Neu, C., 110
Neuwelt, E. A., 4
Newman, B., 106
Newman, R. G., 170, 191, 193
Newton, R. E., 143
Nichols, D. E., 209, 216
Nichols, W. W., 296
Nicolson, G. L., 2
Nicotra, M. B., 106
Nierenberg, A. A., 108
Nies, A., 107, 110
Noall, M. W., 106
Noble, R., 210
Nocks, J. J., 178
Norman, T. R., 109
Norwood, C., 31
Nostrant, T. T., 255
Novelly, R. A., 261
Nowlan, R., 284
Noyes, R., 143
Numberger, J., 100, 121

O'Borman, T., 194
O'Brien, C. P., 83, 182, 194, 210, 258
O'Connell, R. A., 46, 75
Oderda, G. M., 108, 109
O'Donohue, T. L., 303, 310
Ogren, S. O., 266
Ohlsson, A., 274, 275, 284
Okada, T., 138
Okamoto, M., 251
Olajide, D., 143
Oldendorf, S. Z., 249
Oldendorf, W. H., 249
Olinger, L. B., 289
Olson, K. R., 221, 233
Ondrusek, G., 227, 228
O'Neil, I., 154
O'Neill, M. E., 151
Oreland, L., 62, 195
Ornish, S. A., 179
Ornstein, P. L., 303
Orvaschel, H., 98
Orzack, M. H., 143
Osborne, H., 252
Osborn, H., 197
Ostergaard, L., 82
Othmer, S. C., 108, 109
Overall, J. E., 155
Owen, J. A., 249
Owen, R., 63, 142
Oxford, J., 191, 192, 196

Paalzow, L., 249
Padgett, W., 227
Padgham, C., 100
Page, J. B., 286
Pagonis, C., 251, 259
Pahnke, W. N., 288
Palmer, F. B., 150
Palmer, M., 303
Palmer, M. R., 303
Panayiotopoulos, C., 285
Paschelka, G., 134
Pashko, S., 256
Pasternak, G. W., 256
Patel, M. D., 194
Paterson, S. J., 303
Paton, W. D. M., 280, 283
Patrick, K. S., 150
Paul, S. M., 138, 251, 254, 270
Pavlov, L. P., 58
Paykel, E. S., 101, 102, 103, 104, 110
Payne, T. J., 179, 180
Peachey, J. E., 177, 178, 253
Pearlson, G. D., 237, 284
Pearlstein, T., 109
Pearson, H. W., 193
Pechacek, T. F., 179, 238
Pecsok, E. H., 169
Pedroso, J. J., 237, 284
Peele, S., 61, 62, 63, 166, 194, 199, 213
Pellborn, L. A., 62, 195
Peltzman, D. J., 284
Pemow, B., 62, 195
Penn, R. D., 29
Perel, J., 134
Perel, J. M., 105
Perez-Reyes, M., 274, 275, 280, 302
Perlman, T., 152, 157, 158
Peroutka, S. J., 86, 273, 278
Perry, P. J., 84, 89, 143
Pert, A., 237, 240, 303
Pert, C. B., 303
Pertwee, R. G., 280
Petersen, R. C., 300, 303, 304, 305, 307
Petursson, H., 53, 60
Pfohl, B. M., 84, 89
Phelps, M. E., 227
Philip, J., 288
Phillips, G. T., 172, 174
Phillips, R. N., 283
Photiades, H., 290
Pierce, P. A., 273, 278
Pies, R. W., 99, 110
Pikkarainen, P., 178
Pinder, R. M., 109
Pirat, J.-L., 302
Pisani, V. D., 175

Pittman, Q. J., 251
Pitts, F. N., 302
Placidi, G. F., 129
Plant, M., 191, 213
Pleasants, D. Z., 158
Plenge, P., 124
Poland, R. E., 84, 89
Polani, P. E., 288
Pollack, S., 90
Pollard, J. C., 281, 300
Pollard, S., 151
Pollin, W., 233
Pontius, E. B., 280
Pool, J. L., 106
Pope, H. G., 92, 121
Porjesz, B., 252, 260
Post, R., 102
Post, R. D., 280
Post, R. M., 237, 239, 240
Pottash, A. C., 194
Pottash, A. L. C., 167, 169, 172, 174, 183, 285
Potter, W. Z., 100, 104, 107
Poulos, C. X., 59
Povlsen, U. J., 87, 90
Prakash, R., 122
Prange, A. J., 100
Pratt, H., 252, 260
President's Commission on Organized Crime, 193, 212
Preskom, S. H., 108, 109
Price, L. H., 124, 290
Pridmore, S., 90
Prien, R. F., 70, 98, 101, 112, 122, 123, 126
Prusoff, B. A., 110
Przewlocki, R., 252
Puder, K. S., 207
Pullan, L. M., 303
Pyke, R. E., 134

Quiron, R., 303
Quitkin, F. M., 102, 106, 107, 110, 111, 112

Rabkin, J. G., 102, 110
Rafaelsen, O. J., 124, 288
Rafferty, M. F., 303
Raft, D., 107
Rahav, G., 207, 208
Raine, C. S., 2
Rainone, G. A., 207, 208, 209
Raizman, P. S., 179
Rall, T. W., 222, 224, 231, 234
Ranaud, A., 281
Rane, A., 249
Rapaka, R. S., 274, 275, 278, 286

Rapoport, J. L., 150, 152, 154, 157, 288
Rappolt, R. T., 233, 234, 304, 305
Rapport, M. D., 152
Raskin, A., 55, 102
Ravaris, C. L., 107
Raveis, V. H., 193
Rawson, R. A., 171, 174, 182, 227
Read, L. L., 180
Redmond, D. E., 172, 174
Reed, R., 308
Reel, J. K., 303
Reese, C. A., 156
Reeves, R. S., 255
Regan, P., 74
Regier, D. A., 98
Reich, J., 134
Reiman, E. M., 134
Reimherr, F. W., 151, 153, 158
Resch, 37
Resenfeld, E., 193, 199
Resnekov, L., 210
Resnick, R., 210
Resnick, R. B., 172, 174
Reveley, A., 82
Reynolds, D. T., 228
Riblet, L. A., 143
Ricaurte, G., 290
Ricaurte, G. A., 290
Rice, K. C., 303
Richard, K. C., 283
Richards, D. A. J., 212
Richardson, E., 156, 157
Richelson, E., 103, 104
Rickels, K., 102, 112, 135, 137, 139, 140, 141, 142, 143
Rifkin, A., 84, 85, 86, 92, 112
Rinkel, M., 276
Riordan, C. E., 174
Risch, S. C., 25, 45, 54, 82, 86, 93, 283
Ritchie, J. M., 177, 223, 231, 247, 255, 258, 259, 260
Ritson, B., 176
Rivera, M., 106
Rivers, J. E., 262, 263
Rizzo, A. A., 179, 180
Robertson, D., 221
Robins, L. N., 98, 262
Robinson, D. S., 107, 110, 112
Robinson, J., 76
Robinson, J. T., 289
Roche, A. F., 155
Rochford, J., 285
Roessner, S., 62, 195
Roffman, R. A., 286
Rohsenow, D., 256

Roose, S. P., 105, 106, 111
Rosch, C. A., 177, 178
Rosche, J. D., 138
Rosecrans, J. A., 228
Rose, J. E., 276, 280
Rose, N., 68
Rosen, A., 307
Rosenbaum, G., 300, 304, 306, 307
Rosenbaum, J. F., 120
Rosenberg, C. M., 178
Rosenbloom, A., 60, 175, 176
Rosengren, E., 107
Rosenthal, D., 82
Rosenthal, L. N., 120
Rosenthal, N. E., 120
Rosenthal, R., 120
Rosen, W., 9, 213
Rosow, C. E., 253, 257
Ross-Chouinard, A., 94
Ross, D., 102
Ross, E. M., 37, 44, 47, 273
Rothlin, E., 287
Rothman, E., 75, 76
Rotrosen, J., 90
Roufa, D. G., 303
Rounsaville, B. J., 172, 174, 182, 183, 194, 261
Rovenstine, E. A., 299
Rowan, R. C., 175
Rowe, W. T., 197, 200
Rowsell, A. R., 100
Royal College of Physicians, 255
Ruben, D. B., 233
Rudd, P., 172
Rudorfer, M. V., 100, 104, 107
Rugh, J. T., 234
Rush, A. J., 111
Russell, M. A. H., 61, 179
Ruwe, W. D., 251
Ryall, R. W., 38, 42

Sachs, P. R., 256
Sack, E. L. N. S., 289
Sacks, O., 39
Sadzot, B., 278
Safer, R. P., 150, 155
Sagherian, A. A., 183
Salaspuro, M., 178
Saltz, B., 90
Salvatore, S., 281, 282
Sandler, J. N., 301
Sandler, K. R., 139, 141, 142
Sandoval, J., 149
Sanger, D. J., 195
Sanghvi, A., 260
Sani, J.-M., 312
Sannerud, C. A., 138, 263
Sansone, C., 180

Sargent, W. Q., 251, 255
Sassone, D., 149
Satanove, A., 86
Satinder, K. P., 191, 194
Sato, M., 239
Satterfield, J. H., 154
Savage, C., 288, 289
Sawe, J., 249
Sayers, M., 193
Sbriglio, R., 284
Schaeffer, J., 285
Schaffer, C. B., 45, 196
Schaffer, L. C., 45, 196
Schatzberg, A. F., 99, 100, 105, 108, 109
Schecter, M., 278
Scheri, D. J., 46
Schiele, B. C., 107, 108
Schildcrout, S., 25, 29
Schildkraut, J. J., 100
Schless, A., 139, 141, 142
Schneider, J. W., 191
Schneider, N. G., 180
Schnidler, V. H., 280
Schnoll, S. H., 301, 305, 308
Schoepp, D. D., 303
Schou, M., 124, 125, 126, 127, 128
Schreurs, J., 251
Schroff, P., 259
Schuckit, M. A., 208
Schulman, E. A., 267
Schulsinger, F., 82
Schultz, C. B., 212
Schuman, M., 194, 221
Schuster, C., 290
Schuster, C. R., 169, 179, 210, 280, 282, 285, 290
Schwartz, J. M., 227
Schwartz, R. D., 251
Schweiger, A., 180
Schweizer, E. E., 135, 139, 141, 142, 143
Scott, M. E., 181
Scott, P. V., 257
Searles, J. S., 194
Secoff, R., 256
Sedvall, G., 86
Seecof, R., 221
Seeman, P., 41, 86, 89, 251
Sees, K. L., 179
Segal, D. S., 237
Seiden, L. K., 290
Seiden, L. S., 290
Seivewright, N., 63, 138, 142
Selin, C., 227
Sellers, D., 175
Sellers, E., 56, 61
Sellers, E. M., 60, 175, 176, 269
Sellers, M. L., 254

Semple, W. E., 82
Senay, E. C., 170
Seppala, T., 53, 54
Seymour, R. B., 246, 258
Shader, R. I., 176
Shafer, J., 261
Shaffer, H., 191, 213
Shafland, J., 18
Shagass, C., 288, 289
Shah, C., 90, 93
Shah, N. S., 252
Shah, U., 150
Shalev, A., 92
Shand, D., 30
Shapiro, A. P., 58, 61
Shapiro, S., 133
Shaver, M. R., 259
Shaw, B. F., 111
Shaw, S., 178
Shaywitz, B. A., 149, 150
Shaywitz, S. E., 149, 150
Sheiner, L. B., 29, 31, 44
Shelton, R. C., 82
Shenker, R., 149, 152, 157
Shepherd, M., 102, 112
Sherer, M. A., 239
Shick, J., 288
Shilosch, J., 303
Shiono, P. H., 260
Shoemaker, W. J., 123
Shuer, L., 141
Shulgin, A. T., 276, 278
Sideroff, S. I., 171
Sidman, M., 210
Siegelaub, A. B., 208, 260
Siegel, R. K., 192, 307
Siegel, S., 58, 59, 62
Siever, L. J., 100, 104, 121
Siles, C. R., 100
Simeon, J., 289
Simmons, M., 286
Simone, S., 169
Simon, P., 69, 70, 71
Simpson, D. D., 261
Simpson, G., 87
Simpson, G. M., 94, 102
Sinclair, J. D., 175, 178
Singer, P., 208, 286
Singer, S. B., 158
Singer, S. J., 2
Singh, H., 94
Siris, S., 84
Siris, S. G., 84, 87, 92, 105
Sitar, D. S., 249
Sjoquist, B., 270
Skakkeback, N. E., 288
Skinner, B. F., 61, 62
Skinner, E. A., 133
Skolnick, P., 138, 251, 254, 270

Sleator, E. K., 151, 155, 156
Sloane, R. B., 288
Sloman, L., 154
Slomiany, A., 255
Slomiany, B. L., 255
Small, L., 150
Smart, R. G., 192, 223, 231
Smith, B. R., 251
Smith, C. W., 288
Smith, D., 287, 288
Smith, D. E., 194, 207, 246, 258, 263, 264, 286
Smith, J. A., 288
Smith, J. E., 45
Smith-Wright, D., 156
Snyder, S. H., 7, 16, 86, 227, 303
Socaransky, S. M., 251
Sokolovsky, M., 303
Solanto, M. V., 150, 154
Soldin, S. S., 150
Somjen, G. G., 4
Soni, S. D., 90
Sorensen, J. L., 166, 169, 170, 254
Soskin, R. A., 282
Sourkes, T. L., 18
Spealman, R. D., 196
Sperry, R. W., 17
Spiker, B., 70, 71
Sprague, R. L., 150, 151, 155
Spriet, A., 69, 70, 71
Spring, G., 122
Squire, R. F., 254
Staerke, K., 105
Stahl, S. M., 45
Stallone, F., 120, 121, 123
Stanley, B., 70
Stanton, H. C., 143
Stanton, M., 288
Stark, L., 288
Staunton, D. A., 123
Stawarz, R. J., 105
Stefanis, C., 285
Steinfels, G. F., 303
Stein, L., 195
Stein, M. K., 102, 112
Stephenson, P. E., 231, 240
Sterling, G. H., 275
Sterman, M. B., 39
Sternberg, D. E., 92, 122
Stern, E., 281, 300
Stetner, F., 179
Stewart, J., 59, 167
Stewart, J. W., 110, 111
Stillman, R. C., 300, 303, 304, 305, 307
Stimmel, B., 166
Stine, R. J., 233
Stitzer, M. L., 169, 170
Stock, P. G., 305
Stokes, P. E., 100

Stolerman, I. P., 179, 195, 239
Stomgren, L. S., 129
Stowall, A., 178
Strassman, R. J., 281, 287, 288
Straumanis, J., 285
Strauss, L., 290
Strom, B. L., 207, 208, 209
Strunkard, H., 285
Struve, F., 285
Stuchell, R. N., 180
Sturgis, E. T., 176
Sullivan, J. T., 269
Sulser, F., 105
Sumida, R., 227
Sunderland, T., 107
Sunderwith, S. G., 264
Sutherland, E. A., 266
Suzdak, P. D., 251, 270
Sverd, J., 156
Swanson, J. M., 150
Swanson, K. L., 303
Sweeney, D. R., 183
Sweeney, J., 102, 112
Sweeney, J. A., 109
Swenson, C., 139, 141, 142
Sykora, K., 269
Szasz, T. S., 73, 76, 191, 194, 212, 213
Szirmai, M., 275
Szuster, R. R., 280

Tabakoff, B., 56, 251, 255, 259
Tabner, C. M., 90
Tammings, C. A., 93
Tam, S. W., 303
Tant, S., 285
Tarmey, M. F., 176
Tarter, R. E., 194
Tarver, A. L., 182
Tashkin, D. P., 276, 280, 281, 286
Taylor, D. P., 143
Taylor, E., 158
Taylor, J. L., 139, 141
Taylor, K. E., 60
Taylor, K. M., 288
Taylor, P., 40, 41, 45, 225, 232, 234
Teasdale, J. D., 171
Teichman, M., 207, 208
Temes, J. W., 210
Temple, D. S., 143
Tennant, F. S., 171, 174, 182, 183, 221, 256
Tenner, M., 252, 260
Teutsch, G., 259
Thiessen, J. J., 150
Thompson, T., 195, 210
Thompson, T. L., 45
Thrasher, D., 122, 124

Tijo, J. H., 288
Tilkin, J. M., 175
Timmons, M. C., 274
Tinklenberg, J. R., 139, 141
Titeler, M., 278
Tohen, M., 129
Tollefson, G. D., 141
Tonnesen, P., 180
Topazian, M., 174
Torrey, E. F., 94
Trachtenberg, M. C., 251
Travis, L. E., 289
Trebach, A. S., 213
Tresnewksy, O., 258
Tricamo, E., 110
Triesman, D., 286
Trimble, R., 68, 74
Trinkoff, A. M., 276, 278
Troughton, E., 194
Troyer, L. E., 134
True, W. R., 286
Truitt, E. B., 283
Trupin, E., 285
Tso, E., 125, 126, 127
Tsuang, M. T., 108
Turek, I. S., 282
Turk, R. F., 283
Turner, P., 100
Tuttle, R. J., 290
Tyrer, P., 57, 61, 63, 138, 141, 142

Uhde, T. W., 139, 237, 240
Uhlenhuth, E. H., 55, 141, 150
Uhr, L., 281, 300
Ullmann, R. K., 151, 156
Ulman, R., 208, 286
Ungerer, J., 210
Ungerleider, J. T., 282, 285, 289, 298
U.S. Department of Health and Human Services, 179, 180
U.S. Public Health Service, 105

Vaccarino, F., 195, 196, 199
Valenstein, E. S., 68
VanderMaelen, C. P., 143
Van Dyke, C., 210
Vankat, H., 286
van, Putten, T., 84, 89
VanThiel, D. H., 260
Varley, C. K., 149
Vasey, M. W., 180
Veale, W. L., 251
Verebey, K., 251, 252, 276
Vestergaard, P., 124

Vetulani, J., 105
Vicroy, T. W., 303
Viewig, W. V. R., 197, 200
Vignon, J., 303
Vincent, J.-P., 303
Virus, R. M., 290
Volavka, J., 252, 285
Von Kroff, M., 133
Vonnegut, M., 80
Von Neumann, A., 156
Vosmer, G., 290
Voss, C., 102, 112

Wachspress, M., 85, 86
Wager, S. G., 101, 111
Wahlen, A., 274, 275
Wall, M. E., 302
Wall, W. E., 274
Walsh, B. T., 105, 111
Walsh, J. H., 39
Walsh, T., 179
Walters, G., 288
Wang, Y., 303
Warburton, D. M., 191
Warnick, J. E., 303
Warnick, S. E., 303
Washton, A. M., 172, 174, 181, 183
Wasik, J., 107
Waterfield, A. A., 252, 253
Way, E. L., 253, 263
Wechsler, H., 107
Wedin, G. P., 108, 109
Wehr, T. A., 110
Weil, A., 9, 213
Weil, A. T., 284
Weinberger, D. R., 82
Weiner, H., 194, 196
Weiner, N., 41, 45, 273
Weiner, R. I., 25
Weingartner, H., 152
Weinstein, A., 303
Weinstein, S. P., 256
Weise, C. C., 102, 112
Weisel, F. A., 86
Weiss, G., 148, 149, 150, 152, 157, 158
Weiss, K. J., 190
Weiss, M., 155
Weissman, M. M., 98, 110, 194

Weiss, R. D., 194
Weiss, S. R. B., 237, 240
Welch, S. P., 252
Weller, R. A., 287
Welner, J., 82
Wemicke, J. F., 109
Wender, P. H., 82, 148, 149, 151, 153, 154, 155, 156, 158
Wenger, T., 110
Werry, J. S., 44, 155
Wesson, D., 287
Wesson, D. R., 207, 263, 264
Westermeyer, J., 194
West, L. J., 286
West, R. J., 179
Whalen, C. K., 150, 151, 157, 158
Whitebread, C. H., 212
Whitehouse, D., 150
White, T. H., 90, 93
White, W. M., 256
Whitsett, S. F., 134
Whye, D., 125, 126, 127
Wicker, A., 167
Widman, M. A., 275
Widman, M. V., 275, 288
Wikler, A., 210, 251, 263
Wiknokur, A., 140, 141
Wilkins, B., 289
Wilkinson, D. A., 260
Williams, E. E., 176
Williams, G., 82
Wilner, P. J., 109
Wilson, G. T., 256, 260
Wilson, N. C., 152
Wilson, W. H., 69, 82
Winger, G., 262
Winsberg, B. G., 156, 157
Winters, W. D., 300
Wise, R. A., 195, 196, 198
Wishaw, I. Q., 17, 22
Wish, E. D., 207, 208, 211
Wisotsky, S., 212, 213
Witkie, S. M., 182
Witkin, J. M., 194
Wojcik, J., 182
Wolkenberg, F., 150
Wolverton, C. R., 290
Wolverton, W. L., 282
Wood, D. R., 151, 153, 158
Wood, K., 100
Woodley, D. V., 269

Wood, P. L., 303
Woodring, S., 111
Woods, J. H., 210, 262, 303
Woodson, P. P., 238
Woody, G. E., 182, 183, 194
Woolverton, W. H., 306
Wright, H. H., 307
Wright, L. B., 105
Wright, M., 287
Wurtman, J. J., 39, 40
Wurtman, R. J., 39, 40
Wu, T.-C., 276, 280, 281, 286
Wyatt, R. J., 87, 90, 92

Yadalam, K. G., 94
Yamaguchi, K., 311
Yanagita, T., 238, 240
Yassa, R., 90
Yates, W., 134
Yeh, S. Y., 290
Yelen, D., 300, 304, 306, 307
Yen, F. S., 286
Yesavage, J. A., 285
Yoshitake, J., 299, 306
Youdim, M. B. H., 109
Young, M. J., 255
Young, N. L., 156
Young, S. N., 128
Young, T., 300, 303, 304, 305, 306, 307, 308

Zametkin, A. J., 150, 154
Zerbe, R. L., 109
Zhang, A. Z., 303
Zilboorg, G., 68
Zimmerli, 143
Zimmerman, A. M., 31
Zimmerman, D. M., 303
Zinberg, N. E., 27, 45, 46, 52, 59, 61, 62, 193, 194, 199, 209, 212, 213, 262, 284
Ziporyn, T., 261
Zisock, S., 179
Zohar, J., 134
Zuckerman, M., 194
Zukin, S. R., 303
Zweben, J. E., 166, 169, 170, 254
Zwilling, M., 110

SUBJECT INDEX

Abnormal nervous system, 73-74
Abusable drugs, 190-91
  acute use, dangers of, 196-98
    behavioral toxicity, 197
    drug interactions, 196
    organ toxicity, 197
    overdose, 197
  chronic use, dangers of, 198-201
    brain/organ damage, 199
    compulsive use/physical dependency, 198-99
    tolerance/sensitization, 198
    violence/psychosis, 199-200
  degrees of involvement with, 192
  self-administration of, 210
Acetylcholine, 9
Acne rosacea, and long-term alcohol consumption, 260
Action potentials, 6-7
Active metabolites, 32
Acute dyskineasia, and antipsychotic drugs, 87-89
Acute use of abusable drugs, dangers of, 196-98
Adenosine, 9, 227, 234
Administration methods, 25-29
  inhalation, 26-27
  injection, 27
  insufflation, 27
  new technologies, 27-29
  oral, 25-26
  oral/anal/vaginal absorption, 26
Adrenocorticotropic hormone(ACTH), 9
Agonists, 37-38
  long-term effects, 42-44
  short-term effects, 38-40
  See also Long-term agonist/antagonist actions; Short-term agonist actions
AIDS virus, 69

and injection of drugs, 27
Akathisia, 87
Alcohol, 168, 214
  abuse, treatment of, 175-79
    antabuse, 176-78
    antianxiety agents, 175-76
    lithium/antidepressants, 175
  interactions, 259
  overdose, 258
  See also Ethyl alcohol
Alprazolam, and GAD, 135, 141, 143
Amenorrhea, and antipsychotic drugs, 86
Amnesia, and phencyclinoids, 304
Amotivational syndrome, and marijuana, 286
Amphetamine, 214, 221, 222
  and attention deficit disorder (ADD), 150
Anal absorption, 26
Angeldust, *See* Phencyclidine/phencyclinoids
Antabuse:
  and alcohol abuse, 176-78
  pharmacology, 177
Antagonists, 37-38, 253
  long-term effects, 42-44
  short-term antagonist action, 40-42
  See also Long-term agonist/antagonist actions; Short-term antagonist action
Anterior cerebral branches, 18
Anterior pituitary, 19-21
Antianxiety agents, See Benzodiazepine
Antianxiety agents, and alcohol abuse, 175-76
Anticholinergic crisis, 258
Anticholinergic delirium, 273
Antidepressants:
  and alcohol abuse, 175
  and compliance problems, 111

and drug holidays, 112
  long-term antidepressant treatment, 109-12
  and physical dependency, 111-12
  stopping drug treatment, 112
  and tolerance, 111-12
  tricyclic antidepressants, 100-106
  See also Depression
Antidiuretic hormone (ADH), 21
Antihistamines, 214, 247
  interactions, 259
Antipsychotic drugs, 83-94, 169
  administration, 83
  effect on symptoms of schizophrenia, 84-85
    amelioration of specific symptoms, 84
    delayed therapeutic onset, 85
  endogenous systems, interactions with, 85
  long-term maintenance, 93-94
  major side effects, 87-92
  mesolimbic dopamine blockade, 85-86
  minor side effects, 86-87
  therapeutic action, suspected mechanism of, 85-86
  toxicity, 92
Anxiety:
  and atypical depression, 110
  and benzodiazepines, 141, 144
  and caffeine, 139
  and stimulants, 230, 238
  and Valium, 37
Aphrodisiac, alcohol as, 256

Arrhythmias, and tricyclic antide-
    pressants, 106
Aspartate, 303
Atropine, 299
Attention deficit disorder
    (ADD), 148-63
    and bupropion, 158-59
    and caffeine, 158
    differential diagnosis/DSM-
        IIIR, 148-50
    and methylphenidate, 150-57
    nervous system abnormalities
        in, 150
    and pemoline, 158
    symptoms, 148
Atypical depression, 110
Autonomic nervous system, 13-
    16, 232
Autonomy, sense of, 63, 75
Autoreceptors, stimulation of, 41
Axon, 3
Axon hillock, 3, 6

Barbiturates, 246
    interactions, 259
    overdose, 258
Behavioral explanation, of toler-
    ance/sensitization, 58-59
Behavioral medicines:
    effectiveness of, 74
        evaluating, 68-72
    false positives/false negatives,
        68-69
    new drugs, adequate study of,
        69-72
Benzodiazepine:
    compliance problems, 141
    drug holidays, 142
    effects on symptoms of GAD,
        137-38
    endogenous systems, interac-
        tions with, 138
    and generalized anxiety disor-
        der (GAD), 133-47
    intermittency vs. continuous
        treatment, 140-41
    long-term use, 140-43
    pharmacology, 135-37
    physical dependency, 141-42
    psychotherapy, role of, 140
    side effects, 139-40
    stopping drug treatment, 142-
        43
    suspected mechanism of ac-
        tion, 138-39
    tolerance, 141
    toxicity, 140
Beta receptor, 253
Bipolar affective disorder, 68

Bipolar affective disorder (BAD):
    differential diagnosis/DSM-
        IIIR, 120
    incidence/subtypes, 120-21
    and lithium, 121-28
    nervous system abnormalities,
        121
    symptoms, 119
Blockade of reuptake, 39, 43, 303
    and antidepressants, 103, 104
Blocking of drug effects, 168
Blood-borne carrier proteins, 30
Blood-brain barrier, 4, 5, 248
Bradykinesia, 87
Brain damage:
    and chronic use of abusable
        drugs, 199
    ethyl alcohol-induced, 260
    LSD-induced, 287
    marijuana-induced, 285
    phencyclinoid-induced, 308
    stimulant-induced, 236-37
Bufotenine, 273
Buprenorphine, and heroin
    abuse, 254
Bupropion:
    and attention deficit disorder
        (ADD), 158-59
    and depression, 109
Buspirone, and GAD, 143
Butyrophenones, 83

Caffeine, 139, 158, 221, 222
    mechanism of action, 227
    metabolism, 224
    overdose, 234
    pharmacology, 224
    side effects, 231
Cannabis sativa, See Marijuana
Carbamazepine, and
    mania/BAD, 129
Carotids, 18
Catalepsy, and morphine, 256
Categorization, 211-17
    based on full dose-response
        curves, 213-16
    results, 214-15
    synthetic drugs, 216
    within-category differences,
        214
    by legal status, 212-13
Central canal, 18
Central nervous system, 16-18,
    22
    cerebral cortex, 17-18
    hindbrain/midbrain/forebrain, 16
    major NTs/NMs, 18
    reticular activation system, 16
    ventricles/CSF/meninges, 18

Cerebral cortex, 17-18, 22
Cerebrospinal fluid (CSF), 18
Cessation phenomena, 60-61
Challenge dose, 53
Chlordiazepoxide, 135
Chromosomal damage, LSD,
    287-88
Chronic effects:
    abusable drugs, 198-201
    depressants, 259-64
    ethyl alcohol (ethanol),
        259-61
    hallucinogens, 284-92
    LSD, 287-90
    marijuana, 284-87
    MDMA/MDA, 290
    morphine, 261-63
    pentobarbital, 263-64
    phencycldne/phencyclinoids,
        306-8
    stimulants, 236-41
Circle of Willis, 18
Cirrhosis, and long-term alco-
    hol consumption, 260
Client Oriented Data Acquisi-
    tion Process (CODAP),
    208
Clinical trials, 70
Clonazepam, and mania/BAD,
    128
Clonidine:
    and heroin abuse, 172-75
    pharmacology, 173
Clorazepate, 137, 141
Cocaine, 214, 221, 222
    abuse, treatment of, 181-83
        dopaminergic agonists,
            183
        lithium, 181-82
        methylphenidate, 182
        tricyclic antidepressants,
            182-83
    administration, 223
    mechanism of action, 226-
        27
    overdose, 233-34
    pharmacology, 223-24
    side effects, 231
Codeine, 214, 249
Compliance problems:
    and antidepressants, 111
    antipsychotic drugs, 93-94
    benzodiazepine, 141
    lithium, 128
    methylphenidate, 156
Compulsive use:
    of abusable drugs, 198-99
    phencyclidine/phencyclinoids,
        306
    stimulants, 238-39

Compulsive use (con't)
  user control over development
    of, 62-63
  vs. physical dependency, 61-62
Corpus callosum, 17
Cortical atrophy, and schizophre-
  nics, 82
Crack, 223
Craving, 61, 239
Cross-dependency, 60, 167
Cross-over design, 70
Cross-sensitization, 56
  stimulants, 237-38
Cross-tolerance, 54
  stimulants, 237-38
Cylert, *See* Pemoline

Delta-9-/delta-8-tetrahydro-
  cannabinol, *See* Marijuana
Delta receptor, 253
Delusions, and schizophrenia, 80
Dendrites, 2
Depoliticization, 73
Deprenyl, 109
Depressants, 245-71
  acute side effects at low/me-
    dium doses, 255-57
  characteristics of, 245-46
  chronic effects, 259-64
  definition, 214
  interactions, 259
  overdose, 258-59
  pharmacology, 247-50
  sites/mechanisms of action,
    251-55
  subcategories, 246-47
  true within-class differences,
    247
Depression, 98-118, 169
  and bupropion, 109
  compliance problems, 111
  differential diagnosis/sub-
    types/DSM-IIIR, 99
  and fluoxetine, 109
  incidence, 98
  long-term treatment, 109-12
  and maprotiline, 108
  monoamine deficiency hypo-
    thesis, 100
  and monoamine oxidase inhibi-
    tors (MAOIs), 106-9
  psychotherapy, role of, 109-10
  and trazadone, 109
  and tricyclic antidepressants,
    100-106
  See also Antidepressants
Designer drugs, 261, 301
Dialysis:
  removal of alcohol by, 258

removal of lithium by, 126
removal of drugs by, 30
Diazepam, 135
Dibenzoxazepines, 83
Differential cross-tolerance,
  54
Differential sensitization, 55
Differential tolerance, 53-54
Dihydroindolones, 83
Dilaudid, 263
Diphenhydramine, 246-47
Direct agonists, 39, 43
Direct antagonists, 41, 43
Disequilibrium, neurons, 6
Diuretic effect, of caffeine, 231,
  232
Diuretics, 121
DMT, 214, 273
DOM (STP), 273
Dopamine, 9
Dopamine blockade, 85-86
Dopamine hypothesis, schizo-
  phrenia, 82-83
Dopaminergic agonists, and co-
  caine abuse, 183
Dose-response curves, 46-48
  potency/efficacy, 47-48
  qualitative/quantitative
    changes, 47
  toxicity/therapeutic windows,
    47
Double-blind studies, 79, 112,
  122, 128
Drapetomania, 73
Drug absorption, 29-30
Drug abuse, 164-89
  alcohol abuse, 175-79
  cessation/reduction tech-
    niques, 166-69
  cocaine abuse, 181-83
  definition, 164-66
  DSM-IIIR diagnostic criteria,
    165
  heroin abuse, 169-75
  nicotine abuse, 179-81
  pharmacological treatment,
    risks of, 166
  theories of, *See* Drug use, theo-
    ries of
Drug Abuse Warning Network
  (DAWN), 208
Drug actions, 36-51
  agonists/antagonists, 37-38
  dose-response curves, 46-48
  drug interactions, 45
  mechanism of action, 36-37
  physical status of consumer,
    44-45
  previous drug use, 45
  set and setting, 45-46

Drug ca
  riza
Drug distribut
Drug holidays:
  and antidepressan
  benzodiazepine, 142
  lithium, 128
  methylphenidate, 157
Drug preparation, methods
  of, 29
Drug use:
  age differences in, 44-45
  general health differences
    in, 45
  levels of, 192-93
  motivators for, 190-205
    changeability in, 191-92
  scientific theories, problems
    in developing, 190-93
  sex differences in, 44
  theories of, 193-96
    combined approaches,
      195-96
    learning, 194-95
    neurobiology, 195
    personality, 194
    social/cultural factors,
      194

Edema, and antipsychotic
  drugs, 86
Elemicin, 273
Endocrine system, 18-21
  anterior pituitary, 19-21
  posterior pituitary, 21
Endorphins, 9
Enkaphalins, 9
Environmental specificity of
  tolerance, 59
Enzymatic degradation, 39-40
Ependymal cells, 18
Epidemiology, 208
Epinephrine, 9
Estrogen, 19, 21
Ethyl alcohol (ethanol):
  and alcohol abuse, 247
  chronic effects, 259-61
  mechanism of action, 251-
    52
  pharmacology, 247-48
  side effects, 255-56
Excitatory amino acid neuro-
  transmitters, 303
Excitatory postsynaptic po-
  tential (EPSP), 7
Exocytosis, 6
Exogenous precursors, 38-
  39, 43
Exorcism, 67

First-pass metabolism,
5-HT2 receptors, 278, 279, 291
Flashbacks, LSD-induced, 287, 288
Flat affect, 80
Fluoxetine, and depression, 109
Folk medicine, 67-68
Forebrain, 16, 22
Free base, 223
Frontal lobes, 17
Frustrated nonreward, 61

GABA, 9, 134, 138, 144
    neuromodulation of, 138-39
GABA-benzodiazepine receptor complex, 251, 254
Galactorrhea, and antipsychotic drugs, 86
Ganglia, 14
Gastric lavage:
    and depressant overdose, 258
    and phencyclinoid overdose, 305
    and stimulant overdose, 233
Generalized anxiety disorder (GAD), 133-47
    benzodiazepine treatment of, 135-43
    differential diagnosis/DSM-IIIR, 133-34
    nervous system abnormalities in, 134
    nonbenzodiazepine treatment of, 143
Glaucoma, and marijuana, 286
Glia, 4
Glutamate, 9, 303
Glycine, 9, 228-29
Graded potentials, 7
Gynecomastia, and antipsychotic drugs, 86

Half-life, 31
Hallucinations, and schizophrenia, 80

Hallucinogens, 272-98
    acute side effects at low/medium doses, 279-82
    chronic effects, 284-92
    definition, 214-15
    labelling problem, 273-74
    overdose, 283-84
    partial list of, 273
    pharmacology, 274-77
    sites/mechanisms of action, 277-79
Hangover, symptoms of, 255
Hemodialysis, and lithium removal, 126
Heroin, 168, 214, 247, 248, 249
    abuse, treatment of, 169-75
        clonidine, 172-74
        methadone, 169-70
        naltrexone, 170-72
        psychopharmacotherapeutics, 169
    misconceptions about, 262
Hindbrain, 16
Histamine, 254
Hydromorphine (Dilaudid), 263
Hyperactivity, 68
    and methylphenidate, 151-53
Hyperpolarized/hypopolarized neurons, 7
Hypersalivation, and phencyclinoids, 304, 305
Hypnotics, See Depressants
Hypothalamus, 18

Imipramine, and GAD, 143
Impotence, and long-term alcohol consumption, 260
Informed consent, 69
Inhalation, of drugs, 26
Inhibitory postsynaptic potential (IPSP), 7
Injection, 27
Insufflation, 27
Interactions:
    alcohol, 259
    antipsychotic drugs, 85
    benzodiazepine, 138
    depressants, 259
    lithium, 123
    methylphenidate, 153
    monoamine oxidase inhibitors (MAOIs), 107
    stimulants, 235-36
    tricyclic antidepressants, 103-4
Intramuscular injection, 27
Intravenous injection:
    definition, 27
    of cocaine, 223
    of morphine/heroin, 262

Irreversible inhibition, 40

Jimpson weed, 214

Kappa receptor, 253, 254
Ketamine, 300
Kidney, and metabolized drugs, 31
Korsakoff's syndrome, and long-term alcohol consumption, 260, 264
Kuhn, Thomas, 191

Lack of compliance, 75
Lacrimation, and opioid withdrawal, 263
L-DOPA, 39
Legal status of drugs, 212-13
Lipid solubility, 29-30, 33
Lithium, 121-28, 169
    and alcohol abuse, 175
    and cocaine abuse, 181-82
    compliance problems, 128
    drug holidays, 128
    drug interactions, 128
    effects on symptoms of BAD, 122-23
        acute depression, 122
        acute mania, 122
        relapse, 123
    interactions with endogenous systems, 123
    long-term use of, 126-28
        psychotherapy, role of, 126
        therapeutic onset, 127
    pharmacology, 121-22
    physical dependency, 128
    plasma levels vs. dose, importance of, 127
    side effects, 124
    stopping drug treatment, 128
    suspected mechanism of therapeutic action, 123-24
    tolerance, 128
    toxicity, 125-26
Liver, and metabolized drugs, 31
Lobes, 17, 22
Long-term agonist/antagonist actions, 42-44
    cell death, 43-44
    neurotransmitter:
        depletion of, 43
        increased synthesis of, 43

Long-term actions (con't)
  receptor supersensitivity, 43
Long-term antidepressant treatment, 109-12
Lorazepam, 135, 137, 141
LSD, 214, 273, 274
  chronic effects, 287-90
    brain damage, 287
    chromosomal damage, 287-88
    flashbacks, 287, 288
    psychosis, 289-90
    therapeutic potential, 288-89
  mechanism of action, 278
  overdose, 283
  pharmacology, 275-76
  side effects, 281-82
Luteinizing hormone (LH), 20
Lysergic acid diethylamide, See LSD

Maintenance, 167-68
Malignant syndrome, 92, 122
  and antipsychotic drugs, 92
  and Lithium, 122
Mania, 119-32, 169
  See also Bipolar affective disorder (BAD)
Manic-depressive illness, 68
MAO-A/MAO-B, 109
Maprotiline, and depression, 108
Marijuana, 208, 209, 214, 272, 273, 274
  chronic effects, 284-87
    brain, negative effects on, 285-86
    physical dependency, 285
    psychological effects, 286-87
    reverse tolerance, 284-85
    therapeutic potential, 286
    toxicity, 285
  mechanism of action, 277-78
  pharmacology, 274-75
  physical effects, 286
  side effects, 280-81
MDMA/MDA, 273, 274
  chronic effects, 290
  mechanism of action, 278
  overdose, 283
  pharmacology, 276-77
  side effects, 282
Mechanism of action, 36-37
  efficacy vs. potency, 37
  target vs. side effects, 36-37
Medicalization of deviance, 73
Meiosis:
  and morphine, 256, 257, 261
  and opioid depressants, 258

Melanocyte stimulating hormone (MSH), 20
Membrane potentials, stabilization of, 41, 43
Meninges, 16, 18
Menstrual abnormalities, and long-term alcohol consumption, 260
Mental illness, 72
Mescaline, 272, 273
Metabolism, 9
Metabolites, 9
Metabolized drugs, 31-32
  active metabolites, 32
  drug half-life, 31
Methadone, 249
  and heroin abuse, 169-70
Methylphenidate, 150-57, 214, 222
  and cocaine abuse, 182
  compliance problems, 156
  drug holidays, 157
  effects on symptoms of ADD/hyperactivity, 151-53
    amelioration, 151-52
    effectiveness, 152-53
    paradoxical effect, 152
    rate-dependent effects, 152
  interactions:
    with barbiturates, 259
    with endogenous systems, 153
  long-term use of, 156-57
  pharmacology, 150
  physical dependency, 156-57
  psychotherapy, role of, 156
  side effects, 155
  stopping drug treatment, 157
  suspected mechanism of action, 154
  tolerance, 156-57
  toxicity, 156
Methyl xanthines, 214, 221, 224
  See also Caffeine
Midazolam, 135
Midbrain, 16, 22
Middle cerebral branches, 18
Modern behavioral medicines, 68
Monamine deficiency hypothesis, depression, 100
Monoamine oxidase inhibitors (MAOIs), 106-9
  depression, effects on symptoms of, 107
  endogenous systems, interaction with, 107
  interactions, with barbiturates, 259
  pharmacology, 106-7

side effec[...]
suspected m[...]
  action, 10[...]
toxicity, 108
Monoamine oxidase [...]
  153
Morphine, 214, 247
  chronic effects, 261-63
  mechanism of action, 252-54
  metabolism, 249
  overdose, 258
  pharmacology, 248-49
  side effects, 256-57
Motor system, 13
Mu receptor agonists, 253-54, 255
Muscarinic receptors, 16, 232
Myristicin, 273
Myth of Mental Illness, The (Szasz), 73

Naltrexone, and heroine abuse, 170-72, 174
Negative reinforcement, 62
Nervous system:
  anatomy, 12-23
    gross anatomy, 12-21
    organization, 22
  non-neuronal cells of, 4-5
Neurobiology, and drug abuse, 195
Neuroleptic malignant syndrome, and antipsychotic drugs, 92, 122
Neurons, 1-10
  action potentials, 6-7
  convergence/divergence, 4
  intracellular structures, 2
  neuronal membrane, 2-4
    axon, 3
    dendrites, 2
    receptors, 4
    synapse, 3-4
    vesicles, 3
Neurotransmitters (NTs)/neuromodulators (NMs), 3, 7-9
  enzymes in synthesis/degradation, 9
  information transfer, 7-8
  and lithium, 123
  partial list of, 9
New drug studies, 69-72
  analyzing data, 72
  behavior, measuring changes in, 71
  evaluating basic pharmacology in humans, 71

..., 107-8
...echanism of
...
(MAO),

329

... action, 227
...etabolism, 225, 226
overdose, 234
pharmacology, 225
side effects, 232
Nicotinic receptors, 16
NMDA, 303
Nomifensine, 108-9
Non-barbiturate depressants, 247
Non-neuronal cells of the nervous
system, 4-5
Norepinephrine, 9, 39, 104, 123
Nystagmus, and phencyclinoids,
304

Occipital lobes, 17
Opioids, 246, 249, 257
intensity of withdrawal, 262-63
misconceptions about, 262
Opiophobia, 76
Opium, 248
Oral absorption, 26
Oral administration, 25-26
Overdose:
See also Toxicity
abusable drugs, 197
alcohol, 258
barbiturates, 258
caffeine, 234
cocaine, 233-34
depressants, 258-59
hallucinogens, 283-84
lithium, 126
LSD, 283
MDMA/MDA, 283
morphine, 258
nicotine, 234
phencyclidine/phencyclinoids,
304-5
stimulants, 233-35
strychnine, 224-25
Oxazepam, 135
Oxytocin, 21

Parallel processing, 22
Paranoia, and antipsychotic
drugs, 75, 93

Paranoid psychosis, and
benzodiazepine with-
drawal, 142
Parasympathetic nervous system,
13-16
Parent compound, 32
Parietal lobes, 17
Parkinsonism, and antipsychotic
drugs, 87, 92
Partial agonists, 143, 253
PCP, *See* Phencycli-
dine/phencyclinoids
Peak toxicity, 125
Pemoline, and attention deficit
disorder (ADD), 150, 158
Pentazocine, 259
Pentobarbital, 247
chronic effects, 263-64
mechanism of action, 254
pharmacology, 249-50
side effects, 257
Peripheral nervous system, 13-
16, 22
sensory/motor/autonomic, 13
sympathetic/parasympathetic,
13-16
Personality:
alterations in, and LSD, 287
and drug abuse, 194
Pharmacodynamic explanation,
of tolerance/sensitization,
57-58
Pharmacoepidemiology, 208-9
Pharmacokinetic explanation, of
tolerance/sensitization, 56-
57
Pharmacology, 25-35
antabuse, 177
benzodiazepine, 135-37
caffeine, 224
clonidine, 173
cocaine, 223-24
depressants, 247-50
drug absorption, 29-30
drug administration, 25-29
drug distribution, 30-31
drug preparation, 29
ethyl alcohol (ethanol), 247-48
hallucinogens, 274-77
importance of, 33-34
lithium, 121-22
LSD, 275-76
marijuana, 274-75
MDMA/MDA, 276-77
metabolism/excretion, 31
methylphenidate, 150
monoamine oxidase inhibitors
(MAOIs), 106-7
morphine, 248-49
nicotine, 225

pentobarbital, 249-50
phencycli-
dine/phencyclinoids,
301-2
schizophrenia, 83-84
stimulants, 223-26
strychnine, 225-26
tricyclic antidepressants,
100-101
Phencycli-
dine/phencyclinoids,
216, 299-313
acute side effects at low/me-
dium doses, 303-4
chemical diversity, 300-
301
chronic effects, 306-8
brain/organ damage, 308
tolerance/sensitization,
306
history of, 299-300
overdose, 304-5
pharmacology, 301-2
physical dependency/com-
pulsive use, 306
side effects, 303-4
sites/mechanisms of ac-
tions, 303
violence/psychosis, 306-8
Phenothiazine, 83
Phobias, and atypical depression, 110
Photosensitivity, and antipsychotic drugs, 86
Physical dependency, 60-63
on abusable drugs, 198-99
on antidepressants, 111-12
on antipsychotic drugs, 93
on barbiturates, 264
on benzodiazepine, 141-42
cessation phenomena, 60-
61
cross dependency, 60
on lithium, 128
on marijuana, 285
on methylphenidate, 156-57
on phencycli-
dine/phencyclinoids, 306
on stimulants, 238-39
user control over development of, 62-63
vs. compulsive use, 61-62
Physostigmine, 221
and anticholinergic crisis, 258
Piloerection, and opioid withdrawal, 263
Pituitary gland, 18, 22
Placental barrier, 31
Polarity, neurons, 6
Polydipsia, and lithium, 124

Polyneuritis, and long-term alcohol consumption, 260
Polyuria, and lithium, 124
Positron Emission Tomography (PET), 82
Posterior cerebral branches, 18
Posterior pituitary, 21
Postganglionic fibers, 15
Postsynaptic neuron, 4
Postural hypotension, and tricyclic antidepressants, 105
Precursor, 9
Preganglionic fibers, 15
Priapism, and trazadone, 109
Progesterone, 19, 21
Prolactin, 20, 290
Prophylactic, definition, 120
Prospective studies, 206, 209-11
  administration methods, 210
  ethics, 209-10
  subject selection, 211
Prostaglandin, 277
Psilocybin, 214, 273
Psychiatric calvinism, 76
Psychological disorder, 72
Psychopharmacotherapeutics:
  overuse by patients, 76
  overuse by physicians, 76-77
  underuse by patients, 75
  underuse by physicians, 76-77
Psychosis:
  See also Schizophrenia
  and abusable drugs, 199-200
  and chronic use of abusable drugs, 192
  and LSD, 289-90
  and methylphenidate, 155
  and phencyclinoids, 306-8
  and stimulants, 239-40
Punishing of drug consumption, 168

Rate-dependent effects, of methylphenidate, 152
Rebound, 61
Receptors, 4
Reciprocal inhibition, 14
Recreational drugs, See Abusable drugs
Recurrent disorder, 80
Research methodology, 206-19
  pharmacoepidemiology, 208-9
  prospective studies, 209-11
  retrospective studies, 207-8
Resting potential, 6
Reticular activation system (RAS), 16
Retrospective studies, 206, 207-8

case control/case cohort studies, 208
case histories/case series, 207
trend analysis, 207-8
Reuptake, blockade of, 39, 303
Reverse tolerance, and marijuana, 284-85
Reversible inhibition, 40
Rhinorrhea, and opioid withdrawal, 263
Ritalin, See Methylphenidate
Rotary nystagmus, and phencyclinoids, 304

Schizophrenia, 80-97, 169
  basic symptoms, 80
  and chronic phencyclinoid use, 307-8
  differential diagnosis/DSM-IIIR diagnostic criteria, 81
  dopamine hypothesis, 82-83
  incidence/subtypes, 82
  pharmacology, 83-84
  social consequences of, 93
  See also Antipsychotic drugs
Scopolamine, 299
Second messengers, and lithium, 123
Sedation, 139-40
Sedatives, See Depressants
Selegiline, 109
Self-medication, drug abuse as attempt at, 168
Self-reports, experimental subjects, 71
Sensitization, 55-60, 306
  and abusable drugs, 198
  mechanisms of, 56-59
  stimulants, 237
  user control over development of, 59-60
Sensory system, 13
Serotonin, 9, 39, 104
Shamans, 67
Short-term agonist actions:
  blockade of uptake, 39
  direct agonists, 39
  enzymatic degradation, inhibition of, 39-40
  exogenous precursors, 38-39
  facilitated release, 39
Short-term antagonist action:
  autoreceptors, stimulation of, 41
  direct antagonists, 41
  false precursors, 40
  membrane potentials, stabilization of, 41
  synthetic enzymes, deactivation of, 40

vesicle integrity, destruction of, 40-41
Side effects:
  antipsychotic drugs, 86-92
  benzodiazepine, 139-40
  caffeine, 231
  cocaine, 231
  detecting in new drugs, 72
  ethyl alcohol (ethanol), 255-56
  lithium, 124
  LSD, 281-82
  marijuana, 280-81
  MDMA/MDA, 282
  methylphenidate, 155
  monoamine oxidase inhibitors (MAOIs), 107-8
  morphine, 256-57
  nicotine, 232
  pentobarbital, 257
  phencyclidine/phencyclinoids, 303-4
  strychnine, 232
  target effects vs., 36-37
  tricyclic antidepressants, 106
Simultaneous tolerance/sensitization, 55
Somatotropic hormone (STH), 20
Spinal cord, 16
Split-brain patients, 17
Spontaneous abortion, and long-term alcohol consumption, 260
Spontaneous remission, 71, 80
Stereotypies, 214, 230
Sterility, and long-term alcohol consumption, 260
Stigmatizing labels, 72
Stimulants, 214, 220-44
  acute side effects at low/medium doses, 230-32
  chronic effects, 236-41
  commonalities/differences, 220-23
  full dose-response curve, 221
  interactions, 235-36
  overdose, 233-35
  partial list of, 220-21
  pharmacology, 223-26
  sites/mechanisms of action, 226-30
  time-/place-dependent differences, 221-22
  true within-class differences, 222

Stopping drug treatment:
  antidepressants, 112
Stopping drug treatment (con't)
  antipsychotics, 94
  lithium, 128
  methylphenidate, 157
Striated muscle, 228
Strong agonists, 253
Strychnine, 214, 221, 222
  mechanism of action, 227-28
  overdose, 224-25
  pharmacology, 225-26
  side effects, 232
Subclinical insults, 199
Subcutaneous injection, 27
Substance dependence, *See* Drug
  abuse
Supersensitivity psychosis, 94
Suppositories, 26
Sympathetic nervous system, 13-
  16, 222
Sympathomimetic drugs, 153,
  222
Synapse, 3-4
Synaptic gap/synaptic cleft, 3-4
Synesthesia, and LSD, 281
Synthesis, 9
Synthetic drugs, 216
Synthetic enzymes, deactivation
  of, 40
Szasz, Thomas, 73

Tardive dyskinesias, and anti-
  psychotic drugs, 89-90
Target organs, 15
Temporal lobes, 17
Teratogens, 31
Terminal buttons, axons, 3
Testosterone, 19
THC, *See* Marijuana
Theobromine, 224
Theophylline, 224
  and lithium, 128

Therapeutic exclusiveness, 74
Therapeutic potential:
  of LSD, 288-89
  of marijuana, 286
Therapeutic window, 47
Thioxanthenes, 83
Thyroid stimulating hormone
  (TSH), 20
Tinnitus, and lithium, 124
Tolerance, 52-54
  and abusable drugs, 198
  and antidepressants, 111-12
  and antipsychotic drugs, 93
  and benzodiazepine, 141
  cross-tolerance, 54
  differential tolerance, 53-54
  environmental specificity of,
    59
  and lithium, 128
  mechanisms of, 56-59
  and methylphenidate, 156-57
  and phencycli-
    dine/phencyclinoids, 306
  and stimulants, 237
  user control over development
    of, 59-60
Tonic inhibition, and strychnine,
  229
Toxic dose, definition, 47
Tranquillizers, 214
Transdermal patch, 25, 28-29
Trazadone, and depression, 109
Trephining, 68
Triazolam, 135
Tricyclic antidepressants:
  amelioration vs. cure of symp-
    toms, 102
  and cocaine abuse, 182-83
  effects on symptoms of depres-
    sion, 101-3
  acute/chronic depression, 101-2
  dose-/time-dependence, 102
  endogenous systems, interac-
    tions with, 103-4

  non-depressed persons, ef-
    fects in, 102-3
  pharmacology, 100-101
  side effects, 106
  suspected mechanism of
    therapeutic action,
    104-5
  toxicity, 105-6
Tripelennamine, interaction
  with pentazocine, 259
Triple-blind studies, 71

Vaginal absorption, 16
Valium, 37
Vapors, 68
Vasopressin, 9, 21, 251
Vertebral arteries, 18
Vesicle integrity, destruction
  of, 40-41, 43
Vesicles, 3
Violence:
  and abusable drugs, 199-
    200
  phencyclinoid-induced,
    306-8
  stimulant-induced, 239-40
Vomiting:
  and excessive administra-
    tion of drugs, 26
  and lithium overdose,
    126

Wernicke's syndrome,
  and long-term alcohol
    consumption, 260
Withdrawal-induced dyskinesias, 90
Withdrawal symptoms, 60

Zinberg, Norman, 213